Frank A. Nugent
WESTERN WASHINGTON UNIVERSITY

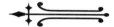

Introduction to the Profession of Counseling

THIRD EDITION

Merrill
an imprint of Prentice Hall
Upper Saddle River, New Jersey   *Columbus, Ohio*

Library of Congress Cataloging-in-Publication Data

Nugent, Frank A.
  Introduction to the professions of counseling / Frank A. Nugent.–3rd ed.
    p.   cm.
  Includes bibliographical references and index.
  ISBN 0-13-260944-4
  1. Counseling. I. Title
BF637.C6N83 2000
158'.3—dc21   99-32596
                                                                         CIP

Executive Editor: Kevin M. Davis
Production Editor: Julie Peters
Editorial Assistant: Holly Jennings
Design Coordinator: Diane C. Lorenzo
Text Designer: Ed Horcharik/Pagination
Cover Designer: Dan Eckel
Cover art: FPG International
Production Manager: Laura Messerly
Electronic Text Management: Marilyn Wilson Phelps, Karen L. Bretz, Melanie N. King
Director of Marketing: Kevin Flanagan
Marketing Manager: Meghan Shepherd
Marketing Coordinator: Krista Groshong

This book was set in Garamond by Prentice Hall and was printed and bound by R.R. Donnelley & Sons Company. The cover was printed by Phoenix Color Corp.

©2000, 1994 by Prentice-Hall, Inc.
Pearson Education
Upper Saddle River, New Jersey 07458

Earlier edition, entitled *An Introduction to the Profession of Counseling*, ©1990 by Merrill Publishing Company.

Printed in the United States of America

10 9 8 7 6 5 4 3 2 1

ISBN: 0-13-260944-4

Prentice-Hall International (UK) Limited, *London*
Prentice-Hall of Australia Pty. Limited, *Sydney*
Prentice-Hall of Canada, Inc., *Toronto*
Prentice-Hall Hispanoamericana, S. A., *Mexico*
Prentice-Hall of India Private Limited, *New Delhi*
Prentice-Hall of Japan, Inc., *Tokyo*
Prentice-Hall (Singapore) Pte. Ltd., *Singapore*
Editora Prentice-Hall do Brasil, Ltda., *Rio de Janeiro*

To My Students

About the Author

Frank A. Nugent, Professor Emeritus of Psychology, Western Washington University (WWU), Bellingham, has more than 50 years' experience in professional counseling. Over the years, he has served as a counselor in schools and universities, as a counseling psychologist in private practice, and as counselor educator, supervisor, and psychology professor. In 1993, the Washington State Counseling Association presented him with the Hank Bertness Award in recognition for his contributions to mental health and to the counseling profession during his long career.

Nugent received his M.A. in vocational counseling at Columbia University (1947), where he worked under Donald Super. He worked, in turn, as a supervising counselor at University of California–Berkeley and Stanford University Counseling Centers and as a counselor at Pleasant Hill High School in California. He completed his Ph.D. in counseling psychology at University of California—Berkeley (1959).

Among Nugent's contributions is the creation of the student counseling center at Western Washington University, where he served as its director from 1962 to 1973. He also initiated and coordinated for WWU's Psychology Department both the M.Ed. program in school counseling in 1963 and the M.S. degree in mental health counseling in 1978. As president of the board for the Whatcom County Mental Health Clinic and, later, for the Lake Whatcom Residential Treatment Center, he helped spearhead the development of new facilities for both agencies.

At the state level, he was influential in gaining certification for school counselors and was recognized for promoting professional and ethical standards for both school and mental health counselors at the state and national levels. He served as president of Washington State Psychological Association in 1968–69 and was initiator, co-founder, and first president of the Washington Mental Health Counselors Association in 1980. At that time, he spearheaded the drive to obtain state licensing for mental health counselors.

He received a Fulbright Senior Research Scholarship in 1982 to study counseling in Germany. Recently, he helped develop WWU's gerontology certificate program and taught courses in the program on psychology of aging. Although officially retired, he continues to teach part-time in WWU's Psychology Department.

Preface

This book presents a comprehensive introduction to professional counseling, a profession that helps individuals, groups, and families work through troubles arising from situational conflicts experienced in everyday life. Professional counselors help people work through transitional periods, an emphasis especially significant during the shift into the new millennium. Counseling as we know it today developed after World War II largely as a result of the need to help veterans cope during the complex transitional period back into civilian life. Although the original focus was on assisting them with vocational exploration and training, the need for attending to their emotional and developmental needs soon became apparent. Up to that time, mental health treatment had been limited to a narrow range of techniques used either for managing persons who were chronically mentally ill or for exploring the neuroses of persons who were well-to-do. Neither approach was sufficient for working with normally functioning individuals, who, as a whole, have many varieties of complex and troublesome symptoms requiring a wide range of treatment options.

I first sensed the need for helping soldiers work through personal conflicts when I was serving in the U.S. Army during World War II as an educational reconditioning specialist at Stark General Hospital in Charleston, South Carolina, one of the army hospitals that received wounded soldiers returning from European battlefields. My task was to help prepare them, through a reeducation process, to return to civilian life. But these soldiers who had physical disabilities were suffering from profound anxieties about going home. None of us on the staff were prepared to cope with their mental anguish. Physicians, nurses, and physical therapists were helping them recover physically, but psychiatrists and psychologists were working elsewhere in the psychiatric wards. In those days, it was thought that only people with mental illness needed psychological help. But times were changing.

My work with the wounded soldiers prompted me, after the war, to enroll in the master's program in vocational counseling at Columbia University. Later, I entered the doctoral program at U.C. Berkeley in the newly formed profession of counseling psychology. Graduate programs such as these were beginning to respond to the psychological needs of the normal population.

The profession of counseling psychology, in its infancy after World War II, evolved from a mix of vocational, developmental, educational, and psychological theories and practices. These divergent roots pulled the fledgling profession in different directions over the years as it struggled to define and redefine itself. As I worked myself through the profession's many transitional stages, confronting developmental conflicts and enduring the turmoils that go along with healthy growth, I developed my own professional outlook as well. The philosophy and content of this text are based on these experiences.

Training programs for counselors have evolved, broadened, and deepened: Programs that once were geared only to vocational trait factor theory or to client-centered theory now include a wide variety of counseling approaches based on psychodynamic, humanistic, cognitive, and cognitive-behavioral theories. Programs expanded to include attention not only to a student's vocational and personal needs but also to the developing self that evolves throughout one's adult life, a self in relation to others, to one's family and to one's community. Training programs attend now as well to a person's holistic concerns—the need to nurture one's body, mind, spirit, and soul. Programs are also including multicultural perspectives. Certain feminist and ethnic counselors are influencing the profession significantly, particularly in their emphasis on the need to address client and family concerns in relation to the social-cultural context and to the community. Increasing numbers of comprehensive neighborhood health care centers are emerging throughout the country to address the needs of individuals and families within the community.

Over the decades, as the counseling profession adapted to the changing needs of society, it has developed approaches to theory and practice that give counselors the flexibility and depth necessary to work with people living in a multicultural society faced with a broad spectrum of concerns and conflicts. Counselors have thus developed a unique ability to help others work through transitions in a changing, pluralistic world, whether they be age-related developmental transitions; family, career, or spiritual transitions; or transitions related to social-cultural-political factors.

During the 1990s, changes in the mental health field again made new demands on counselors. Recent trends have challenged me to reexamine and clarify the role of the counselor, to reexamine more deeply the historical roots and developments in counseling over the past 50 years. Ongoing evaluation of the counselor role helps the profession understand how the counselor makes a special contribution to today's mental health field.

✺ OVERVIEW

As with previous editions, my philosophical and theoretical orientation to counseling is based on a phenomenological, psychosocial, life-span developmental approach. In this approach, counselors help persons resolve or work through situational, developmental transitions and conflicts within a multicultural context. Following is a summary of the text:

- **Part 1: Foundations of Counseling**: I define and clarify the counselor role and describe how the counselor functions in the various counselor work settings in schools, colleges, and community. In the historical overview, I describe the formation of professional guidelines and discuss how the profession incorporated new and more comprehensive theories, techniques, and practices to meet the needs of individuals in a changing multicultural society. I discuss current professional, ethical, and legal issues regarding the profession's responsibility to maintain, monitor, and improve effective counseling practice.

- **Part 2: Counseling Theories and Techniques:** I present a comprehensive coverage of psychological and life-span developmental theories and techniques as applied to counseling, including contemporary psychodynamic and Jungian theories, humanistic and cognitive-behavioral theories, feminist perspectives, spiritual development, and brief counseling. I describe various ways assessment tools are used, depending on the counselor-client context. I show how outreach prevention and intervention activities—psychological education, consultation, crisis intervention—are important adjuncts to counseling.

- **Part 3: The Counseling Process:** Here, in the main section of the book, I first describe individual counseling as a process in which an evolving dynamic counselor-client relationship helps clients develop insights that lead to changes in attitudes and behavior. Then, in separate chapters, I describe how the counseling process is adapted to families, groups, and older adults and to career counseling, multicultural counseling, and substance abuse counseling.

- **Part 4: Counseling Practice:** In this last part, a major feature of the book, I present specific cases and actual counseling programs as examples of how counseling theories, techniques, and professional guidelines are applied in each of the various settings: schools, colleges, and communities.

New Features of the Third Edition

To address the burgeoning needs and trends of professional counseling, I added three new chapters, and made significant revisions and expansions throughout the book. I also reorganized the book to enhance and clarify the four major parts.

New Chapters

- *Assessment: Tools and Processes.* In chapter 6, I discuss the increasing use of tests and assessment tools by counselors, discuss the theory of multiple intelligences, select and evaluate tests most often used by counselors, and assist counselors in learning to distinguish how and when to use assessment tools.

- *The Effective Counselor.* To address the professional counselor's need to adapt to the rapidly changing and increasingly complex needs of a multicultural society, I describe in chapter 8 the characteristics of an effective counselor and the counselor's responsibility to self-evaluate and improve professional practice.

- *Counseling Older Adults.* To meet the counseling needs of the ever-expanding older adult population, I examine in chapter 15 the principles of human development that extend throughout the life span, evaluate societal and counselor attitudes about aging (ageism), explore the potential of older adults to continue leading productive lives, discuss grief and loss, and describe the role and needs of the caretakers of older adults.

Other New Features

- *Part 1:* To meet the changing and complex needs of people in a multicultural society, I expanded and differentiated the increasingly complex ***counselor roles and functions,*** described more comprehensively the ***history of counseling,*** and expanded ***professional and legal issues*** to emphasize the ongoing need for evaluating and monitoring professional practice.

- *Part 2:* I expanded ***feminist*** and ***spiritual developmental*** models and added Ivey's life-span developmental model, ***emotional intelligence,*** and older adult development. I also expanded discussion of the psychological theories that have contributed to ***counseling theories and practice,*** including humanistic person-centered counseling and transpersonal counseling and psychosocial and psychodynamic theories and techniques; expanded discussion of ***feminist theories***; added ***personal construct*** theory and practice; and expanded ***brief counseling*** approaches.

- *Part 3:* I elaborated on the nature of the counseling process and the evolving counselor-client relationship; described how the client's social and situational context influences the nature of the process; expanded discussion of ***multicultural perspectives*** of counseling; expanded family counseling to include emphasis on ***families in relation to their social-cultural environment*** and to their community; and discussed the rapid growth of ***career counseling centers*** in the community, the relation of ***addictive behaviors*** to substance abuse, and the relation of addictive behavior to ***male depression.***

- *Part 4:* In the special section on counseling practice, I expanded and updated examples of new counseling programs in schools, colleges, and communities related to ***careers, multicultural and feminist perspectives, older adults, spiritual concerns, persons at risk,*** and ***victims of social and political upheavals***. I also fully discuss the ***newly emerging comprehensive community health centers*** in low-income neighborhoods and the formation of new liaison programs among school, college, and community counseling centers.

This text is intended for undergraduate and graduate students in introductory courses in counseling. Because of its strong emphasis on applying theory to practice, it can also supplement counseling practicum or internship seminars for graduate students, as well as those courses designed for continuing professional education for practicing counselors. Students in health-related training programs, such as social work and psychiatric nursing, would also benefit from the kind of instructional material this text offers. For professionals who need to study for licensure or certification exams, this text is an excellent resource because it provides comprehensive coverage of all areas included in the exams.

✦ ACKNOWLEDGMENTS

I am thankful to my wife, Ann, for her help in researching new material for this edition, editing the manuscript, and rewriting passages. Her professional contribution, as well as her ongoing encouragement and support as I explored new developments in the field and delved into the literature, helped enrich the text immeasurably. I also appreciate the comments and suggestions made by those professional counselors and therapists who took the time to read different sections of the book: David Sue, Western Washington University, the section on ethnic groups; Sari Dworkin, California State University, Fresno, the section on gays, lesbians, and bisexuals; Candice Wiggum, Western Washington University, and Dana Jack, Fairhaven College, the section on gender concerns of women and feminist developmental theory; and James Hillman, founder of archetypal psychology, Thompson, Connecticut, the sections on archetypal psychology and the mythopoetical men's movement. Appreciation is also due to the following reviewers of the current edition: Grady E. Harlan, University of Mississippi; Aaron W. Hughey, Western Kentucky University; Richard J. Iannelli, University of Missouri, Kansas City; Marcheta McGhee, Auburn University, Montgomery. Thanks also go to the reviewers of the previous edition's manuscript: Sari Dworkin, California State University, Fresno; James Hillman, Thompson, CT; Aaron W. Hughey, Western Kentucky University; Dana Jack, Fairhaven College; Tracy L. Robinson, North Carolina State University; Gerald Spadafore, Idaho State University; David Sue, Western Washington University; and Candice Wiggum, Western Washington University.

Many thanks to Jackie Burley Cummings, who again cheerfully and efficiently typed the numerous drafts of the manuscript. I also express my appreciation to the editorial staff at Merrill/Prentice Hall—Kevin Davis, Holly Jennings, Julie Peters, and Suzanne Stanton—for their support and guidance throughout the project and to Linda Poderski for her careful work in copyediting the manuscript.

F.A.N.

✦ DISCOVER THE COMPANION WEBSITES ACCOMPANYING THIS BOOK

The Prentice Hall Companion Website: A Virtual learning Environment

Technology is a constantly growing and changing aspect of our field that is creating a need for content and resources. To address this emerging need, Prentice Hall has developed an online learning environment for students and professors alike—Companion Websites—to support our textbooks.

In creating a Companion Website, our goal is to build on and enhance what the textbook already offers. For this reason, the content for each user-friendly website is organized by topic and provides the professor and student with a variety of meaning-ful resources. Common features of a Companion Website include:

For the Professor—

Every Companion Website integrates **Syllabus Manager**™, an online syllabus cre-ation and management utility.

- **Syllabus Manager**™ provides you, the instructor, with an easy, step-by-step process to create and revise syllabi, with direct links into Companion Website and other online content without having to learn HTML.

- Students may logon to your syllabus during any study session. All they need to know is the web address for the Companion Website and the password you've assigned to your syllabus.

- After you have created a syllabus using **Syllabus Manager**™, students may enter the syllabus for their course section from any point in the Companion Website.

- Class dates are highlighted in white and assignment due dates appear in blue. Clicking on a date, the student is shown the list of activities for the assignment. The activities for each assignment are linked directly to actual content, saving time for students.

- Adding assignments consists of clicking on the desired due date, then filling in the details of the assignment—name of the assignment, instructions, and whether or not it is a one-time or repeating assignment.

- In addition, links to other activities can be created easily. If the activity is online, a URL can be entered in the space provided, and it will be linked automatically in the final syllabus.

- Your completed syllabus is hosted on our servers, allowing convenient updates from any computer on the Internet. Changes you make to your syllabus are immediately available to your students at their next logon.

For the Student—

- **Topic Overviews**—outline key concepts in topic areas
- **Electronic Blue Book**—send homework or essays directly to your instructor's email with this paperless form
- **Message Board**—serves as a virtual bulletin board to post—or respond to—questions or comments to/from a national audience
- **Web Destinations**—links to www sites that relate to each topic area
- **Professional Organizations**—links to organizations that relate to topic areas
- **Additional Resources**—access to topic specific content that enhances material found in the text

To take advantage of these and other resources, please visit the Companion Website for *Introduction to the Profession of Counseling* at **www.prenhall.com/nugent**.

Brief Contents

Contents

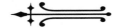

2   A Historical Perspective   25

5   Counseling Theories   104

PART 3   THE COUNSELING PROCESS

11   Group Counseling   253

PART 4   COUNSELING PRACTICE

16   Counseling Programs in Elementary Schools   393

Appendix A

Appendix B

Appendix C

1   The Current Scene

The demand for counseling services for people with normal developmental concerns has rapidly spread from schools and colleges into the community in the last 20 years. Normal conflicts arise when individuals have difficulty fulfilling both their own needs and the expectations of others and of society. Sometimes conflicts emerge because of contradictions or uncertainty regarding a person's motivations, attitudes, or feelings. Individuals may have mixed feelings about premarital sex or about attending college. Conflicts may result from discord between individuals and important persons in their lives. Parents and children or husband and wife may have contradictory values or different role expectations. Financial problems or the illness of a loved one may inhibit the pursuit of a person's life goals.

Counselors help individuals work through transitions and situational conflicts in a complex, multicultural society. Counselors help clients cope with changing family values, family break-ups, shifting job markets, increased demand for high-tech training, and rising cost of education. Increasing numbers of people lack such essentials as food and shelter. These pressures frequently lead to depression, drug and alcohol addiction, and street crimes. Persons with feelings of loneliness or indifference may have difficulty coping effectively with their own needs or with society's demands.

Many families are unduly burdened by having to care for incapacitated older parents. The reverse problem occurs as well when young adults return to live with their parents and when grandparents must take on parenting roles for their grandchildren. Older adults struggle with conflicts of a different nature: Many are often thwarted in their search for new and meaningful roles in society by ageism stereotypes emphasizing deterioration during aging. Such conflicts may cause tension and anxiety that interfere with the ability to make decisions or the will to take action appropriate for the productive growth of self and society.

A dramatic increase in the need for counseling services has also occurred because of the growing numbers of reported cases of child neglect and abuse, domestic violence, and substance abuse. Many persons from dysfunctional families need both counseling and support services. Victims of abuse tend to perpetuate the abuse unless they and their families learn more constructive ways of relating to each other (Brown, 1991).

Developmental conflicts generally represent a healthy recognition that all is not well in one's interactions with others or in one's feelings about oneself. Recognition of the conflict is potentially constructive because it could motivate persons to attempt to change behavioral patterns that are stifling their personal, occupational, or social growth.

⊸❀ WHAT IS PROFESSIONAL COUNSELING?

Professional Counselors Offer a Unique Service

Professional counselors offer voluntary, confidential services that focus on the developmental, situational problems of persons of all ages and of various multicultural backgrounds. Regardless of where they work, counselors help individuals, families, and groups resolve conflicts, solve problems, or make decisions in a social, cultural context.

Counselors are prepared to engage in multiple roles to meet the variety of counseling services required by the public. Their primary role is counseling individuals, groups, or families regarding personal, interpersonal, or career concerns. Their other roles, which are quite distinct from actual counseling, are their involvement in outreach and educational programs, in assessment and diagnosis, and in crisis intervention.

Counseling Is a Process

Professional counseling is a process during which counselor and client develop an effective relationship, one that enables the client to work through difficulties. Following a human development perspective, counselors perceive that individuals go through stages of development throughout their life spans. Client conflicts arise from normal developmental transitions, conflicts that signal an opportunity for clients to reassess and work through factors, attitudes, and feelings contributing to their disequilibrium. This developmental process emphasizes a client's strengths and potential for growth, instead of focusing on a client's symptoms as pathologies or defects that must be eliminated or prevented.

Professional counseling and counseling psychology developed in the 1940s as a reaction to the overemphasis by psychiatrists, psychologists, and social workers on pathology and mental illness. At that time, process-oriented relational therapies emerged, developed primarily by Otto Rank and his followers, including Carl Rogers (1942), who in turn developed his theory of client-centered therapy. Furthermore, counseling psychologist Donald Super (1955) championed the early developmental theories, urging counselors to attend to the developmental needs of normal people, particularly during transitional periods as they struggle with conflicts and anxieties of adjusting to new tasks or roles.

Today, leading counselors reaffirm that the nature of counseling centers around the process of the evolving counselor-client relationship (Ginter, 1989; Guterman, 1994).

According to Ginter (1989), "the single most distinguishing feature we possess that makes us unique is our theoretical grasp of the client-counselor relationship" (p. 83).

Counseling Involves Both Personal and Social Growth

Early counselors of the late 1940s and 1950s were primarily concerned with client situational problems, problems that affect clients' optional functioning in colleges, schools, and workplaces. In later decades, during the 1960s and 1970s, personal problems and self-growth movements eclipsed situational concerns; many counselors, for example, ignored their clients' vocational concerns.

In recent decades, counselors once more are considering the person's well-being in context with his or her environment. The client's relationship with others is now a primary consideration in the therapeutic process. Specially trained counselors are working with families. Career counseling has once again gained recognition as an important service to clients in both the educational setting and the workplace (Isaacson & Brown, 1997).

Increasing numbers of counselors are attending to client concerns in a broader social context. In some cases, counselors from schools, colleges, and community agencies are joining forces to offer family clinics or programs for at-risk schoolchildren and their families. Also emerging are comprehensive neighborhood health care centers that offer counseling, social, and medical services primarily for the uninsured and the poor. Counselors at these centers serve normally functioning individuals with the full range of developmental and situational problems (see chap. 19).

❧ WHAT OUTREACH SERVICES DO COUNSELORS OFFER?

In addition to offering direct counseling, counselors are involved in prevention and intervention activities designed to improve the overall mental health environment in schools and communities. These activities, called *outreach,* include consultation, assessment and diagnosis, psychological education, and crisis intervention.

Consultation

Counselors in schools and colleges offer consultation to parents, faculty, and administrators who may be having difficulty in their interactions with students, parents, or staff. Counselors use their expertise to assess the difficulty and to make suggestions. Community counselors may consult with social agency staff who need professional advice on how to relate to or communicate with the public (Hershenson, Power, & Waldo, 1996).

Assessment and Diagnosis

Some counselors in private practice provide diagnostic evaluations of individuals for community agencies such as the Social Security Administration, the Division of Vocational Rehabilitation, or the courts. In such cases, they provide psychological information to help the agency determine whether an individual's emotional stability or personal abilities qualify him or her for vocational training, Social Security benefits, or parole. Special training in diagnosis and evaluation is needed to carry out this service.

Psychological Education

In all work settings, counselors carry out psychological education intended to improve the overall mental health environment in schools, agencies, or communities. Workshops, classes, or seminars may be offered in parenting skills, assertiveness training, personal growth, career exploration, grief work, or drug and alcohol education (Baker & Shaw, 1987). Counselors in private practice offer psychological education through continuing education programs at universities, community colleges, and professional association conferences.

School counselors' involvement in guidance activities is a form of psychological education specific to the needs of schools. Counselors offer workshops or assemble and disseminate information about scholarships, college admissions, vocational training, school-related work placements, and personal and interpersonal growth.

Crisis Intervention

All counselors, regardless of setting, are involved in intervention when crises arise in the school or community agency in which they work. Should a crisis occur, counselors must be prepared to deal with severe depression, suicide threats, acute shock or trauma, alcohol or drug reactions, psychotic episodes, and even broken love affairs. Counselors must then decide whether a referral is necessary and to whom the referral should be made (Gilliland & James, 1997).

❧ WHO DOES PROFESSIONAL COUNSELING?

Professional Counselors and Counseling Psychologists

Professional counselors are similar to counseling psychologists in that both are uniquely trained to attend to the normal developmental conflicts of clients. They differ in their professional identification and level of training. Professional counselors have master's degrees or doctorates in counseling; those in private practice are credentialed, licensed, or certified by state legislatures or certified as counselors by national professional counseling associations. They are usually trained in one or more of the following specialties:

    school counseling
    mental health
    community
    marriage and family
    rehabilitation
    gerontology
    career

college and university
correctional
pastoral
alcohol and drugs
cross-cultural
creative or expressive arts therapy

Counseling psychologists have doctorates in psychology with a specialty in counseling. Those in private practice are licensed psychologists through state licensing boards. Graduate work in counseling psychology includes more extensive internships and more emphasis in research methodology. Largely because of this emphasis on research, many counseling psychologists have become faculty at universities and colleges where they are engaged in training and supervising counselors and conducting research.

How Counseling Compares with Psychotherapy

As counselors have expanded from working in educational settings to working in the community, and as large numbers of psychotherapists have moved from clinics and hospitals into private practice, considerable overlap has occurred in the services that counselors and psychotherapists offer. In some circumstances, the terms *counseling* and *psychotherapy* are used interchangeably (Brammer, Abrego, & Shostrom, 1993; Gelso & Fretz, 1992; Thompson & Rudolph, 1992).

Counseling and psychotherapy generally differ in terms of severity of the client's problems. Counseling emphasizes short-term counseling processes and focuses more on situational problems of everyday life, particularly during troublesome transitional periods. Psychotherapy specializes in more serious inner emotional problems that require a longer process that often involves reconstructing the client's personality.

Therapists have been criticized for being preoccupied with the client's inner problems without regard for the impact the environment might have on the client's well-being, particularly regarding such adverse conditions as poverty, pollution, violence, and prejudice (Hillman & Ventura, 1992).

Ironically, early in the 20th century, health professionals were aware that adverse environmental conditions affected the individual's well-being. In child guidance clinics of the 1920s, a major treatment method for child behavioral problems was to change the child's environment (Levy, 1971; Rogers, 1939; see also chap. 2). The psychosocial approaches of Alfred Adler (1927) and Karen Horney (1939) emphasized the importance of the interrelationship between individuals and their environment. After the Rogerian client-centered approach became popular, followed by the development of psychotherapy and the rise of the personal growth movement of the 1960s and 1970s, therapists, for several decades, generally lost sight of the importance of considering the environmental impact on the welfare of the individual (see chap. 2).

Other Mental Health Specialists

Other licensed or certified mental health specialists offering counseling or therapy services are clinical or psychiatric social workers, clinical psychologists, psychiatrists, psychoanalysts, psychiatric nurses, and school psychologists. They generally are trained to assess, diagnose, and treat behavior pathology. Most of them tend to view client symptoms as indicators of pathology, which thereby require labeling as a specific type of behavioral disorder; once categorized, symptoms are treated according to a prescribed therapeutic plan.

Clinical or *psychiatric social workers* receive master's degrees in social work with an emphasis in family therapy. They are licensed in most states by state legislation. Their training emphasizes social-cultural factors contributing to client and family problems. Generally serving as case workers, they coordinate therapy services with other services needed by clients, such as health and home-care necessities.

Their professional organization is the National Association of Social Workers (NASW). Historically, social workers have been in the forefront in recognizing the importance of family dynamics when working with dysfunctional persons. They developed and applied a family system approach in various treatment programs for recovering alcoholics, drug addicts, and people in addictive relationships.

Clinical psychologists have Ph.D.'s or Psy.D.'s in psychology. They are trained primarily in the assessment, diagnosis, and treatment of individuals with severe emotional disorders or mental dysfunctions. In training, they are usually required to complete supervised internships in mental health clinics or mental hospitals. They are generally noted for the development and use of cognitive-behavioral therapeutic approaches, although psychodynamic-based professionals have been emerging throughout the country, primarily in private institutes. Clinical psychologists are licensed in all states to do private practice. Their major association is Division 12 of the American Psychological Association (APA).

Psychiatrists are medical doctors with advanced training in psychiatry. They are the only mental health specialists who can prescribe psychotropic drugs. They generally diagnose persons with psychological disorders and treat them with psychotropic medications. Some, but not all, psychiatrists undergo special training as *psychoanalysts*—a program that includes their undertaking long-term analysis. Those who decide to become psychoanalysts generally are trained either in neo-Freudian approaches such as object relations or ego-analytic techniques, or in Jungian analytical psychology (see below).

Jungian psychoanalysts receive Diplomas of Analytical Psychology from the C. J. Jung Institute in Zurich, Switzerland, or from similar Jungian institutes elsewhere in Europe or the United States. Training involves many years of work and includes intensive personal analysis.

Psychiatric nurses take advanced nurses' training that includes counseling and therapeutic skills appropriate for individuals with health problems. Psychiatric nurses are particularly informed about the relationship between physiological symptoms and emotional disorders. They are especially involved in psychological problems of the frail elderly. They also specialize in grief work, which involves counseling those who are dying and those who are suffering from the loss of loved ones. In addition, they work with family members who are caretakers of older persons.

School psychologists generally have master's degrees. Their training emphasizes assessment and diagnosis of students with learning or behavioral disabilities. They assess the intelligence or mental functioning of children having academic or emotional difficulties in school. Although they are sometimes involved in treatment, they generally refer students and families to school counselors or other community mental health professionals for counseling or therapy. They also serve as consultants to school administrators, counselors, parents, and families.

❧ WHERE DO PROFESSIONAL COUNSELORS WORK?

Counseling programs began expanding beyond schools and colleges in the 1970s and 1980s into the community at large. New options and more jobs became available to counselors in community agencies and in business and industry (Baxter, 1990; Hollis & Wantz, 1993). This trend is expected to continue. According to the 1994–1995 *Occupational Outlook Handbook,* which supplies information about occupations in the United States, "Overall employment of counselors is expected to grow faster than the average of all occupations through the year 2005" (U.S. Department of Labor, 1994–1995, p. 151).

By being aware of the similarities of counselors' roles and duties in various work settings, counselors can acquire a feeling of professional unity. In this way, they will be more likely to consult with one another regarding treatment options for clients and more apt to engage in joint psychological-education workshops. Moreover, when counselors are aware of the many specialists among their peers in different work settings, they are more likely to refer clients who need the kind of special help that goes beyond their own expertise to other counselors who are specially trained to work with such cases.

The way counselors apply their training in their various employment settings depends on their area of interest and specialization, the type of counseling or therapeutic services offered in their work setting, and mandates from legislative bodies or other funding agencies about who receives priority in their services.

Local or state institutions or agencies that employ counselors are restricted by legislative bodies, budget agencies, or boards of directors, restrictions that tend to influence the types or range of services that are offered. Legislative bodies, for example, have increasingly been cutting funds for community mental health clinics, so such clinics, for the most part, have now limited their treatment to chronically disturbed persons (Hershenson et al., 1996).

The following descriptions of various work settings cover first the traditional counseling services—those found in schools; colleges; the various public and private community agencies, including mental health clinics and inpatient residential facilities; and federal and state counseling agencies, such as Veterans Administration (VA) hospitals, employment offices, and correctional facilities.

The second section features current trends in community counseling—the newer, community counseling services that have emerged in the past 15 to 20 years, particularly those offered by business and industry, community career centers, managed health care programs, various religious organizations, and various types of comprehensive neighborhood health care clinics.

School Settings

Elementary Schools

When counselors are hired to work in elementary schools, they have good opportunities to counsel students both individually and in groups and to present extracurricular psychological education activities and classes. Because elementary teachers generally have the same children in class all day, the teachers are more likely than those in high schools or colleges to spot potential problems and to refer children to the counselor. Moreover, parents tend to be more involved with their young child's progress in elementary school and to be more available for consultation with counselors than later on, when their son or daughter enters high school.

A survey of 96 outstanding elementary school counselor programs shows how counselors spend their counseling time (Gibson & Mitchell, 1995). Individual counseling was emphasized in 98% of programs, and group guidance and counseling was emphasized in 81%. In 75% of programs, counselors consulted with teachers and parents.

Secondary Schools

According to the standards set by both the American School Counselor Association (ASCA) and the American Counseling Association (ACA), secondary school counselors are trained to offer individual and group counseling, consultation, classroom guidance, and career planning activities. Nevertheless, they have generally found themselves bogged down in clerical duties and crisis intervention duties that leave insufficient time for counseling.

Increasing numbers of secondary school counselors and administrators have shown concern about inappropriate assignments of counselors to clerical or administrative duties and have recommended changes more in line with professional standards. In a national survey of secondary school counseling programs, state guidance directors indicated considerable concern that approximately 85% of school counselors were spending too much time in nonprofessional duties. The directors agreed that high school counselors should spend more time in counseling, group guidance, and career guidance (Peer, 1985).

In another study, reported by Wiggins and Moody (1987), a four-person team (one counselor educator and three experienced counselors) evaluated the effectiveness of counseling programs in seven junior high schools and four senior high schools in four Mid-Atlantic states. The evaluators found that administrators generally considered clerical duties a minor part of the counselor's workload and felt uncomfortable about counselor preoccupation with clerical duties. The evaluators concluded that counselors who agreed to take on heavy loads of clerical work tended to be those who lacked counseling skills or who were unable to object to an excessive amount of noncounseling duties. These findings indicate that well-trained counselors who insist that they should spend the majority of their time in counseling can expect positive responses from reasonable and flexible administrators.

Advantages and Disadvantages of Working in Schools. Counselors in schools obviously have more opportunities than counselors in other work settings to work directly with children and adolescents with normal concerns and conflicts.

Advantages

- Counselors are readily available to students and their families when problems or crises arise. Follow-up counseling is also possible after the original contact.

- Students can receive counseling at no cost.

- Parents are familiar with the school environment; thus, they tend to be comfortable with school personnel who are offering help or guidance.

- Ongoing, intermittent brief counseling can be available throughout the school year and throughout the years that students are in school.

- School counselors are in a good position to make referrals to, and to consult with, mental health counselors in the community and in private practice.

Disadvantages

- Many schools throughout the country are insufficiently staffed with school counselors, especially at the elementary level.

- Secondary school counselors tend to do too much clerical and personnel work at the expense of counseling.

- School counselors in both elementary and secondary schools are being called on to deal with an inordinate amount of students with emotional crises, depression, and drug abuse (Kendrick, Chander, & Hatcher, 1994). This leaves little time for counseling students with normal developmental concerns.

- It is difficult, especially in secondary schools, to schedule ongoing individual and group counseling or to consult with parents because of students' class schedules.

- Maintaining confidentiality in counseling, in accordance with the ACA Code of Ethics, can be a problem for some counselors. Parents, teachers, and administrators may expect or demand feedback from counseling sessions without the permission of the child or adolescent.

- Teaching experience for counselors is mandated in 21 states (Baker, 1994).

Special Training for School Counselors. Elementary school counselors should understand the developmental needs of young children; and of family dynamics. They should have training in counseling techniques such as play and art therapy, sociodrama, and storytelling. Counselors should be prepared to work with a wide variety of multicultural children, many of whom are bilingual. They should be aware of special problems, such as the effects of divorce and child abuse on young children. Knowledge of psychological education techniques is also important. Familiarity with parenting skills is valuable because parents often seek help from elementary counselors about how to communicate with or discipline their children more effectively.

Secondary school counselors should be familiar with multicultural developmental needs of adolescents, such as concerns about identity, sexuality, and dependency/independency. They should also be prepared to work with substance abuse, teenage depression, career or job exploration, parent-adolescent conflicts, and intimate relationships with others.

Both elementary and secondary school counselors need skills in brief, intermittent counseling. They will then be prepared to work with students at different times throughout the years that the students are in school.

College and University Settings

Four-Year Colleges and Universities

Compared with counselors in other settings, counselors in university and college counseling centers are in the best position to apply their training to counseling clients with normal developmental conflicts and concerns. On most campuses, individual and group counseling services are offered with an expected guarantee of confidentiality. More outreach programs—workshops, groups, and other psychological education activities—are offered there than in other counseling settings. As a former college counselor during the late 1940s and 1950s and director of a university counseling center in the 1960s and early 1970s, I have long believed, and other professionals concur (Steenbarger, 1990), that university counseling centers best represent the model of developmental counseling recommended by ACA and APA Division 17.

Budget crunches have led most university counseling staffs to work on short-term counseling approaches that limit each student to about 10 counseling sessions. Students are screened to determine which of them can profit from brief counseling and which of them require referral to other agencies for more intensive help.

Advantages and Disadvantages of Working in Colleges and Universities. In college and university counseling centers, counselors are able to carry out the majority of counseling tasks for which they are trained. Compared with clients in other settings, university students generally live on or near campus, close to the counseling center, and have schedules with enough flexibility that appointments can be arranged fairly easily. College mental health clinics, health centers, career placement bureaus, foreign-student offices, and other resources are generally nearby for referrals. Counselors often have the opportunity to teach and supervise a variety of interns. In large universities, many counselors are able to conduct research.

College and university counselors are often limited in the range of clients they serve: Their clients are usually from a White middle-class background; they rarely see families or work with children; and most seldom see individuals over the age of 30 or 40. At some universities, counselors have difficulties with their professional identity. When they are not given faculty rank, they are often classified as student-personnel administrators—a classification contrary to their non-administrative counseling relationship with students.

Special Training for College and University Counselors. College counselors must be prepared to work with client problems peculiar to university settings, such as uncertainties about choice of major, blocking on exams, homesickness, problems with roommates, and fears of flunking out of school. They also need training in multicultural counseling to work with clients from various ethnic backgrounds. They must be conscious of gender issues, and they must be prepared to work with gay and lesbian clients. They also work with clients who are troubled about AIDS, substance abuse, eating disorders, and sexual harassment.

Most college counselors have either doctorates in counseling psychology or clinical psychology or master's degrees or doctorates in counseling. Professional associations representing college counselors are APA Division 17 and the American College Counseling Association (ACCA), the most recent division of ACA. Psychologists or counselors working in university settings are not required to be licensed or certified, but many of them are licensed through state licensing laws or are certified by national boards for counselors.

Community Colleges

Community college counselors serve a wider range of clients than do counselors at colleges and universities. Many community college students take nondegree technical training, and others take academic courses with the intention of transferring to 4-year colleges. Many of these students are older adults. Because many community colleges are located in inner cities where they are geared especially to meeting the needs of students from various ethnic backgrounds, community college counselors especially need training in multicultural counseling. These counselors must also be especially sensitive to the needs of students who have nonacademic aptitudes and interests and to students who doubt their academic abilities.

Counseling in the Community: Traditional Services

Although services similar to those offered in schools and colleges are needed in the community, most government-funded mental health agencies limit services to dealing with crisis cases or to diagnosing, assessing, and treating the chronically mentally ill and their families. For those who need counseling, help is generally available only if they are affluent enough to pay private practitioners or if they have health insurance that covers services. Escalating costs of treatment, reduction of funds, and limited services since the early 1980s brought about the development of alternative services in mental health care offered by employee assistance programs, career centers, managed health care, and religious organizations. Descriptions of the more recent community counseling settings follow under "Counseling in the Community: Current Trends."

Many counselors work in the more traditional community mental health settings. Each different type of community agency tends to influence and limit the type and degree of counseling services in the particular setting.

Community-Based Mental Health Services

The term *community-based services* is used here to describe services whose funding is dependent on state and/or local resources and whose administrative policies are determined locally. Agencies administered under state and/or federal jurisdiction with local branches are described later.

The innumerable locally based community agencies usually fall into four types of services: (a) public clinics and agencies; (b) private, nonprofit clinics and agencies; (c) private, for-profit clinics and agencies; and (d) inpatient residential facilities.

Local public agencies and private, nonprofit clinics that depend on some county and local funding usually have boards of directors selected from members of the community to help set administrative policies, raise funds, and monitor quality of services. Private services or clinics run by individual counselors or by groups of therapists on a fee basis operate like any other profit-making businesses.

Public Clinics and Agencies.   Two types of outpatient public clinics most common in communities are county-based government-funded comprehensive community mental health clinics (CMHCs) and county youth agencies.

Comprehensive community mental health clinics are the major local mental health services serving a particular region or county in a state. As indicated above, largely because of budget mandates, the staffs of CMHCs work predominantly with individuals who are chronically mentally ill. Community mental health counselors who work in these settings are often frustrated. Even so, because of their training to work with normally functioning people, counselors tend to look for strengths and potentialities in the individual or family that can be used to help resolve problems. They bring a fresh approach to those having severe emotional problems.

County youth agencies are directed to youths who are referred by state child protective agencies or who are wards of the state or in foster homes. Clients may have substance abuse problems, be in trouble with the law for minor violations, or be chronic runaways. Counseling services include individual, group, or family counseling; assessment of behavior for juvenile courts; intake interviews; and educational guidance (Collison & Garfield, 1990).

Private, Nonprofit Clinics and Agencies.   Nonprofit, locally based agencies are dependent primarily on funds or grants from such diverse sources as United Way, corporate foundations, bake sales, or contributions from private donors. They generally have boards whose members, drawn from the community, help the administrators raise funds, set policy, and monitor services. Private, for-profit services generally do not have such boards.

Counselors in private, nonprofit agencies work with individuals, couples, and families. They may offer specialized programs such as those geared for single parents and for adults coping with aging parents. They have been serving primarily those in crises, but more recently, as discussed later in the chapter, comprehensive neighborhood health clinics are emerging in some communities to serve those with situational, developmental problems.

Nonprofit crisis and emergency centers have for many years been available in most communities for individuals who are experiencing acute emotional distress that requires immediate intervention. Counselors in these agencies help such individuals cope with feelings of disorientation and panic accompanying the crises. After clients gain equilibrium, short-term counseling is available in some instances, or a referral is made to other professionals or agencies for follow-up counseling.

Crisis hot lines are available 24 hours a day where individuals experiencing trauma can call paraprofessionals or volunteers trained and supervised by counselors with master's degrees. Suicide prevention is a major activity of these telephone services.

Other emergency centers offer help in specific types of trauma. Rape relief centers provide intervention, offer individual and group counseling, and maintain support groups to help heal trauma and feelings of violation. Centers for victims of domestic violence provide shelter, legal assistance, career counseling, and workshops to build self-esteem. Similarly, centers for juvenile runaways provide shelter, counseling, and consultation. These centers are usually staffed with professionally trained counselors supported by volunteers. (See chap. 19).

Private, For-Profit Clinics and Agencies.   Private, for-profit agencies exist entirely on fees from clients or from clients' insurance. Likewise, counselors in private practice, either independently or in clinics, receive fees from their clients or from clients' health insurance. They offer counseling services for a wide range of problems, and their clients may be individuals and families with normal concerns and stresses or those with more severe emotional trauma requiring longer term treatment. Some private practitioners limit their practice to clients with specific concerns, such as substance abuse, aging, eating disorders, sexual dysfunctions, or vocational rehabilitation.

Currently, 46 states require that counselors be licensed before they can set up private practice. All states require that a person must have a doctorate in counseling or clinical psychology to be a licensed psychologist. Those who are licensed to do private practice are generally the ones who provide psychological evaluation of individuals for government agencies, courts, and other judicial systems.

Inpatient Residential Facilities.   Patients who are chronically mentally ill and require long-term care generally reside in state mental hospitals. Local hospital staffs work with individuals with acute emotional flare-ups that require temporary hospitalization. These professionals offer crisis intervention, emergency treatment, and medication.

Residential treatment centers are available to individuals who are chronically emotionally disturbed but do not need to be committed to a state mental hospital. At these centers, they are given supervised housing, care and management, and the opportunity to live as independently as possible. Unlike those committed involuntarily to state mental hospitals, people in residential treatment centers may choose to leave at any time. They receive counseling, learn social skills to increase their independence and feelings of self-worth, and get help in monitoring psychotropic medications.

Halfway houses, a type of residential treatment facility, are designed to help individuals make transitions to the community after they have been discharged from a state mental hospital. Counselors help them gradually assume responsibility for independent living. They monitor the individuals' psychotropic drugs, help them rejoin their families, and assist them in finding jobs or appropriate training.

Counselors and therapists with special training in expressive arts therapy apply therapeutic skills through music, art, dance, or drama. Such creative outlets as dancing, playing music, painting, enacting dramas, and role playing are beneficial ways of stimulating depressed patients, relaxing agitated patients, or encouraging withdrawn patients to socialize (Collison & Garfield, 1990).

Advantages and Disadvantages of Working in Community-Based Counseling Settings. Working in a local community mental health clinic exposes counselors to a wide variety of counseling, consultation, and assessment techniques. Counselors have opportunities to work with families and with various age-groups, from children to the elderly. Unless counselors are in private practice, however, they are often unable to use their expertise in working with the concerns of normal individuals. Recently, that is changing as comprehensive neighborhood health clinics for the general population are emerging in some communities, as discussed later in the chapter.

Private practice allows counselors the freedom to set up practice the way they want. But establishing a practice can be slow and difficult; one must keep up with all the changing and confusing insurance, taxation, and licensing requirements. Once launched, however, private practice can be financially more lucrative than work in an agency or institution. Yet, the practice can also be isolating unless one joins a group of partners. This concern about isolation has diminished because most managed care organizations, as discussed later, require that mental health care providers combine services under one facility. Clients generally are limited to the White upper middle class. Licensed counselors with master's degrees have difficulty in many states being approved by health insurance companies for services rendered to clients covered by insurance (third-party payments).

Special Training for Community-Based Counselors. To supplement basic counselor training, community agency counselors need more training in diagnostic and evaluative skills, must be knowledgeable about psychotropic medications, and must be familiar with the *Diagnostic and Statistical Manual of Mental Disorders (DSM-IV)*. They must have strategies for working with clients who experience acute emergencies, such as psychotic breakdowns, attempted suicides, or drug reactions. They also need to be familiar with entitlement programs and resources for the poor and the indigent.

Counselors in private practice in most states not only must be licensed but also must take continuing course work to maintain their licenses. They need forensic skills if they wish to testify in court as expert witnesses. They must also be able to handle details of running a business, such as record keeping, billing, and public relations.

Federal and State Counseling Agencies

State and federal agencies provide counseling services in vocational rehabilitation, employment offices, and correctional facilities.

Federal and State Vocational Rehabilitation Services.   VA hospitals offer vocational rehabilitation counseling to veterans who are disabled, with the primary intention of helping them find appropriate careers. VA hospitals typically hire counseling psychologists.

State vocational-rehabilitation centers offer services not only for veterans but for all individuals with disabilities. Counselors with master's degrees in rehabilitation counseling help clients find suitable training programs and employment and help them develop and maintain as independent a living as possible (Herr & Cramer, 1996). Private comprehensive rehabilitation centers have emerged in some cities, in which rehabilitation counseling, social, and medical services are coordinated under one facility or a cluster of facilities (see chap. 19).

Rehabilitation counseling is the only profession established and mandated by a legislative act of the U.S. Congress. Legislative guidelines impose certain expectations on counselors that are different from those of professional counseling associations. These include recruitment of cases, evaluation of a client's eligibility for services, and coordination and case management duties, in addition to the usual counseling functions (see chap. 12).

Employment Offices.   Employment counselors (placement counselors) work in state employment offices to help place individuals in jobs. They are expected to be well-informed about local and state labor market information, occupational trends, and job openings (Collison & Garfield, 1990). Employment counselors may offer workshops or training in searching for jobs, writing résumés, or going on job interviews (see chap. 12). Most employment counselors do not have master's degree training in counseling. State employment agencies differ from privately run career centers, discussed later in this chapter, centers that usually hire trained professional counselors and charge fees for services.

Correctional Facilities.   Correctional counselors work with criminal offenders in state and federal penal institutions, juvenile halls, judicial courts, and parole offices. They use counseling and casework methods to help inmates adjust to living in an institution. Counselors often are the only connection between inmates and the outside world and the only individuals who can help them deal with emotional, economic, and legal concerns (Collison & Garfield, 1990).

Counselors working with individuals on parole assist them in finding job training and placement; they also help parolees reunite with their families and other members of the community.

Correctional counselors are often confronted with a conflict between the role of counselor as a confidential and helping person and the role of law-enforcing disciplinarian (Collison & Garfield, 1990). In some agencies, the counselor role is separated from the disciplinarian role. This separation is consistent with the ethical code of ACA (see chap. 3), which indicates that counselors should not have dual responsibilities with clients.

Advantages and Disadvantages of Working in Federal and State Agencies. Counseling jobs in government agencies are generally stable and provide more job benefits than those in locally run agencies. Counselors may find themselves restricted, however, to services determined by government policies and may be hampered in carrying out counseling duties by administrative red tape.

Counseling in the Community: Current Trends

Counseling services in industry, in career centers, in managed care, in religious organizations, and in local, neighborhood comprehensive health care centers have been gaining prominence in the community.

Business and Industry

Since the early 1980s, counseling employees in business and industry has become one of the most rapidly growing specialties in counseling and in counseling psychology (Lewis & Lewis, 1986; May, 1992). Four programs have developed for employees: (a) employee assistance programs (EAPs), (b) employment enhancement programs (EEPs), (c) career development counseling within the company, and (d) outplacement counseling. EAPs are designed to help employees who have family troubles, substance abuse problems, or other difficulties that interfere with their job performance. EEPs are preventive programs offered by companies to keep workers fit and healthy through exercise, diet, and relaxation techniques. Career development counseling helps employees develop their careers within the company system. Outplacement counselors serve employees who are terminated because their jobs are obsolete or because a company department is shutting down; they help the employees find new jobs and, if necessary, provide ways for them to develop skills for new jobs (see chap. 12).

Although EAPs originally focused on alcohol problems of employees, they have since expanded to serve those with personal, interpersonal, and family problems. In 1982, over half of the companies in *Fortune* magazine's top 500 companies offered EAPs. Since then, increasing numbers of smaller companies have developed EAPs through contracts with mental health clinics, social service agencies, or private practitioners.

In a survey of staffing patterns of 275 EAP organizations in the United States, Hosie, West, and Mackey (1993) found that persons with master's degrees in counseling and social work "were the most frequently employed and constitute the greatest percentage of the professional mental health staff in EAPs" (p. 355).

Advantages and Disadvantages of Working in Business and Industry. In EAPs, counselors can work with the kinds of people they are best trained to serve—those who have situational concerns. Some counselors, however, serve only as intake interviewers who refer clients to other services offered in the community. Moreover, counselors employed by a company are often faced with the problem of being pressured by supervisors to release information about their clients (Dickman, Emener, & Hutchinson, 1985).

Special Training for Business and Industry Counselors. Besides the usual training required of all counselors, EAP counselors need additional training not only in career counseling but also in business, personnel, and management. Because alcoholism is still a major cause of employee problems, training and experience in this area are also important. Training in family counseling is also needed for employees seeking counseling because their problems on the job may be related to family troubles.

Community Career Centers

Career counseling centers emerged during the 1990s, especially in metropolitan areas. They offer individuals opportunities to explore career options and to engage in career planning and develop strategies to find the right job. They offer such educational workshops as how to write résumés, organize a job search, and prepare for job interviews. Workshops are also available to individuals who have lost their jobs, who are having interpersonal conflicts with managers or supervisors on the job, or who want to upgrade themselves in their current jobs. These activities include overcoming anxiety about job loss, managing stress, asserting oneself, or managing conflict with challenging colleagues. These centers generally require yearly membership dues, with additional fees for special workshops or retreats. Counselors who work in these agencies generally have master's degrees in counseling or in career counseling. Career centers are generally open evenings, which is a big advantage for clients.

Managed Health Care Programs

Managed mental health care programs are serviced by a group of health practitioners who contract with employers to provide for counseling, therapy, and psychoeducational needs of their employees (Gelso & Fretz, 1992; Giles, 1993). Regarding managed mental health care, Giles (1993) says, "One should make no mistake about the advent of managed health care; it represents not just an evolution but a revolution in the practice of both in-patient and out-patient care" (p. 1). Because of escalating costs, insurance companies, corporations, and health providers are increasingly turning to health maintenance organizations (HMOs), preferred provider organizations (PPOs), and other managed health care programs (Foos, Ottens, & Hill, 1991). As cited in Bisline, Sheridan, and Winegar (1991), in a health maintenance survey, Boyles (1989) found that 614 HMOs were covering 32.6 million people. In another survey, Masi and Bowler (1988) estimated that nearly two-thirds of commercial corporations offer HMOs as part of their services.

Mental health specialists who work for HMOs may be employed directly by the agencies and offer counseling and therapy at HMO offices. In group model HMOs, in contrast, managed care health organizations contract with groups of private practitioners. Grouping providers together increases efficiency of services and cuts costs (Bisline et al., 1991; Giles, 1993).

Wylie (1994) describes managed care as follows:

> In its broadest sense, managed care usually refers to a corporate, privately run (though often government regulated) system of health care that coordinates and delivers an

entire range of medical and, sometimes, mental health services to a "prepaid" population, while also managing the costs of providing that care. (p. 22)

These health care programs have tailored their services to reduce escalating health costs by limiting the number of sessions covered by insurance. In this way, providers are forced to focus on brief therapy methods.

Wylie (1994) describes how HMOs cut costs in services:

> Typically a managed care company stays within budget by screening medical and mental health services, restricting or denying access to those considered unnecessary or inappropriate and getting providers to agree to reimbursements below what they could get in the free market. (p. 22)

HMOs further cut costs by a process they call *capitation,* in which "bidders submit proposals to provide mental health services on a flat fee per covered HMO members per month" (Giles, 1991, p. 85).

Advantages and Disadvantages of Working for Managed Health Care Programs.

Advantages

- Proponents of managed care services claim that this approach forces mental health providers to be more precise and specific in what they do with clients. This enforced accountability, they say, reduces the chances of exploitation by unscrupulous providers who engage all clients in long-term counseling and therapy, a practice that is costly and unnecessary (Giles, 1993).

- HMOs do not limit contracts with providers to those with Ph.D.'s or M.D.'s. They also include state-licensed master's degree counselors and social workers.

- Short-term brief counseling approaches are generally more compatible with counselors' interests and training.

- Because managed care organizations generally require providers to form into groups, a group of providers has the advantage of engaging in interdisciplinary case conferences, interstaff consultations, and ongoing in-service training. Further, participating providers do not have to build up their own clientele, as do independent practitioners (Bisline et al., 1991).

Disadvantages

- Opponents of managed care argue that HMOs tend to make determinations about type and length of treatment that rightfully should be done by mental health practitioners. They also believe that managed care corporations, in their zeal to cut costs, neglect individual needs of clients, reduce quality of care, and limit eligibility of clients to those diagnosed as needing medical care (Bloom, 1990).

- Critics also point out that HMOs ignore clients who can profit from longer term counseling (Mone, 1994; Whitaker, 1994).

- Ethical considerations are also of concern. Confidentiality and rights of privacy of clients are generally violated when managed care programs require providers to report diagnosis and progress of clients to HMO management.

Special Training for Counselors in Managed Health Care.   Counselors tend to emphasize techniques of brief therapy in HMOs more often than do counselors working elsewhere because of the expeditious nature of the program. Because they traditionally have worked with normal situational concerns of clients, professional counselors are uniquely prepared to use short-term, goal-oriented counseling techniques advocated by HMOs and similar managed health care programs (Foos et al., 1991; Forrest & Affeman, 1986).

Religious Organizations

Religious organizations have developed two major types of counseling services: (a) pastoral counseling provided by pastors and (b) religious-sponsored counseling centers that employ primarily nonpastoral counselors.

Pastoral counselors are ministers who have studied counseling and psychotherapy at the graduate level at a school of theology and have been certified by the American Association of Pastoral Counselors (AAPC). They integrate psychological, religious, and moral theories to help clients work through emotional distress (Young & Griffith, 1989).

Endicott, Greenwalt, Nee, and Jasmine (1983) studied several pastoral counseling centers out of the 260 existing centers in 1983. All had directors who had been parish ministers and had completed graduate training in counseling. The facilities offered individual, family, and couple counseling, as well as group and workshop activities. Most clients were asking for help because of stress, anxiety, depression, or difficulties in social relationships. Clients with psychotic reactions were rare. Clients generally were Protestant and fairly well educated. Most clients indicated they would not have used traditional counseling services if the pastoral counseling center had not been available.

Recently, in larger cities, various religious groups have been offering counseling services; some have networks of services throughout a city. These religious-sponsored counseling centers employ professionally trained counselors who generally do not have a ministerial or theological background. Counseling is available to all individuals in the community who are experiencing normal, everyday problems. These services are offered at fees on a sliding scale and are generally affordable for most people. Spiritual counseling is a special feature. Counselors attracted to these settings are open to and encourage the exploration of spiritual questions with their clients.

Advantages and Disadvantages of Working at Religious-Sponsored Counseling Centers.   In contrast with most other community mental health agencies, counseling services sponsored by religious groups are generally designed to help normally functioning individuals from all socioeconomic backgrounds. Figure 1.1 illustrates these differences. It shows four agencies in Seattle, Washington—two traditional mental health clinics and two religious-sponsored counseling centers. Notice the emphasis of mental health agencies on the chronically ill and on the use of psychotropic drugs, compared with the two examples of religious-sponsored counseling centers. Notice also that the Presbyterian Counseling Services has multiple locations

Publicly Funded Centers:
Emphasis on Chronically Mentally Ill

HIGHLINE-WEST SEATTLE MENTAL HEALTH CENTER
....Intake for all sites: (206) 248-8226
....TTY: (206) 248-8235
C 2600 SW Holden, Seattle 98126 ....(206) 933-7100
C 1010 S 146th, Seattle 98168 ....(206) 241-0990
Special services for enrolled clients: Crisis intervention and aftercare services for clients with acute or chronic mental illness. 24-hour case management service provides psychiatric evaluation, medication monitoring, and a variety of support and referral services. Emergency response team after-hours, weekends, and holidays through Crisis Clinic. *Other services:* Comprehensive outpatient counseling for adults, children, youth, and their families; intake fee $20–125; sessions $20–$85; medical coupons and private insurance accepted. Supervised living services at residential care facilities for severely dysfunctional clients. Chemical dependency treatment for all ages. Parenting and child abuse prevention program and employment assistance. Individual, group, and family case management services for adult clients who are both mentally ill and developmentally disabled. Anger management and shoplifting groups. Community training and consultation.
Partial Hospitalization Program..........(206) 248-8226
Intensive ambulatory treatment program for individuals who have acute or chronic mental illness with acute exacerbation of symptoms.

COMMUNITY PSYCHIATRIC CLINIC ......V/TTY: (206) 461-3614
4319 Stone Way N, Seattle 98103
C 10501 Meridian Ave N #D, Seattle 98133......(206) 461-4544
NOTE: Services vary at each site.
Crisis intervention and outreach for enrolled clients with acute or chronic mental illness. 24-hour case management teams provide psychiatric evaluation, medication monitoring, and a variety of other support and referral services. Emergency response team after-hours, weekends, and holidays reached through Crisis Clinic.
General services: Individual, group, and family counseling: Intake fee: $45–$120, regular sessions: $39–$95; group sessions: $11–$50, medication evaluations: $18–$55. Evening sessions available. Day treatment programs for mentally ill adults and for children ages 6–12. Special evaluation, counseling, and medication monitoring for older adults. Vocational rehabilitation and placement for mentally disabled clients. Residential treatment programs for chronically mentally ill clients, including homeless clients; support services for residents include case management and mental health services.

Religious-Sponsored Centers:
Emphasis on Concerns of Normal Population

PRESBYTERIAN COUNSELING SERVICE ......(206) 527-2266
564 NE Ravenna Blvd, Seattle 98115
    NCES (Multiple sites throughout King County and Seattle)
Individual, couples, and family counseling focusing on stress and conflicts related to relationships, life changes and loss; issues of growth and individual development; also vocational evaluation and counseling. Sliding scale $30–$100. Marriage and Family Training Clinic (MFT) serves low-income families and trains therapists. Couples and families have the option of reflective team therapy (being observed by therapists in training) or one therapist who consults with experienced clinicians. Sliding scale $10–$30 per session. Seminars, workshops and ongoing groups for marriage preparation and parenting.

JEWISH FAMILY SERVICE ....(206) 461-3240
1601 16th Ave., Seattle 98122
    E 606 110th Ave NE, Bellevue 98004 ....(425)-451-8512
Multiservice agency focusing on (but not restricted to) Jewish clients. Individual, group, couple, family, and child counseling; sliding scale fees: $25–$80 per session. Referral to legal, medical, dental, and other community resources. Kosher meals, visits, health care, and case management for older adults. Social programs, tenant support, residential treatment facilities, advocacy and case management for mentally and developmentally disabled Jewish adults. Jewish Big Pals for children in single-parent families. Resettlement of Jewish refugees. Family life education programs are available. Interfaith marriage support is also offered. Employment guidance is available. Food bank 10am–noon, Wednesdays and Fridays; 2pm–4pm Thursdays. Some services are also available in Russian, Hebrew and Yiddish.

FIGURE 1.1
Comparison or representative religious-sponsored counseling centers and publicly funded mental health clinics in Seattle, Washington.

Source: Adapted from *Where to Turn Plus: The Directory of Human Resources,* by Crisis Clinic, Seattle, WA, 1998. Seattle, WA: Author.

throughout the city; notice how the Jewish Family Service Center's comprehensive health care program integrates all aspects of care—counseling, social services, career guidance, and medical care.

Although such counseling programs sponsored by particular religious groups seem to reach an ideal model of community counseling services, there is always the risk that overzealous counselors may try to impose their own religious beliefs on their clients.

This risk is held in check by ethical codes for counselors. The American Association of Pastoral Counselors Ethical Code states that pastoral counselors should avoid any possible imposition of their own theology on clients (AAPC, 1990, p. 22). The ACA code also states that counselors are not to impose their beliefs or values on clients regardless of work setting.

Special Training for Pastoral Counselors.

To be certified in pastoral counseling, ministers enroll in graduate work in counseling at theological schools. AAPC has set up training standards similar to those of ACA and APA Division 17. It requires that pastoral counselors complete courses in the following subjects: counseling theories and techniques, personality development, normal and abnormal behavior, family and marriage counseling, and research. Career or vocational theory is not required. Special courses include the psychology of religious experience and the history and theory of pastoral care. Internships include clinical work under the supervision of a fellow or diplomate of AAPC and participation in a clinic with interdisciplinary supervision (AAPC, 1990). The AAPC Code of Ethics upholds confidentiality.

Counseling at Religious-Sponsored Centers: A Personal View.

Although I do not usually attend church and had the usual secular training in counseling and psychology, I am impressed by how far religious groups have gone to provide services for which the counselor is uniquely trained—that of counseling a wide range of clients with normal developmental concerns. Moreover, unlike most other counseling models, these services, which include spiritual considerations in counseling, emulate a basic goal of professional counseling—working with the whole person.

Comprehensive Community Health Centers and Neighborhood Clinics

Comprehensive community health centers and neighborhood clinics of various kinds are developing throughout the country that combine under one jurisdiction counseling, medical, and social services. In these combined programs, counseling services differ from the comprehensive community mental health clinics, discussed earlier, financed by state and county funds that serve primarily patients with chronic mental illness. These newer centers, designed to service primarily persons who are uninsured, service the full range of situational, transitional problems of clients and families. Emerging in communities from the grass roots, these centers vary widely, depending on the needs of particular communities and neighborhoods. Examples are described in chapter 19 on community counseling.

❧ SUMMARY

The demand for counseling services has increased rapidly because people are experiencing more conflicts in their everyday lives as a result of escalating social, economic, and cultural pressures and upheavals.

Professional counseling is a unique service in the mental health field, one that focuses on developmental social-cultural concerns and conflicts of normally functioning individuals, especially during transitional periods, throughout their life spans. In this process, an experiential relationship develops between counselor and client, an evolving relationship that fosters healing and constructive resolution of personal and interpersonal situational conflicts. This approach generally differs from models used by other mental health providers, models in which providers tend to view client problems as symptoms of pathology that require treatment.

In addition to direct counseling, counselors offer outreach services in all work settings. These include consultation, assessment, psychological education, and crisis intervention.

Professional counseling is done by licensed or certified counselors in public schools, colleges, community agencies, employment agencies, and businesses. Regardless of where they work, counselors perform direct counseling and various outreach services.

Counseling services, which after World War II developed for the most part only in schools, colleges, and rehabilitation centers, gradually expanded during the late 1970s and 1980s into the community. Largely because of limited budgets, however, community mental health services for many years generally had to limit services to persons with severe disturbances.

Increasing numbers of state legislatures have granted licensure to professional counselors, a move that has led to a rapid increase in the number of counselors in private practice and community agencies.

During the 1980s and 1990s, counseling spread into important segments of the community—business and industry through employer assistance programs; career counseling centers; managed care organizations for those covered by health insurance; counseling centers sponsored by religious organizations; and comprehensive neighborhood health care centers predominantly for the uninsured.

❧ PROJECTS AND ACTIVITIES

1. Survey several mental health agencies in your community. Find out how many staff members hold degrees in counseling or social work and how many have psychological or psychiatric training.
2. Attend a meeting of the local, regional, or state counseling association. Do the same for meetings of the social workers' association or the psychological association. Compare the types of issues of each program. Or compare program brochures of scheduled meetings of the associations.
3. Interview the director of the counseling center at your university regarding the history of the center and the current policies and practices.

4. Set up a panel of counselors from schools, colleges, and community agencies, all of whom have training in counseling or counseling psychology. Ask the panelists: What are your major responsibilities? How do these responsibilities tie in with your training? What gaps do you see in services to the general public?
5. Visit a religious-sponsored counseling service near you, or write to such a center for a brochure. Compare its services with those of traditional community agencies. What training do staff members have?
6. Check a directory of community mental health services in a large city, or write for brochures. How many offer mental health services for members of the general public?

REFERENCES

Adler, A. (1927). *Practice and theory of individual psychology.* New York: Harcourt, Brace & World.

American Association of Pastoral Counselors (AAPC). (1990). *Handbook: American Association of Pastoral Counselors.* Fairfax, VA: Author.

Baker, S. B. (1994). Mandatory teaching experience for school counselors: An impediment to uniform certification standards for counselors. *Counselor Education & Supervision, 33,* 314–326.

Baker, S. B., & Shaw, M. C. (1987). *Improving counseling through primary intervention.* Upper Saddle River, NJ: Merrill/Prentice Hall.

Baxter, N. J. (1990). *Opportunities in counseling and developmental careers.* Lincolnwood, IL: V. G. M. Career Horizons.

Bisline, J. L., Sheridan, S. M., & Winegar, N. (1991). Five critical skills for mental health counselors in managed health care. *Journal of Mental Health Counseling, 13,* 147–152.

Bloom, B. L. (1990). Managing mental health services: Some comments for the overdue debate in psychology. *Community Mental Health Journal, 26,* 107–124.

Boyles, W. R. (1989, May 2). Total HMO industry growth steady as a number of HMO outlets exceeds 600 more. *Health Market Survey,* p. 8.

Brammer, L., Abrego, P. J., & Shostrom, E. L. (1993). *Therapeutic counseling and psychotherapy* (6th ed.). Upper Saddle River, NJ: Prentice Hall.

Brown, S. L. (1991). *Counseling victims of violence.* Alexandria, VA: American Counseling Association.

Collison, B. B., & Garfield, N. J. (1990). *Careers in counseling and human development.* Alexandria, VA: American Counseling Association.

Dickman, J. F., Emener, W. G., & Hutchinson, W. S. (Eds.). (1985). *Counseling the troubled person in industry.* Springfield, IL: Charles C Thomas.

Endicott, J., Greenwalt, J., Nee, J., & Jasmine, D. (1983). Pastoral counseling centers: Who goes there, and what services are received? *Journal of Psychiatric Treatment and Evaluation, 5,* 55–61.

Foos, J. A., Ottens, A. J., & Hill, L. K. (1991). Managed mental health: A primer for counselors. *Journal of Counseling & Development, 69,* 332–336.

Forrest, D., & Affeman, M. (1986). The future for mental health counselors in health maintenance organizations. *American Mental Health Counselor Journal, 8,* 60–72.

Gelso, C. J., & Fretz, B. R. (1992). *Counseling psychology.* Fort Worth, TX: Harcourt Brace.

Gibson, R. L., & Mitchell, M. H. (1995). *Introduction to counseling and guidance* (4th ed.). Upper Saddle River, NJ: Merrill/Prentice Hall.

Giles, T. R. (1991). Managed mental health care and effective psychotherapy: A step in the right direction. *Journal of Behavior Therapy and Experimental Psychiatry, 14,* 189–196.

Giles, T. R. (1993). *Managed mental health care: A guide for practitioners, employers, and hospital administrators.* Boston: Allyn & Bacon.

Gilliland, B. E., & James, R. K. (1997). *Crisis intervention strategies.* Pacific Grove, CA: Brooks/Cole.

Ginter, E. (1989). Slayers of monster-watermelons found in the mental health patch. *Journal of Mental Health Counseling, 11,* 77–85.

Guterman, J. T. (1994). A social constructionist position for mental health counseling. *Journal of Mental Health Counseling, 16,* 226–244.

Herr, E. L., & Cramer, S. H. (1996). *Career guidance and counseling through the life span: Systematic approaches* (5th ed.). New York: Scott, Foresman.

Hershenson, D. B., Power, P. W., & Waldo, M. (1996). *Community counseling: Contemporary theory and practice.* Boston: Allyn & Bacon.

Hillman, J., & Ventura, M. (1992). *We've had a hundred years of psychotherapy and the world's getting worse.* San Francisco: Harper.

Hollis, J. W., & Wantz, R. A. (1993). *Counselor preparation 1993–1995: Program and personnel* (8th ed.). Muncie, IN: Accelerated Development.

Horney, K. (1939). *New ways in psychoanalysis.* New York: Norton.

Hosie, T. W., West, J. D., & Mackey, J. A. (1993). Employment and roles of counselors in employee assistance programs. *Journal of Counseling & Development, 71,* 355–359.

Isaacson, L. E., & Brown, D. (1997). *Career information in counseling and career development.* Boston: Allyn & Bacon.

Kendrick, R., Chander, J., & Hatcher, W. (1994). Job demands, stressors, and the school counselor. *School Counselor, 41,* 365–369.

Levy, D. (1971). Beginnings of the child guidance movement. In M. Levitt & B. Rubenstein (Eds.), *The mental health field: A critical appraisal* (pp. 32–39). Detroit, MI: Wayne State University Press.

Lewis, J. A., & Lewis, M. D. (1986). *Counseling programs for employees in the workplace.* Pacific Grove, CA: Brooks/Cole.

Masi, D. A., & Bowler, M. H. (1988). Managing mental health benefits: The changing role of the EAP. *Compensation and Benefits Management, 4,* 129–132.

May, K. M. (1992). Referrals to employee assistance programs: A pilot analogue study of expectations about counseling. *Journal of Mental Health Counseling, 14,* 208–244.

Mone, L. C. (1994). Managed care cost effectiveness: Fantasy or reality? *International Journal of Group Psychotherapy, 44,* 437–446.

Peer, G. G. (1985). The status of secondary school guidance: A national survey. *School Counselor, 32,* 181–189.

Rogers, C. R. (1939). *The clinical treatment of the problem child.* New York: Houghton Mifflin.

Rogers, C. R. (1942). *Counseling and psychotherapy.* Boston: Houghton Mifflin.

Steenbarger, B. N. (1990). Toward a developmental understanding of the counseling specialty: Lessons from our students. *Journal of Counseling & Development, 68,* 434–437.

Super, D. E. (1955). Transition: From vocational guidance to counseling psychology. *Journal of Counseling Psychology, 2,* 3–9.

Thompson, C. L., & Rudolph, L. B. (1992). *Counseling children.* Pacific Grove, CA: Brooks/Cole.

U.S. Department of Labor. (1994–1995). *Occupational outlook handbook.* Washington, DC: Government Printing Office.

Whitaker, L. C. (1994). Managed care: Who cares about psychotherapy? *Journal of College Student Psychotherapy, 9,* 7–17.

Wiggins, J. D., & Moody, A. H. (1987). Student evaluations of counseling programs: An added dimension. *School Counselor, 34,* 353–361.

Wylie, M. S. (1994). Endangered species. *Family Therapy Networker, 18,* 20–28.

Young, J. L., & Griffith, E. E. H. (1989). The development and practice of pastoral counseling. *Hospital and Community Psychiatry, 40,* 271–276.

2 A Historical Perspective

⏚ 1900–1920: THE BEGINNINGS OF COUNSELING

Vocational Counseling and Guidance

In 1908, Frank Parsons opened a vocational bureau, the first of its kind, to offer counseling help to those looking for work. It was more than just a placement center that listed job openings. Unusual for his time, Parsons believed that persons have the right to choose their own vocations rather than, say, follow their fathers' lines of work, assisting on the farm or in the factory. He implemented this idea by creating the role of *vocational counselor.* He countered the prevailing authoritarian society that told young people what to do by listening to what young persons (generally, adolescent boys) had to say about themselves (Parsons, 1909). His belief in the value of listening to their desires and feelings regarding what they wanted to do vocationally in life was a forerunner of what was to become the essential feature of counseling.

In helping the client self-explore, Parsons developed a unique methodology—that of a self-inventory, perhaps the first "questionnaire" of its kind. Comprehensive in scope, it probed a person's interests, aptitudes, limitations, moral character, appearance, bodily characteristics, motivations, and disposition. It was a take-home survey in which the applicant could solicit help from family, friends, and teachers (Parsons, 1909). By today's standards, it was primitive and unwieldy: The many pages of questions would take hours, if not days, to complete. Questions were simplistic; for example, applicants were asked to mark whether they were honest or dishonest, bold or bashful, sensible or foolish. Interpretation of overall responses was time-consuming and difficult.

But Parsons' concept that a self-survey could be useful in matching one's characteristics to a suitable vocation was unique. Moreover, he believed in the importance of client-counselor interaction; together, they interpreted results of the self-survey, going over consistencies and inconsistencies of responses and working together to look for meaningful patterns. Through such interaction, they determined the client's appropriate vocation.

Impressed by Parsons' work, the superintendent of schools in Boston designated 117 teachers as vocational counselors in Boston's elementary and secondary schools. By 1910, approximately 30 cities had programs in vocational planning and job placement. Training in vocational counseling began at Harvard University in 1911. In 1913, the National Vocational Guidance Association was founded (Brewer, 1942).

Parsons and others used the terms *counseling* and *guidance* synonymously, and both methods—counselor-client interaction and advice giver—were used. But after his death in 1909 and after World War I, interest in this method of self-exploration virtually disappeared and was replaced by occupational information centers, a move supported by funds from the federal government through the 1917 Smith-Hughes Act, funds primarily for developing vocational guidance in schools.

The Psychometric Influence

During World War I, the first group standardized tests were developed when the U.S. Army asked psychologists to develop assessment devices to screen out emotionally and intellectually unfit draftees, to place draftees in appropriate jobs, and to select qualified persons for officer training. Psychologists' efforts led to the development of verbal and nonverbal group intelligence tests (the Army Alpha and Beta) and to Woodworth's Personal Data Sheet. Group testing and group assessment proliferated and became a significant force in the growth and direction of applied psychological testing and vocational counseling and guidance (Osipow & Fitzgerald, 1996).

College Services

Vocational guidance centers had not yet developed on college campuses. Some colleges, however, developed psychological clinics to test children who were having difficulties in public school. The first psychological clinic was developed by Lightner Witmer in 1896 at the University of Pennsylvania primarily to diagnose and treat children with learning and behavioral problems. School personnel used this service when their students were experiencing academic, behavioral, or social problems. Other universities opened similar clinics.

The Beginning of Community Clinics

The first psychiatric clinic was established in Chicago in 1908 by Freudian psychiatrist William Healy. It was called the Juvenile Psychopathic Institute, and services were designed to work with juvenile delinquents. The creation of the institute has a remarkable history. Well-to-do philanthropist Ms. Dunner was appalled by the juvenile crime rate in Chicago. Contrary to prevailing opinion, she believed that social conditions were at the root of the problem. She was part of a group of socially concerned women noted for their philanthropic endeavors throughout Chicago, including Jane Addams and her development of Hull House. In search for a director of the institute, Ms. Dunner insisted on finding a physician who was foremost in his profession on the latest theories of modern psychology (Levy, 1971). Fellow supporter Professor George Mead, head of the Department of Philosophy at the University of Chicago, consulted with none other than philosopher William James and psychiatrist Adolf Meyer. They recommended psychiatrist William Healy, who was familiar with Freudian methods of psychoanalysis. Sigmund Freud was hardly known in the United States, and psychoanalysis was not designed for children. Hiring Healy was a bold, innovative step. Treatment was an interdisciplinary approach consisting of a psychiatrist, a psychologist who conducted assessments, and a social worker. In 1917, the Chicago clinic was taken over by the state of Illinois. Healy left for Boston, where he established a similar clinic (Levy, 1971).

·❀ 1920–1940: THE EARLY YEARS

The field of psychometry blossomed and flourished from 1920 to 1940, and along with it emerged psychologists whose primary tasks were developing, administering, and interpreting tests. During the 1920s, the field of educational guidance developed and expanded in schools, but during the 1930s, because of the Depression, the field of vocational guidance expanded in social agencies to serve the needs of large numbers of displaced adults. At the college level, in the 1930s, E. G. Williamson (1939) developed what he called *clinical counseling*, based primarily on techniques of testing and diagnosis. A separate movement emerged as well during the 1930s, a small but significant group of clinical psychologists who practiced relationship therapy in child guidance clinics, a practice that influenced Carl Rogers at this time, from which he was to develop his client-centered therapy.

Growth of the Testing Movement

During this period, the study of individual differences preoccupied applied psychologists throughout the country. At universities and other research centers, psychologists devoted themselves to developing all kinds of tests and measurements. Psychologists who administered and interpreted the tests were called *psychometrists*. Unlike today, psychologists generally did not practice therapy (Gelso & Fretz, 1992).

Tests were developed to cover all aspects of human behavior—intelligence, personality, various aptitudes, and achievement. Arthur Otis, for example, in 1922, developed the Otis Group Intelligence Scale; E. K. Strong, in 1927, published the Strong Vocational Interest Blank; Clark Hull, in 1928, issued his landmark text describing aptitude testing; and Starke Hathaway developed the Minnesota Multiphase Personality Inventory during the 1930s and published it in 1941.

The use of standardized tests took hold in psychological, sociological, educational, and vocational guidance services. Business and industry as well used tests as a means to screen applicants for jobs.

Educational Guidance in Schools

Progressive education, which was introduced into schools in the 1920s by philosopher John Dewey, exerted a strong influence on school curricula (Woodring, 1953). Proponents believed that schools had the responsibility not only to guide children in their personal, social, and moral development but also to modify the school environment for optimal learning. Insisting that all schoolchildren should receive a well-rounded education, they emphasized broadening school curricula to include personal and social development, as well as academic knowledge and vocational skills.

Leading educator John Brewer, in his landmark book *Education as Guidance* (1932), claimed that guidance and education were synonymous. He proposed that the objective of education is to develop skills in living. Schools should guide young people in individual and cooperative activities, and learning should include citizenship, recreation, personal well-being, and moral development. Teachers were considered guidance specialists who should incorporate teaching life skills into their subject matter. Teachers were to help students "relate themselves to the life of the local community and to that of the nation and the world" (Strang, 1953, p. 143).

Vocational Guidance

During the 1920s, most vocational guidance centers were incorporated into school districts and faded from the community as separate agencies. They re-emerged in the community during the Depression in the 1930s, however, to assist the large numbers of unemployed. According to Super (1942), schools had proved inadequate settings for vocational guidance because they "were unable to see beyond the narrow confines of the school" (p. 260). He goes on:

> With the 1930s new trends somewhat reversed the situation, giving the dominant role to nonschool guidance workers. Social agencies, familiar with the problems of the unemployed and frequently closer to the employer than the schools, seemed to be in the key situation for vocational guidance. . . . Social agencies . . . brought a new emphasis into the literature of vocational guidance, an emphasis on community responsibility and organization. (pp. 260–261)

College Counseling

In 1939, E. G. Williamson published *How to Counsel Students: A Manual of Techniques for Clinical Counselors,* a manual that contained the first theory developed specifically for counseling. This book was an outcome of his work at the University of Minnesota's student counseling center, the first of its kind in the country, a center in which students were given educational and vocational counseling. Williamson's clinical counseling theory, a diagnostic prescriptive approach, was based on the assumption that personality consists of measurable traits that can be related to occupational choice and success. His term *clinical counseling* paralleled the diagnostic approach that prevailed at this time among clinical psychologists, social workers, and guidance specialists.

The popularity of Williamson's theory of clinical counseling as applied to vocational counseling can be attributed, in part, to the testing movement that was flourishing in social agencies and schools.

Child Guidance Clinics and the Beginnings of Therapy

In 1921, Child Guidance Demonstration Clinics were established in several strategic cities as a result of increased public interest in the mental health of children. As in Healy's earlier clinics, an interdisciplinary team of psychiatrists, psychologists, and social workers worked with children and parents (Goldenberg & Goldenberg, 1991; Levy, 1971). The team's major task was the testing and diagnosis of children with learning problems and of adults with symptoms of mental illness (Hershenson, Power, & Waldo, 1996). Treatment was primarily that of modifying or changing the environment (e.g., placing the child in a foster home) or psychoanalysis by psychiatrists.

This diagnostic and prescriptive model had a few exceptions. Some child guidance clinics practiced relationship therapy as developed by psychiatrist Otto Rank (1936). Others, such as psychiatrist Frederick Allen and social worker Jessie Taft, popularized this approach (Rogers, 1939, 1942). Some clinics also used play therapy as practiced by child therapists such as Fredrick Allen, Dorothy Baruch, Melanie Klein, and David Levy (Rogers, 1939, 1942). This trend in the use of relationship therapy was given impetus by changes in psychoanalytic treatment made by dissenters of Freud—Alfred Adler and Karen Horney.

Carl Rogers (1939), as a clinical psychologist at a child guidance clinic in Rochester, New York, was also practicing one of the new therapies called *expressive therapy* with children during the 1930s. Although his initial period of training and practice was primarily psychometry, as was customary then for clinical psychologists, he developed a strong interest in the new relationship therapies developed by Otto Rank and his followers (Rogers, 1939, 1942). This, in turn, influenced his theory of non-directive and client-centered counseling, which he was to present in the following decade.

❖ 1940–1960: EMERGENCE OF PROFESSIONAL COUNSELING

A new direction developed in counseling and guidance in the 1940s, one that broke away from the diagnostic prescription approach that had dominated both educational and vocational guidance on the one hand and clinical treatment centers on the other.

The major shift came after Carl Rogers published *Counseling and Psychotherapy* (1942), in which he proposed his non-directive, client-centered therapy. A clinical psychologist with many years of experience working in child guidance clinics in the 1930s, Rogers, as described earlier, was influenced by Rank, Taft, Allen, and others who practiced a process theory of therapy in which the client develops primarily through an evolving relationship with the counselor (Rogers, 1939, 1942). Out of this experience, Rogers developed an approach he called *non-directive* to counteract the directive, diagnostic prescriptive approach prevalent among practitioners at clinical, educational, and vocational guidance clinics. He later changed the term *non-directive* to *client-centered* (1951; see also chap. 5).

In his 1942 publication, Rogers laid out a method of counseling that has influenced counseling and therapy ever since. Counteracting prevailing practice, he claimed that the focus must be on the individual, rather than on the problem, and that counseling is a process that involves developing a trust relationship with the client. Clients learn by exploring their feelings and reflecting on and developing their own insights.

In his early training and practice, Rogers, like other clinical psychologists, had been steeped in testing and diagnosis. But while practicing in this mode, he also indicated his doubts about relying only on testing as a way of diagnosing. Diagnostic testing, he warned, indicates the symptom but never the cause behind it (Rogers, 1939).

Rogers' approach differed significantly from Williamson's traditional model of guidance or clinical counseling, described earlier. Williamson's method was to gather data, evaluate, and diagnose the problem first, and then to "treat" or "counsel" the client (McDaniel, 1956; Nugent, 1981). In later years, Williamson's system came to be known colloquially as the "test 'em and tell 'em" method (Romano & Skovolt, 1998, p. 463). Debates over the relative merits of Williamson's diagnostic prescriptive method versus the Rogerian client-centered approach continued throughout this period. As Zunker (1994) comments: "The center of attention shifted to the client and counseling techniques, with less emphasis given to testing, cumulative records, and the counselor as an authority figure" (p. 10).

While on the one hand Rogers identified with the field of psychology and developed his theory of psychotherapy (see chap. 5), on the other hand his work became very popular and influential in educational and vocational guidance settings. Rogerian theory was readily applicable for counseling normal concerns of persons.

Other influences also contributed to a shift in counseling and therapeutic practice at this time. As a result of the Nazi dictatorship, the Holocaust, and the war, many prominent European existentialists and neo-Freudian, psychosocial analysts immigrated to the United States—Otto Rank, Alfred Adler, Karen Horney, Erich Fromm, Erik Erikson, Victor Frankl. Their approaches counteracted the prevailing American scientific assessment of individual differences, trait factor theory of personality, behaviorism, and classical Freudian psychoanalysis. Their presence in America influenced such leading American psychological theorists as Rollo May, Abraham Maslow, and Carl Rogers.

Coping with Postwar Years

World War II and its immediate aftermath greatly influenced the beginning of professional counseling as we know it today. After the war, the general public and the U.S. government recognized that the millions of returning servicemen needed assistance in coping with the uncertainties during the transition of adjusting to civilian life. Congress, under the G.I. Bill of Rights and through the Veterans Administration (VA), offered full tuition and substantial stipends to returning veterans for the time equal to the months they served in the military.

Emergence of VA College Counseling Centers

The VA provided funding for free vocational counseling for all veterans. Counseling centers sprang up on major campuses, and trained counselors were suddenly needed to fill job openings. These developments supported and promoted the need to provide counseling for normal concerns of people, the aim that is central to counseling theory and practice today.

Origins of Counseling Psychology and Counselor Training Programs

After World War II, the VA initiated and funded university training programs for doctoral degrees in both counseling psychology and clinical psychology. Thus, a new profession termed *counseling psychology* was established (Tolbert, 1982; Whiteley, 1984). Whereas clinical psychologists were trained to diagnose and treat individuals with chronic emotional disorders, counseling psychologists focused on conflicts experienced by normal persons. As Gelso and Fretz (1992) point out, "Counseling psychology was a profession waiting to happen" (p. 37).

Until this time, counseling was virtually synonymous with guidance—educational and vocational guidance in schools and colleges, and vocational guidance in social agencies. Guidance was also closely associated with the use of tests that measured individual differences, assessing various aspects of a person's characteristics. Once a client's personality, intelligence, aptitude, and interests were measured, the guidance counselor typically "guided" the client into a suitable school curriculum and vocation.

Psychological theories focused predominantly on assessing individual differences and personality traits with little regard for developmental processes. The upheavals of the war, however, convinced professionals that social traumas and anxieties during transitional periods influenced and shaped the individual.

Vocational guidance professor Donald Super (1955) readily embraced the new concepts of counseling psychology and promoted the transition from vocational guidance to counseling psychology. When I enrolled in the master's program in vocational counseling at T. C. Columbia University in 1946, Super had just become the director of the program. At this pivotal time in the development of the counseling profession, Super saw himself as part of a new direction for the field of counseling, one that combined vocational assessment, human development theory, social-cultural factors, and the early Rogerian client-centered approach. A long-time specialist in assessment, Super acknowledged the need to shift away from testing as the primary task of the counselor (1949). While I was at Columbia, Super lectured on how the Rogerian client-centered approach could be applied when selecting and interpreting tests in vocational counseling, lectures that were soon to be published in his 1949 text.

Super defined the distinction between counseling psychology and vocational guidance in his article "Transition From Vocational Guidance to Counseling Psychology" (1955). Citing the influence of Rogers' 1942 book, he said that "growth of interest in psychotherapeutic procedures . . . became even greater than interest in psychometrics. . . . [O]ne counsels *people* rather than *problems*" (p. 4). Emphasizing the danger of misusing tests, he made valuable comments regarding how counselors should use and interpret them properly, warning also that counselors shouldn't over-rely on them.

A proponent of one of the earliest human development theories based on the relatively unknown German scholar Charlotte Buehler, Super (1942) expanded the idea of human development into the vocational field. Vocational development was a lifetime process, he said. Different stages have been studied per se, but "with a few important exceptions [Charlotte Buehler and E. K. Strong] no attention has been paid to persons as they pass from one stage to another" (p. 135).

Super (1955) also noted the significant distinction between counseling psychology and clinical psychology:

> *Clinical psychology* has typically been concerned with diagnosing the nature and extent of *psychopathology,* with the abnormalities even of normal persons. . . . *Counseling psychology* on the contrary, concerns itself . . . with . . . the normalities even of abnormal persons, with locating and developing personal and social resources and adaptive tendencies so that the individual can be assisted in making more effective use of them. (p. 5)

Another leading educator who promoted the field of counseling psychology was Gilbert Wrenn (1962), from the University of Minnesota. While Super was influential in the 1950s in shifting vocational guidance over to counseling psychology, Wrenn, whose expertise was in the schools, was instrumental in distinguishing school counseling from the old educational guidance models. Like Super, Wrenn opposed the diagnostic prescriptive model of guidance and supported the new developmental, psychosocial, and self-theories of human behavior promoted by Alfred Adler, Abraham Maslow, and Carl Rogers.

Doctoral Training Programs Emerge for Counseling and Clinical Psychologists

Spurred by VA funding, both counseling and clinical psychology training programs were set up in the early 1950s at universities throughout the country. The first task for new counseling programs was to find faculty with sufficient background to do the training. Thus, most of the newly emerging counseling psychologists were to become the future faculty in counseling programs, the practicing counselors in college counseling centers, and the supervisors of the future master's-level counselors-in-training.

The majority of counseling psychology programs were established in departments of education or educational psychology. Psychology departments, which trained primarily clinical psychologists, tended to specialize in individual differences and testing, or Freudian psychoanalytic approaches, or they were experimentally and behavioristically oriented. Most psychology departments tended to resist the new humanistic, phenomenological, and psychosocial theories of psychology.

Development of Professional Associations

In response to the shift in emphasis away from guidance and toward counseling psychology, and as a result of the VA creating and funding programs for the new field of counseling psychology, Division 17 of the American Psychological Association (APA) in 1953 changed its name from the Division of Counseling and Guidance to the Division of Counseling Psychology (Woody, Hansen, & Rossberg, 1989). Leaders of APA Division 17 were university professors, such as Donald Super and Gilbert Wrenn, "concerned with dealing with the circumstances of normal development in the personal and vocational areas and factors that interfered with that development" (Woody et al., 1989, p. 8).

Professional associations had become very important to the development of counseling at this time because the newly formed, fledgling profession was in need of a unifying force that could define its role, nurture its development, and set and implement standards of training.

Because APA Division 17 was only for psychologists with doctorates, it excluded the bulk of counselors. Recognizing this problem, many leaders, such as Gilbert Wrenn, who helped form APA Division 17, were also instrumental in forming the American Personnel and Guidance Association (APGA) (George & Cristiani, 1986).

APGA, in turn, became an umbrella organization for several existing independent associations (e.g. National Vocational Guidance Association [NVGA], American College Personnel Association [ACPA]). New subassociations soon formed to address the specific concerns of counselors: the American School Counselors Association (ASCA) and the American Rehabilitation Counseling Association (ARCA). Moreover, to break away from their identity with guidance, counselor educators changed the name of their group from the Association of Guidance Supervisors and Counselor Trainers to the Association for Counselor Education and Supervision (ACES).

Counseling Practice: The Struggle to Clarify and Implement Counselor Role

College Counseling

Because of the success of the VA vocational counseling centers on major college campuses, college administrators converted VA centers (which were terminated in the early 1950s) to student counseling centers; most remaining college campuses soon opened similar counseling centers.

College counseling centers were the ideal places for counselors to incorporate into practice the new developmental, process-oriented, self theories, such as those espoused by Rogers and Maslow, existentialist May, and psychodynamic theorists such as Adler and Horney. College students represented the more motivated, goal-oriented segment of the population, all of whom were struggling with normal developmental conflicts.

At the University of California–Berkeley and Stanford University college counseling centers where I was a counselor from 1947 to 1953, we practiced the new counseling approaches. Most of our staff were clinical psychologists eager to abandon the old pathological model of diagnosis and treatment and classical Freudianism and to try the new psychosocial, developmental, process-oriented therapies. They were eager to work with persons with normal situational conflicts, rather than with patients with chronic mental illness. In our counseling sessions, we combined the humanistic Rogerian client-centered approach and the psychodynamic theories of Alfred Adler and Karen Horney. The staff welcomed my developmentally oriented, vocational-counseling training under Donald Super, and I benefited from their psychosocial analytic backgrounds. As were all new counselors, I was closely supervised for 6 months by director Barbara Kirk. Although none of us considered ourselves Rogerian, we were influenced by Rogers' views about the counseling process and counseling relationship, avoiding, for instance, making analytic interpretations of client behavior. Weekly case conferences served as an ongoing training laboratory for us. Sharing cases enabled us to learn from each other, to incorporate new counseling theories into practice, as well as to develop insights into how we were relating to our clients. Psychiatrist Leslie Farber (1966), who later became a well-known existentialist, was part of the team, helping with supervised training, participating at weekly case conferences, and serving as consultant to individual staff members. Perceptive and insightful, with his psychodynamic background, he could sense the underlying dynamics in the counseling relationship.

School Counseling

Spurred by the success of counseling in colleges, many professionals recognized that students in high schools could also benefit from counseling assistance in their academic endeavors and goals. At Pleasant Hill High School in California, where I was a counselor in the late 1950s, our staff members were well-trained counselors with master's degrees. We developed a program similar to the college counseling programs where I had worked earlier—that is, voluntary, confidential, process-oriented counseling that focused on the client's situational, developmental concerns. This was the counseling role that APGA was to adopt in the early 1960s. Recognition of the need for school counseling was fueled by the turmoil of the postwar years: the population explosion, automation in the job market, changing family patterns, and confusion about values (Wrenn, 1962). Equally important was the impact of the new psychological theories that recognized human developmental stages, the crucial transitional stages that young people, especially adolescents, go through.

The demand for school counseling increased again after the Soviet Union launched *Sputnik,* the first space satellite, in 1957. Concerned that the Soviet Union was ahead of the United States in science, Congress pushed through the National Defense Education Act (NDEA; Woody et al., 1989) to encourage scientific and academic development in schools. Funds were provided to upgrade secondary school counseling programs by training counselors through special short-term counseling and guidance institutes.

As a result, the number of secondary school counselors escalated. As with any crash program, however, the effect on the practice of counseling was mixed. Generally, counselor educators were hampered both by federal regulations that limited the scope of the training programs and by the short-term nature of the training.

Community Services

Whereas professional counseling was spreading rapidly in schools, and college counseling centers were springing up throughout the country, this newly defined counseling service, with the exception of vocational rehabilitation centers, was as yet generally unavailable in communities for adults after they left school. Family work continued in clinics, where social worker–psychiatrist teams treated primarily children with disturbances.

❧ 1960–1980: GROWTH IN PROFESSIONAL COUNSELING

Counseling experienced growing pains during the 1960s and 1970s. It spread so rapidly in schools and colleges that supply could not keep up with demand. Counselors lacked a clear understanding of their role and function and, moreover, lacked adequate training. Concerned leaders, through both APGA and APA Division 17, defined the counselor's unique role and function, and developed training standards.

Even so, counseling reached a crisis in the 1970s, as had schools and society in general, triggered in part by the counterculture and personal growth movements and the rise of conflicting values in all segments of society. Many leaders within the profession took sides over humanism versus behaviorism. Many others claimed that psychological education should replace counseling. Out of this challenge, professional counselors again clarified their unique role and primary function as distinct from educators.

Meanwhile, other therapeutic systems, existentialism, and then family systems and cognitive theories gradually broadened the theoretical base for counselors. The need for counseling spread into the community and, along with it, during the late 1970s, the need to develop a terminal master's degree in community mental health counseling as well as national certification and state licensure to back it up.

Professional Associations Set Standards for School Counselors

Counseling boomed during the late 1950s and 1960s, and growth was primarily in public schools. The number of secondary school counselors escalated from 6,700 in the early 1950s to more than 30,000 in 1965 (Aubrey, 1982). Many guidance educators in the 1950s were beginning to recognize counseling in schools as a unique service distinct from other guidance services (McDaniel, 1956; Mortensen & Schmuller, 1959). Although the new counseling model was accepted into practice in the late 1950s in some schools, such as at Pleasant Hill High School, in California, where I was a counselor, most schools were slow to adapt their services to accommodate the new counselor role.

Concerned about the paucity of trained school counselors and the lack of role definition or training standards, APGA asked Gilbert Wrenn to review current counseling practice in schools throughout the country and to make recommendations. His book *The Counselor in a Changing World* (1962), published by APGA, was the outcome. From his preliminary survey, he reached this sobering conclusion: "When the backgrounds of the 1,200 counselors studied for this report are examined, preparation in some vital areas is sparse in spite of the large proportion having a master's degree" (p. 164).

In his book, Wrenn proposed a blueprint that clearly defined the school counselor's role and function and provided guidelines for training programs. In the preface to Wrenn's book, David Wolfle, chairman of the Advisory Commission on Guidance for American Schools, warned:

> The current reality is that most persons employed as school counselors are inadequately prepared to meet these rigorous standards. They are largely recruited from among persons who originally prepared themselves for one career—for example, teaching history—and who later, on the basis of meager additional training, became "counselors." (p. i)

Wrenn's blueprint was a major departure from the old guidance model. He opposed Williamson's clinical counseling model of assessment, diagnosis, and treatment and was in accord with the new Rogerian model of client-centered counseling. He hoped the term *guidance,* in regards to the counselor, would eventually disappear. The counselor, he said, is a specialist whose role is to counsel students and consult with staff and parents. The counselor role should be nondisciplinarian; moreover, counselor tasks should not include programming, advising, keeping student records, clerical work, or lunchroom duty.

Wrenn was a strong advocate of the psychosocial belief that persons develop psychologically in relation to their environment. He was also a follower of human development theories, especially concerned about adolescent transitional stages and accompanying conflicts and anxieties. His proposal for counselor training included a 2-year graduate program with the major core in psychology so students would learn the new psychosocial, developmental, behavioral, and humanistic theories. The proposal also emphasized that students must have adequate and well-supervised practicums and internships.

APGA Assesses Counselor Role

Wrenn's blueprint was revolutionary. As he indicated in his preface, school systems weren't prepared to meet these standards. To obtain a more complete assessment from all school professionals, APGA set up three regional task forces representing APGA, ACES, and ASCA, respectively. From these grassroots task forces and as a follow-up to Wrenn's 1960 blueprint, APGA published a set of guidelines for counselors by Loughary, Stripling, and Fitzgerald (1965) called *Counseling: A Growing Profession.* All statements basically agreed with Wrenn's blueprint.

Emphasizing the importance of the report, particularly regarding training programs, chairman of the APGA task force, Robert Stoughton (1965), said:

> In 1960 there were well over 200 institutions in the United States offering graduate level preparation in counseling. Many of these programs were staffed by a single counselor educator, perhaps supplemented by a part-time staff. In some instances there was no full-

time staff member who had major professional competence in the field of counseling and personnel. A few courses put together in one way or another seemed to justify some colleges to say that they had counselor education programs. (p. 3)

Although the majority of APGA, ACES, and ASCA members supported the task force policy statements, some expressed strong doubts that these role definitions and training standards were applicable or workable in school settings. Others were concerned that most practicing counselors were not prepared to meet these standards.

But despite doubts and objections, Fitzgerald (1965) pointed out: "For the first time there is a statement on the Role and Function of the School Counselor that depicts a consensus from the American School Counselor Association" (p. 41). This statement, he said, could help counselor educators develop appropriate, accredited graduate programs, encourage government agencies to improve counselor certification standards, and stimulate counselors to educate school administrators regarding the professional responsibilities of school counselors.

APGA, in 1961, also published a code of ethics that outlined guidelines for counselors' professional responsibilities to clients. Included was the stipulation that the counseling relationship be voluntary and confidential.

Professional journals were another means of defining for the profession the counselor's unique role. In my early publications (Nugent, 1962, 1966, 1969), for instance, I argued that a counselor was not a guidance specialist, a disciplinarian, a teacher, or an administrator, but rather someone who filled a special role—that of providing voluntary and confidential counseling for students.

Professional association members throughout the country struggled to get state certification of school counselors. In the majority of states, however, certification standards fell short of the criteria recommended by APGA and ASCA. Thus, in many school districts, insufficiently trained persons were assigned counseling jobs.

Counseling Centers Spread on College Campuses

During the 1960s, increasing numbers of universities offered free counseling services to students who were experiencing problems that interfered with their academic work.

As director of Western Washington University's counseling center, I founded a program in 1962 modeled after my experience as a counselor at the UC–Berkeley and Stanford University counseling centers—a program in which counseling was voluntary and confidential, separated from the college administrative and diagnostic testing center. Our program also included weekly case conferences, a practice vital to my earlier counseling experiences. Our consulting psychiatrist, Buell Kingsley, was eager to work with normally functioning clients and to practice the new model of therapy that de-emphasized diagnosis and avoided pathologizing client behavior. His partiality to the new family systems theories offset our staff members who were oriented to behaviorism and humanism. The staff benefited from his attention to the underlying psychodynamics going on between counselor and client during the counseling process. At the same time, Kingsley appreciated learning from the staff's focus on working with client strengths and our emphasis on client situational, developmental concerns.

At annual national meetings of counseling center directors at that time, however, directors were generally confused about the purpose of the college counseling center and the role of the counselor. Concerned about this, another colleague, Nick Pareis, and I conducted a national survey of college counseling centers in 1965 regarding prevailing policies and practices of centers (Nugent & Pareis, 1968). The responses of more than 450 college counseling center directors confirmed that many centers were not complying with either APGA or APA Division 17 statements about the voluntary and confidential nature of counseling and the role and purpose of counselors: 40% of these centers did not maintain complete confidentiality of counseling records, 65% accepted forced referrals, and 40% were allied with university testing services under the office of the Dean of Students, an alignment that contradicts the policy of confidentiality in counseling and confuses students.

In response to this confusion in the early 1970s, APA Division 17 sponsored a task force chaired by my former boss, UC–Berkeley Counseling Center Director Barbara Kirk, to develop guidelines for university and college counseling centers (Kirk et al., 1971). These guidelines reaffirmed that voluntary, confidential counseling was the primary function of counselors.

In the late 1960s and early 1970s, the counterculture movement had its impact on counseling centers. At the college counseling centers where confidentiality was guaranteed, students overwhelmed by conflicting values regarding the draft, free love, or turmoil brought on by encounter groups flocked to the centers for help.

Counseling Theories Multiply in the 1960s and 1970s

The profession of counseling showed a remarkable ability to adapt to the many new theoretical, therapeutic approaches. Humanistic psychology and therapies—Maslow's theory of self-actualizing, Rogerian client-centered or person-centered approach, Gestalt therapy—spread rapidly, becoming a strong contender to the prevailing psychoanalytic and behavioristic schools of psychology. The phrase *third force in psychology* was used to describe humanism as distinct from behaviorism and psychoanalysis.

Out of this grew what came to be known as the *human potential movement.* The emphasis on personal growth became very popular and accessible with the emergence of group counseling. Encounter groups, promoted by Rogers (1970), and sensitivity training groups generated intense experiential atmospheres that released pent-up emotions, methods that were intended to raise consciousness.

At the same time, behavioristic techniques that had proved useful in treating schizophrenics, delinquents, and hyperactive persons were being used with normally functioning persons who wanted to change certain undesirable behavioral patterns. Smoking, overeating, nail biting, and various phobias became suitable concerns for behaviorally oriented counseling. John Krumboltz (1966) edited a book on behavioral counseling with the significant title *Revolution in Counseling.*

Opposing views between humanists and behaviorists about human nature prompted Carl Rogers and B. F. Skinner to hold debates, with Rogers championing the belief in the individual's inner potential to develop and grow, and Skinner arguing that human beings learn only by reacting to outer stimuli. Leaders in the field took sides, and in so doing distinctions within the camps blurred. Gilbert Wrenn (1973), allying with the Rogerian camp, claimed, for example, that humanists and the existentialists were the same.

Existential psychology (see chap. 5) made a strong impact on the profession during the 1960s and 1970s (Wrenn, 1973). Leading existential psychoanalysts Rollo May and Irvin Yalom (1995), however, are careful to clarify distinctions between existentialism and Rogerian humanism. When May was part of a panel of 12 judges evaluating client-centered therapy at the University of Wisconsin, he sharply criticized the Rogerian client-centered approach, pointing out that the so-called permissiveness of the therapist or counselor during the session was controlling. May and Yalom concluded that this style of therapy "is not fully existential in that it does not confront the patient directly and firmly" (p. 269).

Although very influential during the 1960s and 1970s, existential psychology was essentially philosophical and not readily applicable to practice for most counselors and therapists. Rogers' client-centered counseling and Skinner's behaviorism, in contrast, had been developed into therapeutic systems that could be used by practitioners. But both approaches were limited. They agreed only in their rejection of the third camp, psychoanalytic, whose followers were also generally lumped under one person—-Sigmund Freud. At that time, psychoanalytic dissenters of Freud were virtually ignored—psychosocial analysts Alfred Adler, Erich Fromm, Karen Horney, Otto Rank, Rollo May, Erik Erikson, not to mention Carl Jung.

My clinical training and counseling experience, based on a blend of Adler and Horney's psychosocial analytic, Rogerian client-centered, and Super's vocational developmental approaches, kept me from being overly swayed either by the behaviorists or by the human potential movement and Rogerian-promoted encounter groups. Even so, their influence made such an impact on counseling practice that for many years I lost sight of the value of psychodynamic and psychosocial theories.

In the meantime, the polarized and narrow Rogerian and Skinnerian views were quietly being offset by other forces unbeknown to most in the counseling and therapy professions. These forces soon would soften the extreme views and add substantially to the theoretical and practical base for effective counseling and therapy.

Cognitive theories, which focus on a person's thoughts and perceptions that influence how one thinks and acts, soon became influential in psychology. The first to appear at this time was Albert Ellis's rational-emotive therapy (1973). Although he called his book *Humanistic Psychotherapy,* he added a new dimension to humanistic practice by acknowledging that reasoning and emotions are related processes and that one's emotional problems result from illogical or distorted thoughts.

Other developments going on during this period that weren't to influence the counseling and therapy profession until later were psychosocial analyst Erik Erikson's life-span developmental theory; George Kelly's personal construct therapy; Alfred Adler's work with families; family systems theories; and analytical psychology of Carl Jung and his followers.

Psychological Education Emerges

Throughout the 1970s, the counseling profession continued to be unprepared to meet the ongoing counseling boom in schools and colleges. Without enough trained counselors to meet the need, uncertainties arose about counselor effectiveness. Many within the profession who were justifiably unhappy with the quality of both counselor training and counselor practice declared that trained counselors—and all therapists, for that matter—were worse than those with no training at all (Carkhuff, 1972; Rogers, 1973; Szasz, 1971).

In an address presented at the 1972 American Psychological Association (APA) convention, Carl Rogers (1973) said,

> I have slowly come to the conclusion that if we did away with "the expert," "the certified professional," "the licensed psychologist," we might open our profession to a breeze of fresh air, to a surge of creativity, such as it has not known in years. (p. 383)

Many leaders in the field claimed that anyone could be a counselor—teachers, professors, student personnel officers, peers. Impetus in this direction largely came from the human potential movement and the Rogerian approach to human relationships that were in vogue at the time. Rogers' client-centered counseling became person centered (Rogers, 1961). Schools of education responded positively to Rogerian person-centered theory and methods, which Rogers (1951, 1961) claimed could be effective for teachers.

Ivey's interviewing skills (1971) and Carkhuff's relationship skills (1972), based on Rogerian principles, were originally developed for counselor training programs, but they were soon promoted as skills that could be taught to anyone, with the idea that within a short period of time anybody could become a counselor.

Many leading counseling educators published a rash of articles and books supporting the idea of replacing counseling in schools and colleges with psychological education. The old role of the guidance specialist popular in the 1920s and 1930s had emerged once again under a new term: *psychological educators*. Counselors were seen as teaching everyone life skills and relationship skills, rather than as counseling those with personal-social problems.

Concerned about this trend in school and college counseling, I objected, emphasizing that counseling is the counselor's primary role, that psychological education is the counselor's secondary role, and that these two roles and functions must be kept distinct (Nugent, 1981).

Community Counseling Emerges in the 1970s

Although counseling services spread into colleges and schools during the 1950s and 1960s, the need for community counseling lay dormant. But by the 1970s, the popularity of counseling programs in colleges and schools, despite their shortcomings, inevitably led to increasingly felt needs for similar counseling services in the community.

Community mental health had received a boost when Congress passed the Community Mental Health Act of 1963. Federal funds became available to states for constructing community-based mental health programs. The chief characteristic was the centralization in communities of all mental health services, including hospitalization of persons with chronic mental illness and preventive services for the rest of the population, based on a model of "positive mental health" developed by Jahoda (Hershenson et al., 1996; Jahoda, 1958).

At the same time, however, a trend to close state mental hospitals began throughout the country. Federal financing for the comprehensive community mental health programs was gradually decreased, with the idea that communities were supposed to take over the cost. Unfortunately, even with state help, most communities did not have the financial capability to maintain the comprehensive programs proposed by the act. As a result, clinics had to cut staff and programs to treat only clients with chronic mental illness.

As counseling needs increased in the community and state and federal government funds remained tight, nonprofit private organizations emerged, as well as services funded by counties and cities. Crisis centers, drop-in clinics, shelters for battered women, rape relief counseling centers, and centers for runaway youths emerged; these were all run on small budgets and staffed by paraprofessionals and volunteers.

Volunteer help springing up from the grass roots indicated an obvious lack of trained counselors in the community to meet this need. To set up private practice in the community, one had to be a psychologist with a doctorate licensed by the state legislature. Most counseling psychologists, however, became counselor educators or worked in college counseling centers or both; moreover, their research-oriented training was more suitable for academic settings.

As for master's-level psychologists, APA refused to recognize master's degrees as terminal. For this reason, to fill the need for counseling in the community, APGA developed master's-level community and mental health counseling training programs. Along with these trends, I coordinated the development of a master of science (M.S.) mental health counseling program. Our committee succeeded in getting it adopted in 1978 by Western Washington University Psychology Department. Unlike the 1-year master of education (M.Ed.) school counseling program, which we had started in the department 10 years earlier, the 2-year terminal-degree M.S. mental health counseling track was designed for counselors to become licensed practitioners in the community.

Professional Associations Push Licensing

Concerned about unqualified practitioners calling themselves counselors in the community, APGA strongly advocated state licensure for master's degree programs. It developed guidelines in 1976 for licensing of master's degree counselors by state legislation. This packet, called the Licensure Commission Action Packet, was expanded and updated in 1979 and again in 1980. In Washington, several of us established the Washington State Mental Health Counseling Association. After lobbying state legislators for several years, we persuaded them to mandate licensure for professional counselors.

Doctorate psychologists had established licensing laws in some states by the 1970s. Many psychologists started entering private practice because it was no longer necessary that they be supervised by psychiatrists. Psychoactive drugs were being used in mental hospitals to shorten the stays of psychotic patients and were used as well in clinics and in private practices.

THE 1980s: PROFESSIONAL COUNSELING COMES OF AGE

The 1980s witnessed significant changes in counseling and therapy. As counseling in the community increased, the primary focus on the development of professional counseling shifted from school to community. It was gradually being acknowledged that adults of all ages continued to have difficulties adjusting to changes throughout their lives. People of all ages were experiencing increased personal and social stress—drug and alcohol addictions, career changes, increases in divorce rates, job layoffs, midlife crises, homelessness, and unemployment. Vietnam veterans broke silence by expressing in consciousness-raising therapy groups anguish over their war experiences. Their expressed symptoms became known as *posttraumatic stress disorder (PTSD)*.

Counseling was given a substantial boost from the contributions of a wide range of therapeutic approaches. The counseling of the 1970s, dependent primarily on Rogerian client-centered therapy or on behavioristic techniques, had left many counselors disillusioned. The 1980s brought a host of new theories and practices readily adaptable to counseling: Cognitive theories became prominent, with added contributions from Beck (1976) and Meichenbaum (1977). Contributions came from psychodynamic theorists as well: Psychoanalyst Erik Erikson's psychosocial theory of development covering the life span made a strong impact on counseling practice. Family systems theories that had been developed and practiced by psychiatrists and social workers in previous decades now became an important part of counselor training and practice. Out of family systems theory emerged new methods of identifying and working with substance abuse. Another impact on the profession at this time came from gender-based theories and practice raised and developed by the feminist and men's movements and by gays and lesbians. Various ethnic groups began to express counseling needs during this period, each with its own culture-based concerns about traditional methods of counseling and therapy.

Life Span Development Theories Promote Community Counseling

Erik Erikson's psychosocial stages of human development throughout the life span (see chap. 4), a theory he first published in *Childhood and Society* in 1950, made a strong impact on counseling theory and practice during the 1980s. Carl Jung (1931/1962) was the first to present a theory of developmental stages throughout life. Charlotte Buehler, in the 1930s (Buehler & Massarik, 1968), expanded on Jung's ideas. As indicated earlier, vocational counselor educator Donald Super (1942) picked up on her theory and during the 1940s created a developmental model of career stages throughout the life span (see chap. 4).

During the 1980s, counseling theorists and practitioners reaffirmed that human development theory was central to the definition of counseling and to counseling practice. With the above-mentioned exceptions of Jung, Buehler, and Super, most professionals limited their developmental theories to children and adolescents. Developmental theorists gradually increased their attention to the adult developmental stages through midlife, largely through the work of Levinson (1978) and Gould (1978).

Cognitive Therapies Expand

As Albert Ellis's rational-emotive therapy grew in popularity, other cognitive therapies emerged, particularly Beck's (1976), which differed from Ellis's authoritarian approach. While noting the value of the Rogerian client-centered approach, Beck, along with other cognitive therapists, challenged Rogers' view that counselor qualities, congruency, positive regard, and empathy were necessary and sufficient concerns for client change. Beck suggested strategies in which therapists could use the Rogerian client-centered approach while at the same time develop cognitive skills that would enable the client to identify and alter dysfunctional emotions and behaviors (Corey, 1996; see also chap. 5).

Cognitive theories combine well not only with Rogerian theory but also with behaviorism. Recognizing that cognitive theories offered a more comprehensive view of human behavior, behaviorists began developing cognitive-behavioral theories for counseling (Beck, 1976). One of the most successful at this time was Meichenbaum's (1977) cognitive behavior modification (see chap. 5).

Awareness of Pluralism Grows

In the 1980s, awareness of the pluralistic nature of American society increased. Many books and articles on multicultural counseling were published during the 1980s (see chap. 14). McGoldrick, Pearce, and Giordano (1982), for instance, published *Ethnicity and Family Therapy,* in which they describe the need for family counselors to be aware of the special characteristics of each of more than dozen ethnic groups when working with families. Counselors were cautioned to be aware of their potential biases and were encouraged to become aware of differing social and cultural beliefs and special characteristics of each of the varying ethnic groups.

Gender issues related to human development theories arose. Female counselors challenged developmental principles based on male norms. Women presented their own developmental theories that emphasized the importance of the self-in-relation as distinct from the male model of separation and autonomy (see chaps. 4, 5, and 14). At the same time, the men's movement objected to male stereotyping. Increasing numbers of male counselors became aware of the effects of male socialization process on their sense of well-being (see chap. 14).

Counseling in Colleges and Schools

Both college and school counseling benefited from the new multidimensional counseling theories and practices that emerged during this period that became available to counseling training programs and practice—the new developmental theories, cognitive and cognitive-behavioral therapies, family systems theories; methods of dealing with substance abuse; increased availability of gender-based theories and practice regarding special concerns of women, men, gays and lesbians; and diverse multiculture-based theories and practice developed by Blacks, Hispanics, various Asian cultures and other ethnic groups.

College counseling centers were training laboratories for the new therapies and cultural perspectives. At Western Washington University's Counseling Center, we had a fertile mix of cognitive-behaviorists, psychodynamic counselors, humanists, and phenomenologists, many of whom represented different cultural and gender perspectives, including feminist, African American, and Chinese. College counseling centers in the 1980s, however, showed a decrease in career counseling and increases in counseling students with severe personal problems, in time-limited counseling, and in outreach and consultation (Stone & Archer, 1990).

Because of a decrease in funds, both college and school counseling centers curtailed services. College centers, in some cases, began to charge fees for their services. In elementary and secondary public schools, student to counseling staff ratios increased, and fewer districts hired elementary counselors. Baker (1992) comments:

> Basic education and school counseling were bombarded by a range of challenges that . . . demands that the school curriculum be made more rigorous, drug abuse prevented, drug users treated and rehabilitated, exceptional students and culturally different populations integrated and their differences appreciated, dropout rates reduced, children of working parents cared for, students prepared for more complex and challenging jobs, gender equity promoted, and local and state taxes for supporting schools reduced or maintained at existing levels. (p. 10)

Emergence of New Community Counseling Programs

Many new counseling services emerged in the community. The strongest services to appear at this time were the family-oriented counseling and substance abuse programs. Increasing numbers of businesses began to offer employee assistance programs (EAPs) that covered personal and interpersonal stress interfering with job performance. Businesses also offered career development counseling to employees wishing to find more suitable jobs within the company and outplacement counseling to help laid-off employees find new jobs (see chaps. 1 and 19).

Increase in Family-Oriented Therapy

During the 1980s, professional counselors acknowledged the importance of family counseling. Prior to this time, psychiatrists and social workers had for several decades been working with families and as a result developed considerable research and therapy about family dynamics. The new family systems approaches enabled social workers to work effectively with a wide range of dysfunctional families. Counselors made use of this groundbreaking work in developing their own insights and practice in family counseling, theories they gradually incorporated into counselor training and practice (see chap. 10).

Substance Abuse.   In their work with families, counselors became more involved as well in the impact of substance abuse on families. The profession called attention to the dysfunctions of adult children of alcoholics (ACOAs) and developed healing programs. Family counseling was considered an essential component of drug and alcohol treatment. Closer cooperation among professionals, counselors, and Alcoholics Anonymous (AA) developed as well (see chap. 13).

Professional Associations Adapt to Changing Times

Efforts of APGA and ACES in strengthening their professional identities and legal status were given a tremendous boost when APGA and the American Mental Health Counselors Association (AMHCA) agreed in 1979 to merge. AMHCA, which had formed an independent association in 1976, now became APGA's largest division. This merger combined APGA's large membership, financial support, and political clout with AMHCA's enthusiasm and devotion to developing counseling in the community. Their combined strength enabled master's degree programs in mental health counseling to be set up in universities throughout the country.

Consequently, APGA voted in 1983 to change the organization's name to the American Association for Counseling and Development (AACD). This name change reflected the changing emphasis in counseling activity and training, a move away from guidance and personnel, a change that acknowledged counseling the developmental needs of clients. The Association for Adult Aging and Development (AAAD), for instance, was formed as an affiliate of AACD.

While AACD was clarifying the professional identity of the counselor, APA Division 17 was also acknowledging the unique role of the counseling psychologist, an identity whose characteristics are similar to those of AACD. A summary of the general consensus of counseling psychologists at a 1987 annual conference follows:

> . . . attention to promotion of mental health at the level of groups and systems as well as individuals, to development across the entire life span, to adjustment and satisfaction in vocational as well as personal spheres, and to prevention and enhancement as well as remediation. (Rudd, Weissberg, & Gazda, 1988, pp. 425–426)

The difference between APA Division 17 counseling psychology standards and AACD standards lies in their emphasis on academic research. "The training model that has been endorsed by counseling psychologists is the 'scientist practitioner' model" (Gelso & Fretz, 1992, p. 44).

Increase in Licensing, Certification, and Accreditation

The number of states passing licensing laws for master's degree counselors gradually increased during the 1980s. This increase was largely a result of AACD's merger with AMHCA, as well as of the increased cooperation among mental health counselors, social workers, and family counselors, all of whom agreed to work toward omnibus licensing that covered all counseling specialists.

To further upgrade master's degree counselor training programs, the association, then known as APGA, in 1981 established the Council for Accreditation of Counseling and Related Education Programs (CACREP). As an independent arm of APGA, this agency established criteria to evaluate and accredit master's- and doctoral-level counselor training programs.

In 1982, at a time when state legislatures were slow to pass licensing laws for counselors, APGA established the National Board for Certified Counselors (NBCC). This board certified counselors who met standards of training set by the association. Although it did not have the legal status of state licensing, it did help assure consumers that certified counselors met APGA (later known as AACD; now ACA) training standards.

❧ THE 1990s: RECENT TRENDS IN COUNSELING

Professional counselors more or less successfully established themselves during the 1990s in both schools and community. Well-trained master's degree counselors became the norm in many school districts. In the community, increasing numbers of state licensure laws (46) came into effect that allowed mental health counselors to set up private practice. Moreover, many different counseling theories and practices emerged that covered diverse elements of the population, theories that addressed special characteristics of women, men, gays, lesbians, and various cultural and ethnic groups. Comprehensive neighborhood health centers that coordinate counseling, medical, and social services have emerged throughout the country. These centers serve primarily the situational needs of those who are poor or uninsured or both. The overall success of counseling can be attributed to its unique ability to adapt to a wide range of diverse populations in a pluralistic society, including the older population. Counseling recently emerged in the spiritual and religious realm as well.

The development of mental health counselors, along with the development of managed care and insurance benefits, however, gave rise to renewed controversy over the counselor's role and function. Clinical mental health counselors contend that part of the counselor's role and function includes working with pathology, a diagnostic approach that runs counter to what is generally considered the counselor's unique role (see chap. 1). Arguing against the diagnostic, prescriptive illness model are other leading mental health counselors, who reaffirm the long-held definition of counselor as one whose unique therapeutic role is through its process-oriented, evolving, and collaborative relationship with the client (Ginter, 1989).

New theories added substantially to the psychological core of counseling practice. A resurgence of psychoanalytic theories modified for the contemporary world was brought on by rising cases of trauma victims, violence, addictions, and crises. Moreover, many professionals acknowledged *intrapsychic* forces in human nature (Corey, 1996), long denied in the profession because of the dominance of humanistic and behavioristic psychology in the past 50 years. Increasing numbers of counselors also took an interest in post-Jungian studies largely because of the greater numbers of older clients (see chap. 5).

In the cognitive field of psychology, a strong group of counselors and therapists advocated personal construct theory and practice, another field of therapy in practice for the past few decades but until recently not as well received in America as in England and Australia. Personal construct theory claims that humans base their attitudes and behaviors on how they construe events. Each individual, over time, forms her or his unique complex system of constructs. Individuals generally can function well if they are able to perceive their mistakes and thereby modify their system of constructs. They seek therapy when they are unable to avoid repeating debilitating or destructive attitudes and behavioral patterns (G. A. Kelly, 1963; see also chap. 5). According to Guterman (1994), construct therapy works particularly well for the type of above-mentioned, process-oriented counselor-client relationship therapy advocated by Ginter (1989).

Pluralism and the Environment

During the 1990s, professional counselors recognized the depth and complexity of counseling individuals living in a multicultural society (see chap. 14). ACA and APA Division 17 set up task forces and published special editions of journals covering counseling practice with various ethnic groups, women and men, and lesbians and gays.

During the 1990s, multicultural counseling competencies developed by Sue, Arredondo, and McDavis (1992) were adopted by leading counseling professional associations: Association of Multicultural Counseling and Development (AMCD) in 1995; Association for Counselor Education and Supervision (ACES) in 1996; and International Association of Marriage and Family Counseling (IAMFC) in 1997.

Similar to the post-World War II years, increasing numbers of professional counselors once again recognize the deleterious effect of political, environmental, social, and economic conditions on client general well-being. Now taken into account are such social factors as job loss, poor nutrition, abuse, homelessness, and pollution (see chap. 9).

Furthermore, post-traumatic stress, first identified among Vietnam veterans in the late 1970s and 1980s, was acknowledged as a disorder for anyone suffering from trauma—all war veterans, refugees, torture victims, victims of domestic violence. Likewise, the treatment of alcohol and drug addictions spread to the treatment of all addictions or compulsive behaviors—eating disorders, sexual abuse, co-dependency, and gambling (see chap. 19).

Colleges

The 1996 and 1997 annual surveys of college counseling centers showed patterns similar to those of the 1980s—a decrease in career counseling (although separate on-campus career centers are on the rise), an increase in severity of client problems, and an increase in time-limited, brief counseling. New trends for the 1990s were increased cases of alcohol abuse and sexual assault and more demand for crisis intervention. As crisis and severity of student problems escalated, increasing numbers of centers accepted mandatory referrals that required diagnosis and assessment. At the same time, the majority of counselor time has still been spent in individual and group counseling and about one-fourth in consultation and outreach. Outreach programs such as drug and alcohol abuse prevention, multicultural awareness, eating disorder prevention, and stress reduction have continued to be prevalent (Gallagher, 1996, 1997).

School Counseling

As school counselors with master's degrees in counseling became more prevalent in schools, they have been increasingly asked to intervene in student crises resulting from substance abuse, gang violence, family conflicts, and teenage pregnancies. These crises have become so prevalent that counselors unfortunately have often been prevented from serving the normal developmental needs of students (see chap. 17). In many places, school counselors are faced with violent outbreaks in high schools in which students are victims or witnesses. Outbreaks have also occurred in both middle and elementary schools. Because of this, school counselors have had to learn how to intervene in the aftermath of violent outbreaks, as well as to assess violence-prone students and be ready to intervene accordingly.

Increase in Career Counseling and Guidance in Schools

During the 1990s, largely because of federal legislation, school counselors increased their involvement in career counseling and guidance activities, and more school districts hired career counselors to coordinate new programs in career planning. Federal funds also helped school districts improve student career competencies in both technical and academic fields. Eligible students are now able, while still in high school, to attend technical colleges or community college. In some states, such students can obtain an associate of arts (A.A.) degree and a high school diploma simultaneously (see chap. 17).

Community Counseling

The most significant development in professional counseling in the 1990s occurred in community counseling services and in counselor training programs. Managed care programs, with their focus on brief counseling, made a strong impact on community counseling; career counseling centers for adults proliferated, and neighborhood centers offering counseling to the uninsured and the poor emerged throughout the country (see chap. 19). At the same time, increasing numbers of counselor training programs expanded their curricula to include specializations in gerontological counseling and increased course offerings in spiritual counseling.

Managed Care and Brief Counseling and Therapy

As a result of spiraling costs for therapeutic programs, diminishing financial resources, and increased demand for services, managed health care systems such as health maintenance organizations (HMOs) proliferated (Dworkin & Hirsch, 1994). Health providers running these programs emphasized the use of brief counseling and therapy or solution-focused approaches in counseling (Wells, 1994). During the last few years, as these programs mushroomed, increasing numbers of licensed or certified mental health counselors have become eligible to receive insurance payments for services.

Career Counseling in the Community

During the 1990s, increasing numbers of adults changed jobs. Many, for example, were abruptly laid off, or their skills became obsolete. Many new highly technical jobs opened requiring new skills. Consequently, the need for career counseling in the community escalated, and career counseling centers emerged throughout the country. Career counselors offer direct counseling and psychological education workshops and activities in career exploration, career planning, and career management. Career counselor training include master's-level counselors who meet basic requirements plus advanced specialized work in careers.

At the same time, business and industry increased career counseling services as part of their personnel programs that include expanded employee assistance and career counseling services.

Counseling Older Adults

Also in the 1990s, increasing numbers of developmental theorists emphasized that older adults have the potential to continue to grow and develop. This life-span perspective refuted stereotypes about aging that focus on decline and deterioration in one's later years. Counselors started to turn their attention to those 80% of older adults who are self-sufficient and relatively healthy but who nevertheless are experiencing anxiety, depression, or grief resulting from transitions, losses, and sudden changes in life stages (see chap. 15).

Gerontological counseling services increased significantly in the 1990s. "Gerontological counseling is well established as a specialty within the counseling profession" (Myers, 1995, p. 146). Over one-third of counselor training programs include course work in counseling older adults; many of them offer a specialization in gerontological counseling (Myers, 1995). In 1990, NBCC approved a national certification in gerontological counseling as demands for counseling services for older adults increased (see chap. 15).

Spiritual Development

Counseling services sponsored by religious organizations increased steadily (see chap. 1). Services have been offered by both pastoral counselors and mental health counselors in counseling centers sponsored by religious organizations.

Many professional counselors recognized the importance of the client's religious and spiritual concerns and realized the importance of incorporating theories of spiritual development into counseling practice (Ingersoll, 1997; E. W. Kelly, 1995; see also chap. 4). The Association for Spiritual, Ethical, and Religious Values in Counseling (ASERVIC), formerly the Association for Religion and Values in Counseling (ARVIC), is one of the fastest growing divisions in ACA. At a summit conference in 1995, ASER-VIC made recommendations about training in spirituality and counseling. Furthermore, ACES set up a task force on spirituality and counseling. Such professional activities as these on the national level have led to increased awareness and interest among the profession regarding spiritual needs of clients in general (Fukuyama & Sevig, 1997; see also chaps. 1 and 19).

Emerging Comprehensive Health Care Centers and Counseling Liaison Programs

In response to the health needs of the poor and the uninsured, comprehensive health care centers that cover counseling, medical, and social services emerged throughout the country. Typically, they are locally centered, often in ethnic neighborhoods (see chap. 19). Significant for counselors, these centers serve not only the combined needs of persons but also the situational and transitional concerns of persons, such as job adjustment, family conflict, or death of a loved one.

In some areas, counselors from school, college, and community joined forces to work with individuals and families at risk, such as those with problems related to suicide, drug addiction, abuse, and violence.

Professional Issues

The American College Personnel Association (ACPA) voted in 1991 to disengage from the American Association for Counseling and Development (AACD) because ACPA's primary responsibility lies in administrating student affairs, rather than in counseling students. College counselors formed a new affiliate in 1992 called the American College Counseling Association (ACCA). In 1992, AACD voted to change its name to the American Counseling Association (ACA).

In the late 1990s, the AMHCA and ASCA executive boards voted to disaffiliate from ACA. Consequently, in 1998, the ACA Governing Board made a compromise move by changing its structure so as to allow members options: join only their division, join only ACA, or join both. At about the same time, ACA issued a revised definition of counseling that included working with pathology of clients. I comment in chapter 3 on what seems to be unfortunate changes within ACA.

Need for Professional Self-Scrutiny

The practice of counseling and therapy in the 1990s came under critical review by both the general public and professional practitioners. Crises in confidence brought on by such moral issues as those raised over the false-memory controversy motivated the counseling profession to scrutinize and evaluate its members and to assume more responsibility for challenging unethical practices (see chap. 3).

In the meantime, the profession increased its own self- and peer evaluations. States with counseling licensure laws increased the length of supervised experience—as much as 3 years in some states—required for licensure. Increasing numbers of licensed counselors involved in managed care programs have formed group practices with other counselors and mental health providers. Group practice provides counselors opportunities for case conferences and consultations with other professionals, opportunities that are more likely to encourage mutual professional monitoring.

⟡ SUMMARY

Counseling services originated in the early 1900s when Parsons developed a community-based vocational bureau for adolescent boys, a program soon picked up by several school districts. About the same time, the first child guidance clinic opened for juvenile delinquents in response to the effect of adverse social conditions on youths. World War I stimulated the development of group standardized psychological tests for screening U.S. Army recruits.

After World War I, the development of standardized group testing of individual differences became popular for use in schools, colleges, vocational centers, and business and industry. From this emerged the field of psychometry. Educators introduced educational guidance into schools. Vocational guidance expanded into community agencies in the 1930s to serve displaced and unemployed persons. Williamson introduced into schools and colleges a clinical counseling model based on testing for individual differences (traits), diagnosis, and treatment. Counteracting this model, some therapists in child clinics started practicing process-oriented relational therapy, a forerunner of Rogerian client-centered therapy.

During the 1940s, counseling shifted away from the old diagnostic, prescriptive guidance model with the influx of new psychodynamic, developmental, and humanistic theories, including Rogerian client-centered counseling. After World War II, college counseling centers emerged initially to serve the veterans who attended college on VA scholarships. The VA also helped spawn the new profession of counseling psychology, based on a person's situational, developmental concerns.

Whereas college counseling centers flourished during the 1950s, school counseling boomed in the 1960s. Concerned about confusion of counselor role and untrained counselors in schools, leading professionals of APGA, ACES, and ASCA developed policy statements that defined the role of the professional school counselor and proposed training standards that set the model for counseling ever since.

Reacting to the confusion over the role of school counselors in the 1970s and the inadequacy of counselor training programs, many counselor educators urged counselors to become psychological educators. The onslaught of the counterculture movement, the rise of humanistic person-centered counseling and encounter groups, and the opposing rise of behaviorism further contributed to controversies and confusion of values and roles among professional educators.

During the 1980s, as the demand for counseling spread into the community, APGA and AMHCA merged, and with their combined strength promoted the development of master's programs in mental health counseling and lobbied effectively for state licensure of counselors. Erik Erikson's theory of life-span development, new cognitive and family systems theories, and ethnic and gender issues influenced counseling practice. New types of counseling services emerged in the community, including family counseling, employee assistance programs, and substance abuse centers.

Counseling expanded its services in the 1990s to meet the wide range of needs of people in a multicultural society, including career counseling, life skills development, alcohol abuse, sexual assault, and violence. In the community, increasing numbers of counselors joined managed care programs. Counselors offer services to older adults, to those with spiritual concerns, and to those with PTSD. Liaison programs combined school and community counseling services; liaison programs also combined community counseling services with social and medical services in comprehensive neighborhood health centers for the uninsured. New psychodynamic and post-Jungian therapeutic approaches that acknowledge a person's intrapsychic forces emerged to address the general population's increasing stressful and traumatic lives. From the realm of cognitive psychology, personal construct therapy became relevant and applicable to counseling.

·❧ PROJECTS AND ACTIVITIES

1. Trace the influence of federal funding on the development of counseling from its origins to the present. Explore federal programs currently pending in Congress that relate to counseling. How might these programs affect the profession of counseling if they are passed?

2. Describe the differences and similarities in vocational counseling as defined by Parsons (1909) and by Super (1955). How did the notion of vocational development influence the direction of counseling?

3. Super (1955) drew a distinction between clinical and counseling psychologies. Look up preparation programs for each profession at well-known universities. Are the distinctions that Super made consistent with contemporary doctoral and master's degree training programs at these universities?

4. Interview some senior citizens about their perceptions of psychologists, psychiatrists, and counselors. Compare their reactions with those of a group of college students and group of young adults who are not in school.

5. Community mental health clinics originated in the early 1900s. At that time, a psychiatrist, a clinical psychologist, and a social worker constituted the staff in most cases. Their main concerns were working with delinquents and disturbed children and their families. Look up your central regional community clinic, and trace its history in terms of staffing and types of problems handled.

6. Interview a counselor at the college you attend who has been employed there for 15 to 20 years. Ask how the counselor perceives the changes that have occurred and what changes are anticipated.

·❧ REFERENCES

Aubrey, R. F. (1982). A house divided: Guidance and counseling in 20th-century America. *Personnel and Guidance Journal, 61,* 1–8.

Baker, S. B. (1992). *School counseling for the 21st century.* Upper Saddle River, NJ: Merrill/Prentice Hall.

Beck, A. T. (1976). *Cognitive behavior and emotional disorders.* New York: New American Library.

Brewer, J. M. (1932). *Education as guidance: An examination of the possibilities of curriculum in terms of life activ-*

ities, in elementary and secondary schools, and colleges. New York: Macmillan.

Brewer, J. M. (1942). *History of vocational guidance.* New York: Harper & Row.

Buehler, C., & Massarik, F. (Eds.). (1968). *The course of human life.* New York: Springer.

Carkhuff, R. R. (1972). The development of systematic resource models. *Counseling Psychologist, 3,* 4–11.

Corey, G. (1996). *Theory and practice of counseling and psychotherapy* (5th ed.). Pacific Grove, CA: Brooks/Cole.

Dworkin, M., & Hirsch, G. (1994). Responding to managed care: A road map for the therapist. *Psychotherapy in Private Practice, 13,* 1–21.

Ellis, A. (1973). *Humanistic psychotherapy: The rational-emotive approach.* New York: Julian Press.

Erikson, E. (1950). *Childhood and society.* New York: Norton.

Farber, L. (1966). *The ways of the will.* New York: Basic Books.

Fitzgerald, P. W. (1965). The professional role of school counselors. In J. W. Loughary, R. O. Stripling, & P. W. Fitzgerald (Eds.), *Counseling: A growing profession* (pp. 31–41). Washington, DC: American Personnel and Guidance Association.

Fukuyama, M. A., & Sevig, T. D. (1997). Spiritual issues in counseling: A new course. *Counselor Education and Supervision, 36,* 233–244.

Gallagher, R. P. (1996). *National survey of counseling center directors.* Alexandria, VA: International Association of Counseling Services.

Gallagher, R. P. (1997). *National survey of counseling center directors.* Alexandria, VA: International Association of Counseling Services.

Gelso, C. J., & Fretz, B. R. (1992). *Counseling psychology.* Fort Worth, TX: Harcourt Brace.

George, R. L., & Cristiani, T. S. (1986). *Counseling theory and practice* (2nd ed.). Upper Saddle River, NJ: Prentice Hall.

Ginter, E. (1989). Slayers of monster-watermelons found in mental health patch. *Journal of Mental Health Counseling, 11,* 77–85.

Goldenberg, I., & Goldenberg, H. (1991). *Family therapy: An overview* (3rd ed.). Pacific Grove, CA: Brooks/Cole.

Gould, R. I. (1978). *Transformation: Growth and change in adult life.* New York: Simon & Schuster.

Guterman, J. T. (1994). A social constructionist position for mental health counseling. *Journal of Mental Health Counseling, 16,* 226–244.

Hershenson, D. B., Power, P. B., & Waldo, M. (1996). *Community counseling: Contemporary theory and practice.* Boston: Allyn & Bacon.

Hull, C. (1928). *Aptitude testing Yonkers on the Hudson.* New York: World Book.

Ingersoll, R. E. (1997). Teaching a course on counseling and spirituality. *Counselor Education and Supervision, 36,* 224–232.

Ivey, A. E. (1971). *Microcounseling: Innovations in interview training.* Springfield, IL: Charles C Thomas.

Jahoda, M. (1958). *Current concepts of positive mental health.* New York: Basic Books.

Jung, C. (1962). The stages of life. In *Collected works* (pp. 387–403). Princeton, NJ: Princeton University Press. (Original work published 1931)

Kelly, E. W., Jr. (1995). *Spirituality and religion in counseling and psychotherapy: Diversity in theory and practice.* Alexandria, VA: American Counseling Association.

Kelly, G. A. (1963). *A theory of personal constructs.* New York: Norton.

Kirk, B. A., Johnson, A. P., Redfield, J. E., Michel, J., Roster, R. A., & Warman, R. E. (1971). Guidelines for university and college counseling services. *American Psychologist, 26,* 585–589.

Krumboltz, J. D. (Ed.). (1966). *Revolution in counseling.* Boston: Houghton Mifflin.

Levinson, D. (1978). *The seasons of a man's life.* New York: Ballantine Books.

Levy, D. M. (1971). Beginning of the child guidance movement. In M. Levitt & B. Rubenstein (Eds.), *The mental health field: A critical appraisal* (pp. 32–39). Detroit: Wayne State University Press.

Loughary, J. W., Stripling, R. D., & Fitzgerald, P. W. (Eds.). (1965). *Counseling: A growing profession.* Washington, DC: American Personnel and Guidance Association.

May, R., & Yalom, I. (1995). Existential psychotherapy. In R. J. Corsini & D. Wedding (Eds.), *Current psychotherapies* (pp. 262–292). Itasca, IL: F. E. Peacock.

McDaniel, H. B. (1956). *Guidance in the modern school.* New York: Dryden Press.

McGoldrick, M., Pearce, J. K., & Giordano, J. (1982). *Ethnicity and family therapy.* New York: Guilford Press.

Meichenbaum, D. (1977). *Cognitive behavior modification: An integrative approach.* New York: Plenum.

Mortensen, D., & Schmuller, W. (1959). *Guidance in today's schools.* New York: John Wiley & Sons, Inc.

Myers, J. (1995). From "forgotten and ignored" to standards and certification: Gerontological counseling comes of age. *Journal of Counseling & Development, 74,* 143–149.

Nugent, F. A. (1962). Implementing an appropriate counselor image in schools: An educative process. *Counselor Education and Supervision, 2,* 49–51.

Nugent, F. A. (1966). A rationale against teaching experience for school counselors. *School Counselor, 13,* 213–215.

Nugent, F. A. (1969). A framework for appropriate referrals of disciplinary problems to counselors. *School Counselor, 16,* 199–202.

Nugent, F. A. (1981). *Professional counseling: An overview.* Pacific Grove, CA: Brooks/Cole.

Nugent, F. A., & Pareis, E. N. (1968). Survey of present policies and practices in college counseling centers in the United States of America. *Journal of Counseling Psychology, 15,* 94–97.

Osipow, S. H., & Fitzgerald, L. F. (1996). *Theories of career development* (4th ed.). Boston: Allyn & Bacon.

Parsons, F. (1909). *Choosing a vocation.* Boston: Houghton Mifflin.

Rank, O. (1936). *Will therapy.* New York: Knopf.

Rogers, C. R. (1939). *The clinical treatment of the problem child.* Boston: Houghton Mifflin.

Rogers, C. R. (1942). *Counseling and psychotherapy.* Boston: Houghton Mifflin.

Rogers, C. R. (1951). *Client-centered therapy: Its current practice, implications, and theory.* Boston: Houghton Mifflin.

Rogers, C. R. (1961). *On becoming a person.* Boston: Houghton Mifflin.

Rogers, C. R. (1970). *Carl Rogers on encounter groups.* New York: Harper & Row.

Rogers, C. R. (1973). Some new challenges. *American Psychologist, 28,* 379–387.

Romano, J. L., & Skovolt, T. M. (1998). Henry Borow and counseling psychology: A half-century common journey. *Counseling Psychologist, 26,* 448–465.

Rudd, S. S., Weissberg, N., & Gazda, G. M. (1988). Looking to the future: Themes from the Third National Conference for Counseling Psychology. *Counseling Psychologist, 16,* 423–430.

Stone, G. I., & Archer, J., Jr. (1990). College and university counseling centers in the 1990s: Challenges and limits. *Counseling Psychologist, 18,* 539–607.

Stoughton, R. W. (1965). APGA and counselor professionalization. In J. W. Loughary, R. O. Stripling, & P. W. Fitzgerald (Eds.), *Counseling: A growing profession* (pp. 1–17). Washington, DC: American Personnel and Guidance Association.

Strang, R. (1953). *The role of the teacher in personnel work* (4th ed.). New York: Columbia University Teachers College.

Sue, D. W., Arredondo, P., & McDavis, R. J. (1992). Multicultural competencies/standards: A pressing need. *Journal of Counseling & Development, 70,* 477–486.

Super, D. (1942). *The dynamics of vocational adjustment.* New York: Harper Brothers.

Super, D. E. (1949). *Appraising vocational fitness by means of psychological tests.* New York: Harper Brothers.

Super, D. E. (1955). Transition: From vocational guidance to counseling psychology. *Journal of Counseling Psychology, 2,* 3–9.

Szasz, T. (1971). *The myth of mental illness.* New York: Hoeber.

Tolbert, E. L. (1982). *An introduction to guidance* (2nd ed.). Boston: Little, Brown.

Wells, R. A. (1994). *Planned history short-term therapy* (2nd ed.). New York: Free Press.

Whiteley, J. M. (1984). A historical perspective on the development of counseling psychology as a profession. In S. Brown & R. Lent (Eds.), *Handbook of counseling psychology* (pp. 3–55). New York: John Wiley.

Williamson, E. G. (1939). *How to counsel students: A manual of techniques for clinical counselors.* New York: McGraw-Hill.

Woodring, P. (1953). *Let's talk sense about our schools.* New York: Pergamon Press.

Woody, R. H., Hansen, J. C., & Rossberg, R. H. (1989). *Counseling psychology: Strategies and services.* Pacific Grove, CA: Brooks/Cole.

Wrenn, G. (1962). *The counselor in a changing world.* Washington, DC: American Personnel and Guidance Association.

Wrenn, G. (1973). *The world of the contemporary counselor.* Boston: Houghton Mifflin.

Zunker, V. G. (1994). *Career counseling: Applied concepts of life planning.* Pacific Grove, CA: Brooks/Cole.

3 Professional, Ethical, and Legal Issues

✧ WHAT MAKES COUNSELING A PROFESSION?

The profession of counseling is upheld and developed by well-established professional associations—notably, the American Counseling Association (ACA) and American Psychological Association (APA) Division 17. Through these associations, counselors are empowered to define, develop, maintain, clarify, evaluate, and monitor all aspects of the profession, including counselor role, counselor training standards and curriculum, and performance of services according to professional standards. These associations have developed codes of ethics to protect the rights of clients and to monitor the profession; they also abide by client and counselor legal rights and responsibilities and uphold certain rights and responsibilities for minors.

Professional Associations Representing Counselors

The two professional associations whose role definitions and standards are specifically designed for counselors are the American Counseling Association (ACA) and American Psychological Association (APA) Division 17. ACA is the major organization for professional counselors. For psychologists who specialize in counseling, the major organization is APA Division 17, Counseling Psychology. These professional associations are the only ones whose standards are specifically designed for the upholding and training of counselors to counsel people with normal developmental conflicts.

American Counseling Association (ACA)

ACA and its divisions have been responsible for setting standards for counselors since the 1950s. ACA divisions are listed in Appendix C, along with their major publications. ACA was formerly the American Association for Counseling (AACD) and originally the American Personnel and Guidance Association (APGA).

In 1995, the American School Counselors Association (ASCA) and the American Mental Health Counselors Association (AMHCA) executive councils voted to disaffiliate from ACA to pursue their own separate goals.

In a compromise move, the ACA Governing Council, in July 1998, voted to revise the ACA Bylaws that provide new membership options. ACA President Courtland Lee (1997) commented:

> The bylaws were changed to allow a person to have the option of joining ACA only, a division only, or both ACA and a division. Prior to this action, the ACA Bylaws stipulated that all members had to belong to ACA and at least one division. (p. 5)

This seems to be an unfortunate move. Originally, ACA formed to pull disparate forces together (see chap. 2). Creating role definitions and ethical and training standards for counselors, ACA (formerly AACD and APGA) was the unifying force that established and maintained counseling as a unique profession. Providing strength, flexibility, direction, and balance over the years, ACA prevented the profession from giving in to pressures to identify either with diagnostic, pathologizing, clinical models or with psychological education and wellness models.

In the early 1960s, ACA's forerunner, APGA, in conjunction with ASCA and the Association for Counselor Education and Supervision (ACES), developed school counselor role definitions and training standards (Loughary, Stripling, & Fitzgerald, 1965). APGA drew up a code of ethics in 1961 to cover counselors in all settings (see chap. 2). In the late 1970s and 1980s, the association worked with its affiliate, AMHCA, to attain licensure and certification for mental health counselors in the community. ACA also adopted a process of accrediting graduate counseling programs developed by ACES. This accreditation is conducted by the Council for Accreditation of Counseling and Related Educational Programs (CACREP). The standards of ACA and its divisions apply to both master's and doctoral degrees; graduates, however, predominantly have master's degrees in various counseling specialties.

ACA publishes the *Journal of Counseling & Development* (formerly the *Personnel and Guidance Journal*) and *Counseling Today,* which include articles pertinent to all divisions. The organization sponsors yearly conventions at which workshops and papers are presented. ACA coordinates national task forces to study and make recommendations about counseling policy and practice and also lobbies the U.S. Congress to pass legislation to upgrade and fund counseling programs.

APA Division 17

Division 17 (Counseling Psychology) of the American Psychological Association represents psychologists trained specifically to work with the normal concerns of individuals, groups, and families. Members are psychologists with doctorates. The division, which defined the role of the counseling psychologist, continually works on upholding the professional identity of this group (see chap. 2). APA Division 17 developed *Standards for Providers of Counseling Psychological Services* (APA, 1979). It publishes *The Counseling Psychologist,* a journal related to policy and practice; the *Journal of Counseling Psychology,* dedicated to research; and the Division of Counseling Psychology *Newsletter.* APA Division 17 members adhere to the APA (1992) Ethical Principles of Psychologists. Like ACA, this association offers workshops, papers, and panels at national conventions and organizes national task forces to work on issues in the field.

Related Professional Associations

Family therapists, social workers, and clinical psychologists differ from professional counselors in that they generally focus on clients with more serious dysfunctions. Each has separate associations that set standards for training and practice (the American Association for Marriage and Family Therapy [AAMFT], the National Association of Social Workers [NASW], and APA Division 12 [Clinical Psychology]).

Unique Counselor Role

Professional counselor training prepares counselors to engage in counseling with individuals, groups, or families experiencing stress in everyday living that results from normal developmental situational conflicts. Counselor training also prepares counselors to engage in psychological education, assessment and testing, consultation, social change, and crisis prevention and intervention (see chap. 1).

In 1985, members of AMHCA who were certified as clinical mental health counselors by the Academy of Clinical Mental Health Counselors (ACMHC) decided that the definition of *counseling* described by ACA and AMHCA, though basic to all counseling, was too narrow to cover the work of clinical mental health counselors. ACMHC therefore drew up its own special definition of *clinical* mental health counseling that includes treating psychopathology from a developmental point of view, as well as working with normal concerns of individuals (Seiler, Brooks, & Beck, 1987).

This new definition of mental health counseling caused considerable controversy within the profession during the 1990s. The Washington State Mental Health Counseling Association (WMHCA), for example, expressed concerns that the emphasis on pathology runs counter to the principles of ACA and AMHCA, principles that focus on normal developmental concerns. Members of the association argued that this added emphasis on pathology was geared to a small proportion of AMHCA members (2,000 vs. 10,000). Most AMHCA members are primarily oriented toward working with people who have normal concerns.

Those mental health counselors who argue in favor of the pathological model of counseling treatment take a position that harks back to the pre-World War II era of counseling. *Clinical counseling* was a term devised by Williamson (1939) to describe the medical model of assessment, diagnosis, and treatment. After the war, the new developmental theories and such theories as Rogerian (Rogers, 1942, 1951) process-oriented, client-centered therapy enabled counseling to break away from the prewar medical model and form its own unique model.

Speaking for mental health counseling (MHC), Jeffrey Guterman (1994) says:

A seeming consensus has been reached insofar as some writers have suggested that MHC is distinguishable from clinical psychology, psychiatry and social work across key issues. In particular, some have suggested that in contrast with the focus of these other disciplines on psychopathology, MHC takes a developmental approach with clients and is aimed at promoting mental health rather than eliminating mental illness. (p. 226)

Despite this, Guterman (1994) notes that "many researchers have pointed out that MHC, like clinical psychology, psychiatry, and social work, still tends to emphasize psychopathology in its conceptualizing and treatment of clients" (p. 226). Protesting this trend, Guterman continues, "Some researchers have argued that emulating clinically oriented providers has impeded the field's attempt at distinguishing itself as a unique core provider" (p. 226).

He quotes Ginter (1989) in particular as emphasizing the process-oriented nature of counseling in which the counselor-client relationship is fundamental to client developmental change. This is in keeping with the definition of the counselor's unique role that had emerged in the late 1940s (see chap. 2).

The trend toward incorporating the clinical approach, one that tends to pathologize client symptoms, into counseling practice, however, continues. In 1993, the National Board for Certified Counselors and AMHCA, with the approval of ACA, agreed to merge their certification procedures so that AMHCA would represent both community counseling generalists and clinical mental health counselors. Steinhaus (1993), chairman of the Academy Board of Directors, writes, "AMHCA will be free to move into the position of representing the counseling generalists as well as the certified clinician, although not primarily the certified clinician" (p. 4).

In a related move, the ACA Governing Council (1997) revised its definition of *professional counseling* to include strategies that address pathologies, as well as normal developmental concerns. This latest ACA definition of counselor role is as follows:

The Practice of Professional Counseling: The application of mental health, psychological, or human development principles, through cognitive, affective, behavioral or systemic intervention strategies that address wellness, personal growth, or career development, as well as pathology.

ACA's decision to tag the word *pathology* onto the end of the definition of *counseling* is unfortunate. Although I have always been a proponent of working with client conflicts and dysfunctions, I have also held that counselors do not pathologize client symptoms, but rather use client strengths and potentialities to work through difficulties. Abnormal behavior not only is symptomatic of pathology of mental illness but could also signify that the person is suffering from unresolved situational, cultural, developmental conflicts (see chaps. 2, 3, and 5).

Specialized Knowledge and Skills of Counselors

The Association for Counselor Education and Supervision (ACES), a division of ACA, in the late 1970s developed training standards for master's and doctoral work in counseling (ACES, 1978). APA Division 17 did the same for counseling psychology students (APA, 1979).

In both programs, core courses include human growth and development, behavioral dynamics, social and cultural foundations, individual and group counseling theories and techniques, lifestyle and career development, appraisal, research and evaluation, and professional orientation. Family counseling has been added to the curriculum (Richardson & Bradley, 1985). Supervised practicum at the university and internship in agencies in the community are essential training experiences.

Both master's and doctoral students receive these core experiences. Doctoral students generally have longer and more intensive internships, more training in research skills, and more exposure to diagnosis and assessment.

Those AMHCA members described earlier who decided that core experiences in counselor training needed to be expanded for clinical mental health counselors developed a new and separate mental health counseling track for clinical mental health counselors. It includes additional specialized courses in diagnosis and treatment of mental illness.

Counselors-in-training are given a broad philosophical and psychological background, enabling them to assess independently the value of contemporary counseling practices and to evaluate new counseling theories and techniques. As the ACA Code of Ethics (1995) states, it is expected that "Counselors present varied theoretical positions so that students and supervisors may make comparisons and have opportunities to develop their own positions" (Section F.2.f; see also Appendix A). The rationale for this type of preparation is that people who learn only one set of skills are technicians, not professionals, and that their narrow backgrounds limit their ability to expand their knowledge and skills as new discoveries are made in counseling theory and practice.

In the late 1990s, multicultural counseling competencies developed by Sue, Arredondo, and McDavis (1992; see also chap. 14) were incorporated into the training standards of the Association for Multicultural Counseling and Development (AMCD), the Association for Counselor Education and Supervision (ACES), and the International Association of Marriage and Family Counselors (IAMFC).

Increasing interest in spiritual concerns of clients has led ACES to set up a national task force to develop counselor competencies in spiritual counseling to be incorporated into training standards (Fukuyama & Sevig, 1997).

Accreditation

In 1980, the Council for Accreditation of Counseling and Related Educational Programs (CACREP) was created by ACA and its divisions to provide opportunities for accreditation of the various tracks in graduate counseling programs. It accepted the new mental health counselor track and also developed guidelines for community and other agency counseling programs (Seiler et al., 1987).

This accreditation, which is voluntary, covers master's degree programs in community counseling, school counseling, student affairs practice in higher education, mental health counseling, and marriage and family counseling, as well as doctoral programs in counselor education and supervision.

Weaknesses in Practicum and Internship Programs

Counselor training should include two types of supervised experiences: (a) practicum at university clinics under the supervision of university faculty and (b) internships in community agencies or schools under the supervision of agency staff. Effective training experiences work best if both school and community counselors-in-training first engage in practicum at a college training clinic under close supervision by the college faculty. Supervised internship by agency staff at the selected work setting should then follow, and internships should begin with small caseloads that gradually increase over time.

In reality, however, supervised experiences of both types are the weakest part of counselor training. Some colleges and universities do not have counselor educators specifically trained to supervise students and/or facilities or videotaping equipment necessary for quality supervision.

Frequently, school counselors-in-training do not have practicum experience at a university with faculty supervision. Instead, practicum is skipped and students are assigned directly as interns in schools. Worse yet, their internship is often left to an untrained supervising counselor who assigns them to personnel, clerical, or guidance activities, with little actual counseling experience. In community clinics, although counselor interns do see clients, they are often given heavy caseloads with minimal supervision from either the college or the clinic staff.

Certification and Licensure Standards

Certification by Professional Associations

ACA and many of its divisions upgraded professional counseling by setting up national certification procedures whereby individuals with master's degrees in counseling and specified supervised experience take a professional examination and receive recognition from the certifying association. Certification standards are based on ACA professional standards and standards of designated divisions. Certification was set up by the national association before state licensing came into being as a way of indicating to the public that qualified counselors meet standards of practice developed by the profession.

Rehabilitation counselors historically were the leaders in the effort to obtain professional certification. In 1974, the Commission on Rehabilitation Counselor Certification (CRCC) first set up its system of professional certification (Bradley, 1991). In 1985, ACA sponsored the National Board for Certified Counselors (NBCC) to certify counselors qualified to work in all settings. Since that time, the board has expanded certification to six specialized areas: (a) career counselor, (b) gerontological counselor, (c) school counselor, (d) mental health counselor, (e) community counselor, and (f) addictions counselor.

As more and more states set up systems of licensing, the need for national counselor certification by NBCC became less important except for those seeking certification in one of the above-named counseling specialties. Moreover, certification continues to be useful because most state licensure boards use the national certification exams as part of their criteria for licensing. Applying for a state license thus is eased for those certified professionals who must move across state lines.

Credentialing and Licensure by State Legislatures

State legislatures have enacted bills to monitor counselors legally through credentialing for school counselors and licensure for community counselors. Credentialing is regulated by state departments of education, and licensure by state professional licensing boards. All 50 states credential school counselors. Generally, throughout the country, credentials for school counselors are less uniform and stringent than licensure laws for counselors in the community. Increasing numbers of states now require a master's degree for a school counselor credential. As described in chapter 1, master's degrees in community counseling require much higher training standards and supervised field experience than master's degrees in school counseling.

Licensure for community counselors upholds the standards of the profession and protects the client. Licensure generally is required for counselors to qualify for third-party payments from health insurance companies. Agencies also generally hire only licensed counselors.

As of this writing, 46 states have licensing laws for counselors. In 33 states, persons cannot practice counseling unless they are licensed ("Practice Act"). In the other 13 states, licensing laws allow anybody to practice counseling as long as he or she does not use the "title" granted those who are licensed ("Title Act"), such as "professional licensed counselor." (Titles vary from state to state; see Appendix B.) "Practice Acts," obviously, are the preferable licensing law.

My own state of Washington, I'm sorry to say, has one of the weakest licensure laws in the country. Not only is its law just a "Title Act," but the state law also includes another category called "registered" counselor, a license that requires only a bachelor's degree. Clients in Washington are further confused by the fact that a licensed counselor is called "certified mental health counselor," a term that can be confused with the NBCC nationally certified counselor. So, unfortunately, in Washington state, prospective clients, when trying to check the qualifications of a particular counselor, must be readily familiar with the distinctions among "registered," "nationally certified," "certified," "licensed certified," "licensed," and "credentialed."

✎ ETHICAL CODES TO PROTECT THE CLIENT AND MONITOR THE PROFESSION

Ethical codes are developed by professional associations to protect the public from unethical or incompetent professionals, as well as to protect the profession from unethical practices by any of its members (Herlihy & Corey, 1996). As Corey, Corey, and Callanan (1993) warn, these codes are guidelines; they carry no legal weight. At best, the association can reprimand counselors who behave unethically or can drop them from professional membership.

The ACA Code of Ethics (1995; see Appendix A) applies to counselors. The APA's *Ethical Principles of Psychologists* (1992) applies to counseling psychologists. Similar codes have been set by AAMFT (1991) and NASW (1979). Because the ACA code is most representative to general counseling practice, the following pages highlight the major issues addressed in the ACA Code of Ethics.

Ethics Regarding the Counseling Relationship

When establishing a relationship, the counselor's primary obligation is "to respect the dignity and to promote the welfare of clients" (ACA Code of Ethics, Section A.1). Counselors works jointly with clients to encourage client positive growth and development.

Dual Relationships

At times, individuals may ask for counseling from a counselor who is their administrator or supervisor, close friend, or relative. Such requests would require the counselor to serve dual roles; dual roles interfere with professional judgment and inhibit the development of trust necessary for successful counseling. For this reason, dual relations are unethical. The counselor should refer such individuals to another professional (see Appendix A, ACA Code of Ethics, 1995, Section A.6).

Sexual Involvement with Clients

Counselor-client sexual intimacy is forbidden in the ethical codes of all therapeutic professions (Corey et al., 1993). The ACA Code of Ethics states: "Counselors do not have any type of sexual intimacies with clients and do not counsel persons with whom they have had a sexual relationship" (Section A.7.a). Corey et al. (1993) summarize the damage to clients who become sexually involved with therapists and counselors:

> This harm ranged from mistrust of opposite sex relationships to hospitalization and in some cases, suicide. Other effects of sexual intimacies on clients' emotional, social, and sexual adjustment included negative feelings about the experience, a negative impact on their personality and a deterioration of their sexual relationship with their primary partner. (p. 153)

Counselors and therapists who sexually exploit clients not only can be sued for malpractice but also can be jailed on felony charges and lose their licenses, their insurance coverage, or their jobs (Corey et al., 1993).

Countertransference Issues

As the counselor-client relationship develops during the counseling process, the counselor's unconscious, unmet emotional needs invariably arise. This process is called *countertransference.* Counselors must be alert to signs of countertransference and distinguish their affects from those of their clients. Otherwise, their projected needs will have a detrimental effect on their clients.

The ACA Code of Ethics states, "In the counseling relationship, counselors are aware of the intimacy and responsibilities inherent in the counseling relationship, maintain respect for clients, and avoid actions that seek to meet their personal needs at the expense of clients" (Section A.5.a).

Corey (1996) points out, "Ethically, it is essential that we become aware of our own needs, areas of unfinished business, potential personal conflicts and defenses. We need to realize how such factors could interfere with helping our clients" (p. 52).

Counselors' unconscious, unresolved personal needs that interfere with the counseling relationship show up in numerous ways. Counselors who need approval from clients may be oversolicitous toward them; they may also avoid confronting passive clients when necessary. Such counselors may encourage clients' dependence or learned helplessness, or they may exploit clients by delaying appropriate termination of the counseling relationship because they are enjoying a pleasant, need-fulfilling, social interaction with their clients or because they want to continue receiving client fees.

Counselor Values

Values are standards or ethical guidelines that influence an individual or group's behavior, attitudes, and decisions. A person's particular lifestyle is based on a value system derived from his or her particular religious, philosophical, social, cultural, and political background. Values are fostered by families, ethnic groups, religious organizations, or schools, or they may be arrived at through an individual's personal searching. Value issues come up in counseling when clients have mixed motivations about choices they must make or when their choices conflict with the values of family members, peers, or society.

A counselor's job is to help clients search for various alternative behaviors or attitudes and decide which best contributes to their personal satisfaction and development and still permit effective social interaction. The counselor's task is complex because this search may involve several value systems: those of the clients, the counselor, the school, the society, the client's peer group, and the client's family. These value systems may all be different, including the values of each parent. Counseling is further complicated because the counselor cannot always keep personal values out of counseling sessions. A counselor's particular lifestyle and general behavior suggest clues to his or her beliefs about values in general. A counselor should express personal values when appropriate but allow clients to make their own decisions about alternative values (Corey et al., 1993).

One crucial area of potential value conflict lies in counselor reactions to a client's race, ethnicity, gender, or sexual orientation (see chap. 14). The ACA Code of Ethics specifically states that counselors should respect differences in diverse cultural backgrounds: "This includes . . . how the counselor's own cultural/ethnic racial identity impacts his or her values and beliefs about the counseling process" (Section A.2.b). These principles also apply to a person's religious point of view, as well as to older adults, to people with disabilities or handicaps, and to any population that differs in some way from the cultural orientation of the counselor.

According to the ethical codes, counselors must be aware that their own biases might unduly influence a client. In these situations, counselors should decide whether to continue working with the client or to refer the client to another counselor. Counselors who have certain religious beliefs against abortion, for example, find themselves in a moral bind when a pregnant client contemplates abortion. Counselors must determine whether their moral convictions permit an objective discussion of the issue. If not, the counselors should refer the client to another counselor. Similarly, counselors must not try to persuade a client who opposes abortion that abortion is a wise alternative to consider.

Clients' Rights in Counseling

Freedom of Choice and Informed Consent

Both freedom of choice and informed consent relate to the voluntary nature of counseling. They are based on an individual's constitutional right to privacy. Privacy involves "the freedom of individuals to choose for themselves the time and circumstances under which and the extent to which their beliefs, behaviors, and opinions are to be shared or withheld from others" (Siegel, 1979, p. 251).

Regarding freedom of choice, the ACA Code of Ethics (1995) states: "Counselors offer clients the freedom to choose whether to enter a counseling relationship and to determine which professional(s) will provide counseling. Restrictions that limit choices of clients are fully explained" (Section A.3.b).

Besides ethical considerations regarding voluntary counseling, experience has shown that most persons profit more from counseling when they agree to, or voluntarily seek out, counseling. Many counseling theorists and practitioners consider motivation to change behavior a first essential step toward a successful counseling outcome.

Informed consent requires that counselors inform clients of the goals of counseling, the services that will be provided, the potential benefits and risks, fees, length of counseling, degree of confidentiality, qualifications of the counselor, procedures and techniques to be used, and clients' right of access to their files. With this information, clients can make informed judgments about whether or not to enter counseling with a particular counselor. Some state licensing laws require counselors to display disclosure statements that spell out these considerations.

When mental health providers in private practice or in community clinics send a diagnostic classification of a client's problem to a health insurance company without informing the client, the client's rights are violated. The client's problems must fit into a particular category of psychiatric or neurotic dysfunction or adjustment disorder for the insurance company to cover costs. These diagnoses are based on psychiatric and psychological categories of disorders listed in the American Psychiatric Association's *Diagnostic and Statistical Manual of Mental Disorders* (*DSM-IV,* 1994).

Corey et al. (1993) state, "Most clients are not informed that they will be so labeled, what those labels are, or that the labels or other confidential material will be given to insurance companies" (p. 94). Providers of mental health services should obtain consent from clients when it is necessary to diagnose them for insurance reimbursement.

Diagnoses should be shared with clients once agreement is reached. Through sharing, the diagnoses becomes a part of therapy, as well as protect clients' rights.

Confidentiality

Confidentiality means that counselors will not disclose to others what a client has said in counseling sessions without the permission of the client. This protection is guaranteed by the codes of ethics of counselor professional associations, rather than by law. Guaranteed confidentiality enables clients to develop trust in the counseling relationship and to disclose and explore painful or forbidden feelings and experiences during the healing process. In the ACA Code of Ethics, the importance of confidentiality is described as follows: "Counselors respect their clients' rights to privacy and avoid illegal and unwarranted disclosures of confidential information" (Section B.1).

As a consultant to school districts and counseling agencies, I have heard some counselors say that they are better able to understand and help a client when they share information about the client with teachers or parents or with staff members of other agencies. They claim that because they are doing this to benefit their client, they see no need to request client consent because the client may refuse to give it. There is no question that this behavior is not only unethical but also counterproductive to professional practice. Too often, counselors who had taken someone else into their confidence about a client are shocked to find that the client in question was later informed of the interaction by that very person.

Counselors can indicate to a client when they think that sharing client information with others will be helpful to the client. Requesting a client's cooperation keeps that person involved, enhances trust, and makes sharing a productive part of therapy. If the client refuses, exploring the reasons for client reluctance can prove productive.

Exceptions to Voluntary and Confidential Counseling

Enforced Psychological Intervention.   In certain cases, individuals may lose their freedom of choice regarding therapy and have to submit to involuntary commitment if the counselor thinks they may hurt themselves or others; likewise, the guarantee of confidentiality may have to be broken. The counselor is legally bound, for example, to report cases of child abuse or to testify in court when summoned.

If a counselor is in doubt about the necessity of breaking client confidences, consultation with other professionals is recommended, with action taken only after careful deliberation. When, in the counselor's judgment, the client is dangerously suicidal, psychotic, homicidal, or otherwise dangerous to others, the counselor calls on mental health professionals who determine whether involuntary commitment is necessary.

In public schools, a student's behavior may become so disruptive or debilitating, the learning problems so acute, or the home situation so poor that administrators may decide that psychological intervention is necessary to determine administrative or therapeutic action. In such cases, the student and family lose the right to choose.

A school psychologist is the primary resource when behavior or learning difficulties that arise in the classroom require administrative psychological intervention and consultation (Gibson & Mitchell, 1996). After assessing the situation through conferences with the student, teacher, and parents, the psychologist may make specific recommendations about treatment. A social worker who works closely with families can tell when family interactions are so poor or school or home relationships so unproductive that intervention is necessary for the student to function in school (Gibson & Mitchell, 1996). On the basis of the social worker's interaction with the family, a referral to marital and family counseling may result. Counselors are then free to work with the student and family after administrative decisions have been made.

Ethical Duty to Warn.   Counselors have an ethical duty to warn unprotected third parties when clients with a contagious or fatal disease such as AIDS have not informed and refuse to inform partners about their condition (ACA Code of Ethics, Section B.1.d).

Counselor Professional Responsibilities

Counselor Awareness of Degree of Competence

Counselors must be aware of their level of competence. They must not attempt to counsel individuals who have problems that require knowledge or skills beyond their qualifications (see ACA Code of Ethics, Section C.2.a). If a counselor is uncertain about his or her ability to work with a particular client or becomes uncertain after seeing the client a few times, the counselor should consult with another professional or refer the client to another counselor or therapist.

Responsibility to the Agency or Institution

Counselors must abide by the policies and purposes of the institutions in which they work. If their own standards of professional conduct are in conflict with institutional policy, the counselors should try to make such changes in institutional policies that will benefit clients (ACA Code of Ethics, Section D.1). If counselors are not successful in changing institutional policies that violate good ethical practice, they should report these violations to ethical boards and seek employment elsewhere.

Responsibility to Monitor Effectiveness

The ethical standards of all therapeutic professions include the responsibility of the professional associations to assess, monitor, and upgrade therapeutic practice (ACA Code of Ethics, Section C.2.d). In some cases, unfortunately, it takes public outcry, severe criticism from national media, and lawsuits levied against some therapists before the profession scrutinizes questionable practice. Some leading professional journals, however, such as *Family Therapy Networker* and *Professional Counselor,* have been addressing these issues, challenging therapists and counselors to consider tough moral questions.

The issue over false memory is a recent example. A central concept in psychoanalytic theory is that repressed memories of painful childhood traumas contribute to adult client dysfunctions. When therapists help clients recall these experiences and work through their feelings, the clients are generally able to live more productive lives. Therapists have also effectively used repressed-memory recall in working with adult war veterans and torture victims suffering from posttraumatic stress disorder (PTSD).

Some therapists have abused the practice, however, by inappropriately using methods that induce a client to recall memories of abuse that did not actually happen, memories that later were admitted to be false memories. Therapist and memory specialist Michael Yapko (Yapko, 1994; Yapko & Whitfield, 1994) has taken the lead in speaking out on the profession's moral concerns on this issue. Even though he recognizes the therapeutic value of exploring repressed memories and acknowledges the majority of responsible therapists, he also does not refrain from critically assessing some therapeutic practices:

> Many therapists are doing a credible and professional job in their assessment of an individual's sexual history. However, there are also therapists who are unjustifiably inferring a history of sexual abuse on the basis of symptoms that could just as easily be explained in other ways. . . . If the client doesn't accept the diagnosis (of having suffered abuse), he or she is accused of being in denial or worse. . . .
>
> . . . What counselors unwittingly do is foster the belief in clients that they must have been abused, and then create the conditions that are right for recovering specific memories of abuse that are nothing more than confabulations. (Yapko & Whitfield, 1994, p. 37)

Research regarding the nature of repressed memories, their effect on client behavior, and the efficacy of recalling these memories in therapeutic practice is much needed. Memory specialist Elizabeth Loftus (1993) has been the forerunner in exploring the realities regarding repressed memories. Ira Hyman, a cognitive psychologist, has recently joined Loftus in exploring these areas (Hyman & Loftus, 1997, in press).

Controversial issues such as the false memory debate contributed to a crisis in confidence about therapy itself (Butler, 1995; Jacobson, 1995). Such a crisis has been a good opportunity for the profession to engage actively and assess critically all aspects of its therapeutic practices. James Hillman and Michael Ventura's book *We've Had a Hundred Years of Psychotherapy and the World Is Getting Worse* (1992) served as a good model for the 1990s. *Family Therapy Networker* soon followed with a series of special issues over a 4-year period that critically assessed professional practice: November/December 1992; September/October 1993; March/April 1994; and March/April 1995. In the issue "Fallen From Grace" (March/April 1995), for instance, *Family Therapy Networker* discusses how "psychotherapy can redeem its tarnished reputation." Whereas individual mental health workers have taken stands about the need to monitor professional practice, professional associations representing these professionals have been slow to do the monitoring.

Special Ethical Considerations in Family and Marriage Counseling

Green and Hansen (1986, 1989) conducted a survey of family therapists in which they were to rank the most significant ethical dilemmas they faced in practice. They were also asked to indicate whether the AAMFT ethical code was helpful regarding these dilemmas. Corey et al. (1993, p. 310) summarize Green and Hansen's survey. Following are the six most difficult dilemmas in order of rank:

1. Treating the entire family
2. Having values different from those of the family
3. Treating the entire family after one member leaves
4. Professional development activities
5. Imposing therapist values—feminist
6. Manipulating the family for therapeutic benefit

Furthermore, respondents thought that "although the AAMFT ethical code was helpful, it wasn't sufficient as a guide" (Corey et al., 1993, p. 310).

Ethical problems for family and marriage counseling are more difficult than for individual counseling (Huber & Baruth, 1987; Margolin, 1982). Responsibility to each family member or to each partner is complex, particularly if members start out with different purposes.

Marriage and family counselors differ in their views of confidentiality. Some believe that counselors should use professional judgment about whether to disclose a particular communication (Corey et al., 1993). In my opinion, hidden agendas or fears of hidden agendas can block communication within the family or between spouses. If a spouse confesses to the counselor in secret that he or she has had an affair of which the partner is unaware, the counselor who withholds this information as confidential is colluding with the one spouse. To preserve confidentiality and prevent collusion, the counselor, at the outset, could inform family members that he or she will not keep secrets from those participating; family members can then decide whether they want to work with the counselor.

Huber and Baruth (1987) note potential ethical dilemmas in the following cases: (a) when family therapists redefine the presenting problem in terms of their own therapeutic orientation, (b) when therapists refuse to treat willing members of a family because one member refuses treatment, (c) when deceptive paradoxical interventions are used, and (d) when a therapist overidentifies with one marital partner and sets up triangulation in therapy.

⇒ LEGAL ISSUES

Privileged Communication

Both counselors and clients have certain legal rights, responsibilities, and limitations. *Privileged communication* is defined as "the legal right which exists by statute and which protects the client from having his confidences revealed publicly from the witness stand during legal proceedings without his permission" (Shah, 1969, p. 57). Privileged communication is meant to preserve a well-established relationship so that the client can talk freely without fear of disclosure in court. Privileged communication exists in the following relationships: attorney-client, physician-patient, mental health provider-client, husband-wife, and clergy-parishioner. The crucial factor is whether the injury to the relationship from disclosure would be greater than the loss of justice if the information were presented in court (Anderson, 1996).

Counselors should have a clear understanding of the difference between ethical confidentiality and the confidentiality involved in privileged communication. Privileged communication is specific to counselors testifying in a court of law. It is a legal right granted to clients by a state law, rather than a right guaranteed by a professional association's ethical code. Privileged communication is the *client's* right, not the counselor's.

Exceptions to Privilege

Because privilege is a client right, clients can waive the privilege and order a counselor or psychotherapist to testify in court. Other exceptions exist in which testimony must be given if a court demands it. Corey et al. (1993, p. 104) summarize these exceptions in the literature. The following is a paraphrase of their summary:

- When a counselor or therapist is conducting a psychological examination in a court-appointed capacity
- When a client files a lawsuit against the counselor for malpractice
- When a client claims a mental condition as a defense against a committed crime
- When a client under age 16 or with a developmental disability at any age is a victim of sexual abuse, rape, or child abuse
- When a therapist evaluates the sanity of a client and determines that hospitalization is necessary
- When clients are considered dangerous to themselves or others or indicate they intend to commit or have committed a crime

Privileged communication laws do not apply to group counseling or to marital or family counseling (Anderson, 1996; Corey et al., 1993). Knapp, Vandecreek, and Zirkel (1985) argue that family and marital counseling communication should be privileged unless both spouses choose to waive the privilege.

When the statutory privilege does not exist, counselors can be subpoenaed and required to testify in court about communications with clients in counseling sessions. This often happens with school counselors in child custody cases. Herlihy and Sheeley (1987) recommend that counselors attempt to avoid testifying when they believe it would be harmful to their clients or to their image as trusted counselors. They can request that the judge extend privilege because the counseling code of ethics requires confidentiality, or they can request that their testimony be heard in the judge's chambers.

In most states, clients of psychologists and psychiatrists are guaranteed privilege. Counselors, through licensing, are gaining ground. School counselors should also demand privileges for the students they counsel. Students would be more likely to share their concerns about their illegal or asocial acts if the counselor were able to guarantee that he or she can refuse to testify in court about information gained in counseling unless clients agree. Similarly, students involved in issues of child custody in their parents' divorce suits are more likely to seek counseling help if the counselor is not forced to testify in court about their sessions.

Child Abuse: A Requirement to Report

Counselors are faced with a dilemma when clients, in confidence, reveal that child abuse is occurring either to themselves or to someone else. The counselor must report the abuse to child protective services. Laws in all 50 states and the District of Columbia require that a person who suspects child abuse must report it, usually to child protective services, but states vary in detail (Camblin & Prout, 1988).

Child abuse includes physical injury, mental injury, sexual abuse, and neglect. Failure to report child abuse is a misdemeanor. The person reporting is given immunity from any civil or criminal liability for breaking confidentiality. When teachers suspect child abuse, it is their legal responsibility to report it to the child protective agency; the counselor should not do the reporting for teachers. This procedure frees the counselor to develop a counseling relationship with the child and parents after the reporting is done.

Legal Duty to Warn

In the now famous *Tarasoff* case in 1969, a client at the University of California–Berkeley student health services told his psychologist he intended to kill his fiancée. The psychologist contacted the police, who questioned the client and then released him as not dangerous. Subsequently, the client killed his fiancée. The fiancée's parents sued the Board of Regents and employees of the university. The suit was dismissed in a lower court, but the California Supreme Court ruled in favor of the parents, saying that the psychologist should have warned the client's fiancée. This issue stirred controversy throughout the mental health community. In my opinion, the police overrode a psychologist's opinion about a psychological condition that was out of the police's area of expertise. Furthermore, the police, not the psychologist, should be responsible for warning the potential victim. That way, policing would stay in the hands of the police, and therapy would remain with mental health providers. In any case, when a client is dangerous to others, intervention by the authorities is necessary if the client is unresponsive to treatment.

States vary considerably regarding legal duty to warn (Anderson, 1996). Counselors should know their state laws. Consultation with other professionals is suggested when counselors are in doubt about their legal responsibility.

Counseling Liability (Malpractice)

If professional counselors do not follow ethical guidelines or legal statutes related to their profession, clients can sue them for failing to act in good faith or for not taking due care for their clients' welfare. The counselors are then considered professionally negligent, careless, or ignorant in their duties.

In a summary of the literature about malpractice suits, Corey et al. (1993) state that the most frequent grounds for malpractice suits are "violations of confidentiality and sexual misconduct" (p. 130). Other malpractice actions involve failure to consult or refer when a client problem goes beyond the counselor's capability, failure to provide informed consent, misrepresentation of professional competencies, failure to take due precautions with suicidal clients, failure to warn others about violent clients, and making libelous or slanderous statements in public. Other causes of malpractice suits include charging excessive fees, improper diagnosis, and breach of contract.

Counselors can protect themselves from malpractice suits by taking such preventive measures as practicing within professional competence, honoring confidentiality, avoiding dual relationships, and keeping accurate, detailed records (Corey et al., 1993).

MINORS' RIGHTS AND RESPONSIBILITIES: ETHICAL AND LEGAL CONSIDERATIONS

Children and adolescents increasingly have been granted rights to informed consent and privileged communication in counseling. But in practice, these rights remain confusing and complex. To compound the confusion, minors' rights and responsibilities in school differ from those in the community. Minors' rights to seek treatment, to refuse treatment, and to be accorded confidentiality in the schools and in the community are discussed separately.

School Counseling: Free Choice, Informed Consent, and Confidentiality

Although opinions in the literature differ, the general consensus is that children have a right to voluntary counseling in schools even over parents' objections. Schmidt (1987) presents the case of a fourth grader in counseling whose mother objected to the counseling sessions on religious grounds. The director of counseling in the district recommended that if the child wished to continue, the school ethically and legally should continue counseling even if the parent objected. The acceptance of children asking for and receiving counseling in schools has increased because of the recognition in child abuse laws that children need protection from parents who harm or neglect them (Schmidt, 1987). Children also need protection from parental ignorance (Alexander, 1980).

When young children are allowed the same opportunities for free choice that are given older children and adults, their involvement in counseling and their sense of responsibility for their own behavior can increase. These conditions can also enhance relationships among teacher, parents, counselor, and child. When students seek counseling on their own and are treated successfully, parents are encouraged to seek counseling themselves (Ohlsen, Horne, & Lawe, 1988).

In discussing confidentiality in child counseling, Van Hoose (1968) says:

> The fact that the counselee is a child in no way gives the counselor the right to violate or betray confidences. In fact, since the child is almost defenseless, the counselor has an even greater responsibility to make certain that he does not provide the adults with a weapon which can be used against the child. The counselor cannot risk making secret deals with the parents and he cannot align himself with either faction in a conflict. (pp. 135–136)

The counselor's first obligation is to consider the child. If a child does not want confidential information given to his or her parents, the counselor should discuss the matter with the child to discover the reasons for the objections, what information is disputed, and the possible consequences of giving out information. Thus, the child can contribute to the decision.

In many cases, counselors find it important to involve parents in family consultation or family counseling because children's problems generally are part of family interactions (Anderson, 1996). Most parents are cooperative and pleased that counseling is available, but some parents are concerned about their children seeing counselors on their own and about confidentiality. If counselors meet with parents to discuss the value of such an approach, they can reduce parental doubts and resistance. A counseling advisory committee composed of interested parents and teachers can be set up to help implement the policy. A letter emphasizing the voluntary and confidential nature of counseling can be sent to parents at the beginning of the year. If parents object, they can have the opportunity to discuss their objections with a counselor. Counselors can also reach out to parents by making presentations to parent-teacher associations and at parent education programs (Schmidt, 1987).

Regarding these issues, the counselor's domain differs from those of school psychologists or school social workers. For counselors, because the primary client is the *child,* the child's right to confidentiality is honored. For school psychologists and social workers, in contrast, because the *school* is the primary client, the child's right to confidentiality is waived.

Confidentiality of Counseling Records

According to the ACA Code of Ethics, the counselor's notes on counseling sessions are confidential and not part of the school's general student records. Although a student's school records are open to parental review, counseling records are exempt.

Rights of Minors in the Community

In some states, minors over the ages of 12, 13, or 14 have rights to counseling without informing parents in the specific areas of drug and alcohol abuse and venereal disease. These services are often free. A few states have allowed minors free choice to seek counseling on their own in other cases as well (Corey et al., 1993). In California, minors 12 years and older who have been victims of abuse or who are dangerous to themselves or others can receive outpatient help without parental permission or involvement (Corey et al., 1993).

The rationale for permitting children to seek counseling without parental consent is that they may not otherwise receive needed treatment because of their parents' neglect, ignorance, or fears about psychological treatment (Corey et al., 1993). Because of fees, however, most minors will not seek counseling on their own (Melton, 1981).

Regarding informed consent, a Virginia law enacted in 1977 provides minors the same rights that adults have in four areas: venereal disease, pregnancy, substance abuse, and emotional difficulties (Swanson, 1983). Research findings claim that treatment outcome improves when minors have the right to informed consent.

❧ RESEARCH AND EVALUATION

A professional group offering a public service has a responsibility to assess the quality of the service, the degree to which it is helping the public, and its overall effectiveness. In counseling, these assessments generally take the form of research and program evaluations.

Research and program evaluations differ in their contributions to assessment of the profession. *Research* involves the study of the effectiveness of counseling theories and techniques with clients. *Evaluation* involves the study of the usefulness and efficiency of a counseling program in the community from a practical and budgetary standpoint.

Program *evaluators,* who usually are practicing counselors or counselor educators, determine the utility and efficiency of programs and attach values to their findings. They assess programs through questionnaires, surveys, evaluative interviews, and observations. The main questions they address in an evaluation are, Is the program serving the intended populations? and Is the program efficient and effective? (Posavac & Carey, 1985). Decisions about initiating or changing programs arise from evaluations.

At times, *accountability* becomes part of the evaluation. For example, directors are asked to justify whether their programs warrant funding of taxpayers' monies from state or local budgeting agencies.

Counselor training on how to conduct research and evaluation is included in an effective counseling curriculum. Evaluation and accountability procedures, policies, and problems fit well in supervised internship experiences. Each of these assessment activities, however, raises professional and ethical issues.

Ethical Concerns Regarding Research

Ethical problems that arise when conducting research in the fields of counseling and psychology involve lack of treatment-control groups; failure to obtain informed consent of clients; and coercion, deception, and manipulation of subjects. APA (1973) published ethical guidelines for conducting research with humans, and these guidelines have been incorporated into the ACA Code of Ethics.

In all forms of counseling studies, ethical concerns arise about the use of control and experimental groups. It is unethical to withhold therapy or counseling from a control group to determine whether a matched experimental group profits from counseling.

Informed consent means that research subjects, clients or otherwise, have the right to be informed about a proposed study and the right to decide whether they want to participate. To do otherwise is unethical (Corey et al., 1993; Robinson & Gross, 1986). Similarly, it is unethical to deceive research subjects by withholding pertinent material, or otherwise manipulating them so that they will more likely participate in a study (Robinson & Gross, 1986). Another example of unethical behavior is a case in which a family therapist, to determine progress in later sessions, tapes families in the first session without their knowledge.

Need to Improve Research

Many counseling professionals believe that researchers have been devoting too much time and energy to quantitative research and too little time to qualitative research. The *quantitative* method, which has been the most common type of psychological research, studies the causal effect of an isolated, specific, and observable aspect of behavior. The studies are such that the behavior being measured can be counted, or quantified, statistically. The *qualitative* method, in contrast, explores the multidimensional qualities of human beings within the context of their environment through case studies and field observations. Practicing counselors generally ignore the largely quantitative research, which they perceive as irrelevant or useless to practicing counselors (Goldman, 1989; Howard, 1986; Krumboltz, 1986; Lichtenberg, 1986).

Although trained in quantitative methods of research, counseling psychologists in practice generally do not conduct research. Counselors with master's degrees are even less involved in research than those with doctorates. Goldman (1989) recommends that practitioners rely less on experimental, quantitative designs. Krumboltz (1986) argues that students should be encouraged to undertake thesis projects that are relevant to practice. Howard (1986) recommends expanding scientific research to include more practical methods, such as idiographic studies (single cases), historical reviews, and other qualitative research methods.

In a special issue of *The Counseling Psychologist* on qualitative research paradigms, Hoshmand (1989) recommends three approaches: the *naturalistic-ethnographic,* the *phenomenological,* and the *cybernetic.* The first involves research in natural settings; the second focuses on meaning in human experience; and the third is based on understanding social systems and the process of change in the systems.

Other possibilities exist to reduce the gap between research and practice. More joint research programs by university academicians and practitioners could provide meaningful research. The three qualitative research designs that Hoshmand recommends all involve coordination of researchers and practitioners.

⋙ SUMMARY

Over the years, counselors have increased their efforts to obtain recognition from the public as a unique professional group, one that is distinctive from other mental health providers. Role definitions, training standards, and ethical codes have gradually been developed to define and monitor the profession. Professional organizations have contributed to lobbying state legislatures for licensing and certification.

Ethical codes to protect the client and to monitor the profession include matters that involve the counselor-client relationship, such as dual relationships, sexual involvement, and counselor biases; client rights, such as informed consent and confidentiality; and counselor responsibilities, such as competency awareness, responsibility to workplace, and self-monitoring. For marriage and family counselors, AAMFT has developed special codes to cover the ethical complexities of family interactions.

Legal considerations regarding the counselor-client relationship include issues of privileged communication, child abuse, and rights of clients. Privileged communication is a privilege that clients of psychologists have in most states, but for clients of counselors, only a small, though growing, number of states grant such privilege. In cases of child abuse, counselors in all states, like all other mental health providers, are legally required to report their suspicions to a child protection agency. The law protects the rights of clients in several ways; for example, clients can file a malpractice suit if they believe that a counselor violates confidentiality or harasses them sexually.

Certain ethical and legal codes protect minors' rights of free choice and informed consent and confidentiality, but their rights are more protected in the school than in the community.

Counselors have a professional responsibility to assess the quality of their services. A primary way for doing this is through program evaluations that measure the usefulness and efficiency of a program and through research studies that assess the effectiveness of counseling theories and techniques with clients. Professional counselors have suggested that increasing the use of qualitative research designs and reducing reliance on quantitative research would be more meaningful to practitioners.

⟡ PROJECTS AND ACTIVITIES

1. Write or telephone your state attorney general's office, and ask about the legal status of college, school, and community counselors regarding privileged communications. Are minors covered? Do special regulations for minors cover treatment and pregnancy? Ask for copies of any existing statutes. Begin compiling a loose-leaf notebook on legal concerns.

2. Write or telephone the president or executive secretary of your regional or state professional association about procedures for reporting unethical behavior of association members. Find out what sanctions, if any, can be applied. Also explore whether the counseling department of your state department of public instruction has policies on unethical behavior of school counselors.

3. Organize a panel of counselors with master's and doctoral degrees in counseling who are working in private practice, schools, colleges, and community agencies to discuss the licensing of counselors with master's degrees.

4. Check with your state affiliates of ACA about the licensing of counselors in your state. If licensing exists, what are the stipulations for doctoral and master's degree counselors? If licensing does not exist, are plans to license counselors being considered?

5. APA Division 17 has recommended that counseling psychologists distinguish themselves from other professional counselors as described by ACA. Look over the standards and role definitions. In your opinion, do significant differences emerge? If so, what are these differences? Do they outweigh similarities?

6. Select several agencies with different emphases, such as a child guidance clinic, a halfway house, a crisis clinic, and a public school. Find out whether they employ any paraprofessionals. If so, compare their train-

ing programs and duties. How do these duties compare with those of professional persons?

In the following three incidents, assume that you are a school counselor or a licensed community counselor. In each case, write a response indicating what you would say or do.

7. A principal (or agency head) who was once a professional counselor confers with you and tells you that because drug problems in your area have now reached "epidemic proportions," it would be wise for you to let him know about any client who comes to you with such a problem. What do you say to this principal (or agency head)?

8. A 17-year-old comes to see you for the first time. He appears very depressed. He tells you that on May 16, his 18th birthday, he plans to commit suicide; he also tells you in great detail why and how he intends to do so. He further says that he is telling you this because he wants to be sure no one is accused of doing him in and that because he does not belong to any church and has no priest or minister, you are the only person he is telling. In the light of your role as a counselor and considering the ACA Code of Ethics, how do you proceed in the case?

9. The personnel director at a large, local business firm calls you about a former client, now 19 years of age. She apparently is on a trip out of the country with her entire family for at least a month and cannot be reached. She is being seriously considered for a good job, but the director wants to make a decision within 30 days. What the director wishes from you is an evaluation of the woman's personal and emotional adjustment. How do you respond to the company's request for information that could lead to this young woman's getting a good job?

✦ REFERENCES

Alexander, K. (1980). *School law.* St. Paul, MN: West.

American Association for Marriage and Family Therapy (AAMFT). (1991). *Code of ethical principles for marriage and family therapists.* Washington, DC: Author.

American Counseling Association (ACA). (1995). *Ethical standards* (rev. ed.). Alexandria, VA: Author.

American Counseling Association (ACA) Governing Council. (1997). *Definition of professional counseling.* Alexandria, VA, American Counseling Association.

American Psychiatric Association. (1987). *Diagnostic and statistical manual of mental disorders* (4th ed.). Washington, DC: Author.

American Psychological Association (APA). (1973). *Ethical principles in the conduct of research with human participants.* Washington, DC: Author.

American Psychological Association (APA). (1992). *Ethical principles of psychologists* (rev. ed.). Washington, DC: Author.

American Psychological Association (APA), Committee on Standards for Providers of Psychological Services. (1979). *Standards for providers of counseling psychological services.* Washington, DC: Author.

Anderson, B. (1996). *The counselor and the law* (4th ed.). Alexandria, VA. American Counseling Association.

Association for Counselor Education and Supervision (ACES). (1978). ACES guidelines for doctoral preparation in counselor education. *Counselor Education and Supervision, 17,* 163–166.

Bradley, F. O. (Ed.). (1991). *Credentialing in counseling.* Alexandria, VA: American Counseling Association.

Butler, K. (1995). Caught in the cross fire. *Family Therapy Networker, 19,* 24–34.

Camblin, L. D., Jr., & Prout, H. T. (1988). School counseling and the reporting of child abuse: A survey of state laws and practices. In W. C. Huey & T. P. Remley, Jr. (Eds.), *Ethical and legal issues in school counseling* (pp. 160–172). Alexandria, VA: American School Counselor Association.

Corey, G. (1996). *Theory and practice of counseling and psychotherapy* (5th ed.) Pacific Grove, CA: Brooks/Cole.

Corey, G., Corey, M. S., & Callanan, P. (1993). *Issues and ethics in the helping profession* (4th ed.). Pacific Grove, CA: Brooks/Cole.

Note: Activities 7, 8, and 9 were written by Dr. Elvet G. Jones, Professor Emeritus of Psychology at Western Washington University.

Fukuyama, M. A., & Sevig, T. D. (1997). Spiritual issues in counseling: A new course. *Counselor Education and Supervision, 36,* 233–244.

Gibson, R. L., & Mitchell, M. H. (1996). *Introduction to counseling and guidance* (3rd ed.). New York: Macmillan.

Ginter, E. (1989). Slayers of monster-watermelons found in the mental health patch. *Journal of Mental Health Counseling, 11,* 77–85.

Goldman, L. (1989). Moving counseling research into the 21st century. *Counseling Psychologist, 17,* 81–85.

Green, S. L., & Hansen, J. C. (1986). Ethical dilemmas in family therapy. *Journal of Marital and Family Therapy, 12,* 225–230.

Green, S. L., & Hansen, J. C. (1989). Ethical dilemmas faced by family therapists. *Journal of Marital and Family Therapy, 15,* 149–158.

Guterman, J. T. (1994). A social constructionist position for mental health counseling. *Journal of Mental Health Counseling, 16,* 226–243.

Herlihy, B., & Corey, G. (1996). *ACA ethical standards case book* (5th ed.). Alexandria, VA: American Counseling Association.

Herlihy, B., & Sheeley, V. L. (1987). Privileged communication in selected helping professions: A comparison among statutes. *Journal of Counseling & Development, 65,* 479–485.

Hillman, J., & Ventura, M. (1992). *We've had a hundred years of psychotherapy and the world is getting worse.* San Francisco: Harper.

Hoshmand, L. T. (1989). Alternate research paradigms: A review and teaching proposal. *Counseling Psychologist, 17,* 3–79.

Howard, G. S. (1986). The scientist-practitioner in counseling psychology: Toward a deeper integration of theory, research, and practice. *Counseling Psychologist, 14,* 61–103.

Huber, C. H., & Baruth, L. G. (1987). *Ethical, legal, and professional issues in the practice of marriage and family therapy.* Upper Saddle River, NJ: Merrill/Prentice Hall.

Hyman, I. E., Jr., & Loftus, E. F. (1997). Some people recover memories of childhood trauma that never really happened. In P. Applebaum, L. Uyehara, & M. Elin (Eds.), *Trauma and memory: Clinical and legal controversies* (pp. 3–24). New York: Oxford University Press.

Hyman, I. E., Jr., & Loftus, E. F. (in press). Errors in autobiographical memories. *Clinical Psychological Review.*

Jacobson, N. (1955). The overselling of therapy. Family therapy Networker, 19, 40–47.

Knapp, S. J., Vandecreek, L., & Zirkel, P. A. (1985). Legal research techniques: What the psychologist needs to know. *Professional Psychology: Research and Practice, 14,* 435–443.

Krumboltz, J. D. (1986). Research is a very good thing. *Counseling Psychologist, 14,* 159–163.

Lee, C. C. (1997). A new world order. *Counseling Today, 40,* 5.

Lichtenberg, J. W. (1986). Counseling research: Irrelevant or ignored? *Journal of Counseling & Development, 64,* 365–366.

Loftus, E. (1993). The reality of repressed memories. *American Psychologist, 48,* 518–537.

Loughary, J. W., Stripling, R. O., & Fitzgerald, P. W. (Eds.). (1965). *Counseling: A growing profession.* Washington, DC: American Personnel and Guidance Association.

Margolin, G. (1982). Ethical and legal considerations in marital and family therapy. *American Psychologist, 37,* 788–801.

Melton, G. B. (1981). Children's participation in treatment planning: Psychological and legal issues. *Professional Psychology, 12,* 246–252.

National Association of Social Workers (NASW). (1979). *Code of ethics.* Silver Spring, MD: Author.

Ohlsen, M. M., Horne, A. M., & Lawe, C. F. (1988). *Group counseling* (3rd ed.). New York: Holt, Rinehart & Winston.

Posavac, E. J., & Carey, R. G. (1985). *Program evaluation: Methods and case studies.* Upper Saddle River, NJ: Prentice Hall.

Robinson, S. E., & Gross, D. R. (1986). Counseling research: Ethics and issues. *Journal of Counseling & Development, 64,* 331–333.

Rogers, C. R. (1942). *Counseling and psychotherapy: Newer concepts in practice.* Boston: Houghton Mifflin.

Rogers, C. R. (1951). *Client-centered therapy.* Boston: Houghton Mifflin.

Schmidt, J. J. (1987). Parental objections to counseling services: An analysis. *School Counselor, 34,* 387–391.

Seiler, G., Brooks, D. K., Jr., & Beck, E. S. (1987). Training standards of the American Mental Health Counselors Association: History, rationale, and implications. *Journal of Mental Health Counseling, 9,* 199–209.

Shah, S. A. (1969). Privileged communication, confidentiality, and privacy: Privileged communications. *Professional Psychology, 1,* 56–69.

Siegel, M. (1979). Privacy, ethics, and confidentiality. *Professional Psychology, 10,* 249–258.

Steinhaus, J. (1993). I'm not a mind reader. *The Advocate, 16,* 4.

Sue, D. W., Arredondo, P., & McDavis, R. J. (1992). Multicultural competencies/standards: A pressing need. *Journal of Counseling & Development, 70,* 477–486.

Swanson, C. (1983). The law and the counselor. In B. Pate & J. Brown (Eds.), *Being a counselor: Direction and challenges for the 80s* (pp. 26–46). Monterey, CA: Brooks/Cole.

Van Hoose, W. H. (1968). *Counseling in elementary schools.* Itasca, IL: F. E. Peacock.

Williamson, E. G. (1939). *How to counsel students: A manual of techniques for clinical counselors.* New York: McGraw-Hill.

Yapko, M. D. (1994). *Suggestions of abuse: True and false memories of childhood sexual trauma.* New York: Simon & Schuster.

Yapko, M. D., & Whitfield, C. L. (1994). Two experts discuss false memory. *Professional Counselor, 8,* 33–38.

4 Human Development Theories and Counseling

Since the 1950s, human development theories have influenced and shaped counseling philosophy, training, and practice and contributed to counselors' and counseling psychologists' unique professional identity in the mental health field. These theories emphasize helping people of all ages resolve normal conflicts and maintain healthy personal, social, and career development. The Council for Accrediting Counseling and Related Educational Programs (CACREP) mandates that counselors, regardless of specialty, must study human development as part of their requirements. Division 17 of the American Psychological Association (APA) also describes developmental theory as a strong component of counseling psychology practice. Counseling based on human development theories clearly distinguishes it from the remedial emphasis of psychiatrists, clinical psychologists, and social caseworkers.

Many theorists have contributed to the basic principles of life-span developmental theories that underlie counseling practice. In 1916, G. Stanley Hall introduced the concept of developmental stages in childhood and adolescence. Carl Jung and Charlotte Buehler, in the 1930s, expanded these earlier ideas to include adult developmental theories. Twenty years later, Erik Erikson offered a more comprehensive view of developmental stages that extended from childhood through several stages of adulthood. Erikson's view has had significant influence on counseling theory and practice. His work was temporarily overshadowed by Jean Piaget's and Lawrence Kohlberg's stages of development, which focus on children's and adolescents' cognitive and moral development. In the late 1970s, attention to adult development and to Jung and Erikson once again surfaced with the publication of adult developmental theories—notably, those of Daniel Levinson and Roger Gould, who focused on midlife transitions and crises.

Although these various developmental theories have strongly shaped and influenced counseling theory and practice, critics have noted weaknesses in these models and have made recommendations to strengthen them or have proposed developmental theories of their own. Gilligan (1982), Conarton and Silverman (1988), Miller (1976), Jordan, Kaplan, Miller, Stiver, and Surrey (1991), and others pointed out that developmental theories are based on male behavior, and they proposed modifications that helped lay the foundations for feminist developmental theories.

Robert Butler (1975) challenged society's view that adults progressively decline and deteriorate after 65 years of age. Others, like Baltes (1987, 1993), Schaie (1990), and Chinen (1989), support Butler's contention that older adults have the potential to continue to grow and develop intellectually, socially, and psychologically. Ivey (1986) proposed a theory of cognitive development that incorporates adult stages. Spiritual stages of human development are being explored by Kelly (1995), Fowler (1981, 1991), Worthington (1989), and Moody and Carroll (1997). The theory of emotional development has been proposed by Goleman (1995).

Even though important developmental theories have recently been proposed for women's stages of life, for older people, and for stages of spiritual growth, they are only beginning to be incorporated into mainstream developmental theories and into therapeutic practice.

Other critics of the traditional human development model include ethnic groups who contend that such models are based on White, middle-class, male norms. Some also contend that even in life-span approaches, the influence of child experiences on adult behavior is given too much weight. Moreover, critics also assert that human development theorists have ignored the impact of social and environmental conditions on human behavior.

❧ LIFE SPAN HUMAN DEVELOPMENT

Only recently have theorists included in their study of human development the stages and transitions of growth from birth to death, in which they give particular attention to the adult stages of life. Developmental psychologists generally tended to focus only on the stages of growth in children and adolescents. They also tended to believe that adulthood brought about cessation of growth and emotional and social stability. From this perspective, they argued, emotional problems and disorders in adults stemmed predominantly from dysfunctions in childhood and were difficult to change. Not until the late 1970s did adult developmental theorists emerge and show that human development, rather than ceasing after adolescence, is instead a lifelong struggle.

This trend has been consistent with the changes that have taken place in counseling: Initially counselors practiced only in schools and colleges. But now the profession is helping people of all ages in all aspects of their lives in communities, as well as in educational institutions.

Principles of Life Span Development Theory

Considerable differences exist among human developmental theorists about which human processes (emotional, social, cognitive, physical, or moral) they emphasize, the age on which they focus, and the goals at which they aim. Nevertheless, their theories have the following general principles in common:

1. Individuals go through ordered, sequential, developmental stages in which inter-actions of heredity (biological and genetic) and environment (social and cultural) foster growth.

2. Individuals run into difficulties when they do not make a constructive transition from one stage to the next or remain fixed at a stage when change would be productive to growth.

3. During each stage, certain developmental tasks related to individuals' personal needs and society's expectations should be completed successfully.

4. During each stage, individuals experience challenges, crises, conflicts, or disequilibrium as they attempt to complete developmental tasks (Erikson, 1950).

5. Conflicts or crises that one encounters offer opportunities for developmental growth if acknowledged and worked through. (Dabrowski, 1970; Erikson, 1968).

Pioneers in Human Development

Early developmental pioneers theorized only about children or adolescents or both. Sigmund Freud's theory of psychosexual stages (oral, anal, phallic, and genital) was the first to describe certain developmental tasks to be mastered at each stage and the emotional stagnation or upheaval resulting from not moving from one stage to the next. G. Stanley Hall (1916), in the early 1900s, focused on the characteristics of adolescent development. Arnold Gesell (1940, 1948), well known for his study of growth stages of children and adolescents, likewise limited his work to the early stages of life.

Carl Jung, in 1931, at the age of 56, wrote *The Stages of Life* (1931/1962) after experiencing a midlife crisis that included personal and vocational upheavals. In this work, he differed from other developmental theorists not only in extending the scope of developmental study to those experienced in later life but also in his insistence that the years after midlife are a person's most important ones (Jung, 1931/1962; Staude, 1981). He conceived of four stages of development: childhood (birth to puberty); youth (puberty to 35 or 40 years of life); middle age (35 to 60); and old age (65 and up). Jung believed that the process of *individuation,* which involves a person's inner search for meaning in life, occurs after midlife, rather than during youth or childhood. This theory, though not sharply defined or detailed, was a forerunner of later ideas about stages of life. Jung's conception of life stages foreshadowed Erikson's work in the 1950s and 1960s and is the prime force behind the latest adult developmental theorists, such as Daniel Levinson (1978) and Roger Gould (1978).

Charlotte Buehler was probably the first theorist to explore the life cycle systematically (Buehler & Massarik, 1968). In the early 1930s, she collected personal documents, letters, and biographies from about 400 people of varying socioeconomic status, national origin, and occupation and interviewed them. She then identified the following five psychosocial stages in life during which people develop self-realization and goal-seeking behavior:

1. *0 to 15 years:* Goals not self-determined
2. *15 to 25 years:* Exploratory selection of goals
3. *25 to 45 years:* Definite and specific determination of goals
4. *45 to 65 years:* Assessment of results of striving for goals
5. *65+:* Acknowledgment of degree of self-fulfillment and degree of success or failure in life

Buehler is noted for having strongly influenced Donald Super's career development theory, in which he proposed and, over the years, elaborated on the relationship of personal development to vocational development (see chap. 2 and 12). Equally important, however, is her systematic attention to stages in life and her integration of self-theory and human development that underlie a good deal of current counseling theory and practice.

If Buehler expanded Jung's idea about stages of development, Robert Havighurst (1953) did the same for the concept of developmental tasks. Between 1935 and 1950, Havighurst directed studies of individuals at different stages of life. He coined the term *developmental tasks* to describe necessary actions that individuals must take at each stage of life to move to the higher stage of development.

PSYCHOSOCIAL LIFE SPAN DEVELOPMENT: ERIK ERIKSON

In 1950, Erik Erikson, a Freudian psychoanalyst, published his first book, *Childhood and Society,* in which he proposed eight stages of human development throughout life. Erikson's work over the years has been based predominantly on healthy psychological and social-growth processes of normal individuals. As such, his developmental theory undergirded counselors' efforts to establish a unique profession aimed at working with psychologically normal people.

Erikson's theory has influenced counseling theory and practice more than any other developmental theory (Blocher, 1974; Brown & Srebalus, 1988; Keat, 1974; Rodgers, 1984). Although he is best known for his attention to identity crises in adolescence, Erikson has also had a profound influence on adult developmental theories, which are discussed later in this chapter.

According to Erikson (1950, 1963), personality development occurs in eight stages throughout life (see Table 4.1). These stages relate to an individual's struggle to balance inner needs with external cultural forces of the environment. Erikson describes the conflicts that arise in this process as opportunities for positive growth and change.

Erikson perceives these stages as guidelines, and not as rigid steps in human development. He believes that many environmental forces induce variations that complicate an otherwise simple pattern of progressive growth (Coles, 1970).

According to Erikson's theory, the formation and dynamics of each sequential stage are dependent on what occurs in the previous stage. If children develop a basic trust in others and themselves, they can develop the will for self-control and responsibility for their own actions (*autonomy*). This autonomy permits children to

TABLE 4.1
Erikson's Eight Stages of Life Development

Stage	Psychosocial Crisis	Significant Relations	Basic Strengths
1 Infancy	Basic trust versus basic mistrust	Maternal person	Hope
2 Early childhood	Autonomy versus shame and doubt	Parental persons	Will
3 Play age	Initiative versus guilt	Basic family	Purpose
4 School age	Industry versus inferiority	"Neighborhood," school	Competence
5 Adolescence	Identity versus identity confusion	Peer groups and out-groups; models of leader-ship	Fidelity
6 Young adulthood	Intimacy versus isolation	Partners in friendship, sex, competition, cooperation	Love
7 Adulthood	Generativity versus stag-nation	Divided labor and shared household	Care
8 Old age	Integrity versus despair	"Mankind," "my kind"	Wisdom

Source: Reproduced from *THE LIFE CYCLE COMPLETED, A Review,* by Erik H. Erikson, by permission of W. W. Norton & Company, Inc. Copyright © 1982 by Rikan Enterprises, Ltd.

develop initiative and purpose in life and encourages attainment of productive skills and competence. If these developmental challenges are met, adolescents can develop a coherent sense of self (*identity*) that will lead to tendencies to be true to oneself and others (*fidelity*). These firm foundations set in childhood and adolescence permit the adult to develop, over time, love relationships (*intimacy*), altruistic caring for children and concern for the welfare of the next generation (*generativity*), and wisdom about order and meaning in life (*basic integrity*).

Failure to gain adaptive strength at each sequential stage can lead cumulatively to increased behavioral problems. Children who acquire patterns of withdrawal, for instance, are liable to develop confused identities when they reach adolescence and to have tendencies to repudiate themselves and others. As adults, such individuals tend to isolate themselves or to become promiscuous and rejective of others. In later life, they are apt to end up bitter, disdainful, or despairing of life.

Erikson (1968) believes that conflicts between the individual and society are central to his psychosocial theory and are necessary, potentially valuable, instigators of growth. When conflicts are attended to and resolved in a positive manner, individuals are able to move to a higher stage of development. He says:

> I shall present human growth from the point of view of the conflicts, inner and outer, which the vital personality weathers, reemerging from each crisis with an increased sense of inner unity, with an increase of good judgment, and an increase in the capacity "to do well" according to his own standards and to the standards of those who are significant to him. (pp. 91–92)

Erikson (1968) believes that conflicts can be either positive or negative. Positive conflicts result from individuals' awareness that they are distressed over an ongoing conflict—an awareness that motivates them to change themselves or their circumstances in creative and satisfying ways. Negative conflicts, Erikson says, differ: "Neurotic and psychotic conflicts are defined by a certain self-perpetuating propensity, by an increasing waste of defensive energy and by a deepened psychosocial isolation" (p. 163).

Polish psychiatrist Kasimierz Dabrowski (1964, 1970), whose developmental work is cited in the literature (Conarton & Silverman, 1988; Van Hesterin & Ivey, 1990), supports Erikson's beliefs about conflicts. In his theory, called *positive disintegration,* Dabrowski states that tension aroused by conflicts often represents a healthy awareness that all is not well in one's interactions with others or with one's feelings about oneself. This awareness motivates the individual to change patterns of behavior or to change environmental circumstances that are inhibiting her or his personal or interpersonal growth.

Dabrowski's main point is that individuals must be willing to face conflicts and to break down patterns of behavior that are restricting development (*positive disintegration*) in order for growth to take place. Furthermore, if a child's needs are always satisfied by overindulgent and overprotective parents, the chances for growth and development are diminished. He says, "For the development of higher needs and higher emotions, it is necessary to have partial frustrations, some inner conflicts, some deficits in basic needs" (1970, p. 35).

According to Dabrowski, when individuals deny or suppress conflicts and take no action to change stifling behavior or environmental conditions, conflicts can become neurotic or pathological. Passive aggression, chronic depression, destructive behavior, and other debilitating symptoms may arise. Dabrowski calls the process *negative disintegration* or *negative maladjustment* because it perpetuates or exacerbates behavior that is detrimental to healthy development.

In a 1990 article, Steenbarger reaffirms and amplifies the earlier view of Erikson and Dabrowski:

> Development proceeds through periods of challenge and crisis, which generate new sources of meaning and identity for individuals. Far from being a sign of maladjustment, distress is perceived as a constructive prod and precursor to healthy growth. Behaviors linked to distress often contain the kernel of new responses to developmental tasks and, as such, are potentially adaptive. (p. 435)

He also says, "The healthy life is that which uses the upheaval of change to fashion new and vital life structures for the present and future" (p. 435).

The positive potential of conflicts on normal developmental growth has been a consistent underlying theme of counseling since the 1940s and 1950s. Carl Rogers, in *Counseling and Psychotherapy* (1942), rebelled against a pathological emphasis in therapy. In this classic text, he presented a blueprint for a new orientation to counseling philosophy that is consistent with Erikson's psychosocial developmental crises. About counseling the individual, Rogers says, "It is a matter of freeing him for normal growth and development, of removing obstacles so he can again move forward" (p. 29). Referring to the psychosocial aspect of conflict, he says we must recognize "that in all conflict there is a large cultural component, and that in many instances, conflict is created by some new cultural demand which opposed an individual need" (p. 54). About counseling normally functioning individuals, he comments:

> It can be effective only when there is a conflict of desires or demands which creates tension and calls for some type of solution . . . the tension created by those conflicting desires must be more painful to the individual than the pain and stress of finding a solution to the conflict. (p. 54)

✖️ COGNITIVE THEORIES OF HUMAN DEVELOPMENT

Two cognitive theories that made significant impact in the counseling field in the late 1960s and early 1970s were Jean Piaget's cognitive developmental theory and Lawrence Kohlberg's moral developmental theory of children and adolescents. These theories received considerable attention at that time because most counselors were working with children, adolescents, and young adults in public schools and colleges.

Cognitive Development: Piaget

Jean Piaget studied young boys involved in cognitive problem solving (Piaget & Inhelder, 1969). From this research, he and his associates concluded that intellectual development occurred in four developmental stages, with each stage dependent on, and flowing into, the next stage: *sensorimotor* (ages 0–2), *preoperational* (ages 2–7), *concrete operations* (ages 7–11), and *formal operations* (age 11 and over).

Piaget believes that the ability to reason relates to cognitive structures in the mind that become more sophisticated and logical as the individual develops. These structures are responsible for helping individuals move to higher stages of reasoning and solve progressively more complex problems (Drum & Lawler, 1988; Perlmutter & Hall, 1992; Stevens-Long & Commons, 1992). As individuals mature, they move from the infant's preoccupation with sensorimotor interactions with the world, to the capacity to explore concrete objects and specific events in the environment, to the ability to think symbolically, abstractly, systematically, and logically.

Piaget describes two types of processes that occur in cognitive learning at all developmental stages. One, *assimilation,* occurs when individuals incorporate new information cognitively into already existing knowledge. The other, *accommodation,* occurs when individuals actively apply this new knowledge to changes in their behavior.

Although Piaget (1968) does not deal directly with crisis and conflict in development, his theory is based on a similar process of disequilibrium and equilibrium. He believes that intellectual development involves a move from relative disequilibrium or conflict to equilibrium or resolution of a conflict. When a problem arises that causes discomfort, an individual generally tries to resolve it, which then tends to bring about change and growth. Drum and Lawler (1988) believe that Piaget's idea parallels Erikson's theory. They comment that counselors should not move too quickly to intervene and reduce client discomfort and that challenging or disrupting a client's unproductive lifestyle to promote change may have some value.

Piaget influenced counseling theory and practice in several ways. First, his ideas have influenced counseling theorists, like Albert Ellis, Donald Meichenbaum, and Aaron Beck (see chap. 5), who believe that faulty reasoning or distortions in the thinking processes are the major sources of problems. Piaget's work has also influenced psychological-education activities or developmental interventions involving teaching of cognitive skills, problem solving, or reasoning (Drum & Lawler, 1988; Ivey, 1989; see also chap. 7).

Piaget's theory has been criticized because it is limited to children and adolescents. In an attempt to expand Piaget's work to adults, Perry (1970) explored the relationship of Piaget's work to adults and concluded that adults are more flexible than children in their reasoning ability in that they can accept more than one plausible explanation for a set of facts. Ivey (1986) expanded Piaget's concepts to include adult development in his theory, developmental counseling and therapy (DCT), discussed later in the chapter.

Moral Development: Kohlberg

Lawrence Kohlberg (1969, 1981) expanded Piaget's (1932) work on moral development when, in 1958, he embarked on an intensive longitudinal study of the moral reasoning of 50 male children and adolescents. This study, which follows a cognitive developmental model, was continued by Kohlberg's followers (Muss, 1982; Stevens-Long & Commons, 1992).

Kohlberg was primarily interested in the reasons given for judging a behavior right or wrong (Stevens-Long & Commons, 1992). He developed a series of 11 complex hypothetical stories centering on moral dilemmas. In each story, the main character is faced with a conflict between personal interest and the good of society and acts to resolve the dilemma. After reading a story, subjects are asked to judge the behavior as right or wrong, and then they are asked questions to determine the reasoning they used to arrive at the judgment.

According to Kohlberg, morality begins as an idea of justice that relates to primitive, self-centered thinking of children (*preconventional*), then moves to a more conforming socially motivated way of judging (*conventional*), and ends up in judgments that consider values and ethical principles that go beyond oneself and are centered in the good of society (Santrock, 1992; Stevens-Long & Commons, 1992).

The following well-known story about Heinz, who steals drugs to save his wife's life, illustrates the theory. Kohlberg's conclusion is criticized by feminists who challenge his view that moral reasoning based on justice and fairness is more mature than reasoning based on caring for others (see the discussion under "Feminist Human Development Theories" later in this chapter).

In Europe a woman was near death from a special kind of cancer. There was one drug that the doctors thought might save her. It was a form of radium that a druggist in the same town had recently discovered. The drug was expensive to make, but the druggist was charging ten times what the drug cost him to make. He paid $200 for the radium and charged $2,000 for a small dose of the drug. The sick woman's husband, Heinz, went to everyone he knew to borrow the money, but he could only get together $1,000 which is half of what it cost. He told the druggist that his wife was dying and asked him to sell it cheaper or let him pay later. But the druggist said, "No, I discovered the drug, and I am going to make money from it." So Heinz got desperate and broke into the man's store to steal the drug for his wife. (Kohlberg, 1969, p. 379)

After a subject reads the story, the interviewer asks him questions related to the reasoning he used in judging Heinz's behavior. Which is more ethical—saving his wife's life or not stealing the drug? Is Heinz responsible for saving his wife's life? Does the druggist have a right to protect his interests? Figure 4.1 shows examples of reasons given to support or reject Heinz's actions.

Kohlberg and his associates have extended their original work with children and adolescents to adults. Their studies indicate that mature adults show more caring and concern for others, in contrast with the self-preoccupation of children and adolescents.

How does Kohlberg's work influence counseling practice? His work directly relates to value decisions and value conflicts, a crucial component in counseling. Counselors must be aware of their own values, the values of their clients, and the environmental values surrounding both the counselors and their clients. Many client concerns are presented as moral dilemmas or value conflicts. How individuals perceive right or wrong behaviors influences their feelings about themselves or others and has an effect on self-esteem, career choice, and the types of relationships they seek (see chaps. 14–17 on counseling practice).

In addition to its impact on counseling, Kohlberg's work has been basic to values clarification and to Mosher and Sprinthall's (1970) psychological-education activities (Gelso & Fretz, 1992).

❧ ADULT DEVELOPMENT THEORIES

A relatively new field of developmental psychology, *adult development* got its major impetus from the work of Daniel Levinson (1978) and Roger Gould (1975, 1978). Both theorists studied men's development in the later years of life. They based their work on Erikson's ideas about adult ego states and on Jung's writings about life's meaning in the later years of life. Levinson (1986) says, "The study of adult development is, one might say, in its infancy. It has been taken seriously in the human sciences for only the past 30 years or so largely under the impact of Erikson's . . . general writings" (p. 3). In another source (1978), Levinson calls Jung the father of adult development because he was the first to state unequivocally that the years after midlife are the most important in life.

The recent interest in adult development results from counseling professionals' increased awareness that adults continue to develop throughout life. The expansion of counseling from schools and colleges into the community reflects this growing need for adult counseling. The general public is also increasingly aware that adults continue to be met with crises when, for instance, they are laid off from work, get a divorce, need to seek new lifestyles, retire, or are faced with a terminal illness.

FIGURE 4.1
Examples of moral reasoning: Responses to Heinz's theft of the drug.

Stage description	Examples of moral reasoning that supports Heinz's theft of the drug	Examples of moral reasoning that indicate Heinz should not steal the drug
Preconventional morality		
Stage 1: Avoid punishment	Heinz should not let his wife die; if he does he will be in big trouble.	Heinz might get caught and sent to jail.
Stage 2: Seek rewards	If Heinz gets caught, he could give the drug back and maybe they would not give him a long jail sentence.	The druggist is a businessman and needs to make money.
Conventional morality		
Stage 3: Gain approval/ avoid disapproval especially with family	Heinz was only doing something that a good husband would do; it shows how much he loves his wife.	If his wife dies, he can't be blamed for it; it is the druggist's fault. He is the selfish one.
Stage 4: Conformity to society's rules	If you did nothing, you would be letting your wife die; it is your responsibility if she dies. You have to steal it with the idea of paying the druggist later.	It is always wrong to steal; Heinz will always feel guilty if he steals the drug.
Postconventional morality		
Stage 5: Principles accepted by the community	The law was not set up for these circumstances; taking the drug is not really right, but Heinz is justified in doing it.	You can't really blame someone for stealing, but extreme circumstances don't really justify taking the law in your own hands. You might lose respect for yourself if you let your emotions take over; you have to think about the long-term.
Stage 6: Individualized conscience	By stealing the drug, you would have lived up to society's rules, but you would have let down your conscience.	Heinz is faced with the decision of whether to consider other people who need the drug as badly as his wife. He needs to act by considering the value of all the lives involved.

Source: From John W. Santrock, *Life-Span Development*, 4th edition. Copyright © 1992 Wm. C. Brown Communications, Inc., Dubuque, Iowa. All Rights Reserved. Reprinted by permission.

Levinson's Seasons of Life

Levinson studied a small sample (40 subjects) of blue-collar and professional men between ages 35 and 45 with diverse religious and educational backgrounds (Levinson, 1978, 1986; Perlmutter & Hall, 1992). Each subject was interviewed for a total of 10 to 20 hours over a 2- to 3-month period, with follow-up 2 years after the initial interviews. He and his colleagues found that a man's life transitions are closely tied to chronological age.

From this study, Levinson evolved the concept of life structure for men, in which values, beliefs, and principles guide the choices one makes about marriage, work, relationship, and lifestyle (Cavanaugh, 1992). These life structures result from the interaction of three factors; (a) the social-cultural world of the individual, (b) the roles the individual plays (father, husband, citizen, worker), and (c) factors in life that are either expressed or inhibited (a Jungian influence).

Levinson describes four eras, or seasons, in a man's life that constitute a life cycle. In each era, major changes occur, and each transition takes about 5 years. During periods of stability, men build life structures; during transitions, life structures are changed.

In the first early adult transition period (ages 17 to 22), the young adult leaves a childish, self-centered perspective and moves to more mature and independent relationships with family and others. Levinson calls this the novice stage. The second season, or era, lasts from ages 22 to 45. In this period, stress, conflicts, and contradictions are greatest. Important decisions are made about marriage, family, and work. In the last years of this era, during the midlife transition from ages 40 to 45, 70% of Levinson's subjects found life to be particularly painful, distressing, and tumultuous; they began to question or doubt many aspects of their lives. During the last season (ages 65 and up), adults become more caring, compassionate, and attentive to others, much as Erikson describes in his integrity stage. Levinson's discussion of the last season of life, however, is sketchy: No men over age 47 were interviewed.

The focus of Levinson's work is on the midlife transition from ages 40 to 45. He believes that adults have to face four major conflicts at this time, which have persisted since adolescence. These conflicts or polarities follow Jungian thought: (a) inconsistencies or ambivalences about youth and aging, (b) creative and destructive urges in life, (c) masculine versus feminine drives, and (d) the degree of attachment and separation from others (Santrock, 1992).

Major conflicts experienced by so many people at this latter stage of life led Levinson to believe that a midlife crisis is inevitable for almost everyone. The major task at midlife, he believes, is to begin to look inward for meaning and unity in life, rather than to try to find answers to life in external experiences. As with Erikson's latter stage of life, the person then becomes more caring, compassionate, and reflective.

Transformations: Roger Gould

Psychiatrist Roger Gould (1975, 1978) developed a model of adult stages by observing and recording characteristics of 125 men and women, ages 16 through 59, who were in group therapy at the psychiatric outpatient clinic at the University of California–Los Angeles. From these data, he developed a questionnaire that he administered to 524 middle-class individuals in the same age range.

Gould concluded that adult development involves an ongoing struggle against dependencies on others learned in childhood. Drawing from the psychoanalytic views of Freud and Jung, Gould describes six stages of life: childhood, adolescence, young adult, adult, midlife, and beyond midlife. In each stage, he claims, certain issues based on false assumptions need to be worked on to help transform the individual into the next developmental stage, each stage leading to increased maturity.

Of particular significance here are his latter four stages of adult development. From ages 22 to 28, individuals transform into young adults as they become committed to their own careers and to raising children. In doing so, they give up the false assumption that parents have all the answers to life's problems. Between the ages of 29 and 34, individuals learn to face their own shortcomings and false assumptions about themselves, their relationships, and their careers. Between 35 and 45, Gould, like Levinson, says a midlife crisis is apt to occur. Persons at this stage confront the false assumption that there is no evil in the world and in themselves, confront moral issues about love and death; they feel a sense of desperation and urgency in trying to attain something meaningful before time runs out. During the next stage, 45 years and beyond, older adults settle down, accept life as it is, and become less judgmental or demanding of themselves and others.

Gould's and Levinson's ideas about midlife crises inspired Gail Sheehy's (1976) *Passages,* a best-seller in the late 1970s. Sheehy interviewed 115 women and men and described the unsettling transitions adults must pass through to attain authentic identities. Sheehy has been criticized because she does not give information about the selection of her sample, method of interviewing, collection of data, and basis for generalizing her findings to the general population (Santrock, 1992). Nevertheless, her work made "midlife crisis" a household phrase and its problems a cultural expectancy.

Older Adult Development

At the time when Levinson and Gould were emphasizing midlife developmental issues, the prevailing view about older adult development was that of gradual, progressive decline and deterioration. Robert Butler, a renowned gerontologist, challenged this ageism stereotyping of older adults in the landmark publication *Why Survive* (1975). He noted that people over age 65, who were the fastest growing segment of the population, were living longer, healthier lives and that, furthermore, they were demonstrating the potential to continue to grow and contribute to society in unique ways. A decade later, Butler, along with Herbert Gleason, published *Productive Aging* (1985), in which they describe how older adults individually and as a group could contribute to the betterment of society. These leaders urged that society change its negative attitudes about aging and that, moreover, society needs to encourage and foster new social roles and new opportunities for them to continue to be productive.

In the decade following publication of Butler's *Why Survive* (1975), developmental theorists Baltes (1987), Cavanaugh (1992, 1997), O'Connor and Vallerand (1994), and Schaie (1990) conducted research regarding development in older adults. They found that older adults develop capacities in later life quite different from those in their younger days. Tasks involving reflection, judgment, and knowledge relating to meaningful and cultural experiences replaced tasks necessary to younger people, such as abstract reasoning unrelated to experience, timed responses, or rote memorization.

Jungian theorists are especially adept at recognizing the evolving life stages of older adults. Jungian psychiatrist Allan Chinen (1989) proposed three substages of older adult growth: self-confrontation, self-transcendence and self-transformation (see chap. 15).

➤ FEMINIST HUMAN DEVELOPMENT THEORIES

Feminist developmental theorists point out that Erikson, Piaget, and Kohlberg based their research on male norms of behavior. Feminists contend that women's and men's developmental processes differ: Whereas women learn to relate to and connect with others, men learn to separate and become autonomous (Chodorow, 1978; Conarton & Silverman, 1988; Gilligan, 1982; Jordan et al., 1991).

One of the earliest critics of male-dominated theory was Nancy Chodorow, who in the mid-1970s wrote "against the masculine bias of psychoanalytic theory" (Gilligan, 1982, p. 8), a theory that emphasized that persons must separate from others to gain their own identity. Traditional psychology held that women's tendency to want to relate to, and care for, others were signs of inferiority and dependency. From research in which she observed small children and their mothers, Chodorow noticed developmental differences between boys and girls emerging early in childhood. Whereas male children learn to break away from their initial bonding with their mothers to find their male identities, young female children maintain connections with their mothers and learn that it is socially acceptable to model their mothers' caretaking patterns (Gilligan, 1982).

Carol Gilligan's book *In a Different Voice* (1982) brought the issue to public attention. "Her work on women's development reframes developmental models and brings women's and girls' voices into the center of a new psychology" (Jordan et al., 1991, p. 3). Gilligan criticizes Erikson's psychoanalytic theory that humans go through successive stages of separation, an idea influenced by the 19th- and 20th-century American urge to strive for independence and autonomy. She criticizes as well his claim that after having gained independence and autonomy, one suddenly, at midlife, acquires a sense of caring and intimacy. Erikson's notion of intimacy, Gilligan contends, is little more than gaining a sense of trust. Developing patterns of intimacy and caring is a long, extended process; by midlife, a woman has developed, over a long period of time, complex ways of caring for others.

Gilligan (1982) also points out that Kohlberg's hierarchy of moral reasoning is based only on male norms. She asserts that this male perspective about the morality of individual rights and justice cannot be generalized to females. In contrast with males, females view moral decisions from a caring perspective in which relationship and connections with others are crucial. In studies that compared girls' and boys' responses to Kohlberg's story about Heinz's moral dilemma (extracted earlier in this chapter), Gilligan noted the different responses: When judging the dilemma, girls consider the relationships between Heinz and his wife and Heinz and the druggist and propose solutions that go beyond either stealing the drug or letting his wife die.

They suggest, for example, that Heinz continue to appeal to the druggist to delay payment, get a loan, or find other ways of obtaining money (Gilligan, 1982). Such responses do not suit the (male) norms set by Kohlberg, however, so girls generally score lower than boys on Kohlberg's scale. Gilligan objects to the conclusion in the literature that moral decisions of women are somehow inferior to, or less mature than, those of males because of lower scores on such a scale. Instead, she sees their moral perspective as different.

At the Stone Center at Wellesley College, women have been doing research and conducting symposia on women's developmental issues since 1981. Their work centers on trying to reach "a new understanding of psychological development in women" (Jordan et al., 1991, p. 4). *Women's Growth in Connection* (Jordan et al., 1991) is a sampling of the writings from the center. The authors pay tribute to Gilligan's close "analysis of the centrality of connection in women's sense of self" (p. 3). They also note that Jean Baker Miller's work *Toward a New Psychology of Women* (1976) "is the single most significant influence on all our work" (Jordan et al., 1991, p. 4).

Miller (1991), the director of the center, says that the idea that a girl cannot develop a sense of self because she cannot separate from her mother "is an incredible notion" (p. 14). She claims that the literature has ignored the "complexity of the interaction between caretaking and infant" (p. 14). She also says,

> The literature has generally ignored the extraordinarily important character of the interaction—that of attending to and responding to the other. This is the essential feature of what comes to be called "caretaking." It is also the bases of all continuing psychological growth; that is, all growth occurs within emotional connections, not separate from them. (p. 15)

Surrey (1991) uses the term *self-in-relation* to describe women's developmental growth. "The hyphenated phrase 'self-in-relation' implies an evolutionary process of development through relationship" (p. 59). Supporting the theory that a woman's sense of self is enhanced, rather than diminished, through relationships, Surrey says, "the self gains vitality and enhancement in relationship and is not reduced or threatened by connections" (p. 62).

Developmental growth for women evolves in ever more complex modes of relationship throughout one's life. Kaplan and Klein (1991) present core modes of self-development, which they say are laid out by adolescence:

> The relational self grows in complexity, flexibility, sensitivity, and adaptability: The many planes along which this growth occurs include (1) an increased potential for entering into mutually empathic relationships characterized by being able to share one's own affective states and to respond to the affect of others; (2) relational flexibility, or the capacity to permit relationships to change and evolve; (3) an ability and willingness to work through relational conflict while continuing to value the core of emotional connection; and (4) the capacity to feel more empowered as a result of one's inner sense of relational connection to others, particularly to mothers. . . . Thus, the late adolescent woman does not develop "out of" the relational stage, but rather adds on lines of development that enlarge her inner sense as a relational being. (p. 131)

According to Jordan (1991b), the distorted psychological belief that a woman's desire for relationship is a sign of weakness and dependency can be attributed to the early psychoanalytic theory of "needs gratification." Twentieth-century psychology was generally based on this theory:

> The relationship based on need gratification has been the keystone in developmental theory. . . . The needs to receive, to be given to, to depend on, and to be loved are well covered in the psychological literature. Much relational exchange and growth, however, is overlooked in this one-sided model. (p. 87)

Another issue explored at the Stone Center is the meaning of empathy (Jordan, 1991a; Kaplan, 1991). Traditional psychological belief, which emphasizes building and maintaining ego boundaries, warns that a person who feels empathy toward another is experiencing an affective state that generally means a loss of identity. Jordan (1991a) explains that a person who experiences empathy is using both cognitive and affective responses that preclude the risk of losing one's identity. "In order to empathize, one must have a well-differentiated sense of self in addition to an appreciation of and sensibility to the differentness of self as well as the sameness of another person" (p. 29).

Conarton and Silverman (1988) present a theory of developmental stages for women based on Gilligan's work, Dabrowski's theory of positive disintegration, and Jungian processes of individuation involving mythic symbolism (see Table 4.2). Of particular note is the adolescent stage they call "cultural adaptation." During this time, a woman's tendency to develop relatedness is broken because she must imitate male behavior in order to compete, first in high school and higher education and then out in the business world. At midlife, she begins to yearn for a return to her feminine nature that she had to give up or minimize. Conarton uses symbolism to describe the four stages that follow the midlife period, the stages in which a woman journeys into her deep feminine nature. She compares this journey to the four arduous tasks that

TABLE 4.2
Conarton and Silverman's Feminine Developmental Theory

Stage		Characteristic Tasks
Phase 1.	Bonding	Interdependence with mothers
Phase 2.	Orientation to Others	Caring and connectedness to others
Phase 3.	Cultural Adaptation	Imitation of males
Phase 4.	Awakening & Separation	Beginning search for self
Phase 5.	Development of Feminine	Deeper exploration of needs
Phase 6.	Empowerment	Exerting power over their own lives
Phase 7.	Spiritual Development	Experiencing own interest in life
Phase 8.	Integration	Individuation—expanding caring to the world at large

Source: Adapted from "Feminine Development Through the Life Cycle," by S. Conarton and L. K. Silverman, 1988, in M. A. Dutton-Douglas & L. E. Walker (Eds.), *Feminist Psychotherapies: Integration of Therapeutic and Feminist Systems* (p. 38). Norwood, NJ: Ablex.

Psyche, a figure in Greek mythology, had to carry out. In these last stages, a woman seeks and develops empowerment to claim her right to be feminine, her right to be recognized as a caring person, and her right to apply her feminine ways of "cooperation, consensus, and mediation" (Conarton & Silverman, 1988, p. 58).

As Conarton and Silverman (1988) indicate, "The developmental cycle of women must be viewed with the awareness that women's primary striving is for relatedness and connection" (p. 49). Women first bond with their mothers, then expand relationships to others, and then learn to imitate male behavior as they interact in social or business relationships. At Phase 4, they become aware of themselves and their own needs and start the journey toward self-exploration in which they learn to care for themselves as well as others. As they gain empowerment over their own lives, they begin to move toward wholeness and toward integration of their drives to care for themselves and others. Then, in the last stage of life, they turn their caring toward the world, society, and future generations.

➔ IVEY'S DEVELOPMENTAL COUNSELING AND THERAPY (DCT)

Allen Ivey (Ivey, 1986; Ivey, Ivey, & Simek-Morgan, 1997) modified and expanded Piaget's cognitive theory to include development that continues to occur past childhood and adolescence into adulthood. "We usually think of Piaget's theories as primarily relating to the child, yet they serve as helpful metaphors for the construction of therapeutic theory and method that enables us to examine adult change and development" (Ivey, 1986, p. 78).

Ivey modified and expanded Piaget's original four stages of cognitive development by combining Piaget's first two stages into one stage and adding a new fourth stage—*dialectical system*. As Ivey (1986) explains, this new stage is needed because "Formal operational thinking as usually defined by Piaget . . . does not adequately account for the complexity of thinking that starts to occur" (p. 104).

Ivey thus added a postformal model, which he adopted from Kegan (1982) and others. In this fourth stage, individuals develop a propensity for reflection and dialectic within themselves, with their relationships, and with their social-cultural environment. Individuals learn to realize that self-reflection and interactions with family and culture provide for constant change and development. "They can recognize the influence of family and cultural systems and see the complexity and variability of emotions and thoughts, can challenge their own assumptions, can transform their thinking in response to changing circumstances" (Rigazio-Digilio & Ivey, 1991, p. 6).

Pointing out that Piaget's model is formal and thus in danger of being rigid, Ivey's added stage is "postformal," a dialectical stage, in which the emphasis for individuals is "to examine relationships between and among things and objects, awareness of motion and change in development, inclusion of issues of context that change meaning, an open-system orientation, and an actual effort to seek out contradiction" (Ivey, 1986, p. 120). Individuals at this stage are thus in constant dialogue with their previously developed structural system of development. Individuals, in effect, conduct an evolving transformational process within their basic self structures.

Ivey adapted developmental theory to practice by providing a comprehensive counseling and therapy treatment model called *developmental counseling and therapy (DCT)*. Briefly stated, a counselor using DCT essentially (a) assesses the client's developmental level to note the primary level of competency on which the client relies; (b) amplifies and confirms the client's cognitive structural base; (c) helps the client extend out to other levels of cognitive development and to assimilate and accommodate new cognitive structures into the client's basic framework; and (d) helps the client develop the process of dialectics whereby the client effectively moves back through and engages in previously developed cognitive structures and whereby the client effectively engages in interpersonal and interfamilial relations and responds to her or his particular social-cultural environment. Ivey (1986) especially emphasizes the importance of the complex, interactive relationship individuals have with their relations and with their social-cultural environment, "the importance of context" (p. 121). Moreover, this model is particularly valuable for its capacity to encompass both multicultural and older adult developmental issues. Recognizing the dialectical, postformal component in human development and building on it, Ivey has contributed a comprehensive, multidimensional, dynamic approach to cognitive developmental theory.

⟶ RELIGIOUS AND SPIRITUAL DEVELOPMENT

Many counselors and counseling psychologists indicate that interest about, and attention to, client spiritual concerns has been increasing steadily (Bergin, 1989; Fowler, 1981, 1991; Kelly, 1995; McWhirter, 1989; Worthington, 1989). Bergin (1989) says, "The integration of religious perspectives into the professional psychological frame of reference is simply revolutionary" (p. 621). McWhirter (1989) asks, "Might religion, like sexual preference, be coming out of the closet?" (p. 613).

James Fowler (1981, 1991) is a major developmental theorist who has recognized the importance of human spiritual development. He has proposed a faith developmental model that has received a great deal of attention from counseling professionals.

In his book *Stages of Faith* (1981), Fowler describes faith as "the search for an overarching, integrating and grounding trust in a center of value and power sufficiently worthy to give our lives unity and meaning" (p. 5). Kelly (1995) remarks that Fowler's discipline of faith

> is clearly relevant to the spiritual/religious dimension in counseling because it represents peoples' inner or psychodynamic orientation to questions of meaning and value, that is, to questions that for many people are associated predominantly with spirituality and religion. (p. 70)

Fowler proposes six stages of faith that relate closely to Kohlberg's moral developmental stages and that include, as well, "cognitive, affective and behavioral elements of religious development at different life stages" (Kelly, 1995, p. 71).

In the first three stages of faith development, individuals in one way or another rely on some authority outside themselves for spiritual beliefs. Young children, during the first stage of faith (*intuitive-projective*), follow the beliefs of their parents. They tend to imagine or fantasize angels or other religious figures in stories as characters in fairy tales. In the second stage of faith (*mythical-literal*), children tend to respond to religious stories and rituals literally, rather than symbolically. As individuals move through adolescence to young adulthood, their beliefs continue to be based on authority focused outside themselves. In this third stage of faith (*synthetic-conventional*), individuals tend to have conformist acceptance of a belief with little self-reflection on examination of these beliefs. Most people remain at this level (Fowler, 1981; Kelly, 1995).

Those individuals who move to the fourth stage of faith (*individuative-reflective*) begin a radical shift from dependence on others' spiritual beliefs to development of their own. Fowler (1981) says, "For a genuine move to stage 4 to occur there must be an interruption of reliance on external sources of authority. . . . There must be . . . a relocation of authority within the self" (p. 179). Individuals are no longer defined by the groups to which they belong. Instead, they choose beliefs, values, and relationships important to their self-fulfillment.

In the fifth stage of faith (*conjunctive*), persons still rely on their own views but move from self-preoccupation or from dependence on fixed truths to acceptance of others' points of view. They tend to be more tolerant and begin to consider serving others.

Individuals who move to the sixth and last stage of faith (*universalizing*) are rare. As older adults, they begin to search for universal values, such as unconditional love and justice. Self-preservation becomes irrelevant. Mother Theresa and Mahatma Gandhi are examples of people in this form of spiritual development (Fowler, 1981).

In the field of counseling, Ingersoll (1997), Kelly (1995), Fukuyama and Sevig (1997), and Worthington (1989) have been the most outspoken regarding counselors' need to attend to the spiritual development of clients. Worthington (1989) claims that religious and spiritual development has received insufficient attention in counseling. He argues that counselors must become aware of how religious faith relates to both normal development and pathological behavior. Research has shown that more than 90% of U.S. citizens believe in a divine being and that approximately 30% consider themselves strong believers (Spilka, Hood, & Gorsuch, 1985). On the basis of these figures, the majority of clients are embodied with some degree of spiritual and religious belief, conscious or unconscious, as they face emotional crises and try to resolve them. If clients believe that counselors do not sense the significance of religious or spiritual matters, they will either be reluctant to bring up their beliefs or will decide to drop out of counseling.

Worthington discusses how the views of Erikson, Jung, and Piaget relate to the spiritual development of people at every stage of life in his comprehensive article "Religious Faith Across the Life Span: Implications for Counseling and Research" (1989). He also points out how an individual's problems—sexual, substance abuse, marital conflicts, poverty, retirement—often have overtones of religious or spiritual concerns.

He presents five reasons why counselors need to understand how religious faith influences human development:

1. A high percentage of the population identifies itself as religious.

2. Many people who are undergoing emotional crises spontaneously consider religion in their deliberations about their dilemmas even if they have not recently been active.

3. Despite their private consideration of religion, many clients, especially religious clients, are reluctant to bring up their religious considerations as part of secular therapy.

4. In general, therapists are not as religiously oriented as their clients.

5. As a result of being less religiously oriented than their clientele, many therapists might not be as informed about religion as would be maximally helpful to their more religious clients. (pp. 556–557)

Philosopher Harry R. Moody, cofounder and director of the Brookdale Center on Aging at Hunter College, some years ago noted that Erikson's developmental stages omitted spiritual growth (Moody & Carroll, 1997). He gradually came to realize, however, the correlation between life stages and stages of spirituality: "Just as there are age-related stages of maturity in each of our lives, I discovered, so there are sequential stages of spiritual opportunity—*spiritual* passages, as well as social and psychological ones" (pp. 8-9). In *Five Stages of the Soul: Charting the Spiritual Passages That Shape Our Lives*, Moody and Carroll (1997) note that all the great religions of the world speak of developmental stages. "The notion of stages of the soul, in short, is a universal one" (p. 9). Moody proposes five stages of the soul that "typically occur during midlife and beyond" (p. 33) after a person has experienced enough setbacks in life for her or him to question seriously the meaning of life:

1. *The Call.* This stage is familiar to many people: those who experience a conversion, a change of heart, a deep awakening.

2. *The Search.* During this stage, the person seeks a teacher, a guide, a way.

3. *The Struggle.* During this stage, "the soul's true passage begins" (p. 36). This is the most difficult and longest stage, a period in which the person undergoes many arduous trials and tests and suffers numerous defeats and feelings of despair.

4. *The Breakthrough.* Illuminating insights. "There are many levels of breakthrough experiences, some small, some great, some lasting, some temporary" (pp. 37-38).

5. *The Return.* "Life goes on as before. . . . There's still work to do. . . . At the same time we now have special knowledge and experience to give back to the world" (p. 38). Persons now have a compassionate outlook toward others, and many become guides and mentors.

Counseling Clients with Spiritual Concerns

Many counselors find it difficult to work effectively with clients' religious or spiritual concerns because they themselves have not explored their own spiritual needs (Fukuyama & Sevig, 1997). Recognizing the need for counselors to become more aware of spiritual concerns of clients, the Association for Counselor Education and Supervision (ACES) has appointed a task force headed by Eugene Kelly to develop counselor competencies necessary for effective spiritual counseling. In line with this effort, Ingersoll (1997) and Fukuyama and Sevig (1997) have proposed new courses covering spiritual issues in counseling.

❧ EMOTIONAL INTELLIGENCE: A DEVELOPMENTAL LEARNING PROCESS

The concept of *emotional intelligence* emerged as a result of dissatisfaction with the intelligence quotient (IQ) that has dominated psychology since the early 1900s (Goleman, 1995). Critics claim that IQ measures only "a narrow band of linguistic and math skills" (Goleman, 1995, p. 42). Although IQ scores may predict success in school, they are unreliable indicators for predicting performance and productivity in the broader field of one's life work. Addressing this lack, Howard Gardner (1993) proposed that humans have *multiple intelligences* (*MI*). In contrast with the idea that persons acquire an inherently fixed IQ at birth, Gardner proposes that humans, given sufficient learning conditions, are capable of learning various modes of intelligences (see chap. 6). One component is emotional intelligence.

Goleman (1995), in turn, took Gardner's emotional intelligence component, a concept Gardner described from a cognitive perspective, and developed the concept further, describing emotional development from the perspective of emotions. His thesis is that human emotions can operate independently of one's reasoning and thinking capacities.

Proponents of emotional intelligence challenge long-held beliefs that all information gained through sensory experiences goes first to the neocortex, where rational thinking occurs, and then to the amygdala, the seat of emotional responses in the brain. New research shows that when an individual is caught in a dangerous situation, emotional impulses, instinctive fear reactions, are sent directly to the amygdala, impulses that in effect short-circuit the neocortex.

According to Goleman (1995), emotional intelligence is a learned developmental process that begins in infancy and goes through five sequential stages:

1. Developing awareness of one's emotions through effective parental responses to the infant's emotional needs.

2. Managing one's emotions learned by the preschooler as she or he recognizes and accepts boundaries and limitations.

3. Becoming self-motivated, which Goleman calls the *master aptitude*—an inner zeal that drives a person to persist despite disappointments.

4. Recognizing and responding empathically to feelings of others, an essential factor in developing emotional maturity. Empathic development largely unfolds by how well parental figures "attune" to the infant and child, how well parents convey to said child that they know how the child is feeling.

5. Relating well to others, acquiring social intelligence, the rudiments of which one begins to learn in preschool. "These interpersonal abilities build on other emotional intelligences" (p. 119). Persons undeveloped at this stage have difficulty grasping social signals or

what amounts to a learning disability in the realm of nonverbal messages. . . . [T]he problem can be a poor sense of personal space, so that a child stands too closely while talking or spreads their belongings into other people's territory; in interpreting or using body language poorly; . . . or in a poor sense of prosody, the emotional quality of speech, so that they talk too shrilly or too flatly. (p. 121)

Those who experienced severe trauma in childhood tend to feel danger when none exists in any situation that is even vaguely similar to the earlier trauma. Researchers show that even with adults who are traumatized as children, effective emotional relearning can take place.

The National Center for Posttraumatic Stress Disorder sponsors a network of research sites at designated Veterans Administration (VA) hospitals where psychiatrists work with people with PTSD. Those suffering from PTSD have been conditioned to uncontrollable fear reactions at the slightest stimuli, such as a train whistle, stimuli that trigger memories, seated only in the amygdala, of the original trauma. Unlike persons who at an early age were conditioned to be fearful of, say, spiders, and who eventually outgrew their fear reactions, those with PTSD never get over their fear reactions. "Spontaneous relearning fails to occur." (Goleman, 1995, p. 207).

Even so, Goleman (1995) claims, "traumas as profound as those causing PTSD can heal, and . . . the route to such healing is through relearning" (p. 208). Researchers are finding that traumatized children can replay games that "relive a trauma safely, as play" (p. 208). Severely traumatized children replay the trauma over and over again. Reducing psychic numbing is easier for children because they are accustomed to reenacting imaginatively. For the adult, the way for recovery is first to regain a sense of safety and "control over what is happening in their body and to their emotions" (p. 211) during those instances when certain stimuli trigger fear reactions.

➣ OTHER CRITICISMS OF HUMAN DEVELOPMENT THEORIES

Not only have traditional human development models failed to take into account older adult development, women's development, or a person's spiritual development, but critics also contend that they have failed to generalize across cultures, that they overemphasize the influence of child development on adult development, and that they neglect to consider the impact the environment and world conditions have on the individual. Allen Ivey (1986) addressed these shortcomings with a human development model that (a) encompasses the impact of social-cultural influences on one's development and (b) extends cognitive development through adulthood. Even so, the profession still needs to continue to attend to these criticisms.

Limitations of Human Development Theory to Cross-Cultural Counseling

Drum and Lawler (1988) believe that counselors must be cautious about applying current developmental theory cross-culturally. They say that ethnic groups have a right to complain

when they discover that their rich and valid heritage of values, modes of expression and measurements of maturity—when measured only for compliance with a subset of another culture—are found wrong and lacking rather than different and enriching. (p. 44)

These complaints are similar to those of women who object to being judged less mature on the basis of men's developmental norms.

Counselors, then, must be careful about applying the principles of development discussed in this chapter without considering the nature and degree of involvement of the ethnic client in the culture of her or his family origins. For example, Blacks, Hispanics, American Indians, and Asians, though differing in specific family relationships, have more extensive extended-family relationships and family kinship then do most Whites (McGoldrick, 1982; Perlmutter & Hall, 1992). When working with clients from these ethnic groups, counselors need to be aware that timing and progression of developmental crises or concerns may differ from those of most White clients (see chap. 11).

Overemphasis of Childhood on Human Development

Many mental health professionals have criticized developmental theories because of the assumption that the degree of emotional maturity and well-being of adults is determined largely by the quality of relationships they had with parents and family in early childhood (Hillman & Ventura, 1992; Moore, 1992; Steenbarger, 1991). Furthermore, critics argue that developmental theorists who are preoccupied with child development have ignored how environment and world conditions influence the well-being of adults.

Steenbarger (1991) believes that these limitations in human development theory lie in what he calls an *organismic worldview*. In this mode, he complains, human development is described as rigid stages progressing ever onward from immature, less organized, and less differentiated stages of growth to more mature and cohesive stages as a result of inner unfolding potentialities. He argues that this description ignores or minimizes the influences of external forces on human behavior.

Steenbarger presents a more comprehensive model termed *contextual worldview,* in which human development is affected by individuals' interactions with others, the community, and the world at large. In this contextual mode, change is perceived as essential to human growth. Diversity in behavior is welcomed, rather than perceived as deviant or pathological.

Since the early 1980s, Hillman (1983; Hillman & Ventura, 1992) has been the most vocal, persistent, and provocative critic regarding the relationship of child developmental theory to adult behavior. He objects to the basic tenet of developmental psychology that "what happened to you earlier is the cause of what happened to you later" (Hillman & Ventura, 1992, p. 17). Because of this attitude, he says, therapists tend to encourage patients to refer to early family relationships as a cause of every emotional problem.

Hillman emphasizes that socioeconomic, political, and cultural factors generally are more likely to affect an adult's functioning than most childhood experiences. When patients say they are depressed or anxious because of pollution, war, or job uncertainty, Hillman advises therapists to take heed instead of asking them to examine their childhoods for the cause of their anxieties. Although Steenbarger and Hillman make valid criticisms about the rigidity of fixed progressive stage-development theories, these criticisms do not apply to every developmental theorist.

In his definitive biography of Erikson, psychiatrist Robert Coles (1970) points out that Erikson was concerned that his model of stage development would be perceived as fixed and rigid, rather than as a broad, general framework. Coles substantiates Erikson's flexibility. He writes, "We do not acquire trust and forever rid ourselves of mistrust or 'achieve' autonomy and thus spare ourselves continuing doubts and hesitations" (p. 76). Coles further says of Erikson's views:

> What is won can later be lost—and rewon. The body (and in the case of humans, the mind) is not irrevocably set or determined by any one thing—genes, the mother's "behavior," the so-called environment—but by a combination of everything and everyone, both within and outside the flesh. (p. 77)

Both Hillman and Steenbarger believe that developmental theorists ignore immediate concerns of individuals and the impact of world conditions. Yet Eriksonian psychosocial theory is based on personal development occurring within a social context. His close work with American Indians and his personality profiles of people like Mahatma Gandhi and George Bernard Shaw reflect his strong belief that human development relates to history, anthropology, and the state of the world.

⤜➤ SUMMARY

Human development theories have strongly influenced counseling theory and practice. Piaget's cognitive theory of development underlies the use of cognitive theories of counseling with children and adolescents. Kohlberg's theory of moral development is pertinent to the development of values, which have importance in counseling and psychological education curricula and activities.

Jung and Erikson expanded developmental theories to include a life-span perspective. Levinson and Gould published theories about human development through midlife. Butler then challenged the view that people over age 65 progressively declined. He and others, such as Baltes, Cavanaugh, and Chinen demonstrated that older adults have the capacity to continue to grow and develop throughout life. Ivey has since proposed a theory of cognitive development that includes adults.

Feminist developmental theorists Gilligan, Conarton, and Silverman, for instance, and those from the Stone Center, such as Jordan, Kaplan, Miller, Stiver, and Surrey, believe that the developmental processes of women and men differ. Women need to relate and connect with others; men need to separate and gain autonomy. Thus, they claim, developmental theories based on male norms cannot be generalized to women. A woman's need to relate to and care for others is not an inferior or immature state, but rather represents a different developmental process.

The importance of spiritual development has gained recognition in the counseling field after many years of neglect. Fowler and Moody published separate views on spiritual development. Worthington is most prominent in insisting that counselors must give more attention to a client's spiritual concerns.

Human development theories have also been criticized for basing behavior on White middle-class norms, overemphasizing child development, and minimizing the impact of environment and world conditions. Many professionals are addressing these issues in research and practice, including Allen Ivey, with his developmental counseling and therapy (DCT) model.

☞ PROJECTS AND ACTIVITIES

1. Review the literature on conflict in human behavior, and note how conflict is described. Divide the articles into those that describe conflicts as barriers to growth and those that describe them as potential to growth.

2. If male, place yourself in the developmental stage of Erikson that most describes your stage of life. If female, do the same for the stages of Conarton and Silverman. Do you find that the crises or conflicts described by Erikson or by Conarton and Silverman are typical of your age and fit your current circumstances? What is similar, and what is different?

3. Interview some retired men and women over the age of 60 regarding any changes in attitudes or behaviors that have occurred in their lives in the last 40 years. Did they experience any midlife crises? Do you notice differences in men's and women's responses?

4. Organize a class discussion around Heinz's dilemma. Does the group believe that responses given by contemporary children or adolescents will differ from those of children 20 years ago? How much influence do values presented in the media or represented in behaviors of politicians and public figures have on moral judgments and reasoning?

5. Carol Gilligan poses provocative challenges to developmental theories based on men and generalized to women. Do you see evidence in novels, short stories, or the cinema that support or contradict her view?

☞ REFERENCES

Baltes, P. B. (1987). Theoretical propositions of life-span developmental psychology: On the dynamics, growth, and decline. *Developmental Psychology, 23,* 611–626.

Baltes, P. B. (1993). The aging mind: Potential and limits. *The Gerontologist, 33,* 580–594.

Bergin, A. E. (1989). Religious faith and counseling: A commentary on Worthington. *Counseling Psychologist, 17,* 621–624.

Blocher, D. (1974). *Developmental counseling* (2nd ed.). New York: Ronald Press.

Brown, D., & Srebalus, D. S. (1988). *An introduction to the counseling profession.* Upper Saddle River, NJ: Prentice Hall.

Buehler, C., & Massarik, F. (Eds.). (1968). *The course of human life.* New York: Springer.

Butler, R. N. (1975). *Why survive: Being old in America.* New York: Harper & Row.

Butler, R. N. & Gleason, H. P. (Eds.). (1985). *Productive aging: Enhancing vitality in later life.* New York: Springle.

Cavanaugh, J. C. (1992). *Adult development and aging.* Belmont, CA: Wadsworth.

Cavanaugh, J. C. (1997). *Adult development and aging.* Pacific Grove, CA: Brooks/Cole.

Chinen, A. (1989). *In the ever after: Fairy tales and the second half of life.* Wilmette, IL: Chiron.

Chodorow, N. (1978). *The reproduction of mothering.* Berkeley: University of California Press.

Coles, R. (1970). *Erik H. Erikson: The growth of his work.* Boston: Little, Brown.

Conarton, S., & Silverman, L. K. (1988). Feminist developmental theory. In M. A. Dutton-Douglas & L. E. Walker (Eds.), *Feminist psychotherapies: Integration of therapeutic and feminist systems* (pp. 37–67). Norwood, NJ: Ablex.

Dabrowski, K. (1964). *Positive disintegration.* Boston: Little, Brown.

Dabrowski, K. (1970). *Mental growth through positive disintegration.* London: Gryf.

Drum, D. J., & Lawler, A. C. (1988). *Developmental interventions: Theories, principles, and practice.* Upper Saddle River, NJ: Merrill/Prentice Hall.

Erikson, E. H. (1950). *Childhood and society.* New York: Norton.

Erikson, E. H. (1963). *Childhood and society* (2nd ed.). New York: Norton.

Erikson, E. H. (1968). *Identity, youth, and crises.* New York: Norton.

Fowler, J. (1991). Stages in faith consciousness. In F. K. Oser & W. G. Scarlett (Eds.), Religious development in childhood and adolescence [Special issue]. *New Directions in Child Development, 52,* 27–45.

Fowler, J. W. (1981). *Stages of faith.* New York: Harper & Row.

Fukuyama, M. A., & Sevig, T. D. (1997). Spiritual issues in counseling. A new course. *Counselor Education and Supervision, 36,* 233–244.

Gardner, H. (1993). *Frames of mind: The theory of multiple intelligences.* New York: Basic Books.

Gelso, C. J., & Fretz, B. R. (1992). *Counseling psychology.* Fort Worth, TX: Harcourt Brace.

Gesell, A. (1940). *The first five years of life.* New York: Harper.

Gesell, A. (1948). *Studies in child development.* New York: Harper.

Gilligan, C. (1982). *In a different voice.* Cambridge, MA: Harvard University Press.

Goleman, D. (1995). *Emotional intelligence: Why it can matter more than IQ.* New York: Bantam Books.

Gould, R. L. (1975). Adult life stages: Growth toward self-tolerance. *Psychology Today, 8,* 74–78.

Gould, R. L. (1978). *Transformation: Growth and change in adult life.* New York: Simon & Schuster.

Hall, G. S. (1916). *Adolescence.* New York: Appleton.

Havighurst, R. J. (1953). *Human development and education.* New York: Longman, Green.

Hillman, J. (1983). *Archetypal psychology: A brief account.* Dallas, TX: Spring.

Hillman, J., & Ventura, M. (1992). *We've had a hundred years of psychotherapy—and the world's getting worse.* San Francisco: Harpers.

Ingersoll, R. E. (1997). Teaching a course on counseling and spirituality. *Counselor Education and Supervision, 36,* 224–232.

Ivey, A. E. (1986). *Developmental therapy.* San Francisco: Jossey-Bass.

Ivey, A. E. (1989). Mental health counseling: A developmental process and profession. *Journal of Mental Health Counseling, 11,* 26–35.

Ivey, A. E., Ivey, M. B., & Simek-Morgan, L. (1997). *Counseling and psychotherapy: A multicultural perspective* (4th ed.). Boston: Allyn & Bacon.

Jordan, J. V. (1991a). Empathy and the mother-daughter relationship. In J. V. Jordan, A. G. Kaplan, J. B. Miller, I. P. Stiver, & J. L. Surrey (Eds.), *Women's growth in connection: Writings from the Stone Center* (pp. 28–34). New York: Guilford Press.

Jordan, J. V. (1991b). The meaning of mutuality. In J. V. Jordan, A. G. Kaplan, J. B. Miller, I. P. Stiver, & J. L. Surrey (Eds.), *Women's growth in connection: Writings from the Stone Center* (pp. 81–96). New York: Guilford Press.

Jordan, J. V., Kaplan, A. G., Miller, J. B., Stiver, I. P., & Surrey, J. L. (Eds.). (1991). *Women's growth in connection: Writings from the Stone Center.* New York: Guilford Press.

Jung, C. G. (1962). The stages of life. In *Collected works* (Vol. 8, pp. 387–403). Princeton, NJ: Princeton University Press. (Original work published 1931)

Kaplan, A. G. (1991). Empathic communication in the psychotherapy relationship. In J. V. Jordan, A. G. Kaplan, J. B. Miller, I. P. Stiver, & J. L. Surrey (Eds.), *Women's growth in connection: Writings from the Stone Center* (pp. 44–50). New York: Guilford Press.

Kaplan, A. G., & Klein, R. (1991). The relational self in late adolescent women. In J. V. Jordan, A. G. Kaplan, J. B. Miller, I. P. Stiver, & J. L. Surrey (Eds.), *Women's growth in connection: Writings from the Stone Center* (pp. 122–131). New York: Guilford Press.

Keat, D. B. (1974). *Fundamentals of child counseling.* Boston: Houghton Mifflin.

Kegan, R. (1982). *The evolving self: Problem and process in human development.* Cambridge, MA: Harvard University Press.

Kelly, E. W., Jr. (1995). *Spirituality and religion in counseling and psychotherapy: Diversity in theory and practice.* Alexandria, VA: American Counseling Association.

Kohlberg, L. (1966). A cognitive-developmental analysis of children's sex role concepts and attitudes. In E. E. Maccoby (Ed.), *The development of sex differences* (pp. 82–173). Stanford, CA: Stanford University Press.

Kohlberg, L. (1969). Stage and sequence: The cognitive-developmental approach to socialization. In D. Goslin (Ed.), *Handbook of socialization theory and research* (pp. 347–480). Chicago: Rand McNally.

Kohlberg, L. (1981). *The philosophy of moral development.* New York: Harper & Row.

Levinson, D. J. (1978). *The seasons of a man's life.* New York: Ballantine Books.

Levinson, D. J. (1986). A conception of adult development. *American Psychologist, 41,* 3–14.

McGoldrick, M. (1982). Ethnicity and family therapy: An overview. In M. McGoldrick, J. K. Pearce, & J. Giordino (Eds.), *Ethnicity and family therapy* (p. 330). New York: Guilford Press.

McWhirter, J. J. (1989). Religion and the practice of counseling psychology. *Counseling Psychologist, 17,* 613–617.

Miller, J. B. (1976). *Toward a new psychology of women.* Boston: Beacon Press.

Miller, J. B. (1991). The development of women's sense of self. In J. V. Jordan, A. G. Kaplan, J. B. Miller, I. P. Stiver, & J. L. Surrey (Eds.), *Women's growth in connection: Writings from the Stone Center* (pp. 11–26). New York: Guilford Press.

Moody, H. R., & Carroll, D. (1997). *The five stages of the soul: Charting the spiritual passages that shape our lives.* Garden City, NY: Doubleday.

Moore, T. (1992). *Care of the soul: A guide for cultivating depth and sacredness in everyday life.* New York: HarperCollins.

Mosher, R. L., & Sprinthall, N. A. (1970). Psychological education in secondary schools: A program to promote individual and human development. *American Psychologist, 25,* 911–924.

Muss, R. E. (1982). *Theories of adolescence* (4th ed.). New York: Random House.

O'Connor, B. P., & Vallerand, R. J. (1994). Motivation, self-determination, and person-environment fit predictors of psychological adjustment among nursing home residents. *Psychology and Aging, 9,* 189–194.

Perlmutter, M., & Hall, E. (1992). *Adult development and aging* (2nd ed.). New York: John Wiley.

Perry, W. G., Jr. (1970). *Forms of intellectual and ethical development in the college years.* New York: Holt, Rinehart & Winston.

Piaget, J. (1932). *The moral judgement of the child.* London: Kegan Paul.

Piaget, J. (1968). *Six psychological studies.* New York: Viking Books.

Piaget, J., & Inhelder, B. (1969). *The psychology of the child* (H. Weaver, Trans.). New York: Basic Books.

Rigazio-Digilio, S. A., & Ivey, A. E. (1991). Developmental counseling and therapy: A framework for individual and family treatment. *Counseling and Human Development, 24,* 1–19.

Rodgers, R. F. (1984). Theories of adult development: Research, status, and counseling implications. In A. D. Brown & R. W. Lent (Eds.), *Handbook of counseling psychology* (pp. 479–519). New York: John Wiley.

Rogers, C. (1942). *Counseling and psychotherapy.* Boston: Houghton Mifflin.

Santrock, J. W. (1992). *Life span development* (4th ed.). Dubuque, IA: Wm. C. Brown.

Schaie, K. W. (1990). Intellectual development in adulthood. In J. E. Birren & K. W. Schaie (Eds.), *Handbook of the psychology of aging* (3rd ed., pp. 291–309). San Diego: Academic Press.

Sheehy, G. (1976). *Passages: Predictable crises of adult life.* New York: Bantam.

Spilka, B., Hood, W. R., & Gorsuch, R. (1985). *The psychology of religion.* Upper Saddle River, NJ: Prentice Hall.

Staude, J. R. (1981). *The adult development of C. G. Jung.* Boston: Routledge & Kegan Paul.

Steenbarger, B. N. (1990). Toward a developmental understanding of the counseling specialty: Lessons from our students. *Journal of Counseling & Development, 68,* 434–437.

Steenbarger, B. N. (1991). All the world is not a stage: Emerging contextualist themes in counseling and development. *Journal of Counseling & Development, 70,* 288–296.

Stevens-Long, J., & Commons, M. L. (1992). *Adult life: Developmental processes* (4th ed.). Mountainview, CA: Mayfield.

Surrey, J. L. (1991). The self-in-relation: A theory of women's development. In J. V. Jordan, A. G. Kaplan, J. B. Miller, I. P. Stiver, & J. L. Surrey (Eds.), *Women's growth in connection: Writings from the Stone Center* (pp. 51–66). New York: Guilford Press.

Van Hesterin, F. V., & Ivey, A. E. (1990). Counseling and development: Toward a new identity for a profession in transition. *Journal of Counseling & Development, 61,* 524–528.

Worthington, E. L., Jr. (1989). Religious faith across the life span: Implications for counseling and research. *Counseling Psychologist, 17,* 555–612.

5   Counseling Theories

THE PURPOSE OF COUNSELING THEORY

Psychological theories are based on how one perceives human nature and the environment. Assumptions about unconscious and conscious processes, development, learning, and socialization are essential components of psychological theories. The theories of professional counseling and therapy, which are based on these psychological assumptions, present systematic ways of understanding a person's psychological framework, the ways problems arise in the individual's development, and methods for helping persons resolve them.

An integrated system of beliefs about the counseling process can help counselors improve their professional practice, increase their professional knowledge, and enhance their personal development. A well-integrated theory can guide a counselor through the therapeutic process. It provides the basis for making clear-cut counseling goals, a rationale for selection or rejection of particular counseling techniques, a basis for determining ethical counseling procedures, and a framework for evaluating and conducting research on counseling processes and outcomes. Practicing counselors with a sound theoretical basis are able to make evaluations and judgments about new ideas and techniques. Both counselors-in-training and practicing counselors experience personal growth when they explore how their own beliefs and values relate to various counseling theories (Brammer, Abrego, & Shostrom, 1993).

New approaches to psychoanalytic, psychosocial, and psychodynamic theories, the development of humanistic and existential theories, and cognitive-behavioral theories, and the advent of life-span developmental approaches have added many new and challenging possibilities for counselors-in-training and in practice.

Because a wide variety of theories have mushroomed at a bewildering pace in this pluralistic era, practitioners can no longer adhere strictly to one simple theory. Theorists are borrowing ideas from, or combining their views with, other theories. Increasing numbers of counselors and therapists have become eclectic in their practice (see the section "Eclectism" at end of this chapter).

From the numerous and complex counseling theories, I selected those I believe formed the essential historical foundations of counseling and generated activity through the years that contributed to the development of contemporary counseling. I also chose contemporary theories on the basis of the amount of literature they are generating, the degree to which the literature crosses disciplines, and the degree to which their ideas are accessible to counselors and to the lay public. I also based my selection on those theories that have influenced my own point of view as a practicing counselor and educator for more than 50 years since the inception of the counseling profession in the early post-World War II years.

Classification of Theories

Theories are classified in this text under five categories: (a) psychoanalytic and psychodynamic, (b) humanistic, (c) behavioral, cognitive, and cognitive-behavioral, (d) creative and expressive arts, and (e) brief counseling and therapy theories. The first three categories are based on the differing views theorists have about human nature and human behavior. The fourth and fifth categories demonstrate these perspectives in the context of creative and expressive arts and of brief, time-limited counseling sessions.

Psychoanalytic and psychodynamic theorists cover a wide range of beliefs, but basically they all believe that the unconscious is part of the governing process of individuals and that intrapsychic, dynamic forces operate in one's interactions with others. The goal of analysis is to help patients become aware of, and come to terms with, these underlying unconscious dynamic forces.

Humanists generally believe that persons are inherently good and have the power to shape and direct their behavior as they work toward self-actualization. Humans are active and purposeful beings who can make choices and decisions that affect their lives. The goal of counseling is to help clients increase self-understanding and self-acceptance by getting in touch with their inherent positive potentialities.

Behavioral, cognitive, and cognitive-behavioral theorists basically believe that human attitudes and behaviors are learned in response to one's environment. Maladaptive behavior is best corrected by reinforcing appropriate client behavior, or by reshaping or restructuring clients' perceptions and cognitive processes, or both.

❧ PSYCHOANALYTIC AND PSYCHODYNAMIC THEORIES

The theories that follow are based on the assumption that unconscious forces influence behavior. About 100 years ago, Sigmund Freud was developing his theory of psychoanalysis. He believed that a person's unconscious processes are determined by biological, *libidinal,* or *psychosexual* instincts or drives—drives that are potentially destructive unless controlled and channeled. Through psychoanalysis, the analyst helps the patient learn to control his or her unconscious drives.

Carl Jung and Alfred Adler once were followers of Freud but later broke with him over his deterministic concept of human nature. They developed their own theories, each of which is described below. They disagreed with Freud's belief that behavior is determined by psychosexual drives. They claimed that other unconscious forces also govern behavior, such as soul and spirit (Jungian) or the drive to socialize (Adlerian).

Psychoanalysts Karen Horney, Erich Fromm, and Harry Stack Sullivan also objected to Freud's psycho*sexual* model of human nature. Following Adler's belief in the individual's fundamental drive to socialize, they emphasized the individual's psycho*social* or interpersonal development.

Contemporary psychoanalysis is based primarily on significant contributions after World War II in the name of ego-analytic and object relations theories, which, in turn, have been countered more recently by feminist psychodynamic theories on the nature of connections in relationships.

Classical Psychoanalytic Theory

According to Sigmund Freud (1940/1949), human behavior is determined by unconscious, biological, potentially destructive instincts (the *id*). Id impulses (sex and aggression) often clash with a person's need to adapt to society.

As children grow, they develop the *ego* and the *superego*. The *ego* is the conscious part of the mind that acts as a mediator between an individual's instinctive, uninhibited *id* impulses and external reality. As their egos develop, children learn to make compromises between their inner urges and parental and societal controls. The *superego* (conscience) helps persons develop a moral code and an ideal of behavior consistent with traditional values in society.

The ego and the superego develop as part of the personality as children go through psycho*sexual* growth stages—oral, anal, phallic, latent, and genital (Brill, 1938). In the *oral stage* (from birth to about 18 months), gratification centers on feeding. Conflict and anxiety reside in the dependency of the child and the child's demand for immediate gratification. In the *anal stage* (18 months to 3 years), gratification comes from elimination of feces. Toilet training creates conflict and anxiety in child and parent. In the *phallic stage* (3 to 6 years), pleasure centers in the genital area. In this stage, the child experiences sexual impulses toward the parent of the opposite sex and sees the same-sex parent as a rival. In the *latent stage* (6 to 12 years), the impulses are relatively dormant. In the *genital stage* (12 to 18 years), the adolescent begins to develop relationships with members of the opposite sex (Baker, 1985).

As the child experiences *psychosexual* conflicts, the ego runs the risk of becoming overwhelmed either by id impulses or by the superego. To protect the ego, children develop unconscious *defense mechanisms,* which help them survive (A. Freud, 1966). These defenses can become maladaptive if they contribute to the distortion or denial of reality.

Examples of defenses are *repression,* or complete denial of impulses; *projection,* in which people ascribe their own unacceptable behavior to others; *displacement,* in which impulses toward something threatening are redirected toward a safe object or person; and *sublimation,* in which unacceptable drives are channeled into socially acceptable or creative activities.

If parent-child relationships are constructive, children express their impulses in acceptable and satisfying ways. If parents are overly strict, rejecting, or neglectful, children will *repress* impulses and develop defense mechanisms to deny reality. These defense mechanisms may become overly stringent and lead to neurosis or other personality disorders.

Psychoanalysts devote more attention to neuroses than to more severe personality disorders because they believe that persons with neurotic symptoms are more responsive to change. The goal of psychoanalysis is to help clients express, in a safe, therapeutic environment, repressed impulses, fears, and anxieties they had experienced as children and to help them learn to channel those energies into socially acceptable behavior.

The therapist assumes an authoritarian position like that of a parent but is neutral or nonthreatening, unlike parents of neurotics. The analyst maintains neutrality and distance by sitting behind the client, who lies on a couch. The therapist then encourages the patient to let thoughts come out regardless of their content through *free association* (saying whatever comes to mind) and by reporting dreams.

As patients bring out repressed memories and emotions, they begin to attach or transfer early unresolved feelings they had toward parents, such as resentment or admiration, onto the therapists. This *transference* is encouraged by therapists as an essential process in therapy. Analysts respond to these distorted feelings in a nonthreatening or nondemanding way, again unlike parents.

Because of their *defenses,* clients inevitably begin to resist therapy regardless of how motivated they are. *Resistance* is an unconscious process whereby patients prevent repressed impulses and emotions from coming to awareness. Freud believed that resistance blocked efforts of client and therapist to gain client insights necessary for progress in therapy.

As clients free-associate, report dreams, and experience transference and resistance, the analyst interprets the behavior in a process called *working through.* These interpretations include helping patients see hidden meanings in free associations and dreams, understand the distortions and misperceptions involved in transference toward the analyst, and accept resistance as a sign of progress in therapy. This brings about a nondistorted, real relationship with the analyst and increases client willingness to deal with and resolve unconscious conflicts.

Throughout therapy, therapists must be aware of the possibility of *countertransference,* which is an irrational reaction they may have toward clients that results from the therapists' unresolved needs or conflicts. Therapists may find themselves overprotecting, overidentifying with, or feeling unwarranted irritation toward clients as a result of the therapists' earlier unresolved relationships with others who are like the clients.

Psychosocial Neo-Analytic Theories

Alfred Adler: Individual Psychology

Alfred Adler, a contemporary of Freud, rejected Freud's deterministic, instinct-driven view about human nature and emphasized instead a psychosocial, purposeful perspective of behavior. Moreover, he objected to "Freud's belief that the personality is divided: conscious behavior against unconscious, ego against id and super-ego"

(Woodworth & Sheehan, 1964, p. 298). Rather, Adler perceived individuals as unitary, holistic organisms striving to better themselves.

This belief in the unity of personality led Adler to call his theory *individual psychology*—a term that can be misleading, considering his strong advocacy of social forces in human development. The term is clarified, however, in the light of Adler's belief that individuals develop only in the context of their relation to society.

Adlerian theory is best described as follows: "The nucleus of Adler's personality theory is the concept of a unitary, goal-directed creative self which in the healthy state is in a positive constructive, i.e. ethical relationship to his fellow man" (Ansbacher & Ansbacher, 1973, p. 6). This unifying and organizing force shapes the individual's orientation to life, strategies for living, and striving for meaningful goals (Corey, 1996). Individuals have the power to develop their own unique lifestyles. This creative power of self is "Adler's crowning achievement as a personality theorist" (Hall, Lindzey, & Campbell, 1998, p. 13).

Most significant is the individual's *social interest:*

> *Social interest* . . . is probably Adler's most significant and distinctive concept. The term refers to an individual's awareness of being part of the human community and to the individual's attitudes in dealing with the social world; it includes striving for a better future for humanity. (Corey, 1996, p. 137)

Adler believed that individuals strive to develop themselves in relation to their community throughout their lives. Feelings of inferiority or helplessness that all humans experience are instigators for individuals to seek change: "We can seek to change a weakness into a strength, for example, or we can excel in one area of concentration to compensate for defects in other areas" (Corey, 1996, p. 137).

Adlerian counseling involves counselors and clients exploring clients' faulty perceptions about goals. Clients then work toward more constructive goals by developing appropriate social interests, by expanding self-awareness, and by creatively modifying their lifestyles (Corey, 1996).

Adler's views strongly influenced the views of Karen Horney, Erich Fromm, and Harry Stack Sullivan. Each, in turn, elaborated on Adler's psychosocial emphasis:

> Among those who provided psychoanalytic theory with the twentieth century look of social psychology are: . . . Alfred Adler, Karen Horney, Erich Fromm and Harry Stack Sullivan. Of these four Alfred Adler may be regarded as the ancestral figure of the "new social psychological look." (Hall et al., 1998, p. 24)

Adler's views that individuals develop within a social context led him to focus on family interactions—an emphasis later amplified by Rudolf Dreikurs (see chap. 10).

Karen Horney

Unlike Freud, and influenced by Adler, Karen Horney emphasized that social-cultural forces are the major influences in human development. She explored how social influences affect the nature or dynamics of a person's character.

An example of this process of character development is exemplified in her own experience when she became aware of her difference with Freud's views about feminine psychology:

Freud's postulations in regard to feminine psychology set me thinking about the role of cultural factors. Their influence on our ideas and what constitutes masculinity or femininity was obvious, and it became just as obvious to me that Freud had arrived at certain conclusions because he failed to take them into account. (Horney, 1945, pp. 11-12)

Likewise, her views about cultural influences on personality were confirmed after she moved from Germany to the United States and noticed that attitudes and behaviors of neurotic individuals in Germany differed from those in the United States. Horney believes that the tendency for persons to develop either creatively or neurotically depends on the quality of their interpersonal relationships. Parents thus play a crucial role in the development of their children. When parents are neglectful, indifferent, abusive, or otherwise fail to offer loving guidance, the child develops basic anxiety or, as Horney (1945) puts it, "the feeling a child has of being isolated and helpless in a potentially hostile world" (p. 41). The child, feeling unsafe or insecure, develops a basic hostility toward others. These feelings further threaten the child.

To assuage this inner conflict, children must develop strategies to repress their impulses in order to maintain a feeling of security. These strategies take the form of three directional interactions with others: *movement toward* others to gain love, *movement away from* others to gain independence, and *movement against* others to gain power (Horney, 1945).

Horney believes that conflicts are an essential and inevitable part of normal human development. She makes important distinctions between normal or situational conflicts, and conflicts that are neurotic. Normal conflicts arise out of well-defined, stressful problems related to transitions or to everyday problems in work or family relationships. Normal persons are able to resolve these conflicts and learn from them. They may use any or all of the three orientations toward people in a flexible way. Neurotics, in contrast, are unable to resolve their conflicts; they use inflexible and artificial solutions that do not resolve basic anxiety.

The normal conflict is concerned with an actual choice between two possibilities, both of which the person finds really desirable, or between convictions, both of which he really values. . . . The neurotic person engulfed in a conflict is not free to choose. He is driven by equally compelling forces in opposite directions, neither of which he wants to follow. (Horney, 1945, p. 32)

Individuals with either normal or neurotic conflicts can learn to become more adaptive through counseling or therapy. Neurotics, because of strong repressed contradictory impulses, find it more difficult to change. The emphasis in therapy is to help neurotic individuals become aware of their inflexible strategies with people and to help prepare them to risk changing these patterns.

Erich Fromm

Erich Fromm believes that social-cultural, political, and economic forces play a dominant role in personality development. Exploitative trends in a culture are major causes of pathology. Personal growth, then, is stifled by economic or political forces that prevent individuals from being productive in society.

In his first book, *Escape From Freedom* (1941), based on his experiences in Nazi Germany, Fromm presents his view about the human dilemma: As humans have emerged from animal-like dependence on instinctual behavior to that of beings who can reason, think, and choose, they have developed strong ambivalences about this freedom. The world of choices is less secure.

> He has become free but longs for continued dependency and belonging; he has a biological urge to live but his human reason confronts him with the inescapability of death; unlike animals, he has the capacity to solve problems of his world by thought rather than by instinct, but his brief life span makes fulfillment of his potentialities improbable if not impossible. (Woodworth & Sheehan, 1964, pp. 323-324)

Humans try to escape this freedom of choice and the difficulties of solving problems by preferring the security of submitting to authority and to totalitarian systems. People obey orders at the risk of jeopardizing their loved ones; feelings of love for one's neighbor are replaced by feelings of mistrust and meanness: "The person comes to see others as threats to personal existence—as obstacles to be overcome or removed. Under these conditions, the person is alienated from self and from others" (Ryckman, 1993, p. 174).

Individuals can attain positive growth and transcend themselves after they become aware of the societal conditions that have hampered their development. They then can actively work to come to terms with personal values, and beliefs in relation to society (Ryckman, 1993).

Harry Stack Sullivan

Harry Stack Sullivan's psychosocial theory is based on the importance of interpersonal relationships in human development.

> Personality is shaped primarily by social forces, with the child's lengthy period of dependence making it particularly vulnerable to influence by others. He posits a powerful human need for interpersonal relationships . . . And he insists that personality exists, and can be studied, only through its interpersonal manifestations. (Ewen, 1998, p. 213)

Sullivan's lasting contribution is his emphasis on the therapeutic interview as a prime example of an interpersonal interaction. The role of the interviewer in therapy sessions, he claimed, is as important as the behavior of the client. "The interviewer becomes the 'participant observer' systematically noting what the patient does, what he says, and how he says it" (Woodworth & Sheehan, 1964, p. 333). Interviewers must also be aware of their own beliefs or attitudes that are incompatible with their clients' (Woodworth & Sheehan, 1964).

Contemporary Psychoanalytic and Psychodynamic Theories

After a lengthy decline, psychoanalysis has been experiencing a revival. Many new psychoanalytic books have been published; a new journal, *Review of Psychoanalytic Books,* was established; and a new Division of Psychoanalysis was formed in the

American Psychological Association (APA). The renewed activity was further stimulated by the development of contemporary shorter term psychoanalytic theories.

Psychoanalytic theories were overshadowed from the 1950s through the 1970s by the emergence and domination of humanistic, behavioral, and cognitive approaches. Contemporary psychoanalysis received its major impetus with significant revisions of psychoanalytic theories in the name of *ego-analytic* and *object relations* theories. Both object relations theorists and ego-analysts have done much to emphasize that interpersonal relationships are fundamental to human growth and development. As Corey (1996) explains, "The early experiences of the self shift in relation to an expanding awareness of others. Once self-other patterns are established, it is assumed, they influence later interpersonal relationships" (p. 109).

More recently, feminists developed a revisionist psychodynamic theory regarding the essential nature of connection in relationships as fundamental to human growth and development.

Ego-Analytic Theories

Ego-analysts differ from Freud's belief that the id, or instinctive drives, essentially governs human behavior and that the ego is a relatively weak servant of the id. They do not believe that the principal role of the ego is to develop defense mechanisms to protect the individual from being overwhelmed by id impulses. Instead, ego-analysts believe that the ego has energies of its own that are not derived from the id. Remembering, thinking, and perceiving are ego processes that influence behavior (Prochaska & Norcross, 1994). The functions of the ego are to adapt to and master the environment as a way of developing the personality structure (Baker, 1985; Ewen, 1998; Ryckman, 1993).

Maladaptive behavior is described as unresolved conflict that results from ineffective or destructive relationships with parents or guardians at some period in psychosocial development. Such persons have not developed strong enough egos to respond appropriately or have lost the capacity to respond. In either case, persons move from conscious to unconscious control (Hansen, Rossberg, & Cramer, 1994).

Ego-analysts are concerned more with normal conflicts in development than with pathology. Classical psychoanalytic techniques are used but are modified for shorter term treatment. Ego-analytic therapists tend to be more direct, more active, and more accessible to clients than traditional psychoanalytic therapists. Transference and resistance are important parts of the relationship. Current aspects of the relationship, rather than past experiences, are emphasized (Prochaska & Norcross, 1994).

Leading ego-analysts are Erikson (1963), Hartmann (1958), and Rapaport (1958). The best known is Erik Erikson, particularly for his life-span development theory (see chap. 4). A brief description of his theory follows.

Erik Erikson. Erikson (1950, 1963, 1968, 1982), the best known of the ego-analysts, published his first landmark book, *Childhood and Society,* in 1950, and continued developing his theory over many years. Affirming the autonomous nature of the ego, he explains: "The ego keeps tuned to the reality of the historical day, testing perceptions, selecting memories, governing action, and otherwise integrating the individual's capacities of orientation and planning" (1963, p. 193).

Erikson believes that psychosocial or ego developmental forces occur throughout a person's life span. His developmental theory is based on his ego-analytic approach. At each stage of life, humans are confronted with mastering a developmental task that is of critical importance to maintaining and building the ego while making transitions to the next stage of development (see chap. 4).

To master these tasks at each stage of life, individuals must rely on their ego energies to strike an equilibrium between their inner forces and maturational changes and the increasing or changing demands of significant others in society.

Erikson calls such an attempt to master the developmental task at each stage a *crisis* because the task raises conflicts within the individual and between the individual and others in one's life. A crisis is equivalent to a turning point in life when the individual has the potential to progress or regress. At these turning points, one can either resolve one's conflicts or fail to master the developmental task. To a large extent, a person's life is the result of the choice he or she makes at each of these stages.

The individual's success in resolving these conflicts depends on the degree of ego strength developed in previous stages of life, the degree to which the individual actively works to use emerging abilities and strengths, and the degree of favorable influences in the individual's life (Erikson, 1963, 1968; Ewen, 1998; Ryckman, 1993).

Object Relations Theory

One of the most significant contemporary psychoanalytic approaches is *object relations theory,* whose proponents proposed a major restructuring of the classical Freudian instinct-driven theory of human nature. Instead of being governed by id instinctual drives, humans are motivated by their desire to connect or identify with others (objects).

An early proponent of object relations theory is W. R. D. Fairbairn, who claimed that "the ego's main functions are to seek and to establish relations with objects in the external world" (Hall et al., 1998, p. 180). Similar to the ego-analytic view about the autonomous nature of the ego, Fairbairn claimed that

> the ego . . . has its own dynamic structure; and it is the source of its own energy. . . . The ego's main functions are to seek and to establish relations with objects in the external world. . . . The central issue in personality development is not the channeling and rechanneling of instinctual impulses, but the progression from infantile dependence and primary identification with objects to a state of differentiation of self from the object. (Hall et al., 1998, pp. 180–181)

One of the most influential of the object relations theorists was Heinz Kohut (Hall et al., 1998). He stressed more emphatically the necessity of the adequately nurturing family in development of self, one whose primary caretaker can sufficiently serve as the responding object to the infant and child. The primary issue for Kohut is

> the presence or absence of empathic and loving relationships. Healthy mirroring and idealizing afford development of the ideal personality type, the person with an *autonomous*

self. . . . Exposure to deficient self- objects produces children who possess a noncohesive, empty, or injured self. (Hall et al., 1998, p. 182)

Object relations theory has spawned numerous studies and publications. Attention once more has shifted to early childhood relations as a source of malformed sense of self, but with a significant difference in inquiry from earlier psychoanalytic thinking. Attention now is focused on the deficiencies of relatedness and the repair thereof.

Feminist Psychodynamic Theory of Connection

Renewed interest of the developing self from infancy on from the perspective of self in relation to others has had a significant impact on the profession—notably, family therapists (see chap. 10) and feminist perspectives of human development (see chap. 4). A growing number of feminists claim, however, that ego and object relations theories have not gone far enough. Women have been providing new theories of their own on the psychodynamic nature of connection in relationships. Even though their theory is based on women's psychological development, they believe that their insights are relevant to everyone.

This theory has been developed over the years by numerous women researchers, but primarily by a group of four women: psychiatrist Jean Baker Miller and psychologists Irene Pierce Stiver, Judith Jordan, and Janet Surrey at the Stone Center at Wellesley College (Jordan, 1997; Jordan, Kaplan, Miller, Stiver, & Surrey, 1991; Miller & Stiver, 1997). This feminist perspective is based on mutual connection as the primary mode of human growth and development. It is "a relational model organized around the importance of growth-fostering connections in relationships" (Jordan, 1997, p. 4).

Although influenced by the early relations theorists Sullivan, Horney, and Rogers and the contemporary ego-analytic theories of Erik Erikson and object relations theorists, these women researchers differ significantly. Regarding the latter contemporary theories, they disagree with the belief that a human naturally seeks to become an autonomous self (Jordan et al., 1991). To the contrary, they claim that the essential nature of human development is to grow in connection with others. As quoted in Miller and Stiver (1997), Janet Surrey claims, "*Connection* has replaced *self* as the core element or the locus of the creative energy of development" (p. 53).

Moreover, these women disagree with object relations theory that the infant instinctually attaches to an object (food or love object) as the source for growth. In their first major publication, *Women's Growth in Connection* (Jordan et al., 1991), they expressed their differences with traditional contemporary psychoanalytic beliefs and presented a human development model from a women's perspective (see chap. 4). In a subsequent book, *Women's Growth in Diversity* (Jordan, 1997), they extended beyond their earlier, White, middle-class, heterosexual model to include women from different multicultural backgrounds. In 1996, they founded the Jean Baker Miller Training Institute.

The next book, *The Healing Connection* (Miller & Stiver, 1997), describes their theory as it has since evolved and provides more detail on its therapeutic applications. They assert their theoretical position quite strongly:

> This book is about connections between people, about how we create them and how disconnections derail them throughout our lives. Just as disconnections restrict us and block psychological growth, connections—the experience of mutual engagement and empathy—provide the original and continuing source of that growth. (p. 3)

Furthermore, they point out that, "it reflects a major shift in our thinking about what creates pain and psychological problems and what fosters healing and growth" (p. 3).

The theoretical position of Miller and Stiver and their colleagues at the Stone Center is unique in that no one person's name can be associated with it. Unlike traditional psychotherapies that promote the individual (male) along with his theory—Freud, Jung, Sullivan, Rogers, Skinner, Ellis, Erikson, Kelly, and so on—this group of women developed their perspective together, an endeavor that is consistent with their theory: the dynamic nature of mutual connection in relationships. Moreover, they claim that "the powerful role of connections in human growth alters the entire basis of contemporary psychological theory and psychotherapy" (Miller & Stiver, 1997, p. 3).

With connection as the core element of development, other elements specific to this theory include the following: (a) Connections are developed through continual responses and affirmations; (b) relationships involve mutual participants, rather than one person having power over another; (c) all participants become empowered in the relationship; (d) participation, rather than gratification, is the essence; (e) movement occurs in the relationship, a process that evolves over time and provides continuity; and (f) the relationship is something more than the participants and includes what might be called a field or arena, or as Surrey says, "Relationships are *'arenas of growth and learning'*" (Miller & Stiver, 1997, p. 213).

Miller and Stiver (1997), in describing the ideal model of mutual connection, say that, on the one hand,

> we would form images of relationships that are mutually empathic and give us the means and motivation to act—connections that lead us to more knowledge, that make us feel worthwhile and eager for more connections, that help problematic situations resolve into solutions. (p. 40)

On the other hand, one who experiences too many disconnections

> might form an image of relationships in which feelings cannot be heard, understood, or engaged with mutually; in which she is unable to act or to change a situation; in which she feels less worthwhile and which demonstrate that trying to connect with an important person in her life leaves her feeling more isolated and more alone. (p. 40)

Psychoanalytic Psychotherapy

In the first half of the 20th century, psychology and psychoanalysis had little in common. Operating in entirely different camps, each focused on different aspects of human behavior: Psychoanalysts focused on the person's unconscious; psychologists focused on measurement of individual differences and on conscious behaviors. Each worked in different research settings: Psychoanalysts practiced in clinics; psychologists worked primarily as researchers in academic institutions, observing controlled groups of behaviors that could be statistically measured (Hall et al., 1998).

After World War II, a closer relationship developed between psychologists and psychoanalysts as both groups recognized that sharing ideas and concepts would be mutually beneficial. George Klein was a key person who gave impetus to this development between psychologists and psychoanalysts (Hall et al., 1998). Expanding on the ideas of David Rapaport (1960), Klein integrated a typical academic curriculum with psychoanalytic training.

> These individuals brought to psychoanalysis the values of laboratory experimentation and quantification and a respect for theory building as well as a firm grounding in cognitive processes. They received from psychoanalysis the kind of theoretical orientation and insights into the person that were lacking in their educational background. (Hall et al., 1998, p. 184)

This rapprochement was further strengthened when psychoanalytic institutes, such as the Menninger Clinic in Kansas, offered psychoanalytic training to postdoctoral psychologists.

Psychoanalytic psychotherapists make assumptions about behavior similar to those of ego-analysts. They, too, are interested in normal developmental problems; they, too, see maladaptive behavior as resulting from repressed needs and from rejecting parents. They differ from ego-analysts in that they focus on even shorter, less intensive and less regressive treatment. They tend to see a wider range of clients who are less seriously disturbed, see clients less frequently, support useful defenses of clients, use a broader range of intervention strategies, and place more emphasis on resolving specific, present-day problems of clients (Baker, 1985).

Carl Jung: Analytical Psychology

Like Freudian theories, Jungian ideas fell out of favor in the United States for several decades, primarily because the dominating psychological theories followed the empirical approach to behavior. Unconscious forces were not recognized as influencing behavior because they could not be measured or observed. Moreover, Jungian theory was even less acceptable than Freudian because Jungian therapists believed that persons are governed not only by biological forces but by other forces as well—mind, spirit, and soul—forces foreign to the scientific empirical model of behavior.

Carl Jung began his work as a psychiatrist before becoming a Freudian psychoanalyst. Early in his career, Jung broke with Freud primarily because he disagreed with the Freudian theory that a person's sexual drive is the primary force determining psychic life. To distinguish himself from Freudian psychoanalysts, Jung called his theory *analytical psychology*. Jung held that the unconscious contains forces that are potentially positive if they are integrated into consciousness. He believed also that the major force in human behavior is an innate purposive drive to attain wholeness and completeness of self, a process he called *individuation* (Bennett, 1983; Jacobi, 1962; Jung, 1933/1970; Samuels, 1985). Individuation is "a process of integration of the world consciousness with the inner world of unconsciousness. Such action and reaction is inherent in development and growth" (Bennett, 1983, p. 172).

Individuation, or the search for wholeness of self, goes on throughout life and is never completed (Bennett, 1983; Samuels, 1985). Individuation falls into two main stages: the first and second half of life. Jung is primarily concerned with individuation of adults in the second half of life (see chap. 4).

> The task of the first half is "initiation into outward reality." . . . it aims at the adaptation of the individual to the demands of his environment. The task of the second half is a so-called "initiation into the inner reality," a deeper self-knowledge and knowledge of humanity, a "turning back" (*reflectio*) to the traits of one's nature that have hitherto remained unconscious. (Jacobi, 1962, p. 105)

Jung's theory developed out of his observations that the images patients see in their dreams, and the symbols drawn from them, are similar to those found in ancient folklore, myths, legends, art, and rituals (Kaufmann, 1989). From this discovery, Jung hypothesized that the human mind is the storehouse of "latent memory traces inherited from man's ancestral past" (Hall & Lindzey, 1970, p. 83). This part of the mind he called the *collective unconscious,* and the images he named *archetypes.*

Among the many archetypes, some significant ones for personality development are the *persona* (mask) or adaptive behaviors that are necessary for social conformity; the *animus* and *anima,* which are, respectively, the woman's masculine side and the man's feminine side; the *shadow,* a person's dark, unconscious; and the *self,* a person's inherent tendency to strive for wholeness in life (Kaufmann, 1989). Therapists help patients bring the unconscious to consciousness and relate them to archetypal themes.

Jung (1921/1971) also introduced the idea of two major personality types: the *introvert* (a person oriented to introspection) and the *extravert* (a person oriented to the outer world). He noted, however, that persons are too complicated simply to be divided into two types, so he hypothesized that these can each be further qualified by four typical styles of functioning: *thinking, sensing, feeling,* and *intuitive.* Considerable work has since been done on what is known as Jungian *typology* (Samuels, 1985). The personality inventory Myers-Briggs Type Indicator is based on these Jungian types (see chaps. 6 and 12). It should be noted, however, that Jung objected to classifying people into rigid personality types (Bennett, 1983). Jung believed that all these character "types" are inherently in everyone's unconscious. Every person, he claimed, can draw these functions into consciousness, a process that is all part of individuation. One purpose of therapy is to help the person in this process.

Jung's major procedures were dream analysis and *active imagination.* Dreams, he believed, are expressions of the unconscious, expressions attempting to speak to some situation in the person's conscious life (Samuels, 1985). In *active imagination,* therapist and patient plumb the details of a dream, relate the images to ancient myth, and connect them with universal archetypes, as well as with daily events. This process gives meaning to the dream that goes beyond one's ego. Jung distinguished between *fantasy* and *active imagination:*

> A fantasy is more or less your own invention, and remains on the surface of personal things and conscious expectations. But active imagination, as the term denotes, means that the images have a life of their own and that the symbolic events develop according to their own logic—that is, of course, if your conscious reason does not interfere. (Bennett, 1983, p. 107)

Jung was virtually ignored in the United States during most of the 20th century (Kaufmann, 1989). Even so, Hall and Lindzey (1970) remarked, "The originality and audacity of Jung's thinking have few parallels in recent scientific history, and no other man aside from Freud has opened more conceptual windows into what Jung would choose to call 'the soul of man'" (p. 112). Later in the same source, they state, "Certainly his ideas merit the closest attention from any serious student of psychology" (p. 112). More recently, Kaufmann (1989) claimed that "Jung's influence . . . has been enormous, although mostly unacknowledged, and recently there has been a reawakening to his ideas" (p. 126).

Post-Jungians

Post-Jungian psychology has gained national and international attention in many therapeutic circles. According to Samuels (1985), post-Jungian theories have been classified into three schools: classical, developmental, and archetypal. Each school can be thought of, respectively, as first-, second-, and third-generation Jungians. Samuels argues that differentiating and classifying the various post-Jungian theories can generate more dialogue among schools. He says, "a classification . . . into schools can tell us *as much about what is held in common* as about differences of opinion" (p. 18). Adherents of the classical school are those most loyal to Jung, whereas "both the Developmental and Archetypal Schools share an iconoclastic, revisionary attitude that expresses itself empirically in one case, and poetically in the other" (p. 44).

Post-Jungian schools cannot all be discussed in an introductory text. For further reading, start with Samuels' book, *Jung and the Post-Jungians* (1985).

Archetypal psychology is discussed more at length here because it significantly differs from traditional psychoanalysis and psychotherapy. Founder James Hillman (1975, 1983, 1989), a Jungian analyst trained in Zurich, continues to challenge not only the theories and methods of Jungian, post-Jungian, Freudian, behaviorist, cognitive, and developmental thought but also the very foundations of counseling and psychotherapy. Proponents of archetypal psychology also attracted attention by their best-selling books of the 1990s: *Women Who Run with the Wolves,* by Clarissa Pinkola Estés (1992); *Care of the Soul,* by Thomas Moore (1992); and *Iron John,* by Robert Bly (1990). Archetypal psychology stimulated as well the mythopoetical men's movement and creative and expressive arts therapy. Moreover, its complex premises and unfamiliar terminology are often misunderstood.

Hillman (1983) prefers the term *archetypal* over *analytical* because it reflects "the deepened theory of Jung's later work which attempts to solve psychological problems beyond scientific models" (p. 1). More important, he prefers *archetypal* because it "belongs to all culture, all forms of human activity, and not only to professional practitioners of modern therapeutics" (p. 1).

Comparing the principles of archetypal psychology with other psychological theories poses difficulties. The terms central to its understanding—*soul, spirit, psyche, myth, imagination, polytheism*—are foreign to most psychological schools of thought. Moreover, archetypal psychology differs from traditional approaches to psychology in many and complex ways: It focuses on images and imaginal sensibilities, rather than on empirical behavior; relies on a poetic regard, rather than literal analysis of dreams and images; regards an experience in the context of myth, rather than merely as a literal event; emphasizes soul more than spirit; attends to a deepening awareness of soul, rather than to development of self or ego; and accepts the normality of a person's multiple selves, rather than encourages a person to strive toward an integrated self or ego. Archetypal psychology insists as well that patients view themselves as part of a larger myth, the myth of society in which they are living, responsible for the world's health, the soul of the world *(anima mundi)*, rather than their own ego development.

In archetypal psychology, "The aim of therapy . . . is the development of a sense of soul" (Hillman, 1983, p. 4). The term *psychology,* or "logos of psyche," Hillman notes, "etymologically means: reason or speech or intelligible account of soul" (p. 16). Soul is a difficult concept to define. Hillman (1989) says, in part:

> By *soul* I mean, first of all a perspective rather than a substance, a viewpoint towards things rather than a thing itself. This perspective is reflective, it mediates events and makes differences between ourselves and everything that happens. . . . The word refers to that unknown component which makes meaning possible, turns events into experiences, is communicated in love, and has a religious concern. (pp. 20–21)

Hillman does not perceive soul in the strict theological sense. Rather, he says, "Religion approaches Gods with ritual, prayer, sacrifice, worship, creed. . . . In archetypal psychology, Gods are *imagined*" (1983, p. 35). In *Care of the Soul* (1992), Thomas Moore emphasizes how persons can express themselves soulfully in everyday life, whether they are doing dishes, making decisions, cooking, or playing music.

Because imagination is the primary activity of the soul, the major focus in archetypal therapy, similar to that of other Jungians and post-Jungians, is to apply *active imagination* to images sensed in dreams. Instead of analyzing dreams, however, archetypal psychologists help patients deepen their awareness of their dreams or images by reflecting imaginatively on the details of the image. They are encouraged to expand the images, as well, by associating them with particular myths, myths that represent archetypal messages. Image work, however, is not easy. In her cogent and comprehensive article on dream work, "An Approach to the Dream" (1982), Patricia Berry warns, "Our imaginations are untrained, and we have no adequate epistemology of the imagination with which to meet the dream image on its own level" (p. 78).

As with all Jungians, the use of archetypal images is essential in the process of therapy: "Archetypes are the primary forms that govern the psyche. But they cannot be contained only by the psyche, since they manifest as well in physical, social, linguistic, aesthetic, and spiritual modes" (Hillman, 1983, p. 1).

Hillman (1989) says, "The archetypal perspective offers the advantage of organizing into clusters or constellations a host of events from different areas of life" (p. 24). The hero, warrior, lover, and king discussed by R. Moore and Gillette (1990) are examples of archetypes.

Archetypal psychology emphasizes, "For psychology to be possible at all, it must keep the distinction between soul and spirit" (Hillman, 1983, p. 25). The spirit uses scientific objectivity to conceptualize and interpret experiences and to develop rules about behavior (Hillman & Ventura, 1992; Levine, 1992; T. Moore, 1992). According to archetypal psychologists, effective therapy can more likely occur when patients work imaginatively with both soul and spirit together so as to get a better sense of themselves and of the world.

Most therapists, archetypal psychologists argue, try too quickly to free clients from symptoms or problems by explaining or interpreting their behavior, or by using rational problem solving, or by administering psychotropic and tranquilizing drugs. Archetypal psychologists suggest that counselors instead help individuals reflect on the symptoms closely and imaginatively for meaning as part of soul work (T. Moore, 1992).

HUMANISTIC AND EXISTENTIAL THEORIES

All humanists believe to some extent that people possess dignity and worth and are purposeful, active, and capable of directing their own behavior. Existentialism and humanism are similar in their belief that human nature is basically good and that persons have free choice to grow and develop. Existentialists, however, differ significantly from humanists: "They differ in that existentialists take the position that we are faced with the anxiety of choosing to create an identity in a world that lacks intrinsic meaning" (Corey, 1996, p. 199). In counseling practice, they share some basic similarities. Both believe that "the client-therapist relationship is at the core of therapy. . . . Both approaches focus on the client's perceptions and call for the therapist to enter the client's subjective world" (Corey, 1996, p. 200).

Rogers' Client-Centered (Person-Centered) Theory

Carl Rogers (1942, 1951) perceives humans as possessing a basic innate drive toward growth, wholeness, and fulfillment. People have a basic need for high self-regard. If unhampered, individuals will organize their inner and outer experiences into an integrated self through a self-actualizing process. Unhealthy social or psychological influences, in contrast, tend to inhibit individuals from achieving an integrated productive self so that they experience conflicts in expressing their basic needs.

According to Rogerian theory, humans have the ability to resolve conflicts but are limited mainly by lack of awareness about themselves. Conflicts arise when there is a disparity between individuals' basic needs and their needs to gain approval from others.

Rogers (1939, 1942) was impressed with what was called *relationship therapy,* a method he learned in the 1930s during his work as a clinical psychologist in a child guidance clinic in Rochester, New York: "Rooted in many respects in the psychoanalytic concepts of Otto Rank, its development has come almost entirely from the field of social case work, where it has aroused a great deal of interest" (1939, p. 196).

Relationship therapy was promoted by some of Rank's followers, such as psychiatrist Frederick Allen and social worker Jessie Taft. This mode of therapy differed significantly from traditional psychoanalysis in that the therapist does not make intellectual interpretations or conceptual judgments regarding the patient's behavior or expressions aside from clarifying feelings. "This is a different sort of interpretation"

(Rogers, 1939, p. 346). Rogers' landmark book *Counseling and Psychotherapy* (1942) claimed that the counselor role should be *non-directive,* in reaction against the prevailing authoritarian counselors and therapists: "Effective counseling consists of a definitely structured, permissive relationship which allows the client to gain an understanding of himself to a degree which enables him to take positive steps in the light of his new orientation" (p. 18).

Acting on the theory that, in the appropriate environment, individuals self-actualize, the counselor is crucial in providing the right atmosphere that will help clients self-correct behaviors that block growth and, moreover, help clients develop new ways of being that fosters growth. Thus, in counseling, the counselor focuses on the individual, not on the problem; acknowledges the feelings of the client; places more importance on the immediate situation than on the client's past; emphasizes the evolving nature of the counseling process; and perceives the emotional relationship that develops during the process between counselor and client as a therapeutic growth experience.

Rogers' insistence that the counselor assume a non-authoritarian, non-advisory role was a radical departure from conventional therapeutic practice. Without the counselor acting as adviser, the process itself becomes the essence of counseling, a process that can be delineated in a series of stages. The stages indicate the evolving nature of the process itself. The permissive role of the counselor allows the client to explore feelings and develop insights during the ensuing stages; gradually during the process, the client develops feelings of confidence, begins changing dissatisfying behaviors, and risks taking action in unfamiliar ways. Although these stages have been modified over the years of counseling practice, they essentially have remained the same (Rogers, 1942).

Rogers' 1942 book on non-directive counseling influenced the immediate postwar years. In his next book, *Client-Centered Therapy* (1951), however, Rogers virtually eliminated the term *non-directive,* a change that implies he realized the term was misleading, a fear he had noted earlier in his 1939 text. Inexperienced practitioners, he worried, would take *non-directive* to mean that counselors "do nothing" (1939, p. 348). Nevertheless, regarding Rogerian theory, the term *non-directive* stuck for many years.

Rogers' 1951 text describes in more detail his theory that the counseling process itself is the essence. "He focused more explicitly on the actualizing tendency as a basic motivational force that leads to client change" (Corey, 1996, p. 198). Thus, he describes clients' experiences, how their feelings both emerge and evolve during the counseling process as they undergo changes and pass through more complex levels of turbulent feelings, including increased feelings of conflicts, fears, and anxieties.

By focusing on the evolving experiential nature of the therapeutic process itself and by delineating the many characteristic changes the client goes through, Rogers emphasized the sense of movement as the essence of the counseling process: The first part of the counseling session involves changes in client *feelings,* beginning with a movement from feelings of symptoms to self. This is followed by changes of perception about one's feelings of self-worth and of independence; changes in awareness of denial of experience; changes regarding values; changes in development of emotional relationship between client and counselor; and changes in client personality structure and organization. The second part of the counseling session involves characteristic changes in client *behavior,* including increased discussion of plans and behavioral steps to be taken; change from relatively immature behavior to relatively mature behavior; decrease in psychological tension; decrease in defensive behaviors; increased tolerance for frustration as measured in physiological terms; and improved functioning in life tasks (Rogers, 1951).

In 1957, Rogers wrote the article "The Necessary and Sufficient Conditions of Therapeutic Personality Change," in which he elaborated on his earlier views that certain counselor qualities were important in the counselor-client relationship to foster client change. These essential counselor characteristics are *congruency, unconditional positive regard,* and *empathy. Congruency* means the counselor is an authentic, integrated person. *Unconditional positive regard,* often called warmth, is the non-evaluative, nonjudgmental attitude the counselor has toward the client's thoughts, feelings, and behavior. *Empathy* is the counselor's ability to understand the client's world in the way the client does. When these conditions are present, Rogers claimed, clients can arrive at self-understanding and resolve conflicts (see chap. 8).

With the publication of his book *Becoming a Person* (1961), Rogers expanded his theory of the experiential nature of the counseling process into a person's growth experience during the process of life itself. "The process of 'becoming one's experience' is characterized by an openness to experience, a trust in one's experience, an internal locus of evaluation, and the willingness to be a process" (Corey, 1996, p. 199).

In the late 1960s, Rogers turned his attention to human relationships in all spheres of society and consequently changed from individual to group work. The publication of his *On Encounter Groups* in 1970 promoted a wave of encounter groups throughout the country.

At this time, Rogers started calling his theory *person-centered* and wrote books and articles on a person-centered approach to teaching and educational administration, on encounter groups, on marriage and other forms of partnership, and on the "quiet revolution" that he believed would emerge with a new type of "self-empowered person" (Raskin & Rogers, 1995, p. 136).

Largely because of Rogers' influence, most counselors today, regardless of their theoretical framework, generally regard the counseling relationship as a crucial part of counseling. Moreover, many counselors also acknowledge the therapeutic value of the experiential nature of the process itself. "This approach is perhaps best characterized as a way of being and as a shared journey in which therapist and client reveal their humanness and participate in a growth experience" (Corey, 1996, p. 202).

Gestalt Theories

Fredrick ("Fritz") S. Perls (1969) and Laura Perls (1976) were the major developers of Gestalt theories and techniques. After Fritz Perls's death, Walter Kempler (1973) and Yontef and Simkin (1989) became major proponents of this theory. In the Gestalt approach, the purpose is to integrate the person's inner reality (needs, perceptions, emotions) with his or her outer reality (environment). Human experiences always occur in an interactional field (phenomenal field) in which both inner and outer forces are integrated into a whole (called, in German, *Gestalt*). Thus, any inner behavior is immediately responsive to outer behavior and vice versa (Yontef & Simkin, 1989). Humans have potential for functioning in a responsible, genuine way.

Conflict, indecision, or anxiety arises when an inconsistency exists between inner perceptions or needs and demands from the environment. These contradictions can lead to a continual battle between individuals' inherent drive to function authentically, consistent with their inner experiencing self (*self-actualization*), and the need to behave as they believe they should because of expectations of parents and other significant people (*idealized self-actualization*). The goals of counseling are to teach people to become fully aware of themselves and the world and to become mature and responsible for their own lives.

Unlike Rogerians, Gestalt counselors are active teachers who directly confront clients with their inconsistencies. They provoke and persuade clients or manipulate the interview to get clients to correct misperceptions, to express emotions authentically, and to take responsibility for change. The major emphasis is to get clients to respond immediately to experiences. To make clients do so, the counselors confront them with their inconsistencies and with the need to take constructive action regarding unresolved problems related to past experiences (*unfinished business*). This action permits individuals to devote more energy and more awareness to resolving current problems (Corey, 1996).

Besides confrontation, Gestalt counselors use many other techniques, including role playing. In contrast with behaviorists' use of role playing, however, Gestaltists emphasize understanding one's own feelings and the feelings of others, rather than practicing behavior. Another strategy is role reversal, in which clients act out behaviors of individuals with whom they are in conflict. Dialogue games are also used. In these, clients play out both parts of conflicting feelings or attitudes they are experiencing. Empty chair dialogues may also be used. In these dialogues, clients act out conflicts with other persons who are imagined to be in the empty chair. Clients assume both roles and change chairs as they carry out a dialogue. Gestalt counselors encourage their clients to take responsibility for their emotions by using "I" statements, like "*I* am angry," rather than "*It* makes me angry." Body awareness, massage, visual imagery, and dream analysis are also characteristics of Gestalt therapy. Readers interested in more complete discussions can consult Corey (1996), Ivey, Ivey, and Simek-Downing (1993), Levitsky and Perls (1970), and Passons (1975).

Existential Counseling and Therapy

Existential theories are rooted in the European philosophies of Heidegger, Kierkegaard, and Sartre and in the existential practice of European psychiatrists. In the United States, psychoanalyst Rollo May (1961) and psychiatrists Irvin Yalom (1980) and Victor Frankl (1963) have applied the existentialist ideas to their analytic practice.

For existentialists, humans have the self-awareness and the freedom to make choices that will bring meaning to their lives. This freedom and responsibility to live with the consequences of these choices leads to existential anxiety—an essential part of living and being (Corey, 1996; May & Yalom, 1995). "Existential therapists define anxiety more broadly than any other psychotherapeutic groups. *Anxiety arises from our personal need to survive, to preserve our being, and to assert our being*" (May & Yalom, 1995, p. 264).

The well-functioning person is authentically experiencing and expressing needs in a manner not determined by others. People feel guilt and anxiety when they do not take actions they should take or when they do not act responsibly and authentically. Anxieties also arise from an inability to perceive purpose or meaning in life, especially with the realization of death. Existentialists believe that some anxiety is an essential part of life, a condition that encourages people to try to experience life fully and authentically. May (1961) sees awareness of death, for example, as an incentive to live life with zest because people realize that life is only temporary.

Existentialists differ in their view of the dynamics or development of adaptive and maladaptive behavior. May and Yalom (1995) believe that conflict relates to persons' feelings about death, freedom, isolation, and meaninglessness. Frankl's (1963) theory is based on the idea that the unity of an individual has three dimensions—physical, psychological, and spiritual. He emphasizes life's spiritual meaning, including death, love, and suffering. Maladjustment arises when a person has conflicts between various moral or spiritual values.

Frankl's views regarding existential philosophy emerged during his terrible experience in Nazi concentration camps in World War II. Through personal experiences and observations of others in these camps, Frankl came to the conclusion that, in the worst conditions of suffering and torture, humans can maintain spiritual freedom, independent thinking, and opportunities for choice. Meaning and purpose in life are maintained through love and suffering. He says that all things can be taken from individuals except two things—the person's attitude and beliefs.

Several counseling texts were published during the 1960s in which existentialism was applied to counseling practice (Arbuckle, 1967; Dreyfus, 1962; Pine, 1969; Van Kaam, 1967). Existential counselors emphasize subjective inner experiencing and the active, purposeful nature of humans. Human beings develop and experience themselves only in relation to other people in the world (Frankl, 1963; Van Kaam, 1967). Individuals are unique and have not only the capacity but also the responsibility to make choices.

The goal of existential counseling is to help clients explore and develop meaning in life. The counselor can help clients recognize their choice-making potential and understand and accept the consequences of choice for their lives and for the lives of others. Counseling is essentially an encounter between therapist and client. The emphasis is on understanding and experiencing being in an authentic partnership with each other. The problem to be faced is that the world is not necessarily meaningful. Therapists like May and Yalom (1995) and Frankl (1963) believe that confusion and suffering in the world provide opportunity for growth. Existentialist counselors expect clients to commit themselves ultimately to authentic action and to assume responsibility for the consequences of their actions.

Existentialists draw techniques from other psychological theories. For example, May and Yalom (1995) use various psychoanalytic concepts, such as transference and resistance, but interpret them in terms of how they apply to current experiencing. Frankl (1963) developed a technique called *paradoxical intention,* in which clients are encouraged to exaggerate their fears and anxieties, rather than to deny them. Paradoxically, this helps dissolve anxiety. Gendlin (1981) uses a technique now popular with other theorists, called *focusing,* in which clients are taught to become aware of their bodies as a means of bringing forth inner feelings.

Holistic and Transpersonal Counseling

Holistic counselors perceive good mental health as resulting from physical, emotional, intellectual, and spiritual development—all of which are interconnected. Thus, they bring body, mind, and spirit into the counseling arena (Pietrofesa, Hoffman, & Splete, 1984). Physicians, counselors, and psychologists recognize that emotional stress can contribute to or exacerbate many types of physical illnesses, including migraine headaches, asthma, ulcers, back pain, high blood pressure, heart attacks, and cancers. No systematic theories of holistic counseling have been developed.

Techniques are geared to the development of self-awareness and self-monitoring that will promote self-actualization. The best known of these techniques in traditional counseling practice are *biofeedback* and relaxation exercises. Clients are taught to give attention to body functions, such as breathing, body temperature, and body tension, and to mind functions, such as intrusive or negative thoughts. They are then given instructions to relax through controlled breathing, relaxation exercise, meditation, body exercise, visualization of nonstressful scenes, and recitation of poetry. Meditation, yoga, and massage are familiar because of their popularity with health groups and with some Gestaltists and existentialists. Nutrition education is considered crucial because a poorly fed body can interfere with a person's sense of well-being, as well as health.

Transpersonal counseling is the best known holistic approach. According to Walsh (1989), transpersonal therapists believe that the sense of meaningless can best be resolved "by a transformation of one's state of consciousness and sense of identity, such as can occur through meditation" (p. 547). The major goal of transpersonal counselors is to help persons learn to expand personal boundaries and to monitor, facilitate, and unify body, mind, and spirit.

Transpersonal psychology has become very popular among people seeking fulfillment beyond ego development. It emerged out of Abraham Maslow's principle of self-actualization:

> Transpersonal psychology was called the "Fourth Force" psychology by Abraham Maslow in 1969. It has emerged from mainstream psychology and religious studies as the branch of psychology that studies states of consciousness, identity, spiritual growth, and levels of human functioning beyond those commonly accepted as healthy and normal. (Strohl, 1998, p. 397)

This fourth force follows earlier psychological forces—psychoanalytic, behavioral, humanistic (see chap. 2). It adopted various Eastern philosophies and practices of attaining higher states of consciousness. Transpersonal psychology essentially is experiential, rather than intellectual. Many accredited transpersonal training institutions throughout the country offer comprehensive programs of psychological studies and supervised internships. Counseling procedures are similar to humanistic counseling developed by Carl Rogers.

> Transpersonal counselors are generally more concerned with teaching a problem-solving process than with resolving specific problems and complaints. To a transpersonal counselor, conflicts and symptoms are not viewed as illnesses or flaws but as natural consequences of blocked and distorted expressions of one's true identity. They are reminders that the expression of one's deepest truths and potentials are being obstructed by poor choice of thoughts and behaviors. (Strohl, 1998, p. 402)

This humanistically oriented approach tends to overlook or ignore one's unconscious and intrapsychic forces underlying human motivation and behavior. It is often associated with New Age healing, wherein counselors, therapists, and healers engage in a wide variety of mind-altering practices.

New Age spirituality has prompted many professionals to criticize those seeking spiritual enlightenment as a way of escaping their problems and the ills of the world. Clinical psychologist and Buddhist monk Jack Kornfield (1993) warns that most Westerners seeking enlightenment as practiced by Eastern philosophies generally misunderstand such practices. Reaching enlightenment is always temporary, Kornfield says, and only just the beginning of one's spiritual practice, a practice that is a perilous and never-ending discipline.

Depth psychologists working with the unconscious, Jungian psychoanalyst James Hillman (1975, 1983, 1989) and Thomas Moore (1992), described earlier, emphasize that one cannot work with *spirit* without working with *soul*—terms they are careful to distinguish—without grappling with one's shadow or dark side, confronting one's moral dilemmas. Jungian analysts lead the patient down instead of up; they delve into the depths as a way of bringing the unconscious into consciousness, integrating soul with spirit, rather than aim only for higher consciousness.

⤳ BEHAVIORAL, COGNITIVE, AND COGNITIVE-BEHAVIORAL THEORIES

Behavioral and cognitive theories originally developed separately at different times. *Behaviorists,* following B. F. Skinner's theory, which became prominent in the 1950s and 1960s, believe that humans are born *tabla rasa,* a blank slate, without drives or instincts. All behavior is learned. Behaviors that can be scientifically measured constitute the major concern of behaviorists.

Cognitive theorists, who emerged some years later, believe, in contrast, that persons' perceptions are instrumental in processing, selecting, evaluating, and responding to external stimuli. The way a person perceives an event determines his or her response or reaction.

Most behaviorists have since adopted cognitive principles and are now generally known as *cognitive-behaviorists.* Likewise, most cognitive theorists, notably Albert

Ellis (1995), have adopted behaviorist principles and techniques. Ellis changed his rational-emotive therapy (RET) to rational-emotive behavior therapy (REBT). Although all tend now to fall under the term *cognitive-behaviorist,* a few continue to remain primarily cognitive, notably Aaron Beck's (1976a, 1976b) cognitive therapy and George Kelly's (1955, 1963) personal construct theory.

Behavioral Theories

For behaviorists, symptoms in terms of observable behavior are the main concern in the counseling process. Because people react to events in the environment, counselors focus on rewarding positive behavior and extinguishing ineffective behavior by eliminating the conditions that reinforce it. New behavior is then introduced and appropriately reinforced. The counselor is essentially a teacher who helps clients learn new and more adaptive responses to old situations (Corey, 1996).

Operant Conditioning

The first behavioral approach that centered exclusively on observable, overt behavior was developed by B. F. Skinner (1953) and was called *operant conditioning* and *reinforcement theory.* According to Skinner's operant conditioning theory, an individual learns by reacting to observable stimuli. If the response is reinforced through rewards, the behavior will likely be repeated. If the response is ignored or punished, the behavior usually decreases.

This operant approach was popular in the 1960s in working with disruptive children in schools, those with bed-wetting problems, or persons who had mental retardation or schizophrenia (Bijou & Baer, 1965; G. R. Patterson & Guillion, 1968). Since then, key persons who have applied this approach to normal concerns of people in schools and communities are Hosford and DeVisser (1974) and Krumboltz and Thoresen (1976). Counselors have found this theory useful for clients who want to manage or control some undesirable habit or characteristic, such as smoking, overeating, alcohol addiction, or procrastination, or who wish to learn new habits, such as studying effectively, managing time, or improving parenting skills. An important technique is *token economy,* whereby clients gain tokens (positive reinforcement) or lose tokens (penalties), depending on whether they attain a mutually agreed-on target behavior. *Aversive conditioning* also may be used. This conditioning pairs an electric shock or some other unpleasant stimulus with thoughts or pictures of undesirable behavior.

Counter-Conditioning Theory (Desensitization)

Joseph Wolpe (1958, 1969) introduced a behavioral therapeutic approach that reflects the *classical conditioning* work Ivan Pavlov conducted in the 1920s (Wilson, 1995). Pavlov conditioned dogs to salivate at the sound of a bell. At first, Pavlov produced the food, which elicited the salivation, at the sound of the bell. Later, only the bell itself caused the salivation. Using this same learning principle, Wolpe paired anxiety responses with relaxation exercises so that the relaxation exercise gradually extinguished the anxiety response.

Wolpe (1969) demonstrated that emotionally debilitating behavior can be changed by a technique called *systematic desensitization,* a form of classical conditioning called *counter-conditioning. Desensitization* refers to a process that gradually decreases the client's sensitivity to an anxiety-provoking emotion by pairing the emotion with relaxation responses. Wolpe assumed that a person cannot physiologically be anxious and relaxed at the same time. A client, for instance, tells a counselor about an unreasonable fear of dentists. The fear is preventing the client from keeping his or her dental appointments. The client is taught how to relax through a series of relaxation exercises and then is told to imagine gradually increasing anxiety-provoking images about dentists. In this way, the client learns to visualize being worked on in a dentist's chair without anxiety. It is assumed that the person will ultimately be able to see a dentist without fear.

For persons experiencing unmanageable phobic fears, a desensitization technique is used to encourage them to expose themselves gradually to the feared object in real life under the guidance of the counselor. After progressive exposure, clients learn that consequences of facing the fear are not disastrous. *Flooding*—a technique that should be used with care—involves having clients fully expose themselves to the feared situation so that they eventually realize that their fear is unfounded. *Biofeedback* has been used to help clients learn to relax by monitoring their physiological responses: breathing, heartbeat, blood pressure, or muscle tension. Clients are wired to a computerized instrument and are taught to reduce tension by observing feedback from the machine about their biological responses. They ultimately learn to relax by becoming aware of feedback from their own physiological responses without the machine.

Behavioral Self-Control and Management

Thoresen and Mahoney (1974) broadened the base of behaviorism by teaching clients to modify or manage their own undesirable behavior by using self-administered reinforcement. For example, an overweight person is taught to implement changes in his or her environment (keeping records of caloric intake, using smaller plates) and to self-administer a reward if a certain amount of weight is lost in a specific time (give oneself a gift) and to penalize oneself (pay a fine) if the weight is not lost.

Cognitive Theories

Cognitive theorists believe that "how one thinks largely determines how one feels and behaves" (Beck & Weishaar, 1995, p. 229). People's thinking or cognitions relate to their perceptions about themselves and the world around them. Maladaptive thinking results from faulty perceptions or constructs about oneself and others.

Kelly (1955), Beck (1963), and Ellis (1973) were early pioneers in the development of cognitive theories. In the 1990s, Ellis combined his cognitive rational-emotive therapy (RET) with behaviorism and changed its name to rational-emotive behavior therapy (REBT). It thus is discussed in the cognitive-behavioral section of this chapter.

Beck's Cognitive Theory

Aaron T. Beck's (1976a, 1976b) cognitive theory, following Ellis's early RET model, is similar to it in that clients are helped to recognize and change self-defeating thoughts and cognitions that occur in inner *self-talk* (Corey, 1996; Prochaska & Norcross, 1994). It differs from Ellis's approach, however, in that Beck's cognitive therapy is less confrontational. Beck works together with clients to help them discover their own misconceptions. Beck assumes that people live by irrational rules that influence distorted thinking, rather than by irrational beliefs (Beck, 1976a). Beck treats obsessions and phobias but is best known for his work with depression.

In treatment of depression, Beck administers the Beck Depressive Inventory (BDI), based on typical symptoms and beliefs of depressed persons, to assess the severity of the problem. He then teaches systematic skills in self-observation whereby clients observe their thought pattern distortions and their faulty inferences, misperceptions, or exaggerations about external events that are not supported by the evidence (Beck, 1976b).

Next, Beck teaches coping skills. If clients are depressed and are withdrawing from activity, he will help them set up a schedule of activities, beginning with nonthreatening tasks, they can complete successfully. In role playing, he may play the role of the client and display the client's distorted thinking; with self-critical clients, he may use humor. He helps and directs clients to explore and correct misperceptions, list duties and tasks that need to be done, set priorities, and then carry out a realistic plan of action that will reduce depression.

Theory of Personal Constructs

Although George Kelly's landmark book *A Theory of Personality* was published back in 1955 in the United States, his theory of personal constructs and his comprehensive therapeutic system were not generally acknowledged or accepted in professional circles in the United States until about 30 years later (Jankowicz, 1987). Personal construct theory received considerable attention, however, in England and Australia.

Since the 1980s, personal construct theory not only has been acknowledged in the United States by increasing numbers of practitioners but also has been adapted for many specialties. Guterman (1994), for example, explains why it is particularly appropriate for counselors, and Fransella and Dalton's (1990) book *Personal Construct Counselling in Action* describes how this theory can be applied specifically by counselors (see chap. 9); Jankowicz (1987) explains why it works especially well in the corporate business world; Viney (1993) describes how it can be used for older adults (see chap. 15); and Neimeyer (1988) argues how well it works as a theoretical structure for eclecticism (see later in this chapter).

According to Kelly's (1955) theory of personal constructs, individuals look at the world through patterns of constructs. *Constructs* "are ways of construing the world. They are what enables (individuals) . . . to chart a course of behavior" (p. 9). One can improve one's constructs by increasing, altering, and subdividing them. Often, the attempt to alter one's constructs is too great, and individuals seek psychotherapy to help modify or reorganize their construct systems.

Kelly's (1955) basic assumption of his structure or "fundamental postulate" is this: "A person's processes are psychologically channelized by the ways in which he anticipates events" (p. 46). This hypothesis is supported by 11 subsidiary structures or *corollaries*. A person's construct, for example, must replicate itself. Only when a person senses *recurrent themes* does life begin to make sense. Corollaries speak to the evolving, changing nature of one's constructs, that they are individualistic, dichotomous, limited in range, applicable to certain contexts, open to choice as well as to change, part of a complex interrelated system, susceptible to social influences, and subject to incompatibility within the system.

In describing the nature of a construct or the way one uses one's constructs, Kelly (1955) explains quite simply, "A construct is a way in which some things are construed as being alike and yet different from others" (p. 105). One construes events by comparison and contrast, or more basically by noting opposites. White is the opposite of black. A construct is termed *emergent* when several elements start forming around the similarity pole (replication, or recurring patterns). At this point, the individual assigns the pattern a name. The use of symbols, Kelly notes, is "characteristic in the early stages in the formation and use of any construct" (p. 139). "Construct theorists (are) . . . concerned with finding better ways to help a person reconstrue his life so that he need not be the victim of his past" (p. 23).

Much of the emphasis in therapy is acknowledging that one's constructs are incompatible or inappropriate, out of alignment. Normally, on the one hand, an individual is constantly reevaluating his or her system as the individual encounters new experiences. On the other hand,

> if he fails to reconstrue events, even though they keep repeating themselves, he minimizes his experience. . . . If he is prepared to perceive events in new ways, he may accumulate experience rapidly. It is this adaptability which provides a more direct measure of the growing validity of a man's construct system. (p. 172)

A strong advocate of personal construct therapies for counselors is J. T. Guterman (1994). He argues persuasively its merits for counselors because it is a process model, in contrast with a diagnostic prescriptive "realist" approach used by some mental health practitioners.

> Social constructionist theories have . . . been described as process-oriented models because they emphasize change processes rather than formal-theory content. . . . (p. 236)
>
> Social constructionist models . . . take a collaborative approach with clients in contrast with the educative position that is usually assumed within the context of realist models. (p. 236)

Cognitive-Behavioral Theories

In the 1970s, many behaviorists realized that conditioning procedures were too limited to explain behavior adequately and saw the value of combining with cognitive theories. Cognitive-behaviorists aim to change clients' inaccurate, subjective perceptions about themselves and their environment by uncovering faulty assumptions and beliefs that underlie their thinking that are causing them personal or interpersonal problems. The counselors then teach logical reasoning skills to restructure these thinking patterns and correct problems (Corey, 1996). This process is called *cognitive restructuring*.

Ellis's Rational-Emotive Behavior Therapy (REBT)

In the 1970s, Albert Ellis (1973, 1989, 1995) introduced his theory that most human problems relate to irrational beliefs that arise because of illogical reasoning. Believing that thinking and emotion are not separate processes, he claimed that emotional problems result from illogical thought processes. Thus, he coined the term *rational-emotive therapy* (*RET*). About 1995, he changed RET to *rational-emotive behavior therapy* (*REBT*) because he believed that it more accurately describes his approach.

Ellis lists about a dozen irrational beliefs that he believes plague most people in our culture. These beliefs relate to unrealistic ideas or expectations about themselves, about others, and about the world in general. For example, it is irrational to become very upset over other people's problems or to believe that the world is a catastrophic place when things are not as one would like them to be. These ideas form and are reinforced when a child is exposed to parents and others who model irrational thinking. The goal of counseling is to help clients attain logical approaches to solving problems.

Ellis's famous *ABC principle* emphasizes the importance of the perception one has of a stimulus. *A* represents the stimulus, *B* is the belief related to *A* (perception of the stimulus), and *C* is the consequence. For example, a male student comes to counseling complaining that he feels worthless (*C*) because he did poorly on a math test (*A*). The counselor will try to show that the failure (*A*) is not what really caused these feelings, but rather it was his perception of the failure (*B*). Ellis believes that people use illogical internalized sentences, which he calls *self-talk*. In this case, the student thinks, (*A*) I failed my math test; (*B*) I should not have failed, for only worthless people fail; and (*C*) how worthless I am for failing. The counselor helps the student see that belief *B* is irrational.

After clients go through the *ABC* steps, Ellis then helps them change their illogical thinking in a process he calls *disputing* (*D*). During this stage, counselors proceed to teach more rational belief systems. Persuasion, cajolery, provocation, and subtle coercion are used where necessary. Homework assignments are given to help clients practice thinking rationally. REBT counselors use other behavioral techniques when appropriate, including self-management, assertiveness training, relaxation exercises, and systematic desensitization (Ellis, 1973, 1989, 1995).

Social Learning Theory

Social learning theorists counteracted the behaviorists' conditioning model in the 1960s and 1970s by claiming that learning can occur when individuals imitate the behavior of others even though the imitation is not directly reinforced. Albert Bandura (1977) has been a major proponent of social learning theory. Actors, either live or on video, are used to model socially desirable or socially effective behavior. Clients observe and imitate the models' behavior. This approach has been used to treat phobias. Modeling of fearless behavior is often effective for phobias. For example, children fearful of dentists may be shown films of a friendly dentist interacting pleasantly with cheerful children. Or a client who fears snakes observes a model petting a snake. Video- or audiotape recordings, autobiographies, and typescripts can be used to demonstrate the desired behavior.

The emphasis on external factors makes possible a wide range of techniques. Counselors may demonstrate culturally appropriate behavior by serving as models or by using other persons to model behavior. Problem-solving or logical-reasoning skills may be taught. Another popular approach is role playing, in which counselor and client assume the roles of other persons in the client's life and practice appropriate responses. Clients are given reinforcement, or are taught to reinforce themselves, for desired behavior. Clients may also be trained in specific social skills, such as assertiveness. Homework assignments are considered an essential part of counseling (Bandura, 1977).

Meichenbaum's Cognitive-Behavioral Modification

Donald Meichenbaum (1977, 1985) uses a self-instructional technique called *cognitive restructuring*. Like Ellis and Beck, Meichenbaum (1985) believes that distorted thought processes are at the base of stress or emotional problems (Corey, 1996).

Meichenbaum believes that persons are as afflicted by self-talk as they are by explicit comments of others. The goal of counseling, then, is to teach clients the skills to change their maladaptive ways of talking to themselves. Therapy involves teaching clients first to observe their own behavior and listen to themselves, second to develop a new, more adaptive internal dialogue (self-talk), and finally to learn new coping skills so that they will be able to handle stressful situations in real life (Corey, 1996).

A coping-skills learning program usually starts by exposing clients to an anxiety-provoking situation through role playing or imagery. Clients then evaluate their anxiety level and become aware of their anxious self-statements. Next, they make changes in their self-talk and note the decrease in level of anxiety after the evaluation (Corey, 1996). This procedure is effective for working with those with social or sexual dysfunctions, test or speech anxieties, phobias, or addictions (Meichenbaum, 1977, 1985).

Meichenbaum (1985) teaches stress management skills by means of what he calls *stress-inoculation therapy (SIT)*. As in desensitization approaches, clients are taught to use a graded system in evaluating stress: They start by imagining the simplest stress situations they can manage and then try progressively to imagine more intense, stressful situations. At each stage, they are taught various problem-solving skills: defining the problem, choosing alternatives, making decisions, and verifying outcomes. He encourages clients to use various kinds of relaxation exercises similar to those used by holistic counselors—meditation, breath control, yoga, jogging, gardening, and walking. He believes that stress management training is useful in assertiveness training, anger control, treatment of depression, improving creativity, and treating health problems.

Coping skills learned in the sessions are practiced in real-life situations through increasingly difficult assigned exercises and homework. These activities prepare clients to apply these new learnings after they terminate counseling.

Lazarus's Multimodal Therapy

Arnold Lazarus (1976, 1995) developed a multimodal therapy in which counseling or therapy is tailored to the individual client's need by the use of techniques taken from all the theories—cognitive-behavioral, psychoanalytic, psychodynamic, and humanistic. Lazarus classifies himself as a social and cognitive-learning theorist because his beliefs are based on empirical principles of learning. He makes the point, however, that he is not theoretically eclectic, but rather technically eclectic.

Maladaptive behaviors or problems are assumed to result from deficient or faulty social learning. The goals of counseling are to bring about, in an efficient and humane way, client-desired change in behavior that will be enduring (Lazarus, 1995).

Using the acronym *BASIC I.D.,* Lazarus describes seven major areas of personality: (a) **b**ehavior (observable action), (b) **a**ffective (emotional), (c) **s**ensation (feelings), (d) **i**mages (imagination), (e) **c**ognitions (thought process), (f) **i**nterpersonal relationships (social), and (g) **d**rugs/biological (physical). A counselor must consider each of these modalities in assessing a person's problem and prognosis. An important feature of this approach is that every individual is considered unique, with his or her own *BASIC I.D.,* so no one theory or set of techniques can work with everyone.

Clients first fill out a life history questionnaire and rate themselves on each modality of the BASIC I.D. Profile. The counselor, after making an assessment based on the client's responses and the counselor's observations, uses a procedure called *bridging.* Bridging means that the counselor first focuses on the client's preferred personality mode before exploring the other modalities. If the client functions predominantly from a cognitive mode, the counselor at first interacts and then responds, also in a cognitive way.

Among the wide variety of techniques used by behavioral and cognitive-behavioral counselors, multimodal counselors may use reinforcement procedures, assertiveness training, desensitization, biofeedback, and cognitive restructuring, especially in behavioral, affective, and cognitive modes. In physical and imagery modes, multimodal counselors may add Gestalt and holistic techniques, such as empty chair or role reversal dialogues, confrontation, abdominal breathing, positive visual imagery, and focusing. In the interpersonal mode, they may use self-management, instruction in parenting, and social skills. In drug and biological considerations, they make certain that appropriate medication is available and that inappropriate medication is curtailed. Like holistic counselors, multimodal counselors will encourage good nutrition, physical fitness, and exercise.

➾ THEORIES OF CREATIVE AND EXPRESSIVE ARTS THERAPY

Creative and expressive arts therapies are based on the belief that many persons express themselves nonverbally in ways they are unable to do otherwise. Thus, expressive arts, used therapeutically, in one way or another can reveal one's nature as it evolves over time; reveal feelings; release defenses that block or inhibit growth; and as symbolic expression, reveal one's inner self or soul.

Creative and expressive arts therapies are rapidly gaining favor among counselors and therapists in a wide range of therapeutic settings. Much has been written about creative arts counseling and therapy in which the client works with imagery, drawing, dancing, music, drama, or poetry during counseling and therapy sessions (Levine, 1992; McNiff, 1988). The therapeutic use of storytelling is gaining attention among professionals. Especially helpful in describing how stories are used therapeutically are Clarissa Pinkola Estés's book *Women Who Run with the Wolves* (1992) and Michael Meade's book *Men and the Water of Life* (1993).

Fleshman and Fryrear (1981) comment, "The art therapies, to a very great extent, have grown from the early seed planted by Jung" (p. 33). Carl Jung's theory of active imagination and archetypes, as well as his use of creative arts in his own life and in his therapy, were strong influences in the development of art therapies. Kaufmann (1989) says, "In Jung's consulting room, people danced, sang, acted, mimed, played musical instruments, painted and modeled with clay, the procedures limited only by Jung's inventiveness and ingenuity" (p. 132). Dalley et al. (1987) tie Jung's early work to current creative arts practice. They say, "His technique of active imagination which deliberately mobilized the patient's creativity is an approach that many art therapists use today" (p. 9). Douglas (1995) comments that Jung encouraged arts therapy "as a conscious way to express elements of the unconscious" (p. 118).

Creative arts therapist Stephen Levine (1992) indicates how archetypal psychology, discussed earlier in the chapter, has given impetus to creative arts therapy:

> Given this conception of psychotherapy and its relation to the imagination, it becomes clear why the arts need to enter into the therapeutic process and why, in recent years, different expressive arts therapies have emerged with such vigor. (p. 3)

Unlike Jung, Freud was ambivalent about the idea of using creative arts in therapy and did little with it in practice (Dalley et al., 1987; Levine, 1992). Even so, some of his followers used creative art techniques, primarily drawing and painting, with children (Robbins, 1980).

Among the humanists, those most closely aligned with the concepts and techniques of art therapies are the Gestaltists, followed by the self-theorists (Dalley et al., 1987; Fleshman & Fryrear, 1981). Because of their emphasis on wholeness of body and mind and the connections between feelings and actions, Gestaltists encourage body movements, dance, massage, drama, acting out dreams, and the use of imagery. Self-theorists also encourage their clients to express themselves in poetry writing, drawing, or dance.

Behaviorists, because of their focus on observable actions of clients and external factors influencing these actions, tend to use creative activities as reinforcements or rewards. Cognitive-behaviorists, such as Lazarus, Meichenbaum, and Wolpe, who are concerned about perceptions and distorted thought processes, use imagery as a way of helping clients change behavior (Corey, 1996; Fleshman & Fryrear, 1981; Robbins, 1980).

Personal construct counselors use numerous creative arts therapies to help nonverbal clients become aware of their self-perceptions—the way they construe themselves. Drawings, including interactive drawings between counselor and client, have been effective for those clients who have difficulty talking. Working with clay, music, and dance are also effective. Of particular value is what personal construct counselors call *enactment.* The client acts the part of a significant person in his or her life. Or client and counselor together act certain parts and then exchange parts (Fransella & Dalton, 1990).

➛ ECLECTICISM

The 1980s saw a growing trend toward eclecticism among practitioners. In an overview of research, Lambert, Shapiro, and Bergin (1986) said that "there is a major trend toward eclecticism or integration of diverse techniques and concepts into a broad, comprehensive, and pragmatic approach to treatment that avoids strong allegiance to narrow theories of schools of thought" (p. 157). Neimeyer (1988) cites several studies indicating that about 40% of practitioners called themselves eclectic.

More recently, however, researchers have criticized eclecticism, charging that inexperienced counselors are apt to adopt eclecticism because they are inadequately trained: "A frequent charge leveled at eclectic practitioners is that they employ various techniques indiscriminately, to the detriment of their clients. . . . there is a tendency to assume that haphazard eclecticism results from an atheoretical orientation" (Neimeyer, 1988, p. 285).

Although attempts have been made to achieve a unified, integrated system to counteract the randomness of eclecticism, Neimeyer (1988) does not support this approach. "The unificationist view . . . is objectionable because it directly contradicts the relativistic, narrative view of social reality" (p. 293).

Neimeyer (1988) argues instead that personal construct theory, described earlier, could provide a basis, a coherence to eclecticism. He cites authors who acknowledge "personal construct therapy to be *technically eclectic but theoretically consistent*" (p. 290).

Although eclecticism should not consist of a haphazard use of various techniques from different theoretical approaches, I believe there is value in developing a carefully considered eclectic approach. No one theory is applicable to all clients, to all types of client problems, or to clients who come from various socioeconomic and multicultural backgrounds. To develop a sound, eclectic point of view, counselors must be aware of their own underlying assumptions about human nature and human psychological growth and development. They can then select concepts and techniques from the various theories that are consistent with their own philosophy.

My eclecticism has gradually evolved and developed over many years of practice. It is based predominantly on a psychosocial, psychodynamic, phenomenological view about human development, combined with humanistic and cognitive-behavioral concepts that are consistent with and that amplify this perspective. In the early days of counseling, I was trained in a combination of humanistic and existential theories; the psychosocial, psychodynamic theories of Adler, Horney, and Sullivan; and the early vocational development theories as they applied to situational problems and concerns of normal individuals.

I responded to humanistic and existential views that humans have the capacity to determine their purpose in life and to make choices and that they have the potential to grow and the responsibility to acknowledge their behavior and make changes when necessary. The phenomenological, humanistic, client-centered approach of Rogers helped me drop the prevailing authoritarian role of the counselor and participate in a process-oriented counseling experience with clients, one that fosters clients' ability for self-exploration. Moreover, I found the existential view that a person's anxieties, which arise from the conflicts of free choice, is useful as a catalyst for change. I have trouble, however, with the inherently automatic nature of the self-actualizing principle and with the belief that minimal interactions with others are beneficial for one to self-actualize freely. Neither can I accept the Gestaltist's belief that persons are responsible only for themselves and, consequently, their minimizing attention to the interactive dynamics between persons.

From psychodynamic approaches, I gained depth in my counseling as I developed awareness of unconscious intrapsychic forces that influence a person's attitudes and behaviors and are part of the dynamics of human interaction. Furthermore, these theories helped me recognize that resistance, transference, and countertransference are essential components of counseling relationships. I also learned early from psychosocial theorists to focus on the social context in which the client experiences the problem. However, I found the tendency of psychoanalytic theories to conceptualize and interpret behavior inhibiting to the kind of counselor-client collaborative relationship that fosters client growth and development.

I was later drawn to Erik Erikson's ego-analytic, life-span developmental theory based on individuals passing through transitional stages in which the conflicts they experienced were commensurate with the particular stage in life; it was a theory consistent with earlier psychosocial views of Adler and Horney.. The work of ego-analytic therapies with families has been very influential to my approach. Erikson's theory is limited, however, in that it excludes women's experience, as well as the developmental experiences of various cultural and ethnic groups. Women at the Stone Center, however, have since compensated for this lack by contributing their own psychodynamic developmental theories that emphasize the mutuality of connections in relationships as essential to growth.

At the same time, I find that certain cognitive and cognitive-behavioral theories are compatible with my phenomenological approach to working with clients' situational problems, particularly the strategies of helping them become aware of faulty, illogical reasoning or faulty perceptions of reality that may be interfering with their ability to cope and to relate to others. The emphasis on specifying goals and using motivational techniques is particularly helpful in the latter stages of counseling. Cognitive-behavioral approaches, however, may be so involved in cognitive processes that emotional responses and underlying dynamics in relationships are ignored.

Certain post-Jungian and archetypal theories have helped me consider human behaviors and symptoms symbolically, reflect on spiritual needs and needs of the soul, think imaginatively about dreams or other events in one's life, and gain a sense of the kind of myth in which one is living. At the same time, trained as I was by secular, scientific, and empirical psychologies, it is difficult for me to understand the concepts of psyche, soul, and spirit and to imagine these psychological phenomena in a mythical context.

My eclectic approach is demonstrated more clearly later in the text, particularly chapter 9, on the counseling process, and chapters 16 to 19, where I present case studies and describe various counseling practices in the field.

✦ THEORIES OF BRIEF COUNSELING AND THERAPY

Brief counseling and therapy has increased rapidly in community mental health practice. As the demand for mental health services increased in the community in the 1980s and funding for these services declined sharply, the idea of planned short-term therapy developed. Health maintenance organizations (HMOs) and employee assistance programs (EAPs) emerged with a deliberate emphasis on "brief, highly-focused therapeutic services" (Wells, 1994, p. 3). Managed care soon followed; because it was related to third-party payments, it deliberately shortened the treatment period. With the rise in popularity of managed health care, brief therapy became a standard model.

In contrast with traditional counseling theories, therapists using brief counseling set specific goals and specify that the number of sessions will be limited. Counselors, moreover, focus on helping clients develop coping skills that will enable them to anticipate and manage future problems, as well as resolve immediate concerns.

Intermittent counseling is another form of brief counseling. In this approach, clients see counselors or therapists off and on over the years as problems arise, rather than spend long periods of time trying to make general personality changes. This model is consistent with the way patients see physicians or dentists. An individual experiencing a particular difficulty sees a therapist or counselor for a limited time until the problem is resolved and then returns when the problem recurs or another problem arises.

Short-term therapy and counseling has a long history. The chief difference with brief therapy now is that therapy is deliberately planned and sessions are determined in advance to be completed within a set period of time. The beginnings of short-term therapies go back to the earliest Freudian analysts: "At that time, the prevailing mood among psychoanalytic thinkers was that therapeutic intervention could be brief, concise, and effective. Examples abound of therapies being successfully completed in several visits" (Budman & Gurman, 1988, p. 1). Freud at first limited his analysis with patients to 6 to 12 visits, but analysis became more prolonged as clients brought in more complex concerns and as the goals of analysts became more ambitious (Phillips, 1985). As analysis became longer, psychoanalysts Alfred Adler, Otto Rank, and Sandor Ferenczi objected (Garfield, 1989). In later years, Alexander and French (1946) noted that as analysts focused more on the client's immediate conflicts rather than the client's childhood traumas, fewer sessions of analysis were needed.

A great impetus for brief counseling came with the emergence of the profession of counseling in the late 1940s and 1950s. The emphasis on working with developmental concerns of normally functioning individuals was geared to short-term approaches. In the late 1940s, when I counseled at UC–Berkeley Counseling Center, we found that the majority of our clients could be helped on a short-term basis. In the high school where I practiced in the 1950s, our counseling was naturally brief, and it was naturally intermittent as well because students kept returning to see their counselor over the 4-year period they were enrolled. So, right from the beginning, college and school counseling typically engaged in short-term work because counseling problems centered on transitional, situational concerns that were limited to a person's effectiveness in school.

Many counselors and other mental health providers object to agencies deliberately limiting the number of sessions for all clients. Although it is true that many clients profit from short-term therapy, others need longer term help to resolve their problems. A more effective policy is one in which the number of sessions is determined by the client's particular problem, with an extension of sessions when the client needs it.

Brief therapy is used in both psychodynamic and cognitive-behavioral therapies. Counselors and therapists who use short-term psychodynamic approaches focus on the therapeutic relationship and, unlike long-term analysts, work only with the client's current circumstances. Short-term cognitive-behavioral therapists set specific goals, teach new learning skills, and emphasize practice of new behavior. Psychodynamic theories appear more frequently in the literature, but in practice, particularly in managed care settings, cognitive and cognitive-behavioral approaches are more commonly used (Koss & Butcher, 1986).

Common themes for all approaches are that clients have a prior history of adequate adjustment and an adequate ability to relate; moreover, a situational difficulty has arisen that has provoked a dilemma, anxiety, or crisis, such as loss of a job or sudden weight gain.

Psychodynamic Brief Counseling and Therapy

Lewis Wolberg's (1980) *A Handbook of Short-Term Psychotherapy* presents a comprehensive and thorough discussion of how psychodynamic concepts can be adapted to brief therapy. Wolberg indicates that it is important to "focus on what is of immediate concern to the patient, such as incidents in life that have precipitated the symptoms for which he seeks help" (p. 99). Thus, therapists focus on some particular situational problem of the client. Transference feelings and dream content are related to the client's current concerns and circumstances.

Psychodynamic theories getting the most attention are Strupp and Binder's (1984) time-limited dynamic psychotherapy, Sifneos's (1979) short-term dynamic psychology, Davenloo's (1978) short-term dynamic psychotherapy, and Mann's (1973) time-limited psychotherapy. Mann's time-limited psychotherapy (TLP) relates particularly well to counselors: "This psychoanalytic approach is compatible with counseling psychology's emphasis on client strengths, is suited to intact personalities, and places a premium on brevity" (Gelso & Fretz, 1992, p. 210). Further, this approach is consistent with Eric Erikson's human development theory in that Mann recognizes that conflicts happen during transitions that occur throughout life.

Mann's (1973) approach is limited to 12 sessions. He focuses on a central issue, the crisis of separation and individuation that reoccurs in different forms throughout the individual's life. "There are countless experiences throughout life that revive repeatedly the sense of loss and anxiety related to separation-individuation phase. Loss of money, of power, of a relationship, of self-esteem and of a job . . . are obvious examples" (Gelso & Fretz, 1992, p. 212).

The therapist in TLP focuses on the client's feelings of loss and anxiety, rather than develops a diagnosis about underlying conflicts and repression that are contributing to the anxiety (Mann, 1973; White, Burke, & Havens, 1981). Although the therapist explores the client's past and relates it to the present, this exploration is limited to those experiences that are relevant to the client's central problem (Gelso & Fretz, 1992; Mann, 1973).

Therapists employ an empathic approach throughout the 12 sessions, using the counseling process as a positive experience of union and separation. They are understanding of the client's pain but at the same time are unequivocal in maintaining 12 sessions to resolve the client's dilemma.

> The two opening moves by the therapist, setting up an empathic bond for which the patient has yearned and then announcing that it will be terminated, build a structure for the therapy that will continue throughout its course with the oscillation between magical fantasies and harsh reality. (White et al., 1981, p. 250)

This experience, according to Mann (1973), will make "separation a genuine maturational event" (p. 36).

Some Cautions About Brief Dynamic Therapies

Strupp and Binder (1984) developed *time-limited dynamic psychotherapy (TLDP)*, involving 25 to 30 sessions, a system similar to Mann's theory. Earlier, Strupp (1981) had expressed cautions about the limitations of psychodynamic brief therapies:

> We have not gone far enough in this endeavor. . . . I believe there are definite limits to what time-limited dynamic psychotherapy . . . can accomplish, and that outcomes depend importantly on patient selection, the goals to which the therapist (and the patient) aspire, and the nature of the therapeutic changes the therapist is able to engender. (p. 238)

Recent criticism of time-limited, brief therapy is discussed later in this section.

Cognitive and Cognitive-Behavioral Brief Counseling and Therapy

Cognitive and cognitive-behavioral theories generally are easily adapted to brief counseling and therapy because they are goal oriented and focus on presenting issues or symptoms of relatively short duration. The major brief cognitive and cognitive-behavioral approaches used in mental health practice today are based on the strategic theories of Jay Haley (1977) and Milton Erickson (1980) (see also chap. 10).

Brief Strategic Therapy

Early strategic counselors and therapists used intervention strategies to direct or manipulate changes in client repetitive, nonproductive behavior without regard for client emotions or situational factors. Strategic therapists now attend to both client emotions and social context (Cade & O'Hanlon, 1993). They also refrain from using manipulative interventions the way they used to; they are careful now to avoid using interventions that are unethically deceptive or potentially harmful to clients. Cade and O'Hanlon (1993) say, "We have become more concerned with the resourcefulness of our clients and with avoiding approaches that disempower either overtly or covertly" (p. xii).

Two forms of brief strategic therapy are described here: Donald Genter's brief strategic therapy and solution-focused brief therapy.

Genter's Brief Strategic Therapy. In Genter's (1991) brief strategic model, the counselor defines the problem, establishes goals, designs an intervention, assigns a strategic task, emphasizes positive new behavior changes, and then, before termination, helps the client learn to incorporate new behaviors gradually into everyday living.

Counselors ask specific and systematic questions to learn client perceptions of the problem and about social circumstances related to the problem. They also explore attempts the client has made to try to resolve the problem. Goals are specific—only those that can be observed and measured directly. Intervention strategies focus on constructive reframing of the problem and on strategic tasks assigned to encourage the client to make gradual, progressive, positive changes in behavior. The client is then encouraged to try out new behaviors and experiences in everyday life.

Solution-Focused Brief Therapy. Solution-focused brief therapy has been particularly adaptable to limited therapy as practiced in managed care. Steve de Shazer (1988), one originator of this approach, acknowledges that major influences were Weakland, Fisch, Watzlawick, and Bodin (1974), Haley (1977), and Erickson (1980).

Unlike brief strategic and traditional cognitive-behavioral approaches, counselors using a solution-focused brief model do not analyze or investigate presenting problems of clients. Talking only about constructing solutions has shortened the time necessary to bring about client change. Counselors "realized that only solution goal talk was necessary, that solution construction was independent of problem processes" (Walter & Peller, 1992, p. 8).

Counselors focus on client strengths and on solutions that are different from unsuccessful methods that clients have been attempting. They look for exceptions to client problem behavior and aim for small changes. Therapists work with clients who are able to cooperate and who have the ability to solve their problems. They start with changes the clients want, help them select goals that will work for them, and help them choose different tasks when client attempts are not successful (Walter & Peller, 1992).

Traditional Cognitive-Behavioral Models Adapted to Brief Therapy

Burbach, Borduin, and Peake (1988) describe how cognitive and cognitive-behavioral theories have traditionally been based on goal-oriented, short-term procedures: "Cognitive approaches have much to offer the practitioners of brief psychotherapy" (p. 57).

Two cognitive-behavioral theorists described earlier in the chapter—Ellis (REBT) and Lazarus (multimodal therapy)—have adapted their approaches to fit into a brief therapy model. Ellis (1992, 1995) perceives little change from his original position that clients learn to reframe or reconstruct and dispute beliefs that are causing emotional or behavioral problems.

In a similar vein, Lazarus (1989) published an article, "Brief Psychotherapy: The Multimodal Model," in which he uses a technical eclecticism to help clients solve problems in the modalities (BASIC I.D.) that are causing difficulties. He advocates an intermittent short-term approach so that clients, once they solve a certain set of problems, may seek further help as new problems arise.

When Is Brief Therapy Enough?

Increasing numbers of counselors and therapists, including advocates of brief therapy, are acknowledging that some clients with more severe symptoms or whose symptoms are susceptible to relapse require some form of longer therapy. Erica Goode (1998) discusses the importance of distinguishing those clients needing longer term treatment from those who profit best from brief therapy. She recommends that more studies be conducted to determine to what degree length of counseling depends on the type of client and/or client problem.

In addition to considering increasing the number of counseling sessions, more therapists are suggesting intermittent counseling. Psychiatrist Simon Budman, an advocate of brief therapy, is a proponent of this sort of arrangement. Clients, he says, "may benefit from a longer term with a therapist even if they come in for a session every few months, or a few weeks or every few years" (Goode, 1998, p. 10). Budman may see some patients over a period of years, "but intermittently dealing with different problems as they come upon the patient's life" (Goode, 1998, p. 10).

Goode (1998) predicts that exerted efforts by both frustrated practitioners and dissatisfied patients eventually will change policy so that allowances for longer term treatment will be granted when necessary.

⇥ SUMMARY

Counseling theories represent rationales about human nature and development that provide counselors with the means by which they can create a framework that determines the way they view the counseling process, their clients and the way they interact with them, and their goals and techniques. Counseling theories are divided in this text into five categories: (a) psychoanalytic and psychodynamic, (b) humanistic and existential, (c) behavioral, cognitive, and cognitive-behavioral, (d) creative and expressive arts, and (e) brief therapies.

Psychoanalytic and psychodynamic theorists believe that unconscious, intrapsychic forces within individuals are central to behavior. Freud proposed that instinctual, psychosexual (id) forces shape behavior; later psychoanalytic theorists Adler, Horney, and Sullivan emphasized instead that behavior developed within a psychosocial context.

Following them, ego-analytic theorists, notably Erikson, proposed that the ego has its own energies that drive individuals to develop the skill necessary to become autonomous and to master their environment. Object relations theorists added that one's relationships help one grow and become autonomous. Women at the Stone Center, contrary to ego-analytic and object relations theories, believe that growth develops through mutual connections in relationships.

Jung parted company with the Freudian theory that the unconscious is basically deterministic and destructive, theorizing instead that the unconscious can be positive and productive when it is integrated into one's consciousness, an endeavor that can be done through imaginative activity related to myths and archetypes. Post-Jungian archetypal psychologists focus more on a metaphorical awareness of one's experience, one that connects with archetypal images. They acknowledge as well the process of depth psychology that involves developing a sense of soul and moral commitment.

Humanists and existentialists believe that humans have potentialities for positive growth. Humanists emphasize that a self-actualizing process moves individuals to increased self-awareness and development. Existentialists assume that individuals' freedom to determine meaning in life creates anxiety, an anxiety that potentially can become a growth force.

Behavioral theorists believe that behavior is shaped through reinforcement or imitation. Cognitive and cognitive-behavioral theorists assume that one's perceptions influence one's thinking, feeling, and actions. They both emphasize that learning is central to development. Personal construct theorists believe that individuals develop constructs that shape the way they perceive (construe) events and experience, a process that evolves by reshaping one's constructs through new experiences.

According to creative arts theorists, individuals' nonverbal expressions through art, dancing, music, or other creative activities help them express underlying feelings blocking their growth.

Brief therapy and counseling theories, developed by both psychodynamic and cognitive-behavioral theorists, have become prominent in practice because of rising costs of mental health, limited budgets, and increased demand for counseling in schools, colleges, and the community.

❧ PROJECTS AND ACTIVITIES

1. Compare Rogers' later writings with his original client-centered theory published in 1942. What are the similarities and differences?
2. Interview counselors in a college, in a school, or in the community concerning how they arrived at their current views about counseling theories.
3. Review the work of the women at Stone Center, Wellesley College regarding their views about the importance of connections in women's development. Do you agree with them that this perspective could apply equally to men's development? Why or Why not?
4. Both social learning theorists and phenomenologists agree that perception is an important dimension of behavior. How do they differ in their definitions of the process of perception and the way it relates to behavior or attitudes?

5. Compare a cognitive-behaviorist with a humanist in terms of their views about human nature and their definition of counseling. How do their beliefs and definitions influence their counseling goals and the type of relationship they establish with clients?

6. List techniques used by each of the following: Personal construct theorists and Gestaltists. Determine differences in type and use of the techniques, and indicate how these differences tie in with philosophical views on human nature and reality.

7. Interview several mental health specialists who classify themselves as psychoanalytic counselors or therapists. Compare their views of the therapeutic process with Freud's original descriptions of psychoanalysis. Find out why they classify themselves as psychoanalytic practitioners.

8. Select the theory you like most and the one you like least. Review the current research about the effectiveness of each theory. Does this research change your attitudes or confirm them?

✦ REFERENCES

Alexander, F., & French, T. M. (1946). *Psychoanalytic therapy: Principles and applications.* New York: Ronald Press.

Ansbacher, H. L., & Ansbacher, R. R. (Eds.). (1973). *Superiority and social interest: A collection of later writings.* New York: Viking.

Arbuckle, D. (Ed.). (1967). *Counseling and psychotherapy: An overview.* New York: McGraw-Hill.

Baker, E. L. (1985). Psychoanalysis and psychoanalytic therapy. In S. J. Lynn & J. R. Garske (Eds.), *Contemporary psychotherapies: Models and methods* (pp. 19–67). Upper Saddle River, NJ: Merrill/Prentice Hall.

Bandura, A. (1977). *Social learning theory.* Upper Saddle River, NJ: Prentice Hall.

Beck, A. T. (1963). Thinking and depression: Idiosyncratic content and cognitive distortions. *Archives of General Psychiatry, 9,* 324–333.

Beck, A. T. (1976a). *Cognitive therapy and emotional disorders.* New York: New American Library.

Beck, A. T. (1976b). *Depression: Clinical, experimental, and theoretical aspects.* New York: Harper & Row.

Beck, A. T., & Weishaar, M. E. (1995). Cognitive therapy. In R. J. Corsini & D. Wedding (Eds.), *Current psychotherapies* (5th ed., pp. 229–261). Itasca, IL: F. E. Peacock.

Bennett, E. A. (1983). *What Jung really said.* New York: Schocken Books.

Berry, P. (1982). An approach to the dream. In P. Berry, *Echo's subtle body: Contributions to an archetypal psychology* (pp. 53–79). Dallas, TX: Spring.

Bijou, S. W., & Baer, D. M. (1965). *Child's development* (Vol. 2). New York: Appleton-Century-Crofts.

Bly, R. (1990). *Iron John: A book about men.* Reading, MA: Addison-Wesley.

Brammer, L., Abrego, P. J., & Shostrom, E. L. (1993). *Therapeutic counseling and psychotherapy* (6th ed.). Upper Saddle River, NJ: Prentice Hall.

Brill, A. A. (1938). *The basic writings of Sigmund Freud.* New York: Modern Library.

Budman, S. H., & Gurman, A. S. (1988). *Theory and practice of brief therapy.* New York: Guilford Press.

Burbach, D. J., Borduin, C. M., & Peake, T. H. (1988). Cognitive approaches to brief psychotherapy. In T. H. Peake, C. M. Borduin, & R. P. Archer, *Brief psychotherapies changing frames of mind* (pp. 57–86). Newbury Park, CA: Sage.

Cade, B., & O'Hanlon, W. H. (1993). *A brief guide to brief therapy.* New York: Norton.

Corey, G. (1996). *Theory and practice of counseling and psychotherapy* (5th ed.). Pacific Grove, CA: Brooks/Cole.

Dalley, T., Case, C., Schaverien, J., Weir, F., Halliday, D., Hall, P. N., & Waller, D. (1987). *Images of art therapy: New developments in theory and practice.* New York: Tavistock.

Davenloo, H. (Ed.). (1978). *Basic principles and techniques in short-term dynamic psychotherapy.* New York: Spectrum.

de Shazer, S. (1988). *Clues: Investigating solutions in brief therapy.* New York: Norton.

Douglas, C. (1995). Analytical psychotherapy. In R. J. Corsini & D. Wedding (Eds.), *Current psychotherapies* (5th ed., pp. 95–127). Itasca, IL: F. E. Peacock.

Dreyfus, E. (1962). Counseling and existentialism. *Journal of Counseling Psychology, 9,* 128–132.

Ellis, A. (1973). *Humanistic psychotherapy: The rational-emotive approach.* New York: Julian Press.

Ellis, A. (1989). Rational-emotive therapy. In R. J. Corsini & D. Wedding (Eds.), *Current psychotherapies* (4th ed., pp. 197–240). Itasca, IL: F. E. Peacock.

Ellis, A. (1992). Brief therapy: The rational-emotive method. In S. H. Budman, M. F. Hoyt, & S. Friedman (Eds.), *The first session in brief therapy* (pp. 36–58). New York: Guilford Press.

Ellis, A. (1995). Rational-emotive behavior therapy. In R. J. Corsini & D. Wedding (Eds.), *Current psychotherapies* (pp. 162–196). Itasca, IL: F. E. Peacock.

Erickson, M. H. (1980). *Innovative hypnotherapy: Collected papers of Milton H. Erickson and hypnosis* (Vol. 4, E. L. Rossi, Ed.). New York: Irvington.

Erikson, E. H. (1950). *Childhood and society.* New York: Norton.

Erikson, E. H. (1963). *Childhood and society* (2nd ed.). New York: Norton.

Erikson, E. H. (1968). *Identity, youth, and crisis.* New York: Norton.

Erikson, E. H. (1982). *The life cycle completed.* New York: Norton.

Estés, C. P. (1992). *Women who run with the wolves.* New York: Ballantine Books.

Ewen, R. B. (1998). *An introduction to theories of personality* (5th ed.). Mahwah, NJ: Lawrence Erlbaum.

Fleshman, B., & Fryrear, J. L. (1981). *The arts in therapy.* Chicago: Nelson-Hall.

Frankl, V. (1963). *Man's search for meaning.* New York: Washington Square Press.

Fransella, F. & Dalton, P. (1990). *Personal construct counselling in action.* Newbury Park, CA: Sage.

Freud, A. (1966). *The ego and mechanisms of defense.* New York: International Universities Press.

Freud, S. (1949). *An outline of psychoanalysis* (J. Strachey, Trans.). New York: Norton. (Original work published 1940)

Fromm, E. (1941). *Escape from freedom.* New York: Rinehart.

Garfield, S. L. (1989). *The practice of brief psychotherapy.* New York: Pergamon.

Gelso, C. J., & Fretz, B. R. (1992). *Counseling psychology.* Fort Worth, TX: Harcourt, Brace & Jovanovich.

Gendlin, E. T. (1981). *Focusing.* New York: Bantam Books.

Genter, D. S. (1991). A brief strategic model for mental health counseling. *Journal of Mental Health Counseling, 13,* 59–68.

Goode, E. (1998, November 24). When is brief therapy enough? *New York Times,* p. 10.

Guterman, J. T. (1994). A social constructionist position for mental health counseling. *Journal of Mental Health Counseling, 16,* 226–243.

Haley, J. (1977). *Problem-solving therapy.* San Francisco, CA: Jossey-Bass.

Hall, C. S., & Lindzey, G. (1970). *Theories of personality* (2nd ed.). New York: John Wiley.

Hall, C. S., & Lindzey, G., & Campbell, J. B. (1998). *Theories of personality* (4th ed.). New York: John Wiley.

Hansen, J. C., Rossberg, R. H., & Cramer, S. (1994). *Counseling: Theory and process* (5th ed.). Boston: Allyn & Bacon.

Hartmann, H. (1958). *Ego psychology and the problem of adaptation.* New York: International Universities Press.

Hillman, J. (1975). *Re-visioning psychology.* New York: Harper & Row.

Hillman, J. (1983). *Archetypal psychology: A brief account.* Dallas, TX: Spring.

Hillman, J. (1989). *A blue fire: Selected writings.* New York: Harper Perennial.

Hillman, J., & Ventura, M. (1992). *We've had a hundred years of psychotherapy and the world's getting worse.* New York: Harper.

Horney, K. (1945). *Our inner conflicts.* New York: Norton.

Hosford, R. E., & DeVisser, L. (1974). *Behavioral approaches to counseling: An introduction.* Washington, DC: APGA Press.

Ivey, A. E., Ivey, M. B., & Simek-Downing, L. (1993). *Counseling and psychotherapy: A multicultural perspective* (3rd ed.). Boston: Allyn & Bacon.

Jacobi, J. (1962). *The psychology of C. G. Jung* (6th ed.). New Haven, CT: Yale University Press.

Jankowicz, A. D. (1987). Whatever became of George Kelly? Applications and implications. *American Psychologist, 42,* 481–487.

Jordan, J. V. (Ed.). (1997). *Women's growth in diversity: More writings from the Stone Center.* New York: Guilford Press.

Jordan, J. V., Kaplan, A. G., Miller, J. B., Stiver, I. P., & Surrey, J. L. (1991). *Women's growth in connection: Writings from the Stone Center.* New York: Guilford Press.

Jung, C. G. (1970). *Modern man in search of a soul* (W. S. Dell & C. F. Baynes, Trans.). New York: Harcourt Brace Jovanovich. (Original work published 1933)

Jung, C. G. (1971). *Psychological types* (H. G. Baynes, Trans.; rev. R. F. C. Hull). (Bollingen Series XX, vol. 6). Princeton, NJ: Princeton University Press. (Original work published 1921)

Kaufmann, Y. (1989). Analytical psychotherapy. In R. J. Corsini (Ed.), *Current psychotherapies* (4th ed., pp. 119–152). Itasca, IL: F. E. Peacock.

Kelly, G. A. (1955). *The psychology of personal constructs.* New York: Norton.

Kelly, G. A. (1963). *A theory of personality: The psychology of personal constructs.* New York: Norton.

Kempler, W. (1973). Gestalt therapy. In R. J. Corsini & D. Wedding (Eds.), *Current psychotherapies* (pp. 251–286). Itasca, IL: F. E. Peacock.

Kornfield, J. (1993). *A path with heart: A guide through the perils and promises of spiritual life.* New York: Bantam Books.

Koss, M. P., & Butcher, J. N. (1986). Research on brief psychotherapy. In S. L. Garfield & A. E. Bergin (Eds.), *Handbook of psychotherapy and behavior change* (pp. 627–670). New York: John Wiley.

Krumboltz, J. D., & Thoresen, C. E. (1976). *Counseling methods.* New York: Holt, Rinehart & Winston.

Lambert, M. J., Shapiro, D. A., & Bergin, A. E. (1986). The effectiveness of psychotherapy. In S. L. Garfield & A. E. Bergin (Eds.), *Handbook of psychotherapy and behavior change* (3rd ed., pp. 157–211). New York: John Wiley.

Lazarus, A. (1976). *Multimodal behavior therapy.* New York: Springer.

Lazarus, A. (1989). Brief psychotherapy: The multimodal model. *Psychology: A Journal of Human Behavior, 26,* 7–10.

Lazarus, A. (1995). Multimodal therapy. In R. J. Corsini & D. Wedding (Eds.), *Current psychotherapies* (5th ed., pp. 322–355). Itasca, IL: F. E. Peacock.

Levine, S. K. (1992). *Poiesis: The language of psychology and the speech of the soul.* Toronto: Palmerston Press.

Levitsky, A., & Perls, I. (1970). The rules and games of Gestalt therapy. In F. Gagan & I. Shepherd (Eds.), *Gestalt therapy now* (pp. 140–149). New York: Harper & Row.

Mann, J. (1973). *Time-limited psychotherapy.* New York: McGraw-Hill.

May, R. (1961). *Existential psychology.* New York: Van Nostrand Reinhold.

May, R., & Yalom, I. (1995). Existential psychotherapy. In R. Corsini & D. Wedding (Eds.), *Current psychotherapies* (5th ed., pp. 272–292). Itasca, IL: F. E. Peacock.

McNiff, S. (1988). *Fundamentals of art therapy.* Springfield, IL: Charles C Thomas.

Meade, M. (1993). *Men and the water of life: Initiation and the tempering of men.* San Francisco: Harper.

Meichenbaum, D. (1977). *Cognitive behavior modification: An integrative approach.* New York: Plenum.

Meichenbaum, D. (1985). Cognitive-behavioral therapies. In S. J. Lynn & J. P. Garske (Eds.), *Contemporary psychotherapies: Models and methods* (pp. 261–286). Upper Saddle River, NJ: Merrill/Prentice Hall.

Miller, J. B., & Stiver, I. P. (1997). *The healing connection: How women form relationships in therapy and in life.* Boston: Beacon Press.

Moore, R., & Gillette, D. (1990). *King, warrior, magician, lover: Rediscovering the archetypes of the mature masculine.* San Francisco: Harper.

Moore, T. (1992). *Care of the soul: A guide for cultivating depth and sacredness in everyday life.* New York: HarperCollins.

Neimeyer, R. A. (1988). Integrative directions in personal construct therapy. *International Journal of Personal Construct Psychology, 1,* 283–297.

Passons, W. R. (1975). *Gestalt approaches in counseling.* New York: Holt, Rinehart & Winston.

Patterson, G. R., & Guillion, M. E. (1968). *Living with children.* Champaign, IL: Research Press.

Perls, F. S. (1969). *Gestalt therapy verbatim.* Lafayette, CA: Real People Press.

Perls, L. (1976). Comments on the new directions. In E. Smith (Ed.), *The growing edge of Gestalt therapy* (pp. 221–226). New York: Brunner/Mazel.

Phillips, E. L. (1985). *A guide for therapists and patients to short-term psychotherapy.* Springfield, IL: Charles C Thomas.

Pietrofesa, J. J., Hoffman, A., & Splete, H. H. (1984). *Counseling: An introduction* (2nd ed.). Boston: Houghton Mifflin.

Pine, G. J. (1969). The existential school counselor. *Clearing House, 43,* 351–354.

Prochaska, J. O., & Norcross, J. C. (1994). *Systems of psychotherapy: A transtheoretical analysis* (3rd ed.). Pacific Grove, CA: Brooks/Cole.

Rapaport, D. (1958). The theory of ego autonomy: A generalization. *Bulletin of Menninger Clinic, 22,* 13–55.

Rapaport, D. (1960). *The structure of psychoanalytic theory: A systematizing attempt* [Psychological Issues Monograph No. 6]. New York: International Universities Press.

Raskin, N. J., & Rogers, C. R. (1995). Person-centered therapy. In R. Corsini & D. Wedding (Eds.), *Current psychotherapies* (5th ed., pp. 128–161). Itasca, IL: F. E. Peacock.

Robbins, A. (1980). *Expressive therapy: A creative arts approach to depth-oriented treatment.* New York: Human Sciences Press.

Rogers, C. R. (1939). *The clinical treatment of the problem child.* Boston: Houghton Mifflin.

Rogers, C. R. (1942). *Counseling and psychotherapy.* Boston: Houghton Mifflin.

Rogers, C. R. (1951). *Client-centered therapy: Its current practice, implications, and theory.* Boston: Houghton Mifflin.

Rogers, C. R. (1957). The necessary and sufficient conditions of therapeutic personality change. *Journal of Consulting Psychology, 21,* 95–103.

Rogers, C. R. (1961). *Becoming a person.* Boston: Houghton Mifflin.

Rogers, C. R. (1970). *Carl Rogers on encounter groups.* New York: Harper & Row.

Ryckman, R. M. (1993). *Theories of personality* (5th ed.). Pacific Grove, CA: Brooks/Cole.

Samuels, A. (1985). *Jung and the post-Jungians.* New York: Routledge.

Sifneos, P. E. (1979). *Short-term dynamic psychotherapy.* New York: Plenum Press.

Skinner, B. F. (1953). *Science and human behavior.* New York: Macmillan.

Strohl, J. E. (1998). Transpersonalism: Ego meets soul. *Journal of Counseling & Development, 76,* 397–403.

Strupp, H. H. (1981). Toward the refinement of time—limited dynamic psychotherapy. In S. H. Budman (Ed.), *Forms of brief therapy* (pp. 219–242). New York: Guilford Press.

Strupp, H. H., & Binder, J. (1984). *Psychotherapy in a new key: A guide to time-limited dynamic psychotherapy.* New York: Basic Books.

Thoresen, C. E., & Mahoney, M. J. (1974). *Behavioral self-control.* New York: Holt, Rinehart & Winston.

Van Kaam, A. (1967). Counseling and psychotherapy from the viewpoint of existential psychology. In D. Arbuckle (Ed.), *Counseling and psychotherapy: An overview* (pp. 20–52). New York: McGraw-Hill.

Viney, L. L. (1993). *Life stories: Personal construct theory with elderly.* Chichester, UK: John Wiley.

Walsh, R. (1989). Asian psychotherapies. In R. J. Corsini & D. Wedding (Eds.), *Current psychotherapies* (4th ed., pp. 547–560). Itasca, IL: F. E. Peacock.

Walter, J. L., & Peller, J. E. (1992). *Becoming solution-focused in brief therapy.* New York: Brunner/Mazel.

Weakland, J. H., Fisch, R., Watzlawick, P. & Bodin, A. (1974). Brief therapy: Focused problem resolution. *Family Process, 13,* 141–168.

Wells, R. A. (1994). *Planned short-term treatment* (2nd ed.). New York: Free Press.

White, H. S., Burke, J. D., & Havens, L. L. (1981). Choosing a method of short-term therapy: A developmental approach. In S. H. Budman (Ed.), *Forms of brief therapy* (pp. 243–267). New York: Guilford Press.

Wilson, G. T. (1995). Behavior therapy. In R. Corsini & D. Wedding (Eds.), *Current psychotherapies* (5th ed., pp. 197–228). Itasca, IL: F. E. Peacock.

Wolberg, L. R. (1980). *Handbook of short-term psychotherapy.* New York: Thieme-Stratton.

Wolpe, J. (1958). *Psychotherapy by reciprocal inhibition.* Stanford, CA: Stanford University Press.

Wolpe, J. (1969). *The practice of behavior therapy.* New York: Pergamon.

Woodworth, R. S., & Sheehan, M. (1964). *Contemporary schools of psychology* (3rd ed.). New York: Ronald Press.

Yalom, I. D. (1980). *Existential psychotherapy.* New York: Basic Books.

Yontef, G. M., & Simkin, J. S. (1989). Gestalt therapy. In R. J. Corsini & D. Wedding (Eds.), *Current psychotherapies* (4th ed., pp. 323–361). Itasca, IL: F. E. Peacock.

6   Assessment: Tools and Processes

Counselors use assessment tools such as tests, interviews, and observations to help clients in their exploration about themselves and their problems. Although ambiguity in the use of the terms *assessment* and *testing* exists and some individuals use them interchangeably, most experts make a distinction. Cohen, Swerdlik, and Smith (1992), distinguish the terms as follows. *Psychological assessment* is "the gathering and integration of psychology-related data for the purpose of making a psychological evaluation through the use of tools such as tests, interviews, case studies, behavioral observation and specially designed apparatuses and measurement procedures" (p. 11). By contrast, "a *test* may be defined simply as a measuring device or procedure" (p. 11); psychological testing is "the process of measuring psychology-related variables by means of devices or procedures designed to obtain a sample of behavior" (p. 13).

These psychological tests, called *standardized tests,* originated during World War I when psychologists developed screening tests for the U.S. Army. They flourished with the popularity of psychology of individual differences in the 1920s and 1930s (see chap. 2).

Tests are but one form of assessment among many other devices used by counselors. Assessment of one kind or another occurs throughout the counseling sessions. *Evaluation* is another term used frequently in the assessment procedure. Evaluation refers to a process that counselor and client use to integrate test scores, results of other measurement devices, and counselor-client interview comments and observations to help the client gain insight into feelings and evaluate progress in resolving those concerns.

In the early pre-World War II days of guidance counseling, the primary task for counselors was that of making vocational assessments of a client through the use of standardized tests. Their approach was based on a diagnostic model in which clients were perceived as having fixed personality traits that could be measured through standardized interest and aptitude tests and personality inventories.

Carl Rogers (1942, 1951) objected to counselors using a diagnostic testing and prescriptive approach because such an approach counteracts the belief that humans are dynamic individuals capable of change. The popularity of his client-centered counseling during the 1950s through the 1970s resulted in a sharp decline in counselor use of tests and assessments.

This change from diagnosing traits to facilitating self-exploration dramatically influenced the direction of counseling. Those counselors who used standardized tests and inventories did so only after a counseling relationship was established and then only to enhance client self-exploration. Effective counselors still hold to this practice today.

Counselors who continued to use standardized tests in a predictive way were later challenged by testing and assessment specialist Leo Goldman, who, in his classic article "Tests and Counseling: The Marriage That Failed" (1972), questioned the predictive power of standardized tests. In a more recent article (1994) in which he summarized his 1972 declaration of the "failed marriage," he explains:

> The main problem with tests was that they had been developed in the first place for *selection* purposes, and that the typical level of predictive validity that made tests useful for selecting college students or employees had a very different meaning and value when used in *counseling*. (p. 214)

Noting in 1972 that standardized tests were also narrow and limited in scope, Goldman suggested that different types of tests should be designed and published that could be used to help clients explore their potentialities.

Subsequently, Goldman (1990) recommended that a qualitative assessment approach in counseling be emphasized instead of standardized tests:

> Qualitative assessment methods typically are holistic and integrated. . . . Compared with standardized tests, they offer a more active role for clients, a more intimate connection between assessment and the counseling process, and greater adaptability to ethnic cultural, age, gender, and other individual differences. (p. 205)

He suggested that counselors who use tests need to integrate client scores with client self-reports as a way of increasing client self-understanding. This is a position I have upheld as counselor/educator throughout my career (Nugent, 1981).

Goldman (1972, 1992) has also objected over the years that most counselors are not adequately trained to use tests. Either they have had insufficient course work in test selection, administration, and interpretation, or they have had courses that emphasize using tests in a diagnostic, predictive manner.

❧ NEW EXPECTATIONS FOR COUNSELORS

Since the 1980s, a dramatic upsurge has occurred in the numbers and types of tests used in counseling. "Nearly ten million counselors each year complete 'tests,' 'inventories' and other 'assessments'—and that estimate does not include school achievement tests or college entrance exams" (Prediger, 1994, p. 228).

One only need observe the huge booths displaying testing and assessment tools at counseling and psychological conventions or notice the catalogs from over a dozen testing companies to realize how many thousands of psychological tests are now available and being used. Moreover, these companies offer computerized scoring and canned interpretations that make tests so very easy and efficient for anyone to use.

Although tests are easier to administer and score, the vast array of types of tests makes selection and interpretation more confusing than ever—especially to the inexperienced and minimally trained counselor. Inexperienced counselors or those with inadequate training are apt to overuse or misuse tests or to misinterpret their results. Goldman (1994) has been so dissatisfied with the lack of adequate courses in tests and measurements in counseling programs that he recommends "Standardized tests would be best used by perhaps 10% of counselors who are well qualified in quantitative methods, whereas the 90% would make better use of qualitative assessment methods" (p. 217).

Testing specialist Dale Prediger responds to Goldman in the article "Tests and Counseling: The Marriage That Prevailed" (1994). A long-time advocate of Goldman's position, he concurs with Goldman's feelings of discouragement about the use of testing in counseling. Prediger agrees with Goldman that the poor quality of tests and the lack of adequate training for counselors in the selection, use, and interpretation of tests persists today. "We are still in the snake-oil era of testing" (p. 229). "I invite evidence that professional practice has improved" (p. 229).

Prediger (1994) does not think that all is lost, however, in the alliance between testing and counseling. Although he concurs with Goldman's preference for using qualitative testing in counseling, he does argue that using only qualitative assessment measures is unrealistic for most counselors because it is too time-consuming. Furthermore, he believes that client self-estimates without confirming data may be inaccurate or incomplete. He suggests instead that test score interpretations be used to help clients make more informed and accurate self-estimates: "Ability test scores should not be used as substitutes for ability self-estimates. Instead, they should be used to inform self-estimates/concepts" (p. 232).

It is especially gratifying that testing specialists have acknowledged the value of combining the use of tests and client knowledge about themselves as a means of helping clients explore and clarify their self-concepts. This view is consistent with those of us who, in the early days, were trained under Donald Super to relate vocational counseling to one's self-concept and who incorporated Rogerian self-theory into their practice. Integrating clients' insights about themselves with test scores in career counseling applies as well with counseling all kinds of client concerns.

➤ DIFFERENT WAYS COUNSELORS USE ASSESSMENT

Today, the use of assessment has become much more complex as counselors have spread into the community, working in a variety of agencies and in private practice. Counselors need to develop or upgrade their assessment skills for the following reasons:

- Counselors have sharply increased their use of standardized and nonstandardized tests and inventories because they have proliferated and are readily available in the market and easy to use.

- Increasing numbers of counselors are expected to conduct intake interviews for prospective clients to determine the most suitable counseling plans for them.

- In all work settings, counselors are increasingly involved in crisis intervention as the number of individuals experiencing emotional upheavals has escalated.

- Increasing numbers of counselors, particularly clinical mental health counselors, are conducting diagnostic psychological evaluations for community and government agencies.

- Increasing numbers of clinical mental health counselors are employed in managed care programs that require the use of the *Diagnostic and Statistical Manual of Mental Disorders* (*DSM-IV*; American Psychiatric Association, 1994).

The types of assessment used in intake interviewing, in counseling, and in career centers are quite different from those used in crisis intervention and in diagnostic evaluation for outside agencies. The primary distinction is that, in the first group, assessment remains confidential to the client. Other basic distinctions: In the *intake interview*, counselors use structured interviews to make preliminary judgments to determine counseling plans suitable for the prospective clients. Intake interviews may be used to assess degree of severity of alcohol abuse, degree of suicidal threat, or history of sexual or domestic abuse for prospective clients. In *career centers*, counselors make assessments with clients regarding career choice and job placement. In *counseling sessions*, assessment is used nonjudgmentally as part of the counseling process to help clients clarify and work through their problems.

Crisis intervention and *diagnostic evaluation* differ in that, besides being non-confidential to the individual being assessed, information is generally not shared with the individual. In a very short period of time, usually one session, counselors must quickly make psychological diagnoses of individuals, with specific recommendations regarding treatment or eligibility for benefits or placement. In *crisis intervention*, counselors must intervene where individuals are experiencing emotional crises requiring immediate attention, assistance, and possibly referral for therapeutic help. In *diagnostic evaluations for agencies*, counselors, at the request of an outside agency, assess the psychological or intellectual functioning of individuals. In these circumstances, the counselors' "clients" are the agencies, rather than the individuals being assessed.

It is important that counselors who are involved in multiple roles of assessment not mix or confuse their roles. For example, they should not diagnose an individual for another agency who happens to be one of their own clients. They also should not agree to take the person on as a client while they are doing the diagnostic evaluation. This separation of duties helps counselors maintain non-evaluative, trust relationships with their clients. It also helps counselors maintain a non-evaluative image for the sake of all people who seek counseling help. For similar reasons, university counseling centers should be kept separate from university testing centers. If centers combine the two services, they assume dual roles; dual roles are apt to confuse and inhibit students from using the counseling center because they would perceive counseling as an evaluation center that submits reports to the administration.

Intake Interviewing

An intake interview is used to help determine the most suitable counseling plan for a prospective client. After conducting the interview, the intake counselor assigns the individual to an appropriate counselor.

Intake interviewing involves a structured exploration to gain information about a client's presenting problem. Questions typically include the nature of the problem, how long the problem has persisted, whether the individual has had previous counseling, a bit about the individual's current career or educational status, and some input about current and past interactions with her or his family.

Intake interviewers then determine which of the counseling staff has the personal characteristics or professional specialization that best fits the prospective client's particular needs. Intake interviewers may recommend that a client be referred to another counseling service that better suits the needs of the individual. A client with a chronic eating disorder, for example, might be referred to a clinic specializing in addictions.

If the center has a waiting list, intake interviewers determine when persons can be seen, depending on the urgency of their problems. Information gained in intake is confidential to the intake interviewer and to the assigned counselor.

During the Counseling Process

The primary method of assessment that counselors use during the counseling process is interviewing. In many cases, this assessment method is sufficient to help clients self-explore and also to help them develop joint strategies to resolve problems.

Counselors may decide that information from standardized tests would help supplement and augment information from interviews—whether or not client concerns are related to career choice, interpersonal relationships, and/or self-awareness. Counselors often differ in the extent and type of assessment they use during counseling or therapy, depending on their theoretical orientation. Humanists, as a rule, depend almost entirely on the interviewing process, with only occasional use of self-exploratory measures. Psychoanalysts or psychodynamic counselors or therapists more readily use projective techniques, drawings, stories, or inventories that tap clients' unconscious. Behaviorists and cognitive-behaviorists tend to use structured interviews and instruments that measure observable behavior. They tend to use behavioral rating scales or checklists, rather than standardized tests, to assess client behavior. Cognitive behaviorists may use self-monitoring devices to help clients, for example, manage caloric intake or quit smoking.

If testing is agreed on, counselors select appropriate tests of high quality, arrange for administration and scoring of these measures, and make appropriate, meaningful interpretations. Counselors may administer tests themselves or have psychometrists do them. In public schools, scores from standardized tests, which are administered schoolwide, are generally available in student cumulative records.

As indicated earlier, most standardized tests have been computerized; in some cases, they give not only scores or patterns of scores but also computerized interpretations. Some self-inventories can be easily scored by counselors or clients. A measure like Holland's Self-Directed-Search (SDS) is designed to be self-administered and self-scored.

Interpreting Assessment Measures

Learning how to select standardized tests and other assessment methods is only part of the training program in assessment. Learning how to interpret results of assessments and how to interpret clinical observations is the most crucial part of the assessment process. It is also the most misused and neglected. Interpretation involves integrating results from test scores, interviews, and personal observations into a meaningful, accurate pattern that contributes to a greater understanding of the individual and the individual's problem.

Test results should not be used to label clients in ways that will determine or shape the direction of the counseling process. This caution applies especially to computerized interpretations supplied by testing corporations. Assessments of an individual's responses and personality characteristics may change during the counseling process. The counselor makes nonjudgmental, tentative assessments on an exploratory level and gives feedback to the client that will contribute to the clarification of the client's feelings and encourage deeper self-exploration. Counselor and client together make a working hypothesis about assessing the client's problem, an assessment that will help determine a plan of counseling action. Interpretation often focuses on unraveling and reshaping the client's distorted opinions about her or his behavior.

The timing of the interpretation of a client's apparent behavioral characteristics is crucial. Counselors generally withhold making judgments in the initial sessions of counseling, although they are keenly attentive to observing their clients' behavior. These observations provide tentative assessments that will be useful in later interactions with the clients during the counseling process.

The mode of interpretation of standardized tests differs from that of nonstandardized tests. Interpreting standardized tests is fairly simple and clear-cut. The counselor compares client scores with those of an appropriate norm group on which the test was standardized. Percentile scores indicate how well the individual ranks compared with the norm group. This simplicity has its dangers, however. Counselors must be careful not to rely only on test scores or on commercial canned interpretations, but rather to integrate them with other assessments.

Nonstandardized assessment is more complex. Counselors must attend to clients' verbal comments, body language, and degree of nervousness; they must avoid making snap judgements about individuals, but instead observe clients' comments and behavior within the context of the overall counseling experience.

Career Counseling Centers

Counselors in career centers in colleges and in communities are the ones who most often use vocational interest inventories, aptitude tests, and personality inventories. Their primary focus is to help clients find job placement in the workforce appropriate to their interests, aptitudes, and personality traits. They arrange for clients to take batteries of tests, based on client need; integrate results into occupational profiles for the clients; and then match these profiles with occupations that require worker traits similar to those of the clients.

Crisis Intervention

In crisis intervention, counselors are suddenly called on to work with individuals who are unable to cope. Such individuals are generally not the counselors' clients. The counselors' job involves assessing the persons, determining the degree or severity of their conditions, and then making referrals based on the assessments.

Crisis counselors must first help disoriented or out-of-control individuals regain their equilibrium as much as possible. To accomplish this, counselors direct the interviews appropriately. They must identify and clarify the severity of the precipitating problems while at the same time helping the individuals release emotions and calm down (see "Counselors and Crisis Intervention" in chap. 7).

Because there is no time to use standardized tests, counselors rely on structured interviews and observations. Counselors need to recognize signs of suicidal intentions, psychotic breakdown, or drug overdose. In these cases, assessment checklists are available detailing behaviors related to severity of the crises.

At times, a crisis intervention may involve one or two meetings to enable an individual to stabilize and regain coping skills. Then, the crisis counselor can determine whether ongoing counseling or more intensive therapy is needed. In such a case, the individual will be referred to another counselor in the agency or to a psychiatric service at another agency. In some cases, it may be necessary to recommend mandatory psychiatric services to protect individuals from harming themselves or others (see chap. 7).

Diagnostic Evaluation for Agencies

Some counselors and mental health workers include in their practices various kinds of psychological evaluations of individuals for community agencies when these agencies need to make psychological decisions about individuals. These decisions may require clinical assessment of individuals to determine, for example, whether they need to be involuntarily committed to a mental institution; whether they are emotionally or mentally competent to stand trial; and whether they are qualified for vocational rehabilitation or for Social Security disability benefits.

In the past, master's degree counselors generally were not involved in diagnostic evaluations for agencies. But as licensing and private practice have increased and diagnostic evaluations have become a lucrative business, more counselors have become involved in this activity. Diagnostic evaluations require special training in the use and interpretation of individual psychological measures. A counselor's recommendations can have a profound and lasting effect on the lives of the individuals being assessed. Clinical mental health counselors now include diagnostic evaluation of pathology in their training programs and list this form of evaluation as one expected competency. Other counselors who want to use the *DSM-IV* should also take special training.

⊰❧ TYPES OF ASSESSMENT

Counselors and therapists assess clients in basically two ways: *nonstandardized* or qualitative measures, and *standardized* or quantitative measures. *Nonstandardized measures* are informed observations about client behavior or clients' self-reports about their feelings, interests, attitudes, and experience. The assessments are specific to a particular client. There are no formal procedures for administering and scoring these assessments. In qualitative assessment, counselors use their clinical skills to interpret their observations and self-reports and share the results with clients.

Learning theorists prefer behavioral observations, rather than tests or inventories, when they assess a problem. They emphasize assessing a person's behavior, rather than using tests or measures that infer underlying personality traits or personality dynamics of clients. They use three general assessment approaches: self-reports, direct behavioral observations, and physiological recordings. Self-monitoring schedules, in which clients collect and record data of their own behavior, are used frequently. Examples of questionnaires and scales that involve self-reports are the Social Anxiety Inventory, Agoraphobic Questionnaire Cognitions, and the Fear Survey Schedule (Kleinknecht, 1986).

Standardized measures are based on statistically derived norm groups, with formal procedures for administering and scoring, procedures that remain the same any time they are used. Interpretations are based on comparing clients' scores with scores of individuals on whom the measure was standardized.

Statistical Versus Clinical Interpretation of Tests

Counselors can use two different approaches to interpret standardized tests. One is an actuarial or statistical approach; the other is a clinical approach (Cohen et al., 1992; Cronbach, 1990). Cohen et al. (1992) compare these methods as follows:

> The *actuarial* approach . . . is distinguished by its exclusive reliance on statistical procedures, empirical methods, and formal rules as opposed to reliance on the interpreter's own judgment in evaluating the data. By contrast, the *clinical* approach is characterized by less formal rules and reliance on the clinician's own intuition, judgment and experience. (p. 429)

Following is an example comparing the use of these two approaches in interpreting a profile of the Minnesota Multiphasic Personality Inventory (MMPI) to a client. In an *actuarial* approach, a counselor would generally use a computerized interpretation of a client's profile, provided by a test-scoring company and based on extensive statistical data about clients with similar profiles. Counselors using a *clinical* approach, in contrast, would use their knowledge about, and experience with, MMPI profile patterns. They would integrate this information with clients' observations and comments about themselves and with counselor-client insights gained during the counseling process.

According to Cohen et al. (1992), the actuarial or statistical approach emphasizes efficiency in making predictions about client behavior, whereas the clinical approach emphasizes more flexibility, more attention to the client's overall functioning in life, and more acknowledgement of the client's individual needs.

Nonstandardized or Qualitative Assessment Skills

Observation

Client observation is an important skill counselors use to assess clients' emotional frame of mind and readiness to interact with counselors. Clients' degree of anxiety, depression, uncertainty, or resentment can often be gauged by their body behavior: Do they sit slumped in a chair? Do their hands or voices tremble? Are they alert or distracted? Counselors should guard against automatically perceiving a client's body behavior as a sign of emotional distress, however. A squirming client, for example, may be sitting in an uncomfortable chair or may have a back problem.

Counselors often record their observations in their case notes. Those interested in systematic recording of client behavior can use checklists to mark off whether a client is demonstrating some particular behavior that is considered significant. Some may even use rating scales ranging from *never* to *always*. Behavioral and cognitive-behavioral counselors who are particularly interested in observable behavior are more likely to use checklists and rating scales.

Self-Reports

Some counselors use client self-reports of various types to encourage client self-observation and self-exploration. These self-reports are as diverse as questionnaires designed to obtain background information, autobiographical or personal essays, or journal keeping. Client self-observations thus contribute to counselors' understanding of client needs or conflicts.

Standardized Tests and Inventories

Unlike informal intuitive procedures, standardized tests and inventories are systematically and statistically designed to give objective information about certain specific client characteristics or behaviors. The two basic types of measurements are *tests* and *inventories*. *Tests* entail right or wrong answers and measure a person's cognitive, intellectual, or achievement levels. *Inventories*, in contrast, are not concerned with correctness of response, but rather measure descriptive aspects of the client: personality characteristics, values, needs, or degree of emotional well-being or pathology.

A client's scores on a particular standardized test or inventory are compared with scores of particular groups of people on whom the test was standardized. These comparative representative scores, called *norms,* add meaning to a client's raw scores. Clients' scores on an intelligence test, for example, can be compared with those of an appropriate norm group to determine whether clients' scores are higher, at the same level, or lower than other representative individuals like themselves. Norms are usually nationally based, but they can also be regionally or even locally based.

Effective counselors are aware of the possible abuse of norm grouping, particularly with ethnic groups. Multicultural groups have criticized standardized tests whose item choices and norm groups are based on White, middle-class, male youth populations. Of particular concern are intelligence tests and personality inventories. D. W. Sue and Sue (1990) say: "The improper use of such instruments can lead to an exclusion of minorities in jobs and promotion, to discriminatory educational decisions, and to biased determination of what constitutes pathology" (p. 12). Cohen et al. (1992) explain:

> Items on tests of intelligence tend to effect the culture of the society where such tests are employed; to the extent that a score on such a test reflects the degree to which the test takers have been integrated into the society and the culture, it would be expected that members of sub-cultures would score lower. (p. 25)

To work toward decreasing test bias, psychologists attempted to develop *culture-fair* and *culture-specific* tests, but they have not proved successful. *Culture-fair tests* include items common to all cultures. A *culture-specific test* contains items expressly related to a specific subculture. Culture-fair tests have had little success as accurate measures for minority groups. Culture-specific tests have low predictive value for the specific cultural group (Cohen et al., 1992). Work is continuing on constructing nonbiased tests. Meanwhile, counselors are being alerted to their own biases in selecting and interpreting tests for minorities.

Counselors must also be aware of the reliability and validity of standardized tests. *Reliability* "refers to the degree to which test scores are consistent, dependable and repeatable" (Drummond, 1996, p. 48). *Validity* refers to the degree to which a test score measures what it claims to measure. For example, individuals who score high on a measure of mechanical ability should be expected to do well on mechanical jobs or in mechanical training.

Reliability can be assessed in three ways: *retest,* in which one administers the same test twice; *parallel form,* in which one administers an equivalent form; and *split-half,* in which two or more equivalent portions are given to determine the internal consistency of the tests (Thorndike, 1997).

Validity, too, can be assessed in three ways: *Content validity,* often referred to as *face validity,* indicates to what extent a test measures what it is supposed to measure. This form is most often used in achievement and ability testing. *Criterion-related validity* measures how well an individual's scores compare to a particular criterion of success. For example, individuals' scores on a spatial aptitude test may be compared to their success as draftsmen. *Construct validity* indicates whether a test measures the particular construct it is supposed to measure. This form of validity is particularly applicable to unobservable constructs, such as personality and interest variables (Cohen et al., 1992; Thorndike, 1997).

Counselors generally use five types of standardized measures: three are tests—intelligence, aptitude, and achievement; and two are inventories—interest and personality.

Intelligence Tests

Intelligence tests are designed to measure general academic ability or the ability to perform successfully in academic settings. They fall into two categories: (a) intelligence tests that are designed to be administered only to an individual by a specially trained mental health worker and (b) intelligence tests that are designed to be administered to groups but can be given to an individual. Also discussed is the theory of multiple intelligences (MI). Many researchers have criticized traditional intelligence tests—most notably, Howard Gardner (1993), who challenges the assumption that intelligence is based only on a person's intellectual capacity to perform academically.

Individually Administered Intelligence Tests.   The two major individually administered intelligence tests are the Stanford Binet and the Wechsler Intelligence Scales. The Stanford Binet grew out of an intelligence scale developed by Alfred Binet in France in 1905 to screen mental retardation in children. It was designed only for use with children and adolescents because of its content and because it is standardized on children and adolescents. It relies only on verbal responses. The Wechsler scales are a variety of tests designed for all ages, including the Wechsler Intelligence Scales for Adults (WAIS-III) for ages 16 years and over; the Wechsler Intelligence Scales for Children III (WISC-III) for ages 6 to 16 years 11 months; and the Wechsler Preschool and Primary Scale of Intelligence-Revised (WPPSI-R) for ages 4 to 6 ½ years. The Wechsler scales also differ from the Binet in that they include performance tasks, as well as verbal responses. For these reasons, the Wechsler scales are used more often in measuring intelligence (Walsh & Betz, 1995).

Group Intelligence Tests.   Group intelligence tests are often used when counselors and clients decide it is important to obtain a measure of scholastic aptitude. These tests usually measure a component of intelligence. Verbal reasoning and numerical reasoning are most often used in school and college settings. A client may be having academic difficulties in college or in a school setting, or a client may be contemplating college when her academic record is mediocre. The client or the counselor or both may believe that the client's academic record underestimates her true ability, so an intelligence test is used to make comparisons. The most commonly used are the Otis-Lennon School Ability Test, the Henmon-Nelson Tests of Mental Ability (K-12), the California Short Form of Mental Ability, the School and College Ability Tests (SCAT), and the Scholastic Aptitude Test (SAT). A group intelligence test often used by counselors working in business or in government agencies to help in selecting individuals for job placement is the Wonderlic Personnel Test (Walsh & Betz, 1995).

Multiple Intelligences (MI).   Gardner (1993) challenges the traditional measurements of intelligence, claiming they measure only an individual's intellectual capacity to perform academically. Years ago, he began questioning the method of assessing intelligence: "There must be more to intelligence than short answers to short questions—answers that predict academic success" (p. 4).

> The problem lies . . . in the ways in which we customarily think about the intellect and in our ingrained views of intelligence. Only if we expand and reformulate our view of what counts as human intellect will we be able to devise more appropriate ways of assessing it and more effective ways of educating it. (p. 4)

Thus, Gardner (1993) spends considerable time inquiring into the nature of intelligence, challenging the traditional assumption that a person's intelligence is a single entity that is inherited. He and other researchers propose that "there exists a multitude of intelligences, quite independent of each other; that each intelligence has its own strengths and constraints" (p. xix).

In his naming of several human intelligences—linguistic, musical, logical-mathematical, spatial, bodily-kinesthetic, and personal—Gardner (1993) warns that these names are only convenient constructs: "These intelligences are fictions—at most, useful fictions. . . . [T]hey exist not as physically verifiable entities but only as potentially useful scientific constructs" (p. 70).

The theory of MI proposes that humans are limited by their cultural *domain* and by their *field*. Development of intelligences is constrained by the context in which one lives:

> Human beings are born into cultures that house a large number of *domains*—disciplines, crafts, and other pursuits in which one can become enculturated and then be assessed in terms of the level of competence one has attained. (p. xvi)
>
>   . . . Once one achieves a certain competence, the *field* becomes very important. The field—a sociological construct—includes the people, institutions, award mechanisms, and so forth that render judgments about the qualities of individual performances. (p. xvii)

MI assessment measures, Gardner emphasizes, are radically opposed to the standard systems of measuring intelligence. First, MI cannot be obtained by a single test taken in an hour or so and out of the context of one's life. Assessment of MI must be conducted over time by observing individuals in context with their performances in real-life situations. Furthermore, MI can be measured at different times in one's life.

MI criteria, differing from those of standard intelligence tests, focus primarily on the person's problem-solving ability in various situations. Criteria, moreover, vary across human cultures:

> To my mind, a human intellectual competence must entail a set of skills of problem solving—enabling the individual *to resolve genuine problems or difficulties* that he or she encounters and, when appropriate, to create an effective product—and must entail the potential for *finding or creating problems*—thereby laying the groundwork for the acquisition of new knowledge. (Gardner, 1993, pp. 60–61)

Although the process of developing adequate MI assessment measures is fairly new, Gardner is very optimistic. Assessment procedures to measure MI would be very useful, he says, because they would measure a much broader aspect of human abilities; moreover, they would present a much broader, clearer picture of the individual's multiple capacities to learn.

Aptitude Tests

Aptitude tests, like intelligence tests, measure an individual's ability to learn but are more specific to given areas of performance. These tests usually include some form of verbal, abstract reasoning, numerical, spatial, mechanical, and clerical ability. Counselors tend to use aptitude tests in career counseling in a variety of settings— schools and colleges, community career centers, employment agencies, and personnel services in business and industry.

Multiple aptitude batteries provide a comparative profile of scores based on the same norm group. The three multiple aptitude batteries most often used by counselors are the Differential Aptitude Tests (DAT), the Armed Service Vocational Aptitude Battery (ASVAB), and the General Aptitude Test Battery (GATB). Aptitude batteries are developed to predict how well one will do in specific jobs or training programs. Their content is determined out of analyses of numerous jobs on the assumption that different aptitudes relate to different jobs (Thorndike, 1997).

The DAT is specifically designed for high school students exploring career or curricular choices. The ASVAB, originally developed to classify armed services recruits, is now offered to high school students by the U.S. Department of Defense in 15,000 schools at no cost to the students or the school districts.

The GATB, used predominantly in state employment services, has for many years been the most widely used battery in career counseling and placement. The GATB also includes performance tests measuring finger dexterity, manual dexterity, and motor coordination—abilities necessary in jobs requiring skills in working with one's hands and with small objects. The GATB currently is administered only in government employment agencies. Counselors in other settings can obtain the results, however, through a written request and with the consent of the client.

Achievement Tests

Counselors use achievement tests primarily in educational settings to help clients explore curricular or career options when proficiency in a specific subject is important. Achievement batteries are given to students in most school districts at specified grade levels. All states use some form of state-wide standardized achievement tests in public schools (Thorndike, 1997). The same tests are used either for the entire student body or at a specified grade level. Results are placed in students' cumulative files. Counselors and clients can then make use of them in counseling sessions when students want information about their competencies in various subject areas. Examples of these batteries are the Iowa Tests of Basic Skills (ITBS), used in elementary schools; and the Metropolitan Achievement Tests (MAT), the Stanford Achievement Tests, and the Iowa Tests of Educational Development (ITED), used in elementary and secondary schools.

An achievement test often used by community counselors is the Wide Range Achievement Test (WRAT). This battery, which measures reading, spelling, and arithmetic competencies, has norms from kindergarten age to 75 years of age. It is individually administered and used along with individual intelligence tests to determine whether an individual has a learning disability.

Interest Inventories

When clients are concerned about career choices or are seriously dissatisfied with their jobs, counselors often use vocational interest measures to help clients decide a more satisfying choice of job or career. The three major interest measures are Holland's Self-Directed Search (SDS) for high school and college students and adults; the Strong Interest Inventory (SII), for high school seniors, college students, and adults; and the Kuder Occupational Interest Survey Revised (KOIS-R) for high school students. These inventories, in one form or another, compare client vocational interest scores with those of persons in business, professional, scientific, artistic, technical, and social service occupations.

In recent years, the SDS Form R has become the most widely used interest measure in counseling practice (Drummond, 1996; Walsh & Betz, 1995). The SDS was published in 1971 and revised several times. This self-administered, self-scored, and self-interpreted inventory measures an individual's self-reported occupational interests and classifies responses into six personality types: *r*ealistic, *a*rtistic, *i*nvestigative, *s*ocial, *e*nterprising, and *c*onventional (RAISEC). These personality types are then related to more than 1,000 occupational groups representing these personality types (see chap. 12). Although the SDS is designed for individual self-interpretation, as Thorndike (1997) points out, it is best used in counseling sessions where the counselor assists in the interpretation.

The Strong Interest Inventory (SII) is the granddaddy of interest measurement tests. Originally published in 1927, it has gone through innumerable revisions. The inventory compares an individual's profile of scores to more than 200 occupational scales and relates them to Holland's six occupational themes (RAISEC). Originally based primarily on professional occupations, its latest revision (1994) added significantly more nonprofessional or vocational technical occupations. The two separate women's and men's forms were combined into one form to allow responses free of gender bias (Walsh & Betz, 1995).

Another pioneer interest inventory, the Kuder Occupational Interest Survey Revised (KOIS-R), introduced in 1934 and revised several times, has 119 occupational scales and 48 college major scales. It has norms for high school, college, and adult populations. Compared with the SII, Kuder scales cover a wider range of occupations and include more nonprofessional and technical occupations.

Personality Measures: Objective Inventories and Projective Tests

Counselors use personality measures (a) to assess client personality traits or characteristics, (b) to compare client characteristics with those of individuals in various occupations or careers, and (c) to assess client degree of emotional trauma or pathology.

Personality measures are of two forms: *objective inventories* and *projective techniques*. Objective inventories are self-reports in which clients respond to a series of statements related to their personality characteristics. Projective techniques are used to tap a person's unconscious reactions to ambiguous pictures or images or through storytelling or drawing.

Objective Inventories.   Examples of objective personality inventories used by counselors are the California Psychological Inventory–Revised (CPI–R); the Myers-Briggs Type Indicator (MBTI); the Minnesota Multiphasic Personality Inventory 2 (MMPI-2); and the Edwards Personal Preference Schedule (EPPS).

Effective counselors use scores on these measures as indicators of client predispositions capable of change, rather than as fixed, static traits. For example, clients who have low sociability scores and are concerned about their ineffective relationships can be helped to develop social skills; or clients showing obsessive-compulsive behavior can learn to modify their behavior through counseling and therapy.

The California Psychological Inventory–Revised (CPI–R) is used with clients 13 years of age and older. Personal characteristics in the inventory focus on social interactions and feelings of adequacy. Scales presented in terms of desirable characteristics include such areas as sociability, social presence, self-acceptance, sense of well-being, and self-control.

The Myers-Briggs Type Indicator (MBTI) is based on Carl Jung's theory of typology. The MBTI was developed by a mother-daughter team, Isabel Briggs Myers and Katherine C. Briggs. Many counselors in colleges and in the community use the inventory to help their clients gain some understanding of how their typology relates to career choices or to personal and social functioning.

Jung's theory of typology is complicated, but basically persons are perceived as either extraverted or introverted. A person is also governed by four functions that are divided into two oppositional pairs: sensory/intuitive and thinking/feeling. Jung's typology is not intended to categorize individuals into personality types that determine their behavior (Pascal, 1992). It is meant to help explore one's inner world, the world of the unconscious, a task usually reserved for the latter part of life. It serves as a theoretical base from which the analyst can work to help clients develop their inferior functions. In this way, clients make changes that lead to wholeness and individuation.

Why is the MBTI so popular among young, career-minded people? Myers-Briggs expanded on Jung's typology system by adding another set of oppositional scales: judgment/ perceiving. Thus, the patterns of typology are more applicable to how one functions in the external world. Spoto (1989) says:

> By developing the perceiving-judging polarity as a separate criterion and then combining it with Jung's basic typological theory and principles, Briggs-Myers implicitly urges users of Jung's original typological theory to be more careful observers of those patterns of behavior relating specifically to the external world. (p. 131)

The Minnesota Multiphasic Personality Inventory (MMPI) is one of the most widely used personality measures in community clinical mental health practice. The inventory consists of eight clinical scales based on psychiatric-psychological symptoms of neurosis or psychosis: hypochondriasis (Hs), depression (D), conversion hysteria (Hy), psychopathic deviate (Pd), paranoia (Pa), psychasthenia (Pt), schizophrenia (Sc), and hypomania (Ma). Scales also measure masculinity and femininity (MF) and social introversion (SI). Four validity scales are scored to detect faking and distorted responses.

The MMPI (revised edition known as MMPI–2) is used in a variety of counseling and therapeutic settings to assess the degree and nature of an individual's emotional distress. Counselors and other mental health practitioners in private practice and those who work in mental health clinics or mental hospitals most often use the MMPI.

The Edwards Personal Preference Schedule, with norms for college students and adults, is used when the counselor wants to help clients explore unfulfilled needs that are interfering with their personal, interpersonal, or career functioning. Based on Henry Murray's need theory of personality, it has 28 scales tapping such areas as need for achievement, need for dominance, and need for autonomy.

Projective Tests.   Projective tests are based on psychoanalytic or psychodynamic views about the importance of assessing a person's unconscious motives. Clients react unconsciously to ambiguous pictures, images, or incomplete sentences, or they may draw human figures or objects that are projections of their self-image.

The most commonly used projectives in counseling practice are the Thematic Apperception Test (TAT), the Rorschach, the Rotter Sentence Completion Blank, the House-Tree-Person (HTP), and the Draw a Person (DAP). These projective techniques are most likely to be used by doctorate-level mental health practitioners trained in psychodynamic theory and practice.

The TAT consists of picture cards that show one or more individuals in ambiguous settings. The client tells a story about each picture that assumedly reveals something about the person's conflicts or social constraints (Walsh & Betz, 1995). The Rorschach is a set of cards with inkblot images; clients are asked what they see in each image.

Counselors using the Rotter Sentence Completion Blank ask individuals to respond to sentence stems such as "I like" and "I want to know." The Rotter gives an overall adjustment rating and is used for assessing both how well an individual is functioning and psychiatric disturbances.

The HTP and the DAP asks clients to draw pictures to indicate unconscious projections about their self-image. These tests are sometimes used by elementary school counselors and community counselors in their work with children. Counselors using these tests need special training in psychodynamic theory, as well as in the use of projective tests.

Another drawing test, the Bender Visual-Motor Gestalt Test, commonly called the Bender-Gestalt, is used to assess whether personality disturbances are a result of brain damage. Individuals copy nine abstract designs consisting of dots, curves, and lines; protocols of individuals being assessed are compared with protocols of individuals with brain damage. Clinical mental health counselors in the community or in private practice are most likely to use the Bender-Gestalt for this type of diagnostic evaluation.

Most Frequently Used Standardized Tests and Inventories

The tests discussed in the previous sections were selected from hundreds of standardized measures used by counselors. The selection was based on reviews of leading texts on tests and assessment and on two surveys regarding the most frequently used standardized instruments used by counselors in the community.

In Watkins, Campbell, and McGregor's 1988 survey, 66% of counseling psychologists surveyed used tests. In Bubenzer, Zempfer, and Mahrle's 1990 survey of use of tests by counselors in the community, 70% of doctorate-level counselors and about 50% of master's-level counselors used tests.

Watkins et al. (1988) found that the six most frequently used tests by counseling psychologists were, in order, (a) the Strong Campbell Interest Inventory (SCII), (b) the Minnesota Multiphasic Personality Inventory 2 (MMPI-2), (c) the Wechsler Adult Intelligence Scale Revised (WAIS-R), (d) the Rotter Sentence Completion Blank, (e) the Bender-Gestalt, and (f) the Thematic Apperception Test (TAT). These were followed by the (g) Sixteen Personality Factor Questionnaire (16PF), (h) the California Psychological Inventory (CPI), (i) the Wechsler Intelligence Scale for Children Revised (WISC-R), and (j) the Edwards Personal Preference Schedule (EPPS). These researchers found that vocational interest and objective personality tests were used predominantly in university counseling centers, and the WISC-R in community agencies; projectives were used more often in private practice, community clinics, and hospitals.

Bubenzer et al. (1990) found that the MMPI was by far the most commonly used instrument; the next four highest were the SCII, the WAIS-R, the MBTI, and the WISC-R. Rounding out the top 10 were the 16PF and the TAT (tied in ranking), the Bender-Gestalt, the Wide-Range Achievement Test (WRAT), and the Rorschach and the Multiaxial Clinical Multiple Inventory (MCMI) tied for 10th position. The researchers also compared the use of the MMPI, SCII, WAIS-R, MBTI, and TAT by counselor educational degree and by counselor use (diagnosis, treatment planning, and evaluation). They found that although both doctorate-level and master's-level counselors used these tests, master's-level counselors used them less. They also reported that both master's and doctorate counselors administer all these tests and use them for assessment and diagnosis, treatment planning, and evaluation.

Diagnostic and Statistical Manual of Mental Disorders (DSM-IV)

For those clients covered by health insurance, community counselors and therapists must use the *DSM-IV,* a classification of the various mental disorders, to determine whether a client is eligible for insurance coverage. The *DSM-IV* is a manual in book form that classifies mental disturbances into 16 categories including dementia, substance abuse, schizophrenia, mood disorders, anxiety disorders, physical symptoms rooted in psychological problems, intentional faking of disorders, dissociative disorders, sexual and gender disorders, eating disorders, sleep disorders, lack of impulse control, adjustment disorders, and chronic, or pervasive personality disorders. The counselor or therapist working with normally functioning individuals experiencing stress classify them as having adjustment disorders.

A unique feature of the *DSM-IV* is the use of five axes to classify client problems in a comprehensive and informative way. The axes assume a biophysical-social etiology. Axis I describes the major clinical symptom the client is experiencing. Axis II describes a personality disorder that may accompany the major clinical symptom. Axis III describes any medical condition that may exacerbate the emotional disorder. Axis IV denotes any psychosocial or environmental problems the client has experienced during the past year that complicate the emotional disturbance. As a final note, the clinician makes a global assessment and a rating of the client's current psychological, social, and occupational functioning at the time of the evaluation. The rating scale runs from 1, *severe impairment,* to 100, *superior functioning with absence of symptoms.*

Following is an example of a *DSM-IV* diagnostic assessment of a particular depressed client, one who suffers from diabetes, recent loss of a job, and divorce:

Axis I:	Clinical Disorder: depression
Axis II:	Personality Disorders: obsessive-compulsive
Axis III:	General Medical Conditions: diabetes
Axis IV:	Psychosocial and Environmental Problems: divorce, loss of job
Axis V:	General Assessment of Functioning: 50 (current)

A major criticism of the *DSM-IV* is that it has a strong medical orientation even though more than half of the classified disorders are unrelated to physical disorders (D. Sue, Sue, & Sue, 1994). The manual also focuses heavily on symptoms of severely disturbed individuals, which limits its use by counselors or therapists working with normally functioning clients experiencing unusually stressful conflicts.

The advantage of the *DSM-IV* is the inclusion of various physical, psychosocial, or environmental circumstances influencing the client's dysfunction.

Whether counselors use the *DSM-IV* or not in their counseling practice, they should be familiar with *DSM-IV* classifications. They can better dialogue with other mental health specialists who use the *DSM-IV.* Further, knowledge of patterns of emotional distress as described by the *DSM-IV* can be useful in intake interviewing or crisis intervention to determine type of treatment needed and whether a referral is necessary.

❧ NEED FOR QUALITY TRAINING IN ASSESSMENT

The increase in the use of tests by counselors and the more varied purposes for their use have raised concerns regarding the quality of counselor training, concerns Goldman (1972, 1982) has expressed for decades. Prediger (1994) concurs: "Unfortunately, the response to student preferences by some counselor educators has been to water down courses, to confine measurement instruction to units in other courses" (p. 228). Bubenzer et al. (1990), after surveying mental health counselors' use of standardized tests in agencies and private practice, concluded that counselor education programs need to improve and strengthen curricular offerings in tests and measurements:

> If master's degree practitioners are using both objective and projective tests and use personality, career, intelligence, and special problem tests for diagnostic and treatment pur-

poses, then it appears that we need to assure, through our accreditation and licensing practices, that they have adequate training and skill. (p. 65)

Counselor training programs need to include comprehensive exposure to tests and measures in ways more complex than the simple testing methods used in the early days. Increasing numbers of counselors are working in private practice, managed care, and community agencies where insurance companies require a diagnosis from the *DSM-IV* before they will reimburse clients for treatment. Counselors are also exposed to a wide variety of theoretical orientations in which some form of assessment is part of the counseling process. Counselors in private practice are called on to make diagnostic evaluations for agencies. All counselors, regardless of their work setting, are expected to intervene and assess in crisis situations as the stresses in everyday living have escalated. The need for using assessment in intervention, family systems, substance abuse, and child abuse has also increased.

As assessment measures have proliferated and are now easily available in the market, and as the ways they are used have become more varied and complex, counselors-in-training need to be made aware of resources regarding quality of tests and their appropriate ethical use. Resources regarding types, descriptions, and evaluation of tests include *The 12th Mental Measurement Yearbook* (Conoley & Impara, 1995) and standardized tests like Anastasi (1996), Cohen et al. (1992), Thorndike, (1997), and Walsh and Betz (1995).

Guidelines for ethical and appropriate use of tests are included in codes of ethics of counseling and related professional associations. For example, ACA (see Appendix A) and APA codes include sections on evaluation and assessment covering this, such as competence to use and interpret tests, interpretation of tests, and test selection and administration. Both codes include the importance of maintaining test security that will uphold integrity and validity of the tests. Test items and content cannot be modified or reproduced without permission of the publishers.

An invaluable resource that promotes the ethical use of tests in education and psychology is the *Standards for Educational and Psychological Testing* (1985), developed jointly by the American Educational Research Association (AERA), the American Psychological Association (APA), and the National Council on Measurement in Education. As of this writing, a revision is being developed. Anyone using tests should be knowledgeable about these standards (Thorndike, 1997).

☙ SUMMARY

In the early days of counseling, the counselor's primary task was to assess the vocational aptitudes and interests of clients through the use of standardized tests. Rogers (1951) and others challenged counselor overreliance on testing, claiming it was a diagnostic, prescriptive approach to counseling. Rogers claimed that the counselor's role is to develop a trusting counseling relationship to encourage client self-exploration. His views led to a decline in the use of tests for the next three decades. Those counselors who continued to use tests to assess clients first developed a relationship and then used tests to help their clients self-explore.

For many decades, testing specialist Leo Goldman has criticized the profession for not adequately training counselors in the selection, use, and interpretation of tests and assessment. The need for quality training in assessment methods is all the more essential now because the use of tests by counselors has escalated dramatically in recent years. Not only are counselors using more assessments, but they are also becoming involved in new types of assessment with individuals who are not their clients. These newer duties with nonclients are intake interviewing, crisis intervention, and diagnostic evaluation of individuals for outside agencies.

Counselors in counseling sessions use tests and assessment in a nonjudgmental manner to help clients clarify their problems and to enhance their self-exploration. Test results are confidential to clients. Appropriately interpreting test results is a key factor in the assessment process in counseling. It requires the skills and wise judgment of a trained counselor, one who can integrate information gathered from client test scores, interviews, and personal observations into meaningful patterns and use their appraisals to enhance client self-exploration.

In intake interviews, counselors screen prospective clients to determine the best plan of therapeutic action. In crisis intervention, counselors use structured interviews first to help the traumatized individuals gain some equilibrium and then, if necessary, make an appropriate referral for treatment. In diagnostic evaluations of individuals, counselors work for outside agencies that request their assistance in determining individuals' eligibility for benefits, training, or legal disposition.

Counselors use both nonstandardized and standardized types of assessments. Nonstandardized measures include informal observations of client behavior or self-reports of clients about themselves. Counselors use standardized measures based on statistically derived norm groups. Counselors use five types of standardized measures, three of which are tests—intelligence, aptitude, and achievement; the other two are inventories—interest and personality.

Gardner challenged the use of I.Q. as the method of measuring intelligence by proposing a theory of multiple intelligences. Increasing numbers of counselors are using the *DSM-IV* for diagnostic classification as part of the expectations in managed care programs.

✒ PROJECTS AND ACTIVITIES

1. Visit your university counseling center and determine the type of assessment procedures the staff uses most often.
2. Talk with a counselor whose major responsibility is crisis intervention. Discuss with him or her procedures used and referral sources available.
3. Interview the counselor or mental health worker assigned to intake interviewing in a community mental health clinic. What are the major assessment tools used? What are the advantages and disadvantages of being an intake interviewer?
4. Survey your class by using an anonymous questionnaire about the types of tests they have taken and their opinions about the value of these measures.

❧ REFERENCES

American Psychiatric Association. (1994). *Diagnostic and statistical manual of mental disorders* (4th ed.). Washington, DC: Author.

American Educational Research Association (AERA), American Psychological Association (APA), & National Council on Measurement in Education. (1985). *Standards for educational and psychological testing.* Washington, DC: Author.

Anastasi, A. (1996). *Psychological testing* (7th ed.). New York: Macmillan.

Bubenzer, D. L., Zempfer, D. G., & Mahrle, C. L. (1990). Standardized individual appraisal in agency and private practice: A survey. *Journal of Mental Health Counseling, 12,* 51–66.

Cohen, R. J., Swerdlik, M. E., & Smith, D. K. (1992). *Psychological testing and assessment: An introduction to tests and measurement.* Mountain View, CA: Mayfield.

Conoley, J. C., & Impara, J. C. (Eds.). (1995). *The 12th mental measurement yearbook.* Lincoln: University of Nebraska, Buros Institute of Mental Measurement.

Cronbach, L. J. (1990). *Essentials of psychological testing* (5th ed.). New York: Harper & Row.

Drummond, P. J. (1996). *Appraisal procedures for counselors and helping professions.* Upper Saddle River, NJ: Prentice Hall.

Gardner, H. (1993). *Frames of mind: The theory of multiple intelligences.* New York: Basic Books.

Goldman, L. (1972). Tests and counseling: The marriage that failed. *Measurement and Evaluation in Guidance, 4,* 213–220.

Goldman, L. (1982). Assessment in counseling: A better way. *Measurement and Evaluation in Guidance,* 15, 70–73.

Goldman, L. (1990). Qualitative assessment. *Counseling Psychologist, 15,* 205–213.

Goldman, L. (1992). Qualitative assessment: An approach for counselors. *Journal of Counseling & Development, 70,* 616–621.

Goldman, L. (1994). The marriage is over . . . for most of us. *Measurement and Evaluation in Counseling and Development, 26,* 217–218.

Kleinknecht, T. (1986). *The anxious self.* New York: Human Services Press.

Nugent, F. (1981). *Professional counseling: An overview.* Pacific Grove, CA: Brooks/Cole.

Pascal, E. (1992). *Jung to live by.* New York: Warner Books.

Prediger, D. J. (1994). Tests and counseling: The marriage that prevailed. *Measurement and Evaluation in Counseling and Development, 26,* 227–234.

Rogers, C. R. (1942). *Counseling and psychotherapy.* Boston: Houghton Mifflin.

Rogers, C. R. (1951). *Client-centered therapy: Its current practice, implications, and theory.* Boston: Houghton-Mifflin.

Spoto, A. (1989). *Jung's typology and perspective.* Boston: SIGO Press.

Sue, D., Sue, D., & Sue, S. (1994). *Understanding abnormal behavior* (4th ed.). Boston: Houghton Mifflin.

Sue, D. W., & Sue, D. (1990). *Counseling the culturally different* (2nd ed.). New York: John Wiley.

Thorndike, R. M. (1997). *Measurement and evaluation in psychology and education* (6th ed.). Upper Saddle River, NJ: Merrill/Prentice Hall.

Walsh, W. B., & Betz, N. E. (1995). *Tests and assessments* (3rd ed.). Upper Saddle River, NJ: Prentice Hall.

Watkins, C., Campbell, V., & McGregor, P. (1988). Counseling psychologists' uses of and opinions about psychological tests: A contemporary perspective. *Counseling Psychologist, 16,* 476–486.

7 Counseling Outreach: Prevention and Intervention

Besides time spent in direct counseling with individuals, groups, and families, counselors in all work settings are involved in prevention and intervention activities designed to improve the overall mental health climate for everyone in schools and the community. These activities are called *outreach* because counselors usually leave their offices and literally reach out. Their major purposes are to broaden the knowledge and skills of individuals in personal, social, educational and career development; to improve the school or community environment so that good mental health practices will be encouraged and enhanced; and to assist crisis victims. Thus they serve both a preventive, educational role to improve the mental health of a community and an intervention role to attend to those experiencing crises.

Since the 1970s, the number and variety of outreach programs have been increasing in all settings. This is largely a result of the recent proliferation of counseling theories and techniques, including psychological education, holistic approaches, wellness preventive programs, and the improvement in crisis intervention programs.

This is not to say that effective and appropriate outreach activities will necessarily decrease the number of requests for counseling. Instead, they tend to increase them. As a counseling center's staff becomes better known and more trusted, more persons may ask for counseling or be referred by other persons. As teachers or work supervisors become more effective in communication and in relationship and behavioral skills, they not only improve the classroom or work climate but also become more aware of when individuals need professional counseling. Outreach activities may prevent the development of some problems but may also spark the recognition that some individuals are experiencing conflict and can profit from counseling.

The following four categories are helpful in establishing or evaluating outreach activities of a counseling staff: (a) consultation, (b) psychological education, (c) social change activities, and (d) crisis intervention.

COUNSELORS AS CONSULTANTS

Gelso and Fretz (1992) define *consultation* as "a professional service that uses knowledge of human behavior, interpersonal relationships, and group and organizational processes to help others become more effective in their roles" (p. 515).

Consultation activities have certain characteristics regardless of work settings:

- The consultation involves three parties—client, consultant, and consultee.
- The consultation is voluntary and nonjudgmental.
- The focus is on specific issues regarding the client's problem.
- The consultee is free to accept or reject any or all recommendations (Hershenson, Power, & Waldo, 1996; Kurpius & Fuqua, 1993).

In their consulting work, counselors maintain confidentiality and protect rights of privacy of consultees just as they do with their clients in counseling. The ACA Code of Ethics (1995) says: "Information obtained in a consulting relationship is discussed for professional purposes only with persons clearly concerned with the case . . . and every effort is made to protect client identity and avoid undue invasion of privacy" (Section B.6.a). Consultation differs from supervision, teaching, and counseling; each serves a different role.

The Consultation Process

Professional counselors offer consultation in their areas of expertise—personal and interpersonal relationships, behavior dynamics, occupational knowledge, appraisal information, and communication skills. In the consultation process, the consultant listens to the concerns that consultees have about their interactions with third parties (clients). For example, a consultee (a fellow counselor) may wonder whether he has sufficient background to work with a client with a severe eating disorder. He may be perplexed about the lack of client response in the counseling sessions. Or he may be experiencing countertransference feelings he does not recognize. The consultant helps the consultee gain insight into the situation and suggests ways to work through it. In some cases, consultant and consultee may agree that the client's problem goes beyond the consultee's particular expertise. In these instances, the consultee refers the client to another professional.

The Consultation Relationship

Blackham (1977) says, "The desirable relationship between a consultant and consultee is best termed a 'colleague' or equal relationship rather than a relationship of authority to subordinate" (p. 393). Mutual respect and trust characterize their interactions.

The goal of consultation is to identify jointly the consultee's problem and to collaborate in helping the consultee make use of existing skills or attitudes or upgrade skills to improve interaction with a third party. In the process, the consultee's concerns about the third party are specified. Both explore whether the problem relates to a breakdown in communication, a difference in values, or a feeling of inadequacy by the consultee about handling the problem.

The consultee first describes strategies that have been used to manage the situation. For example, when a counselor consults with parents about a child with a behavioral problem, the counselor usually asks the parents to describe their unsuccessful attempts to discipline or communicate with the child. Consultant and consultee then explore different or modified strategies to resolve the problem. Recommendations may include referring the child and/or parent to individual or family counseling.

Types of Consultations

Consultation activities include the following types:

- With other counselors, other mental health professionals, and other professionals in related disciplines (psychologists, psychiatrists, social workers, physicians)
- With faculty, administrators, parents, or families in educational settings
- With administrators of community organizations serving mental health needs (directors of crisis centers, senior citizen centers, rape relief services, women's shelters)
- About an ongoing client

Consultation with Other Counselors and Other Professionals

When counselors experience problems or need specialized information in working with clients, they may consult with other counselors on their staff or elsewhere in the community. They request consultations when questions about a client arise, or when they are having persistent countertransference, ethical concerns, or concerns about appropriate training to handle the case. When counselors are uncertain or dubious about their work with clients, they have an ethical responsibility to check with a consultant (ACA, 1995).

At times, counselors want technical assistance from an expert in a particular phase of counseling. For example, they may consult with someone who specializes in bulimia, alcoholism, or vocational rehabilitation. In these cases, clients should be informed about the need, and their permission should be obtained prior to the consultation.

Consultation in Educational Settings

Faculty, parents, and administrators seek consultation with school counselors when they have confidence in the counselors' professional expertise.

Consultation with Faculty.   Faculty may have problems with individual students or in their overall classroom interactions. A student may not be handing in work and may look depressed or agitated, or a student may be disclosing personal concerns beyond what the teacher is prepared to handle. Teachers may have personal or marital concerns that are interfering with their class performance, or they may be depressed or anxious about their lives in general (Baker, 1996; Nugent, 1981).

For problems with students, the process of clarifying the difficulties and determining alternative action follows the consulting procedure discussed earlier (see "The Consultation Relationship"). For a teacher who consults with a counselor because of problems dealing with a student, sometimes the issue is too difficult to be worked out within a classroom. In such cases, the counselor will suggest that the teacher refer the student directly to the counselor (Nugent, 1981). In cases of a desire for disciplinary action or a formal evaluation of the student's abilities in public schools, the teacher should be directed to the administrator, school psychologist, or social worker (Nugent, 1969, 1973, 1981). In these same circumstances at the college level, faculty should be referred to the dean of students or to the chairs of their departments.

When a faculty member wants to consult about a student, it is wise ethical policy for the teacher to maintain the student's right to privacy and not identify the student. If the student under discussion is referred to counseling or comes in independently later, the counselor will not have prior knowledge about the student. Also, the teacher will be more likely to generalize suggestions about one student's particular behavior to similar behaviors of others.

This approach is feasible in college counseling and larger high schools because anonymity is fairly easy to maintain. In small schools, however, preservation of anonymity becomes more difficult. Nevertheless, it is good policy that students' names be of secondary importance unless it is determined that the identity of an individual be known because that student's behavior is injurious to him- or herself or to others.

Teachers who have personal problems may find it valuable to consult with a counselor for a few sessions. Together, they can evaluate the severity of the problem and decide whether counseling help is needed. Most often, consultees are apprehensive about whether they need counseling and where to go for the kind of help they need. If counseling is decided on, the counselor can refer the teachers to a professional person whom the counselor respects. It is not considered wise professional practice for counselors to involve themselves in counseling relationships with colleagues. Counselor and teacher may find it difficult to disengage social and/or business interactions from the counseling relationship. Establishing a relationship of the kind necessary for effective counseling would be difficult (G. Corey, Corey, & Callanan, 1993; Nugent, 1981).

Consultation with Parents.   Considerable agreement exists about the importance of effective parent-counselor consultations (Baker, 1996; Gibson & Mitchell, 1995; Strother & Jacobs, 1986). Parents may request a consultation with a school counselor. They may be concerned about their child's or adolescent's poor academic work, lack of friends, poor motivation in school, or unmanageable behavior at home. In these instances, it is most effective that the parents or counselor let the child know that a consultation has been requested and the reason for the request. If the child objects, the parents may need to resolve the objections before seeing the counselor. The counselor might also talk with the child about the objections, and that discussion in itself might help communication between parents and child. By establishing at the outset effective communication processes based on the right to privacy and confidentiality, the counselor and parents reduce the possibility that the child will perceive intrigue between the adults. This approach is particularly important because a counseling relationship with the child or with the family often arises out of effective consultation (Baker, 1996; Nugent, 1981).

After the consultation, if more intensive work with the family is needed, a referral to a family counseling service is in order. If a psychological evaluation of the child or an evaluation of home conditions seems warranted, a referral to the school psychologist or social worker can be made (Nugent, 1973, 1981).

Consultation with Administrators.   Administrators are often faced with conflicting demands and pressures from students, parents, and teachers concerning student behavior and school policy, student rights and responsibilities, and teacher or parent rights and responsibilities. They may, for example, have difficult interactions with parents or with individual teachers or groups of teachers, or they may face a gap between curricular offerings and student needs. Testing programs, appropriate use of school records, and changes in laws about administrator-student interactions are also areas in which school administrators may want consultation.

The counseling staff can offer information and guidelines about potential consequences of certain administrative actions on the student body or the teaching staff. Counselors can also use their expertise to ensure that testing and record-keeping policies are in line with the rights and responsibilities of students and adults. Guidelines on handling the administrator's interactions with parents and teachers can be discussed.

It is not wise professional practice, however, for counselors and administrators to discuss a specific teacher's interaction with students or the teacher's proficiency in teaching. This sort of evaluative interview can raise ethical dilemmas for counselors who are inviting referrals from teachers. If a teacher and an administrator request a joint consultation with a counselor about their interaction, a consultation may be useful as long as it has no evaluative overtones. When an administrator is concerned about a teacher suffering from an emotional breakdown (or the safety of others), a consultation with the counselor is in order.

Consultation in the Community

Individual consultations may be requested from counselors or directors at mental health community facilities or from staff at various mental health-related services in the community, such as crisis clinics, rape relief centers, senior centers, teenage counseling centers, or women's shelters. Consultations may be requested about individual clients, a particular type of client, ethical policies, or referral services of the organization. Professionals from various work settings also seek similar consultations—educators, physicians, lawyers, and people from business, industry, government agencies, and religious groups (Boytim, 1986).

In business, supervisors may ask for consultation—usually through an employee assistance program (EAP)—about a staff member, or they may want to learn how to refer an employee to counseling (Lewis & Lewis, 1986; Quayle, 1985).

At times, family members will ask for consultation with counselors in community agencies regarding a concern about a family member, such as an aging parent with Alzheimer's disease. Family members may also request consultation from employee assistance counselors about a relative's alcohol problems or undue emotional strain on the job that is affecting the family (Gerstein & Sturmer, 1993; Hutchison, 1985; Lewis & Lewis, 1986).

Consultation About a Client

If anyone asks to meet with a counselor about a client, the counselor should agree to consult *only* with the permission of the client (ACA, 1995). If the client is not involved in the decision, the trust relationship described earlier could be jeopardized (Nugent, 1981).

➤ PSYCHOLOGICAL EDUCATION

Psychological education is another form of outreach in which the counselor educates people in areas of personal, social, career, and educational development (Baker, 1996; Baker & Shaw, 1987; Brooks & Weikel, 1986).

Counselors can offer the following psychological education activities:

- Teaching courses
- Leading workshops and groups
- Training paraprofessionals
- Providing wellness activities
- Offering career education programs

Teaching Courses

Counselors have the background to teach courses in vocational, personal, and social areas. Professional counselors can offer elective, nongraded courses in public schools, colleges, and the community. They can teach classes in conjunction with the regular instructors, or they may be invited into classrooms to cover certain topics within their areas of expertise. Counselors typically offer courses in community colleges and in extension and extended day programs at colleges and universities.

Courses or units dealing with career awareness, personal development, and social interactions are pertinent. Also appropriate are courses on such social issues as race relations, cultural differences, mental health issues, sex and marriage, family relationships, individual rights and responsibilities, the changing roles of men and women, and alcohol and drug abuse.

Humanistic Education

Activities that increase the affective content of school and college curricula are generally called *humanistic education* to differentiate them from academic or intellectual subject matter. Commercial kits, canned teaching units, recordings, and videotapes are available to counselors and teachers. Some of the more popular programs are the following:

- Valuing processes, also called *values clarification*
- Processes in moral development (Kohlberg's moral development)
- Activities to improve personal growth and social interactions (Besell and Palmores's Sructured Human Development Program for elementary grades and Dinkmeyer's Developing Understanding of Self and Others (DUSO) kits of puppets and games to develop understanding of self and others for Grades 4 to 6)
- Games to change a behavior (achievement motivation)
- Various strategies to change the classroom environment (sensitivity modules) (Baker & Shaw, 1987)

Counselors who teach courses in personal and social development must be cautious about pushing their personal beliefs or social attitudes on their students. Psychological education courses such as these should not be considered a substitute for professional counseling. The following considerations are offered as guidelines for determining the appropriateness of various humanistic programs and systems in education.

1. Are participants permitted to choose whether they want to be involved in a particular class exercise?
2. Are families' and group members' rights to privacy protected?
3. Are safeguards included so that participants' attitudes are not shaped according to some predetermined values or moral beliefs?
4. Are discussions or exercises of such a nature that they do not provoke psychological or emotional reactions that the instructors are not professionally prepared to handle?
5. Are games or units regarding self-disclosure designed to protect individuals from indulging in intimate revelations that may subsequently lead to psychological distress?
6. Are precautions included to ensure that the program does not foster superficial resolutions of student problems or lead to superficial relationships among class members?

Leading Workshops and Groups

Workshops and educational group experiences differ from the instructional units just discussed in that they are usually short term, do not involve academic credit, and are less structured than classroom activities.

Counselors often survey students, staff, or members of the community about the types of workshops or group experiences they would like. Workshops or groups are offered by the counseling staff, or the staff arranges for outside consultants to run an activity.

Workshops are typically offered on vocational development, decision-making processes, women and careers, job-seeking skills, assertiveness training, development of self-esteem, communication skills, and parental skills (Hershenson et al., 1996). Leaders of local or regional ethnic groups are often invited to the school or community agency to discuss means of improving communication and the understanding of differing value systems. Workshops on the use and abuse of alcohol or other drugs might be developed by the local alcohol referral center, or the staff of a Planned Parenthood clinic could be invited to present the clinic's function in the community.

It is important that skill workshops be based on the needs expressed by the population being served, rather than on the belief of a counselor or counseling staff that everyone needs training in some skill. Thus, if all groups were offered assertiveness training, values clarification, or skills in listening to others, regardless of request, one could legitimately wonder whether the counselor was pushing one system of skills rather than tailoring these experiences to specific concerns expressed by various groups.

Some counselors lead workshops or groups based on techniques of major counseling theories. For example, counselors may use Gestalt techniques when running workshops on assertiveness training, increasing body awareness, or learning to confront others constructively. Other counselors may develop stress management, study skills, or weight-control workshops based on cognitive-behavioral approaches. Further examples are Gordon's (1975) Parent Effectiveness Training (PET), which follows Rogerian views, and Dinkmeyer's (1976) Systematic Training for Effective Parenting (STEP), based on Adlerian therapy. Gordon's PET is briefly discussed here.

Gordon calls his system the "no-lose" method of resolving conflicts. Parents learn effective management of conflicts by learning how to listen in a non-evaluative way and how to communicate feelings honestly. The system also spells out techniques to change unacceptable behavior by changing the environment. Parents learn how to identify the conflict, generate and evaluate alternative solutions, and decide on the best solution. Then ways are worked out to implement the solution, and follow-up is arranged. Gordon (1977) has applied similar steps to working with Teacher Effectiveness Training (TET) and Youth Effectiveness Training (YET) (Baker & Shaw, 1987).

Groups that develop social interaction skills are sometimes called *sensitivity training* or *organizational development groups.* They are similar to other workshops except they have less structured leadership and less emphasis on developing a particular social skill. These groups, whose members learn to develop their own system of democratic processes, their own leadership, and their own methods of developing social cooperation, have been used extensively in schools and colleges. They can be used to help student governments function more equitably and can be developed to help improve student-faculty interactions. They also work well in community agencies and businesses.

Structured groups are designed to help group members focus on specific social skills training, such as stress management, eating disorders, test anxiety, assertion, and other developmental life skills (M. S. Corey & Corey, 1992; Gazda, 1989). As the name implies, these groups are highly structured, with predetermined, specific goals accomplished through the use of training and exercises. The process is based on a skill deficit model. The procedure is to teach appropriate skills to eliminate the deficiency, thereby increasing social interaction and social use.

Training Paraprofessionals

Counselors provide in-service training for those who want to become paraprofessionals in counseling. These paraprofessionals are also called *paracounselors* or *counselor aides.* Paraprofessionals receive training by a professional to perform specific auxiliary duties related to professional duties. Some, for example, act as librarian aides in information resource rooms. Others learn basic interviewing skills so that they can serve at referral and information desks. Still others are trained to score simple paper-and-pencil tests used in counseling interviews (Hershenson et al., 1996).

Some are trained for somewhat higher skill levels. In colleges, for example, students are often hired as aides in the residence halls to act as resource persons for students. Through in-service training with professional counselors at the counseling center, these students can learn how to be alert to students' problems as they arise in the dormitories and about consultation procedures with a counselor about whether to refer students.

Counselor aides can also be helpful to the professional when they are trained to provide information about, and make referrals to, such specific community services as drug or alcohol referral centers or pregnancy counseling centers. In these more complex positions, aides should be forewarned that they are not counselors; training includes knowing how to avoid becoming overly involved in a person's problems and knowing when and how to refer an individual to a professional.

Ivey's (1994) interviewing and human relationship skills (discussed in chap. 8) are commonly used in workshop and affective curricula to train paraprofessionals or interviewers, receptionists, and other nonspecialists serving the public in mental health or mental health-related jobs.

Providing Wellness Activities

Counselors who follow wellness models teach individuals how to maintain good health by attending to their physical, emotional, intellectual, and spiritual development. This holistic approach can be applied to groups in educational settings, the workplace, and the community (Hershenson et al., 1996; Myers, 1992).

Wellness outreach programs are commonly found in the workplace as part of employee enhancement programs (see chap. 12) and in universities as part of counseling center or health services. Although less common in schools, school counselors have started offering preventive workshops recommended by wellness advocates.

In industry, employees are encouraged to develop healthy lifestyles through educational workshops that cover subjects such as managing stress, developing a healthy diet, learning about the hazards of smoking or misuse of alcohol, monitoring weight and blood pressure, and doing exercises to keep physically fit (Lewis & Lewis, 1986; Witmer & Sweeney, 1992). Some industries provide fitness rooms where employees can do aerobic exercises.

In universities, wellness components of student counseling services and/or student health services offer similar types of group experiences. Information and workshops about avoiding sexually transmitted diseases, using safe-sex practices, and reducing chances of date rape are available. Support groups for individuals grieving over losses through death, divorce, or breakups with lovers are common.

Omizo, Omizo, and D'Andrea (1992) discuss the importance of developing wellness activities for elementary students because effective or ineffective lifestyles develop in the early formative years. Omizo et al. conducted a study in which one class of fifth-grade students (the experimental group) were given 10 weekly guidance sessions that covered exercise, nutrition, stress management, relaxation exercises, and good health habits. When compared with another fifth-grade class that received no wellness instruction (the control group), the experimental class showed statistically significant better scores on measures of general self-esteem, anxiety level, and knowledge about wellness. Stress management skills can be easily integrated into existing school curricula by using a variety of techniques such as proper breathing, muscle relaxation training, imagery and visualization, and biofeedback training (Romano, 1992).

Other programs that contribute to individual wellness are those that teach people to honor the welfare of the planet by encouraging recycling and suggesting ways to help reduce pollution and protect natural resources.

Offering Career Education Programs

During the 1990s, increasing numbers of counselors in educational settings and in the community became active in developing career education and career outreach programs. This increased activity in schools stemmed mainly from federal and state funding for career education. In communities, the numbers of career counseling centers for adults increased in response to the demands of the general public for career information and exploration.

Through federal incentives, counselors in schools developed curricular activities, workshops, and projects that help students see how their personal characteristics and environmental factors in their lives influence their occupational choices. These programs focus on career awareness in elementary schools, career exploration in middle schools, and career preparation in senior high schools (Isaacson & Brown, 1993). For high school seniors, these activities include training in writing job applications, developing résumés, practicing job interviews, and visiting, observing, or interning at job sites.

In colleges and universities, career education activities are often offered jointly by counseling center and placement center staffs. Typically, these activities are workshops or all-day seminars that include computerized occupational exploration programs, panels of speakers from a variety of occupations, and hands-on workshops to give students practice in writing job résumés and preparing for job interviews. Placement center staff also provide information about job openings and arrange for student-employer job interviews.

Career counseling centers for adults in the community provide numerous career education services to their clients, including developing job résumés, preparing for job interviews, and becoming more marketable. Community career centers also provide workshops for clients wishing to change or upgrade jobs or desiring to develop their own businesses. Support groups are also formed to help individuals who are displaced homemakers, who suddenly lose their jobs, or who are trying to work through uncertainties about changing jobs.

⟶ SOCIAL CHANGE ACTIVITIES

Most outreach programs are social change activities in that they attempt to educate staff in the schools or officials in the community so as to improve general mental health for everyone. In some cases, it is appropriate for counseling staffs to make specific suggestions to change the social environment. For example, in a high school, a counselor might suggest changes in the curriculum because of ethnic stereotyping, and in a community, a counselor might propose ways that area businesses can offer better child care.

Counseling staffs may also affect the social environment in other ways: by helping individuals or groups become aware of a need for change in policy, curricular offerings, or services and by helping others become aware of their right to work for change and to learn procedures by which they can make changes. Counselors can try to carry out a particularly important social change in circumstances where administrative policies violate counselor ethical codes, such as instances that break confidentiality or ignore rights of privacy. A need for change can be pointed out through workshops in which policies and procedures can be discussed and recommendations for change made to the appropriate officials. Examples of important issues are gender and racial stereotyping, minors' rights and responsibilities, and child care services in colleges and businesses.

It is important that the counselor let clients know that clients will not always be successful with authorities in making changes and that they may come out of the interactions somewhat bruised. Nevertheless, individuals who decide to try to make changes should be given help. They can be shown how to proceed in a fair and firm manner that will best convince the persons in charge that a change is necessary. Although counselors should support clients' efforts, they should not try to persuade or pressure them in any way to take action. Decisions to take action and the consequences of the decisions are the responsibility of the clients.

⟶ CRISIS INTERVENTION

A *crisis,* or sudden unexpected trauma, can happen to any normally functioning individual. It can cause that person to experience disequilibrium or immobility accompanied by panic, debilitating anxiety, hopelessness, or helplessness; the person may lose the capacity to use coping skills to master his or her responses to overcome the trauma.

Two major categories of stress—external and internal—are liable to produce crises. In *external stress,* something or someone in the environment unexpectedly causes disruption, which brings out severe emotional reactions. Examples of these stressors are sudden death of a loved one, sudden onset of terminal or serious illness, unexpected loss of a job, rape, assault, abandonment by a loved one, or natural disasters such as floods or earthquakes. *Internal stress* include suicidal thoughts, severe depression, severe generalized panic, acute alcohol or drug reactions, or psychotic reactions.

Counselors and Crisis Intervention

Crises occur in educational, community, and business settings. A student may panic in class or on school or college premises and be brought to the counseling center by a faculty member or another student. Similarly, a person in crisis may be brought to the community agency by family or a friend. The counselor must be available immediately to intervene (Gilliland & James, 1997).

Counselors must assess quickly whether individuals might harm themselves or others. If so, they have an obligation to take appropriate action to protect others or to arrange protective care for the client (G. Corey et al., 1993). If no immediate danger exists, counselors then can take steps to help the individuals cope with the crises.

Crisis intervention is not synonymous with counseling. Goals are immediate and specific to the crisis. Belkin (1984) aptly and succinctly remarks that "crisis intervention is to counseling what first aid is to medicine, a temporary but immediate relief for an emerging situation presented by an incapacitated client" (p. 423).

Process in Crisis Intervention

The principal goal of crisis intervention is to restore the person to the way he or she was before the crisis occurred. Counselors must be supportive, empathic, and willing to direct the interview (Brammer, Abrego, & Shostrom, 1993; Gilliland & James, 1997). Their views, along with mine, can be summarized as follows:

1. Help the person express and release emotions through support and empathy
2. Identify and clarify the precipitating problem and the extent of its severity
3. Gather information about the event that caused the crisis
4. Help the client identify his or her coping skills, emphasizing strengths that can help overcome the problem
5. Assess the degree of support for the client from family, colleagues, and friends
6. Explore strategies to improve or resolve crisis-inducing stress
7. Decide whether further counseling is needed and whether a referral to a psychiatrist or another specialist is required

Gilliland and James (1997) specify counselor strategies and degree of counselor direct action (see Figure 7.1). The more immobilized the client, the more directive the counselor should be.

FIGURE 7.1

The six-step model of crisis intervention.

ASSESSING:

Overarching, continuous, and dynamically ongoing throughout the crisis; evaluating the client's present and past situational crisis in terms of the client's ability to cope, personal threat, mobility or immobility, and making a judgment regarding type of action needed by the crisis worker. (See crisis worker's action continuum, below.)

Listening →

LISTENING: Attending, observing, understanding, and responding with empathy, genuineness, respect, acceptance, nonjudgment, and caring.

1. *Define the problem.* Explore and define the problem from the client's point of view. Use active listening, including open-ended questions. Attend to both verbal and nonverbal messages of the client.

2. *Ensure client safety.* Assess lethality, criticality, immobility, or seriousness of threat to the client's physical and psychological safety. Assess both the client's internal events and the situation surrounding the client, and, if necessary, ensure that the client is made aware of alternatives to impulsive, self-destructive actions.

3. *Provide support.* Communicate to the client that the crisis worker is a valid support person. Demonstrate (by words, voice, and body language) a caring, positive, nonpossessive, nonjudgmental, acceptant, personal involvement with the client.

Acting →

ACTING: Becoming involved in the intervention at a nondirective, collaborative, or directive level, according to the assessed needs of the client and the availability of environmental supports.

4. *Examine alternatives.* Assist client in exploring the choices he or she has available to him or her now. Facilitate a search for immediate situational supports, coping mechanisms, and positive thinking.

5. *Make plans.* Assist client in developing a realistic short-term plan that identifies additional resources and provides coping mechanisms—definite action steps that the client can own and comprehend.

6. *Obtain commitment.* Help client commit himself or herself to definite, positive action steps that the client can own and realistically accomplish or accept.

Crisis Worker's Action Continuum

Crisis worker is nondirective	Crisis worker is collaborative	Crisis worker is directive
(Threshold varies from client to client)	(Threshold varies from client to client)	
Client is mobile	Client is partially mobile	Client is immobile

The crisis worker's level of action/involvement may be anywhere on the continuum according to a valid and realistic assessment of the client's level of mobility/immobility.

Source: From *Crisis Intervention Strategies*, 3rd Ed., by B. E. Gilliland and R. K. James. Copyright 1995 by Wadsworth Inc. Used by permission of Brooks/Cole Publishing Co., Pacific Grove, CA 93950.

In some cases, one, two, or three meetings with a client may suffice. But in others, the decision to carry out postcrisis counseling may be agreed on either with the counselor or with another mental health specialist.

When a person experiences the death or dying of a loved one, after the initial trauma is eased, the client may need to work through a grief process for persons facing death. Kûbler-Ross (1975) developed a system of working with dying people that has also been found appropriate for other losses, such as that of a loved one, a job, or a treasured possession. The stages generally proceed first with denial and isolation (in which persons do not accept reality); followed by feelings of anger at their fate; then attempts to bargain with life; followed by feelings of depression as reality is faced; and finally acceptance. Most persons going through grief stages move back and forth many times between the stages (see chap. 15 sections on grief work).

Hershenson et al. (1996) point out that a crisis can be a positive growth experience, rather than a disastrous event, if the counselor helps the client cope successfully during the crisis and use it as a learning experience.

Suicide Intervention

Suicide intervention is an area of concern for counselors in all settings. An alarming number of teenagers in the United States attempt or commit suicide every year. Among teenagers, 15% have seriously considered suicide (Comer, 1996). Resnick (1989), Burbach, Kaskani, and Roseberg (1989), and Shaffer (1993) cite figures that show the suicide rate among young adults (15-24%) is now the third leading cause of death for this group.

Suicide is the highest, however, among the elderly. Almost 25% of individuals who commit suicide in the United States are over age 65. This group also has the highest percentage of completed suicides (Cavanaugh, 1997; see also chap. 15).

In instances where someone threatens suicide, the counselor must assess the situation carefully (see Figure 7.1). The counselor must determine the intensity of the depression, anxiety, or disorientation; the frequency of suicidal thoughts; the amount of withdrawal; and the responsiveness to counselor overtures to give help. The counselor also needs to check whether the individual has made a specific plan to carry out suicide (Gilliland & James, 1997; Moursund, 1993). Counselors should be particularly concerned when suicidal persons start telling others about their specific plans to kill themselves. When the amount of risk is moderate, counselors can try contracting with clients to delay any action until alternatives can be discussed and to encourage them to contact a counselor if they feel strong destructive urges. In severe cases where persons seem determined to take their lives, contacting family or friends is in order. Counselors should consult with a psychiatrist to determine whether a person needs involuntary commitment to a hospital (G. Corey et al., 1993).

The same procedures apply in assessing persons who have sudden psychotic breakdowns and are disoriented or with persons who are severely depressed. In these cases, the counselor should consult with a psychiatrist.

⫸ LIAISON WITH OTHER COMMUNITY AGENCIES AND SPECIALISTS

By maintaining good professional relationships with other community agencies and specialists, the counseling center can expand its service to clients. Referrals to these agencies and specialists can then be made with a minimum of delay or red tape. It is advisable to have lists of referral sources available for clients or consultees.

Joint outreach programs in such areas as drug education, AIDS, and career problems for persons at various stages of development can be arranged through communitywide workshops or seminars. School counselors can also have a variety of consultants available for use in the schools.

⫸ SUMMARY

In addition to direct counseling, counselors offer outreach services designed to improve the mental health climate for individuals within the community. These services involve prevention and intervention programs that augment and supplement the direct counseling duties of the counseling staff. The four types of outreach most commonly provided by counselors are consultation, psychological education, social change activities, and crisis intervention.

In consultation activities, counselors often act as consultants with each other to help gain insights or different perspectives regarding a particular case. They likewise act as consultants with faculty, parents, administrators, and employers regarding matters relating to counseling.

Counselors also offer psychological education activities in the form of prevention and intervention to educate the population they are serving in the areas of personal, social, career, and educational development. Counselors may teach courses, offer workshops, or teach groups in schools and in the community. They may also teach personal and social skill building to improve one's feelings about oneself, to improve one's ability to relate better in social interactions, or to prepare oneself for effective job searches. Other psychological education activities include training paraprofessionals to serve as aids to the counseling staff.

Counselors may also take direct social action to improve or change administrative policies or procedures that are impeding or stifling good mental health in the community or institutional setting. This step is particularly important if these administrative policies involve actions that violate the ethical codes of the counselor.

Regarding crises, direct intervention becomes necessary when individuals experience a sudden unexpected crisis or trauma that causes panic, severe depression, helplessness, or suicidal thoughts that render them incapable of overcoming the trauma by themselves. Intervention strategies include assessing the problem, calming down the individual, and determining follow-through measures or referrals.

PROJECTS AND ACTIVITIES

1. A school counselor receives a call from a parent concerned that her son is going with the wrong crowd. The student is not, and has not been, a client of the counselor. The parent asks the counselor to call in her son to set him straight. She requests that the counselor not tell her son that she called. How should the counselor respond?

2. Develop an educational and informational program focusing on the culture and customs of a minority group in your locality or in a locality in which you might like to work. How could you involve leaders and other members of the group in the development of the program?

3. Select two psychological education programs that have been proposed in the literature for counselors to use in educational institutions, the community, or both. Evaluate these programs on the basis of theoretical orientation, consideration of rights to privacy, protection against psychological harm, and appropriateness to age level.

4. Discuss how a birth control agency and a counseling center staff in a school, college, or community center could develop a cooperative educational program that would appeal to both females and males.

5. Select and organize a list of books, pamphlets, and films about drug education, sex education, careers, and self-help. Consider the criteria you would use in selecting the material.

6. Interview a career counselor at your university and another at a community career counseling center regarding their outreach activities. Compare the activities in each agency. What are the similarities and differences? Compare also the training and experience of the professional staff at each of these settings.

REFERENCES

American Counseling Association (ACA). (1995). *Ethical standards of the American Counseling Association.* Alexandria, VA: Author.

Baker, S. B. (1996). *School counseling for the 21st century* (2nd ed.). Upper Saddle River, NJ: Merrill/Prentice Hall.

Baker, S. B., & Shaw, M. C. (1987). *Improving counseling through primary prevention.* Upper Saddle River, NJ: Merrill/Prentice Hall.

Belkin, G. S. (1984). *Introduction to counseling.* Dubuque, IA: William C. Brown.

Blackham, J. G. (Ed.). (1977). *Counseling: Theory, process, and practice.* Belmont, CA: Wadsworth.

Boytim, J. A. (1986). The mental health counselor as a consultant. In A. J. Palmo & W. J. Weikel (Eds.), *Foundations of mental health counseling* (pp. 229–232). Springfield, IL: Charles C Thomas.

Brammer, L. M., Abrego, P. J., & Shostrom, E. L. (1993). *Therapeutic counseling and psychotherapy* (6th ed.). Upper Saddle River, NJ: Prentice Hall.

Brooks, D. K., Jr., & Weikel, W. J. (1986). History and development of the mental health counseling movement. In A. J.

Palmo & W. J. Weikel (Eds.), *Foundations of mental health counseling* (pp. 3–28). Springfield, IL: Charles C Thomas.

Burbach, D., Kaskani, J., & Roseberg, T. (1989). Parental bonding and depressive disorders in adolescence. *Journal of Child Psychology and Psychiatry, 30,* 417–430.

Cavanaugh, J. C. (1997). *Adult development and aging.* Pacific Grove, CA: Brooks/Cole.

Comer, R. J. (1996). *Fundamentals of abnormal psychology.* New York: W. H. Freeman.

Corey, G., Corey, M. S., & Callanan, P. (1993). *Issues and ethics in the helping professions* (4th ed.). Pacific Grove, CA: Brooks/Cole.

Corey, M. S., & Corey, G. (1992). *Groups: Process and practice.* Pacific Grove, CA: Brooks/Cole.

Dinkmeyer, D. (1976). *Systematic training for effective parenting.* Circle Pines, MN: American Guidance Service.

Gazda, G. M. (1989). *Group counseling: A developmental approach* (4th ed.). Boston: Allyn & Bacon.

Gelso, C. J., & Fretz, B. R. (1992). *Counseling psychology.* Fort Worth, TX: Harcourt Brace.

Gerstein, L. H., & Sturmer, P. (1993). A Taoist paradigm of EAP consultation. *Journal of Counseling & Development, 72,* 178–184.

Gibson, R. L., & Mitchell, M. H. (1995). *Introduction to counseling and guidance* (4th ed.). Upper Saddle River, NJ: Merrill/Prentice Hall.

Gilliland, B. E., & James, R. K. (1997). *Crisis intervention strategies* (3rd ed.). Pacific Grove, CA: Brooks/Cole.

Gordon, T. (1975). *Parent effectiveness training.* New York: New American Library.

Gordon, T. (1977). *Teacher effectiveness training.* New York: McKay.

Hershenson, D. B., Power, P. W., & Waldo, M. (1996). *Community counseling: Contemporary theory and practice.* Boston: Allyn & Bacon.

Hutchison, W. S., Jr. (1985). The importance and criticalness of the family systems component of employee assistance programs. In J. F. Dickman, W. G. Emener, Jr., & W. S. Hutchison, Jr. (Eds.), *Counseling the troubled person in industry* (pp. 30–37). Springfield, IL: Charles C Thomas.

Isaacson, I. E., & Brown, D. (1993). *Career information, career counseling, and career development* (5th ed.). Boston: Allyn & Bacon.

Ivey, A. E. (1994). *Intentional interviewing and counseling: Facilitating client development* (3rd ed.). Pacific Grove, CA: Brooks/Cole.

Kûbler-Ross, E. (1975). *Death: The final stage of growth.* Upper Saddle River, NJ: Prentice Hall.

Kurpius, D. J., & Fuqua, D. (1993). Fundamental issues in defining consultation. *Journal of Counseling & Development, 71,* 598–600.

Lewis, J. A., & Lewis, M. D. (1986). Counseling programs for employees in the *workplace.* Monterey, CA: Brooks/Cole.

Moursund, J. (1993). *The process of counseling and therapy* (3rd ed.). Upper Saddle River, NJ: Prentice Hall.

Myers, J. E. (1992). Wellness, prevention, development: The cornerstone of the profession. *Journal of Counseling & Development, 71,* 136–139.

Nugent, F. A. (1969). A framework for appropriate referrals of disciplinary problems to counselors. *School Counselor, 16,* 199–202.

Nugent, F. A. (1973). School counselors, psychologists, and social workers: A distinction. *Psychology in the Schools, 10,* 327–333.

Nugent, F. A. (1981). *Professional counseling: An overview.* Pacific Grove, CA: Brooks/Cole.

Omizo, M. M., Omizo, S. A., & D'Andrea, M. J. (1992). Promoting wellness among elementary school children. *Journal of Counseling & Development, 71,* 194–198.

Quayle, D. (1985). American productivity: The devastating effect of alcoholism and drug use. In J. F. Dickman, W. G. Emener, Jr., & W. S. Hutchison, Jr. (Eds.), *Counseling the troubled person in industry* (pp. 20–29). Springfield, IL: Charles C Thomas.

Resnick, M. (1989). *The state of adolescent health in Minnesota.* Minneapolis: Minnesota Department of Public Health, University of Minnesota.

Romano, J. L. (1992). Psychoeducational interventions for stress management and well-being. *Journal of Counseling & Development, 71,* 199–202.

Shaffer, D. R. (1993). *Developmental psychology: Childhood and adolescence* (3rd ed.). Pacific Grove, CA: Brooks/Cole.

Strother, J., & Jacobs, E. (1986). Parent consultation: A practical approach. *School Counselor, 33,* 292–295.

Witmer, J. M., & Sweeney, T. J. (1992). A holistic model for wellness and prevention over the life span [Special issue: Wellness through the life span]. *Journal of Counseling & Development, 71,* 140–148.

8   The Effective Counselor

Far more is expected of an effective counselor now than in the 1950s and 1960s, the early days of counseling. Since then, the roles and expectations of the counselor have steadily become more varied and complex as counseling theories multiplied, theories now based on humanistic, behavioral, cognitive, cognitive-behavioral, and new contemporary psychosocial and psychoanalytic and psychodynamic approaches. Furthermore, life-span developmental theories extended counseling beyond the schools and colleges to include counseling older adults throughout the life span.

So, the question, What makes an effective counselor for the 21st century? has become very complicated. One would expect the effective counselor to measure up to the ideally well-developed individual that psychological theorists have formulated. But each of the different psychological theories—humanistic, cognitive-behavioral, contemporary psychodynamic, and post-Jungian—tends to present its own ideals and set of criteria regarding human nature. Moreover, each describes differing processes that help individuals overcome patterns that block effective ways of being.

These various theories on what constitutes the well-developed person challenge counselors who aspire to be as effective as possible with their clients: Psychoanalysts, for instance, focus on a person's intrapsychic forces, whereas humanists focus on self-actualizing development; cognitive-behaviorists focus on a person's cognitive structure, perceptions, and behavior; and certain feminists focus on the psychodynamics of mutual connections.

Not only have counselor educators and counselors in the field needed to adapt to the steady stream of new theoretical approaches over the years, but they also have had to acquire new and varied competencies as they expanded services beyond schools and colleges to the community. As the number of master's degree programs in counseling spread throughout the country and as states established licensure requirements, increasing numbers of counselors began working in private practice and in community agencies. To be effective in these new settings, they have had to acquire competencies in working with families, substance abuse cases, trauma victims, clients with spiritual concerns, and older adults. Ethnic and feminist counselors emphasize the importance of becoming more aware of one's cultural and gender differences. Increasing needs for crisis intervention and requests from agencies for diagnostic psychological evaluations of individuals have added to the load of expectations for being an effective counselor.

Because of budget cuts, reduced services, streamlined sessions, and the rise of managed care, a sharp rise in brief-therapy programs has occurred, requiring counselors to adapt counseling theories and techniques to short-term counseling sessions. To further complicate the expectations of well-trained counselors, the use of standardized tests, which had declined sharply in the 1960s and 1970s, escalated dramatically in the 1990s, requiring counselor competencies to include effective use of assessment tools.

With these many new and varied expectations of counselors, their job of making sound moral and value judgments in their counseling relationships have become more complex. This, in turn, has made it increasingly important that counselors attend to and cultivate their own personal and professional growth and development. Being aware of their own ongoing developmental processes, they would know when to seek professional consultation, when to seek professional counseling or therapy, and when to participate in relevant workshops, seminars, and retreats.

❧ PERSONAL QUALITIES OF EFFECTIVE COUNSELORS

Effective counselors are well-integrated individuals committed to their own continued growth and change. They tend to be open to new experiences, aware of their own motivations, values, vulnerabilities, and unmet needs. They know when to seek counseling or therapeutic help themselves to maintain growth and meaning in life. These qualities enable counselors to empathize and support clients struggling through the often painful steps of self-examination and self-exploration necessary for change and development.

In the 1950s, Carl Rogers (1951, 1957) proposed that counselors need to establish effective relationships with their clients that would lead to client self-actualization. He presented core characteristics essential to an effective counselor-client relationship: *empathy* (understanding), *congruency* (genuineness), and unconditional *positive regard* (warmth) (see chaps. 2 and 5). To review briefly, *empathy* describes counselors' ability to experience a client's inner world without identifying with the client. *Congruency* refers to the basic integrity of counselors that permits them to be authentic and honest with clients. Unconditional *positive regard* involves warm, accepting, nonjudgmental attitudes toward clients.

Carkhuff (1969, 1971) proposed two additional core characteristics: *respect* and *immediacy*. *Respect* refers to counselor attitudes that convey the counselor's high regard for a client's worth as a person. *Immediacy* refers to the counselor's sensitivity to the immediate experiencing of the client.

After a review of the literature, Gelso and Carter (1985) concluded that whereas most researchers generally agree that these core characteristics are necessary to facilitate a counseling relationship, they do not see them as sufficient qualities to ensure successful counseling outcome.

Counseling theorists have presented other qualities that also contribute to an effective counselor: *self-awareness, open-mindedness, flexibility, objectivity, trustworthiness,* and *personal integrity* (Belkin, 1984; Corey, 1996; Cormier & Cormier, 1991; Kottler & Brown, 1992).

Self-awareness refers to counselors' understanding and acceptance of their own feelings, attitudes, and values; recognition and acceptance of their own vulnerabilities and personal inadequacies; and awareness of the impact these have on others.

Open-minded counselors are those open to new ideas and experiences that stimulate personal and professional growth. They are alert to noting preconceived notions they may have about a client's experiences, feelings, and values; they are accepting of client views different from their own. Counselors who are open-minded and unbiased tend to maintain clearer and more accurate perceptions of clients' feelings and actions.

Counselors who are *flexible* are not bound to one theoretical view, nor do they impose one set of techniques on all clients at all times in all contexts. They are thus able to work with a wide range of clients and client problems.

Trustworthy counselors hold confidences shared by clients. They do not deceive clients by misrepresenting their areas of expertise or their theoretical views about counseling. Nor do they experiment with new or untried techniques outside their areas of expertise. If a counselor wants to try a new technique within her or his specialty, the counselor should first get the consent of the client.

Objectivity refers to counselors' ability to understand a client's struggles and pain. Because of their own self-awareness, counselors do not overidentify or become oversolicitous with their clients, nor do they underestimate and ignore their clients' feelings.

Counselors with *personal integrity* who are aware of their own inadequacies, vulnerabilities, and defenses do not project their own unresolved emotions on their clients. They are able to accept clients' emotional reactions toward them objectively. They are aware of their position of power with vulnerable, dependent clients and do not abuse it by attempting to control or manipulate client behavior. They are comfortable with intimacy but are aware of appropriate boundaries in the counseling relationship.

Regarding *values,* effective counselors are aware of value differences between themselves and clients when clients present value conflicts. Counselors help clients seek resolutions that are consistent with client self-growth and with client effective interactions in society. They do not impose their own values on clients.

Multicultural Awareness

Multicultural counselors have insisted over the years that all counselors must become aware of their own ethnic- and gender-related biases. Counselors should become aware of their own cultural values and beliefs and how they may differ from those held by others, especially their clients (Arredondo, 1998; Lee, 1995; Locke, 1995; Sue, 1996; Sue & Sue, 1990).

The efforts of the leaders cited above and others like them have led to the inclusion of multicultural competencies in counselor training standards (see chaps. 2 and 14). In addition, they have been instrumental in emphasizing the moral and ethical considerations for counselors who lack cultural awareness and/or cultural competencies necessary to be effective in multicultural counseling. Largely because of their influence, the ACA Code of Ethics (1995) includes in its preamble the following statement: "Association members recognize diversity in our society and embrace a cross-cultural approach in support of the worth, dignity, potential and uniqueness of each individual" (p. 1).

Sue (1996) presents three goals that are essential characteristics of effective, professionally ethical counselors:

> First, we need to become more culturally aware of our own biases, values, and assumptions about human behavior. Second, we need to become increasingly aware of the cultural values, biases and assumptions of diverse groups in our society. Third, we need to begin to develop culturally appropriate individual and system intervention strategies. (pp. 196–197)

Effective counselors are open and responsive to the different socialization and cultural processes and the different views about human nature that exist among the diverse cultures in our multicultural society. They are aware that the traditional human developmental stages presented by Erikson, Piaget, Kohlberg, and others tend to exclude the majority of the population because they are based on young, White, secular, middle-class, male norms. Counselors open to their own self-development are familiar with other developmental models (see chap. 4) that take into account women, persons from the various ethnic cultures, older adults, and a person's spiritual development. To accommodate multicultural values and traditions, Ivey and colleagues' (Ivey & Ivey, 1999; Ivey, Ivey, & Simek-Morgan, 1997) publications describe interviewing skills from multicultural perspectives.

Personal Counseling and Therapy for Counselors

Many people now entering the counseling profession have probably had some sort of counseling or therapy themselves. A successful therapeutic experience would enable counselors to understand the process of growth and transformation expected in a therapeutic relationship.

If personal counseling were an expected part of their professional development, counselors-in-training would more likely become aware of their own limitations and strengths; they would experience the process of delving into themselves, a process that could help them relate to clients in more authentic or non-exploitative ways. Learning how to recognize their own unmet needs, counselors-in-training prepare themselves to deal with countertransference reactions when they are working with clients (Corey, 1996).

In the light of what is now expected of an effective counselor, it makes sense that all counselors would benefit from intermittent or periodic counseling or therapy themselves as they experience transitions, losses, or conflicts in their own lives. In this way, they would continue to develop and maintain the self-awareness necessary to remain effective with their clients.

Self-Growth Activities for Counselors

Many opportunities are possible for counselors to expand their self-awareness and to learn new perspectives about relating to clients. Regular case conferences and case presentations can help counselors become aware of countertransference issues and acquaint them with counseling approaches different from their own. Personal-growth workshops and seminars are expected of counselors and therapists on an ongoing basis as a way for them to continue to develop and maintain effective relationships with their clients. Professional associations offer a multitude of workshops at their annual conferences. Professional counselors and therapists should also partake in therapeutic workshops, seminars, or retreats offered outside their associations or outside their expertise to broaden their outlook. Schools of social work, spiritually oriented groups, and the Society of Aging, for example, are apt to address issues that many counseling and psychological associations are probably unaware of.

✦ PROFESSIONAL COMPETENCIES: KNOWLEDGE AND SKILLS

Professional competencies considered essential for counselors fall into four major categories: (a) knowledge about counseling theories and strategies, (b) interviewing skills, (c) assessment skills, and (d) sound ethical judgment. Additional competencies necessary for counselors in specialty areas such as family, career, or substance abuse or, in particular, work settings such as schools, colleges, or community agencies are described in separate chapters in parts 3 and 4.

Knowledge About Counseling Theories and Strategies

It is important for counselors to be aware of the differences among the various theoretical approaches and the value of using these approaches under different client circumstances. It is necessary for counselors to learn all major theories before they eventually decide to specialize in one theoretical orientation. Students in those graduate counseling programs that adhere to professional training standards are thus expected to acquire knowledge of various counseling theories—humanistic, cognitive-behavioral, and psychodynamic. They also learn the various strategies these theories propose (see chap. 5). Humanists, for example, use strategies to increase clients' insights about themselves and their environment. Among the humanists, Rogerians use interviewing and relationship skills to help clients self-actualize, and Gestaltists use strategies such as visual imagery, body work, or confrontation to provoke feeling responses in clients. Cognitive-behaviorists use strategies such as reinforcement, social modeling, cognitive restructuring, and reframing to correct clients' distorted perceptions about the nature of their problems. Psychodynamic therapists help clients integrate conscious and unconscious processes by helping them become aware of dynamic, intrapsychic processes underlying their perceptions and interactions.

Although many counselors and therapists eventually specialize in applying certain strategies based on one particular theoretical view, many counselors tend to be eclectic and draw on techniques from a variety of theoretical orientations, depending on the nature of the problem, varying client characteristics, social context and environment, and the counselor's work setting (Lazarus & Beutler, 1993; see also chap. 5). Even though an eclectic approach allows counselors more flexibility in working with a wide range of clients and client problems and their particular situations, eclecticism can be dangerous in the hands of inexperienced or minimally trained counselors or therapists. Such persons are apt to be injudicious in using techniques that go beyond their expertise and training. When inappropriately applied, techniques that are otherwise potentially beneficial to clients can become damaging.

An eclectic approach is acquired over time as counselors gradually develop a broad and comprehensive understanding of counseling theories and strategies. Through practice and participation in periodic postgraduate training programs, counselors gradually draw on techniques stemming from the different theoretical approaches that are consistent with their fundamental assumptions about human growth and development. They are cautious about using a technique unless they have acquired sufficient training and expertise. They are willing to take intensive training to learn new strategies that fit their own theoretical model (see chap. 5).

More important, effective counselors know when to refer clients to specialists when client problems require use of techniques that go beyond their expertise. For example, a counselor who thinks a particular client needs to explore deeper unconscious processes through prolonged therapy would know enough to refer the client to an appropriate psychoanalyst or psychodynamic therapist. Similarly, if a counselor has a client who has agoraphobic reactions, she or he might refer the client to a cognitive therapist specializing in treating phobias.

Interviewing Skills

A significant part of counselor training is the development of effective interviewing skills—a basic component in the counseling process. Allen Ivey (1971) and his colleagues (Ivey & Ivey, 1999; Ivey & Authier, 1978) have been most active in describing the types and uses of interviewing skills that contribute to an effective counseling process.

Ivey took Rogers' listening and attending concepts that he emphasized in the counseling relationship and turned them into specific interviewing skills that could be taught to counselors (see chap. 5). During the ensuing years, Ivey expanded and refined these skills and added some new skills. He pointed out that although listening and attending skills were useful in establishing a relationship early in the counseling process, additional skills, which he called *social influencing skills,* were necessary to help move the counseling process along and to encourage clients to change behavior and take action during the latter stages of counseling (Ivey & Authier, 1978).

In later writings, Ivey and his colleagues (Ivey & Ivey, 1999; Ivey et al., 1997) have taken the lead in applying these skills to multicultural clients that include attention to their social-cultural, contextual world; specifically, the counselor should "examine factors such as his or her family, school, and neighborhood, and the impact of broader social issues such as unemployment, poor housing, racism, and ageism" (Ivey & Ivey, 1999, p. 17).

Listening and Attending Skills: Establishing a Relationship

Listening and attending skills, though important throughout the counseling session, are particularly necessary during the beginning stage because they are central to establishing a relationship (see Table 8.1). When counselors listen intently, clients get the feeling that what they are saying is important. They then feel encouraged to talk more about themselves—the first step in self-exploration. The counselor who is listening attentively is less likely to make premature judgments about the client or the client's problem or to give premature advice. Such interferences would spoil the counseling process.

Listening and attending skills serve two different but related functions: The counselor uses *listening skills* to gain information and encourage clients to talk about themselves and to help clients express how they perceive themselves and their problems (*open* and *closed questions* and *encouragers*). The counselor uses

TABLE 8.1
The Basic Listening Sequence

Skill	Description	Function in Interview
Open questions	"What": facts "How": process or feelings "Why": reasons "Could": general picture	Used to bring out major data and facilitate conversation.
Closed questions	Usually can begin with "do," "is," "are," and can be answered in a few words.	Used to quickly obtain specific data; close off lengthy answers.
Encouraging	Repeating back to client a few of the client's main words.	Encourages detailed elaboration of the specific words and their meanings.
Paraphrasing	Repeating back the essence of a client's words and thoughts using the client's own main words.	Acts as promoter for discussion; shows understanding; checks on clarity of counselor understanding.
Reflection of Feeling	Selective attention to emotional content of interview.	Results in clarification of emotion underlying key facts; promotes discussion of feelings.
Summarization	Repeating back of client's facts and feelings (and reasons) to client in an organized form.	Useful in beginning interview; periodically in session to clarify where the interview has come to date; and to close the session.

Source: From Allen E. Ivey, Mary Bradford Ivey, and Lynn Simek-Morgan, *Counseling and Psychotherapy: A Multicultural Perspective,* Copyright © 1997, by Allyn and Bacon. Reprinted by permission.

attending skills, in contrast, to understand and clarify clients' feelings and to convey the counselor's feelings of understanding to clients (*paraphrase, reflection of feeling,* and *summarization*). Counselors who attend closely to their clients use appropriate eye contact, body language, and tone of voice (Ivey & Ivey, 1999; Ivey et al., 1997; Young, 1992).

When using listening and attending skills with multicultural clients, counselors tend to shift focus from facilitating client self-expression or self-understanding to facilitating client understanding of self in situational context, or as Ivey puts it, one's "system." Multicultural counselors tend to listen for family and contextual issues that affect client expression of self (Ivey et al., 1997, p. 73). Attending skills, for example, require an awareness of what is appropriate within the client's culture. "With some clients, direct eye contact will be personally or culturally inappropriate, the use or body language will be different, vocal tone may vary" (Ivey & Ivey, 1999, p. 42).

Facilitative Skills: Social Influencing

Additional skills are necessary to help clients explore ways to change behavior once the relationship has developed. Ivey and Ivey's (1999) *social influencing skills* allow counselors to help clients more deeply explore their problems and take actions that will lead to change (see Table 8.2). These techniques help both inspire and empower clients to change undesirable attitudes and behaviors and alter their interactions in detrimental environments. Although these social influencing skills are meant to encourage the client to take action, counselors should not allow their own needs to interfere. In other words, they should not determine for the client what that action should be.

Confrontation is a facilitative tool used to increase client insights and motivations so as to change self-defeating behavior. The counselor may confront clients when they show persistent discrepancies between what they say and how they behave or when they give mixed or garbled messages about their feelings and actions. The intention of counselor confrontation is to invite clients to face themselves realistically so as to examine behaviors or attitudes that are blocking their growth and development (Egan, 1994; Young, 1992).

Egan (1994) prefers the term *challenge* to *confrontation* to avoid the idea of a client-counselor battle. Young (1992) cautions that confrontation, though a powerful tool to elicit change, must always be used judiciously and not out of counselor frustration or impatience. Ivey and Ivey (1999) describe effective confrontation as supporting clients while challenging discrepancies or mixed messages in their comments. All authors agree that if confrontations are done in a way that would damage self-esteem or humiliate or shame the client, the client's defenses will become even more impenetrable.

Counselors use *focusing skills* to direct discussions to areas they believe will improve clients' perspectives about themselves, about their problems, and about the influence of others in their environment. They usually focus first on their clients and their clients' problems. Later, counselors change the focus to other persons in the clients' lives, to the counselor-client relationship, or to cultural-environmental or contextual (situational or historical) conditions (Ivey & Ivey, 1999).

TABLE 8.2
Influencing Skills

Skill	Description	Function in Interview
Interpretation/ reframing	Provides an alternative frame of reference from which the client may view a situation. May be drawn from a theory or from one's own personal observations. *Interpretation may be viewed as the core influencing skill.*	Attempts to provide the client with a new way to view the situation. The interpretation provides the client with a clear-cut alternative perception of "reality." This perception may enable a change of view that in turn may result in changes in thoughts, constructs, or behaviors.
Directive	Tells the client what action to take. May be a simple suggestion stated in command form or may be a sophisticated technique from a specific theory.	Clearly indicates to clients what action counselors or therapists wish them to take. The prediction with a directive is that the client will do what is suggested.
Advice/information	Provides suggestions, instructional ideas, homework, advice on how to act, think, or behave.	Used sparingly, advice and related skills may provide client with new and useful information. Specific vocational information is an example of necessary use of this skill.
Self-disclosure	The interviewer shares personal experience from the past or may share present reactions to the client.	Emphasizes counselor "I" statements. This skill is closely allied to feedback and may build trust and openness, leading to a more mutual relationship with the client.
Feedback	Provides clients with specific data on how they are seen by the counselor or by others.	Provides concrete data that may help clients realize how others perceive behavior and thinking patterns, thus enabling an alternative self-perception.
Logical consequences	Explains to the client the logical outcome of thinking and behavior. "If, then."	Provides an alternative frame of reference for the client. This skill helps clients anticipate the consequences or results of their actions.
Influencing summary	Often used at or near the end of a session to summarize counselor comments; most often used in combination with the attending summarization.	Clarifies what has happened in the interview and summarizes what the therapist has said. This skill is designed to help generalization from the interview to daily life.

Source: From Allen E. Ivey, Mary Bradford Ivey, and Lynn Simek-Morgan, *Counseling and Psychotherapy: A Multicultural Perspective,* Copyright © 1997, by Allyn and Bacon. Reprinted by permission.

In some instances, counselors may find it helpful to refer briefly to their own beliefs and experiences, a technique called *self-disclosure*. Sharing something about themselves can deepen client-counselor relationships or facilitate client insight or action. Counselors might say, "I get angry at my husband at times," or "I, too, had troubles concentrating in college, but I settled down once I picked a major." Research shows that a moderate amount of counselor self-disclosure, rather than too much or too little, has a positive effect on the relationship. Counselors must be judicious in the timing, depth, and length of time spent in self-disclosure. The sharing must be directed toward helping the client's progress and not occur because the counselor is anxious about the client's feelings or because the counselor overidentifies with the client (Cormier & Cormier, 1991).

Ivey et al. (1997) emphasize that counselors using social influencing skills with multicultural clients tend to pay particular attention to the family and cultural context in which the client is experiencing a problem. Counselors are also more likely to encourage multicultural clients to participate, become involved in their community as a way of empowerment.

Use of Skills Depends on Theoretical Orientation

Counselors vary in how they use interviewing skills during counseling, depending on their theoretical orientations (Ivey et al., 1997, see Figure 8.1). All theorists use listening and attending skills, but there are differences in the use of questions: Rogerians tend not to use questions; at the other extreme, behaviorists and Gestaltists frequently ask questions. Behaviorists tend to ask closed questions; Gestaltists ask open questions.

Although all counselors tend to use listening and attending skills, they differ in their choice of social influencing skills. Behavioral and cognitive-behavioral counselors tend to use directives or explanations of logical consequences; psychodynamic and Gestalt counselors tend to use interpretation (see Figure 8.1).

Assessment Skills

In the 1930s, 1940s, and 1950s, when the major focus was on vocational and educational guidance and counseling, most counselors were trained to use standardized tests and inventories. During the 1960s and 1970s, largely because of the influence of Carl Rogers, the use of standardized tests declined dramatically. Most counselors used only those interviewing skills that helped clients assess and clarify their problems.

During the 1990s, the use of standardized tests increased steadily. Effective counselors need to maintain an awareness of the increasing numbers of assessment materials available on the market. To meet new and expanded roles and duties, professional counselors must develop or upgrade competency skills in the selection and use of standardized tests (see chap. 6, "Assessment: Tools and Processes").

Competent counselors learn to distinguish how and when to use assessment interviewing and tests in counseling and in diagnostic evaluations. During the counseling process, counselors may use assessment tools to help clients conceptualize

FIGURE 8.1
Examples of skills used by interviewers of differing theoretical orientations.

		Nondirective	Modern Rogerian encounter	Behavioral (Assertiveness training)	Psychodynamic	Gestalt	Rational-emotive therapy	Feminist therapy
ATTENDING SKILLS	**MICROSKILL LEAD**							
	Open question	○	○	◐	◐	●	◐	◐
	Closed question	○	○	●	●	◐	◐	◐
	Encourager	◐	◐	◐	◐	◐	◐	◐
	Paraphrase	●	●	◐	◐	○	◐	◐
	Reflection of feeling	●	●	◐	◐	○	◐	◐
	Reflection of meaning	◐	●	○	◐	○	◐	●
	Summarization	◐	◐	◐	○	○	◐	◐
INFLUENCING SKILLS	Feedback	○	●	◐	○	◐	●	◐
	Advice/information/ and others	○	○	◐	○	○	●	●
	Self-disclosure	○	●	○	○	○	○	◐
	Interpretation	○	○	○	●	●	●	◐
	Logical consequences	○	○	◐	○	○	●	◐
	Directive	○	○	●	○	●	●	◐
	Influ. summary	○	○	◐	○	○	◐	●
	CONFRONTATION (Combined Skill)	◐	◐	◐	◐	●	●	●
FOCUS	Client	●	●	●	●	●	●	◐
	Counselor, interviewer	○	◐	○	○	○	◐	◐
	Mutual/group/"We"	○	◐	○	○	○	○	◐
	Other people	○	○	◐	◐	◐	○	◐
	Topic or problem	○	○	◐	◐	○	◐	◐
	Cultural/ environmental context	○	○	◐	○	○	○	●
	ISSUE OF MEANING (Topics, key words likely to be attended to and reinforced)	Feelings	Relationship	Behavior problem solving	Unconscious motivation	Here and now behavior	Irrational Ideas/logic	Problem as a "women's issue"
	AMOUNT OF INTERVIEWER TALK-TIME	Low	Medium	High	Low	High	High	Medium

Legend

Frequent use of skill ●   Common use of skill ◐   May use skill occasionally ○

Source: Adapted from Allen E. Ivey, Mary Bradford Ivey, and Lynn Simek-Downing, *Counseling and Psychotherapy: Integrating Skills, Theory, and Practice,* Copyright © 1987, by Allyn and Bacon. Reprinted by permission.

their problems and to encourage deeper self-exploration. In diagnostic evaluations, counselors need to know how to assess individuals in three different circumstances: intake interviewing, crisis intervention, and psychological diagnosis for outside agencies (see chap. 6).

Sound Ethical Judgment

Effective counselors work with clients in an ethical and professional manner. Although counselors-in-training learn the codes of ethics of professional behavior, the codes give only guidelines. Counselors must rely on their own good judgment in knowing how to use those guidelines. As discussed in chapter 3, counselors must exercise professional and ethical behavior in the following ways: They must maintain confidential relationships, not impose their values on clients, avoid satisfying their own unmet needs in the counseling relationship, and above all, respect the integrity and welfare of the client.

Kitchener (1984) has developed a critical evaluation model to help counselors learn to improve their ethical judgments. This model is based on four underlying moral principles involved in counselor-client relationships: autonomy, beneficence, nonmaleficence, and justice or fairness. *Autonomy* means that clients have the right to self-determination, *beneficence* refers to counselors' intent to foster growth in clients, *nonmaleficence* means that counselors avoid taking actions that can harm clients, and *justice* refers to treating clients equally regardless of race, gender, age, or other social or economic differences (Corey, Corey, & Callanan, 1993; Cottone & Tarvydas, 1998).

Feminists and ethnic minorities caution that counselors should not strictly abide by ethical principles laid out in ethical codes. Rather, they say, counselors need to consider as well what is best for a particular client (Cottone & Tarvydas, 1998). Corey et al. (1993) say, "Simply stated, principle ethics ask 'Is this situation unethical?' whereas virtue ethics asks 'Am I doing what is best for my client?'" (p. 8).

Effective training programs use case studies and case conferences to acquaint students with ethical dilemmas and to give them practice in exercising good judgment. When faced with perplexing complex ethical dilemmas, effective counselors will consult with other professional colleagues to help them resolve these dilemmas (Stadler, 1990).

Counselors who function best in their professional practice are those who work at resolving their own unmet needs and who learn to cope with their own emotional traumas (Guy, 1987). Effective counselors also recognize that because counseling is a stressful profession, they are ethically responsible for recognizing their own stress symptoms and must take steps to deal with or prevent undue stress that could impair their ability to work with clients (Stadler, 1990).

Effective counselors must be aware of their own countertransference reactions that inevitably arise during counseling: "Working with clients who are in pain often opens up therapists to their own pain, and if these countertransference issues are not recognized, they can have ethical implications" (Corey et al., 1993, p. 48). Effective counselors are able to work through countertransference issues regarding their clients' struggles and not assume too much responsibility for clients' progress. When necessary, as was discussed earlier, they seek professional consultation or participate in self-growth activities. They also are willing to turn to professional help, if necessary, to resolve undue stress or countertransference issues in their personal or professional life that, if not dealt with, can impair their effectiveness with clients (Stadler, 1990).

✎ EFFECTIVE COUNSELORS-IN-PRACTICE: THE WHOLE COUNSELOR

Counselors-in-practice become effective in counseling when they are able to integrate personality characteristics, personal growth experiences, and professional competencies learned in training into a cohesive counseling approach consistent with their values and purposes in life. Put in another way, the effective counselor cannot be described through lists of favorable personal characteristics or through lists of professional competencies. On the one hand, counselors who have well-developed personalities but inadequate professional skills may be able to develop rapport with clients but may ineffectively or inappropriately use techniques. On the other hand, counselors who are highly knowledgeable of the various psychological theories but lack essential personal characteristics may be unable to relate to clients; they may rely on a set of techniques without regard for their suitability for a particular client. Nor is it simply a matter of a combination of personal characteristics and professional competencies.

Counselors are effective when they integrate personal attributes and professional competencies in an ethical manner that benefits the client. Because student counselors learn skills in separate courses and in isolation from the actual counseling experience, they need opportunities to integrate their personal and professional competencies. Extended supervised practicum and internships under well-qualified supervisors provide student counselors the first of such opportunities.

Effective counselors are not self-satisfied, intransigent, or ego-centered about who they are and what they know. They are open and flexible to new ideas and to learning new techniques based on sound judgment and moral principles that safeguard the client's welfare. They are cautious, however, about shifting their attitudes or changing their skills impulsively according to the current fads.

✎ SUMMARY

Effective counselors are well-integrated individuals committed to their own continued growth and development. They have personal qualities and professional competencies that enable them to develop trusting counseling relationships that foster mutual counselor-client interactions and encourage therapeutic developmental changes.

Personal qualities of effective counselors are warmth, congruency, and positive regard supplemented by self-awareness, open-mindedness, flexibility, objectivity, trustworthiness, and personal integrity.

Professional competencies acquired by effective counselors are knowledge and skills learned in training necessary to help them guide or encourage clients during the counseling process. These professional competencies include counseling theories and techniques, interviewing skills, and assessment skills.

Effective counselors are knowledgeable about the three major counseling theoretical orientations: humanistic, cognitive-behavioral, and psychodynamic. They are aware of the different helping strategies inherent in each of these orientations. They select strategies that fit their theoretical orientation and the needs of their clients.

The two major types of interviewing skills used by counselors are listening and attending skills and social influencing skills. Listening and attending skills are used to establish a trusting relationship to encourage clients to clarify problems and begin self-exploration. Social influencing skills are used to encourage clients to take action to change attitudes and behavior.

Competent counselors know that assessment skills are used in two fundamentally different ways: in counseling and in diagnostic evaluations. During counseling, assessment focuses on helping clients clarify their concerns and explore themselves more deeply. Diagnostic evaluations determine and classify behavior symptoms.

Effective counselors abide by ethical standards that ensure clients' integrity and welfare by maintaining confidentiality with clients, by refraining from imposing their values on clients, and by avoiding exploiting clients to satisfy their own unmet needs. To remain effective, mature counselors engage in self-growth activities and personal counseling intermittently, thus maintaining and enhancing their self-awareness.

⇥ PROJECTS AND ACTIVITIES

1. Select a counselor who you have reason to believe is effective with a variety of clients. Interview the counselor and ask what she or he believes are important characteristics in effective counselors.
2. Talk with the director of the university counseling center or community mental health counselors. Find out what evaluative roles counselors are expected to carry out.
3. Interview two or three counselors who call themselves eclectic. Ask them about their views on counseling and about the techniques they use most often.
4. Visit a school counseling program. Ask the staff how counselors treat emotional crises of students.
5. Role-play two beginning interviews: one in which the client is nontalkative, and the other in which the client, with the same presenting problem, is talkative. Note the differences in listening skills.

⇥ REFERENCES

American Counseling Association (ACA). (1995). *Ethical standards of the American Counseling Association.* Alexandria, VA: Author

Arredondo, P. (1998). Integrating multicultural counseling competencies and universal helping condition and culture-specific contexts. *Counseling Psychologist, 26,* 592–601.

Belkin, G. S. (1984). *Introduction to counseling.* Dubuque, IA: William C. Brown.

Carkhuff, R. (1969). *Helping and human relations* (Vols. 1 & 2). New York: Holt, Rinehart & Winston.

Carkhuff, R. (1971). *The development of human resources.* New York: Holt, Rinehart & Winston.

Corey, G. (1996). *Theory and practice of counseling and psychotherapy* (5th ed.). Pacific Grove, CA: Brooks/Cole.

Corey, G., Corey, M. S., & Callanan, P. (1993). *Issues and ethics in the helping professions.* Pacific Grove, CA: Brooks/Cole.

Cormier, W. H., & Cormier, L. S. (1991). *Interviewing strategies for helpers: Fundamental skills and cognitive behavioral intervention* (3rd ed.). Pacific Grove, CA: Brooks/Cole.

Cottone, R. R., & Tarvydas, S. (1998). *Ethical and professional issues in counseling.* Upper Saddle River, NJ: Merrill/Prentice Hall.

Egan, G. (1994). *The skilled helper: A systematic approach to effective helping* (5th ed.). Pacific Grove, CA: Brooks/Cole.

Gelso, C. J., & Carter, J. A. (1985). The relationship in counseling and psychotherapy: Components, consequences, and theoretical consequences. *Counseling Psychologist, 13,* 155–243.

Guy, J. D. (1987). *The personal life of the psychotherapist.* New York: John Wiley.

Ivey, A. E. (1971). *Microcounseling and psychotherapy: Innovations in interviewing training.* Springfield, IL: Charles C Thomas.

Ivey, A. E., & Authier, J. (1978). *Microcounseling innovations in interviewing, counseling, psychotherapy, and psychoeducation* (2nd ed.). Springfield, IL: Charles C Thomas.

Ivey, A. E., & Ivey, M. B. (1999). *Intentional interviewing and counseling: Facilitating client development in a multicultural society* (4th ed.). Pacific Grove, CA: Brooks/Cole.

Ivey, A. E., Ivey, M. B., & Simek-Downing, L. (1987). *Counseling and psychotherapy: Integrating skills, theory, and practice.* Boston: Allyn & Bacon.

Ivey, A. E., Ivey, M. B., & Simek-Morgan, L. (1997). *Counseling and psychotherapy: A multicultural perspective.* Boston: Allyn & Bacon.

Kitchener, K. S. (1984). Intuition, critical evaluation, and ethical principles: The foundation for ethical decisions in counseling psychology. *Counseling Psychologist, 12,* 43–55.

Kottler, J. A., & Brown, R. W. (1992). *Introduction to therapeutic counseling* (2nd ed.). Pacific Grove, CA: Brooks/Cole.

Lazarus, A. A., & Beutler, L. E. (1993). On technical eclecticism. *Journal of Counseling & Development, 71,* 381–385.

Lee, C. C. (Ed.). (1995). *Counseling for diversity.* Boston: Allyn & Bacon.

Locke, D. C. (1995). Counseling interventions with African American youth. In C. C. Lee (Ed.), *Counseling for diversity: A guide for school counselors and related professionals* (pp. 21–40). Boston: Allyn & Bacon.

Rogers, C. (1951). *Client-centered therapy: Its current practice, implications, and theory.* Boston: Houghton Mifflin.

Rogers, C. (1957). The necessary and sufficient conditions of therapeutic personality change. *Journal of Counseling Psychology, 21,* 95–103.

Stadler, H. A. (1990). Counselor impairment. In B. Herlihy & L. Golden (Eds.), *AACD ethical standards casebook* (4th ed., pp. 177–187). Alexandria, VA: American Counseling Association.

Sue, D. W. (1996). Ethical issues in multicultural counseling. In B. Herlihy & G. Corey (Eds.), *ACA ethical standards casebook* (5th ed., pp. 193-204). Alexandria, VA: American Counseling Association.

Sue, D. W., & Sue, D. (1990). *Counseling the culturally different.* New York: John Wiley.

Young, M. E. (1992). *Counseling methods and techniques: An eclectic approach.* New York: Macmillan.

9   Individual Counseling

Individual counseling is a process in which a professional counselor and a client develop an interactive relationship, one that fosters client self-awareness and empowers that person to resolve his or her particular situational problems effectively. Many complex variables influence the nature, intensity, and duration of the counseling process: the counselor's effectiveness, the counselor's particular theoretical point of view, the setting in which the counseling takes place, the client's characteristics, and the nature of the client's problem.

Personal and professional counselor characteristics essential for effective counseling are discussed in chapter 8. Effective counselors vary in their theoretical approaches; clients need to be aware of the counselor's particular approach to determine whether it is suitable to their needs. My own point of view, my theoretical framework described earlier in the book (see chap. 5), governs to a large extent how I describe the nature of the counseling process in this chapter, a model I have developed over the years in the various settings in which I have worked. It is based on working with normally functioning clients who volunteer to engage in counseling; moreover, it is based on those clients who experience situational conflicts or dilemmas resulting from transitional changes or losses in their lives.

In the next six chapters, this model is adapted to fit special needs of clients—families, groups, careers, substance abuse, multicultural issues, gender issues, and older adults. Likewise, in the last four chapters, this model is adapted to practical applications in different counseling work settings—schools, colleges, and communities.

⤞ THE COUNSELING SETTING

Clients either are in settings—school, college, or workplace—where they can seek counseling help, or they come to a certain counseling agency in the community because of special needs. As discussed in chapter 1, the counseling setting significantly influences the type of counseling offered in that setting. In assessing the particular counseling treatment for a client, counselors need to consider the policies of their particular agency or institution regarding type, length, and intensity of services. They also need to inform the client of the limitations of their services.

These decisions about length and type of treatment have been important considerations in all counseling settings. Many college counseling centers, because of tight budgets, have for some time limited the number of sessions. School counselors have also had to determine whether to work with individuals themselves or to refer them to community agencies for more intensive work. In the community, health maintenance organizations and other managed care services advocate and mandate brief counseling and therapy (see chaps. 1 and 5).

⋙ CLIENT CHARACTERISTICS

Research about client characteristics that contribute to effective counseling outcome has proved inconclusive. This finding is not surprising because the criteria that typically have been used to describe effective clients are those that generally apply to optimally functioning individuals: willingness to admit problems, verbal fluency, ability to cope, and flexibility (Brammer, Abrego, & Shostrom, 1993; Brown & Srebalus, 1987; Heilbrun, 1982; Rogers, 1942). Researchers have overlooked the fact that clients who seek help, rather than being optimally coping individuals, instead tend to be anxious, doubtful, uncertain, or defensive, especially in an initial therapeutic encounter.

Clients differ considerably in their attitudes about starting counseling with a counselor. Many clients these days have had previous counseling: Older clients and those who have attended college may have had a series of counseling experiences and have been exposed to a variety of counseling approaches; some may have had counseling for specific needs, such as career counseling or weight-loss counseling; some may be therapy-wise, cynical, and wary; some may have formed certain opinions about therapy and about themselves from reading self-help books or taking self-administered personality surveys; those who have never had counseling may have heard varying reports from friends. No matter the individual case, however, clients generally will approach any initial counseling session with apprehension.

In addition to being nervous about the initial meeting, client apprehensions are compounded by anxieties that compelled the clients to seek counseling in the first place, symptoms that typically surface when individuals are going through transitions or changes in their lives—times in which they feel particularly vulnerable. One significant characteristic can generally be assumed for all clients, at least those who voluntarily seek counseling: They recognize that they have difficulties and have the insight, strength, and motivation to seek help.

While developing relationships with clients and planning effective counseling sessions, counselors should consider basic client personality characteristics that might influence the counseling process: values, view of human nature, worldview. Are they shy or outgoing, articulate or glib or inarticulate? Do they have positive or negative views about human nature, about themselves, and about the world in general?

Other client characteristics that might influence counseling are the extent to which clients believe they have basic or ultimate control of their lives, whether they tend to blame others for their problems, or whether they tend to blame themselves. Attitudes such as these are apt to influence the degree to which clients can bring about changes within themselves or in their environment necessary for growth. Still other client characteristics—the degree of insight they have about their problems, their stated goals, the strength of their defenses—give clues to the degree to which they are able to confront and explore their problems.

These factors are all apt to influence how clients will respond to counseling—how they will interact with counselors, what they expect to happen in the counseling sessions, and how well motivated or capable they are of making changes within themselves for growth. In turn, these characteristics will help counselors decide what goals are realistic for clients and what type of strategies will best help the clients attain those goals.

✎ THE COUNSELING PROCESS

In the counseling process, counselor and client develop a trusting, dynamic, interactive relationship that helps empower the client to resolve his or her problem. Counselors and therapists generally agree that a successful counseling outcome occurs when an effective relationship between counselor and client is established (Gelso & Carter, 1985). Moreover, most counselors recognize that an essential role of the counselor is to enable clients to self-explore and develop self-awareness as a way for them to resolve their problems.

The counseling process evolves through several stages, from the first interview through termination. This process is similar regardless of counselor orientation (Brammer et al., 1993; Egan, 1994; Sexton & Whiston, 1994).

This process can generally be divided into three major stages: In the initial stage, counselor and client develop a relationship that will foster client self-exploration, and they clarify the nature of the problem and set goals and treatment plans. In the middle stage, the counselor helps the client explore inwardly more deeply to increase insight and understanding of the problem. In the last stage, counselor and client work together in helping the client take action to change behavior or attitudes in everyday living; they then proceed toward terminating counseling sessions.

Tracey (1984) points out that the dynamics of the counselor-client relationship changes during each of the three stages: In the initial stage, counselors relate to clients on client terms, developing rapport, listening, and attending to their needs; in the middle stage, they challenge clients to explore deeper emotions; in the last stage, counselors relate to clients collaboratively as peers.

Initial Stage: Developing a Relationship and Clarifying Client Presenting Problem

In the early sessions, counselor and client begin to develop a mutual relationship necessary to carry them along on a journey together to resolve the client's problem.

Counselors, right from the start, through their overall manner, must convey to each client that they are accepting and understanding. They must also assure the client that they will maintain confidentiality throughout the counseling sessions. Further, counselors must create an ambience that assures the client that his or her welfare is their primary concern during this time: No telephone calls or interruptions are allowed during sessions, counselors are on time for appointments, and counselors' offices are inviting, comfortable but not fancy, and soundproof.

First Interview: Setting the Tone and Defining Parameters

In the crucial first interview, counselors lay the foundation and set a climate for an effective working relationship. In doing so, they have a somewhat paradoxical task. They must immediately convey an aura of understanding and warmth with the client, one that assures trust. At the same time, they must clarify the parameters of counseling with the client, as well as gather information about the client so as to make an initial assessment of the problem.

Clients arrive at the first interview feeling uncertain and ambivalent about talking intimately to a counselor. Clients may wonder whether they have sufficient strength to undertake the often painful experience of self-exploration. Along with their fears, they come with certain expectations about the counselor and counseling (Moursund, 1993). They hope the counselor will not make negative judgments about them, they wonder whether the counselor will hold what they say in confidence, they sense the potential power of the counselor and the possibility of abuse of that power, and they hope the counselor will have the personal characteristics and expertise to help them.

The first interview can be awkward, particularly when a client is shy or reserved. Making social chit-chat in the first interview to set a client at ease is not recommended. This delay in getting to the reason for counseling can increase anxiety (Tyler, 1969). Usually, a simple statement will suffice, such as, "Tell me what brings you here for counseling." If the counselor has already talked on the telephone with the client when setting up the appointment, it would be helpful to review that conversation: "Last week, you called and said you had split up with your wife," or, "The other day when you phoned, you said you were feeling depressed." If the person has been referred, it is usually helpful to go over how the referral occurred and what the client's expectations are.

During the first interview, the counselor generally relies on what is known as *open questions* (to bring out general information) and *closed questions* (to obtain more specific information). In the following interchange, for example, the counselor obtains information from the client while also responding to the client's feelings:

Counselor:	Have you ever had counseling before? (closed question)
Client:	Yes, I saw a counselor about a year ago.
Counselor:	What do you think you gained from that experience? (open question)
Client:	Nothing much. I was disappointed. My counselor didn't hear what I was saying.
Counselor:	You didn't get what you had hoped for, an understanding counselor. (reflection of feeling)

Besides setting a climate of acceptance and warmth and determining appropriateness of service, counselors explain to clients what they can expect in counseling; they also describe their qualifications and the policies of the agency they work for. They may ask clients what they are hoping for. Confidentiality, rights of privacy, and other ethical and legal considerations also need to be clarified (see chap. 3).

The counselor must make time at the end of the first session to discuss whether the client's concerns are within the counselor's expertise or whether the client believes that the counselor can best serve his or her needs. For example, if the client's main concern is alcohol addiction and the counselor does not work with this problem, then it is necessary to refer the client to someone who does. If the client needs more intensive help than the counselor or agency is prepared to provide or if the agency in which the counselor works limits intensive therapy, then the counselor can suggest an appropriate referral.

Clients at this time may also decide that the counselor's theoretical orientation or approach is not what they were expecting. If so, the counselor can suggest someone more in line with the clients' preferences.

In states where counselors are licensed for private practice, it is mandatory that counselors disclose their educational background, theoretical orientation, and types of techniques they may use. This procedure, even when not mandated, is a sound idea because counselor and client then have a better idea about their potential compatibility.

The counselor also needs to discuss length of sessions, fees, and payment of fees and to arrange regular meeting times. Those counselors in private practice who are eligible for third-party insurance payments also need to explain the expected diagnosis required by the insurance company.

Developing a Mutual Relationship

An effective counseling relationship occurs when trust develops between a counselor and a client and is maintained throughout the counseling process. Trust develops when clients believe that their counselor accepts them as worthy persons with dignity and value regardless of what they disclose to the counselor about themselves. Bordin (1975) calls the counselor-client relationship a *working alliance*. He divides the working alliance into three parts: (a) an establishment of an emotional bond, (b) mutual agreement about goals, and (c) mutual agreement about tasks.

While client and counselor are getting to know each other and are beginning to establish mutual trust in the early stage of counseling, the counselor listens to the client's concerns and encourages him or her to express those feelings and thoughts that are bothersome; moreover, the counselor fully accepts what the client has to say. This client-centered approach encourages clients to talk more freely and also gives counselors important information to use later when they explore problems more deeply (Young, 1992).

A counselor's accepting, nonjudgmental attitude helps clients reveal more about the hurt, pain, or anxiety they are experiencing. In a warm, accepting atmosphere, the counselor demonstrates understanding and genuineness and attention to client feelings even as he or she focuses on cognitive processes regarding what is happening or how clients perceive what is happening in their lives.

The counselor might respond to a client's concerns with a reflection of feeling intended to encourage the client to express more feelings:

Client (a 30-year-old divorcee):   My whole life collapsed when my husband left me and the children without warning. I'm not sleeping well. I don't have job skills to take care of myself, and my two children.

Counselor: You are feeling overwhelmed by it all.

Client: Yes, I do, and I see no way out unless I get some training.

Counselors may also rephrase a statement by the client to show they are listening and to help the client focus on the concern:

Client: I know it doesn't help my grades when I procrastinate and start projects the night before they are due, but I keep doing it.

Counselor: You know your grades won't improve if you wait until the last minute to begin your project, but up to now you feel unable to change that behavior.

Client: Yes, that's why I decided I need help. I see the problem but not the solution.

To help a client elaborate the problem, the counselor might ask for clarification:

Client: Sometimes I get a peculiar feeling about myself and my life.

Counselor: Can you tell me more about what you mean by peculiar feeling?

Client: Yes, I sometimes feel as though nothing in my life is real, as though I'm in a dream.

Toward an Understanding of the Client's Problem

Counselors consider several factors about a client and his or her situational concerns: the severity and complexity of the problem, length and persistence of symptoms, and past stability of the client. They also consider the context in which the client is experiencing the problem: social and cultural factors, degree of environmental support, and family relationships. These and other client characteristics described earlier help determine the way counseling will proceed.

Client Problem in Context.   The context in which clients' problems develop and persist in their current lives and circumstances is important in determining the types of counseling strategies that will be most effective. Counselors need to consider how functional or dysfunctional clients' families of origin are, the nature of clients' current familial interpersonal and personal relationships, how well clients function in their careers or schoolwork, and the types of environmental support available to them. Counselors must also assess how clients' changes in attitudes and behavior will be received by persons close to them. In other words, what will be the consequences of their change?

Counselors must also consider the client's cultural background, particularly those from ethnic groups—Hispanic, Asian, African American, Native American, as well as the numerous cultural subgroups. Asians, for instance, are made up of distinctly different ethnic groups—Chinese, Japanese, Thai, Korean, Vietnamese, and so on. Moreover, for recent immigrants, one's ethnic identity also depends on whether one is first, second, or third generation. Where one lives also influences one's cultural identity: Growing up in California is considerably different from growing up in New York City or Alabama. And for Native Americans, growing up on a reservation, a semi-sovereign tribal nation, is a significantly different experience from that of all the other cultural groups. Yet again, growing up on, say, the Sioux Reservation is culturally different from growing up on the Swinomish Reservation (see chap. 14).

Forming a Working Hypothesis and Making a Tentative Diagnosis

An important step begins in the first interview and continues during the initial stage of counseling: forming a hypothesis of the client's problem. Using information gained by observation and interviewing of the client, the counselor assesses the nature and complexity of the problem to make a tentative hypothesis or diagnosis of the problem.

For those clients covered by mental health insurance, counselors and therapists must make diagnoses as quickly as possible because diagnoses are required to qualify for services. In many college counseling centers and community agencies, determining whether clients qualify for services is first made in intake interviews.

Counselors determine whether clients require a considerable number of sessions or only a few. If a client's symptoms are mild and of short duration, motivation is high, environmental disruption is at a minimum, and the problem is specific and can be resolved in a reasonable amount of time, the counselor can assume that short-term counseling is sufficient. If a client has long-term symptoms, complicated or vague problems, strong defenses, confused values, or complex, immobilizing social-cultural conditions, the counselor can assume that deeper, more intensive work is needed before client-desired change will occur.

To help in these decisions, many counselors use assessment devices, such as tests, inventories, behavioral surveys, or schedules.

Use of Tests, Inventories, or Behavioral Assessments.   During the first stages of exploration, a self-inventory may be helpful for clients who have difficulty expressing their needs or talking about their feelings. Nonthreatening personality inventories that measure normal personality characteristics may be used (see chap. 6).

Cognitive-behaviorists tend to use behavioral observations and self-monitoring scales, rather than standardized or nonstandardized tests or inventories, to help them assess clients' problems. Many counselors prefer to make a tentative assessment of a client's difficulty over several sessions in the early phase of counseling. Client-centered counselors do little, if any, diagnosis, considering it unnecessary and a block to the effective relationship (Rogers, 1951).

Many counselors do not label clients diagnostically, but rather prefer to view diagnosis as a continuous, ongoing process that focuses on understanding clients and on helping them understand themselves. In this approach, the counselor develops a working hypothesis to help him or her set goals with the client and establish a productive, flexible plan of helping (Brammer et al., 1993; Corey, 1996; Tyler, 1969).

Personal construct therapists and counselors (Fransella & Dalton, 1990; Kelly, 1963) likewise object to labeling client behavior, claiming that such conceptualizations are indications only of the counselor's own theoretical constructs and say little about the client. Personal construct counselors and therapists aim at understanding how clients perceive themselves so as to plan a way to make the necessary changes the clients think are necessary.

> The counsellor must find avenues in the client's construing of the world along which he and the client may move towards a solution of the client's problem. This all leads to our construing any diagnosis as *the planning stage for client reconstruction.* Kelly calls this "transitive diagnosis." (Fransella & Dalton, 1990, pp. 31–32)

The term *diagnosis,* Kelly warns, is not meant in the usual sense of categorizing with a set prescribed treatment for everyone who is similarly diagnosed. Thus, he uses the term *transitive diagnosis* for a special reason. As cited in Fransella and Dalton (1990), Kelly (1955) says:

> The term suggests that we are concerned with transitions in the client's life, that we are looking for bridges between the client's present and his future. Moreover, we expect to take an active part in helping the client select or build the bridges to be used and in helping him cross them safely. (p. 32)

In determining "transitive diagnoses," counselors help clients search for and determine their own personal constructs—that is, self-assessments of the way they see themselves and others. Because Kelly believes he wanted a precise description of how clients view themselves, he and other personal construct practitioners who followed him have created an elaborate system for helping clients explore their world. They use numerous techniques, such as repertory grids, laddering, and pyramiding, in which clients in various ways explore and discover their system of personal constructs. Thus, for personal construct counselors and therapists, exploring the client's world in the initial stages can be very time-consuming. The grids and other techniques are optional, however. Counselor can select among them or not use them at all, depending on the client and on circumstances (Fransella & Dalton, 1990).

Use of the* DSM-IV *for Diagnosis. The *Diagnostic and Statistical Manual of Mental Disorders* (*DSM-IV;* American Psychiatric Association, 1994) has become a prominent instrument used by counselors and therapists for those clients covered by health insurance. Community counselors and therapists must use diagnostic categories in the *DSM-IV* to justify that a client is eligible to receive insurance benefits (Corey, Corey, & Callanan, 1993). They may also use this instrument to help in assessing the nature and severity of the emotional disorder to determine appropriate treatment or referral (see chap. 6).

Setting Goals and Designing a Plan of Action

Once client presenting problems have been discussed and conceptualized, counselor and client work together to set goals and to develop a plan of action. Goals need to be as clear and specific as possible, considering the complexity of the problem. They must be realistic, consistent with client resources and capabilities, stated in a way that permits continual evaluation of progress toward goals, and possible to accomplish in a realistic amount of time (Egan, 1994). Consideration must be given to whether any external circumstances are hindering the stated goal of a client. For example, a client who desires a particular type of training that is only available 3,000 miles away but who cannot leave his family will have to come to terms with his conflicting goals.

Contracts. Some counselors, particularly behaviorists and cognitive-behaviorists, find it productive to develop contracts with clients. These contracts may be written agreements or may be verbally agreed on. Goodyear and Bradley (1980) say that all relationships, written or oral or simply implied, are in some way contractual.

In such cases, a contract that includes statement of goals, techniques to be followed, and length of time to accomplish goals can serve as a useful working model for both counselor and client. Goals and treatment plans, however, must be flexible enough to be modified if deeper exploration of client problems or circumstances warrant a change.

Middle Stage: Exploring More Deeply

In the middle stage of counseling, a shift occurs in the counseling process. Once counselor and client have discussed preliminaries, reached an initial understanding of each other and of the client's problem, and agreed on their purpose for working together, they then move into deeper explorations.

For brief, solution-focused, or time-limited counseling, the middle stage is fairly short. Also, for those clients who are seeking counseling to solve a particular problem, who have a fairly well developed sense of themselves, and who don't need to go through the complicated process of self-exploration at this time or for this particular purpose, counseling with a brief middle stage is all that is necessary. Counselors and clients can then proceed to the last stage, where they focus on turning new client attitudes and insights into effective behavioral changes in everyday life.

For counseling needs that take more time, the process in the middle stage becomes complicated and unpredictable and thus is difficult to describe. As Moursund (1993) points out, in contrast with the fairly predictable first and last stages, the middle stage can go in any number of directions, and moreover, the counselor needs to allow clients to explore the numerous avenues at their own volition and pace. At the same time, the counselor must also lead clients back on track if they wander too far afield. This seeming contradiction is inherent in the counseling role:

> The apparent contradiction is resolved when we realize that our clients operate at many levels and can move in many directions at once. For both client and therapist, one of the signals of middle-phase work may be a sense of confusion, of muddledness, of not really knowing what is going on. The therapist needs to be able to step back from the muddle far enough to sense the overall direction in which the work is proceeding and to invite the client to explore material which will further that overall direction. (Moursund, 1993, p. 68)

Noting Movement and Gaining Emotional Insights

A major characteristic in the counseling process is the sense of movement, accelerating especially in the middle stage of the counseling process (Miller & Stiver, 1997; Rogers, 1942, 1951). Rogers was one of the first to note this (1942), describing in particular the client's gaining of new insights and feelings of increasing emotional intensity and turbulence. Expanding on this sense of movement in the therapeutic process in his 1951 text, Rogers alerted the counselor to watch for the various aspects of movement, or changes that occur in the client during the counseling process. Counselors should watch for client changes in perception and changes of feelings; increasing feelings of self-worth and independence; less denial of experience; and changes in values. He also noted the changing emotional relationship between client and counselor.

Since then, counselors and therapists have confirmed, over the years, this movement or evolving process the counselor and client experience in counseling, particularly the shift from client concerns about external problems to client exploration of inner feelings and emotions:

> The shift from early- to-middle-phase work, then, is marked by a shift from primarily cognitive concerns to an emphasis on emotional work, from focusing on external to focusing on internal events, from looking at relationships outside of therapy to experiencing relationships within the therapy session itself. (Moursund, 1993, p. 69)

In this move from cognitions to emotions, clients begin to take more risks disclosing their feelings and actions toward themselves and others, and the process shifts to the client-counselor relationship: "Emotional issues begin to take precedence over cognitive ones, and the therapeutic relationship itself is often the arena in which these issues are worked through" (Moursund, 1993, p. 69). Therapists and counselors are recognizing that, in the evolving client-counselor relationship during the counseling process, the counselor experiences feelings and new insights as well. These are discussed further in the section "Transference and Countertransference."

Miller and Stiver (1997), representing the women at the Stone Center at Wellesley College, who emphasize developing and maintaining mutual connections in relationships, also note movement as a primary indicator in the therapeutic process. They believe that commencement of movement begins with the awareness of a mutual empathic relationship between patient or client and therapist or counselor. This bonding elicits motion itself. It commences precisely when the patient[1] notices that the feelings he is sharing has an impact on the therapist. The therapist, feeling moved by the patient's experience, responds. Because the patient's dysfunction is based on denial of feelings by others, therapist responsiveness, Miller and Stiver explain, is a new experience for a client and precisely what moves them both. With the focus on developing mutual empathic connections, the counseling process commences.

---

[1]Miller and Stiver (1997) prefer to use the term *patient* because *client* implies someone in a business transaction. They do not like using the term *patient,* but they say, "it's the best of bad choices" (p. 217). Its original meaning is "one who suffers," stemming from the Latin "to endure."

Participating together . . . is very different from struggling alone without a sense of impact or response, or, alternatively, feeling that you have to hold back parts of yourself because you don't know 'where the other person is' psychologically. This is what we mean by building increasing mutual empathy and mutual empowerment in therapy. (Miller & Stiver, 1997, p. 133)

Personal construct theorists also recognize motion or movement similar to taking a journey: After the client ascertains his or her current constructs and those parts that are dissatisfactory, client and counselor embark on the path of reconstruing the client's personal constructs in ways that are compatible with the client's circumstances (Fransella & Dalton, 1990).

Personal construct counselors note that an increase of emotional reactions is inevitable for the client during the therapeutic transitional phases, phases they call the *cycles of change.* They watch for increased client feelings of anxiety, threat, guilt, hostility, and aggression. The client's emerging feelings are signs that he or she is experiencing changes, and the feelings occur in increasing and decreasing cycles of intensity during the cycles of change (Fransella & Dalton, 1990).

During the cycles of change, clients alternate between loosening and tightening their constructs. They loosen constructs when they lower cognitive awareness, give into experience, and participate without judgment or without holding back. They use relaxation techniques or engage in free association or dream work. The counselor uncritically accepts client trial behaviors. In tightening constructs, clients raise cognitive processes to a high level by keeping logs of their new experiences, summarizing what happens, evaluating and comparing them to other experiences, and putting them into historical context. Counselors may challenge what the clients mean, being careful not to impose their own differing point of view or their own constructs on them (Fransella & Dalton, 1990).

The counselor's primary role is to help guide clients between alternating loosening and tightening constructs because of the hazards inherent in going too far either way. On the one hand, becoming too loose brings on strong anxieties as clients try unfamiliar ways and experiences chaotic reactions. With premature tightening of constructs, on the other hand, clients are apt to conclude that their experience was bad, and they will revert back to the safety of former familiar old constructs.

Transference and Countertransference.   As clients increase their self-disclosure and self-awareness, counselors and clients begin to develop emotional interactions that need to be acknowledged and worked through for counseling to proceed. These interactions are called *transference* and *countertransference.* These emotional interchanges are described in chapter 5 as cornerstones of psychoanalysis. To recapitulate briefly, *transference* refers to clients transferring on the therapist emotions developed toward significant others during their lives. *Countertransference* describes therapists projecting their own emotional reactions on clients. Although these concepts are well known as essential elements in psychoanalysis, many counseling professionals believe that they are universal in all relationships (Brammer et al., 1993; Gelso & Carter, 1985; Young, 1992).

Because these concepts and dynamics were considered the province of deeper levels of psychoanalysis, most counselors, in their focus on a client's short-term situational problems, historically did not deal with these issues. Recently, both counselors and therapists have been attending to problematic transference and countertransference issues, as well as to client resistances (discussed later), that emerge during this stage.

Transference.   *Transference* refers to clients transferring on the therapist emotions developed from early age toward significant others in their lives. When clients trust the counselor and are encouraged to become aware of emotions, they begin to express transference feelings: anger, dependency, admiration, love, or hate toward counselors. "To varying degrees, transference occurs in probably all relationships. The therapeutic situation, however, with its emphasis on a kind of controlled help-giving, magnifies and intensifies this natural reaction" (Gelso & Carter, 1985, p. 169).

Rogers (1951) discouraged counselors from fostering transference reactions from clients because he feared it would encourage client dependency on the counselor. He thus urged counselors to depersonalize themselves and to avoid making interpretations and giving advice. But his theory has been criticized. Rollo May, for example, points out that this approach is not only unnatural but also controlling (May & Yalom, 1995).

Regarding transference, Corsini (1995), a student of Rogers, says that counseling has come a long way since Rogers' time. Attention has been given to the value of transference issues for counselors, for example, by Watkins in 1983. Clients with transference issues, he explains, are predisposed to react to others in a set way. "Consequently, the counselee enters a relationship—be it of an impersonal, friendly, or therapeutic nature—with a fixed bent in perceptions and feelings" (Watkins, as cited in Dryden, 1998, p. 75). Clients with transference issues thus tend to distort reality. Moreover, a client's set of reactions acts as a defensive mechanism and thus prevents the client from self-development. For these reasons, Watkins explained, it is important that counselors address transference issues.

Counselors now generally recognize the value of transference as a natural process. In a therapeutic situation, clients who have been projecting feelings and attitudes onto parents and other authority figures start transferring feelings onto the counselor; with therapeutic help, they become aware of similar transference feelings toward other significant persons in their lives.

Counselors and therapists help clients express strong feelings without reacting negatively or making judgments—in contrast with how parents might respond. This accepting attitude reduces client defensiveness and reduces anxiety about expressing forbidden feelings.

Brammer et al. (1993) offer suggestions on working through feelings of transference. The counselor might ask a *clarifying question,* such as, "You seem to be angry with me today. Why is that?" A counselor could also *reflect* a client's feelings if the client denies them: "You think these feelings might upset me?" Or the counselor may *interpret* the transference, demonstrate that the client's earlier interpersonal interactions relate to current behavior while reassuring the client that these feelings are normal: "Perhaps you become anxious when you show anger at people. Perhaps you are afraid that you are showing too much anger toward me."

Two recent alternative approaches to the concept of transference are the *psycho-dynamic therapies* of Miller and Stiver (1997) and others who represent the women at the Stone Center, and the *personal construct therapies* (Fransella & Dalton, 1990). Miller and Stiver, because their therapeutic philosophy is based on developing a relationship in which therapist and client engage in a mutual connection (see chap. 5), believe that transference experiences are natural and should not be avoided:

> We believe that if the therapist is able to create a new relational context that is empathic and empowering, she will provide a more fertile ground for the essentials of transference to emerge. . . . We see transference as an avenue to learning some of the essentials of past relationships and to seeing how they impact the current therapy relationship. (p. 139)

Moreover, Stiver (1997) emphasizes that "focused attention to transference phenomena provides the central work of the therapy" (p. 38).

Miller and Stiver (1997) point out two objections to traditional approaches to transference. First, they object to the therapist/counselor adopting a neutral role, a role that runs counter to their theory of mutual connections in relationships. They also object to the therapist/counselor making interpretations of client responses:

> We are not at all persuaded that the therapist offering interpretations about the transference to the patient is necessarily as effective as we were taught it would be. These formulations can often be experienced as highly intellectualized, or as criticisms, and often they are not very meaningful to the patient. (p. 140)

Personal construct counselors also view transference as a useful part of the process if transference is seen as the client casting the counselor in various roles during the changing cyclical process. If, however, the client literally sees the counselor as an object the client has become dependent on, attached to, the counselor needs to reevaluate the relationship and be alert to such a possibility before it happens. The counselor needs to guide the client into projecting onto imaginary figures who symbolize persons in his or her life or to enact roles.

Countertransference. It is equally important for counselors to recognize their own irrational feelings they have projected on clients. When counselors feel uncomfortable or experience irritation or resentment toward clients or when they foster dependence in their clients or become too emotionally involved, they must ask themselves why these feelings exist. If these feelings persist, counselors should consult with another professional. If feelings of countertransference persist with more than one client, the counselor may need counseling or therapy.

Attention has been given to how counselors can use their irrational feelings toward clients to enrich the counseling relationship. In his article "In Praise of Countertransference: Harvesting Our Errors," Taffel (1993) notes that when counselors become aware of and accept their seemingly irrational or inappropriate feelings about clients, they can perceive their projected feelings as "enlightening mistakes and fruitful errors and can make them part of a richer and more realistic vision of the therapeutic experience" (p. 57).

Countertransference issues are a primary consideration for Miller and Stiver (1997) and the women at the Stone Center. They view the therapists' emotional reactions that surface with clients as positive signs, signals for them to come to terms with their own unresolved emotional issues. "Especially when a particular therapy relationship is difficult or confusing the therapist needs to make certain she has a growthful relational context of herself" (Surrey, 1997, p. 45). They also urge the therapist who experiences countertransference reactions to share them with other professionals, "not as signs of failure but often as necessary arenas for growth and relationship movement" (Surrey, 1997, p. 45).

Personal construct counselors believe that countertransference is a more important issue than transference. "It is even more vital to be aware of any counter dependency transference, with the counsellor projecting his or her own needs on to the client" (Fransella & Dalton, 1990, p. 98).

The Difficult Phase: Coping with Impasse

During the middle stage, clients begin to make significant positive changes in their attitudes and outlook and to gain new insights into their problems. They have bonded well with their counselor and developed trust. The counselor or therapist feels good about progress. Then, suddenly, right after positive improvements have occurred, clients react, there's a breakdown. Clients revert back to old ways. An impasse develops in the client-counselor relationship that is very frustrating to the counselor (Miller & Stiver, 1997).

Some therapists and counselors have recently been dwelling on this period at length because they acknowledge that it is the most difficult stage; moreover, they have been reconsidering the traditional assessment of client impasses and resistances.

Resistance.   Impasses as a sign of client defenses have long been known in psychoanalysis and have been considered typical of the therapeutic process. Over the years, therapists have developed strategies to work with client defenses and resistances. Historically, they have perceived client resistance as a negative factor impeding progress in counseling. More recently, resistance has been recognized as an expected part of therapy that can be used to produce more effective counseling (Brammer et al., 1993; Cormier & Cormier, 1991).

Assuming the client voluntarily comes to counseling, counselors can recognize that the client's resistance may be signaling that important sensitive feelings are being tapped, feelings that may be defenses against anxiety or pain. Similarly, when a physician pokes a sensitive spot in the anatomy, the patient winces, withdraws, or cries out in pain. Clients naturally will be ambivalent about change, uncomfortable about the need to disclose painful or shameful things about themselves, and afraid to face what the therapist is trying to help them explore.

Client resistance ranges from open hostility or antagonism to more subtle, passively resistant behavior, such as being late for an appointment, skipping appointments, misinterpreting what the counselor says, or agreeing with everything the counselor suggests. These manifestations may be perplexing to new counselors, particularly when the client initiates counseling and is paying a fee for the sessions. Such behaviors make sense when counselors recognize that these behaviors are means of preventing disturbing feelings from coming into awareness.

Counselor strategies with client resistance. Many counselors use what is known as *social influencing skills* suitable for this stage, such as *interpretation, confrontation,* and *self-disclosure,* to help clients in their self-exploration (Ivey & Ivey, 1999; see also chap. 8). Through this approach, they attempt to increase the depth of clients' understanding or to encourage clients to comment on the causes of their behavior, the amount of control they have over their circumstances, or the meaning behind their remarks (Cormier & Cormier, 1991).

Counselors may offer *interpretations* regarding clients' defensive attitudes and behaviors that keep the clients from becoming aware of painful experiences (Brammer et al., 1993). Interpretations should be done only after clients have become at least aware of the particular emotions they are experiencing and the context in which the feelings arose. Brammer et al (1993) suggest that it is wise to focus on attitudes or behaviors that are subject to a client's control, rather than to point out difficulties the client is experiencing that he or she cannot change. They also recommend tentative positive interpretations, rather than a dogmatic, negative approach.

Counselors may also use *self-disclosure* to encourage clients to explore feelings. Self-disclosure must be appropriate to a client's goals, must not burden the client, must not be done too frequently, and must be adapted to the particular client's feelings or circumstances (Egan, 1994).

> *Client:* I'm in a new job, have a new exciting relationship, am moving to a bigger and better apartment. Things are going great, but I feel sick to my stomach.
>
> *Counselor:* So many major transitions going on in your life all at once can be unsettling and stressful even when positive. I recall having butterflies in my stomach when I started my first job in counseling in a new city right after I married.

Other examples of social influencing skills to facilitate client insight are *encouragement,* in which the counselor praises clients' efforts in disclosing more about themselves, and giving *directives* or *information* or *advice* when one client's apparent lack of movement seems to relate to his or her lack of appropriate information or experience.

Alternative approaches to resistance. Both psychodynamic feminist therapists Miller and Stiver (1997) and the cognitive-oriented personal construct therapists and counselors such as Fransella and Dalton (1990) object to traditional therapeutic approaches to resistance, in which the therapist or counselor blames the client for not cooperating. They also object to the various strategies that are then employed to break down client resistances, from outright confrontation to subtle and not-so-subtle manipulative strategies.

Miller and Stiver (1997) have been dwelling on the midstage period at length. They note that after successful emotional bonding and connecting between patient and counselor and after the patient shows definite signs of improvement, he or she will suddenly disconnect. "The movement into more connection itself leads to the most difficult parts of therapy because it threatens the person's strategies for disconnection" (p. 149).

Miller and Stiver (1997) are emphatic about the necessity of therapists being aware of patients' need to hold on to their defenses. The aim of a therapist in a therapy session is to be aware of the patient's strategies of disconnection. They emphasize the importance of "respecting these strategies of disconnection rather than viewing them as what therapists typically call defenses—something the therapist hopes to get rid of as quickly as possible" (p. 149). It is so crucial that the therapist remain empathic with patients when they shift away and disconnect that Miller and Stiver call their therapy the *therapy of honoring the client's disconnecting strategies.*

> Indeed, one way to describe therapy is to say that it is a special place designed for working on disconnections (that's why it can be so hard)—and for learning to move on through the pain of disconnection to new connections, that's why it can be so fulfilling and enlarging for both people involved. (p. 149)

Personal construct practitioners believe that when a client gets defensive, shows signs of resistance, counselors should back off and reevaluate their strategies:

> A client may sometimes appear to 'resist' attempts to persuade her to loosen her construing. . . . It means that the counsellor has not got a clear enough view of what the client is being asked to do. There is a failure of communication between the client and counsellor. There may be too much threat. The client may be having too great a struggle to keep anchors firmly embedded in reality readily to countenance loosening their hold. (Fransella & Dalton, 1990, p. 90)

Although increasingly intense feelings of fear, threat, anxiety, and guilt are signs of moving in transitions, if they are too intense, the client will revert back, resist, and raise defenses. Such signs of resistance alert the counselor to pause and try to understand more where the client is coming from.

Counselors have a particularly difficult time working with clients' hostile feelings. Although these feelings can be recognized as part of the transitional process, they may also be signs of feelings of threat and chaos. After venturing out aggressively when they have been passive most of their lives, clients may react adversely, become guilty, and retreat back into former old patterns. "The client who is maintaining his grasp on the world by holding his construing under a tight rein can easily be faced with a world of chaos with an over-zealous counsellor bent on loosening at all costs" (Fransella & Dalton, 1990, p. 91).

In such cases, the counselor can ask clients to describe areas in their lives where they feel secure, where they feel most a sense of themselves. Fransella and Dalton (1990) cite the case of a client who enjoys stamp collecting and who reacts defensively in most situations. Because the client feels very secure collecting stamps, he can risk trying new possibilities in this domain.

Last Stage: Integrating Client Changes Into Daily Life

As a result of deeper exploration about themselves and development of a positive relationship with counselors, clients become more self-confident, more assertive, and more authentic in counseling sessions. A "real" counseling relationship emerges in which the client perceives the counselor without distortion (Gelso & Carter, 1985). This new, "real" relationship, according to Gelso and Carter (1985), permits clients to express feelings more authentically, assert their needs, continue to be insightful, and gain understanding of themselves and others.

The counseling relationship in the last stage becomes collaborative; counselor and client are peers working together to help the client reach agreed-on goals (Tracey, 1984). Counselors become more real themselves. They feel free now to offer their own opinions, give advice, and instruct clients in coping or adopting social and self-management skills.

Counselors and clients focus primarily on reaching the goals they originally laid out in the initial stage. The social contexts in which clients will apply their new attitudes and behaviors become a primary counselor-client consideration. With the counselors' help, clients' major task now is to apply changes in perception, feelings, and behavior generated during counseling sessions to relationships and circumstances in everyday life.

Clients should be alerted that spouses, family members, and colleagues, rather than welcoming client changes, may be puzzled, resistant, resentful, or hostile to changes. Whereas the counselor has provided an accepting atmosphere to foster and nurture client changes, these same accepting conditions generally do not exist in the typical client's world. Clients may be asserting their new feelings in ways that offend others.

Counselors can help clients consider more effective and less aggressive ways to relate to significant others who are resisting client changes. At the same time, they can keep clients from reverting back to their former ways. Counselors can, for example, rehearse with clients effective ways of asserting themselves with others. After clients make trial attempts, counselors can give feedback about the effectiveness of their actions.

Hansen, Rossberg, and Cramer (1994) point out that this is an important stage, a "working through" stage in which the client's new insights and self-understanding are put into constructive action. "The client gains little in the long run from an intellectual understanding of the problem unless she or he is able to try out new methods of behaving" (p. 239).

Counselors differ in the degree of action-oriented strategies and techniques they use, depending on their theoretical orientation (see chap. 5). Client-centered counselors, for instance, tend not to use techniques. Psychodynamic counselors tend to focus only on fostering changes going on within counseling or therapy sessions. Gestaltists use dramatic enactments—role playing, visual imagery, empty chair techniques—as ways for clients to practice changing behavior, but these practices also are confined only to counseling sessions.

Cognitive-behavioral counselors, in contrast, use many instructional and directive techniques to help clients apply new learning to their everyday actions and relationships. Some begin earlier, in the middle stage. Personal construct counselors, for example, integrate restructuring strategies into behavioral action earlier in the counseling process, as described in the middle stage, because they emphasize the importance of clients applying new insights and attitudes to behavior as they go along in the therapeutic process. "It is in action, in the person's experiments with ways of *behaving* differently that new constructions of events are tried and tested" (Fransella & Dalton, 1990, p. 105).

As an eclectic counselor, I select strategies and techniques consistent with my theoretical orientation that are best suited to the particular client and to his or her situation.

Strategies to Implement Behavioral Changes

Cognitive-behaviorists have taken the lead in developing strategies to help clients take action in their everyday lives. Egan (1994) lists criteria that contribute to effective action strategies: They must be (a) specific and realistic, (b) powerful enough to lead to client changes and move clients toward stated goals, and (c) actions that clients decide on themselves and that are consistent with client values.

It is also important to consider the context in which changes in behavior and attitude are practiced. For example, those who have just stopped drinking alcohol should avoid social interactions that center on drinking alcohol. Clients should also try out new behaviors in gradual steps.

Counselors can motivate clients to take action by using the social influencing skills described in the previous stage. But whereas in the middle stage, counselors were influencing clients to explore and express emotions, this time, in the last stage, counselors are influencing clients to take action. They first use strategies that encourage or influence clients to be willing to take appropriate actions, and then once the clients are willing, the counselors teach them certain skills to carry out the actions effectively.

The numerous social influencing strategies include confronting, probing, offering information, providing feedback about specific behaviors and attitudes, and considering logical consequences of one's actions. In the following case, the counselor raises the question of *logical consequences* when a client impulsively decides to make a major change in life:

> *Client:*   I'm fed up. I'm going in tomorrow to let them know I quit.
>
> *Counselor:*   This is the first time you've mentioned this, yet you've not explored alternative jobs. How will you support yourself and your wife?

If a client takes no initiative to change after he or she has expressed a strong desire to change, the counselor might *confront* the client.

> *Counselor:*   You have expressed dissatisfaction with your work, and you mentioned some alternative jobs. Yet, you've said nothing about changing. What's going on?
>
> *Client:*   I've just been too busy to think about it.
>
> *Counselor:*   Are you feeling ambivalent about leaving your job?

Once the client is ready and willing to take appropriate action, the counselor can instruct the client in various skills or strategies to help him or her make changes in daily life. These include conducting behavioral rehearsals in which clients rehearse new behaviors with the counselor; using coping or adaptive skills, such as self-management or self-monitoring skills; modeling behaviors of others; writing journals; engaging in relaxation exercises; completing homework assignments; and getting feedback from counselors.

Self-management and self-monitoring strategies help clients direct and control their own behavioral change. "Self-management methods involve a combination of behavioral and cognitive-behavioral strategies to increase a client's self-control and ability to change his or her behavior" (Brammer et al., 1993, p. 194). These methods are particularly useful for clients with such concerns as weight loss, anxiety, insomnia, poor interpersonal and communication skills, and nicotine addiction (Cormier & Cormier, 1991).

Meichenbaum's (1985) stress-inoculation therapy, described in chapter 5, is a good example of self-management strategy. Clients learn and practice coping skills in which they replace nonadaptive self-statements that accompany stress with more adaptive ones.

Counselors can help clients explore community facilities that offer training in skills they may need—assertiveness training, self-management, weight control— courses that can be taken as an adjunct to counseling. Counselors can also help clients search for and evaluate social support systems in the community, such as single-parenting or eating disorder groups.

Close collaboration between counselors and clients is crucial to the success of these programs. Not only are clients expected to initiate changes, but they are expected to monitor their progress as well.

> Self-management programs rely on therapist and client negotiated tasks and homework assignments to both enhance client motivation and structure the change program. . . . Self-monitoring is used to measure progress over time and as an activity that can produce change itself. Clients are taught to administer both verbal and material reinforcers for personal progress. (Brammer et al., 1993, pp. 194–195)

Termination of Counseling Sessions

Effective termination of counseling sessions is a key factor in how successful the counseling outcome will be. An otherwise productive interaction with clients can be marred if the process is terminated before clients are ready or if sessions continue beyond what clients need. Successful counseling outcomes are more likely to occur when counselors and clients jointly decide when termination is appropriate, prepare to end sessions, and attend to emotional responses that go along with termination.

During the termination stage, counselors help clients review major themes that have emerged during counseling and help them assess progress in attaining goals; they consider how clients can apply and generalize their new learning and insights to problems that may arise in the future. Counselors can also encourage clients to express feelings regarding the ending of the counseling relationship.

> The major themes, conflicts, and fantasies of the entire therapeutic process are reworked in the context of termination, of ending. Part of this reworking has to do with uncovering new issues that may bubble up . . . another part involves . . . taking in reinforcement for the new behaviors and responses that he has acquired. Yet a third factor is the therapy relationship itself: the reality . . . of ending an interaction which has been a meaningful and important part of their lives. (Moursund, 1993, p. 90)

Appropriate Time to Terminate

Counselors and clients can determine whether the clients are ready to end sessions by assessing whether the original symptoms or presenting problems have been resolved. In what specific ways has client stress been reduced? What skills have been developed to help clients cope with concerns? In what ways are clients relating more effectively with others or functioning more constructively in their jobs, academics, or home life? Do clients feel more positive and more comfortable with themselves?

Personal construct counselors also emphasize the importance of the preparation for ending:

> The ending of a period of counselling needs as much, if not more, careful preparation. As at all stages, we need to make predictions about this important part of the process, to ensure that clients are aware of the implications of moving on and able to take into the future the changes in construing which have helped them to overcome current difficulties. (Fransella & Dalton, 1990, p. 131)

Fransella and Dalton (1990) list several aspects of client changes to look for: sufficient psychological movement; changes in the nature of construing, ability to loosen and tighten construing appropriately, and ability to cope with transitional periods of rising feelings of anxiety, threat, guilt, and hostility; and tendency to "move away from the client's 'problems' and his immediate personal concerns into a more dilated field of interest" (p. 133).

Terminating Too Soon

At times, counselors or clients initiate termination before the clients have attained counseling goals. Counselors may end a relationship prematurely because they feel resentful toward the client or anxious because they think they cannot help the client—difficulties relating to countertransference issues discussed earlier. Clients' desire to terminate prematurely may arise from feelings of a lack of progress in the counseling sessions. It may also signal that clients' resistances have not been completely worked through and that clients are not ready for the last stage.

Resistance to Appropriate Termination

When they have been in a close and satisfactory relationship, counselor or client or both may resist ending counseling even though all indications show that the client is ready to go. Clients may resist leaving the safety of the relationship because they are anxious about being on their own. Clients with unstable relationships may want to hold on to the counselor. When they resist terminating, their symptoms may flare up, or they may bring in other problems. Counselors need to attend to clients' feelings and reassure clients if termination still seems advisable (Moursund, 1993).

Counselors may resist termination because they are reluctant to end a satisfactory relationship, are particularly attached to the client, or are overly anxious about the client's ability to function adequately on his or her own. In these cases, counselors must assess their own countertransference feelings.

Leading Up to the Last Session

Sudden termination can be disruptive to client progress in counseling even when it is appropriate. More than one session should be devoted to termination issues before counselor and client say their good-byes in the final session. Cormier and Cormier (1991) believe that counselors should spend as much time terminating the relationship as they did building it in the initial stages. Young (1992) believes that the length of preparation for ending counseling depends on the length and quality of the relationship. If the counselor believes that the client's problem has been resolved, he or she may raise the issue directly: "I have observed some positive changes in your attitudes, behavior, and relationships. You've made a decision about school, your relationship with your wife has improved, and your work is going well. I wonder if you need any further counseling at this time." If the client agrees, then a termination process can be worked out.

The client may also bring up the idea of termination: "I seem to be doing well on my job and in my relationships. I am sleeping better, and I don't have as many headaches. Maybe I no longer need to see you." If the counselor thinks the client is not quite ready for termination, they can discuss whether it is advisable to terminate at this time.

Personal construct counselors recommend gradually phasing out, stretching meeting times to every 3 weeks, and then more infrequently, depending on the case.

Moursund (1993) emphasizes that, during the review of progress and feelings about therapy, the material brought up must be considered in the context of separation. Communication must focus on what it means to the client "who is ending a supportive/confrontive growth-producing relationship" (p. 97). Moreover, counselors should acknowledge and honor client expressions of positive feelings about the counseling relationship, the counseling experience, and the progress they have made in gaining new insights and in resolving problems.

The closure of counseling will mean a transition to a new phase, and transition means some loss, a loss that is usually accompanied by feelings of anger, fear, guilt, or sadness. Moursand (1993) discusses these various client emotions that might emerge as counseling winds to an end. If anger occurs, it may be a defense against feelings of anxiety or a substitute for the more difficult expressions of sadness. At this point, Moursand notes, counselors need to help clients see the positive and energizing aspects of their anger. Fear may also emerge prior to termination. Counselor acceptance of client fear reactions can help reassure clients of their ability to manage their lives.

Sadness occurs most often at this time. Not only is there sadness about parting from the counselor, but the experience may also evoke sadness of earlier partings (Moursund, 1993). As Moursund (1993) points out, however, there is a difference between therapeutic grief and grief over other losses. Here is an opportunity to talk about and work through the client's feelings of loss.

In my experience, feelings of poignancy describes more aptly what may be felt during this period; poignancy does not imply the sense of finality that grief does. Although counseling sessions do end, the possibility of the client returning is left open, such as in intermittent counseling.

In personal construct counseling, clients are encouraged to report back 2 years hence and give a progress report. They are also encouraged to renew contact if necessary at any time. So, the loss is not a final one, but rather part of the ongoing life cycle of loss and renewal (Fransella & Dalton, 1990).

Many therapists nowadays, including Dr. Simon Budman, assistant professor of psychiatry at Harvard Medical School, view therapy as intermittent and ongoing, discussed in the chapter 5 section on brief counseling, in which they work with different problems as they arise in one's life, much like the way one sees the family doctor (Goode, 1998).

✺ RESEARCH STUDIES ON COUNSELING OUTCOME: META-ANALYSIS

The quantity of research on counseling and psychotherapy outcomes is overwhelming. As an aid, results of outcome studies have been reviewed and summarized through a process called *meta-analysis* (Ivey, Ivey, & Simek-Morgan, 1997; Parloff, London, & Wolfe, 1986). In this process, investigators conduct a systematic search of the literature by using predefined criteria for including studies. Important characteristics of each study—such as client population, type of theory or technique, or type and severity of client problem—are systematically recorded. Varied statistical devices are used to obtain summary statements about the significance of the results based on a common key question being studied (Lambert, Shapiro, & Bergin, 1986).

Meta-analysis has been criticized because of insufficient attention to quality of research designs, but in general, most counselors and therapists believe that its strengths outweigh its limitations and that improved methods of meta-analysis will be forthcoming (Ivey et al., 1997).

After reviewing outcome studies, Lambert et al. (1986) say, "Psychological treatments are, overall and in general, beneficial, although it remains equally true that not everyone benefits to a satisfactory degree" (p. 158). They found little evidence of meaningful superiority of one form of psychotherapy over another. Behavioral and cognitive-behavioral approaches seem more effective with phobias and compulsions. Garfield (1986) criticizes outcome research because the studies have not dealt with such variables as counselor-client interactions or with the impact of external life events on the outcome of therapy.

✺ SUMMARY

In the process of individual counseling, counselors and clients develop a mutual relationship to help clients gain self-awareness that will enable them to resolve problems effectively.

Factors that influence the counseling process are the counselor's professional and personal characteristics; the type of services provided in the counseling setting; the client's personal attributes, including age, social-cultural background, ethnic identity, and views about gender role; and the overall context in which clients are experiencing problems.

The individual counseling process generally goes through three stages. In the initial stage, a counselor-client relationship is established that focuses on understanding clients and their problems. Problems are assessed, tentative working hypotheses are developed, and goals are set. In the middle stage, a shift occurs in which the client turns inward, exploring feelings and developing insights. Client and counselor experience a sense of movement as they work through client emotional turbulence, client and counselor transference and countertransference, and client resistance.

In the last stage, the counselor helps clients apply their new insights and attitudes into their behavior in everyday life. As clients and counselors focus on attaining client goals, the relationship becomes more authentic, collaborative, and instructive. Counselors and clients then work toward effective termination by reviewing what they have accomplished and sharing feelings about ending the relationship.

Meta-analysis of counseling outcome research indicates that counseling, overall, is beneficial to most clients.

-※ PROJECTS AND ACTIVITIES

1. Compare the resistance of a client who has been persuaded to seek counseling against his will with resistance of a client who volunteers for, and comes regularly to, counseling. How would you handle them differently?
2. Interview counselors in a public school, in a college, and in a community setting. How do they think the policies of their agency or institution affect their work with clients?
3. What client characteristics do you think would make it difficult for you to develop a working relationship—for example, a macho male, a militant feminist, a person with fundamentalist religious views, an atheist, a spouse abuser, a spouse having an extramarital affair, an obnoxious client, a very passive client. Play the role of a client who has one of these characteristics.
4. Interview a male counselor and a female counselor with similar background and expe-

rience. Ask each of them to describe the major gender issues. Ask them in what way, if any, male and female clients differ. Compare responses. Do you see any evidence of cultural biases?
5. Interview students from two or three different ethnic groups and from a group of multiracial students regarding the major problems they experience. How willing are they to use counseling services to help them resolve problems?
6. Select a study about counseling outcome from the reviews of research in the chapter. Go to the original source, and evaluate the study. Does it include type of client problem, client characteristics, counselor theoretical views, and techniques used? Was a control group used? How would you improve the study?

-※ REFERENCES

American Psychiatric Association. (1994). *Diagnostic and statistical manual of mental disorders* (4th ed.). Washington, DC: Author.

Bordin, E. S. (1975). The generalizability of the psychoanalytic concept of the working alliance. *Psychotherapy: Theory, Research and Practice, 16,* 252–260.

Brammer, L. M., Abrego, P. G., & Shostrom, E. L. (1993). *Therapeutic psychology: Fundamentals of counseling and psychotherapy* (6th ed.). Upper Saddle River, NJ: Prentice Hall.

Brown, D., & Srebalus, D. S. (1988). *An introduction to the counseling profession.* Upper Saddle River, NJ: Prentice Hall.

Corey, G. (1996). *Theory and practice of counseling and psychotherapy* (5th ed.). Pacific Grove, CA: Brooks/Cole.

Corey, G., Corey, M. S., & Callanan, P. (1993). *Issues and ethics in the helping professions* (4th ed.). Pacific Grove, CA: Brooks/Cole.

Cormier, W. H., & Cormier, L. S. (1991). *Interviewing strategies for helpers: Fundamental skills and cognitive behavioral interventions* (3rd ed.). Pacific Grove, CA: Brooks/Cole.

Corsini, R. J. (1995). Introduction. In R. J. Corsini & D. Wedding (Eds.), *Current psychotherapies* (5th ed., pp. 1–14). Itasca, IL: F. E. Peacock.

Dryden, W. (Ed.). (1998). *Key issues for counselling in action.* London: Sage.

Egan, G. (1994). *The skilled helper: A systematic approach to effective helping* (5th ed.). Pacific Grove, CA: Brooks/Cole.

Fransella, F., & Dalton, P. (1990). *Personal construct counseling in action.* London: Sage.

Garfield, S. L. (1986). Research on client variables. In S. L. Garfield & A. E. Bergin (Eds.), *Handbook of psychotherapy and behavior change* (pp. 213–256). New York: John Wiley.

Gelso, C. J., & Carter, J. A. (1985). The relationship in counseling and psychotherapy: Components, consequences, and theoretical antecedents. *Counseling Psychologist, 13,* 155–243.

Goode, E. (1998, November 24). How much therapy is enough? It depends. *New York Times.* pp. D1, D10).

Goodyear, R. K., & Bradley, F. O. (1980). The helping process as contracted. *Personnel & Guidance Journal, 58,* 512–515.

Hansen, J. C., Rossberg, R. H., & Cramer, S. H. (1994). *Counseling: Theory and process* (5th ed.). Boston: Allyn & Bacon.

Heilbrun, A. B., Jr. (1982). Cognitive factors in early termination: Social insight and level of defensiveness. *Journal of Counseling Psychology, 29,* 29–38.

Ivey, A. E., & Ivey, M. B. (1999). *Intentional interviewing and counseling: Facilitating client development in a multicultural society* (4th ed.). Pacific Grove, CA: Brooks/Cole.

Ivey, A. E., Ivey, M. B., & Simek-Morgan, L. (1997). *Counseling and psychotherapy: A multicultural perspective* (4th ed.). Boston: Allyn & Bacon.

Kelly, G. A. (1955). *The psychology of personal constructs* (Vols. 1 and 2). New York: Norton.

Kelly, G. A. (1963). *The psychology of personal constructs.* New York: Norton.

Lambert, M. J., Shapiro, D. A., & Bergin, A. S. (1986). The effectiveness of psychotherapy. In S. L. Garfield & A. E. Bergin (Eds.), *Handbook of psychotherapy and behavior change* (pp. 157–211). New York: John Wiley.

May, R., & Yalom, I. (1995). Existential psychotherapy. In R. J. Corsini & D. Wedding (Eds.), *Current psychotherapies* (pp. 262–292). Itasca, IL: F. E. Peacock.

Meichenbaum, D. (1985). Cognitive behavioral therapies. In S. J. Lynn & J. P. Garske (Eds.), *Contemporary psychotherapies: Models and methods* (pp. 261–286). Upper Saddle River, NJ: Merrill/Prentice Hall.

Miller, J. B., & Stiver, I. P. (1997). *The healing connection: How women form relationships in therapy and in life.* Boston: Beacon Press.

Moursund, J. (1993). *The process of counseling and therapy* (3rd ed.). Upper Saddle River, NJ: Prentice Hall.

Parloff, M. B., London, P., & Wolfe, B. (1986). Individual psychotherapy and behavior change. *Annual Review of Psychology, 37,* 321–349.

Rogers, C. R. (1942). *Counseling and psychotherapy: Newer concepts in practice.* Boston: Houghton Mifflin.

Rogers, C. R. (1951). *Client-centered therapy: Its current practice, implications, and theory.* Boston: Houghton Mifflin.

Sexton, T. L., & Whiston, S. C. (1994). The status of the counseling relationship: An empirical review, theoretical implications, and research directions. *Counseling Psychologist, 22,* 6–78.

Stiver, I. P. (1997). What is the role of transference and the unconscious in the relational model? In J. V. Jordan (Ed.), *Women's growth in diversity* (pp. 37–41). New York: Guilford Press.

Surrey, J. L. (1997). What do you mean by mutuality in therapy? In J. V. Jordan (Ed.), *Women's growth in diversity* (pp. 42–49). New York: Guilford Press.

Taffel, R. (1993). In praise of countertransference: Harvesting our errors. *Family Therapy Networker, 17,* 52–57.

Tracey, T. J. (1989). The stages of influence in counseling. In W. Dryden (Ed.), *Key issues for counselling in action* (pp. 63–72). London: Sage.

Tyler, L. E. (1969). *The work of the counselor* (3rd ed.). New York: Appleton-Century-Croft.

Watkins, C. E. (1983). Transference phenomena in the counseling situation. *Personnel and Guidance Journal, 62,* 206–210.

Young, M. E. (1992). *Counseling methods and techniques: An eclectic approach.* New York: Macmillan.

10   Family and Marriage Counseling and Therapy

Family counseling and family therapy involve an interaction between a professional counselor or therapist and a family during which family members are helped to improve their relationships with one another; improved relationships, in turn, foster growth and development of each member. During the counseling process, family members learn to confront and resolve conflicts more productively so that both individual and family development are enhanced.

The terms *family counseling* and *family therapy* are used interchangeably by many professionals writing and practicing in the field (Passmore & Horne, 1991). Generally, *family therapy* designates work with more severe family dysfunctions. *Family counseling* is for those suffering from normal situational concerns and conflicts.

In the early decades, psychoanalysts (most of whom were Freudians) did not work with families. They worked only with individual patients. The therapeutic intention was to help patients break away from their families, psychologically and literally.

One of the first to break with Freud, Alfred Adler, in the 1920s, perceived individuals as being influenced by social interactions. Emphasizing the influence of parental behavior on the child, Adler worked with parenting skills.

Not until the 1950s was the term *family systems* used to describe family social interactions. Building on Adler's early work, psychiatrists and social workers explored the idea that if family influences were contributing to an individual's problems, then working with the family would contribute to the resolution of the individual's problems. For example, while conducting research on schizophrenic behavior in the 1950s at Stanford University, Don Jackson, Jay Haley, Virginia Satir, and others found that schizophrenia arose from schizophrenic patterns of behavior in the family (Foley, 1989; Satir, 1982).

From these explorations, family systems therapy, based on the family as a social unit, took hold and since the 1970s spread throughout the therapeutic and counseling community. The term *family systems* was coined to represent the idea that when one member of a family shows signs of trouble, the symptoms represent problems in and among all members of that family. Although one person is designated as the *identified patient* (IP), the family is perceived as the source of the problem, and the whole family is treated. Currently, the family systems model underlies all schools of family therapy.

⟶❀ FAMILY SYSTEMS THEORIES

The family systems model is based on the general systems theory developed by biologist Ludvig von Bertalanffy (1974), who believed that humans are living systems composed of subsystems that are connected together and dependent on one another; any change in one subsystem produces change in the others. In this model, the whole system is greater than the sum of its parts. Family subsystems include smaller units of individual family members who interact and affect the total system. Examples of these subsystems are interactions between parents, various interactions among siblings, and interactions between a parent and each child.

In equating family systems with general systems theory, Foley (1989) describes three important characteristics: wholeness, relationship, and equifinality. He says, "*Wholeness* means the system is not just the sum of its parts taken separately, but it also includes their interaction" (p. 456). Thus, a family does not consist simply of separate individuals, but rather includes the complex interactions occurring among them. *Relationship* describes the types and quality of interactions going on among family members who are in different subsystems in the family. *Equifinality* is based on the idea that any problem a family member or family is experiencing results from numerous causes, rather than from one particular cause. If an adolescent girl is experiencing an eating disorder, for example, one cannot simply say it is caused by a rejecting mother. Complex interactions between parents, between parents and daughter, and among daughter and her siblings all contribute. For this reason, family systems therapists believe that they can intervene at any time to resolve the family problem. "Regardless of the origin of a problem, any difficulty can be removed if a change is made at any point in time in the system" (Foley, 1989, p. 456). Because of this belief, family therapists do not search for underlying causes of family dysfunction, but instead focus on the current interactions in the family that are perpetuating the problem.

Murray Bowen (Papero, 1991), who began his work in the 1950s, was the first family therapist to apply systems theory to family therapy. He originally called his theory "family systems" but in the 1970s changed the name to the *Bowen theory* because the term *family systems* had become widely used to describe numerous family theories.

Family therapists, regardless of theoretical orientation, follow the general principles of systems theories. They attend to current problems in family dynamics. They explore relationships, alliances, and conflicts within the family and their effects on each member of the family and on the family as a whole. In applying these principles, family therapists tend to be active in the sessions, often acting as instructors, directors, or guides in reorganizing family patterns of interaction. Family therapists differ, however, in the way they work with a family because of differing theoretical positions they have about human behavior.

Acknowledging that family classification systems are numerous and complex, I have selected eight family systems theories that represent the basic theoretical approaches presented in chapter 5: (a) object relations, (b) Bowen's family systems, (c) Adlerian family therapy, (d) Satir's process model, (e) Minuchin's structural family therapy, (f) strategic therapy, (g) social learning family therapy, and (h) cognitive-behavioral family therapy.

Object Relations Theory

Object relations has its psychoanalytic roots in ego psychology. Unlike Freud, who specified that instinctual gratification of sexual drives residing in the id is a person's primary drive, object relations theorists believe that humans relate primarily to others. Children develop strong attachments to significant people (called *objects*) to fulfill this need (Atwood, 1992b).

> According to this theory, human beings have a fundamental motivation to seek out objects—that is, people for the purpose of relationships. . . . An **object** is a significant other (for example, a mother during infancy) with whom children form an interactional, emotional bond. As they grow, children will often internalize (interject) good and bad characteristics of these objects within themselves. (Gladding, 1995, p. 111)

Thus, early psycho*social* rather than psycho*sexual* relationships influence the development of the child and, later, the adult (M. B. Thomas, 1992).

James Framo (1982) is a well-known advocate of this theory. He believes that the emotional responses of each family member and the effects these various emotional expressions have on family interactions are at the crux of family dynamics and family functioning. Any unresolved conflicts that exist in either *parent's family of origin* result in conflicts in relationships in the current *nuclear family.*

Another important proponent of object relations, Robin Skynner (1981), believes that the family as a unit fosters individual development to the degree that both parents have worked through their own development in their families of origin. When parents request counseling for a problem child, the child's unresolved behavioral problems represent the parents' failure to develop emotional maturity. Skynner believes that when two people marry, each partner brings to the marriage fears and distorted expectations related to blocked developmental processes; moreover, each partner tries to re-create circumstances where the undeveloped experience can be reencountered and worked through. He sees these attempts as a great potential for growth in the marriage relationship. But also, he warns, these undeveloped experiences can lead partners to resist individual changes; such rigid reactions result in unresolved family tensions and dysfunctions.

Object relations practitioners tend to combine treatment of the whole family with treatment of subgroups and individual members of the family. A man and a woman often work together as co-therapists.

First, the therapist assesses the whole family to determine the nature and severity of the problem. One family member, usually a child, as said earlier, is designated as the identified patient (IP). After the initial assessment, the therapist decides whether to work with the whole family, a subgroup, or the parents alone. If assessment shows that serious marital conflict exists that would impede progress in family counseling, the therapist may first do marital counseling with the parents and bring in the rest of the family later.

The family and the therapist agree on goals, which are usually quite specific. Therapy consists of attending both to the personal problems of each family member and to family dysfunctional patterns. Both parents' unresolved conflicts with their families of origin are included as well.

Therapists recognize that transference and resistance will occur among family members because the members are expressing unresolved feelings of anxiety or anger blocked by either the nuclear family or the parents' families of origin. At the same time, therapists are observing and interpreting family rules and family transactions that are causing family breakdown. Skynner (1981) attempts to let family members express their concerns as spontaneously as possible with a minimum of direct guidance or prompting. By strengthening the ego functioning of each member, therapists help the family reduce dysfunctional family transactions and communications so that healthy interpersonal (object) relations can develop (Goldenberg & Goldenberg, 1991).

Bowen's Family Systems

Murray Bowen (1978) originated the term *family systems* in the 1950s when he developed his theory of family therapy. He believes that an emotional system exists within a family and that this system influences the degree of separateness (*differentiation of self*) and togetherness (*fusion*) of family members. Bowen's major goal is to develop differentiation or independence among family members (Atwood, 1992b).

Differentiation of self, according to Bowen, is crucial for the effective functioning of each family member and the family as a whole. Members of a dysfunctional family fuse identities, become emotionally dependent on one another, and lose their individual selves. Growth, maturity, and emotions are stifled. In an emotionally mature family, he believes, an effective balance of differentiation and togetherness is maintained. Members attain sufficient individuality to make their own decisions without becoming fused, while at the same time they show consideration for others. Bowen claims that it is a mistake for a person to try to resolve fusion problems by isolating from the family through emotional withdrawal, denial of problems, or running away. People who use these escape mechanisms behave immaturely and impulsively and fuse with others (Papero, 1991; Singleton, 1982).

Bowen believes that fusion between members of a family leads to the development of triangles. When two members of a family who are fused enter into conflict with each other, one or the other tries to move out of this locked-in relationship by involving a vulnerable third party who inevitably take sides with one of the fused partners (Becvar & Becvar, 1986). In a triangle, two members of the family align while the third becomes an outsider and a scapegoat (Singleton, 1982). When tension becomes really unbearable, a fourth person may be drawn in, forcing realignment of the triangle.

When a family first comes in for therapy, members usually blame the family discord on one of the following: (a) One spouse has a problem (drinking, gambling, or adultery), (b) serious marital discord exists, or (c) a child's behavior is disrupting the marriage and family harmony (Bowen, 1978). Bowen believes that marital conflict in itself does not cause problem children but rather that problems arise when parents project their anxieties onto children. This is called *family projection process.*

Bowen believes that patterns of differentiation, fusing, triangulation, and projection are passed from generation to generation in a *multigenerational transmission* process. Problems in a nuclear family can be understood and resolved only if therapy includes exploration of relationships in the families of origin for three generations. In therapy, then, Bowen traces dysfunctional patterns through the use of a *genogram* that demonstrates three generations of family structure and family triangulations and alignments. (A *genogram* is a structural chart showing the relationship of family members for three generations, including dates of birth and death, marriages and divorces, and number and gender of siblings.)

Once family members understand this pervasive fusing and triangulation, Bowen's main goal is to help all involved differentiate themselves from one another and break the tendency to triangulate. Because triangles are interlocking, a change in one triangle will cause a change in all triangles.

On the basis of his assessment of the family, Bowen may work with the whole family, with individual family members, or with various combinations of family members representing a family subsystem. If he thinks the conflict between husband and wife is the major factor contributing to a child's symptoms, he may work with the marital discord first before seeing the whole family. If the conflict between spouses is very severe, he may see each one separately until they are able to work together.

Bowen does not give the IP special attention. He believes that the so-called stronger members of the family play a part in fostering and maintaining sickness in a weaker member. He helps all members become aware of their roles in the family dynamics.

Adlerian Family Therapy

Alfred Adler, originally a follower of Freud, broke with him because Adler believed that a social drive to belong and to relate to others, rather than biological instincts, directed human behavior. He contended that all behavior is purposeful and that the goal is to attain social status in the family and the community (see chap. 5). In the 1920s, Adler applied his principles of psychotherapy to work with families in schools and in the community. He emphasized the importance of family dynamics, sibling rivalry, and birth order of children. He used consultations with nonpathological families struggling with practical problems in rearing and relating to children. Parents were taught appropriate ways of disciplining children (Dinkmeyer & Dinkmeyer, 1991).

Alfred Adler, who started working with families in the early 1920s, rightfully can be considered the originator of family counseling and therapy. He was ignored for many years, however, overshadowed by the monopoly of Freudian psychoanalysts and the domination of humanists and behaviorists among counselors and therapists. A resurgence of Adlerian thought has profoundly influenced psychology in the United States (Mosak, 1995).

Having once again gained professional attention, Adlerian psychology has become a viable, flourishing system. Rudolf Dreikurs and then Don Dinkmeyer have been primarily responsible for carrying on Adlerian thought. The worth and viability of Adlerian psychology can be measured by the amount of research and development it continues to generate and the many Adlerian institutes, professional societies, journals, family-education centers, and study groups. Counselors and therapists have come to recognize the value of Adler because they have become more socially conscious, have moved beyond treating the family in isolation, and are now treating families in context with their social-cultural environment.

In the 1940s, Dreikurs updated Adler's pragmatic theory and style and his focus on nonpathological families struggling to bring up children effectively. A manual on Adlerian family counseling centers, published in 1959 by Dreikurs, Lowe, Sonstegard, & Corsini, 1959, became "the bible of Adlerian family counseling" (Dinkmeyer & Dinkmeyer, 1991, p. 385). According to Dreikurs (1968), children are motivated for growth most effectively in groups. They try to attain a place in the group, and if they don't, they develop feelings of inferiority. In severe cases, they become discouraged and withdraw from efforts to cooperate.

Even discouraged children, however, try to use creative powers to attain social status. Dreikurs (1968) claims that discouraged children take one of four goal-directed behaviors. They may try to (a) get attention, (b) prove their power, (c) get revenge, or (d) display deficiencies to get special service or exemptions. He does not advocate punishment for misbehavior. He proposes instead that children should experience either natural or logical consequences of their actions. *Natural consequences* apply when the activity involves only the child—when the child spends all her or his weekly allowance the first day, for example, and has no money the rest of the week. *Logical consequences* occur when two or more people are involved; for instance, children who are frequently late for dinner will not be served dinner whenever they are late.

Dreikurs (1968) points out that when parents, after World War II, began following a permissive style of raising children, they were at a loss about how to guide or discipline them. Elaborating on Dreikurs's views, Lowe (1982) points out that children in such cases, believing that they can make any demand they please, become irresponsible tyrants, and adults adopt the children's roles. Lacking new methods of disciplining children in a democratic way, parents need help in establishing order. Counseling is meant to give parents these methods.

For many years, professionals used the term *Dreikurs/Adlerian family counseling and therapy.* Recently, they have been calling it simply *Adlerian family counseling and therapy.* Adlerian theory has been used as a basis for a system of parenting skills called *Systematic Training for Effective Parenting* (STEP), developed by Don Dinkmeyer (Dinkmeyer & McKay, 1976). Christensen (1975), Dinkmeyer and Dinkmeyer (1991), Fine (1980), and Lowe (1982) are among the family counselors who have applied Adlerian principles to school settings and to parenting groups. Dinkmeyer and Dinkmeyer (1991), Sherman and Dinkmeyer (1987), and Sweeney

(1989) have published texts describing Adlerian family therapy as a systems approach in both educational institutions and community practice.

Dinkmeyer and Dinkmeyer (1991) emphasize the social aspect of Adlerian therapy. Individuals, they say, strive to gain significance by belonging to a social system, beginning with the family. Family members develop feelings of inferiority when they believe that other family members reject them or deem them unworthy. "All behavior attempts to overcome feelings of inferiority. We seek superiority in part because our earliest experiences surrounded us with superiors" (p. 388). Power struggles then emerge in the family as each member tries to gain social status.

Adlerian counselors and therapists act as teachers, advisers, and facilitators. They help families understand some dynamics in family transactions and how each member contributes to the family problems. They help family members recognize their mutual interdependence by directing them to attend to one another's needs and to cooperate in constructive give-and-take relationships.

Satir's Process Model

Virginia Satir's model holds that family dysfunction results from faulty communication, a condition directly related to each individual's feelings of low self-esteem. She originally called her theory *conjoint therapy* (1967) to describe the idea that the therapist works with the total nuclear family in counseling sessions.

After completing her work on conjoint therapy, Satir spent time at the Esalen Institute, a humanistic growth center in California. Her exposure to Gestalt therapy, altered states of consciousness, body therapies, and sensory awareness had a profound influence on her personally and professionally. From this rich combination of experiences, she developed the *process model* of family therapy (Satir & Bitter, 1991).

Satir moved away, then, from an emphasis on pathology, which had characterized her earlier family therapy, to an emphasis on maintaining the healthiness of normally functioning individuals and wholeness in the family. She used the process model to describe her methods of interacting with individual and family members to help them improve communication styles and feelings of worth. Satir (1982) wrote, "I feel the name 'Process Model' fits how I see what I do. The model is one in which the therapist and family join forces to promote wellness" (p. 12).

Communication and self-esteem are the cornerstones of process therapy (Goldenberg & Goldenberg, 1995; Satir, 1982). Any symptoms displayed by family members result from problems that have blocked their emotional growth. Satir's theory holds that all members of the family and the family itself have within them the resources necessary to overcome these emotional blocks. It emphasizes that the absence of ill health is not the same as the presence of good health. Thus, removing a symptom-producing sickness is not sufficient to ensure positive growth. Well-being is directly related to a sense of vitality and to the development of self-esteem.

Because improving communication among family members is the key factor in Satir's approach, congruency between an event and a person's perception of the event is crucial. Dysfunctional family members continually misperceive the behaviors of other family members, which results in considerable distortions in family communication. Poor communication can result from family members finding it difficult to accept differences in another member of the family.

When symptoms are observed in families, those following Satir's model look for family rules determining the communication that governs the family system. These rules form the patterns by which children develop their own self-esteem. The system is maintained to preserve members' sense of self-esteem. As such, these symptoms have a survival function.

During therapy sessions, therapists become models of communication and growth and act as facilitators for each family member and for the family as a whole. They observe interactions, transactions, and messages of communication and responses. They intervene to ask whether messages are clear and correct and how family members feel about a particular comment made by another family member. They may interrupt dialogue to check whether each person thinks the communication is correct (J. H. Brown & Christensen, 1986). They see themselves as guides, companions, and nourishing educators, rather than as authoritative changers or manipulators. They help families see their nonproductive or destructive patterns and help them engage in health-producing processes.

The goals of Satir's process model are to help each of the family members develop self-esteem and to enable them to grow. Therapists work to change or correct four elements in a family: (a) feelings of self-worth, (b) communication skills, (c) the system of alliances and coalitions, and (d) rules governing the family (Satir, 1982). No one is blamed for the family disturbance; the focus is on the multiple interactions in families. When parents are in conflict, a child often becomes the third angle in a family triangle. The child must take sides with one parent or another to avoid unbearable conflict.

A major contribution to family therapy is Satir's (1972) classification of styles of communication (Figure 10.1) and her use of them in therapy or counseling. She believes that each individual in a dysfunctional family communicates with the others in one of four ways:

- *The Placater.* Tries to smooth things over, takes blame, apologizes, and tries to please so that other persons do not get angry
- *The Blamer.* Accuses others and finds fault in order to appear strong
- *The Computer.* Gives intellectual reasons; is super-reasonable so as to be immune to threats
- *The Leveler.* Tries to be genuine and straightforward in communicating with others; helps resolve conflict

Satir developed a technique called *sculpting,* in which family members take physical postures that indicate how they are relating and communicating in the family system. Family members exaggerate postures to represent the four communication styles. The sensory responses help them become visibly and tactually aware of their communication styles. Family members may switch roles to experience other persons' styles. Communication styles of close friends, employers, household help, lovers, and former spouses may also be role-played.

FIGURE 10.1

Satir's communication stances.

Source: From *Peoplemaking* (p. 83) by
V. Satir, 1972, Palo Alto, CA: Science &
Behavior Books. Copyright 1972 by
Science & Behavior Books. Adapted by
permission.

The family often enacts a current conflict occurring at home and then uses communication games to help members see how family rules or patterns are contributing to the conflict. In doing so, Satir uses props such as blindfolds and ropes. For example, family members might use ropes to tie themselves to each other to represent the prevailing pattern so that they become aware of the complexity and dissonance of their relationships.

> Satir might literally tie a rope around all members' waists, bending them together, and selectively ask one or another member to move. In this way, family members would experience what it is like to be tied together so as to become a single entity. They would also feel for how the movement of one family member influences the rest of the family. (Gladding, 1995, p. 147)

The family might also role-play a system whereby all members are either blamers or distracters and then change to a more productive way of communication.

Minuchin's Structural Family Therapy

Structural family therapy, one of the most influential theories in the 1970s, originated in the work of Salvador Minuchin at the Philadelphia Child Guidance Clinic. Minuchin was trained as a psychoanalytic psychiatrist and became interested in families in the 1950s when he was working with juvenile delinquents and with lower socioeconomic minority groups (Atwood, 1992b; Gladding, 1997).

When analyzing faulty family patterns, Minuchin (1974) explores how members of families interact, how faulty communication—repetitive and highly rigid patterns and habits—contributes to family dysfunction. He is also interested in how families under stress use these ineffective behaviors as a means of survival.

According to Minuchin, the family is a social system that develops *transactional patterns,* or family rules, that determine how each member relates to other family members and under what conditions or at what times certain transactional patterns occur (Minuchin, 1974; Minuchin, Lee, & Simon, 1996). In transactions occurring in family subsystems, three factors are involved: boundaries, alignments, and power. *Boundaries* are the rules determining who will participate in a family interaction or transaction and what role each member will play. *Alignments* refers to how various family members form coalitions or alliances to join or oppose another member of a subsystem. *Power* relates to the degree of influence each person has on the family system. A healthy, functioning family has clearly defined generational boundaries; parents are the executives in the family. Alignments are also clear between parents on crucial issues such as discipline; rules about power are defined, so children know that the orders parents give them will be enforced. These firm generational boundaries ensure that children will not inappropriately take over parental functions and that grandparents will not interfere (Goldenberg & Goldenberg, 1991). Also, in a healthy family, boundaries and alliances are flexible, and the family can adapt to inevitable changes, such as births, deaths, marriages, or job changes.

Minuchin, like Bowen, believes that family dysfunctions occur when family members are either *enmeshed* or *disengaged.* In the *enmeshed* family, whose boundaries are diffused, members are tightly interlocked, and any change brought about by one member causes quick resistance from another; family members become fused and lose personal identity. In the *disengaged* family, in contrast, boundaries are rigid, and family ties are weak. Members are isolated or disconnected from each other; they seldom communicate or make contact with one another (Gladding, 1995). Children run the risk of developing antisocial behavior. In both enmeshed and disengaged families, the power of family members is unclear or inappropriate. Children may either have insufficient opportunity to express themselves or tyrannize the family.

Dysfunctional families are resistant to change; when stress arises because of changes in the family, conflict avoidance occurs. In enmeshed families, disagreements are rare because conflicts are seen as a sign of disloyalty and as a refutation of love and closeness. In disengaged families, the distance that prevents confrontations between members gives a false impression of independence and harmony (Colapinto, 1991). Minuchin believes that whenever conflicts arise, such families use repetitive, stereotyped reactions without modification to preserve family equilibrium at all costs. Instead of resolving conflicts, these rigid responses solidify the dysfunctional family patterns.

A family usually asks for help because of concern about a particular family member (the IP). Minuchin's therapeutic goal is to restructure transactional rules of the family so that members can communicate and relate in a way that is growth producing for the family and for each of its members. He either tightens or loosens boundaries and helps families make changes in their stereotyped, rigid positions or roles so that they become more flexible in their ways of relating, resolving conflicts, and managing stress related to change. He works on current symptoms and does not involve himself in patterns from the family of origin or in multigenerational transmission of family patterns.

Minuchin is very active in therapy. He uses two basic strategies and a variety of techniques within these strategies. In the first strategy, he joins with, and accommodates to, the family patterns existing at the beginning of therapy. For example, he may ask the family to enact a conflict that is occurring at home. Using a tactic called *mimesis,* he imitates or models how family members interact with each other. Then, in the second strategy, he begins to restructure the family. He may use the technique of *reframing* by putting a positive interpretation on a person's negative behavior. For example, the attempts of a child to run away may be reframed as an attempt to pull the family together in a crisis. Minuchin may use manipulative intervention if he believes it will alter rigid, unworkable family structures. He may encourage conflicts and actively join alliances or coalitions against other family members to try to induce the family to interact in healthier ways (Minuchin et al., 1996; Roberts, 1992). Therapy is completed when both the therapist and the family think a new and more effective structure exists that the family can use in coping with future transactions and stress.

Strategic Therapy

Strategic therapy is defined as "a family therapy in which the therapist devises and initiates strategies for solving the family's presenting problem" (Schilson, 1991, p. 142). Therapists give family members directives or orders to carry out certain strategic tasks the therapists believe will eliminate the presenting problem.

Strategic therapy is best represented in the work of Jay Haley (1987), a pioneer in family therapy. Haley describes his approach as problem-solving therapy. The goal of therapy is to solve the family's presenting problem by using specific techniques and skills within the family structure.

Haley believes that changes in families come not through family members gaining their own insights through the counseling process, but from directives given by the therapist. Symptoms are the problem to be treated. Current interactions of the family are paramount. No attention is given to historical antecedents in nuclear families or families of origin or to multigenerational patterns. He accepts that family symptoms are attempts at survival by family members (Atwood, 1992a). He also agrees with most other family systems theorists that symptoms arise and are maintained because a family cannot deal with changes, such as death, marriage, divorce, illness, or loss of a job. Families cannot solve problems because they are locked into repetitive and nonproductive communication patterns (Foley, 1989).

The problems (symptoms) of one family member, the IP, may lead the family to seek help. In confronting the problem behavior, Haley focuses on power struggles in the family, on the assumption that maneuvering for power is inherent in families. He defines *power* as a struggle to determine who is in charge of the relationship. All forms of symptoms—depression, drinking, agoraphobia, work addiction—influence a person's behavior (Goldenberg & Goldenberg, 1991). Thus, the problem of the IP controls family social activities, as well as interfamily interactions.

Rules governing family functioning come under close scrutiny. In a healthy family, rules are clear. If parents become angry with each other, family survival is not threatened. Children do not become involved in their arguments. In a dysfunctional family with ambiguous or unclear relationships, clear-cut rules about who is in power do not exist. Alliances cross generational lines, so triangulations may occur between a parent and a child that prevent resolution of parental conflict. Parents' fights may become violent; children feel threatened and often develop symptoms of anxiety and rebelliousness or depression.

Haley (1987) contends that the family and the therapist are in a power struggle just as family members are. Gladding (1998) notes that strategic family therapists like Haley perceive themselves as experts who have no need for "collaborative input from client families" (p. 240). The key factor, then, in therapy is therapist control. The therapist works to restructure the family system by reestablishing boundaries, changing hierarchies of power and family triangulations, and improving family communication. The therapist does this by using two forms of directives—straightforward and paradoxical. *Straightforward directives* are called *positive cooperative tasks* because they are based on what the therapist has learned about the family, with the expectation that the family members will carry them out and profit from completing them. For example, the therapist tells a husband and wife they each need more privacy and directs them to spend specific time by themselves. *Paradoxical directives* are called *negative cooperative tasks* and are used on families highly resistant to following the therapist's directives. "The directives are paradoxical because the therapist has told the family that he wants to help them change but at the same time he is asking them not to change" (Madanes, 1981, p. 26).

Three *paradoxical interventions* have been recommended for use in family therapy by Weeks and L'Abate (1982): (a) reframing the symptom, (b) escalating or inducing a crisis, and (c) redirecting the occurrence of the symptom. *Reframing* refers to relabeling the problem behavior in a positive way. For example, the therapist will describe a child who refuses to do her assigned household chores as someone who may be expressing an urge for independence, a desire that has not been sufficiently recognized. If the child's needs are recognized, then she will probably be willing to do the chores. *Escalating* refers to a strategy called *prescribing the symptom,* in which the client is told to increase the behavior that is presented as a problem. If a child is lying, the child is told to continue lying at every opportunity, to make up better and bigger lies, and to keep a chart indicating success. In *redirection,* the client is encouraged to continue the symptom but in altered circumstances. If spouses are continually bickering, for example, they are directed to bicker only at a certain time of day, every day, and to continue bickering without stopping for, say, 2 hours. Clients find it impossible to carry out these directives and end up reducing or giving up the problem behavior.

Weeks and L'Abate (1982) believe that these approaches are best with very resistant families who have severe or chronic problems. They caution against using these techniques, however, in acute crisis situations or with dangerous persons—those who are suicidal, homicidal, sociopathic, or paranoid. For moderately resistive families with less severe or chronic problems, they suggest modifying the procedures and using them with some caution. For example, the therapist might tell the family what is intended to be accomplished with such a paradoxical intervention.

Behavioral and Cognitive-Behavioral Family Counseling

There has been some controversy over whether behavioral and cognitive-behavioral family counseling theories are forms of family systems. Behavioral and cognitive-behavioral family theories were considered outside the circle of family systems until fairly recently because they had emphasized working with the individual who was designated as the problem in the family. Contemporary theorists with behavioral and cognitive-behavioral leanings have since moved into a systems approach (Atwood, 1992a; Horne, 1991).

While acknowledging that these theorists tend to emphasize the identified patient, Goldenberg and Goldenberg (1991) nevertheless say, "There are efforts by some . . . to accommodate a systems/behavioral/cognitive perspective" (p. 212). According to Horne (1991), social learning behavioral counselors are "incorporating systems theory and looking at more interactional circular explanations for behavior change" (p. 472). Atwood (1992c), in her systemic cognitive-behavioral approach to family therapy, also describes cognitive-behavioral models as definitely being within a family systems model. Most contemporary cognitive-behavioral family therapists now perceive the family within a social system and are attentive to family members' interactions. The theories presented here are classified as forms of family systems.

Behavioral and cognitive-behavioral family theories are based on some form of learning theory and are focused on overt, observable behavior. Learning occurs when the individual's response to external stimuli is reinforced or when the individual models the behavior of others. Behavioral family therapists teach and reinforce more adaptive and constructive ways for families to interact. Cognitive-behavioral theorists believe that dysfunctional family members have inaccurate perceptions about themselves and other family members. Misperceptions then lead them to develop illogical or faulty thoughts about their interactions. Counselors following this approach help families correct their perceptions and teach them new reasoning skills.

Social Learning Family Therapy

One of the most prominent groups working with a family behavioral approach is the staff at the Oregon Social Learning Center, directed by Gerald Patterson and John Reid (Horne, 1991). They base their belief on the concept that behavior is affected primarily by *social learning*. This group began their work in an experimental laboratory where they studied parents and children. Using social learning concepts, they trained parents and teachers to become agents of change. Here at the Oregon Social Learning Center, they applied modeling, time-out, and reinforcement techniques (M. B. Thomas, 1992). They then began working with children and families in their natural environment and with children and teachers in schools, focusing on those children with socially aggressive and antisocial behaviors that were of particular concern to parents and teachers.

Patterson has had a lasting influence in behavioral family counseling:

> Overall, Patterson is credited as playing a critical role in the extension of learning princi-
> ples and techniques to family and marital problems. His practical application of social
> learning theory has made a major impact on family therapy. He has influenced other
> behaviorists to work from a systemic perspective in dealing with families. (Gladding,
> 1995, p. 168)

Patterson (1971) describes two types of parent-child interactions that he observed most frequently—*reciprocity* and *coercion.* He uses *reciprocity* to describe a person's behavior that is followed by a similar behavior from the other person. A positive move elicits a positive response; a negative action is followed by a negative response. The other type of parent-child interaction, *coercion,* describes situations that involve either punishment or negative reinforcers. For example, a parent spanks a child who later hits a younger or weaker sibling (Lynn & Garske, 1985). The aggressive behavior of the parent serves as a model for the child, and the child imitates it.

Counselors meet with the family and make a behavioral assessment in which they identify the problem as precisely as they can. They determine with the family the specific behavior needing change. They consider it essential to establish a therapeutic environment and a relationship in which the family will feel safe and comfortable while discussing family problems.

After counselors determine the problem and establish baseline data, they begin a program of intervention or change in which all positive or desirable behavior is reinforced. Goals are specific and are limited to changing specific behavior or eliminating presenting symptoms. They use behavioral techniques, such as time-out, modeling, and reward systems, to extinguish undesirable behavior. Contracts between family members and the problem child may be made that detail expected decreases and increases in certain behaviors. After the initial interview, counselors help parents learn parenting skills without having the child present.

Behaviorist counselors are basically teachers. They teach skills to parents and train them in reinforcement techniques. Parents may watch a counselor's child-management procedures and then reproduce them at home with the child (Goldenberg & Goldenberg, 1991). Parents do most of the actual work with the child.

The counselor helps parents make decisions about changing the behaviors of a problem child. Parents and child negotiate a contract specifying behaviors to be changed; the contract includes rewards or punishments to be given when the child complies or fails to comply (M. B. Thomas, 1992). Behaviors to be targeted are specific—lying, stealing, or bullying siblings, for example. Parents monitor the child and give out rewards and punishments. The counselor does a follow-up after therapy is completed.

Cognitive-Behavioral Family Therapy

As discussed in chapter 5, cognitive-behavioral theorists like Beck (1976), Ellis (1982), and Meichenbaum (1985) expanded behavioral counseling approaches to include the influences that cognitive processes—thoughts, beliefs, and attitudes—have on client behavior. These ideas have since been applied to family counseling.

In his *rational-emotive* family therapy, Ellis (1991) uses principles and techniques similar to his individual RET approach (now called rational-emotive behavior therapy—REBT, 1995). Ellis is active, persuasive, and directive; he emphasizes correcting illogical or irrational thoughts. He assesses family members' illogical ways of relating to one another and explores destructive or irrational inner talk that family members direct toward themselves or others. He teaches them how to relate reasonably, logically, and constructively without becoming over- or underinvolved. He assigns homework when necessary.

Alexander and Parsons (1982) developed a cognitive-behavioral family system called *functional family therapy (FFT)*. Therapists help family members understand and change thought processes and emotional states that are causing problems in the family system (Fenell & Weinhold, 1989).

Therapists follow three stages in the family counseling process: (a) assessing, (b) facilitating change in the family, and (c) maintaining changes. During the assessment period, therapists observe how each family member perceives the problem and how everyone relates to one another. To facilitate change, therapists interpret and clarify family dynamics, reduce blaming, and encourage listening to one another. To maintain changes, families are taught communication skills, ways of monitoring their behaviors, and methods of constructive interactions (Alexander & Parsons, 1982; Fenell & Weinhold, 1989).

❧ THE FAMILY LIFE CYCLE

Human development theorists (see chap. 4) assume that individuals go through stages of development throughout their life spans. At each stage, individuals usually experience disequilibrium or conflict.

In family counseling, these stages are called the *family life cycle* (Carter & McGoldrick, 1988; L'Abate, Ganahl, & Hansen, 1986; M. B. Thomas, 1992). Families go through stages or transitions, as do individuals. Individual, family, or environmental changes occur periodically that require adjustment or realignment among family members. This realignment often involves changes in attitudes and behaviors, which, in turn, increase family stress and upset family equilibrium.

Carter and McGoldrick (1988) believe that, at each developmental stage in a family life cycle, each family member and the family as a whole experience changes in status that involve emotional and behavioral consequences. For example, the first stage is when the newly married couple learn to commit to a new relationship together, as well as to the extended families of both partners. In the next stage, when children come along, the married couple learn to make space for their children, learn to assume joint responsibility for child rearing and for housekeeping tasks. When children become adolescents, the couple must adjust to the next stage, one that requires increased flexibility in family boundaries to give adolescents more independence. When adult children leave home, the family must adjust yet again. In later years, grandchildren enter the family, involving new relationships between the older adults and their children and grandchildren. Everyone must learn to adjust to each other's new lifestyles, losses, illnesses, and social roles.

This model readily fits the family systems concept of the family as a social unit; it fits as well the multigenerational concepts of psychoanalytic family therapists. It also is suitable for cognitive-behaviorist family counselors, who can use the model to assess target tasks for their clients.

➣ FAMILY COUNSELING AND THERAPY IN PRACTICE

Family counseling relationships follow predictable stages. Although family specialists may not agree on what specifically should occur in each stage, they describe the following similar processes:

Stage I:	Initial stage—developing a relationship and assessing the family problem
Stage II:	Middle stage—developing emotional awareness and acceptance of family dysfunctional patterns
Stage III:	Last stage—learning how to change the family system
Stage IV:	Termination—separating from therapy

Initial Stage: Developing a Relationship and Assessing the Family Problem

Family counseling or therapy usually begins with one family member making the initial contact by telephone. A person may be calling about a family member, the IP, whose ongoing misbehavior is disrupting the family—an unruly or despondent adolescent, a hyperactive child, an alcoholic spouse. Or persons may call on their own behalf because they have problems with their families.

Examples of problems presented are "My husband is depressed, and I am worried about him"; "I feel depressed, and my family is upset about my condition"; "My husband is threatening to divorce me"; and "The children are completely out of hand, and my wife and I disagree on how to discipline them."

Family counselors usually try to have all family members living in the home together at the initial interview. Later, decisions can be made whether to see only certain family members, whether to involve children, or whether to have separate sessions at times for some family members (Goldenberg & Goldenberg, 1991).

At this stage, counselors explain the purpose and process of therapy, the counselor's role, and the family members' responsibilities in the session. A counselor might say:

> You are all here because you believe your family is not working together well, and you want to change that. My role is to help you. First, I must learn more about you as a family, hear some history, and find out how you work together. I also want to learn what each of you sees as the major problems in your family. Then, we can discuss what changes you'd like to make and work together to make changes.

In the beginning sessions, family counselors or therapists establish rapport, confidence, and trust. They also assess family dynamics or interactions and clarify the central problem. The development of rapport is complex because counselors must develop trust relationships between themselves and each member of the family while at the same time helping family members trust one another. As in individual counseling, a warm, empathic, and genuine relationship is essential in family counseling. Counselors treat each family member as important; they insist that members speak for themselves and listen to one another respectfully. For this reason, counselors ask family members to tell what they think is the major problem and to say what they expect of the family.

Counselors observe family dynamics, conflicts, and quality of relationships. They determine who is allied with whom, what the power structure is, what triangles are present, and what boundaries and rules implicitly function in the family. How enmeshed or disengaged are family members? Faulty communication patterns arising from, and contributing to, relationship problems are of particular interest. In this assessment of family behavior, counselors must also look for positive resources and strengths in the family (Satir, 1982).

In addition to assessment of family dynamics, counselors may explore family history and the reactions of family members to significant earlier family events (Goldenberg & Goldenberg, 1991). During this time, it is also important to assess the family's interaction with their extended family, including grandparents and other relatives.

As the family explores itself, counselors begin to reframe the problem as a total family problem and not just the problem of the IP. Resistance to this reevaluation must be met with firmness, patience, and tact. Counselors point out faulty interactions in current relationships and help the family shift to more constructive patterns.

Once the problem has been refocused successfully, counselors help the family set goals for change, clarify the commitment of each family member, and determine whether family members will be seen together or whether separate sessions for individual members are necessary.

Middle Stage: Developing Emotional Awareness and Acceptance of Family Dysfunctional Patterns

In the middle stage, the counselor or therapist helps family members explore and analyze their dynamics to get an understanding of what is causing the problem. The counselor is usually more confrontational, and family members usually experience and acknowledge hurt, pain, shame, frustration, and loss. Anxiety increases with emotionally charged self-disclosures, and resistance arises in this middle stage.

In family counseling, as in individual counseling (see chap. 9), resistance is generally seen as a positive sign, one that either indicates the family is closer to confronting its problems or alerts counselors they are moving too quickly. Fear of change contributes to this resistance. Family members may resist counseling or therapy by remaining silent or by discussing only superficial matters. They may also question the counselor's ability to understand the problem, come late to sessions, or complain about the counseling fees. Other types of resistance common at this stage are instances when one family member refuses to speak to another or when one family member interrupts another who begins to reveal something meaningful. At times, the whole family might resist by withholding a family secret pertinent to the problem or by denying that the IP is improving (Solomon, 1969). Transference may also arise as family members project unresolved emotions onto the counselor. The counselor helps family members work through resistance and transference by being patient with the clients and by being sensitive and empathic with the anxiety or fear generated by disclosures.

Therapists with a psychodynamic orientation, like Framo (1982) and Bowen (1978), help parents see that some of their problems stem from unresolved conflicts in their families of origin. Role playing or psychodrama may be used. In psychodrama, for example, a parent may reenact an experience when, as a child, she was ridiculed by her parents.

Expression of grief is encouraged in this stage of therapy, when families have unresolved feelings about losses such as the death of a loved one, divorce, failure in school, loss of a job, or realization of loss of childhood (Brock & Barnard, 1988; Middleton-Moz & Dwinell, 1986). Shame is another pervasive, unresolved emotion common to dysfunctional families. Shame needs to be acknowledged and worked through as family members disclose secrets about themselves that they have hidden from others because of deep feelings of unworthiness. For example, a man who has professed only love for his mother may reveal long-standing resentments about her manipulation of him that he has felt ashamed to admit. Once he admits shame, he can begin to explore his feelings and move from self-hate to self-respect (Fossum & Mason, 1986). In his book *Taming Your Gremlin: A Guide to Enjoying Yourself,* Richard Carson (1983) presents a humorous and keenly perceptive view of how people can become aware of the self-defeating consequences of shame and learn to live more productively.

In this middle stage, the family begins to accept that relationships can change and that destructive alliances can be broken without undue loss of security. These acknowledgements lead to changes in family structure. Roles are less rigid, communication becomes more direct and constructive, and feedback to one another about new behaviors within the family is more authentic.

Last Stage: Learning How to Change the Family System

As family members understand and accept how they each have contributed to the origin and perpetuation of problems, they begin to see alternative ways of behaving and communicating. Needing less prompting from the therapist, they begin to intervene, to confront one another constructively, and to give one another feedback on more effective ways of interacting (Perez, 1979).

Counselors encourage family members to generalize these changes they have made during the counseling session to interactions at home. Counselors may assign homework to practice new behaviors. For example, a mother who has learned to declare in session her need for boundaries and her own space may be directed to take time off, go on a weekend retreat. Satir (1982) developed communication exercises to help families compare ineffective ways of communicating with effective ways. For example, two members may sit back-to-back and try, without success, to communicate authentically and then in gradual stages move to looking into each other's eyes and touching hands while communicating fully.

At this point, counselors can help the family become aware of resources in the community that can support their efforts to continue new patterns of behavior. For example, a single parent can be encouraged to join a group working on parenting skills.

Counselors can also help the family look ahead to upcoming transitions and changes that are likely to occur. Counselors can then help family members consider how to make use of their new attitudes and skills to cope with the anticipated changes.

Termination: Separating From Therapy

Most counselors believe that termination in family counseling is less difficult than in individual counseling (Goldenberg & Goldenberg, 1995). In successful family counseling, the family has learned to work as a unit to solve its own problems and to give members support. Family members have practiced working on communication skills and relationship issues during the sessions. Feeling less dependent on the counselor, they thus have fewer problems with termination than do individual clients.

In successful treatment, family members show signs that they are ready to terminate when they begin to solve family conflicts at home and when presenting complaints or symptoms are no longer present. Counselor and family members notice more independent activities, more constructive conflict, and better ways of resolving problems among family members.

Even so, the counselor needs to prepare the family for separation by allowing the last two sessions for the process of termination. A review of what has happened during counseling is helpful. The counselor can also arrange for a follow-up session with the family and convey that the members can return at any time if they feel the need for more help. The advantage of a well-thought-out termination is summed up as follows:

> If conducted over time and with sensitivity, it can help families and family members recognize their growth and development during treatment. It can also help families and their members recognize and accept their feelings, thoughts, behaviors, failures, and accomplishments. (Gladding, 1998, p. 109)

❧ MARRIAGE AND COUPLE COUNSELING THEORIES

Family counseling and marriage or couple counseling overlap considerably, particularly when couples start having children or when young couples are having difficulty disengaging appropriately from their extended families. Most practitioners who identify themselves primarily as family counselors thus include marriage and couple counseling with family therapy. Some of them indicate they will work with the marriage problem first if they think the marital discord is so severe that it would be impossible to work with the whole family. Some counselors also work with spouses first if they think the IP's problems are primarily a result of marital discord.

Those who specialize only in marriage and couple counseling, however, make certain distinctions between their type of counseling and family counseling. Many couples seeking help do not have children, are undecided about whether to have them, or have decided to remain childless. Other couples have older children who are not living at home and are not available for family counseling even if it seems advisable. They seek help because they are not happy with their relationship, rather than because they are having trouble with problem children. These couples may be having conflicts over gender roles, finances, infidelity, religious values, sexual disharmony, in-laws, retirement, alcoholism, careers, or other problems not related to children.

Some marriage and couple counselors work with premarital couples, cohabiting unmarried couples, or lesbian and gay couples. Some specialize in sex therapy.

Theories designed especially for couple counseling come predominantly from the social learning school, which emphasizes learning skills and educational information. Social learning counselors Liberman, Wheeler, DeVisser, Kuehnel, and Kuehnel (1980), Stuart (1980), Jacobson and Margolin (1979), and E. J. Thomas (1977) have developed specific approaches to working with couples. Therapist and couple assess the problem, decide on specific changes in behavior, and set specific goals. The couple is asked to collect data about their presenting problems, to explore the causes of the undesirable behaviors, and to consider what keeps them going despite negative consequences.

Stuart (1980) developed an 8-step model of couple counseling. Both partners of a couple independently fill out a Marital Precounseling Inventory to assess how they perceive their own general goals, their satisfactions with the marriage, the goal changes they desire, and their commitment to the marriage. Areas of agreement and disagreement, as well as actual responses, are used in setting goals and tasks during the sessions that follow. The counselor then persuades the partners that the best way to resolve their difficulties is to increase positive behaviors toward each other. Both partners specify what behaviors they want in their partner. They begin what Stuart calls "caring days," in which they carry out the request of the other partner to demonstrate caring behavior for each other. They are then taught to communicate honestly and constructively and to argue more productively. As skills of communication and decision making improve, the couple practice specific relationship skills in the therapy sessions. During the last stage, the counselor encourages the couple to practice the new skills and attitudes outside the sessions.

✎ CHANGING FAMILY AND MARRIAGE PATTERNS

Counselors and therapists need to be aware that family counseling theories and practices are generally based on the traditional American (White, middle-class) nuclear family. Such a model is no longer typical for most American families. In the traditional idealized model, a married couple raise their own biologically related children, the father acts as head of household and provider, and the mother is the family's homemaker and nurturer. Nowadays, a majority of children grow up in quite different family patterns. In the majority of families, both parents work outside the home; one-third of American children are raised by single parents (usually women); and many families are blended together from remarriages.

Dual-Career Families

In 1988, nearly 75% of women with school-age children were employed—two and one half times the rate in 1950 (Basow, 1992). The causes for this sharp increase are many: feminists' objections about traditional gender roles (see chap. 14), rising divorce rates, rising costs, and lower ratio of income for most wage earners (Hershenson, Power, & Waldo, 1996).

As a result, women are spending less time with their children, and men are expected to spend more time in child caretaking (Atwood, 1992c). In addition to job stress for both parents, stress occurs at home. Men, as well as women, experience stress in dual-career families, but women's stress is greater because of expectations that women should continue to handle more domestic responsibilities than men (Basow, 1992). Conflicts in managing a dual role of homemaker and out-of-home worker have made it especially difficult for women to meet their own needs (Zunker, 1994).

With the increase in dual-career families, more than 2 million schoolchildren ages 6 to 13 are *self-care (latch key)* children, left to themselves after school with little or no supervision (Cole & Rodman, 1987). The professional literature indicates that those children whose mothers work outside the home do not, as a rule, become emotionally disturbed as long as they have had adequate day care and if parents are caring and responsive when they and their children are together (Shaffer, 1993). Shaffer (1993) warns, however, that the research focuses primarily on the ideal norm of the two-parent, middle-class family.

Family counselors must be alert to parents' changing gender roles and to the stresses resulting from lack of adequate and affordable child care. They must also be aware that family conflicts are exacerbated because the marketplace and communities have not made allowances for dual-career families. Hoffman (1990) and Zucal (1992) urge that family therapists pay attention to Carol Gilligan's views about the differences in women's and men's development (see chap. 4) to become more "gender sensitive" in their counseling approaches when family conflicts arise.

Single-Parent Families

Single parents head about one-third of all families—more than double the number in 1970 (Gladding, 1998). Divorce is by far the leading reason for one-parent families (70%), followed by death of a spouse (14%) and by never-married women (10%) (Atwood, 1992c); 90% of these families are headed by women. Major sources of stress for single mothers are low income, disapproval from society, and lack of a co-parent to help with domestic chores, discipline, and child welfare in general (Basow, 1992).

Single-parent homes differ from two-parent homes: Single parents try to assume the roles of both parents, financial worries are usually worse, children may be expected to assume more responsibilities, and child care services are more necessary (Baruth & Burggraf, 1991).

Walters (1988) says that therapists must help single parents see their problems more as a family issue than as a personal one. The counselor or therapist can help single parents learn to reconstruct their families so that all members, to the extent of their abilities, are involved in overall family functioning.

Atwood (1992c) proposes using a cognitive-behavioral family systems approach to help single parents resolve problems with their children. In this approach, the counselor teaches behavior management skills to single parents whereby children are rewarded for completing tasks and for taking care of some of their own needs. Single parents are also helped to schedule time in ways that provide nurturing to their children while still maintaining appropriate roles and boundaries. "Part of the family counselor role is to teach the family good child-rearing practices and to help them learn age-appropriate behaviors" (Atwood, 1992c, p. 204).

Attention is given as well to helping single parents work through feelings of abandonment, develop social support groups, and when possible, work toward and maintain civil and respectful contact with former spouses for the benefit of the child or children.

Remarried (Blended) Families

Remarried or blended families are formed when two previously married individuals with children marry each other. Between 40% and 50% of recent marriages will end in divorce, with 80% of men and 75% of women remarrying within a few years. These figures show that increasing numbers of families will be reconstituted into ones in which multiple parents, stepparents, multiple grandparents, and stepsiblings interact (Nystul, 1993; Shaffer, 1993). Because mothers usually gain custody of children, the stepfamily in which the children live with their mother and her second husband is most common.

Betty Carter (1988), a well-known family therapist who is discussed later, notes the new family patterns that have arisen from complex relationships and roles in remarried families. Role conflicts often occur between the realigned members. Confusion arises over a stepparent's role as disciplinarian. Remarried families may exclude a biological parent or children not living in the new household.

In her counseling model for remarried families, Carter (1988) recommends helping the family develop a flexible system in which it forms permeable boundaries between all family members, including those who do not live together.

❧ CHILD ABUSE AND NEGLECT

The four major types of child abuse are (a) physical or bodily injury, (b) emotional or psychological damage, (c) sexual abuse, and (d) neglect of physical and emotional needs of the child (S. L. Brown, 1991; Thompson & Rudolph, 1992). Children are often victims of multiple abuse. Sexual abuse, which involves molestation, fondling, or penetration, generally carries with it emotional abuse and physical abuse. Physical abuse, besides inflicting physical injuries, causes emotional damage. Another form of abuse—verbal assaults, threats, and terrorizing of children—also causes emotional damage to children, as well as indirect, internalized, physical harm.

Neglected children suffer from feelings of abandonment; persistent neglect leads to emotional disorders. With physical neglect, parents do not provide adequate supervision of children or safe conditions in the home, or they fail to provide nourishing food or adequate clothing or medical care. Emotional neglect includes parents' withdrawing loving contact with the child, ignoring or dismissing the child's feelings, and preventing the child from developing emotional boundaries.

Incidence of Abuse

Almost 3 million cases of child abuse and neglect were reported in 1992, and 1,261 children died as a result, according to the National Committee for the Prevention of Child Abuse. The number of cases increased by 8% from the previous year. Most instances of child abuse, however, go unreported. The majority of abused children are under 3 years of age (Sroufe, Cooper, & DeHart, 1992).

Both male and female parents abuse children physically, emotionally, and through neglect. Sexual abuse occurs more frequently in father-daughter or stepfather-stepdaughter relationships than in any other family relationship. In a survey, Russell (1986) found that 38% of women in his sample of 930 reported being sexually abused before 18 years of age. Most female abuse happens in the family; male abuse is more likely outside the family.

On a more optimistic note, Shaffer (1993) points out that many abused or neglected children develop a great deal of resiliency, especially if a supportive, secure relationship is established with a nonabusive parent, grandparent, or other adult in the family. Counselors, then, when working with abused children, should look for and cultivate the children's positive strengths.

Characteristics of Families in Which Abuse Occurs

Abusers in a family tend to dominate the family and often are substance abusers, have poor relationships outside the family, and often have been abused themselves (S. L. Brown, 1991; Sroufe et al., 1992). There are numerous exceptions. Many who are abusive to spouse and children are not substance abusers, and many abusers seemingly have good relationships outside the home.

Families in which abuse occurs usually have a multitude of stressors: financial problems, lack of jobs, family breakups. Boundaries are unclear or unspecified, and communication is woefully inadequate, with secrecy predominant (S. L. Brown, 1991).

Effects of Abuse

If counseling interventions for abused children and their families are not provided, the children can develop serious emotional disorders that carry into adulthood. These disorders include depression and anxiety, codependency, eating disorders, learning disorders, multiple personalities, and sexual or drug addictions (S. L. Brown, 1991; Shaffer, 1993). Abused children tend to be either aggressive or overly withdrawn with other children, which results in their being rejected by their peers. Posttraumatic stress disorder, including nightmares and flashbacks, often develops and continues when they become adults. The likelihood is also strong that abused children, when they grow up, will abuse their children. Emotionally abused children also maintain a low self-image and gravitate to those who confirm their feelings of worthlessness (Cooney, 1991).

Requirement to Report Child Abuse

In all 50 states, family counselors, mental health workers, teachers, principals, and any other professional person working with children must report evidence of child abuse to child protection agencies. When clients reveal that child abuse is happening to them or to others, the counselor has a legal responsibility to inform child protection services, which can take steps to prevent further abuse of the child (see chap. 3).

Counseling Families with Abuse

Regarding counseling families in which parents have been shown to be abusive, S. L. Brown (1991) emphasizes that treatment must first focus on individual family members. Brown is adamant about the necessity of removing the abused child from the family home. During this time, the counselor works individually with each member of the family until the counselor is fairly certain that abuse will not recur when the child returns to the family or that abuse will not be directed toward other children in the family. Brown further recommends that, after placement in foster homes, children should receive counseling to help process the traumatic experiences and work through shame, guilt, anger, or grief.

Rencken's (1989) comments regarding family dynamics and intervention strategies for sexually abused children, abusers, and their families can be generalized to working with victims of all kinds of abuse. He describes three patterns of boundary breakdowns in families in which sexual abuse occurs. The first is the possessive father who considers his spouse and children to be possessions and does not differentiate among them. He views his daughter in the same way as a wife. Second is the immature, irresponsible father, who becomes like one of the children. Third is the child who is pushed into becoming a pseudo-adult; the child is described as "parentified" (Rencken, 1989, p. 20) when the child assumes the substitute mother role, for example, which the mother has abdicated.

In treating families in which abuse occurs, Rencken works with what he terms three dyads in the following order: mother-child, husband-wife, and father-child. He then works to shift the dyad into a triad of child-mother-father. Finally, he helps clients view their family unit as a whole.

⟿ CRITICISMS OF FAMILY SYSTEMS THEORY

The major criticism of family systems theory comes from therapists concerned that the systems theory has neglected to consider the impact of the social system on the family. Minuchin was a significant exception. His early work with juvenile delinquents in inner-city ghettos was groundbreaking. In retrospect, family therapists, including

Minuchin, however, admit that his method of taking youths out of the slums and treating them away from the community mostly failed. After the boys returned to their families and communities, recidivism rates were high. "The overall recidivism rate . . . was high . . . because the moment those kids came back to Harlem, they were sucked into the allure of the streets and the chaotic drama of their families" (Markowitz, 1997, p. 8).

Psychiatrist and family therapist Ramon Rojano, director of DSHS in Hartford, Connecticut, has expanded Minuchin's ideas and family therapy into what he calls *community family therapy* (Markovitz, 1997). Working with predominantly ethnic families, he emphasizes the value of families working things out within their cultural neighborhoods and communities. He believes that family therapists should focus on helping clients and their families become empowered within their communities. Family therapists help clients use resources in the community, such as schools, public assistance agencies, and employment offices. Some clients are encouraged to take leadership training to enable them to confront inadequacies and injustices in their communities in such matters as inadequate school programs or abuse of police power. Others are encouraged to enroll in job-training programs (Markowitz, 1997).

In a similar vein, Allen Ivey and his colleagues (Ivey & Ivey, 1999; Ivey, Ivey, & Simek-Morgan, 1997) also discourage the practice of the traditional therapeutic approach of pressuring the client to gain autonomy and separation from family influences. They instead encourage counselors to help multicultural clients gain new ways to interact with their families and their communities (see chaps. 4 and 14).

Feminist therapists are concerned that problems that arise from gender stereotyping (see chaps. 4, 14, and 19) are not being given sufficient attention in family systems therapy. They believe that family therapists tend to use an outdated model of the overinvolved, overnurturant mother and the distant, uninvolved father as the accepted cultural pattern. By doing so, the family system is perceived as not being connected to the larger social system. Thus, family therapists, they say, do not pay sufficient attention to the inferior power status of women, thereby perpetuating the inequality of women in our culture (Zucal, 1992). Zucal (1992) believes that if family therapists are aware of these socialized gender differences, then they will be less likely to blame either parent for perpetuating the family problem.

Marianne Walters, Betty Carter, Peggy Papp, and Olga Silverstein, members of the Women's Project in Family Therapy, are family therapists who also have taken into account socialized gender differences. The primary role of the Women's Project over the past 20 years has been to "persuade the field to move beyond the interior of the family to incorporate social and cultural issues into main stream clinical thinking" (Simon, 1997, p. 60).

Known as the "Fearless Foursome" (Simon, 1997, p. 60), the women got together at a time when family therapies were run primarily by men. These women criticized the dominant male perspectives promoted by Bateson, Haley, Bowen, and Minuchin, claiming that the men's views are "more of the same old sexism done up in fancy terminology. . . . Family therapists were too often guilty of perpetuating the same cultural myths about men and women that got families in trouble in the first place" (Simon, 1997, p. 60). In their landmark book *The Invisible Web* (1988), Walters, Carter, Papp, and Silverstein claim their feminist perspectives have yet to make significant changes in mainstream family therapy.

> With regard to these changes in the family, and in women's roles in the family, family therapy theory lags behind the culture as a whole. It is now imperative that there be new approaches in family therapy built on new assumptions about what constitutes a viable family. (p. 15)

In their work with families, Walters, Carter, Papp, and Silverstein focus on issues other than blaming parents, especially the mothers, for the family dysfunction. They concentrate instead on helping family members improve relations with each other and with their extended family, such as the grandparents, and on helping family members work on forming and maintaining positive connections, rather than trying to encourage them to become separate and autonomous (see also chap. 19).

❧ RESEARCH IN FAMILY AND MARRIAGE COUNSELING AND THERAPY

Gurman, Kniskern, and Pinsof (1986) and Bednar, Burlingame, and Masters (1988) critiqued research reviews on family systems and on behavioral marital and family therapy (BMFT). Here is a summary of these reviews:

- Regardless of approach, family therapy is more effective than none at all.
- Success rates in marital therapy (61%) and family therapy (73%) are comparable to those of individual therapy.
- When both parents are involved, outcomes tend to be more positive.
- The therapist's degree of relationship skills shows a relatively high correlation with effective outcomes.
- Both behavioral and nonbehavioral approaches have been shown to be equally effective.
- Brief family counseling and therapy has proved to be as effective as long-term family therapy.

In a review of the literature, White and Allers (1994) note a renewed interest in play therapy (PT) for abused children. Although strongly advocating the value of PT, they found inconsistencies in the research regarding the definition of abuse, the definition of play therapy, the play therapist's training, and the effectiveness of play therapies. They suggest that more consistent research studies and outcomes are necessary before any definite therapeutic system can be recommended.

❧ SUMMARY

Family therapy has flourished in the mental health field since the 1960s when psychiatrists and social workers first perceived the family as a social unit, or *family system*. Family systems therapists focus on the family as a whole, rather than on an individual identified patient (IP). As a natural social system, the family is composed of alliances, sets of rules, assigned roles for each family member, and prescribed modes of communication.

Because the family is a social unit, when one family member develops problems, the symptoms represent dysfunctions among all family members. Dysfunctional families are enmeshed with or disengaged from one another, cannot communicate directly and authentically, and form alliances among themselves when conflicts arise. Therapists help family members learn to communicate directly and to respect one another's boundaries and privacy.

Counselors who specialize in marriage and couple counseling work with married or unmarried couples with or without children, lesbian or gay couples, and those wanting premarital counseling.

Changing family patterns have brought about new considerations for family counselors and therapists. The traditional family pattern, with father as breadwinner and mother as caregiver of their biologically related children, is no longer predominant. In the majority of homes now, both parents work, and about one-third of American families are led by a single parent (mostly women) or are composed of remarried families with multiple parents, stepparents, and stepsiblings.

Child abuse includes neglect and physical, emotional, and sexual abuse. Family counselors tend to treat the abused child first and then the member of the family who committed the abuse separately before they treat the family together as a unit. Family sessions include issues about boundaries, assuming responsibility for changing behavior, developing support systems, and working to reunify the family.

Critics of family systems theory believe that theorists do not consider the influence of social forces in the family. Feminists object that the effects of gender cultural stereotyping on family roles is ignored while multicultural counselors believe that, for ethnic families, therapy should focus on empowering family members within the community system.

❧ PROJECTS AND ACTIVITIES

1. Interview some counselors who specialize in family counseling. Compare their theoretical backgrounds and the techniques each prefers to use.
2. Practice the technique called *sculpting*, as used by Virginia Satir. Using other classmates to act roles of a family, pose the family to demonstrate its pattern of relating (see Figure 10.1).
3. Interview counselors and social workers in nearby school districts. Find out what family services are offered to parents and students.

If none exist, ask how families with problems receive help.
4. Role-play a telephone conversation in which a parent calls to get counseling for an adolescent daughter with "problems." During the conversation, it becomes obvious to you that the whole family needs counseling. How would you make this clear to the parent?
5. Consider the pros and cons of using a family systems approach with a single-parent family or with a blended family.

⊰⊱ REFERENCES

Alexander, J. F., & Parsons, B. V. (1982). *Functional family therapy.* Pacific Grove, CA: Brooks/Cole.

Atwood, J. D. (Ed.). (1992a). *Family therapy: A systemic-behavioral approach.* Chicago: Nelson-Hall.

Atwood, J. D. (1992b). The field today. In J. D. Atwood (Ed.), *Family therapy: A systemic-behavioral approach* (pp. 29–58). Chicago: Nelson-Hall.

Atwood, J. D. (1992c). A system-behavioral approach to counseling the single-parent family. In J. D. Atwood (Ed.), *Family therapy: A systemic-behavioral approach* (pp. 191–205). Chicago: Nelson-Hall.

Baruth, L. G., & Burggraf, M. Z. (1991). Counseling single-parent families. In J. Carlson & J. Lewis (Eds.), *Family counseling: Strategies and issues* (pp. 175–188). Denver, CO: Love.

Basow, S. (1992). *Gender stereotypes and roles* (3rd ed.). Pacific Grove, CA: Brooks/Cole.

Beck, A. (1976). *Cognitive therapy and the emotional disorders.* New York: International Universities Press.

Becvar, D. S., & Becvar, R. J. (1986). *Family therapy: A systemic integration.* Boston: Allyn & Bacon.

Bednar, R. L., Burlingame, G. M., & Masters, K. S. (1988). Systems of family treatment: Substance or semantics? *Annual Review of Psychology, 39,* 401–434.

Bowen, M. (1978). *Family therapy in clinical practice.* New York: Jason Aronson.

Brock, G. W., & Barnard, C. P. (1988). *Procedures in family therapy.* Boston: Allyn & Bacon.

Brown, J. H., & Christensen, D. N. (1986). *Family therapy: Theory and practice.* Monterey, CA: Brooks/Cole.

Brown, S. L. (1991). *Counseling victims of violence.* Alexandria, VA: American Association for Counseling Development.

Carson, R. D. (1983). *Taming your gremlin: A guide to enjoying yourself.* New York: Harper & Row.

Carter, B. (1988). Remarried families: Creating a new paradigm. In M. Walters, B. Carter, P. Papp, & O. Silverstein (Eds.), *The invisible web: Gender patterns in family relationships* (pp. 333–368). New York: Guilford Press.

Carter, B., & McGoldrick, M. (1988). Overview: The changing family life cycle: A framework for family therapy. In B. Carter & M. McGoldrick (Eds.), *The changing family life cycle* (2nd ed., pp. 3–28). New York: Gardner Press.

Christensen, O. C. (1975). Family education: A model for consultation. In D. Dinkmeyer & J. Carlson (Eds.), *Consultation: A book of readings* (pp. 226–238). New York: John Wiley.

Colapinto, J. (1991). Structural family therapy. In A. M. Horne & J. L. Passmore (Eds.), *Family counseling and therapy* (2nd ed., pp. 77–103). Itasca, IL: F. E. Peacock.

Cole, C., & Rodman, H. (1987). When school-age children care for themselves: Issues for family life educators and parents. *Family Relations, 26,* 92–96.

Cooney, J. (1991). Counseling and child abuse: A developmental perspective. In J. Carlson & J. Lewis (Eds.), *Family counseling: Strategies and issues* (pp. 225–242). Denver, CO: Love.

Dinkmeyer, D., Jr., & Dinkmeyer, D., Sr. (1991). *Adlerian family therapy.* In A. M. Horne & J. L. Passmore (Eds.), *Family counseling and therapy* (2nd ed., pp. 383–402). Itasca, IL: F. E. Peacock.

Dinkmeyer, D., & McKay, G. D. (1976). *Systematic training for effective parenting.* Circle Pines, MN: American Guidance Services.

Dreikurs, R. (1968). *Psychology in the classroom.* New York: Harper & Row.

Dreikurs, R., Lowe, R., Sonstegard, M., & Corsini, R. J. (Eds.). (1959). *Adlerian family counseling: A manual for counseling centers.* Eugene: University of Oregon.

Ellis, A. (1982). Rational-emotive family therapy. In A. M. Horne & M. M. Ohlsen (Eds.), *Family counseling and therapy* (pp. 302–328). Itasca, IL: F. E. Peacock.

Ellis, A. (1991). Rational-emotive family therapy. In A. M. Horne & J. L. Passmore (Eds.), *Family counseling and therapy* (2nd ed., pp. 403–434). Itasca, IL: F. E. Peacock.

Fenell, D. L., & Weinhold, B. K. (1989). *Counseling families: An introduction to marriage and family therapy.* Denver, CO: Love.

Fine, M. J. (1980). The parent education movement: An introduction. In M. J. Fine (Ed.), *Handbook on parent therapy* (pp. 3–26). New York: Academic Press.

Foley, V. D. (1989). Family therapy. In R. J. Corsini & D. Wedding (Eds.), *Current psychotherapies* (4th ed., pp. 455–500). Itasca, IL: F. E. Peacock.

Fossum, M. A., & Mason, J. J. (1986). *Facing shame: Families in recovery.* New York: Norton.

Framo, J. L. (1982). *Explorations in marital and family therapy.* New York: Springer.

Gladding, S. T. (1997). *Community and agency counseling.* Upper Saddle River, NJ: Merrill/Prentice Hall.

Gladding, S. T. (1998). *Family therapy: History, theory, and practice* (2nd ed.). Upper Saddle River, NJ: Merrill/Prentice Hall.

Goldenberg, I., & Goldenberg, H. (1991). *Family therapy: An overview* (3rd ed.). Pacific Grove, CA: Brooks/Cole.

Goldenberg, I., & Goldenberg, H. (1995). Family therapy. In R. J. Corsini & Wedding, D. (Eds.), *Current psychotherapies* (5th ed., pp. 356–398). Itasca, IL: F. E. Peacock.

Gurman, A. S., Kniskern, D. P., & Pinsof, W. M. (1986). Research on marital and family therapies. In S. L. Garfield & A. E. Bergin (Eds.), *Handbook of psychotherapy and behavior change: An empirical analysis* (3rd ed., pp. 565–624). New York: John Wiley.

Haley, J. (1987). *Problem-solving therapy* (2nd ed.). San Francisco: Jossey-Bass.

Hershenson, D. B., Power, P. W., & Waldo, M. (1996). *Community counseling: Contemporary theory and practice.* Boston: Allyn & Bacon.

Hoffman, L. (1990). Constructing realities: An art of tenses. *Family Process, 29,* 1–12.

Horne, A. M. (1991). Social learning family therapy. In A. M. Horne & J. L. Passmore (Eds.), *Family counseling and therapy* (2nd ed., pp. 463–496). Itasca, IL: F. E. Peacock.

Ivey, A. E., & Ivey, M. B. (1999). *Intentional interviewing and counseling: Facilitating client development in a multicultural society* (4th ed.). Pacific Grove, CA: Brooks/Cole.

Ivey, A. E., Ivey, M. B., & Simek-Morgan, L. C. (1997). *Counseling and psychotherapy: A multicultural perspective* (4th ed.). Boston: Allyn & Bacon.

Jacobson, N., & Margolin, G. (1979). *Marital therapy.* New York: Brunner/Mazel.

L'Abate, L., Ganahl, G., & Hansen, J. C. (1986). *Methods of family therapy.* Upper Saddle River, NJ: Prentice Hall.

Liberman, R. P., Wheeler, E. G., DeVisser, L. A. J. M., Kuehnel, J., & Kuehnel, T. (1980). *Handbook of marital therapy: A positive approach to helping troubled relationships.* New York: Plenum.

Lowe, R. N. (1982). Adlerian/Dreikursian family counseling. In A. M. Horne & M. M. Ohlsen (Eds.), *Family counseling and therapy* (pp. 329–359). Itasca, IL: F. E. Peacock.

Lynn, S., & Garske, J. (1985). *Contemporary psychotherapies.* New York: Macmillan.

Madanes, C. (1981). *Strategic family therapy.* San Francisco: Jossey-Bass.

Markowitz, L. (1997). Ramon Rojano won't take no for an answer. *Family Therapy Networker, 21,* 24–35.

Meichenbaum, D. (1985). Cognitive-behavioral therapies. In S. J. Lynn & J. P. Garske (Eds.), *Contemporary psychotherapies: Models and methods* (pp. 261–286). New York: Macmillan.

Middleton-Moz, J., & Dwinell, L. (1986). *After the tears.* Pompano Beach, FL: Health Communications.

Minuchin, S., Lee, W., & Simon, G. M. (1996). *Mastering family therapy: Journeys of growth and transformation.* New York: John Wiley.

Minuchin, S. T. (1974). *Families and family therapy.* Cambridge, MA: Harvard University Press.

Mosak, H. H. (1995). Adlerian psychotherapy. In R. J. Corsini & D. Wedding (Eds.), *Current psychotherapies* (5th ed., pp. 51–94). Itasca, IL: F. E. Peacock.

Nystul, M. S. (1993). *The art and science of counseling and psychotherapy.* Upper Saddle River, NJ: Merrill/Prentice Hall.

Papero, D. V. (1991). The Bowen theory. In A. H. Horne & J. L. Passmore (Eds.), *Family counseling and therapy* (2nd ed., pp. 47–76). Itasca, IL: F. E. Peacock.

Passmore, J. L., & Horne, A. M. (1991). Introduction. In A. M. Horne & J. L. Passmore (Eds.), *Family counseling and therapy* (2nd ed., pp. 1–12). Itasca, IL: F. E. Peacock.

Patterson, G. R. (1971). *Families: Application of social learning to family life.* Champaign, IL: Research Press.

Perez, J. F. (1979). *Family counseling: Theory and practice.* New York: Van Nostrand Reinhold.

Ratican, K. L. (1992). Sexual abuse survivors: Identifying symptoms and special treatment considerations. *Journal of Counseling & Development, 71,* 33–38.

Rencken, R. H. (1989). *Intervention strategies for sexual abuse.* Alexandria, VA: American Association for Counseling Development.

Roberts, E. (1992). The role of fun in family therapy. In J. D. Atwood (Ed.), *Family therapy: A systemic behavioral approach* (pp. 70–87). Chicago: Nelson-Hall.

Russell, D. E. (1986). *The secret trauma.* New York: Basic Books.

Satir, V. M. (1967). *Conjoint family therapy.* Palo Alto, CA: Science & Behavior Books.

Satir, V. M. (1972). *Peoplemaking.* Palo Alto, CA: Science & Behavior Books.

Satir, V. M. (1982). The therapist and family therapy: Process model. In A. M. Horne & M. M. Ohlsen (Eds.), *Family counseling and therapy* (pp. 12–42). Itasca, IL: F. E. Peacock.

Satir, V. M., & Bitter, J. M. (1991). The therapist and family therapy: Satir's human validation process model. In A. M. Horne & J. L. Passmore (Eds.), *Family counseling and therapy* (2nd ed., pp. 13–46). Itasca, IL: F. E. Peacock.

Schilson, E. A. (1991). Strategic therapy. In A. M. Horne & J. L. Passmore (Eds.), *Family counseling and therapy* (2nd ed., pp. 141–178). Itasca, IL: F. E. Peacock.

Shaffer, D. R. (1993). *Developmental psychology: Childhood and adolescence* (3rd ed.). Pacific Grove, CA: Brooks/Cole.

Sherman, R., & Dinkmeyer, D. (1987). *Systems of family therapy: An Adlerian integration.* New York: Brunner/Mazel.

Simon, R. (1997). Fearless foursome. *Family Therapy Networker, 21,* 58–68.

Singleton, G. (1982). Bowen family systems theory. In A. M. Horne & M. M. Ohlsen (Eds.), *Family counseling and therapy* (pp. 75–111). Itasca, IL: F. E. Peacock.

Skynner, A. C. R. (1981). An open-systems group analytic approach to family therapy. In A. S. Gurman & D. P. Kniskern (Eds.), *Handbook of family therapy* (pp. 39–84). New York: Brunner/Mazel.

Solomon, M. (1969). Family therapy dropouts: Resistance to change. *Canadian Psychiatric Association Journal, 14,* 22–23.

Sroufe, L. A., Cooper, R. G., & DeHart, G. B. (1992). *Child development: Its nature and course* (2nd ed.). New York: McGraw-Hill.

Stuart, R. B. (1980). *Helping couples change: A social learning approach to marital therapy.* New York: Guilford Press.

Sweeney, T. (1989). *Adlerian counseling: A practical approach for a new decade* (3rd ed.). Muncie, IN: Accelerated Development.

Thomas, E. J. (1977). *Marital communication and decision making: Analysis, assessment, and change.* New York: Free Press.

Thomas, M. B. (1992). *An introduction to marital and family therapy: Counseling toward healthier family systems across the life span.* New York: Macmillan.

Thompson, C. L., & Rudolph, L. B. (1992). *Counseling children* (3rd ed.). Pacific Grove, CA: Brooks/Cole.

von Bertalanffy, L. (1974). General systems theory and psychiatry. In S. Aristi (Ed.), *American handbook of psychiatry* (Vol. 1, pp. 1095–1117). New York: Brace Books.

Walters, M. (1988). Single-parent, female-headed households. In M. Walters, B. Carter, P. Papp, & O. Silverstein (Eds.), *The invisible web: Gender patterns in family relationships* (pp. 289–332). New York: Guilford Press.

Walters, M., Carter, B., Papp, O., & Silverstein, O. (Eds.). (1988). *The invisible web: Gender patterns in family relationships.* New York: Guilford Press.

Weeks, G. R., & L'Abate, L. (1982). *Paradoxical psychotherapy: Theory and practice with individuals, couples, and families.* New York: Brunner/Mazel.

White, J., & Allers, C. T. (1994). Play therapy with abused children: A review of the literature. *Journal of Counseling & Development, 72,* 390–394.

Zucal, B. (1992). Gender issues in couples therapy. In J. D. Atwood (Ed.), *Family therapy: A systemic behavioral approach* (pp. 59–69). Chicago: Nelson-Hall.

Zunker, V. G. (1994). *Career counseling: Applied concepts of life planning* (4th ed.). Pacific Grove, CA: Brooks/Cole.

11   Group Counseling

Group counseling became popular in the 1960s when counselors began to realize that individuals who were having problems in their relationships could benefit from sharing their concerns and resolving their problems with others having similar problems. The definition of *group counseling* by George Gazda (1978), one pioneer in group counseling, remains one of the clearest explanations of the process:

> Group work refers to the dynamic interaction between collections of individuals for prevention or remediation of difficulties or for the enhancement of personal growth/enrichment through the interaction of those who meet together for a commonly agreed-on purpose and at prearranged times. (p. 260)

Corey and Corey (1992) point out:

> The broad purpose of a therapeutic group is to increase people's knowledge of themselves and others, help them clarify the changes they most want to make in their life, and give them some of the tools necessary to make these desired changes. (p. 9)

Group counseling can be useful to persons who are either shy or aggressive in their interpersonal interactions, anxious or uncomfortable in groups, or unduly resistant or overconforming to social expectations. They may be having difficulty making or keeping friends, or they may be experiencing friction with peers, parents, faculty, or bosses. Special groups who can benefit from group counseling include abused women, adult children of alcoholics, and men needing to learn to control their anger (Corey & Corey, 1992).

Group counseling is inappropriate and inadvisable for individuals experiencing personal or interpersonal conflicts too private to share in a group; it is also unsuitable for those with strong fears about social interactions, for those who might find a group experience traumatic, or for those with low impulse control who might constantly disrupt group interactions (Burlingame & Fuhriman, 1990; Gladding, 1995; Nystul, 1993). In these cases, individual counseling may be more suitable until the individuals feel more confident or more in control of themselves.

When clients' problems relate to interpersonal awkwardness, insecurities, or conflicts, group counseling has the advantage of giving members an opportunity to work out their problems in a structured social setting. In this setting, they can experiment with and practice new behaviors and receive support for their efforts and feedback from other group members and the counselor. Each member becomes, or is made, aware of the feelings and experiences of other persons (Nystul, 1993). Each has a chance to help others in the group improve social interactions. Counselors can both observe clients interact with other group members, as well as interact themselves with each group member (Corey, 1995).

Another value unique to group therapy and counseling is that individuals often experience feelings of isolation as they suffer pain, despair, and/or guilt, even if they share with an understanding counselor or therapist. Expressing painful emotions in a supportive group among those who have experienced similar pain and traumas removes feelings of isolation an individual otherwise suffers and, moreover, validates one's trauma as a communal experience, thus relieving the overwhelming emotional burden carried by lone individuals.

Working psychotherapeutically with depressed males, Terence Real (1997) emphasizes that groups provide significant support for participants. When ready, a volunteer goes to the center of the group circle, where he sits alongside the therapist. Here, in the presence of others, he delves into his deepest fears, conflicts, rage, pain. In one example, Real asks a man who enters the circle for the first time how he feels being surrounded by so many others. The man responds:

> "Well, I'm nervous, believe me. But I also feel buoyed up. *Like, I feel their energy, man,*" he clowns. Some men laugh. "No really, though," he continues, "like floating in the ocean."
>
> "It's called support," I say.
>
> "Well, I like it," he says. (p. 215)

Groups have some disadvantages. Clients receive less direct attention from counselors who must focus on group concerns and group interactions. Some clients may find it difficult to develop the trust in other group members that is necessary for constructive self-disclosure. They may experience direct or subtle pressure to conform to group norms. If the leadership is weak, group members may experience psychological distress when they reveal more than they are ready to or when they are confronted inappropriately by other group members (Corey, 1995).

Groups differ in purposes, goals, and intensity, depending on the severity of the clients' problems or the degree of the clients' dysfunctions. In group counseling literature, these various types of group work are described as falling along a continuum (Gazda, 1989). *Growth groups,* designed for persons who feel fairly satisfactory but want more meaning in life, are at one end of the continuum. *Group counseling,* in the middle of the continuum, serves persons who are not living as effectively as they could, who have learned maladaptive ways of interacting with others, or who have negative views of themselves but are able to manage their lives adequately. *Group psychotherapy,* at the other end of the continuum, includes persons who are more emotionally disturbed and who require intensive remedial work. The goals of *growth groups* are to educate and train persons in skills and attitudes; the goals of *group counseling* are to help persons solve problems, develop self-awareness, and improve interpersonal relations. The goal of *group psychotherapy* is remedial work. In a similar way, Corey (1995) differentiates between group counseling and group therapy: "Whereas counseling groups focus on growth, development, enhancement, prevention, self-awareness and releasing blocks to growth, therapy groups typically focus on remediation, treatment, and personality reconstruction" (p. 18).

As with individual counseling and psychotherapy, some overlap exists between group counseling and psychotherapy. Thus, at times, the terms *group counseling* and *group psychotherapy* are used interchangeably by theorists and practitioners (Vander Kolk, 1985).

This chapter focuses on *group counseling* and *group psychotherapy. Growth groups,* which emphasize specific social skill training (*structured* groups), interpersonal interactions (*sensitivity training* or *T*-groups), and personal awareness (*personal growth* and *encounter* groups), are discussed in the section "Psychological Education Activities" in chapter 7 and in the counseling practice chapters in part 4.

✦ ETHICAL GUIDELINES WITH GROUPS

Ethical guidelines specific to group counseling have been developed by the Association for Specialists in Group Work (ASGW, 1989) and the American Psychological Association (APA, 1973). These guidelines are consistent with the American Counseling Association (ACA) code of ethics for individual and group counseling (1995).

Counselors must face different ethical considerations with groups than with individuals. Some of the more important ethical considerations are screening for appropriateness for group counseling, allowing freedom to leave the group, monitoring confidentiality among group members, and guarding against group members manipulating or abusing each other (Corey, Corey, & Callanan, 1993).

Screening of Group Members

Group counselors have an ethical responsibility to screen clients as to their suitability for the group. If, in a counselor's judgment, an individual is not psychologically ready for the group or has purposes different from those of the group, the counselor should let the individual know and refer him or her to individual counseling or to a more appropriate group. Otherwise, the choice of joining a group should ultimately rest with the client on a voluntary basis (Corey, 1995).

Voluntary Participation and Freedom to Leave the Group

Group counseling is most effective when members voluntarily enter a group and have the freedom to leave it (Carroll & Wiggins, 1997; Corey, 1995). According to the ASGW Code of Ethics (1989), members of a voluntary group "have the right to exit a group; but it is important they be made aware of the importance of informing the counselor and the group members prior to deciding to leave" (Section 5.d). The code recommends that counselors and the group discuss with exiting members the advantages of remaining with the group and encourage them to give their reasons for wanting to leave.

Like most ethical questions, the issue is whether individual or group rights take precedence. One can argue that a leader has no way of forcing a member to explain why he or she wants to leave the group. Moreover, for a member who has never asserted him- or herself before, it may be a sign of newly found strength to leave a group suddenly without explanation. Furthermore, such a disruption allows the group to tussle with an actual problem that occurred within the group. For example, when such an incident happened in a group I was leading in a university setting, the members contemplated sending angry letters to the young man who abandoned the group. After working through their feelings and discussing group and individual rights, group members decided to send him cards thanking him for his contributions, telling him they missed him, and letting him know he was welcome back if he so chose. Although he did not return, he did send the group a letter thanking them for understanding him. He explained that he had learned to assert his needs for the first time in this group, which gave him the courage to break away.

Confidentiality

Concerns about whether group members will hold in confidence self-disclosures and group interactions are expressed frequently in the literature (Corey, 1995; Forester-Miller & Rubenstein, 1992; Gladding, 1995). If counselors clarify the group's responsibilities regarding confidentiality and give reasons for its importance, problems do not often arise (Corey et al., 1993). Because members tend to want to share their group experience with close friends or loved ones outside the group, Corey and Corey (1992) suggest that they not share who is in the group or reveal what other members have brought up. Confidentiality poses more problems in those educational institutions or agencies where members know one another and share mutual associates and friends (Corey & Corey, 1992). Confidentiality and rights of privacy require that counselors get written consent from each member if group sessions are to be recorded or if research based on the group experience is being conducted (Gazda, 1989).

Coercion and Psychological Risks

Attempts by a group counselor or group members to persuade an individual member to behave in a manner the group thinks is desirable is a greater potential problem in groups than is confidentiality. Consistent with professional ethical guidelines (ASGW, 1989), each member in group counseling has the right and obligation to make the ultimate decision about how and when he or she wants to participate. Similarly, counselors have an ethical responsibility not to indoctrinate groups with the counselors' values.

Group counselors must always be alert to the psychological risks inherent in group counseling and must conduct groups in a way that minimizes client trauma.

Counselors must monitor the group, intervening whenever someone puts pressure on another to self-disclose more than that person is ready for. Counselor intervention is also necessary when someone makes hostile attacks on another person in the guise of confrontation or when someone makes fun of or scapegoats another person.

⁓ GROUP COUNSELING THEORIES

Group counseling theories are classified in an order similar to that of individual and family theories: psychodynamic (transactional analysis and psychodrama), humanistic (group-centered and Gestalt), cognitive-behavioral, and developmental.

Psychodynamic Group Counseling

In psychodynamic group counseling, exploration and analysis of members' unconscious intrapsychic dynamics are emphasized (Hershenson, Power, & Waldo, 1996). Feelings generated by unresolved childhood conflicts with parents and family are reexperienced, reenacted, and related appropriately to present-day relationships. A counselor must resolve feelings of transference, countertransference, and resistance that arise from each member of the group, as well as from the total group (*group transference*). Because these same feelings occur among group members, they also need to be acknowledged and worked through (Brammer, Abrego, & Shostrom, 1993).

The counselor shares his or her interpretations of individual and group emotional reactions with the members of the group. As counseling progresses, members—with guidance from the counselor—share insights about their own behavior and emotional expressions. Insights and understandings lead to more realistic perceptions of early relationships, as well as of themselves, of other group members, and of the counselor. These new and more accurate perceptions help each group member learn more appropriate ways to express and satisfy authentic, legitimate needs in group sessions. In the final stage of counseling, members are encouraged to apply these new insights and learnings to everyday living (Gazda, 1989).

Transactional Analysis

Eric Berne (1961), a psychoanalyst, developed *transactional analysis (TA)* specifically for groups. TA is based on analysis and understanding of social communication. A *transaction* refers to the way two people communicate or exchange ideas or feelings, and *analysis* refers to interpretation of how adaptive or maladaptive these social exchanges are and how to make them more constructive (Gross & Capuzzi, 1992).

In TA, personality structure is seen as consisting of three ego states: Parent, Adult, and Child. The *Parent* is the conscience or a group of dos and don'ts learned as a child; the *Adult* is the commonsense, reality-oriented portion of the personality; and the *Child* is composed of spontaneous, impulsive feelings—the creative part of the personality. Individuals tend to move from one state to another in their transactions with others.

In 1964, Berne published a best-selling book called *Games People Play,* in which he describes how people behave to get attention, recognition, and physical contact (strokes) in order to flourish and survive. Positive strokes from parents (warmth and acceptance) lead to healthy functioning; negative strokes (rejection or severe criticism) lead to dysfunctions; and indifference often results in pathology or severe dysfunctions. Healthy persons give and receive positive strokes in authentic, open, social transactions; maladjusted persons use repetitive sets of social manipulations called *games* to elicit strokes they received as children. Through reinforcement by strokes similar to those learned from, and further reinforced by, games they play, persons develop *life scripts* that control or shape their lives (Berne, 1972).

Counselors use four progressive stages of analysis to help clients: structural, transactional, game, and life script. Most people complete the first three. Few go on to life script analysis, in which they desire to change personality (Berne, 1966). In *structural analysis,* individuals are taught to understand their own personality structures and to be aware when one ego state is excluding another or when one state is intruding on or contaminating another. The Adult who always denies the Child may become computerlike or develop into a workaholic; the Child who always intrudes on the Adult may lead the Adult to expect immediate gratifications all the time.

In TA, what people say to each other (*transactions*) is analyzed in the group. Transactions may be either complementary or crossed. In *complementary transactions,* comments, questions, or requests from one person elicit appropriate and healthy responses in another. *Crossed transactions* inhibit communication. A request from an adult is responded to as if the initiator were a parent and the responder a child. In TA, crossed transactions are converted to complementary ones (Patterson, 1986).

In *game analysis,* people are made aware of games they play to get strokes (Berne, 1964). In analysis, game playing is exposed and more authentic relationships taught (Dusay & Dusay, 1989). *Life script analysis* helps group members first recall and reenact childhood experiences and then discover how they acquired and maintained the dysfunctional life script (Steiner, 1974).

Psychodrama

Jacob Moreno (1946) was one of the most influential figures in the development of group work. He coined the terms *group therapy* and *group psychotherapy.* In 1946, he introduced *psychodrama,* which has had considerable impact on group counseling and therapy in hospitals, community settings, and schools (Blatner, 1995). Psychodrama was the forerunner of several current group theories, including Gestalt, encounter, and some behavioral groups that emphasize action-insight and immediate experiencing.

The purpose of psychodrama is to build a therapeutic setting using life itself as a model. Clients act out conflicts instead of talk about them. Ideally, it is carried out on a psychodrama stage, but more often it takes place in an informal room where staging can occur. The actor-client is aided by a director (the counselor or therapist) and by one or more *auxiliary egos* (other group members) who act out either persons in the client's life who are not present or imaginations, fantasies, or dreams of the actor (Gazda, 1989).

Psychodrama consists of three parts or stages: the warm-up, the action, and the post-action or sharing and discussion stage (Z. T. Moreno, 1983). In the *warm-up stage,* the director describes the procedure, interviews each member briefly, and asks whether the members have present, past, or future situations or relationships they would like to explore. The group may break into smaller groups and practice sharing a conflict. In the *action stage,* a member volunteers to present and act out his problem. His enactment is directed by the counselor (the *director*), and the client-actor can choose one or more persons from the group (*auxiliary egos*) to help in his presentation.

In writing about Jacob Moreno, Blatner (1995) describes certain principles of psychodrama. The client must act out conflict rather than talk about it. The actor acts in the immediate present regardless of when the incident happened or might happen in the future. The client acts out how he feels regardless of how distorted his perceptions may seem to anybody else.

Clients are encouraged to play roles of other persons in their lives, as well as their own. They may use soliloquy with side comments to group members. A double, played by an *auxiliary ego,* may act out the client's feelings, or multiple doubles may portray ambivalent feelings that are hindering free expression by the client-actor. Sometimes an *auxiliary ego* mirrors the actor's behavior, with the actor observing offstage. Dream work, as in Gestalt groups, involves persons enacting, rather than analyzing, the dreams. The director interprets or suggests changes in scripts or use of auxiliary egos when necessary. After the performance, group members share observations and reactions to the psychodrama in a supportive manner. The actor is encouraged to practice new behavior.

Jacob Moreno introduced psychodrama and sociodrama into schools in 1949. Using these ideas, Heathcote (1971) introduced a model for child drama in schools in 1971. Increasing numbers of elementary school counselors are now using psychodrama with groups of elementary school students (Thompson & Rudolph, 1992). John Allan (1988), a Jungian counselor, has integrated the principles and processes of psychodrama with Jungian concepts of imagination and individuation to use with elementary schoolchildren who act out.

Humanistic Group Counseling

Person-Centered or Group-Centered Counseling

In their work with clients, Rogerian counselors, as they do in individual counseling, develop warm, accepting, and authentic relationships with each group member they believe will facilitate positive personal growth. Rogerian counselors accomplish this personal growth by modeling warm, empathic, and congruent attitudes and behaviors toward not only the group but also each member. Thus, an atmosphere is created that fosters these same facilitative characteristics in group members in their interactions with both the counselor and one another. The group works toward building trust and nonjudgmental support for one another. This nonjudgmental atmosphere permits members to drop protective masks and defenses and to face the anxiety of bringing up painful thoughts or shameful acts.

As trust deepens, the counselor helps group members let others know when they are not being genuine, authentic, understanding, or supportive. Rogerian counselors believe that if unconditional positive regard is established, substantial personal growth occurs. Misperceptions about self and others are thus corrected, enabling each person to express appropriate needs and to relate authentically with others (Corey, 1995; Gazda, 1989).

The counselor expects group members to decide on their individual and mutual group goals. The counselor's only direction is that they ask group members to decide what they want to accomplish. Techniques and games are used sparingly. Trust exercises may be engaged in, but only if the group decides to do so.

Gestalt Group Counseling

Gestalt is an unusual form of group work and in a sense is quite similar to individual counseling because the counselor emphasizes one-to-one interactions with group members, as well as focuses on group dynamics (Corey, 1995; Gross & Capuzzi, 1992; Perls, 1969).

In the sessions, the counselor asks for a volunteer to present a problem he or she is experiencing. Other group members encircle the client and counselor and observe the interaction. The person may be put on the hot seat and be confronted by the counselor about contradictions or inconsistencies or may be asked to describe a recent dream and act out the dream or to role-play with the counselor. The counselor may initiate group interactions by asking the group member to interact with other group members. The counselor allows spontaneous interactions among group members (Vander Kolk, 1985).

As in individual Gestalt counseling, counselors expect group members to attend to immediate experiencing in the sessions. They also expect members to be responsible for themselves. Confrontation and games and gimmicks designed to encourage or goad members to give up dependency and to assume self-responsibility are often used (Gladding, 1995). Through developing awareness in themselves and in others, group members correct distortions in self-perception and perceptions of others.

Cognitive-Behavioral Group Counseling

Cognitive-behavioral group counseling is task oriented. To start off a group session, the counselor first clarifies group procedure, establishes a working relationship, and then assesses each client's problem with input from the other group members. The counselor sets up specific goals with each member for behavioral changes. At the same time, group goals consistent with individual goals are determined (Varenhorst, 1976). As counseling progresses, the counselor teaches and models effective behavior, helps members clarify cognitive misperceptions about themselves and others, and helps change faulty habit patterns by appropriate negative and positive reinforcement (Ohlsen, Horne, & Lawe, 1988). Group members experiment with and try new behaviors in the sessions and help one another by modeling effective behavior and by giving appropriate feedback and reinforcement to one another. Through these interactions, members learn new attitudes, ideas, behaviors, and skills to help them cope and adapt. In the final stages, group members learn to generalize the new attitudes and skills developed in group sessions to real life through role playing, behavior rehearsal, and assignments for applying specific new skills at home.

Albert Ellis, a cognitive-behavioral theorist, has been active in group work for many years (Ellis, 1995; Ellis & Grieger, 1977). His rational-emotive therapy (RET, now called rational-emotive behavior therapy, REBT) approach has been used frequently in schools (Belkin, 1984). Ellis attempts to have group members work together under his direction to pick out one another's irrational beliefs, encourage one another to stop self-defeating self-talk, and teach one another to think rationally. He encourages and persuades them to practice newly learned behaviors outside the sessions (see "Ellis's Rational-Emotive Behavior Therapy (REBT)" in chap. 5).

Arnold Lazarus (1976, 1995), another cognitive-behaviorist, believes that his multimodal BASIC I.D. pattern (see chap. 5) works particularly well with groups. He argues that a nonpunitive, nonthreatening group atmosphere enhances the opportunity for group members to correct maladaptive responses across the seven modalities (**b**ehavior, **a**ffect, **s**ensation, **i**magery, **c**ognition, **i**nterpersonal, and **d**rugs/biological). Under his direction, group members can practice new attitudes and behaviors and receive support, feedback, and reinforcement from one another. As in individual work, the counselor is active, uses and teaches numerous techniques that reinforce positive behavior and increase realization, and models appropriate emotional expression and logical thinking.

Developmental Group Counseling

The developmental group counseling approach is based on concepts similar to those discussed in chapter 4. Theorists assume that persons must complete developmental tasks by learning coping skills and by playing social roles at different stages in their lives. These tasks arise out of individual biological and psychological needs and out of society's expectations of certain behaviors at certain ages. If persons fail to perform expected tasks adequately, maladjustment will occur.

Gazda (1989), the major proponent of this approach, perceives group counseling as an attempt to provide a group counseling system applicable to clients at all age levels. Groups are formed around problems related to particular developmental tasks expected for the age-group. Gazda describes the application of developmental group counseling for four groups of different ages: children, preadolescents, high-school-age persons, and adults.

Since developmental theorists have subdivided the adult level into several stages, effective groups have also been forming around the needs of young adults, adults at mid-life and older adults. The demand for group counseling with older adults has been increasing, but services have not kept up with demand.

Older adults, because of their age, are good candidates for group work. They have a lot of experience on which to draw, and many have developed extraordinary capacities of introspection, deep thinking, and compassion. Group counseling with older adults can be an effective way to help them confront myths of ageism.

> Counseling groups can do a lot to help older people challenge these myths and deal with developmental tasks that they, like any other age group, must face in such a way that they can retain their integrity and self-respect . . . and offer the elderly the encouragement necessary to find meaning in their lives. (Corey, 1995, p. 10)

Corey and Corey (1992) pay particular attention to groups for grief and bereavement:

> Bereavement is a particularly critical developmental task that older people must often cope with, not only because of the loss of others who are close to them but also because of the loss of some of their capacities. Although death strikes at children as well as the elderly, facing one's own death and the death of significant others takes on special significance with aging. (p. 424)

⊸֍ THE GROUP EXPERIENCE

Forming a Group

In university counseling centers, public schools, and community agencies where group counseling has already been established as a service, counselors form groups by announcing that a group will be starting at a particular time with a particular purpose. Potential clients then sign up for the group, and other counselors working with individual clients who could profit from group counseling refer them to the group.

If the center, school, or agency has not yet developed a group counseling program, the interested counselor can make a proposal indicating a need for the group, the anticipated goal, the leader's background, and the procedures that will be used. In public schools particularly, the proposal should indicate which topics will or will not be explored and the risks to the clients.

The recommended number of group members varies with the group's age range. For college students or adults, the optimal size is 8 persons, according to Corey (1995), or from 5 to 10 members, according to Vander Kolk (1985). Adolescent groups function best with 6 to 8 members. A smaller number (3–5) is recommended for groups with elementary children because of their shorter attention span (Corey & Corey, 1992). Some experienced counselors and therapists working with special groups are able to work effectively with large numbers of people. Real (1997), for example, describes working with 40 depressed male clients in a group that meets weekly.

Screening of Group Members

As discussed earlier, careful screening of candidates is necessary for ethical and professional reasons. Screening avoids having group members who would be jeopardized by the experience; who might, because of their personality or behavior, inhibit progress in the group; or who have different purposes from the group's purpose (Brammer et al., 1993; Corey, 1995).

Prescreening prospective group members in individual sessions is the optimal procedure. Where the setting does not permit individual screening, potential group members can complete questionnaires and be interviewed in small groups. If neither of these options is feasible, a pregroup session can be used as both a screening and an informational procedure (Corey, 1995).

Composition of Groups

Grouping clients with similar concerns and purposes facilitates a working bond and a more cohesive group relationship (Hershenson et al., 1996). Special groups are effective for those with specific problems, such as alcoholism. Grouping in a similar age range permits the group to focus on developmental concerns appropriate for all members (Gazda, 1989). Groups exclusive to men or to women are effective ways of exploring gender issues. Special groupings are also effective for abused spouses or spousal abusers.

Frequency and Duration of Sessions

The setting in which group counseling occurs determines the frequency and duration of sessions. In a community agency or college or in private practice, 2-hour weekly sessions are optimal. In school settings, shorter times twice a week may be more suitable because of the shorter attention span of students and because clients miss less class time (Ohlsen et al., 1988).

In colleges and universities, groups usually run about 10 or 14 weeks—the length of a quarter or a semester—because of convenience to the students and the counselor and because this is a reasonable amount of time for a group to attain goals. In communities, from 10 to 20 sessions seems reasonable. Table 11.1 presents a summary of guidelines for forming groups.

Co-Leaders

Some group counselors prefer to work with co-leaders, for several reasons. First, there is apt to be less leader burnout and closer attention to group interaction. Second, co-leaders can benefit from each other's perceptions of group dynamics and from each other's observations and comments on their emotional responses. Third, they can use the way they relate to each other as a model for the group. Fourth, male and female co-leaders can, in some cases, better deal with gender concerns (Corey, 1995; Yalom, 1985).

One disadvantage of co-leaders is the possibility that the group may suffer if co-leaders act as rivals, do not trust each other, or try to work out their own relationship struggles in the sessions (Corey, 1995). As in families (see chap. 10), triangulation may occur if a leader sides with a group member against the co-leader or if group members work one leader against the other in a power struggle (Vander Kolk, 1985).

TABLE 11.1
Guidelines for Forming a Group

Selection of Clients
> Counselor publicizes a group is forming.
> Prospective clients sign up for groups.
> Counselors refer individual clients to groups.

Screening of Clients for Group Suitability
> Counselors conduct individual interviews with each applicant.
> Counselors hold precounseling meeting with group for further screening.

Group Size
> Adults: 5 to 10 members.
> College students: 5 to 10 members.
> Secondary students: 6 to 8 members.
> Elementary students: 3 to 5 members.

Frequency and Duration of Sessions
> Adults: 2 hours once a week for 10 to 20 sessions.
> College students: 2 hours once a week for a quarter or a semester (11 to 15 weeks).
> Secondary students: 40 to 45 minutes once a week.
> Elementary students: 30 minutes once or twice a week.

Yalom (1985), who sees both advantages and potential hazards to co-leadership, emphasizes that if co-leaders are incompatible or of unequal ability, the group will suffer from split loyalties.

Group Stages

Corey (1995) divides the group counseling process into four stages: initial stage (orientation and exploration), transition stage (dealing with resistance), working stage (cohesion and productivity), and final stage (consolidation and termination). Gazda (1989) outlines exploratory, transition, action, and termination stages, and Vander Kolk (1985) describes a beginning and building stage, a conflict and dominance stage, and a cohesive and productive stage. The stages used here are a composite of the above models: (a) initial exploratory stage, (b) transition stage marked by resistance and conflicts, (c) working stage marked by cohesiveness and productivity, and (d) consolidation and termination.

Initial Exploratory Stage

In the beginning sessions, group members are often strangers to one another. They may be ambivalent about groups. They want help but may be fearful of sounding stupid or dumb or may think they might disclose too much about themselves. So, the leader often finds many in the group reluctant to talk or only able to bring up superficial topics in an intellectual manner. Members may expect leaders to have authoritative answers to their problems. Some may focus on themselves and not on other members.

At the beginning of the sessions, counselors generally respond to the group as a whole to foster group feeling; they also allow time for group members to get to know one another (Vander Kolk, 1985). They can be paired off, learn something about one another, and then introduce each other to the group. Group members can also be asked to share their feelings about being in a group.

It is important to discuss and set goals in the first session. Group members can help one another clarify goals. For example, a member who says, "I'd like to be less aggressive," can be asked to explain what he or she means by being aggressive.

In the beginning stage, counselors facilitate the development of trust, just as is done in individual and family counseling. As in family counseling, group counselors must engender trust between themselves and group members and among all the members as well. Counselors accomplish this by modeling genuineness, warmth, and nonjudgmental attitudes to group members and by listening carefully.

Counselors also work on developing those communicative attitudes and skills among group members that will contribute to group cohesiveness. Self-disclosure and constructive feedback are considered important therapeutic communication skills by a majority of group leaders (Kaul & Bednar, 1986). The leader who discloses immediate feelings and reactions occurring in the group helps the group focus on the immediate experience. When leaders react with positive and negative feedback to concrete, specific, and observable behaviors in a nonjudgmental way, group members more readily accept the feedback (Morran, Robison, & Stockton, 1985).

Transition Stage: Resistance and Conflicts

As the group moves into the second stage, members begin to realize or are confronted with the need to explore more deeply, to self-disclose more intensively, and to interact more with other group members. Although some trust has been established, the feeling is still tentative, and group members are ambivalent, anxious, and defensive as they realize that they are expected to explore painful emotions and feelings even more deeply. Some wonder whether the group will reject them if they reveal too much, some are afraid that they may lose control and reveal more than they intend, and some are suspicious that the counselor or others might ridicule or shame them (Corey & Corey, 1992).

Group counseling professionals describe this stage as characterized by conflict or rebellion resulting from a struggle for power, control, or dominance among the members and with the counselor (Brammer et al., 1993; Schultz, 1973). Schultz (1973) sees it as a time of competition and rivalry, with members testing whether they can trust the leader and other group members. Group members tend to criticize each other more frequently, and clashes occur as some members become judgmental or dogmatic in presenting ideas or views (Corey, 1995; Vander Kolk, 1985).

At this time, verbal attacks on the leader may occur, with some members expressing doubts about his or her leadership ability, and others reacting negatively to the counselor's attempts to help them explore their problems. Counselors must recognize that these behaviors represent the resistance to exploring painful feelings that is expected in any form of therapy. Resistance is a sign that members are getting closer to the core of their problems (Ohlsen et al., 1988). Resistance manifests itself in such behaviors as giving intellectual advice, missing sessions, not participating, using other members as scapegoats, or talking about oneself with no mention of feelings (Corey, 1995).

As group members feel freer to express anger, resentment, dependency, or erotic feelings toward counselors, counselors must be aware that transference is occurring (Ohlsen et al., 1988). They must recognize and accept that these feelings toward them stem from unresolved conflicts in their relationships (see chap. 5). Corey and Corey (1992) say,

> Regardless of the value you may place on exploring transferences, you should be aware of the expectations that members are likely to have of you as their group leader. Unless their feelings about you are dealt with in the group, meaningful work may never occur. (p. 175)

When resistances arise, counselors need to challenge group members to work through conflicts so that they can move toward more authentic self-explorations and more attention to group interactions and to the problems and feelings of the others in the group.

Working Stage: Cohesiveness and Productivity

In the third stage, group members develop intimacy and cohesiveness. Group identity is high, and members feel close to one another and more aware of one another's problems. Trust has increased, so they are more willing to take risks in sharing feelings and thoughts that occur within the group and to give constructive feedback to one another.

Group intimacy may lead to a false cohesiveness in which members protect one another (Vander Kolk, 1985). An overly supportive group may not confront one another authentically, may suppress negative emotions in the group, or may not challenge one another to make changes in their everyday living. Many groups become stuck in this loving, nonproductive lethargy and never move on.

Plenty of work is yet to be done in the third stage, however. Known as the *working stage,* it is often regarded as the most productive stage in group development and is characterized by its constructive nature and the achievement of results (Gladding, 1995).

When a group attains cohesiveness and stability yet does not allow itself to remain in a comfortable, secure state, the lengthy working process can begin to help group members change. When the group becomes productive, group members are more committed to delving into significant problems and to giving attention to interchanges in the group. Group members should challenge one another to convert insights they have learned into action. For example, someone can confront a member who says he recognizes the need to assert himself but remains passive in the group and in his interactions outside the group.

Group members depend less on the leader, and the group begins to focus on working toward specified individual goals and group goals. Group members feel free to confront one another and are more willing to accept confrontations as a constructive challenge to change. They are more willing to risk experimenting with new behaviors and giving honest, spontaneous feedback without passing judgment. Conflict among members is effectively being dealt with in sessions. As group interactions bring about attitudinal and behavioral changes in the group, members accept challenges to make changes in everyday life.

Group leaders will use a variety of techniques related to their theoretical beliefs to help group members explore their problems, confront one another, and make behavioral changes. Eclectic counselors might use Gestalt techniques such as confrontation, empty chair, hot seat, psychodrama role playing, or role reversal to get clients more in touch with their feelings. They might use cognitive-behavioral techniques to help persons concentrate on changing self-defeating self-talk, as Ellis does, or by clarifying thoughts through cognitive restructuring. Transactional analysis might be used to improve group members' communication skills. Behavioral rehearsal or assertiveness exercises in anticipation of an encounter outside the sessions or a homework assignment to carry out a specific new learning can help members apply new insights to real-life situations.

Consolidation and Termination

Yalom (1985) writes emphatically, "Termination is more than an act signifying the end of therapy; it is an integral part of the process of therapy and, if properly understood and managed, may be an important force in the instigation of change" (p. 365).

Most groups have a termination date fixed in advance of the session, particularly in educational settings and in clinics. It is wise to start discussions about separation approximately three sessions before the final one to allow time for members to handle psychological or emotional feelings, to work toward transferring new group experiences to the outside world, to work through any unfinished problems in group relationships, and to review what happened in the group to each member and how each one can build on these changes after the group ends (Ohlsen et al., 1988).

Feelings of anxiety, loss, sadness, or anger about losing those with whom group members feel close, safe, and supported must be discussed; it is, after all, the death of the group. Psychological or emotional reactions of significant persons outside the group need to be discussed, with suggestions about how to deal with feelings. Family or close friends may resist or be disturbed at changes. Suggestions for further therapy can be made when necessary. Specific suggestions—joining a support group or another, more advanced group, reading, attending workshops—increase chances that learning will continue.

Not all groups will run smoothly through all stages to a clear-cut, successful termination. Some groups never pass the comfortable stage. Other groups, because of the personality mix of group members or leader or both, may not succeed in becoming cohesive. Like individuals, groups have different capacities for growth.

❧ TRENDS IN GROUP WORK

Group work is being used more frequently in business and industry to reduce conflict, increase cooperation among coworkers, and encourage higher satisfaction and greater productivity among employees (Gladding, 1995). One type of group that is effective with coworkers is the "quality circle." Members are employees in the same work area who meet weekly to try to solve problems related to their joint work efforts (Hershenson et al., 1996). Quality circles are described as follows: "Leaders function in a caring capacity offering members support as they examine conflicts and detriments to effective co-worker relations and explore solutions" (Hershenson et al., 1996, p. 220).

Other trends are the increasing numbers of groups that focus on special needs, such as groups for victims of domestic violence, those with PTSD, those with spiritual needs, male depression, grief work, and debriefing witnesses of public violence (see chap. 19).

❧ RESEARCH IN GROUP COUNSELING AND PSYCHOTHERAPY

Kaul and Bednar (1986), who surveyed approximately 900 periodicals and 1,500 books and monographs published between 1977 and 1983, found 477 studies about group counseling and group psychotherapy outcomes. Of these studies, they judged 17 to be statistically significant and valid.

Although positive results on outcome were found, Kaul and Bednar (1986) expressed concern that these articles did not include conditions in the group process contributing to outcome, such as quality or type of leader, composition and duration of the group, theoretical orientations and techniques, and similar pertinent factors. They did note, however, that researchers did attend to the three factors in group process described earlier: self-disclosure of the counselor, type of counselor feedback, and cohesiveness in the group.

In a study on self-disclosure, Frielander, Thibodeau, Nichols, Tucker, and Snyder (1985) found no reliable differences in type and amount of self-disclosure and cohesiveness of the group. They did find, however, a positive relationship between low-self-disclosing leaders and counseling outcome. In a similar study, Kirshner, Dies, and Brown (1978), working with undergraduate volunteers, found self-disclosure to be related to the degree of cohesiveness in the group.

Kaul and Bednar (1986) made three generalizations in their evaluation of feedback studies: (a) Clients seem to prefer positive feedback to negative feedback, (b) group members accept negative feedback more readily if it is preceded by positive feedback, and (c) group members are more comfortable giving positive feedback than negative feedback.

Kaul and Bednar (1986) acknowledge that the majority of group therapists consider group cohesiveness crucial to successful group outcome, but they found little in the literature to support this. Yalom (1985) claims that research evidence does show a relationship between cohesiveness of groups and positive group outcome. Kaul and Bednar have found cohesion a complex factor that is difficult to define and measure. They recommend that researchers give more attention to leadership quality, constitution of the group, and type of treatment when studying cohesion in groups.

In another review of research, Gazda (1989) analyzed 641 studies on group counseling, 68% of which were outcome studies. From 1976 to 1987, 79 of the outcome studies reported significant positive results.

Research on groups has lagged behind research on individual counseling, a lag attributable to the complexity of studying groups, the lack of effective instruments to measure group process, and the lack of ongoing research by researchers who investigate group processes (Gladding, 1995). Improvement, however, is occurring in group research methods: "Increased concern and attention is being devoted to this area. . . . For instance, awards for group-work research are constantly being given out by professional group-work associations" (Gladding, 1995, p. 418).

❧ SUMMARY

Group counseling is helpful to persons having difficulties in interpersonal relationships and with social skills. The group counseling environment, which is generally safe and accepting, gives members the opportunity to self-disclose, to interact with others, and to receive constructive feedback. Group counseling theories are adaptations of theories described in chapter 5—psychodynamic, humanistic, cognitive-behavioral, and developmental, or age-related, approaches.

Ethically, group participation should be voluntary, and group disclosures must be kept in confidence by the group leader. The group leader must also alert group members about the need to maintain confidentiality about group interchanges. Persons who are vulnerable, too aggressive, or destructively antisocial are inappropriate candidates for groups. Group leaders screen group candidates and generally exclude persons who are highly vulnerable emotionally, overly aggressive, or antisocial. It is unethical for a group leader or group members to persuade or coerce individuals to participate when they are reluctant to do so.

Groups go through stages. The initial stage is exploratory, in which group trust is developed so that clients feel safe enough to participate. This is followed by a transition stage, in which resistance develops among members that must be worked through. A cohesive working stage follows in which trust is high, self-disclosure is authentic, and feedback is productive. This is followed by the final stage of consolidation and termination of the group sessions.

Trends show increased activity in group work in business to improve worker morale and productivity. Increasing numbers of groups are focusing on persons with special problems—for example, victims of domestic violence, those with PTSD, male depression, grief work, and those with spiritual needs.

❧ PROJECTS AND ACTIVITIES

1. Check with a university counseling center and a community clinic regarding the type of groups offered. Do they distinguish group counseling, group therapy, and personal growth groups?
2. Assume that you are a leader of a group of college students. One member tells you he thinks another member has been talking about personal revelations of group members outside the group. He thinks he knows who the person is but isn't sure. How would you handle this complaint?
3. A husband and wife, both psychologists, are co-leading a group. Some group members ask very personal questions about the husband-wife relationship. The co-leaders think they have some right to privacy. How do you think the co-leaders should respond to the request for intimate self-disclosures in the group? Role-play a group with co-leaders with this type of problem.
4. Trace the history of group counseling. What social, cultural, and psychological factors contributed to the movement?
5. Select a group population with whom you would like to conduct a group experience, such as the elderly, children, adolescents, or battered spouses. Search the literature for group counseling research findings with this population. Find two studies that you think are statistically sound and two that you think are poorly designed.
6. Debate the merits of having one group leader versus using co-leaders. Would the type of group problem, age-group, or work setting make a difference?
7. Contact an elementary and a secondary school counselor and ask whether they handle groups and, if so, what types of groups. What do they see as advantages or disadvantages of group counseling at these age levels?
8. Role-play a group in which a member says she has decided to leave the group because it is a waste of time, the group leader isn't directive enough, and group members are not leveling with one another.

❧ REFERENCES

Allan, J. (1988). *Inscapes of the child's world: Jungian counseling in schools and clinics.* Dallas, TX: Spring.

American Counseling Association (ACA). (1995). *Ethical standards.* Alexandria, VA: Author.

American Psychological Association (APA). (1973). Guidelines for psychologists conducting growth groups. *American Psychologist, 28,* 933.

Association for Specialists in Group Work (ASGW). (1989). *Ethical guidelines for group leaders.* Falls Church, IA: Author.

Belkin, G. S. (1984). *Introduction to counseling* (2nd ed.). Dubuque, IA: William C. Brown.

Berne, E. (1961). *Transactional analysis in psychotherapy.* New York: Grove Press.

Berne, E. (1964). *Games people play.* New York: Grove Press.

Berne, E. (1966). *Principles of group treatment.* New York: Oxford University Press.

Berne, E. (1972). *What do you say after you say hello?* New York: Grove Press.

Blatner, A. (1995). Psychodrama. In R. J. Corsini & D. Wedding (Eds.), *Current psychotherapies* (5th ed., pp. 399–408). Itasca, IL: F. E. Peacock.

Brammer, L. M., Abrego, P. J., & Shostrom, E. L. (1993). *Therapeutic counseling and psychotherapy* (6th ed.). Upper Saddle River, NJ: Prentice Hall.

Burlingame, G. M., & Fuhriman, A. (1990). Time-limited group therapy. *Counseling Psychologist, 18,* 93–118.

Carroll, M. R., & Wiggins, J. (1997). *Elements of group counseling: Back to basics* (2nd ed.). Denver, CO: Love.

Corey, G. (1995). *Theory and practice of group counseling* (4th ed.). Pacific Grove, CA: Brooks/Cole.

Corey, G., & Corey, M. S. (1992). *Groups: Process and practice* (4th ed.). Pacific Grove, CA: Brooks/Cole.

Corey, G., Corey, M. S., & Callanan, P. (1993). *Issues and ethics in the helping professions* (4th ed.). Pacific Grove, CA: Brooks/Cole.

Dusay, J. M., & Dusay, K. M. (1989). Transactional analysis. In R. J. Corsini & D. Wedding (Eds.), *Current psychotherapies* (4th ed., pp. 405–453). Itasca, IL: F. E. Peacock.

Ellis, A. (1995). Rational-emotive behavior therapy. In R. J. Corsini & D. J. Wedding (Eds.), *Current psychotherapies* (5th ed.). Itasca, IL: F. E. Peacock.

Ellis, A., & Grieger, R. (1977). *Handbook of rational-emotive therapy.* New York: Springer.

Forester-Miller, H., & Rubenstein, R. L. (1992). Group counseling: Ethics and professional issues. In D. Capuzzi & D. R. Gross (Eds.), *Introduction to group counseling* (pp. 307–323). Denver, CO: Love.

Frielander, M. L., Thibodeau, J. R., Nichols, M. P., Tucker, C., & Snyder, J. (1985). Introducing semantic cohesion analysis: A study of small talk. *Small Group Behavior, 68,* 285–302.

Gazda, G. M. (1978). *Group counseling: A developmental approach.* Boston: Allyn & Bacon.

Gazda, G. M. (1989). *Group counseling: A developmental approach* (4th ed.). Boston: Allyn & Bacon.

Gladding, S. T. (1995). *Group work: A counseling specialty* (2nd ed.). Upper Saddle River, NJ: Merrill/Prentice Hall.

Heathcote, D. (1971). *Drama in education of teachers.* Newcastle, UK: University Printing.

Hershenson, D. B., & Power, P. W., & Waldo, M. (1996). *Community counseling: Contemporary theory and practice.* Boston: Allyn & Bacon.

Kaul, T. J., & Bednar, R. L. (1986). Experiential group research: Results, questions, and suggestions. In S. L. Garfield & A. Bergin (Eds.), *Handbook for psychotherapy and behavior change* (3rd ed., pp. 671–714). New York: John Wiley.

Kirshner, B. J., Dies, R. R., & Brown, R. A. (1978). Effects of experimental manipulation of self-disclosure on group cohesiveness. *Journal of Consulting and Clinical Psychology, 46,* 1171–1177.

Lazarus, A. (1976). *Multimodal behavioral therapy.* New York: Springer.

Lazarus, A. (1995). Multimodal therapy. In R. J. Corsini & D. Wedding (Eds.), *Current psychotherapies* (5th ed., pp. 322–353). Itasca, IL: F. E. Peacock.

Moreno, J. L. (1946). *Psychodrama.* Beacon, NY: Beacon Press.

Moreno, Z. T. (1983). Psychodrama. In H. I. Kaplan & B. J. Sadock (Eds.), *Comprehensive group psychotherapy* (2nd ed., pp. 158–166). Baltimore: Williams & Wilkins.

Morran, D. K., Robison, F. F., & Stockton, R. (1985). Feedback exchange in counseling groups: An analysis of message content and receiver acceptance as a function of leader versus member delivery, session, and value. *Journal of Counseling Psychology, 32,* 57–67.

Nystul, M. S. (1993). *The art and science of counseling and therapy.* Upper Saddle River, NJ: Merrill/Prentice Hall.

Ohlsen, M. M., Horne, A. M., & Lawe, C. F. (1988). *Group counseling* (3rd ed.). New York: Holt, Rinehart & Winston.

Patterson, C. H. (1986). *Theories of counseling and psychotherapy* (4th ed.). New York: Harper & Row.

Perls, F. (1969). *Gestalt therapy verbatim.* New York: Bantam Books.

Real, T. (1997). *I don't want to talk about it.* New York: Fireside.

Schultz, W. (1973). *Elements of encounter.* Big Sur, CA: Joy Press.

Steiner, C. (1974). *Scripts people live: Transactional analysis of life scripts.* New York: Grove Press.

Thompson, C. L., & Rudolph, L. B. (1992). *Counseling children* (3rd ed.). Pacific Grove, CA: Brooks/Cole.

Vander Kolk, C. J. (1985). *Introduction to group counseling and psychotherapy.* Upper Saddle River, NJ: Merrill/Prentice Hall.

Varenhorst, B. (1976). Behavioral group counseling. In G. M. Gazda (Ed.), *Theories and methods of group counseling in the schools* (2nd ed., pp. 215–246). Springfield, IL: Charles C Thomas.

Yalom, I. D. (1985). *The theory and practice of group psychotherapy* (3rd ed.). New York: Basic Books.

12   Career Counseling

Career counseling involves helping individuals or groups explore career options, make career plans, prepare for appropriate training, and resolve career-related problems. Client concerns include career indecision and uncertainty, dissatisfaction on the job, unsatisfactory integration of life roles, and conflicts with others about career choice or development.

The number of community career centers has been increasing rapidly to meet the growing demand of those reentering the job market, those reappraising their work skills, and those searching for employment in fields unrelated to their former work experience and training. Isaacson and Brown (1997) comment that this practice

> will grow because adults on our society seem to be relying increasingly in career counselors for assistance. . . . Because of the number of people changing jobs voluntarily and involuntarily, it seems likely that increasing numbers of people will seek assistance from private practitioners in the future. (p. 475)

Supporting this view is a recent Gallup poll sponsored by the National Career Development Association. Responses indicate that approximately 11 million people paid fees to a career counseling agency to get help with their careers (Hoyt & Lester, 1995; Isaacson & Brown, 1997).

Commenting on the rapid increase in these services in the community, Isaacson and Brown (1997) say:

> Career counselors offer a wide variety of services including career counseling with individuals and groups, consultations, job placement, testing, outplacement, resume development, and the development of other employability skills, retirement planning, career/life role integration counseling, spousal relocation training, program evaluation, work adjustment counseling, and vocational appraisal services. (p. 478)

⁂ HISTORICAL PERSPECTIVE

Historically, counseling was initiated in colleges and schools to help students with vocational and career concerns (see chap. 2). Early vocational counseling in the 1930s and 1940s was primarily influenced by the prevailing emphasis among psychologists and educators on measuring individual differences. The basic assumption underlying this theory is that individuals have unique inherent abilities, interests, and personality traits that can be assessed through standardized tests and matched with certain types of occupations.

As the history chapter shows, in 1942, Donald Super, himself a psychologist specializing in vocational assessment and guidance, introduced a different philosophical approach, one that believes persons develop vocationally throughout life, an amplification of Charlotte Buehler's theory of human development. Carl Rogers then introduced a client-centered approach and the emphasis on personal growth.

Leading vocational counseling professionals at the time—Super (1951, 1955), Ginzberg, Ginzburg, Axelrad, and Herma (1951), Holland (1959), and Roe (1957)—believed that vocational counseling should be integrated with personal and interpersonal counseling. Vocational choice and development, they emphasized, are influenced by, and related to, personality development. Super (1955), in particular, proposed a theory that could ameliorate these opposing approaches, a theory that integrated vocational development with self-development and that related personality factors to vocational concerns.

In my various experiences as a counselor in college and high school counseling centers, as a supervisor of counseling interns, and as a private practitioner, I, and those with whom I worked, found this integrated approach to work well. We were able to distinguish when a client's concerns were specific to career exploration and when client personal conflicts or emotional disequilibrium were interfering with client career exploration. This practice was compatible with the counseling services at the time, which existed almost exclusively in school and college settings, settings that encompassed the normal population with their typical conflicts and concerns related to school and thus to vocational issues.

Even so, during the 1970s, many college counselors began to focus only on a client's personal growth issues and tended to ignore the client's vocational or career concerns. Humanistic and behavioral theories of psychology prevailed; these did not address problems related to career development. Moreover, counseling expanded to address such issues as family and substance abuse, in which career concerns were generally not the issue.

Consequently, at many colleges and universities, placement centers developed into career centers to assist students who needed help in making career choices. Those college counseling centers that no longer attended to clients' career issues referred students with career concerns to the college career centers (Gallagher, 1996).

This primary emphasis on a client's personal and interpersonal concerns was augmented in the late 1970s when the American Mental Health Counselors Association was formed and the master's degree in counseling emerged as a terminal degree. Most agencies that hire mental health counselors in private practice tend to limit their services to the client's personal and interpersonal concerns. Moreover, managed care generally does not allow insurance coverage for those who need career counseling.

✖ THE CURRENT SCENE

Both the American Counseling Association (ACA) and Division 17 (Counseling Psychologists) of the American Psychological Association (APA) have consistently specified that the counseling profession, which is unique in its emphasis on normal developmental conflicts, take a holistic approach and consider career concerns as part of the counseling process. Leading professionals continue to claim that general counseling and career counseling are inseparable, rather than independent, processes (Betz & Corning, 1993; Brown & Lent, 1984; Krumboltz, 1993). Professionals supporting integration have generally been those with specialized interests in career counseling (Brown, 1985; Gysbers & Moore, 1987; Isaacson & Brown, 1997; Osipow & Fitzgerald, 1996; Zunker, 1994).

Counseling psychologists, whose professional identities originally emerged out of the field of vocational counseling in the early 1950s, have also continued to uphold the importance of integrating career and personal counseling, whether or not they are career specialists. These beliefs have been reiterated not only by myself but also by counseling psychologists Betz and Corning (1993), Brown and Lent (1984), Herr and Cramer (1996), Holland (1985), and Osipow (1987).

Community and mental health counselors, however, generally do not include career counseling in their practice, preferring to keep the services separate. They cite several factors that they believe prevent mental health counseling and career counseling from being integrated. They claim, for example, that counselors have the right to specialize; that career issues are too complicated for nonspecialists; that associations are organized around specialties; and that work settings in schools, universities, and communities preclude integrating general counseling and career counseling (Krumboltz, 1993). Krumboltz (1993), in response to their claims, insists that such arguments do not justify separating a client's career concerns from personal and interpersonal concerns.

Need for Professional Training

Career counselors now generally have graduate degrees in counseling or counseling psychology with specialization in career development, career assessment, and career planning. They are trained to be alert to signs that a client's vocational concerns might relate to personal or interpersonal conflicts. They are prepared to help a client explore personal concerns as she or he works toward career decisions or, in more serious cases, to refer the client for personal counseling. Brown and Brooks (1991) point out that "many people bring very complex career-related problems to counselors, and the assistance they need requires the career counselor to be highly skilled in both personal and career counseling" (p. 4).

In 1997, the NBC television news magazine *Dateline* presented an exposé about "career counselors" who were not professionally trained who were charging exorbitant fees for placement services that actually did not provide expected services. In response, the president of the American Counseling Association (ACA), and the president of the National Career Development Association (NCDA) sent a joint letter to *Dateline*. The letter was also published in *Counseling Today*. A portion of the letter follows:

> Unfortunately the term 'career counseling' is widely used by persons who have no training or experience to provide professional counseling services. . . .
>
> Career counselors offering their services to the public should, at minimum, have a master's degree in counseling . . .
>
> Consumers should also ask if the individual is licensed or certified. (Lee & Shahnasarian, 1998, p. 18)

Leading career counseling professionals emphasize the need for professional counseling training (Brown, 1995; Brown & Brooks, 1991; Gysbers & Moore, 1987; Isaacson & Brown, 1997; Krumboltz, 1993). Isaacson and Brown (1997) emphasize the "interrelationship of mental health and career concerns" and assert that "counselors and psychologists need to be prepared to deal with both" (p. 496). They also state the National Board for Certified Counselor's (NBCC) position: "NBCC (1996) has reiterated its stand on the need for generic counseling preparation by reaffirming its requirement that professionals seeking certification as National Certified Career Counselors first obtain certification as NCCs, National Certified Counselors" (p. 496).

Such recommendations for career counselors, however, are not enforced by licensing or by certification laws. Unlike mental health counselors and school counselors, career counselors and placement counselors, unfortunately, are allowed to practice without being either licensed or certified.

Trends in Career Counseling

After surveying the literature, Isaacson and Brown (1997) predicted the following trends in career counseling that will influence the future of the specialty:

- Career counseling will continue to develop as a counseling specialty requiring training in both personal and career counseling.

- Increasing attention will be given to certification of career counselors by counselors and psychologists.

- Career counseling techniques for women and men and for ethnic groups will become more similar.

- John Holland's career counseling theory will continue to dominate theory and practice.

- The use of computer-assisted guidance programs (CAGS) will escalate dramatically.

❧ THEORETICAL APPROACHES TO CAREER COUNSELING

Career counseling theories are based on the idea that one's personal development influences one's choice of, and satisfaction in, a career.

Early Career Developmental Theories

As said earlier, Super (1942) was one of the first persons to relate personality factors and developmental stages to career development. In 1951, using Buehler's concept of developmental life stages, he described vocational adjustment as an implementation of a person's self-concept. He then outlined (1953) a series of developmental stages throughout life that relate to occupational development (see chap. 2).

Ginzberg et al. (1951) published one of the earliest theories of vocational choice based on developmental stages. They described the process of career choice as following three stages: (a) *fantasy period* in early childhood, composed of unrealistic ideas; (b) *tentative period,* when children begin to sort out activities they like and can do well; and (c) *realistic period,* when individuals explore realistically and make a specific choice. In 1972, Ginzberg revised his ideas and concluded that vocational choice is lifelong and always open to change.

Super (1961) continued to develop his vocational theory, extending it to include *vocational maturity.* Ultimately, through choices considered mature at each life stage, adults find and establish themselves in appropriate vocations. In 1980, Super expanded his theory further, in what he calls a *life-span, life-space* approach. He proposed that people play numerous roles throughout their life spans that help shape their careers in a broad sense. He described how various roles interrelate to contribute to career development over the life span (Osipow & Fitzgerald, 1996).

Typology Approach

Holland's typology is considered the most widely used and most influential theory in career counseling practice (Isaacson & Brown, 1997; Osipow, 1987; Weinrach & Srebalus, 1990). His approach assumes that we can classify individuals into the following six personality types: realistic, investigative, artistic, social, enterprising, and conventional (Holland, 1985). Further, he believes that individuals in each personality type will select jobs or careers that fit their interests, thus forming six matching work environments composed of members who enjoy similar activities and respond to tasks and to people in similar ways. Vocational success, satisfaction, and stability, he assumes, depend on how well the individual's personality (as described by interest inventories) matches work environments selected by the individual.

Table 12.1 classifies descriptions of each personality type with matching work environment. From the initial letters of the six personality types, Holland coined the acronym RIASEC to portray the total interest pattern. He combines these letters to code dominant personality types resulting from an individual's interest inventory profile. Few people are only one type, Holland says, so he combines the three most dominant types a person shows on an interest inventory and classifies accordingly. For

TABLE 12.1

Holland's Personality Styles and Occupational Environments

Personal Type	Personality-Job Theme	Working Environment
Interested in machinery and working with things; not interested in people	Realistic	Skilled trades (machinist, carpenter, mechanic, cook)
Interested in science and abstract analytical tasks; not sociable; independent	Investigative	Scientific/technical job (engineers, chemists, mathematicians, medical technicians)
Interested in creative and imaginative activities; enjoys self-expression	Artistic	Artistic jobs, (artists, musicians, designers, writers)
Interested in helping people and solving social problems	Social	Social service jobs (educators, counselors, nurses, ministers)
Interested in persuading others, leading others; extroverted, dominant	Enterprising	Marketing and promotional jobs (salespersons, public relations specialists, real estate)
Enjoys systematic repetitious tasks and manipulating data	Conventional	Office work (secretary, file clerk, bookkeeper)

Source: Adapted and reproduced by special permission of the Publisher, Psychological Assessment Resources, Inc., 16204 North Florida Ave., Lutz, FL 35549 from *The Self-Directed Search* by John L. Holland, Ph.D. Copyright 1985 by Psychological Assessment Resources, Inc. All rights reserved.

example, IAE would show *investigative* interests strongest, followed by *artistic* and *enterprising*. He also classifies working environments by using the same three-letter combinations. These he has listed in a pamphlet called the "Occupations Finder."

Holland has conducted extensive longitudinal studies, and results show that personal types and occupational environments do differentiate people. He has used his research to revise his theory over the years (Zunker, 1994).

➣ CAREER COUNSELING PROCESS

Although many college counseling centers no longer offer career counseling, many still do. Leading proponents, including myself, reaffirm the value of offering career counseling along with regular counseling for reasons described earlier. Although both types of centers potentially can offer quality career counseling, there are distinctions between the counseling that goes on in career centers and the counseling that is offered in general counseling centers.

While reaffirming that career counseling and personal counseling are related, Super (1993) proposed that they entail distinct approaches, approaches that are treated as a continuum ranging from *career counseling* and its focus on "situational" concerns to *personal counseling* and its focus on the person's inner self-exploration.

> There are in fact two fields: situational counseling, which has subspecialties that focus on differing types of situations (career, family, etc.), and personal counseling, in which the focus is on individuals whose problems are based primarily in their own approach to and coping with situations, not on factors in the situations they encounter. In accepting this dichotomy one should not actually treat it as a dichotomy, but as a continuum of which these are the extremes. (p. 135)

With these differences in mind, well-trained counselors generally function similarly in both settings. As with counseling in general, career counseling requires that the counselor establish a "positive, productive relationship" with clients (Gysbers & Moore, 1987, p. 173). Counselors, in any case, must be able to respond meaningfully to a client's expressed feelings, behaviors, and attitudes (Isaacson, 1986). Counselors must help the client make use of new insights and understandings to develop more constructive attitudes and behaviors she or he can use to make decisions and implement them.

Yost and Corbishley (1987) have developed a career counseling process in which they emphasize a procedure similar to the individual counseling process described in chapter 9. First, counselor and client develop rapport, assess client needs, and establish goals. Next, the counselor works to promote client self-understanding through interviews and aptitude and interest inventories. The counselor then helps the client develop appropriate career alternatives, making use of occupational information such as *Occupational Outlook Handbook (OOH),* which is described below under "Occupational Information." From these possibilities, the counselor helps the client choose a career. Throughout the sessions, the counselor helps the client work through obstacles that impede her or him from making choices, such as too few alternatives, not enough information, inappropriate options, or interference from family. Once a choice is made, the counselor helps the client develop job search skills, write résumés, and prepare for job interviews.

Types of Problems

The relationship between career and personal concerns related to career is evident in the types of problems clients present to counselors regarding choosing or maintaining a career. These types of problems are as follows:

- Need for career exploration
- Conflict between themselves and others over choice of a career or performance on a job
- Personal doubts or conflicts about choice of career or continuing with a career, or apprehension about losing one's job
- Conflicts arising from transitions in life that are causing problems affecting a career

Exploration of Careers

When clients seek counseling help in exploring careers in schools, colleges, universities, and communities, their primary goals are to make both appropriate occupational choices and to look into related training programs. In high schools, clients are in their formative stages of career exploration. They are exploring types of careers and trying to determine whether to find a job or seek further training. In universities, clients seek assistance in choosing majors or in making plans for after they graduate. In community settings, clients seek help in exploring the possibility of switching to new jobs, in finding job opportunities that fit their interests and training, or in seeking further schooling or training.

When a client requests help in exploring career choice, the counselor uses a goal-oriented approach. Together, they review occupational history and experience, consider the use of occupational testing, and explore data about occupations or training possibilities as part of client self-exploration and environmental exploration.

As said earlier, few counselors rely solely on tests and inventories to predict appropriate choices in occupations. Most professional career counselors take into consideration social, cultural, and developmental factors when helping persons make career choices.

Conflict with Others About Careers

Conflicts because of others' expectations about one's career often contribute to vocational concerns. In high schools, colleges, and communities, parents, spouses, or peers may pressure clients to make choices that are incompatible with their own interests or abilities. In the community, job demands in two-career families or a husband's objection to his wife's desire to start a career may cause marital strife. Conflicts with bosses, supervisors, colleagues, or family may be interfering with a client's progress or satisfaction on the job.

When clients express strong feelings of anxiety or uncertainty related to work, counselors tend to switch to a client-centered approach in which interviewing skills are used to help clients explore feelings and develop insights. An unemployed woman without work experience might ask for counseling because of marital conflict. Her husband is unwilling to come to counseling. Conflicts about leaving the marriage may relate to her fears about her ability to support herself and her children if she divorces her husband. A young man comes to counseling ostensibly for career counseling. He would like to major in music but is confused because his parents will not give him financial or emotional support. Their support will come, however, if he enters into a computer training program. In family or marriage counseling, a wife's decision to start a career is causing dissension, or a husband's discontent with his job is contributing to conflicts with his wife and children. In all these cases, both career and personal concerns must be met.

To accomplish an integration of personal and career considerations, counselors must think holistically. In her work with the client, the counselor skillfully integrates the client's career-related concerns with the client's personal concerns. (For clients in acute emotional distress, career exploration is delayed.) Rather than interpreting a whole battery of occupational test results all at once, for example, the counselor discusses with the client each test result whenever one fits into what the client is working through in the counseling session. In the final stages, a decision about, say, staying with a marriage may include career plans whether or not a divorce occurs. Or a decision about staying with one's own career interest might include changing one's attitudes toward parents.

Personal Doubts About Careers

Clients come to counselors about career concerns when they are experiencing a conflict or confusion about their choice of career. A client with strong interests and abilities in two or more areas becomes confused about which way to go, especially if one choice appears to exclude the others. Clients may experience discrepancies between their interests and aptitudes and their career choices. They may have interest in an occupation but insufficient aptitude, or they may have strong interest in one field and strong aptitude in a different field. Clients' personal values may be at odds with their career choices. For example, an individual may have a strong leaning toward business but believe that the corporate world discriminates against women and minorities.

Life Transitions Affecting Careers

Changes in lifestyles, family moves, or family changes may lead to requests for counseling. A husband who has been the sole provider may suddenly divorce, or desert his wife, or die. His wife, who has not worked outside the home for years, needs help finding employment to support herself and her family. Occupations become obsolete, and individuals must find new careers. Those considering retirement want to explore new possibilities. A stay-at-home mom, after her children are in school, decides to begin a new career outside the home. An employed worker dissatisfied with a job wants to explore a more satisfying career. A client laid off from her job experiences uncertainty, apprehension, and bewilderment about how to find a new job.

When clients' personal concerns interfere too much with career issues, the counselor refers these clients to an outside agency for personal counseling or therapy before proceeding with career counseling. Brown (1995) points out that although it is possible for counselors to address career and personal problems at the same time, this becomes impossible when clients' emotional or psychological distress prevent them from engaging in career exploration.

⇒ OUTREACH

Counselors in career counseling centers offer clients a wide range of psychological education and outreach activities. They refer clients with personal concerns regarding careers to workshops or group activities related to stress reduction, assertiveness training, or feelings of loss. They offer, as well, seminars and workshops on preparing job résumés, preparing for job interviews, or learning skills and strategies to improve relationships with supervisors or fellow workers on the job (see chaps. 7 and 19).

The Career Action Center (1997) in Cupertino, California, offers numerous outreach activities as well as counseling. This center is a nonprofit organization staffed by approximately 70 full- and part-time staff. About a third of them are master's-level counselors, most of whom are specialists in career counseling. A few are nationally certified counselors. The rest are specialists in business and are experienced in career-related concerns such as organizational development, human resources, human relations, and business management. The organization has membership fees that cover free workshops or discounts on workshops for members.

Besides offering counseling for self-awareness related to careers, this center offers workshops on how to market oneself when looking for jobs or changing careers, career management and work strategies for those working to improve their status in their current jobs, and strategy workshops for those wanting to be self-employed. Examples of workshops focused on marketing oneself are conducting a work search, canvassing the area for prospective employers, practicing job interviews, and writing effective job résumés. Career management workshops cover skills in conflict management, active listening, writing skills, assertiveness training, and overcoming anxiety on the job.

⊰ SPECIAL TOOLS IN CAREER COUNSELING

Innumerable vocational interest and personality inventories and aptitude tests can help counselors and clients explore client characteristics related to careers. Occupational information resources are also valuable aids to help counselors and clients gather data about occupations, jobs, educational opportunities, or vocational training.

Inventories and Tests

Vocational Interest Inventories

Vocational interest inventories, in which clients compare themselves with groups of people in various occupations, are the most popular measures used in counseling. The Strong Interest Inventory (SII), the Kuder Occupational Interest Survey (KOIS), and Holland's (1994) Self-Directed Search (SDS) are examples of widely used interest inventories (see chap. 6). Other commonly used interest inventories with descriptive data can be found in Isaacson and Brown (1997).

The SII is designed for counseling with adults, college students, and high school seniors. The client's profile of interests is compared with those of people employed successfully in a wide variety of occupations. These occupations are grouped according to Holland's personality types and environmental structures (RIASEC).

The KOIS also compares an individual's scores with those of people in various occupations, but it includes more occupations in skilled trades and semiprofessions than does the SII. It also includes scores for college majors. The Kuder General Interest Survey—with broad interest classifications, such as mechanical, clerical, scientific, and social service—is appropriate for students in middle schools and the first 2 years of high school.

Holland's SDS is a self-administered, self-scored, and self-interpreted instrument that can be completed in less than an hour. Clients then compare their personal responses with occupations on the basis of Holland's RIASEC categories using the "Occupations Finder."

Personality Inventories

Some counselors administer *personality inventories* if they sense that personal conflicts are interfering with clients' career resolution. The California Psychological Inventory (CPI), the Edwards Personal Preference Schedule (EPPS), the Omnibus Personality Inventory, and the Minnesota Counseling Inventory are representative of personality inventories used in vocational counseling (see chap. 6).

The Myers-Briggs Type Indicator (MBTI), based on Jungian personality types (introvert-extravert, sensing-intuition, thinking-feeling, and judgment-perception), is of interest to counselors who relate lifestyles to career development (Brown & Brooks, 1991; Gysbers & Moore, 1987). Many Jungians have expressed concerns about an oversimplified use of typology based on the idea that individuals have inherent, unalterable tendencies that determine their lives (Samuels, 1985; see also chap. 5).

Ability Tests

Two aptitude batteries are predominant in vocational counseling: the Differential Aptitude Test (DAT), given widely in high schools, and the General Aptitude Test Battery (GATB), administered most often by state employment offices to the general population. Other aptitude tests commonly used are described in Isaacson and Brown (1997).

The Armed Services Vocational Aptitude Battery (ASVAB) was developed for use in career counseling in the military. It is now used in high schools for exploration of both civilian and military careers (Zunker, 1994). When used in high schools, the battery should be administered and interpreted by school counselors and not by armed services recruiters, because recruiters tend to be biased toward selection of military careers.

Occupational Information

Occupational information is available in resource libraries at centers offering career counseling. Innumerable pamphlets, monographs, audiovisual materials, programmed instruction, computer-based systems, and simulated career games cover occupations, jobs, job families, and occupational fields (Herr & Cramer, 1996; McWhirter, 1991).

Government agencies—particularly the U.S. Departments of Labor and Commerce—and private companies are the major sources for this information. Educational institutions, professional associations, and commercial outlets also publish information about technical schools, colleges, and continuing education. State employment agencies can provide information on trends in the labor market, including projections of future job openings.

Two sources that counselors and clients use most frequently for career information are the *Dictionary of Occupational Titles (DOT)* and the *Occupational Outlook Handbook (OOH;* Isaacson & Brown, 1997). The *DOT,* published by the U.S. Department of Labor, provides important client information about almost any occupation in the United States. Included are definitions of occupations, descriptions of jobs in typical industries, and lists of specific skills and worker traits essential to perform these jobs. The *OOH* describes the occupations in more detail, including educational and experience prerequisites, places of employment, employment outlook, earnings, working conditions, chances for advancement, and lists of government resources that provide additional information.

Computer-Assisted Programs

Computer-assisted programs are very useful for counselors and clients who are ready to search for career information. It is almost impossible for counselors to gain access on their own to the tremendous amount of information available on occupations, occupational characteristics, and occupational requirements. Computer databases can help counselors keep up with the ever-changing trends, projections about jobs, and job descriptions (Zunker, 1994).

Computers are also helpful in counseling when clients are ready to compare what they know about their abilities, interests, and personality with occupational lists provided by the computer that match these characteristics (Isaacson, 1986). Some computer-assisted systems help clients plan by providing educational and training programs consistent with the clients' personal characteristics. Some programs offer help in planning job search procedures.

Computers can give only limited help to clients, however, in their explorations about themselves and about their interactions with others. Clients generally need a counselor's help in expressing their interests or in clarifying perceptions about their own abilities before using a computer. Moreover, material gained from computer-assisted programs is best synthesized and integrated in counseling sessions.

Computers do not replace counselors. For this reason, Sampson, Shahnasarian, and Reardon (1987) argue that the term *computer-assisted* be used, rather than *computerized,* a term that implies a counselor is not needed. They found that 95% of all institutions using computer-assisted programs provide counselor assistance.

Types of Computer-Assisted Programs

Three major computer-assisted programs are discussed here briefly. Readers interested in comprehensive descriptions of major computer-assisted programs should consult Isaacson and Brown (1997) and Zunker (1994).

DISCOVER, developed for Grades 7 to 12, includes information about self, a systematic exploration of occupations, decision-making skills, the relationship of information about self to various occupations, and assistance in choosing an occupation.

SIGI, used for persons considering enrolling or already enrolled in 2- and 4-year colleges, is based on the assumption that a person's values relate to choice of occupation. Included are lists of values and related occupations, predictions about grades in required courses, programs for entering training, and help in selecting occupations that fit certain values.

CHOICES, available in colleges and placement offices, follows a practical, step-by-step counseling sequence. The counselor first interviews a client, and then the client fills out a self-assessment inventory of interests, aptitudes, and temperament. Then, with the counselor's help, the client decides whether to use the computer to locate specific occupations, to compare them and find related ones, or to explore occupations generally if the client has limited knowledge about them.

✺ COUNSELING PROGRAMS FOR EMPLOYEES IN BUSINESS AND INDUSTRY

Counseling employees in business and industry has become one of the most rapidly growing specialties in counseling and in counseling psychology (Lewis & Lewis, 1986).

As discussed in chapter 1, four programs have developed for employees: (a) employee assistance programs (EAPs), (b) employee enhancement programs (EEPs), (c) career development counseling in the industry, and (d) outplacement counseling. *Employee assistance programs (EAPs)* offer counseling to employees and their families when personal or social conflicts or problems are interfering with work performance. *Employee enhancement programs (EEPs)* emphasize preventive services to improve overall mental and physical health of employees and their families. *Career development counseling programs* help employees in making career choices within the organization in which they work. *Outplacement counseling programs* help employees who have been laid off in assessing their employment experience and skills and search for new jobs (Herr & Kramer, 1996; Zunker, 1994).

Employee Assistance Programs (EAPs)

As early as the 1940s, a few companies—Dupont, Consolidated Edison, and Eastman Kodak—started offering counseling services for employees who were alcoholics. They realized that it was more profitable and effective to rehabilitate alcoholic workers with good records than to fire them and retrain new workers. These programs were called occupational alcoholism programs (OAPs) (Dickman, 1985). In the 1960s, this service spread to other companies. Kemper Insurance Group expanded its alcoholism program to include marriage and family problems and emotional, financial, or legal concerns. This expansion led to the formation of employee assistance programs (EAPs). In the 1970s and 1980s, EAPs continued to expand their services to include employees whose job performance was affected by other personal problems (Smith, Salts, & Smith, 1989). By 1995, the number of EAPs offered in businesses were between 12,000 and 14,000 (Gladding, 1997).

As Figure 12.1 shows, the original alcoholism programs expanded services first to EAPs, known as the broad-brush approach, and then to EEPs (Dickman, 1985).

FIGURE 12.1

Types of employment counseling programs in business.

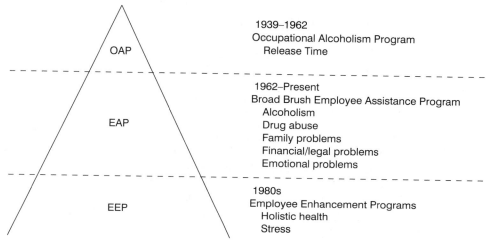

1939–1962
Occupational Alcoholism Program
Release Time

1962–Present
Broad Brush Employee Assistance Program
Alcoholism
Drug abuse
Family problems
Financial/legal problems
Emotional problems

1980s
Employee Enhancement Programs
Holistic health
Stress

Source: From "Employee Assistance Programs: History and Philosophy" (p. 7) by J. F. Dickman, in J. F. Dickman, W. G. Emener, Jr., & W. S. Hutchison, Jr. (Eds.), *Counseling the Troubled Person in Industry,* 1985. Courtesy of Charles C Thomas, Publisher, Springfield, Illinois.

Purpose of EAPs

The major purpose of an EAP is to provide professional counseling for employees and their families when the employees are experiencing conflicts or problems that are leading to poor work performance, absenteeism, accidents, or conflicts with supervisors that could result ultimately to job termination if not corrected.

Characteristics of EAPs

In the 1980s, representatives of labor and management, national associations concerned with alcoholism, and occupational consultants jointly developed standards for EAPs throughout the United States. Although these standards are voluntary, most practitioners adhere to them (Lewis & Lewis, 1986).

According to these standards, EAPs must have written policies about their philosophy and intent; procedures to orient employees, employers, and supervisors; guarantees of confidentiality to clients; and freedom of choice concerning whether an employee will use the service. Moreover, procedures for individuals referred by supervisors or union representatives must be clear-cut. Counselors need to be located in offices that are fairly accessible to all employees.

Counseling with employees and their families is usually relatively short term. When long-term counseling is necessary, EAP counselors refer such clients to community agencies or private practitioners.

Counselor Characteristics for EAP Counseling

Besides the training required of all counselors, EAP counselors need additional experience and training in business organizations and personnel management. Because alcoholism is still a major source of employee problems, training and experiences in this area are important. Family counseling methods are also needed to meet the increased demand to work with families when individuals are having problems.

Internal and External Programs

Some EAPs are based within the organization (*internal model*); some are run by outside consultants under contract with the company (*external model*); (Lewis & Lewis, 1986). Each model has advantages and disadvantages. Smaller companies usually use outside consultants because they are less expensive.

Almost all early programs were internal, with services provided by counselors who were employees of the company. The advantages are that the EAP counselor is familiar with the organization, its potential strengths, and its potential problems. The counselor may be more trusted by employees, more joint consultation with supervisors and employees is possible, and more realistic solutions may emerge. Preventive educational programs might be more easily developed. Confidentiality might be a problem, however, if counseling facilities are close to administration offices, or supervisors might make demands to know about the client's progress.

When companies use outside mental health services, counselors find it easier to maintain confidentiality and to be more professionally objective about company policies and procedures. But they might find it more difficult to integrate these services into the total organizational work environment.

Hosie, West, and Mackey (1993) surveyed staffing patterns of EAPs throughout the country. They found that professionals with master's degrees in counseling and in social work were employed more frequently than individuals with doctoral degrees in the mental health field.

Services Offered

Whether a company runs an EAP or contracts out, EAP counselors offer services paralleling those offered in other counseling services. In addition to individual, group, and family counseling, counselors offer consultation and skills workshops to supervisors and provide psychological education programs promoting good mental health in the work setting. They may also act as agents of social change in suggesting changes in policies and procedures in supervisor and employee relationships and expectations. EAP counselors are also trained to make appropriate referrals to mental health agencies or private practitioners when the client's problems require more intensive or extensive work than allowed by the EAP counselor. EAP counselors anticipate they will be offering more comprehensive services in the future, including child care, care for older adult relatives, and planning for retirement (Zunker, 1994).

Employee Enhancement Programs (EEPs)

EEPs are preventive, or wellness, programs that may be an arm of an EAP or offered as a separate package of services. These programs, combined with counseling services offered by EAPs under one jurisdiction, can supplement each other as they do in other counseling services.

The purpose of EEP preventive programs, also known as psychological education, is to educate workers about drug and alcohol use, teach stress management and relaxation skills, and provide workshops in other life skills, such as parenting, marriage enrichment activities, and communication and relationship skills (Lewis & Lewis, 1986; see also chap. 7).

In addition to providing psychological education programs and wellness activities, EEP counselors can explore and help alleviate stressful work conditions:

> Environmental characteristics to examine include physical stressors such as noise level or crowding, as well as such job situations as lack of control, ambiguity and insecurity, family reward systems, overly repetitive work, poor communication patterns, and too little opportunity for growth and development. (Lewis & Lewis, 1986, p. 13)

Job Adjustment Counseling

Career counselors hired by an industry work primarily on helping clients find appropriate placement or job adjustment within the company, including helping them explore the possibilities of changing to a more satisfying job or advancing within the company (see chap. 19).

A career counseling unit can help employees identify career paths in an organization leading to advancement or to more satisfying jobs. At times, career plans do not involve new positions. Sometimes employees realize they need to broaden skills or learn new competencies to be successful and satisfied in a particular job. Large companies often have in-service or on-the-job training to enhance and improve employees' skills. Some provide tuition for employees to take college-level courses or technical school training. These programs are expanding in business and industry. "Increasingly, evidence suggests that both employers and employees benefit from these programs" (Isaacson & Brown, 1997, p. 473).

Retirement is one of the most potentially distressing transitions unless planning is started a few years before work officially ends. Organizations need to provide pre-retirement counseling services to employees, covering both emotional concerns and practical consideration about benefits (Zunker, 1994).

Other painful transitions occur when a worker is suddenly transferred to a new job, promoted, demoted, or moved to a new branch within the company, perhaps requiring a move to another part of the country. Those who have just graduated from technical school and are starting their first real job often experience transition anxiety. Counselors in the workforce who are aware of the vocational pressures and the personal stresses can be of help to both employees and company management in easing the strain of those workers in transition.

Outplacement Counseling

An increasing number of companies have become interested in helping employees whose jobs were terminated because of bankruptcy, company cutbacks, obsolescence, or other reasons for which the workers are not responsible (Isaacson & Brown, 1997; Zunker, 1994).

Companies most often use outside career consultants to help displaced employees find new jobs and adjust psychologically (Herr & Cramer, 1996). It is important to help these employees, individually or in groups, express their anger. In these situations, counselors give personal counseling assistance and help employees learn job-seeking skills, develop effective résumés, and conduct themselves with confidence in job interviews (Zunker, 1994).

✒ EMPLOYMENT COUNSELORS

Employment counselors specialize in helping people find jobs. They work in state employment offices and in college and private placement agencies. These workers are often called *occupational information specialists* or *career information specialists.* As said earlier, although the national professional association strongly recommends that employment and placement counselors be certified, this is not required by law.

Most placement agencies accumulate job listings from employers through telephone calls or visits, or they receive them directly from employers. Effective placement counselors spend considerable time cultivating relationships with personnel directors and other hiring officials so that their placement offices will be contacted when firms have job openings.

Counselors, particularly those in colleges and private placement offices, also teach clients job search techniques and job interview skills and give them tips on developing résumés (Herr & Cramer, 1996). By role playing with clients before they go on interviews, the counselor helps them reduce anxiety, as well as teach them how to respond and assert themselves constructively with the person in charge of hiring.

Employment counselors in state employment agencies work with challenging and difficult groups of clients, particularly those who have been laid off from their jobs. Clients need urgent help, especially if they have families to support. Those who have suddenly lost jobs may experience shock, denial, grief, and anger. Those who cannot find work over a long period of time may feel defeated, resigned, desperate, or resentful. Another group, the chronically unemployed, are often difficult to place because of alcoholism, marginal intelligence, or borderline personality functioning. Their motivation is low, and their employment histories are erratic, at best.

To help the special needs of unemployed clients, it is essential that agencies hire certified or licensed career counselors. Professional counselors then can consider clients' emotional conflicts as they try to help the clients find work. When the employment counselor finds that a client is so distraught that she or he is not ready for placement, a referral to a mental health counselor or to a counseling psychologist is in order.

✎ VOCATIONAL REHABILITATION COUNSELING

Rehabilitation counselors help clients with disabilities find appropriate employment and aid them in developing and maintaining as much independence as possible (Herr & Cramer, 1996; Leahy & Szymanski, 1995). State rehabilitation agencies differentiate the terms *disabled* and *handicapped*. Zunker (1994) defines a *disability* as a physical or mental impairment that limits functioning in one or more bodily systems. A *handicap* is described as an inability, related to the disability, to function on a job because of some barrier in the work environment. For example, elevators are unavailable for a paraplegic worker.

Rehabilitation counselors, besides having typical course work expected of all counselors, have course work in medical and psychological aspects of disability, worker compensation policies, environmental and attitudinal barriers related to disabilities, special considerations in job placement of those with disabilities, and knowledge about psychological, medical, social or behavioral services and interventions needed by clients with disabilities (Jenkins, Patterson, & Szymanski, 1992; Leahy & Szymanski, 1995).

The majority of rehabilitation counselors work in public rehabilitation agencies for federal and state governments. These include rehabilitation centers, state employment services, Veterans Administration facilities, prisons and correctional agencies, mental health clinics, hospitals, and Social Security and worker compensation agencies. Recently, privately run rehabilitation services have developed that contract their services with public agencies or the government. In addition, private schools for students with disabilities and some colleges employ rehabilitation counselors.

Rehabilitation counselors are now being hired in EAPs, university-based services for students with disabilities, school-to-work transition programs, and disability management programs in business and industry (Leahy & Szymanski, 1995).

Parker and Hansen (1981) were among the first to describe rehabilitation counseling as a multistep process. Others have followed with similar proposals (Jenkins et al., 1992; Leahy & Szymanski, 1995). This process-oriented counseling generally proceeds as follows: (a) case finding, (b) eligibility determination for services, (c) career counseling, (d) career placement, (e) case management, and (f) termination.

Case Finding

Rehabilitation counselors find potential clients by contacting and setting up referral procedures with other agencies and health professionals who come in contact with persons with disabilities. After a client and the counselor have an initial interview, they review the client's medical, psychological, educational, and vocational background. The counselor is still in the case-finding stage. Eligibility of the client for rehabilitation services has yet to be determined.

Eligibility Determination for Services

Before counseling proceeds, the counselor must evaluate the extent of the disability, how much the disability is handicapping the person at work, and whether handicapping problems can be corrected through rehabilitation.

The counselor coordinates and evaluates the medical, psychological, and vocational assessment and decides on eligibility. If eligibility is denied, the counselor must inform the client of the reason and of the right to appeal. A claim may be denied because the client is employable without need for rehabilitation, the disability is not sufficient to warrant benefits, or the client is so severely disabled that vocational rehabilitation would not help. If eligibility is established, the counselor develops written plans that include long-term and intermediate goals and services to be provided.

The client may be eligible for one or more of the following services: counseling, medical treatment, physical restoration (prosthesis, hearing aid), psychiatric help, prevocational or vocational training, maintenance expenses, transportation, and such provisions as reader services and guide dogs for the blind.

Career Counseling

Throughout the rehabilitation process, counselors must work with the emotional impact individuals experience because of their incapacitating disability. Strategies to accomplish this task must be included in counselor training (Livneh & Sherwood, 1991).

Livneh and Sherwood (1991) discuss how counselors can use any number of theoretical approaches with clients with disabilities: *psychoanalytic, Adlerian, person-centered, Gestalt, behavioral,* and *cognitive-behavioral.* They recommend that counselors select interventions congruent with their own theoretical orientation and with the nature and setting of client disability. Using these interventions, counselors help clients with disabilities gain insight into the psychosocial impact of the disability.

Livneh and Sherwood (1991) point out that those persons with disabilities go through phases of adjustment. "Adaptation to disability is not a static concept. It is a dynamic and often protracted process that is composed of several fluctuating and overlapping phases" (p. 525). Synthesizing from models presented by other researchers, Livneh and Sherwood describe eight phases of adjustment, named in the following sequence: "*shock, anxiety, denial, depression, internalized anger, externalized hostility, acknowledgment,* and *adjustment*" (p. 525). These feelings must be acknowledged and worked through if appropriate vocational rehabilitation is to occur.

Career Placement

Placement is considered a major focus of rehabilitation counseling (Jenkins et al., 1992). Complications in placement of these workers may arise because of negative attitudes of employers, fellow employees, and the clients themselves regarding the disability (Isaacson & Brown, 1997).

Some placement agencies have a rehabilitation counselor who specializes in placing persons with disabilities. Such a specialist places clients in jobs after the counselor has helped the clients become ready for the jobs (Parker & Hansen, 1981).

Case Management and Termination

After placing a client on a job, the rehabilitation counselor monitors the client for a few months to see how well she or he is adapting and adjusting to the new work setting. The counselor also consults with the employer and the client's supervisor about how the new employee is functioning on the job. The counselor may suggest changes that are needed in the work setting.

When the counselor, client, and employer are satisfied with the client's progress on the job, the case is terminated. At that time, the counselor lets the client know that her or his case can be reopened if further assistance is needed.

⟡ RESEARCH IN CAREER COUNSELING AND DEVELOPMENT

Considerable research has been conducted by counseling psychologists in the area of career development theory, career measurement, and career interventions (Osipow, 1987). Interest measurement and vocational development represent some of the best-developed research areas in counseling psychology (Borgen, 1984).

Comprehensive reviews of career research have been presented by Borgen (1984), Brown and Lent (1984), Osipow and Fitzgerald (1996), Spokane and Oliver (1983), and Walsh and Osipow (1983). Presented here are overall trends. Readers interested in specific research areas can refer to the resources listed.

Much of career theory began in the 1950s with Super's research on career development and career maturity. These concepts have been listed empirically and have received support from researchers (Osipow, 1987).

Holland's person-environment theory has generated more research than any other career theory (Osipow, 1987). Weinrach (1984) comments, "Probably no theory of career development or vocational choice has been researched or commented on as extensively as Holland's" (p. 71). Osipow (1987) sums up research on Holland's theory as follows: "Most of the findings point to the theory's vitality and validity for the purposes for which it was designed" (p. 263).

Research on outcomes of career counseling or vocational interventions has been summarized by Spokane and Oliver (1983). They present an integrative analysis of 52 studies about the outcome of vocational intervention. They concluded that career counseling leads to positive outcomes. Herr and Cramer (1988) concur that "research studies have repeatedly demonstrated that career interventions do yield positive results and that their general utility is clear" (p. 478).

EAPs have consistently shown remarkably high degrees of success in increased worker productivity and improved physical and emotional health of alcoholic workers (Quayle, 1985). The rapid increase in the number of companies developing these programs attests to more productive, satisfied, and healthier workers (Dickman, 1985).

✤ SUMMARY

Career counseling relates to personal and social counseling because the development, choice, and establishment of a career are closely tied to personal needs, social and environmental influences, and personality development. The number of career counseling centers has greatly expanded in the past decade or so in the community and in business and industry.

The major theories influencing the career counseling process are those that relate career development to personal development and those that relate one's personal developmental characteristics to occupational environments compatible with the individual. Typical client problems related to careers are the need for career exploration, conflict with others regarding career choices, doubts about choosing or remaining in a career, and disruptive conflicts arising out of transitions in work and family.

Community career counseling centers offer numerous and varied outreach workshops and seminars to help clients develop strategies in job searches, to upgrade themselves in current jobs, and to deal with anxieties or uncertainties during job transitions.

Increasing numbers of counselors are hired by businesses to work with employees whose concerns interfere with their work productivity. Some businesses also hire counselors to help employees find the most suitable career path in the company or to find jobs in other companies when their jobs are terminated. Rehabilitation services to help individuals with disabilities in career and educational planning have spread from government agencies to private agencies in the community and to schools and universities.

✤ PROJECTS AND ACTIVITIES

1. Ask one or more people in their 50s who are well-established in jobs why they chose their fields, how they entered them, and what steps they took to get to their current jobs.
2. Sigmund Freud once said that work and love are two of the most important experiences in life. Alfred Adler, another psychoanalyst, agreed. How does this view relate to the theories of career development currently popular?
3. Explore your university's computer-assisted programs for information about careers. Ask to use the program to gain information about professional counseling. Evaluate the quality and quantity of information obtained.
4. Interview counselors at your local state unemployment and Division of Vocational Rehabilitation offices. From their comments, indicate how you might make use of these agencies as referral sources if you were a counselor in the community.
5. Interview a college placement counselor and a placement counselor in the state employment service. Compare their functions, attitudes, and resources.
6. Explore what employee assistance programs are available in your community. Try to interview both a counselor who works in an internal program and one who is employed in an external agency.
7. Select one career theory or one vocational interest measure (e.g., Strong, Kuder, or SDS), and read a review of the research. Select a study considered a sound one and one the reviewer considers faulty. Analyze the strengths and weaknesses.

⋙ REFERENCES

Betz, N. E., & Corning, A. F. (1993). The inseparability of "career" and "personal" counseling. *Career Development Quarterly, 42,* 137–142.

Borgen, F. H. (1984). Counseling psychology. *Annual Review of Psychology, 35,* 579–604.

Brown, D. (1985). Career counseling: Before, after, and instead of personal counseling? *Vocational Guidance Quarterly, 33,* 197–201.

Brown, D. (1995). A value-based approach to facilitating career transitions. *Career Development Quarterly, 44,* 4–11.

Brown, D., & Brooks, L. (1991). *Career counseling techniques.* Boston: Allyn & Bacon.

Brown, S. D., & Lent, R. W. (Eds.). (1984). *Handbook of counseling psychology.* New York: John Wiley.

Career Action Center. (1997). *Career action connections: A resource guide to career self-reliance bimonthly.* Cupertino, CA: Author.

Dickman, J. F. (1985). Employee assistance programs: History and philosophy. In J. F. Dickman, W. G. Emener, & W. S. Hutchison (Eds.), *Counseling the troubled person in industry* (pp. 7–12). Springfield, IL: Charles C Thomas.

Gallagher, R. P. (1996). *National survey of counseling center directors.* Alexandria, PA: International Association of Counseling Services.

Ginzberg, E. (1972). Toward a theory of occupational choice: A restatement. *Vocational Guidance Quarterly, 20,* 169–176.

Ginzberg, E., Ginzburg, S. W., Axelrad, S., & Herma, J. I. (1951). *Occupational choice: An approach to theory.* New York: Columbia University Press.

Gladding, S. T. (1997). *Community and agency counseling.* Upper Saddle River, NJ: Merrill/Prentice Hall.

Gysbers, N. C., & Moore, E. J. (1987). *Career counseling: Skills and techniques for practitioners.* Upper Saddle River, NJ: Prentice Hall.

Herr, E. L., & Cramer, S. H. (1988). *Career guidance and counseling through the life span: Systematic approaches* (3rd ed.). Boston: Scott, Foresman.

Herr, E. L., & Cramer, S. H. (1996). *Career guidance and counseling through the life span: Systematic approaches* (5th ed.). Boston: Scott, Foresman.

Holland, J. L. (1959). A theory of vocational choice. *Journal of Counseling Psychology, 6,* 35–45.

Holland, J. L. (1985). *Making vocational choices: A theory of vocational personalities and work environments* (2nd ed.). Upper Saddle River, NJ: Prentice Hall.

Holland, J. L. (1994). *The Self-Directed Search: Professional manual.* 3rd ed. Odessa, FL: Psychological Assessment Resources.

Hosie, T. W., West, J. D., & Mackey, J. A. (1993). Employment and roles of counselors in employee assistance programs. *Journal of Counseling & Development, 71,* 355–359.

Hoyt, K. B., & Lester, J. L. (1995). *Learning to work: The NCDA Gallup survey.* Alexandria, VA: National Board for Certified Counselors.

Isaacson, L. E. (1986). *Career information in counseling and career development* (4th ed.). Boston: Allyn & Bacon.

Isaacson, L. E., & Brown, D. (1997). *Career information, career counseling, and career development* (6th ed.). Boston: Allyn & Bacon.

Jenkins, W., Patterson, J. B., & Szymanski, E. M. (1992). Philosophical, historic, and legislative aspects of the rehabilitation counseling profession. In R. M. Parker & E. M. Szymanski (Eds.), *Rehabilitation counseling: Basics and beyond* (2nd ed., pp. 1–41). Austin, TX: PRO-ED.

Krumboltz, J. D. (1993). Integrating career and personal counseling. *Career Development Quarterly, 42,* 143–148.

Leahy, M. J., & Szymanski (1995). Rehabilitation counseling: Evolution and current status. *Journal of Counseling & Development, 74,* 163–166.

Lee, C. C., & Shahnasarian, M. (1998). Setting the record straight. *Counseling Today, 40,* 18.

Lewis, J. A., & Lewis, M. D. (1986). *Counseling programs for employees in the workplace.* Pacific Grove, CA: Brooks/Cole.

Livneh, H., & Sherwood, A. (1991). Application of personality theories and counseling strategies to clients with physical disabilities. *Journal of Counseling & Development, 69,* 525–538.

McWhirter, E. H. (1991). Career counseling: An introduction. In D. Capuzzi & D. R. Gross (Eds.), *Introduction to counseling: Perspectives for the 1990s* (pp. 133–157). Boston: Allyn & Bacon.

Osipow, S. H. (1987). Counseling psychology: Theory, research, and practice in career counseling. *Annual Review of Psychology, 38,* 257–278.

Osipow, S. H., & Fitzgerald, L. F. (1996). *Theories of career development* (4th ed.). Boston: Allyn & Bacon.

Parker, R. M., & Hansen, C. E. (Eds.). (1981). *Rehabilitation counseling: Foundations—consumers—service delivery.* Boston: Allyn & Bacon.

Quayle, D. (1985). American productivity: The devastating effect of alcoholism and drug abuse. In J. F. Dickman, W. G. Emener, & W. S. Hutchison (Eds.), *Counseling the troubled person in industry* (pp. 20–29). Springfield, IL: Charles C Thomas.

Roe, A. (1957). Early determinants of vocational choice. *Journal of Counseling Psychology, 4,* 212–217.

Sampson, J. P., Shahnasarian, M., & Reardon, R. C. (1987). Computer-assisted career guidance: A national perspective on the use of DISCOVER and SIGI. *Journal of Counseling & Development, 65,* 416–419.

Samuels, A. (1985). *Jung and post-Jungians.* New York: Tavistock/Routledge.

Smith, T. A., Jr., Salts, C. J., & Smith, C. W. (1989). Preparing marriage and family therapy students to become employee assistance professionals. *Journal of Marital and Family Therapy, 15,* 419–424.

Spokane, A. R., & Oliver, L. W. (1983). The outcomes of vocational intervention. In B. W. Walsh & S. H. Osipow (Eds.), *Handbook of vocational psychology: Applications* (Vol. 2, pp. 99–136). Mahwah, NJ: Lawrence Erlbaum.

Super, D. (1942). *The dynamics of vocational adjustment.* New York: Harper Brothers.

Super, D. E. (1951). Vocational adjustment: Implementing a self-concept. *Occupations, 30,* 88–92.

Super, D. E. (1953). A theory of vocational development. *American Psychologist, 8,* 185–190.

Super, D. E. (1955). Personality integration through vocational counseling. *Journal of Counseling Psychology, 2,* 217–226.

Super, D. E. (1961). Consistency and wisdom of vocational preference as indices of vocational maturity in the ninth grade. *Journal of Educational Psychology, 52,* 35–43.

Super, D. E. (1980). A life-span, life-space approach to career development. *Journal of Vocational Behavior, 22,* 191–226.

Super, D. E. (1993). The two faces of counseling: Or is it three? *Career Development Quarterly, 42,* 132–136.

Walsh, W. B., & Osipow, S. H. (Eds.). (1983). *Handbook of vocational psychology* (Vols. 1 & 2). Mahwah, NJ: Lawrence Erlbaum.

Weinrach, S. G. (1984). Determinants of vocational choice: Holland's theory. In D. Brown & L. Brooks (Eds.), *Career choice and development.* San Francisco: Jossey-Bass.

Weinrach, S. G., & Srebalus, D. J. (1990). Holland's theory of careers. In D. Brown & L. Brooks (Eds.), *Career choice and development* (2nd ed., pp. 37–67). San Francisco: Jossey-Bass.

Yost, E. B., & Corbishley, M. A. (1987). *Career counseling: A psychological approach.* San Francisco: Jossey-Bass.

Zunker, V. G. (1994). *Career counseling: Applied concepts of life planning* (4th ed.). Pacific Grove, CA: Brooks/Cole.

13 Substance Abuse Counseling

Substance abuse occurs when a person overuses alcohol, illegal street drugs, or prescribed painkillers, tranquilizers, or stimulants over a sustained period of time, resulting in an impairment in personal and social functioning (Nystul, 1993). These substances are *psychoactive,* in that they alter mood, behavior, and perceptions and affect the nervous system through chemical changes in the brain. All these substances can lead to physical or psychological dependence (*addiction*) with repeated use; withdrawal from them can be devastating to the physical, psychological, and social functioning of the individual (American Psychiatric Association, 1994; Comer, 1998).

The addicted person also develops a *tolerance* to the effects of the substance. To maintain a certain level of euphoria requires increasing dosages, which can lead to more physical and mental damage and more financial burdens (Porter, 1998).

Although alcohol, like the other substances mentioned, is technically a drug, society has viewed its consumption differently from other drugs. Alcohol is not illegal for adults, and it does not require a prescription, as do most other drugs. Thus, alcohol problems and addictions warrant a separate discussion.

Although this chapter addresses substance abuse addictions, other addictions are increasingly prevalent in society, such as eating disorders, compulsive gambling, and sexual addictions. According to Fossum and Mason (1986) and Kasl (1989), as discussed later in this chapter, all addictive behaviors have the common underlying feelings of shame that stem from shame-based families. All members of such families participate in and maintain the system of shame and addiction. "One of the most clearly identifiable aspects of shame in families is addictive behavior. The addiction becomes a central organizing principle for the system, maintaining the system as well as the shame" (Fossum & Mason, 1986, p. 123).

Adding to this theory, Terence Real (1997), speaking on male depression, argues that all addictive behaviors—substance abuse, workaholism, excessive workouts, womanizing, overeating, gambling—act as defenses against male depression.

✸ COUNSELING PERSONS WITH ALCOHOL PROBLEMS

An estimated 13 million adults and 3 million people under the age of 21 can be classified as alcoholics or as problem drinkers. More than 70% of teenage suicides are related to alcohol. In half of all automobile accidents and deaths, the driver has been drinking (Comer, 1998; Stevens-Smith, 1998a). About $30 billion a year is lost in business because of the absenteeism or poor work performance of alcoholics (Quayle, 1985). Moreover, many diseases are frequently related to alcohol addiction: cirrhosis of the liver, pancreatic disorders, malnutrition, heart disease, problems of the nervous and muscular-skeletal systems, brain damage, and psychiatric reactions such as depression and paranoia (Goodwin, 1992; Porter, 1998). Serious interpersonal problems resulting from alcohol abuse include domestic violence, child abuse, marital conflict, sexual dysfunctions, and dysfunctional social relationships (L. W. Bennett, 1992; Stevens-Smith, 1998c).

How Do Alcoholics, Problem Drinkers, and Social Drinkers Differ?

The differences among alcoholics, problem drinkers, and social drinkers are indicated by the degree of dependency persons have on the substance. *Alcoholics* are both physically and psychologically dependent, *problem drinkers* are psychologically dependent, and *social drinkers* are not dependent on alcohol at all (Metzger, 1988; Peer, Lindsey, & Newman, 1982; Stevens-Smith, 1998a).

Alcoholics physically and psychologically depend on alcohol to such an extent that they spend most of their waking hours drinking to reduce psychological tension and to prevent *withdrawal symptoms* (severe physiological reactions when alcohol is withheld). They have trouble holding jobs because of poor attendance and poor performance. Alcoholics are chronically intoxicated; their drinking is obvious to friends and to the public. They deteriorate physically because of malnutrition and the toxic effects that alcohol has on their bodies.

Problem drinkers have a psychological dependence on alcohol. They are apt to drink every day and often excessively. Like alcoholics, they feel compelled to drink as part of their daily routine to reduce tension or anxiety. They differ from alcoholics in that they do not need alcohol to prevent withdrawal symptoms. They do not need a drink, for instance, when they first wake up in the morning to prevent the "shakes." But they sometimes cannot remember what they said or did for brief periods the night before. They may not start drinking until after 5:00 p.m., so they may seem normal most of the time. But their need for a drink every evening is still based on a compulsive urge that is persistent and repetitious. Problem drinkers often deny that they drink excessively and that the drinking causes any problems. Yet, their drinking leads to negative physical, economic, and social consequences (Forrest, 1978). According to Belkin (1984), alcoholism is a progressive disease, and problem drinkers are just "one step from alcoholism" (p. 416). Regarding the problem drinker's compulsion to drink at social events, he says, "If you need a drink to be social then you're not a social drinker" (p. 416).

Social drinkers drink a moderate amount of alcohol—perhaps one or two drinks a few times a week—and intoxication rarely occurs (Peer et al., 1982). Social drinkers feel no compulsion to drink; even at parties, they are often able to accept or refuse drinks as they please.

In the literature, problems of alcoholics are typically considered more serious than those of problem drinkers. For instance, in comparing the two groups, Belkin (1984) says that "the alcoholic is by far the worse" (p. 416).

Because the difficulties of problem drinkers are less obvious, they are more easily ignored, and thus their problem becomes more insidious. Families of alcoholics are often forced to seek help because of the severity of the problem: Alcoholics may pass out in public or on kitchen floors, they may lose jobs, or they may be hospitalized for cirrhosis of the liver. Friends, easily recognizing the problem, are more ready to lend support.

Families of problem drinkers are in a more ambiguous position. They are uncertain about the severity of the problem because problem drinkers are often sober a good part of the day. Without certain clear-cut evidence, families are less able to counter the problem drinkers' denials that they have a problem. Friends and relatives, often unaware of the problem, are less ready to understand the family's concerns. Problem drinkers, then, continue their compulsive drinking, and dysfunctional family patterns develop and persist.

What Causes Alcoholism?

Disease Theory

Most commonly, alcoholism is described as a disease caused by genetic or biological multigenerational factors that render persons susceptible to alcohol addiction or compulsive uncontrolled drinking (Erickson, 1998; Gilliland & James, 1997). Goodwin (1979) compared adopted children whose biological parents were alcoholics with adopted children whose biological parents were not alcoholics. He found that a significantly higher number of children whose biological parents were alcoholics became alcoholics themselves even though a higher percentage of these children had adoptive parents who were not alcoholics than did the group with nonalcoholic biological parents.

Alcoholism, when defined as a disease, is described as follows: "a chronic, primary, hereditary, eventually fatal disease that progresses from an early physiological susceptibility into an addiction characterized by tolerance changes, physiological dependence, and loss of control over drinking" (Mueller & Ketcham, 1987, p. 9). As in other diseases, a process of deterioration and destruction is based on specific causes, and specific characteristic symptoms are evident. Under this description, abstinence is essential for recovery.

Psychological Theories

Psychoanalytic and cognitive-behavioral theorists have given more attention to the psychological causes of alcoholism than have humanists (Price & Lynn, 1986). Freudian theorists assume that alcoholism is related to self-destructive tendencies or to intensive, inappropriate dependency (G. Bennett & Woolf, 1983). According to this view, the dependent oral character uses alcohol as a pacifier. Object relations proponents emphasize the alcoholic's need to alleviate and deny underlying personal and interpersonal conflicts. (Price & Lynn, 1986) Cognitive-behavioral and social learning counselors believe that alcohol addiction occurs because drinking habits are learned and maintained by sociological, psychological, and physiological factors (P. M. Miller & Eisler, 1976). They hypothesize that drinking serves the seemingly useful purpose of reducing discomfort, anxiety, and tension. This tension reduction reinforces drug usage and increases the possibility of continued usage.

Social-Cultural Theories

Social-cultural theories are based on observing drinking habits and patterns of differing cultural groups. Studies show that Jews and Italians have low alcoholism rates, whereas the Irish and French are high on the scale of alcoholism (Calahan, Cisin, & Crossley, 1969; Comer, 1998; Valliant & Milofsky, 1982). Other culture-specific theories attribute high rates of alcoholism in specific groups to prejudice or other forms of oppression against those groups. According to these theorists, oppression of a group contributes to its poverty and stagnant socioeconomic status, causing its members to suffer depression or to take refuge in alcoholism (Forrest, 1978; Stevens-Smith, 1998a). Native American Indians, who have the highest rate of alcoholism in the United States, are an example (Trimble, 1991).

Biopsychosocial Theories

Recently, biopsychosocial theories of substance abuse have emerged that incorporate biological, psychological, and social factors in assessing individuals who are predisposed to substance abuse (Erickson, 1998). These factors include "individual differences in pleasurable reactions to alcohol, psychophysiologic differences, neuro-chemical differences, temperament or personality differences, and environmental differences within the family, school, community and peer groups" (Erickson, 1998, p. 53).

These trends are gaining increasing support from those involved in treatment of substance abuse. This view is in accord with a multifaceted, comprehensive approach that includes attention to the individual's environment and family dynamics, as well as genetic and biochemical predisposition (Erickson, 1998).

Pretreatment of Persons with Alcohol Problems

Confronting a Person with an Alcohol Problem

Both alcoholics and problem drinkers deny that they have a drinking problem, so they most often respond negatively to suggestions or pleas that they seek treatment. They continue to deny the problem even though family members worry about their secret drinking, gulping of drinks, poor school or work attendance, bad nutrition, or family violence.

When family members decide that the excessive drinker must get treatment, they can—with consultation of alcoholism counselors—confront the alcoholic or problem drinker in a caring way with the necessity for treatment (Dickman & Phillips, 1985; Gilliland & James, 1997). This confrontation may convince the drinker to abstain from drinking, join Alcoholics Anonymous (AA), seek counseling, or take a combination of actions.

If the alcoholic or problem drinker continues to deny the problem, then a more forceful intervention technique may be necessary. An alcoholism counselor and, at times, very close friends may join with the family in confronting the person with the alcohol problem about the effects drinking is having on the individual's health and well-being and on the well-being of family members and friends (Mueller & Ketcham, 1987). If treatment is still refused, then alcoholism counselors recommend that the family break away from the excessive drinker for the sake of the family's mental health (O'Keefe, 1988).

Confrontation may also occur on the job when work performance is poor or when absenteeism is high because of the worker's alcoholism. Supervisors may confront the worker or may intervene jointly with a counselor in an employee assistance program (EAP) to convince the worker to seek treatment. Such interventions are usually effective because job security is involved (Dickman & Phillips, 1985).

Researchers caution against heavy-handed coercion in confronting the abuser. Making accusations or exhorting confessions from the abuser can lead to increased defensiveness and denial (Gilliland & James, 1997). R. H. Miller and Rollnick (1991) have developed a client-centered approach called *motivational interviewing*. Instead of forcing the issue, they discuss the problem with the abuser at an appropriate time and place and give advice rather than make demands. Such an approach gives the person in question a chance to make the decision to remedy the problem. This approach is most successful as an initial step when persons are being approached for the first time and if they are willing to listen.

Some alcoholics and problem drinkers may be able to abstain from alcohol for a while when they recognize the problem or are confronted. For alcoholics, spontaneous abstinence is rare because of withdrawal symptoms; for problem drinkers, it is difficult to do so for any length of time because environmental pressures from the family or the job often induce persons to revert to drinking. In most cases, alcoholics and problem drinkers need counseling help to recover; their families need counseling as well to give up behavioral patterns that are reinforcing the addiction.

Assessment and Detoxification

When the person with an alcohol problem agrees to go into treatment, an alcoholism counselor interviews the family and makes an assessment. If the alcoholism is chronic and severe, the person may need to be hospitalized to go through withdrawal under medical supervision. Withdrawal reactions can be severe and even fatal. This precursor to treatment is called *detoxification*. At times, the drug disulfiram (Antabuse) is used. It causes nausea and vomiting when taken with alcohol and helps the person attain abstinence (W. R. Miller & Hester, 1980). Detoxification may take from 3 or 4 days to a week, at which time the person is ready for treatment.

During assessment, the alcoholism counselor discusses with the spouse and other appropriate family members their own counseling and support needs. The counselor also indicates when and where these services are available.

Treatment Settings and Goals

Recovering alcoholics and problem drinkers can be rehabilitated at inpatient, outpatient, or partial hospitalization (day care) services at general or psychiatric hospitals with alcoholic units or at private, nonprofit alcoholism treatment centers. They may also choose to see private practitioners who have expertise in alcohol treatment, or they may receive treatment in community mental health clinics. Frequently, these programs are offered through EAPs, as described in chapter 12. Manfrin (1998) notes the diverse settings in which substance abuse treatment is offered:

> As opposed to mental health settings, which have a moderate range of facility differences, chemical dependency services can be delivered in hospitals, converted houses, basements of nonhospital detoxification centers, jails and prisons, youth centers, community centers, locked and unlocked psychiatric units, rural dwellings, and almost any setting that will house an alcohol or drug counselor with clients. (p. 135)

Inpatient treatment usually lasts about 4 weeks but can last as long as 6 months. Partial hospitalization often runs 5 or more hours a day, 5 days a week, for 4 to 6 weeks.

Although some professionals suggest that some alcoholics can continue drinking if they learn control (G. Bennett & Woolf, 1983), most researchers and clinicians believe that abstinence is the primary and essential goal in alcohol treatment. According to Nathan (1984), "Few clinicians would recommend a controlled drinking goal for an alcoholic" (p. 101). Erickson (1998) claims that research to support controlled drinking for alcoholics is meager and unsubstantiated. Whether or not problem drinkers can learn to control drinking has been a controversial issue for some time. Even so, research data have yet to show that problem drinkers can successfully control their alcohol consumption (Smith, 1998). My position, as expressed in this text, supports those clinicians who believe that abstinence, except in rare cases, should be the primary goal for both alcoholics and problem drinkers who intend to overcome alcohol abuse.

After alcoholics and problem drinkers stop drinking, they and their families need counseling help and for good reason. The term *recovering alcoholic* is often used for both alcoholics and problem drinkers who have stopped drinking. For convenience, my use of the term *recovering alcoholic* includes the recovering problem drinker. Some professionals claim that these people will always remain in the recovery stage because they will always be addicted to alcohol. Moreover, abstinence alone is insufficient to resolve the alcoholic's or the family's problems. Abstinence does not resolve the underlying problems of the alcoholic or those of the family members; nor does it immediately improve family relationships. Instead, family problems often become exacerbated when the denial patterns surrounding the alcoholism and the sedative effects of alcohol no longer exist. Because alcohol is no longer used as a cover-up for family dysfunction, personal problems of family members and family discord erupt. Moreover, family members often unconsciously or subconsciously resist changes in the recovering alcoholic who begins to assert needs and to display strengths. Continued counseling is needed to help both the alcoholic and the family form new patterns of behavior.

Counseling services and support groups for both alcoholics and family members can help change former dysfunctional family patterns. These services not only help recovering persons abstain but also help them and their family members learn to interact with one another in more productive ways. Counseling helps them understand old behaviors and attitudes, develop coping skills for new experiences in the present, and build a framework for continual future growth individually and as a family.

Spouse and Family Need for Treatment

Once the alcoholic agrees to treatment, the spouse and other family members also need counseling help. "The attitude structure, and function of the family system have been shown to be perhaps the most important variables in the outcome of treatment" (Gilliland & James, 1997, p. 387). As discussed in chapter 10, when one member of the family has a problem, this represents a problem in the total family system. In the typical family of an alcoholic or problem drinker, the spouse and children have been caught up in a family dynamic of intrigue in which the alcohol problem has been denied and rarely discussed so that feelings of shame permeate the family. Family boundaries are unclear, family members are enmeshed, and authentic communication is infrequent.

Families then hide their secret and unwittingly assume roles of *enablers* that allow the alcoholic to continue drinking and not suffer consequences. The spouse covers up for the alcoholic, takes over duties the spouse should handle, makes excuses for the drinking, pretends the spouse is ill (not drunk), and ends up acting like a martyr (Hogg & Frank, 1992; Schaef, 1986). Meanwhile, children assume different roles to help themselves and the family survive emotional stress while maintaining secrecy and denial. One may play the hero who hopes to redeem the family by being successful. Another may hide the pain by acting like the family clown, joker, or mascot. Still another may play the role of scapegoat and act out the family problems. Others may withdraw from stress and act like lost children (Ackerman, 1987; Woititz, 1983).

The goals of treatment of spouses and families are to work through their own problems and attitudes and gain sufficient independence so that they can drop their caretaking or enabling roles in which they control, manage, or manipulate one another or the alcoholic (Metzger, 1988; Nace, 1987). They also need help in overcoming their tendency to continue blaming the recovering alcoholics for all the drinking-related problems they had caused in the past. To compound the problem, as recovering alcoholics regain strength, family members are apt to feel stronger rage and resentment against them. The members may begin to act out, become physically ill, or develop an emotional disorder (Stevens-Smith, 1998b). "Paradoxically, if the alcoholic makes a commitment to stop drinking, the maladaptive family may become threatened enough to try to reinstitute the perceived homeostasis of alcoholism" (Gilliland & James, 1997, p. 387). This can be quite a problem for recovering alcoholics, and one main reason why many take refuge in AA groups is to protect themselves and get the necessary support to remain sober because little support is available from their families.

Codependency

According to alcoholism counselors, the enabling behavior described above occurs because family members have developed mutual codependent relationships (Beattie, 1987; Subby, 1987). In a codependent family, family members have not developed their own independence, cannot express their own needs, and cannot communicate genuine feelings. These characteristics originated in the early experiences of each parent in his or her family of origin.

Codependency is defined as an addiction to a relationship that stifles self-growth and self-expression. According to Wegscheider-Cruse (1985), the codependency addiction closely resembles the alcoholic's addiction to alcohol. Wegscheider-Cruse defines codependency as being dependent on others to such an extent that the dependent person becomes dysfunctional. Subby (1987) more generally sees codependency as arising from prolonged exposure to oppressive family rules that prevent open expression of feelings and straightforward discussion of personal problems. Cermak (1986) describes codependence as a pattern of maladaptive mechanisms in alcoholic families in which control of self and others' feelings and needs is the major way to reduce free-floating anxiety. Shame generated in shame-based families, as discussed later, is considered a major contributor to codependent behaviors (Fossum & Mason, 1986; Subby, 1987). Codependency involves a lack of clearly defined boundaries within a family, resulting in a loss of personhood.

Scores of characteristics have been published to describe the codependent (Beattie, 1987; Subby, 1987; Wegscheider-Cruse, 1985). Some common behaviors are typical of codependency (Cermak, 1986). Hogg and Frank (1992, p. 371) list some of these common behaviors as follows:

- *Martyrdom:* Giving up one's own needs in order to meet the needs of others
- *Fusion:* Losing one's identity in an intimate relationship
- *Intrusion:* Controlling the behavior of intimates through excessive caretaking, guilt, or manipulation
- *Perfection:* Holding unrealistic expectations of oneself and others
- *Addiction:* Using compulsive behaviors to manage one's emotions

Concerned about the proliferation of characteristics and the potential of overdiagnosis of codependency, Myer, Peterson, and Stoffel-Rosales (1991) urge that research about the etiology and characteristics of codependency be carried out by mental health counselors.

Alcohol Treatment

As said earlier, many professionals believe that best results occur if counselors insist that clients with an alcohol problem abstain from drinking as soon as counseling begins. Otherwise, the counselor becomes an enabler by giving tacit permission for continued drinking. If alcohol abusers continue to drink, the toxic effects of alcohol on their psychological and physical well-being inhibit the development of a counseling relationship and interfere with or distort communication (Forrest, 1984). After assessment of the severity of the individual's alcohol abuse and, if necessary, after detoxification treatment is completed, the majority of treatment programs, regardless of setting, include individual counseling, family counseling, group counseling, auxiliary services, and support groups (Manfrin, 1998).

Individual Counseling

In individual counseling, recovering alcoholics or problem drinkers and their spouses and appropriate family members receive help to develop feelings of self-worth and responsibility for their own behavior. They learn, most important, to express their own needs more directly. Through exploration of childhood experiences, they get in touch with unresolved feelings of anger, grief, or shame that are affecting their current behavior. They also learn new ways of dealing with stress.

Recovering alcoholics and problem drinkers learn not to depend on alcohol during times of stress. Spouses learn not to assume responsibility for persons recovering from excessive alcohol use so that they feel compelled to control or manage them. Above all, spouses must learn not to treat recovering alcoholics as inferior persons.

Individual counseling approaches vary. Psychodynamic approaches may be used to get at the issues and needs underlying abuse. Cognitive-behavioral strategies may be used to help the abuser develop self-control and prevent relapses. To help the client break the habit of drinking, behaviorists may apply an aversion technique in which an unpleasant stimulus is paired with drinking. Social skills practice or stress management are offered in counseling sessions (Comer, 1998; Stevens-Smith, 1998b).

Family Counseling

In family counseling sessions, family counselors—using a family systems approach as described in chapter 10—help family members become aware of their mutual dependency, dysfunctional communication, and family roles that have exacerbated and perpetuated both the alcohol and the codependent addictions. Family members learn to develop appropriate boundaries by expressing their individual needs for independent action and privacy. They practice communicating personal needs, feelings, and emotions in a direct and authentic manner. They work at giving up the enabling or manipulating roles characteristic of their former dysfunctional interactions. "Just as the family learned to organize itself around the substance abuse, it must now reorganize itself when there is no substance abuse in the family. This will require the restructuring of family rituals, roles, and rules" (Stevens-Smith, 1998c, p. 185).

Through these sessions, family members move from shame to respect for themselves and each other (Fossum & Mason, 1986). They respond to new behaviors with healthy expressions of feelings, rather than with old stereotyped protective interactions. They learn how to live more independently of one another and to get on with their own lives.

Nace (1987) uses a family systems approach, as well as psychological-education activities, insight-oriented therapy for individual family members, and group therapy for family members.

Walters, Carter, Papp, and Silverstein (1988) of the Women's Project, as discussed in chapter 10, criticize the traditional approach to treating family dysfunctions, claiming that gender-based, social-cultural roles are imposed on mothers, fathers, daughters, and sons, roles that cause and perpetuate family dysfunctions. Supporting their position, Real (1997) argues persuasively that family dysfunctions are caused by socially determined masculine and feminine roles.

Group Counseling

Group counseling has always been a very popular and preferred type of treatment for recovering substance abusers. Group therapy is especially effective with those recovering from substance abuse because groups provide social support, empowerment, encouragement to counteract ongoing social pressures to take drugs, and resistance to falling back into addictive behaviors (Stevens-Smith, 1998c). Group counseling is equally effective for other members of the recovering alcoholic's family. Typically, persons with a drinking problem meet with other alcoholics or problem drinkers in one group, and spouses and/or other family members meet with other spouses and family members in a different group (Nace, 1987).

In a group setting, clients get feedback from peers, experiment with new behaviors and social skills, experience emotional closeness to others, learn to assert themselves and confront others, and develop spiritual strength helpful to recovery (Gilliland & James, 1997).

Auxiliary Services and Support Groups

All types of auxiliary services are available for recovering drinkers: psychological education, recreational and occupational therapy, nutritional guidance, vocational rehabilitation and employment counseling, and Alcoholics Anonymous, Al-Anon, and Alateen support groups.

In psychological education, information about the destructiveness of alcohol to health, survival, and relationships is presented in lectures, slides, videotapes, and films. The goal of education is to generate, increase, or sustain motivation for treatment.

Recreational or occupational therapy helps clients cultivate new interests and hobbies or renew old ones. Programs often include arts and crafts, organized games, and trips. Nutritional guidance helps clients gain healthy eating habits.

Vocational rehabilitation services and employment counseling help clients either return to their previous jobs successfully or explore and seek different jobs. If referrals for treatment began within an EAP, this rehabilitation is built into treatment.

Alcoholics Anonymous (AA) and related groups have been very successful over the years in persuading alcoholics to give up alcohol and in helping recovering alcoholics maintain sobriety. Many counselors and therapists, in working with recovering alcoholics, now use AA as an adjunct to their therapy (Fossum & Mason, 1986).

Most counselors insist that the alcoholic join AA (Geller, 1992). Family members are encouraged to join affiliates: Al-Anon for spouses, and Alateen for teenagers. AA helps build the confidence needed to remain sober and the skills necessary to interact with family members. The affiliates help family members relate and interact with the person recovering from alcohol abuse. Al-Anon and Alateen help spouses and children learn how to live with nonrecovering alcoholics or when and how to confront them.

AA has developed a spiritually based system to help alcoholics remain sober. This system has 12 steps in which alcoholics acknowledge that they need a power greater than themselves to maintain abstinence (see Table 13.1). They give themselves into the care of a higher power, acknowledge wrongs, make amends, and continue to admit mistakes. They then help other alcoholics find this spiritual help.

Many professionals believe that AA involvement is the most important factor in recovery. Some, however, criticize or express caution about its effectiveness. In evaluating overall AA effectiveness, Stevens-Smith (1998b) summarizes the pros and cons of AA programs. Some complain that AA success has been based on White, middle-class groups. Little in the research, however, indicates that AA is successful only with

TABLE 13.1
The Twelve Steps of AA

1. We admitted we were powerless over alcohol—that our lives had become unmanageable.
2. We came to believe that a Power greater than ourselves could restore us to sanity.
3. We made a decision to turn our will and our lives over to the care of God as we understood Him.
4. We made a searching and fearless moral inventory of ourselves.
5. We admitted to God, to ourselves, and to another human being, the exact nature of our wrongs.
6. We were entirely ready to have God remove all these defects of character.
7. We humbly asked Him to remove our shortcomings.
8. We made a list of all persons we had harmed, and became willing to make amends to them all.
9. We made direct amends to such people wherever possible, except when to do so would injure others.
10. We continued to take personal inventory and, when we were wrong, promptly admitted it.
11. We sought through prayer and meditation to improve our conscious contact with God as we understood Him, praying only for knowledge of His will for us and the power to carry that out.
12. Having had a spiritual awakening as the result of these steps, we tried to carry this message to alcoholics, and to practice these principles in all our affairs.

Source: The Twelve Steps are reprinted with permission of Alcoholics Anonymous World Services.

this population. Others criticize the 12-step approach as reinforcing the powerlessness of women. In response to this criticism, some groups have modified the AA steps. Despite criticisms, AA is still regarded as a significant force in the successful treatment of alcoholics.

Therapists Fossum and Mason (1986), at the Family Therapy Institute in St. Paul, Minnesota, believe that all members of a shame-based family are inherently addictive; family members need to become aware of, and endeavor to overcome, their own addictive behaviors before other members of the family can successfully stay in recovery. Fossum and Mason use the various 12-step groups as an adjunct to their own therapy. "These mutual help groups meet regularly and focus on a single problem such as alcoholism, bulimia, narcotics, overeating, etc., with one stipulation for membership, the desire to abstain from the compulsive behavior" (p. 124). They point out that many other groups modeling AA have formed—Narcotics Anonymous, Overeaters Anonymous, Gamblers Anonymous, Sex Addicts Anonymous.

Tables 13.2 and 13.3 indicate similarities and differences between treatment procedures of AA and professional counselors.

Adult Children of Alcoholics and Codependency

Approximately 30 million adults have come from alcohol-dependent families and can be classified as *adult children of alcoholics (ACOAs)* (Ackerman, 1987). ACOAs are three or four times more likely to become alcoholics than persons from nonalcoholic families. Some 50% of women ACOAs with alcoholic fathers marry alcoholics (Wegscheider-Cruse, 1985). Also, about 55% of people receiving help in EAPs are ACOAs (Ackerman, 1987).

Personality characteristics of ACOAs are similar to those described earlier for codependents. Some writers use the terms *codependent* and *ACOA* interchangeably. After reviewing the literature, Gilliland and James (1997) summarized what professionals generally consider to be ACOA characteristics:

> Upon reaching adulthood, the majority of children of alcoholics continue to experience problems related to trust, dependency, control, identification, and expression of feelings. They are people-pleasers who are not able to trust their feelings or instincts about others. They have difficulty saying no and may be manipulated by others and extend themselves beyond any reasonable human capacity. (p. 349)

Ackerman (1987) and Goodman (1987) are concerned that many counselors perceive ACOAs only negatively. Ackerman claims that many positive characteristics of ACOAs are not acknowledged. He sees them as survivors and believes that counselors have much to learn from ACOAs.

The degree and type of maladjustment of the ACOA depend on the severity and type of alcoholism, birth order, gender of the ACOA, gender of the alcoholic parent, stress tolerance of the ACOA, childhood perceptions of the problem, current perception of his or her adjustment, and influence of important persons in the ACOA's life. The need for and type of treatment should be based on assessment of all these factors (Ackerman, 1987).

TABLE 13.2

General Similarities Between Alcoholics Anonymous and Professional Counselors Treating Alcoholism

1. Alcoholism is a disease.
2. Since it is a disease, no one is to blame.
3. The disease involves the whole person—body, mind, and spirit.
4. The disease involves the whole family, with those close to the alcoholic deeply affected by, and affecting, its course.
5. It cannot be cured, but it can be arrested and its damage healed.
6. To arrest it, the alcoholic must stop drinking immediately, completely, and permanently.
7. He also must change both his attitudes and his behavior, literally transforming his life.
8. The responsibility for these changes rests on the alcoholic himself because only he can make them.
9. He cannot make them, however, without help.
10. One powerful source of help is the caring concern of another person, one who cares enough to risk being honest.
11. Another source of help is the group, where the alcoholic can hear the experiences of other alcoholics, share his own, and get frank feedback.
12. The alcoholic must learn to be honest with himself, feeling his true feelings and seeing his actions as they really are.
13. He must learn to be honest with others as well, saying what he really feels and letting them say what they feel.
14. An important part of recovery is rebuilding the alcoholic's shattered self-worth.
15. Lasting recovery requires continuing effort by the individual with support from friends and family.
16. Literature, films, and lectures are valuable aids in teaching the alcoholic about his disease, motivating him to change, and facilitating his attempts to do so.
17. All the above principles, except number 6, apply equally to other members of the alcoholic family.

Source: From *Another Chance: Hope and Health for the Alcoholic Family* (p. 208) by S. Wegscheider, 1981, Palo Alto, CA: Science and Behavior Books. Copyright 1981. Adapted by permission.

Goodman (1987) makes two further points: (a) One cannot assume that all problems of ACOAs can be attributed to the alcohol problem in the family of origin; and (b) other emotional repressive factors, such as overcontrol, rejection, severe discipline, or overindulgence by parents, may contribute to ACOA dysfunction.

Treatment for ACOAs

Fossum and Mason (1986), Gravitz and Bowden (1986), and Middleton-Moz and Dwinell (1986) have written specifically about counseling and therapy for this group.

Middleton-Moz and Dwinell (1986) emphasize helping ACOAs reclaim personal childhood losses by guiding them through depression, experiences of loss, and

TABLE 13.3
Some Practical Differences Between Alcoholics Anonymous and Professional Alcoholism
Treatment

Alcoholics Anonymous	Professional Alcoholism Treatment
Basis: personal experience of other alcoholics.	Basis: scientific research and theory; accepted psychotherapeutic practice.
Program: The Twelve Steps	Program: planned course of medical and psychological treatment.
Trust placed in "Higher Power."	Trust placed in counselor.
Individual totally responsible for recovery.	Individual totally responsible but initially motivated by intervention and later assisted by professional counseling.
Milieu: nonprofessional and social.	Milieu: professional and clinical.
Caring offered in a personal relationship.	Caring offered in a professional relationship.
Individual help given in informal private conversations.	Individual help given in structured private counseling.
Sharing in leaderless group.	Sharing in group led by trained counselor.
Individual participation in meetings optional.	Individual participation in treatment program expected.
Dependent and family attend separate groups.	Dependent and family treated together in some stages of treatment.
Help available any time.	Help available by appointment.
Individual takes Twelve Steps at his own pace.	Individual progresses according to treatment program timetable.
Individual assesses own progress and readiness to take next step.	Counselor assesses individual's readiness to take next step.
Period of participation open-ended.	Period of participation limited.

Source: From *Another Chance: Hope and Health for the Alcoholic Family* (p. 210) by S. Wegscheider, 1981, Palo Alto, CA: Science and Behavior Books. Copyright 1981. Adapted by permission.

expression of grief. The first step is the development of an intellectual understanding of what their lives were like in alcoholic families. Clients make genograms to help attain a perspective of the families of origin. They may draw pictures of how they saw themselves during earlier parts of their lives and as they expect themselves to be in the future. These activities help them move to the next step, to a deeper emotional experience. Clients are helped to stop denying their feelings, emotions, and pain about past experiences and to develop a trusting relationship with the counselor. This relationship gives the emotional security necessary for clients, as they move to the third step, to work through the grief processes about their losses. These losses, which clients are asked to list, include the love and acceptance they did not receive from parents, loss of the chance to be a child, and loss of friendships, toys, home, and similar deprivations. Particular attention is paid to the effect of anniversaries, holidays, and birthdays on their feelings of loss. Once grieving has been worked through, behavior and attitudes become more productive.

Gravitz and Bowden (1986) divide ACOA recovery into four stages: (a) survival, (b) emergent awareness, (c) core issues, and (d) integration. In the *survival* stage, clients feel pain but do not link it to alcoholism in the family of origin. In the *emergent awareness* stage, they begin to identify as ACOAs and break out of the taboo against talking about family interactions. In the *core issues* stage, clients are ready to explore feelings and behaviors that led them to seek help. Gravitz and Bowden believe that the primary issue to correct is the "all or none," or black-and-white, way of thinking about behavior and feelings. Once flexibility is attained, clients move to the *integration* stage, wherein they begin to accept themselves, express needs and wants, and have fun without feeling guilty.

As said earlier, Fossum and Mason (1986) believe that shame based on dysfunctional interactions within a family is at the core of the development and perpetuation of codependent addictive relationships. This idea is considered a major breakthrough in the treatment of alcoholic addiction and resultant codependent relationship. Subby (1987) writes, "The private shame and mistaken troubled past festers on into adulthood creating an infection of codependent anxiety" (p. 95).

Fossum and Mason (1986) distinguish guilt from shame. *Guilt* involves acknowledging a specific inappropriate or destructive behavior and making amends. This attitude leaves self-esteem intact. *Shame* is a feeling that one is fundamentally unworthy, bad, or inadequate. An inappropriate behavior that hurts others or impinges on others is considered so bad by the offender and is accompanied by painful humiliation so deep that the individual feels rejected as a person. This pervasive feeling of shame leaves little room for repairing damage to others or for learning or growing from a mistake.

Shame is fostered, reinforced, and perpetuated in alcoholic families, so children carry these feelings into adult relationships. As adults, then, intimate relationships are difficult to establish.

Fossum and Mason (1986) use a family-of-origin approach to help shame-bound families move from shame to respect for themselves. First, they explore early patterns of communications, interactions, rules, and early sources of shame that existed in the original family. Next, they move to a deeper stage in which emotions are the focus. They confront denial of family problems, distinguish guilt from shame, and expose old compulsive patterns of controlling. New feelings and behaviors are experienced and practiced in the group and then generalized to life.

A structured group experience for ACOAs described by Gelso and Fretz (1992) includes helping group members learn to trust others, identify and express feelings, and search out patterns in their dysfunctional families that contribute to their own dysfunction. Genograms are used to demonstrate basic family patterns and to facilitate discussion of their own roles in the family. Characteristics of ACOAs are also presented and analyzed.

Recovering ACOAs and Recovering Parents

The relationship between parents who are recovering from alcohol abuse and codependency and their adult children who are ACOAs is an important, complex, and often neglected relationship. Wegscheider-Cruse (1985) insists that recovering parents and ACOAs must treat each other with dignity and respect. Counseling help is especially recommended for those ACOAs who continue to blame the recovering alcoholic and the codependent spouse for all the problems they caused in the past. ACOAs need help in working through anger and grief to reach understanding and forgiveness.

It is unusual for recovering parents and recovering ACOAs to receive family counseling together. Often, they live miles apart, and each ACOA may have his or her own nuclear family. Nevertheless, counselors can develop effective ways to help both parties engage in long-distance healing.

The characteristics described here for ACOAs, such as codependency and shame, were developed by counselors working with adults who grew up in alcoholic families. Mental health professionals have been noticing these same characteristics in adults who were raised in dysfunctional families where alcohol was never consumed. In such families, children were similarly deprived emotionally or abused (Fossum & Mason, 1986; Woititz, 1983).

⇘ COUNSELING PERSONS WITH DRUG ABUSE PROBLEMS

Types of Drugs

Psychoactive drugs besides alcohol that alter mood and affect the nervous system are marijuana, stimulants, opiates, depressants, and hallucinogens (Comer, 1998; Palfai & Jankiewicz, 1991; Porter, 1998). This list includes not only illegal street drugs such as marijuana, cocaine, and heroin, but also prescription drugs used to help people relax, sleep, decrease pain, or lose weight.

Similar to alcohol abuse, tolerance develops with increased use of these drugs, requiring increased dosages for the desired effects. Overuse can lead to physical or emotional impairment and generally leads to addiction and physical dependency, with withdrawal causing physical and emotional disorientation (Comer, 1998).

Many mental health professionals, government officials, and the general public consider illegal drug use the number one problem in the United States (Nystul, 1993). The sharp rise in street crime—robbery, assaults, murder, and gang wars—is attributed to the trafficking in illegal drugs.

Marijuana

Marijuana is the most widely used drug after alcohol and is the most socially accepted of the illegal drugs. It is well known that chronic marijuana users often suffer from listlessness and lack of motivation (Comer, 1998; Palfai & Jankiewicz, 1991).

Moreover, persons intoxicated from marijuana can suffer from such side effects as "delusions and paranoia, or outright terror" (Palfai & Jankiewicz, 1991, p. 465).

Regular use of marijuana can damage the body. Similar to heavy drinking of alcohol, extended marijuana use causes bloodshot eyes and increases heart rate and blood pressure (Comer, 1998; Palfai & Jankiewicz, 1991). Similar to smoking cigarettes, marijuana causes bronchitis and asthmatic reactions. "Smoking grass [marijuana] contributes to heart and lung damage, cancer, and damage to unborn babies" (Nielsen, 1987, p. 634). Furthermore, users are often unaware that marijuana bought off the street can be laced with other, more potent and toxic drugs (Nielsen, 1987; Palfai & Jankiewicz, 1991).

Stimulants

Stimulants increase arousal in the nervous system. Amphetamines, such as Dexedrine and Benzedrine, are stimulants obtained by prescription and commonly known as speed, uppers, or bennies. Moderate doses increase alertness and reduce fatigue; some students, truck drivers, and athletes use them to endure stress. Stimulants also curb appetites and are used in prescribed and over-the-counter drugs to help people lose weight (Comer, 1998).

Persons taking amphetamines develop tolerance quickly and need dosage increases as high as 200 times or more to attain a desired effect. When drugs are not available or are withdrawn, users become irritated and suspicious, which can lead to violence.

Cocaine, which comes from the *coca* (not cocoa) plant, is an illegal stimulant taken to develop euphoria. It can be inhaled, injected intravenously, or smoked in a highly dangerous compound called *crack*. In the 1970s and 1980s, cocaine was the glamorous status drug used by upwardly mobile young people, business and professional persons, and professional and college athletes who believed it to be safer than heroin (Burnett, 1979). Early in that period, cocaine was considered nonaddictive, and dangers of the drug were minimized. Research has since shown cocaine to be addictive. Tolerance increase and withdrawal effects occur. As with amphetamines, after an initial euphoric state, restlessness, irritability, and paranoia follow, ending in severe depression (Porter, 1998). Several prominent athletes have died from brain convulsions or cardiovascular failure after ingesting cocaine. Their deaths dramatically changed public opinion about the danger of cocaine addiction.

Opiates (Narcotics)

Opiates (opium, morphine, and codeine) derive from the opium poppy. Opium has been used for centuries to reduce pain and to induce relaxation (Porter, 1998). Codeine is also used in medicine to control coughs and diarrhea (Landy, 1987).

Heroin was developed in the late 1800s as a nonaddictive form of opium. After two decades, it was found to be addictive and was declared illegal. Today, it is an illegal street drug ingested by smoking, injecting under the skin, or injecting into the bloodstream (*mainlining*).

It is estimated that about 500,000 heroin addicts live in the United States. After feeling euphoric for a few hours, heroin users become lethargic and lose interest in food, their health, and personal and sexual relationships (Palfai & Jankiewicz, 1991).

All opiate users are highly susceptible to physical dependence on the drug and require high dosages to maintain euphoria. Overdose on heroin can be fatal (Comer, 1998).

Depressants (Sedatives-Hypnotics)

Depressants are pharmaceutical drugs prescribed either to sedate or to tranquilize people. Barbiturates, such as Seconal and Nembutal, help persons with insomnia, and minor tranquilizers, like Valium, Miltown, and Librium, are used to reduce anxiety.

Barbiturates are addictive, causing withdrawal symptoms similar to those of alcohol. Accidental overdosage can lead to death. They are particularly lethal because the death-producing dose remains the same even though addicts must take higher and higher dosages to get an effect. More than 5,000 deaths were reported in 1986 as a result of accidental or deliberate overdosage. Minor tranquilizers can be addictive for persons prone to avoiding problems and painful situations. Physicians have been criticized for prescribing Valium and Miltown too readily without considering their addictive qualities (Price & Lynn, 1986).

Hallucinogens (Psychedelics)

Hallucinogens include the drugs lysergic acid diethylamide (LSD) and phencyclidine (PCP, angel dust); mescaline, derived from peyote cactus; and psilocybin, derived from a type of mushroom. They produce major alterations in sensation, emotions, and perceptions. Although many users have described their experiences as wonderful "mind-altering trips," these drugs have also caused psychotic reactions requiring extended hospitalization. In addition to psychotic reactions, LSD has caused panic attacks lasting from 2 to 4 days and flashbacks in which a previous LSD trip is repeated even though a person has not taken the drug for months or years. "Flashbacks may occur days or even months after the last LSD experience . . . some people report flashbacks five years or more after taking LSD" (Comer, 1998, p. 422).

Treatment of Drug Abuse

Physical addiction to prescribed drugs occurs when physicians too quickly prescribe or overprescribe stimulants, sedatives, or tranquilizers for persons expressing anxiety or experiencing pain or depression. Some patients, when they become dependent on a drug or need higher dosages, obtain duplicate prescriptions from several physicians. Others will shop for a physician who will prescribe a drug if their own physician refuses to do so. Drugs, if taken over a long period without treatment for emotional or physical disorders, mask a person's turmoil and pain and inhibit opportunities for the person to confront and improve or resolve the cause of the problem.

People become addicted to, or dependent on, illegal street drugs because the drugs fulfill their needs to withdraw or escape from painful reactions to life. Temporary feelings of euphoria and of power inhibit confrontation of problems they are experiencing. A further complication arises when addicts, desperate to buy increasing dosages, end up stealing, selling drugs, or becoming prostitutes to maintain their drug habit. Thus, they are involved in dual criminality—illegal drug use and the resultant criminal acts. Treatment and rehabilitation become even more complex when they are combined with prison terms.

Drug abusers must now also contend with the high probability of becoming afflicted with the human immunodeficiency virus (HIV), the virus that causes acquired immune deficiency syndrome (AIDS) from contaminated needles used to inject drugs (see chap. 14).

Types of Treatment

Treatment programs for drug abuse parallel those of alcohol abuse described earlier. Individual, group, and family counseling are essential components of treatment. Some drug abuse counselors put heavier emphasis on inpatient residential treatment programs with a highly structured and protected environment. In part, they believe that these settings protect drug addicts from the influences of drug pushers and peer pressure.

Synanon, the best-known residential treatment center for drug addicts, is run by recovering addicts. The center emphasizes aggressive confrontation, shaming techniques, and complete isolation of addicts until they attain abstinence. After completion of the project, counselors believe that recovering addicts must maintain attachment to Synanon for the remainder of their lives. Other residential treatment programs—Phoenix House and Day-Top Village, for example—are less aggressively confrontational. They encourage addicts to involve themselves in community programs and patients to disengage from the residence after they complete the program (Comer, 1998).

Residential or semiresidential treatment centers for drug addiction commonly practice behavior modification and social learning theory. Aversion techniques, described in chapter 5, are sometimes used to extinguish need for drugs. Electric shocks may be administered while a person takes the drug or views someone taking the drug. Also, modeling and social reinforcement techniques are used to substitute activities or experiences other than drugs to satisfy needs (Erickson, 1998).

Methadone, an addictive drug, is used to combat heroin addiction. Persons gradually transfer addiction to the less dangerous or less physically damaging methadone. Dosages are administered to addicts at clinics on a prescribed schedule. Although controversial, methadone treatment is still commonly used with heroin addicts. Outcome research indicates that methadone treatment is more effective when combined with counseling or therapy, family involvement, career counseling, and education (Comer, 1998).

YOUTHS AND SUBSTANCE ABUSE

Concern about teenage substance abuse began in the late 1960s. At that time, adolescents were following a trend in American society and experimenting with drugs.

Since that time, teenagers' use of drugs has more than tripled. After reviewing the literature, Comer (1998) and Smith (1998) summarized the extensive data that point to the seriousness of the problem of alcohol consumption among young people. Smith says, for example:

> Youths involved with alcohol and drugs pose a major problem not only to themselves, but the community as a whole. It has been estimated that at least 15% of students age 12–17 have serious problems with alcohol or drugs. Another 5% become chemically dependent. Furthermore, about 25% of all school-age youths are children of alcoholics. (p. 200)

Marijuana use among young people dropped during the 1980s and early 1990s, apparently because of drug education programs. Recently, however, despite continued drug education, marijuana use has been increasing among young people. According to the National Institute on Drug Abuse (NIDA, 1995, as cited in Comer, 1998), more than 5% of high school seniors smoke marijuana every day.

Substance abuse, particularly alcohol, the leading cause of teenage deaths, clearly points to a crisis in schools and communities. The crisis is exacerbated now that many youngsters have easy access to automatic weapons.

Counselors and health professionals are concerned as well about the effects this abuse has on adolescent development and health. Adolescents who learn patterns of avoidance during formative years will find them difficult to change. Nutritional deficiencies arising from substance abuse are more damaging physically to the growing adolescent than to the mature adult. Adolescents, more than adults, are often away from home when they drink, which means they probably drive while drunk more often than adults. Although federal, state, and local agencies have been funded to set up clinics, directors of these clinics complain that funds that would be better spent on treatment are being used to test people for drug use.

Counseling services in public schools, colleges, and communities have developed educational and therapeutic programs that focus on teenage substance abuse. These programs are discussed in chapters 16, 17, and 18.

Almost all drug use begins in preadolescent or adolescent years. Oetting and Beauvais (1988) propose a theory that combines individuals' social and environmental activities with their personal characteristics, a concept these authors call the *peer-cluster theory*. Peer clusters are groups to which individuals gravitate—gangs, church groups, Boy Scouts, best friends, and relatives, for example. Such groups contribute to socialization and identity in positive ways, but some also contribute to initiating and maintaining drug use. Drug prevention programs must consider the influence of peer clusters on the drug abuser. These programs will only be successful if new peers are chosen or if peer clusters themselves discourage drug use.

After a review of treatment programs for adolescents with substance abuse problems, Polcin (1992) presented a comprehensive model of treatment that integrates the various programs. The program offered at Thunder Road Adolescent Treatment Center in Oakland, California, is an inpatient facility. Its phases of treatment include orientation and education, dealing with emotional core issues in counseling and family groups, and preparation to leave. Clients are able to practice new coping mechanisms before returning to the community.

❧ SUBSTANCE ABUSE IN OLDER ADULTS

Substance abuse among older adults has become an increasing problem in our society, especially as greater numbers are living longer. The areas of concern are abuse of alcohol, use and misuse of prescription drugs, and indiscriminate use of over-the-counter drugs to self-medicate (Schliebner & Peregoy, 1998).

Lack of structured activity, separation from family, and loss of spouse and friends can lead to depression, anxiety, and insecurity in older adults, which in turn can lead to substance abuse. According to the Hazelden Corporation (as cited in Schliebner & Peregoy, 1998), "20 percent of hospitalized older adults are diagnosed with alcoholism, and nearly 70 percent are hospitalized with alcohol-related problems" (p. 209).

Physicians, reinforced by managed care's emphasis on treatment efficiency, are quick to prescribe medication. According to Stall (as cited in Schliebner & Peregoy, 1998), one third of the annual 1.5 billion prescriptions are for the elderly. Older adults average 13 different prescriptions per year. Assuming that most of these prescriptions serve ongoing chronic conditions of older age, the average older person takes many pills every day. Often, no one monitors the interaction of various medicines prescribed by different physicians or over-the-counter drugs purchased by older adults. This sort of substance abuse not only can be addictive—it can be fatal.

Both older adults and their families need to be educated about the risks involved in substance abuse and self-medication. Type and amount of medication require monitoring. When substance abuse is diagnosed in older adults, it is crucial that they be referred for treatment: "If the problem is acknowledged and treated, older adults have a very high rate of success in treatment. It is getting them into treatment that is difficult" (Schliebner & Peregoy, 1998, p. 211).

❧ RELAPSE PREVENTION

One of the most difficult problems in the treatment of substance abuse is helping abusers maintain abstinence. Therefore, strategies to prevent relapse are essential components of treatment plans (Annis & Davis, 1991; Nystul, 1993; Peel, 1988).

After clients leave a supportive treatment environment, they may be influenced by social pressures, increased personal stress, or a return to low self-esteem. If their coping skills are not sufficiently developed, if they have a pessimistic attitude about their ability to control themselves, or if family and community are not supportive, abusers may relapse into substance abuse.

AA, as discussed earlier, is designed to prevent alcoholic relapse. Social learning and cognitive-behavioral techniques have also been used to prevent relapses (Stevens-Smith, 1998b). Social learning helps clients build up their own capacities to monitor themselves through keeping logs and journals about their feelings and behaviors. In this way, they are more able to anticipate problems and check with counselors. Cognitive-behavioral models focus on helping clients make comprehensive changes in lifestyle—changes that involve exercise, relaxation, diet, and cognitive restructuring that will bring about new coping skills. In this way, positive habits replace negative ones (Stevens-Smith, 1998b).

Persons with few complicating emotional problems tend to avoid a relapse if they have good jobs, have adequate living conditions, and take care of their physical well-being (Svanum & McAdoo, 1989). Availability of counseling to families of former abusers also cuts back on the possibilities of relapse.

Recognizing and Treating Addictive Patterns

Innumerable complicating factors contribute to relapse. Some researchers believe that until issues underlying addictive behaviors are addressed and remedied, relapse is inevitable for most recovering addicts. As said early in this chapter, according to Fossum and Mason (1986) and Kasl (1989), feelings of shame underlie addictive behaviors, feelings that stem from shame-based families. All members of such a family share and maintain the addiction. Although one family member is, for example, an alcoholic, the addictive behaviors of other members, such as eating disorders, compulsive spending, gambling, sexual compulsions, or overwork, may not be noticeable; all compulsive behaviors are similar in that they are meant to overcome feelings of the family-held shame. Real (1997) concurs with these underlying issues of addiction, claiming further that, among males, all addictive behaviors are defenses against male depression (see chap. 14).

Some persons have multiple addictions; others will fall into a new addictive behavior after overcoming another or will develop an addictive behavior after the primary addict in the family, the identified patient (IP), has abstained and is in recovery. Recognizing and treating the underlying feelings of family shame, as well as overcoming the various addictions within the family system, are necessary in preventing relapse (Fossum & Mason, 1986; Kasl, 1989).

⊸❦ OUTCOME RESEARCH: SUBSTANCE ABUSE TREATMENT

Until Alcoholics Anonymous began in the early 1930s, alcoholism was considered incurable. Currently, alcoholism is considered one of the more treatable problems.

Evaluations of success of alcohol treatment programs have been carried out mainly by alcohol treatment centers, AA, and companies using EAPs. Although criteria for what constitutes success differ, all agree that abstinence is the foremost essential element in recovery. Other indications of successful treatment are improvements in clients' relationships with others and improvements in their school or work performance.

Heinemann and Smith-DiJulio (1982) state that, in general, from 30% to 60% of persons entering treatment recover from alcoholism. Quayle (1985) estimates that successful outcomes of alcoholism treatment in EAPs are as high as 90%, with most programs about 50%. Jerrell and Rightmeyer (1985) indicate that outcomes of treatment in industry show 40% to 60% reduction in accidents on the job; they discuss studies that show improved attendance and decreased tardiness on jobs, improved worker morale and production, and improved worker satisfaction after treatment for alcoholism.

Most experts agree that more carefully controlled studies of recovery and more follow-up studies are needed. The phenomenal increase in EAPs discussed earlier in the book, however, leads one to believe that businesses and industry have found that these programs make a difference in production and worker morale.

Nevertheless, research studies on treatment of substance abuse are, by and large, limited in number and scope (Smith, 1998). Studies are limited because the causes of substance abuse are complex, treatment methods are varied and not standardized, many substance abusers are involved in different treatments at the same time, and centers using multidimensional approaches often cannot specify which modality is contributing to client change (Smith, 1998).

More outcome research has been done on alcohol treatment than on other drug treatments. Alcohol treatment programs have also demonstrated more effective results, compared with other drug treatments (Smith, 1998).

Smith (1998) reviews recent substance abuse outcome research in seven areas: (a) inpatient programs, (b) outpatient programs, (c) 12-step programs, (d) individual, (e) group, and (f) family counseling, and (g) multidimensional treatment. His conclusions are as follows:

1. The longer the outpatient treatment, the more effective it is. More frequent counseling sessions are needed than in traditional counseling (Gerstein & Harwood, 1992).

2. Inpatient programs have been found to be more successful in treating alcohol abuse than in treating other drug abuses. Studies on effectiveness of inpatient treatment for drugs other than alcohol have been limited.

3. The general consensus is that AA programs are important and often essential adjuncts to other treatment modalities. When attendance at AA meetings is voluntary and members participate actively, AA is highly successful in participants maintaining sobriety (Nace, 1987).

4. Individual counseling is effective in reducing drug use and in improving employment performance. More controlled studies about the effectiveness of individual counseling are needed, however.

5. Group counseling has not been sufficiently studied. What studies have been done indicate that group work maximizes the effect of treatment (Fram, 1990).

6. When therapy programs include marital and family therapy, alcohol abusers tend to stay longer in treatment and to maintain sobriety (Todd & Selekman, 1991).

7. Methadone maintenance programs, used for heroin addicts, have been shown to be effective especially when higher dosages are used (Gunne & Grombladh, 1984).

8. Studies have shown that cocaine addicts can be treated successfully in both inpatient and outpatient facilities when accompanied by intensive after-care treatment (Washton, 1989).

Smith (1998) points out that multidimensional programs are the most often recommended treatment of choice but that research regarding their effectiveness is lacking:

Most substance abuse treatment programs currently favor a multidimensional approach when dealing with addictions. Multidimensional or multimodality treatment approaches include detoxification, individual counseling, group counseling, family therapy, in-patient treatment, education and so on. . . . Research studies demonstrating treatment combinations that might work best as a multidimensional model are nonexistent. (p. 271)

Issues needing more research include exploring the validity of the disease model; defining what constitutes a diagnosis of substance abuse; determining whether abstinence is the only acceptable goal; determining gender differences in drinking characteristics, substance abuse, and consequences; and determining who should be eligible as substance abuse counselors (Smith, 1998).

❧ SUMMARY

As many as 13 million adults and 3 million youths under 21 years of age can be classified as alcoholics or problem drinkers who have an uncontrollable desire to drink. Alcoholism is viewed by many experts as a progressive disease. The major characteristic is a physical dependency on alcohol, which leads to serious physical reactions when alcohol is withdrawn. Problem drinkers drink excessively and are psychologically dependent on alcohol. Both alcoholics and problem drinkers strongly deny having a drinking problem and resist treatment. Their families may need to confront the alcohol abusers about their problem and to explain that they must get treatment if they expect family members to remain with them.

Many researchers claim that substance abuse is one of many addictive behaviors used to mask or alleviate deeper emotional feelings of shame generated and maintained by shame-based families and, with males in particular, used to mask or deny feelings of male depression. Individuals must therapeutically work through underlying issues of shame and depression to overcome addictive behaviors.

Spouses and families of alcohol abusers also need treatment because they typically are involved in family dynamics that enmesh them in a dysfunctional, codependent relationship, a relationship that enables the alcoholic to continue drinking.

Abstinence is the primary pretreatment condition for alcoholics and for the majority of problem drinkers. Individual, group, and family counseling is offered by counselors in outpatient and inpatient treatment centers, by counselors in private practice, or by counselors employed in EAPs in business. Support groups such as Alcoholics Anonymous (AA), Al-Anon, and Alateen are valuable adjuncts to psychological treatment. Collaboration between professional counselors and AA has been increasing.

Considerable attention has been given to the problems of adult children of alcoholics (ACOAs) and their codependency in their relationships. Most recently, the influence of shame generated in shame-based families has been recognized as a major contributor to codependency.

Drug addiction has reached epidemic proportions. Street crime has increased because addicts may rob, assault, or murder others to get money to pay exorbitant fees demanded by drug dealers. Treatment for drug addiction parallels that of alcohol treatment, except that for drug addicts heavier emphasis is placed on inpatient residential care.

Counseling and educational services directed to the prevention and treatment of alcohol and drug abuse have been developed in public schools, colleges, and the community because of the current crisis in substance abuse among young people.

➣ PROJECTS AND ACTIVITIES

1. Survey the community in which you live to determine what programs are available for treatment of alcohol and drug dependency.

2. Interview a school counselor in a junior high school and one in a senior high school. Ask for their impressions about the seriousness of the problem of substance abuse in their school districts.

3. Visit an alcohol center and ask the director what procedures are used to confront alcoholics when families request help. Do you consider them consistent with effective counseling procedures?

4. Develop a plan you might use if you were a counselor in a school, college, or community to help prevent alcohol or drug abuse.

5. Contact a counselor in a community clinic and one in a school to ask how they handle a client who comes in with a drinking problem or whose drinking problem emerges during the counseling sessions.

6. Try to discover what type of relationship exists between Alcoholics Anonymous, Alateen, and Al-Anon, and professional counselors and therapists in schools, agencies, and private practice.

7. The latest theorizing about alcoholism focuses on the family relationships in an alcoholic family. Are agencies or private practitioners in your area involving families in alcohol and drug counseling? What kinds of problems do you see, if any, in involving the family? How can these problems be resolved?

➣ REFERENCES

Ackerman, R. J. (1987). Adult children of alcoholics. *EAP Digest, 7,* 25–29.

American Psychiatric Association (APA). (1994). *Diagnostic and statistical manual of mental disorders* (4th ed.). Washington, DC: Author.

Annis, H. M., & Davis, C. S. (1991). Relapse prevention. *Alcohol Health & Research World, 15,* 175–177.

Beattie, M. (1987). *Codependent no more.* New York: Harper & Row.

Belkin, G. S. (1984). *Introduction to counseling* (2nd ed.). Dubuque, IA: William C. Brown.

Bennett, G., & Woolf, D. S. (1983). *Current approaches to substance abuse therapy.* In G. Bennett, C. Vourakis, & D. S. Woolf (Eds.), *Substance abuse: Pharmacologic, developmental, and clinical perspectives* (pp. 341–369). New York: John Wiley.

Bennett, L. W. (1992). Linking domestic assault and addictions. *The Counselor, 10,* 18–22.

Burnett, M. (1979). Understanding and overcoming addictions. In S. Eisenberg & L. E. Patterson (Eds.), *Helping clients with special concerns* (pp. 343–362). Chicago: Rand-McNally.

Calahan, D., Cisin, I. H., & Crossley, H. M. (1969). *American drinking practices: A national study of drinking behaviors and attitudes.* New Brunswick, NJ: Rutgers Center of Alcohol Studies.

Cermak, T. L. (1986). Children of alcoholics and the case for a new diagnostic category of codependency. In R. J. Ackerman (Ed.), *Growing in the shadow: Children of alcoholics* (pp. 23–31). Pompano Beach, FL: Health Communications.

Comer, R. (1998). *Abnormal psychology* (3rd ed.). New York: Freeman.

Dickman, J. F., & Phillips, E. A. (1985). Alcoholism: A pervasive rehabilitation issue. In J. F. Dickman, W. G. Emener, Jr., & W. S. Hutchison, Jr. (Eds.), *Counseling the troubled person in industry* (pp. 99–115). Springfield, IL: Charles C Thomas.

Erickson, S. (1998). Etiological theories of substance abuse. In P. Stevens-Smith & R. L. Smith (Eds.), *Substance abuse counseling: Theory and practice* (pp. 25–63). Upper Saddle River, NJ: Merrill/Prentice Hall.

Forrest, G. G. (1978). *The diagnosis and treatment of alcoholism* (2nd ed.). Springfield, IL: Charles C Thomas.

Forrest, G. G. (1984). *Intensive psychotherapy of alcoholism.* Springfield, IL: Charles C Thomas.

Fossum, M. A., & Mason, M. J. (1986). *Facing shame: Families in recovery.* New York: Norton.

Fram, D. H. (1990). Group methods in the treatment of substance abusers. *Psychiatric Annals, 20,* 385–388.

Geller, A. (1992). Rehabilitation programs and halfway houses. In J. H. Lowinson, R. Ruiz, R. B. Millman, & J. B. Langrod (Eds.), *Substance abuse: A comprehensive textbook* (pp. 458–466). Baltimore, MD: Williams & Wilkins.

Gelso, C. J., & Fretz, B. R. (1992). *Counseling psychology.* Fort Worth, TX: Harcourt Brace.

Gerstein, D. R., & Harwood, H. J. (Eds.). (1992). *Treating drug problems.* Washington, DC: National Academy Press.

Gilliland, B. E., & James, R. K. (1997). *Crisis intervention strategies* (3rd ed.). Pacific Grove, CA: Brooks/Cole.

Goodman, R. W. (1987). Adult children of alcoholics. *Journal of Counseling & Development, 66,* 162–163.

Goodwin, D. W. (1979). Alcoholism and heredity. *Archives of General Psychiatry, 36,* 57–64.

Goodwin, D. W. (1992). Alcohol: Clinical aspects. In J. H. Lowinson, R. Ruiz, R. B. Millman, & J. B. Langrod (Eds.), *Substance abuse: A comprehensive textbook* (pp. 144–151). Baltimore, MD: Williams & Wilkins.

Gravitz, H., & Bowden, J. (1986). Therapeutic issues of adult children of alcoholics: A continuum of developmental stages. In R. J. Ackerman (Ed.), *Growing in the shadow: Children of alcoholics* (pp. 187–207). Pompano Beach, FL: Health Communications.

Gunne, L., & Grombladh, L. (1984). The Swedish methadone maintenance program. In G. Serban (Ed.), *The social and medical aspects of drug abuse* (pp. 205–213). Jamaica, NY: Spectrum.

Heinemann, M. E., & Smith-DiJulio, K. (1982). Care of the chronically ill alcoholic person. In N. J. Estes & M. E. Heinemann (Eds.), *Alcoholism: Development consequences and interventions* (2nd ed., pp. 283–293). St. Louis, MO: C. V. Mosby.

Hogg, J. A., & Frank, M. L. (1992). Toward an interpersonal model of codependence and contradependence. *Journal of Counseling & Development, 70,* 371–375.

Jerrell, J. M., & Rightmeyer, J. F. (1985). Evaluating employee assistance programs: A review of methods, outcomes, and future directions. In J. F. Dickman, W. G. Emener, Jr., & W. S. Hutchison, Jr. (Eds.), *Counseling the troubled person in industry.* Springfield, IL: Charles C Thomas.

Kasl, C. D. (1989). *Women, sex, and addiction: Search for love and power.* New York: Harper & Row.

Landy, F. J. (1987). *Psychology: The science of people* (2nd ed.). Upper Saddle River, NJ: Prentice Hall.

Lewis, J. A., & Lewis, M. D. (1986). *Counseling programs for employees in the workplace.* Pacific Grove, CA: Brooks/Cole.

Manfrin, C. (1998). Treatment settings. In P. Stevens-Smith & R. L. Smith (Eds.), *Substance abuse counseling: Theory and practice* (pp. 135–165). Upper Saddle River, NJ: Merrill/Prentice Hall.

Metzger, L. (1988). *From denial to recovery.* San Francisco: Jossey-Bass.

Middleton-Moz, J., & Dwinell, L. (1986). *After the tears.* Pompano Beach, FL: Health Communications.

Miller, P. M., & Eisler, R. M. (1976). Alcohol and drug abuse. In W. E. Craighead, A. E. Kazdin, & M. J. Mahoney (Eds.), *Behavior modification principles, issues, and applications* (pp. 376–393). Boston: Houghton Mifflin.

Miller, R. H., & Rollnick, S. (1991). *Motivational interviewing: Preparing people to change addictive behavior.* New York: Guilford Press.

Miller, W. R., & Hester, R. K. (1980). Treating the problem drinker: Modern approaches. In W. R. Miller (Ed.), *The addictive behaviors* (pp. 11–141). New York: Pergamon.

Mueller, L. A., & Ketcham, K. (1987). *Recovering: How to get and stay sober.* New York: Bantam.

Myer, R. A., Peterson, S. E., & Stoffel-Rosales, M. (1991). Codependency: An examination of underlying assumptions. *Journal of Mental Health Counseling, 13,* 449–458.

Nace, E. P. (1987). *The treatment of alcoholism.* New York: Brunner/Mazel.

Nathan, P. (1984). The length and breadth of alcoholism. *Contemporary Psychology, 29,* 101–103.

National Institute on Drug Abuse (NIDA). (1995). *Facts about teenagers and drug abuse.* Rockville, MD: Author.

Nielsen, L. (1987). *Adolescent psychology: A contemporary view.* New York: Holt, Rinehart & Winston.

Nystul, M. S. (1993). *The art and science of counseling and psychotherapy.* New York: Macmillan.

Oetting, E. R., & Beauvais, F. (1988). Common elements in youth drug abuse: Peer clusters and other psychosocial factors. In S. Peel (Ed.), *Visions of addiction: Major contemporary perspectives on addiction and alcoholism* (pp. 141–161). Lexington, MA: Lexington Books.

O'Keefe, P. (1988). When the alcoholic refuses treatment. *Alcoholism and Addiction, 9,* 14.

Palfai, T., & Jankiewicz, H. (1991). *Drugs and human abuse.* Dubuque, IA: William C. Brown.

Peel, S. (1988). A moral vision of addiction: How people's values determine whether they become addicts. In S. Peel (Ed.), *Visions of addiction: Major contemporary perspectives on addiction and alcoholism* (pp. 203–233). Lexington, MA: Lexington Books.

Peer, G. G., Lindsey, A. K., & Newman, P. A. (1982). Alcoholism as a stage phenomena: A frame of reference for counselors. *Personnel and Guidance Journal, 60,* 465–469.

Polcin, D. L. (1992). A comprehensive model for adolescent chemical dependency treatment. *Journal of Counseling & Development, 70,* 376–382.

Porter, J. (1998). The major drugs of abuse and their addictive properties. In P. Stevens-Smith & R. L. Smith (Eds.), *Substance abuse counseling: Theory and practice* (pp. 65–96). Upper Saddle River, NJ: Merrill/Prentice Hall.

Price, R. H., & Lynn, S. J. (1986). *Abnormal psychology* (2nd ed.). Chicago: Dorsey Press.

Quayle, D. (1985). American productivity: The devastating effect of alcoholism and drug abuse. In J. F. Dickman, W. G. Emener, Jr., & W. S. Hutchison, Jr. (Eds.), *Counseling the troubled person in industry* (pp. 20–29). Springfield, IL: Charles C Thomas.

Real, T. (1997). *I don't want to talk about it.* New York: Fireside.

Schaef, A. W. (1986). *Codependence: Misunderstood—mistreated.* San Francisco: Harper & Row.

Schliebner, C. & Peregoy, J. J. (1998). Working with selected populations: Treatment issues and characteristics. In P. Stevens-Smith & R. L. Smith (Eds.), *Substance abuse counseling: Theory and practice* (pp. 193–217). Upper Saddle River, NJ: Merrill/Prentice Hall.

Smith, R. L. (1998). Research and contemporary issues. In P. Stevens-Smith & R. L. Smith (Eds.), *Substance abuse counseling: Theory and practice* (pp. 259–282). Upper Saddle River, NJ: Merrill/Prentice Hall.

Stevens-Smith, P. (1998a). Introduction to substance abuse. In P. Stevens-Smith & R. L. Smith (Eds.), *Substance abuse counseling: Theory and practice* (pp. 1–24). Upper Saddle River, NJ: Merrill/Prentice Hall.

Stevens-Smith, P. (1998b). Maintaining behavior change: Relapse prevention strategies. In P. Stevens-Smith & R. L. Smith (Eds.), *Substance abuse counseling: Theory and*

practice (pp. 241–258). Upper Saddle River, NJ: Merrill/Prentice Hall.

Stevens-Smith, P. (1998c). Treatment modalities in substance abuse. In P. Stevens-Smith & R. L. Smith (Eds.), *Substance abuse counseling: Theory and practice* (pp. 169–191). Upper Saddle River, NJ: Merrill/Prentice Hall.

Subby, R. (1987). *Lost in the shuffle: The codependent reality.* Pompano Beach, FL: Health Communications.

Svanum, S., & McAdoo, W. G. (1989). Predicting rapid relapse following treatment for chemical dependency. A matched-subjects design. *Journal of Consulting and Clinical Psychology, 57,* 222–266.

Todd, T. C., & Selekman, M. (1991). *Family therapy with adolescent substance abusers.* Boston: Allyn & Bacon.

Trimble, J. E. (1991). The mental health service and training needs of American Indians. In H. F. Myers, P. Wohlford, L. P. Guzman, & R. J. Echemendia (Eds.), *Ethnic minority perspectives on clinical training and services in psychology* (pp. 43–48). Washington, DC: American Psychological Association.

Valiant, G. E., & Milofsky, E. S. (1982). The etiology of alcoholism: A prospective viewpoint. *American Psychologist, 37,* 494–503.

Walters, M., Carter, B., Papp, O., & Silverstein, O. (Eds.). (1988). *The invisible web: Gender patterns in family relationships.* New York: Guilford Press.

Washton, A. M. (1989). *Cocaine addiction: Treatment, recovery, and relapse prevention.* New York: Norton.

Wegscheider, S. (1981). *Another chance: Hope and health in the alcoholic family.* Palo Alto, CA: Science and Behavior.

Wegscheider-Cruse, S. (1985). *Choice making.* Pompano Beach, FL: Health Communications.

Woititz, J. G. (1983). *Adult children of alcoholics.* Pompano Beach, FL: Health Communications.

14 Counseling in a Pluralistic World

Acknowledging that the United States is a pluralistic society, the counseling profession has been making efforts to address the multicultural needs of the population by attending to the social-cultural characteristics of the various ethnic groups (Blacks, Hispanics, Asians, American Indians), to the particular gender issues of women and men, and to the special concerns of lesbians, gays, and bisexuals. The professional counseling literature has been giving increasing attention to ways counselor training can be improved so that counselors can work more effectively with clients from these groups. The major emphasis is on helping counselors become aware of their potential biases, accept those with differing social and cultural beliefs, and adapt techniques and skills to the special characteristics of persons from diverse groups.

ETHNIC GROUPS: MULTICULTURAL COUNSELING

Ethnic groups has been defined as those who, by virtue of race, language, religion, and cultural values, differ from the predominant cultural group where they live. Because of these differences, ethnic groups often experience discrimination when they interact with others outside their group. Although each ethnic group and each individual within each ethnic group experience varying and different degrees of discrimination, three common reactions result from these negative interactions: (a) a feeling of powerlessness, (b) a feeling of lack of control over one's environment, and (c) a loss of personal identity (Ponterotto & Casas, 1991; A. Smith & Stewart, 1983).

No other nation in the world has the ethnic diversity of the United States (McGoldrick, Giordano, & Pearce, 1996). In their book on counseling minority client populations, Pedersen, Draguns, Lonner, and Trimble (1996) discuss the four major ethnic groups in the United States: American Indians, Hispanics, Asian Americans, and Blacks. McGoldrick, Giordano, and Pearce (1996) include not only these groups but also immigrants from Europe, Jewish families, and Slavic families.

Multicultural professionals emphasize that minority groups should not be equated with low-income groups, as is commonly done by the White majority. They say that minority groups are represented at all socioeconomic levels. Although proportionally more low-income people are in minority populations, in absolute figures more Whites than non-Whites are poor.

For minorities, the everyday stresses that all people experience are exacerbated by political, economic, or religious discrimination. To further the difficulty, if counseling is sought, most ethnic clients see counselors who are from the White middle class.

Ethnic counselors and psychologists emphasize that their professions must attend to the concerns of ethnic minorities. Ponterotto and Casas (1991) and D. W. Sue, Arredondo, and McDavis (1992) indicate that early in the 21st century, the White majority will become a minority because of increasing immigration rates and because White birthrates are decreasing. D. W. Sue et al. comment:

> The 1990 U.S. Census reveals that the United States is fast undergoing some very radical demographic changes. Projections show that by the year 2000, more than one third of the population will be racial and ethnic minorities, with even higher numbers (45%) in our public schools. By the year 2010, fewer than 20 years from now, racial and ethnic minorities will become a numerical majority, with white Americans constituting approximately 48% of the population. (p. 478)

During the late 1980s and 1990s, following nearly two decades of growing awareness about the civil rights of ethnic groups, racial slurs and violence toward ethnic minorities escalated in the United States. The intensity of racial strife was demonstrated in the 1992 Los Angeles riots after a jury acquitted four police officers of beating Rodney King, a Black male, in an incident that had been videotaped by a local resident and shown on television stations across the country.

Definition of Multicultural Counseling

Multicultural counseling, also known as *cross-cultural counseling,* is defined by D. W. Sue et al. (1982) as "any counseling relationship in which two or more participants differ with respect to cultural background, values and life style" (p. 47). Similarly, Pedersen (1988) defines *multicultural counseling* as "a situation in which two or more persons with different ways of perceiving their social environment are brought together in a helping relationship" (p. viii). All counseling is, to some degree, multicultural because in every counseling relationship counselors and clients bring different cultural values and influences and different social roles into the sessions. Speight, Myers, Cox, and Highlen (1991) point out that a White counselor working with an ethnic client is only one example of multicultural counseling. They say, "Female counselors with male clients, lesbian counselors with straight clients, Jewish counselors with Buddhist clients, elderly counselors with teenaged clients all must answer the question of how to effectively work together regardless of differences" (p. 30).

Pedersen (1991) and Ponterotto and Casas (1991) claim that because multiculturalism is relevant throughout counseling, it qualifies as a fourth force in psychology, joining psychoanalysis, behaviorism, and humanism.

Lee and Richardson (1991) are concerned about broadening the definitions of multiculturalism: "As the term has been increasingly stretched to include virtually any group of people who consider themselves *different*, the extent of multicultural counseling theory and practice has become unclear" (p. 6). Locke (1990) cautions that an overgeneralized view of multiculturalism suggests "racism is no different from problems experienced by white persons who suffer from social devaluation" (p. 20).

My own view is that counselors need to be aware of multicultural differences with all their clients—differences in values, socioeconomic status, gender, and age. At the same time, the uniqueness of each client, regardless of race, gender, or age, needs to be acknowledged to prevent stereotyping.

Early Work

Before the 1970s, counseling ethnic individuals received very little attention. Few persons from ethnic groups were using available mental health services, and those who did showed a significant dropout rate. In a 1977 survey, S. Sue found that 50% of ethnic clients dropped out of counseling after the first interview, compared with 30% of Caucasian clients.

At first, ethnic psychologists made three overall recommendations to reduce the resistance of ethnic minorities to counseling. First, they urged improving counselor training so that counselors would become more aware of cultural differences between the White middle class and ethnic groups. Second, they suggested that counselors be highly directive with ethnic clients by giving advice and specific suggestions on how to resolve a problem, rather than by talking with clients about their feelings. Third, they advocated that counselors and clients be matched ethnically to improve the chances of successful counseling outcome.

Although these suggestions made some improvements in mental health services for ethnic groups, research has shown that they also contributed to a different set of problems. According to Margolis and Rungta (1986), counselor educators and counselors, in their early efforts to overcome stereotypes, only perpetuated the problem. Counselors began responding to ethnic clients as members of a group with specific stereotypical characteristics, rather than treating clients as individuals (A. Smith & Stewart, 1983). Counselors were perceiving minority differences as deficits, which further contributed to clients' feelings of alienation and powerlessness.

Moreover, in their attempts to use special directive counseling techniques for their minority clients, counselors neglected their clients' individual needs. For example, E. J. Smith (1977), in writing about Black clients, objected to the frequency with which direct, task-oriented intervention techniques were recommended specifically for Blacks. Her view is that "once the members of the counseling profession start proposing techniques on the basis of race and socioeconomic class alone, they are surely treading in dangerous waters" (p. 393). She continues, "Black clients should be treated as individuals first and secondly as members of a particular racial group" (p. 394).

Professional Issues

Professional counselors and therapists are now giving considerable attention to the following issues in ethnic counseling:

- Counselor characteristics
- Individual and cultural characteristics of ethnic clients
- Differing worldviews of counselors and clients
- Racial/cultural identity of ethnic clients
- Theories and techniques of multicultural counseling
- Training in multicultural counseling

Counselor Characteristics

The common core elements in a counseling relationship apply to ethnic clients, as well as to White, middle-class clients. Trust must be built in a counseling relationship in which the ethnic client is seen as a unique individual to whom the counselor responds with warmth, sincerity, and empathy (Draguns, 1996; Thomason, 1993). As in any counseling relationship, counselors need to be open to the values and beliefs of ethnic clients and aware of how the clients' values relate to their own values.

Jones (1985) asserts that empathy and countertransference are two key factors in counseling with Blacks. Empathy permits the White counselor to go beyond superficial cultural understanding to deep cultural insights in which the counselor apprehends more fully the ethnic client's feelings about cultural values, dilemmas, and conflicts. Countertransference often occurs when White counselors react to Black clients with fear, guilt, or denial of differences. White therapists or counselors become more empathic and effective with Black clients when they explore their own needs or motivations that lead to negative countertransference.

D. W. Sue et al. (1992) propose standards for multicultural counselor competencies based on a 1991 document approved by the Association for Multicultural Counseling and Development (AMCD). Culturally skilled counselors are described as follows:

1. They are aware of their own assumptions, values, biases, and limitations and how these can affect the minority client.
2. They understand the worldviews of culturally different clients and how these worldviews relate to oppressive social-political forces in the United States and to traditional counseling theories.
3. They develop a wide repertoire of appropriate intervention strategies that include verbal and nonverbal communication and out-of-office activities when necessary.

In October 1996, the Association for Counselor Education and Supervision (ACES) endorsed these competencies, followed by an endorsement from the International Association for Marriage and Family Counseling (IAMFC) in 1997.

Individual and Cultural Characteristics of Ethnic Clients

Counselors who are sensitive to the needs of ethnic clients consider both individual and cultural characteristics important to developing an effective relationship. The major characteristics specific to ethnic clients listed below are discussed in some detail by McGoldrick (1982).

Individual Characteristics.

1. Degree of facility with English language
2. Perception about one's ethnicity
3. Whether client lives with parents, lives with an extended family, and/or lives in an ethnic neighborhood
4. Degree of cohesion of family

Cultural Characteristics.

1. Socioeconomic status, educational level, acculturation, and upward mobility of the client and family
2. Degree to which the client has value conflicts with the majority society, with another minority group, or with the extended family
3. Family's facility with the English language
4. Whether the client is first, second, or third generation
5. Attitudes of ethnic group or family about mental health services
6. Whether the client is married to, or is a partner of, a person outside her or his culture
7. Degree of loyalty expected in nuclear and extended families
8. Degree of family ties to country of origin or to cultural traditions or religion
9. Whether an ethnic group designates certain persons as healers

Factors regarding immigration status are very important to many groups (Lee & Richardson, 1991). For example, many refugees who left their countries because of repressive or life-threatening governments are trauma victims suffering from post-traumatic stress disorder (see chap. 19).

Differing Worldviews of Counselors and Clients

D. W. Sue and Sue (1999) discuss worldview orientations under four dimensions: (a) perception of time (past, present, future), (b) human activity (being, being in becoming, doing), (c) social relationships (lineal, collateral, individualistic), and (d) people's relationship to nature (subjugation, harmony, mastery). In presenting examples of different worldview orientations, Sue and Sue caution that one cannot apply them to all members in a particular ethnic group because of individual differences in such factors as socioeconomic status, religious beliefs, and gender. With these cautions in mind, Sue and Sue observe that White people tend to be future-oriented, active individuals who seek autonomy and try to exert control over nature. In contrast, they claim, ethnic minorities tend to be either past or present oriented, to be more involved in communal relationships, and to hold to the belief that they are in harmony with nature (see Table 14.1).

Racial/Cultural Identity of Ethnic Clients

Racial/cultural identity refers to the degree to which members of an ethnic group have assimilated values and behaviors of the majority culture and the degree to which they hold to the beliefs, customs, and values of their ethnic culture or heritage (Sabnani, Ponterotto, & Borodovsky, 1991; D. W. Sue & Sue, 1999). Awareness that each minority client will differ on this degree of assimilation can reduce the chances of treating every member of an ethnic group in a stereotypical way.

Atkinson, Morten, and Sue (1993) propose a minority identity development model (MID) in which members of an ethnic group go through five stages. At first, they attempt to identify with the majority culture (*conformity*). Then, conflicting self-doubts emerge within the group (*dissonance*). In the third stage (*resistance and immersion*), they become disillusioned, resentful, and rebellious. The next is the *introspective* stage, in which they reconsider majority and minority values. In the last stage (*synergistic*), they develop a balanced, integrative awareness of strengths and weaknesses of both majority and minority cultures.

Theories and Techniques of Multicultural Counseling

Contemporary ethnic counselors are less concerned about special theories and techniques for minority clients than were earlier ethnic professionals. Most counselors now attend to both inner reality and environmental factors in a client's life.

TABLE 14.1
Cultural Value Preferences of Middle-Class White Americans and Ethnic Minorities: A Comparative Summary

Area of Relationships	Middle-Class White Americans	Asian Americans	American Indians	Black Americans	Hispanic Americans
People to Nature/ Environment	Mastery over	Harmony with	Harmony with	Harmony with	Harmony with
Time Orientation	Future	Past-present	Present	Present	Past-present
People Relations	Individual	Collateral	Collateral	Collateral	Collateral
Preferred Mode of Activity	Doing	Doing	Being-in-Becoming	Doing	Being-in-Becoming
Nature of Man	Good & Bad	Good	Good	Good & Bad	Good

Source: From *Family Therapy With Ethnic Minorities* (p. 232) by M. K. Ho, 1987, Newbury Park, CA: Sage. Copyright 1987 by Sage Publications. Reprinted by permission.

Regardless of counseling theory, counselors can develop credibility and trust with ethnic clients if they can work with their clients in a way that is compatible with the clients' beliefs about the culture (S. Sue & Zane, 1987).

After trust has been established, counselors can help clients reframe the way they perceive their problems. Awareness of clients' individual and cultural characteristics also helps determine whether culture-specific techniques are needed and, if so, which kind should be used. S. Sue and Morishima (1982) used a culture-specific technique when they asked an older uncle to act as intermediary to help resolve a conflict between an immigrant Chinese daughter and her immigrant mother-in-law—a common practice in Chinese culture. If the client and the mother-in-law had been third- or fourth-generation Chinese Americans, this culture-specific technique probably would have been inappropriate.

Ivey's (1986) developmental counseling therapy theory (DCT) is especially appropriate in multicultural counseling. Ivey emphasizes the importance of moving away from client focus on self-development to developing self in relationship to others, a process in counseling he calls a *dialectical/system approach*. Clients who perceive their problems within a situational context of family and culture become aware of how these factors increase the complexity of their experiences, emotions, and thoughts. Problems then are best resolved within these systems (Ivey, Ivey, & Simek-Morgan, 1997; see also chap. 4).

This view is particularly pertinent to ethnic groups in which family and cultural ties are close and influential. It is consistent as well with feminist views regarding self-development through mutual connections with others (see chaps. 4, 5, and 9).

Ivey et al. (1997) recommend using *network therapy* with ethnic groups that include counselor intervention with the individuals, their family members, and "key figures from the community such as the priest, the teacher, the police, and perhaps even the local bartender" (p. 183). Network therapy addresses not only changes in the individual and family but also attitude changes in the community that are influencing individuals and families. Ivey et al.'s network therapy is remarkably similar to Rojano's community family therapy, discussed later.

Training in Multicultural Counseling

D. W. Sue and Sue (1999) express concerns that deficiencies in the cross-cultural components of counselor education programs are contributing to ineffective mental health services for ethnic minorities. They comment, "One of the major reasons for therapeutic ineffectiveness lies in the training of mental health professionals" (p. 11). They argue that counselor training generally does not include the influences of culture on personality development, career and educational concerns, or behavioral disorders. In addition, they say that counselor-training programs are deficient in teaching counseling skills relevant to the culturally different, use inappropriate training packages of helping skills for ethnic clients, and neglect to give trainees a chance to explore their own subconscious racism.

Suggestions have been made to upgrade multicultural counselor training. Copeland (1982, 1983) recommends that training programs for cross-cultural counseling include four components: (a) consciousness-raising, (b) cognitive understanding, (c) affective experiencing, and (d) skill building. In *consciousness-raising,* the counselor is helped to become familiar with a cultural group. *Cognitive understanding* involves teaching counselors to assess demographic data. *Affective experiencing* consists of training counselors to become aware of client and counselor emotions. Counselors are also trained in *skill-building* techniques appropriate for ethnic clients, including interviewing and assessment.

Margolis and Rungta (1986) recommend that an overall course on multicultural counseling be added to the required core courses for all counselors rather than a course on each of the predominant ethnic groups, because it is economically unfeasible to require several core courses on ethnic counseling. Moreover, they claim, a course that covers the issues of multicultural counseling as a whole is the more effective approach.

D. W. Sue et al. (1992) summarize the following new model of cross-cultural training in their proposal to reform multicultural counselor training:

1. Culturally different does not mean deviancy, pathology, or inferiority.
2. Biculturalism in racial and ethnic minority groups is acknowledged.
3. Biculturalism involves positive and desirable characteristics that enhance and enrich humans.
4. Obstacles or difficulties interfering with the development of the individual are perceived as existing within the environment and with social-political oppressive forces, rather than within the individual or the minority group.

Several models of multicultural training in counseling and counseling psychology have been summarized by Kiselicka (1998):

> Collectively, these models were designed to promote the following: (a) self-knowledge, especially an awareness of one's own cultural biases; (b) knowledge about the status and cultures of different cultural groups; (c) skills to make culturally appropriate interventions, including a readiness to use alternative counseling strategies that better match the cultures of clients than do traditional counseling strategies; and (d) actual experiences in counseling culturally different clients. (p. 6)

The following four sources give suggestions for improving training in multicultural counseling:

Pedersen, P. B. (1988). *A handbook for developing multicultural awareness.* Alexandria, VA: American Counseling Association.

Pedersen, P. B. (Ed.). (1991a). Multiculturalism as a fourth force [Special issue]. *Journal of Counseling & Development, 70.*

Myers, H. F., Wohlford, P., Guzman, L. P., & Echemendia, R. J. (Eds.). (1991). *Ethnic minority perspectives on clinical training and services in psychology.* Washington, DC: American Psychological Association.

Multicultural counselor training [Special issue]. (1998). *Counseling Psychologist, 26.*

Counseling with Representative Ethnic Groups

Because ethnic groups number more than 20, it is not possible to cover them all in an introductory text. The four largest ethnic groups in the United States—Blacks, Hispanics, American Indians, and Asian Americans—have been selected. Because these groups can also be subdivided, depending on geographic origins, country of origin, and in many cases, language, this is only a general overview. In their book *Ethnicity and Family Therapy*, McGoldrick et al. (1996) cover not only subgroups within Blacks, Asians, Hispanics, and American Indians but also more than a dozen other ethnic groups, including Italians, Greeks, Germans, Poles, Jews, Irish, Portuguese, and Puerto Ricans. Each section of their book is written by professional counselors or therapists who represent specific ethnic groups and who work primarily with clients from these groups. They give insights into intercultural family role behaviors and show how these influence the types of problems that individuals and families might experience. For those particularly interested in counseling with ethnic minority children and adolescents, read *Working With Culture: Psychotherapeutic Interventions With Ethnic Minority Children and Adolescents* (Vargas & Koss-Chioino, 1992).

Various names are used by members of ethnic groups to designate their cultural identity: African Americans, Blacks, Black Americans; Hispanic Americans, Hispanics, Latinos, Chicanos; American Indians, Native Americans; Asian Americans, Asians/Pacific Islanders. I have selected the names used most often in the ethnic literature.

Counselors also need to be aware that members within each group often come from different geographic locations or countries of origin, may speak different languages, and may adhere to different customs (Atkinson et al., 1993). Awareness makes counselors more sensitive to individual preferences for how they wish to be called. When in doubt, counselors should ask their clients.

Counseling African Americans (Blacks)

In the United States, African Americans (Blacks) are the largest ethnic group, totaling approximately 36 million people (Baruth & Manning, 1999). Cross and Fhagen-Smith (1996) observe, "The combinations and permutations of Black life are as infinite as the imagination, and healthy Black adjustment should be expected to vary from one context to another" (p. 122).

Ponterotto and Casas (1991) emphasize that Blacks are a heterogeneous group. Some U.S. Blacks grew up in the rural South; others in northern cities; some are recent immigrants from the Caribbean.

Dillard (1983) and Wilson and Stith (1993) claim that the literature often ignores the strengths of African Americans and their families while emphasizing broken homes and other problems inherent with lower socioeconomic status. As a group, they say, Blacks are unusually resourceful, having survived centuries of discrimination and oppression. Their strengths lie in their kinship bonds and loyalty to family (Gladding, 1997). Family boundaries are elastic and often include an extended family of aunts, uncles, and other relatives. Children are readily accepted into the family regardless of the marital status of their parents.

Work and education are highly valued. Parents expect children to take advantage of education and to seek mental health services because they are very concerned about their children's progress in school. Garreau (1988), who sees the emerging Black middle class as a historic change, points out that 81% of Blacks finish high school, compared with 30% in 1960.

Richardson (1991) emphasizes that religion plays an important part in the lives of African Americans, with the church playing a vital role in providing or supporting some sort of mental health service (see chap. 19). He strongly recommends that counselors consider the clergy and church networks to be support resources for families in crises.

Regardless of the socioeconomic status of an African American client, counselors must be aware of the possibility of feelings of powerlessness and rage the client may have regarding environmental barriers related to discrimination. African Americans of higher socioeconomic status will bring in problems similar to those of Whites, which often include self-actualization, improvement of self-esteem, career concerns, and family problems (see chap. 19). Lower income African Americans are often concerned about factors related to physical and economic survival, such as poverty, unemployment, housing, and health care. Their problems center on depression, alcohol and drug abuse, poor academic performance, acting-out behavior, and juvenile delinquency. Behind all this is often a desire to improve their quality of life. According to Hines and Boyd-Franklin (1982), a family systems approach, particularly following that of Minuchin (discussed in chap. 10), works well with African American lower income groups. Wilson and Stith (1993) strongly recommend using family therapy with African American families.

Psychiatrist and family therapist Ramon Rojano objects to this approach. Although Minuchin's system of therapy was initially valuable for attending to the needs of ethnic families in inner-city ghettos, his theory of removing clients from the ghettos to better environments for treatment essentially failed in most cases, Rojano claims, because as soon as individuals returned to their home communities, they fell back into old patterns (Markovitz, 1997). Rojano, originally from Colombia, who is director of DSHS in Hartford, Connecticut, encourages individuals and families to become empowered within their communities. He believes that *family systems* therapy must change into a *community systems* therapy. Rojano's theory emerges out of his culture-specific, Hispanic background that emphasizes close family and community ties, and his programs work particularly well in ethnic neighborhoods (Markovitz, 1997). Because his work has to do primarily with families and their relations to their communities, Rojano's theory and programs are discussed more at length in the chapters on family and community counseling (chaps. 10 and 19).

In any case, Jones (1985) says that counselors must pay attention to client characteristics and to the individuality of each client. He states, "There is enormous within-group variability. The question is not how to treat *the* black client but how to treat *this* black client" (p. 175).

Schools must start with the premise that African American students are capable of succeeding and want to succeed in school. School officials must then develop alternative strategies to educate these students and to encourage parents to exert a positive influence on their children (Locke, 1995):

> If school counselors are to make significant contributions to the education of African-American students, they must develop an awareness of African and African-American cultures. They must also understand how students are influenced by those cultures. From such awareness, counselors can develop specific strategies that address the unique needs of African-American students. (p. 38)

Counseling Hispanics (Latinos)

Hispanics represent the second largest ethnic minority in the United States. They are one of the fastest growing groups and are expected soon to be the largest (Casas & Vasquez, 1996; Ponterotto & Casas, 1991). They are a very diverse group coming from Mexico (63%), Puerto Rico (12%), Cuba (6%), and Central and South America (12%; Comas-Diaz, 1993). A large proportion live in substandard housing in metropolitan areas and are poor and unemployed (Ponterotto & Casas, 1991; D. W. Sue & Sue, 1999).

Mental health services have been underused by Hispanics because strong family caring reduces the need for outside help (Ponterotto, 1987). Even though families help buffer stress, at the same time pressures for commitment with large extended families can intensify difficulties (Padilla & DeSnyder, 1985). Nevertheless, family is the most important social unit for Hispanics, superseding personal identity. Casas and Vasquez (1996) say,

> In traditional Hispanic culture, the family unit (including the extended family) is given great importance; consequently, in that cultural context it is "normal" to deal with the reality and necessity of valuing the welfare of the family higher than one's individual welfare. (p. 57)

Children and adult children thus tend to submerge their needs to parents' needs, behaviors that are reinforced by the teachings of Catholicism—the dominant religion among Hispanics—about respect for parents and family.

Alcohol and drug abuse, as well as unemployment, are serious problems for low-income Hispanics. School dropout rates are high, often because of language barriers—barriers that often interfere with school-family interactions. Hispanic families encourage their children to speak Spanish at home and at school as a means of maintaining cultural identification, whereas school officials generally insist they speak English.

Hispanic Americans tend to tie emotional difficulties to physical illness, and they often take psychological problems to physicians rather than to mental health professionals (Comas-Diaz, 1993). They also tend to seek help from relatives, friends, or spiritualists or faith healers (De La Cancela & Guzman, 1991).

De La Cancela and Guzman (1991) believe that a social action view of therapy must be included in working with mental health problems of Latinos. This approach emphasizes the impact of societal or world sickness on the mental health of the ethnic client, rather than focuses on internal sources of maladjustment. This theory is similar to Rojano's community systems theory and Ivey et al.'s network therapy theory for multicultural communities, discussed earlier.

Casas and Vasquez (1996) caution counselors not to neglect the history of Hispanic clients: "The past and present interrelate in such a complex manner, that, for most Hispanics, it is impossible to understand the total individual without an understanding and appreciation for his or her sociohistorical reality" (pp. 158–159). Ponterotto (1987) recommends using a multimodal counseling approach as developed by Lazarus (see chap. 5) because it has the flexibility to be adapted to the wide cultural diversity of Hispanics.

Counseling Native American Indians

The terms *Native American Indian, Native American,* and *American Indian* are used interchangeably in the literature:

> As most scholars know, the term *American Indian* is an imposed ethnic category with little relevant meaning. . . . Somehow, and no one is really certain why, the category continued to be used to the extent that almost all indigenous, native people of the Western Hemisphere are referred to as Indians. . . . For better or worse, the term has become institutionalized and even accepted by the native people themselves. (Trimble, Fleming, Beauvais, & Jumper-Thurman, 1996, pp. 178–179)

According to the 1990 census, approximately 2 million people in the United States declare themselves to be either Native American Indians or Alaska Natives (Trimble et al., 1996). La Fromboisa (1993) and Ponterotto and Casas (1991) indicate 511 federally recognized American Indian tribes and an additional 365 state-recognized tribes. Estimates are that about 750,000 Native Americans live on or near reservations, the only minority group to do so (Trimble, 1991). Because most Indian tribes are recognized as nations by treaties with the U.S. government, they have certain sovereign rights and are under federal jurisdiction. Conflicts among state, federal, and local governments regarding the rights and jurisdictions of Native Americans occur at many levels. For instance, these jurisdictional conflicts can lead to confusion about who will fund mental health services. The result frequently is lack of adequate funding.

According to Trimble (1991) and Yates (1987), American Indians, who are lowest on the socioeconomic scale, have very serious problems of survival, poverty, and unemployment that relate often to discrimination and stereotyping of groups. On reservations, unemployment generally averages about 40%; poverty, about 48%. School dropout rates are as high as 60%. American Indians resist Anglo American education when it ignores the Indian culture (Dillard, 1983). Adolescents in the culture have higher rates of suicide and substance abuse than do any other group of adolescents.

Many problems of Native Americans are affected by recent changes in the socioeconomic status and upward mobility among some of their people. Those who have college degrees not only have problems similar to those of middle-class Whites but also often find themselves in conflict with members of their tribes. They are often seen as having abandoned their people and their heritage.

Counselors should be aware of the strong extended family system on Indian reservations. Aunts, uncles, and grandparents often serve as parents to nieces, nephews, and grandchildren. Most play a significant part in the upbringing of children; others take over completely (Attneave, 1982). Family counseling is an effective approach to use with American Indians because of their strong family orientation and kinship (Trimble et al., 1996). The traditional healing approaches of shamans and medicine men are also used frequently among the American Indian tribes on the reservations (Thomason, 1993; Trimble, 1991). Thomason (1993) and Trimble (1991) both recommend that counselors cooperate with these healers.

Counseling Asian Americans

Asian Americans are not a homogeneous group, although they are often perceived that way. Asians who live in the United States come from many cultural heritages, each with a distinct language—Chinese, Taiwanese, Japanese, Filipinos, Koreans, Samoans, Vietnamese, Cambodians, and Laotians, for example (Kitano & Maki, 1996; D. Sue & Sue, 1993). Further, large differences exist within Asian American groups in terms of socioeconomic status, primary language, and whether they are recent immigrants or second- or third-generation Asian Americans. The Asian American population is about 6 million, and like the Hispanics, Asian Americans are one of the fastest growing groups in the United States because of increasing ratios allowed for Asian immigration (D. Sue & Sue, 1993; Zane & Sue, 1991). Projections are that Asian Americans will number 20 million in 2020 (Org, 1993).

When working with Asian Americans, the counselor must be particularly aware of their social class, geophysical origin, and level of generation. A bimodal socioeconomic grouping exists in some Asian groups. Half of them are competitive high achievers scholastically, and half are recent immigrants who live in poverty and are unemployed. Because Asian high achievers are more visible to the public, many non-Asians tend to develop a stereotype of Asian Americans as successful, well-educated, and relatively free from mental health problems (Gladding, 1997; D. W. Sue & Sue, 1985).

Strong emphasis is placed on the specific role of each family member. Personal needs of the individual are superseded by the needs of both the elders and the family (D. Sue & Sue, 1993). Shame is used to reinforce family expectations about appropriate behavior (Kitano & Maki, 1996).

Asian Americans generally feel shame about the need to seek outside help, because they believe that the family is supposed to deal with personal problems. In a study of counseling preferences of Asian American college students, Atkinson, Wampold, Lowe, Matthews, and Ahn (1998) found that whereas they underuse personal counseling services, they tend to use vocational counseling services more than do college students in the general population. In personal counseling, this shame persists in the form of resistance to talking about themselves (D. W. Sue & Sue, 1999). A common stereotypical view is that Asian Americans are nonassertive, a characteristic that is thought to be an inherent part of their personalities. D. W. Sue and Sue (1999) claim, however, that such behaviors actually depend on certain situations.

Problems brought to counseling by Asian Americans of higher socioeconomic status relate to career choice, educational opportunities, independence versus loyalty to family, pressure to succeed, and social isolation (Baruth & Manning, 1999). Immigrant groups have problems with language, depression, unemployment, and housing typical of other low-income groups.

When working with first-generation Asian American clients, counselors must be aware of cultural values that influence the clients' views about mental health. Clients' religious beliefs and traditions are closely tied to attitudes about mental health and mental illness (Gladding, 1997). Many Asian American clients are familiar with the use of mediation or negotiation to solve problems. Thus, they often respond well to counselors who use mediation processes in counseling sessions. These clients also believe in the Asian value that family unity comes before the individual's welfare. Counselors need to be aware of these influences when helping clients resolve family conflicts (Kitano & Maki, 1996).

Research on Multicultural Counseling

In a survey of articles published between 1983 and 1988 in leading counseling journals, Ponterotto and Casas (1991) found 183 articles related to multicultural counseling and categorized them into five topic areas. In this survey, the number of articles about Blacks exceeded the total number of articles in the three other major ethnic groups. Only a few articles were on American Indians, and these were narrowly focused on alcoholism, depression, suicide, and substance abuse.

Ponterotto and Casas (1991) also gathered data from five leading counselor journals during the years 1983 to 1988 on 80 empirical studies on North American racial/ethnic groups. They then evaluated these articles on the basis of 10 criticisms that have been consistently presented in the literature as weaknesses in ethnic research. As Table 14.2 shows, six criticisms were supported by the data, two were only partially supported, and two were disputed.

In 1998, Ponterotto reevaluated the above criticisms of multicultural counseling research. He comments, "I believe that in the past decade many of these criticisms have been addressed by researchers to some degree" (p. 63). These criticisms are so pervasive, however, that they still warrant attention.

Ponterotto (1998) emphasizes once again the importance of upgrading research methods, particularly the need for more qualitative research studies. "I am an advocate of qualitative research methods. The qualitative tradition has been, until quite recently, undervalued in counseling psychology and seldom used in multicultural counseling research" (p. 64).

Ponterotto (1998) also recommends that research in the next decade focus on five themes: (a) racial identity development (e.g., oral histories, case studies); (b) multicultural competency assessment; (c) mentoring (e.g., assessing characteristics of effective mentors); (d) model programs (e.g., assessing programs that offer "clinical experience with culturally diverse clients" [p. 61]); and (e) the role of program

TABLE 14.2
Results of Survey on Criticisms of Racial Ethnic Research

Six Criticisms Supported by the Data

Lack of conceptual/theoretical frameworks to guide research.

Disregard for within-group or intracultural differences.

The use of easily accessible college student populations.

Reliance on culturally encapsulated psychometric instrumentation.

Failure to adequately describe one's sample in terms of socioeconomic status (SES).

Overreliance on paper-and-pencil measures as dependent variables.

Two Criticisms Only Partially Supported by the Data

Overemphasis on simplistic counselor/client process variables and a disregard for important psychosocial variables within and outside the culture that might impact counseling.

Lack of adequate sample sizes.

Two Criticisms Disputed by the Data

Overreliance on experimental analogue research.

Failure to delineate study's limitations.

Source: Adapted from J. G. Ponterotto and J. M. Casas, *Handbook of Racial/Ethnic Minority Counseling Research* (p. 94), 1991. Courtesy of Charles C Thomas, Publisher, Ltd., Springfield, Illinois.

diversity in training effectiveness (e.g., taking into account the ratio of culturally diverse students in multicultural classes).

✥ COUNSELING WOMEN AND MEN: GENDER ROLE STEREOTYPING

Women and men suffer from stereotypical roles in different ways. Although the prevailing culture expects women's primary role to be nurturer and caretaker, such a role is considered inferior to the male role. Women are devalued for their emphasis on developing relationships and connections with others. In the workforce, women generally are placed in subordinate positions and experience job discrimination, unequal pay for equal work, and sexual harassment (Basow, 1992; Richmond-Abbott, 1992). Consequently, women feel diminished, trivialized, and disempowered. Emotional problems, such as feelings of lack of power and control over their lives, lack of self-confidence and assertion, eating disorders, phobias, and depression, arise from these socialized roles. Such women often become victims of domestic violence, rape, and other forms of sexual abuse (Cook, 1990).

Stereotypical roles imposed on men lead them to become overzealous in achieving success whereby they must strive at all times to appear competent, assertive, and invulnerable. They are trained to disregard emotions related to tenderness, fear, and grief (Kelly & Hall, 1992). They minimize and devalue both their inner self and relationships. Consequently, their zealous striving for achievement and devaluing relationships lead to aggression, heart attacks, impotency, violence, and addictive behaviors.

Women and men have organized into various groups to reexamine and modify gender roles and regain the sense of well-being and a caring regard for themselves and others. For women, one such group, the National Organization for Women (NOW), works through established channels in society, such as legislative action, to obtain civil rights for women. Another, more radical type of group believes it necessary to revolutionize society in order to bring about equal rights for women (Basow, 1992). Many women have formed academic research centers for women's studies. Among these women are feminist clinicians who have formed research centers to reevaluate traditional psychological theories and to propose therapeutic approaches from a feminist perspective. Two such groups are the women at the Stone Center at Wellesley College, and the Women's Project in Family Therapy, discussed in chapters 5 and 10.

The men's movement has also formed into various groups, including profeminist and promasculine groups. Profeminists believe that working with women to equalize gender roles will profit men as well as women. Promasculine groups believe that men's foremost need is to form groups with other men to improve their roles (Clatterbaugh, 1990).

Male therapists are also presenting new perspectives of male psychology and masculinity. Terence Real (1997), for example, argues that male dysfunctions are the result of coercing boys to adopt so-called masculine behaviors. Other examples are Kenneth Clatterbaugh (1990) and Warren Steinberg (1993).

Although women's and men's groups have differed in their aims and methods to improve gender relationships, they agree that traditional counseling theories and practice have contributed to gender role stereotyping, and they have made moves to change counseling processes. In recent years, women's and men's groups have become remarkably similar in acknowledging that the development of relationships is fundamental and primary for both genders for healthy human growth and development:

> Just as for many depressed women recovery is inextricably linked to shedding the traces of oppression and finding empowerment, for many depressed men, recovery is linked to opposing the force of disconnection, and reentering the world of relationship—to the "feminine," to themselves, and to others. (Real, 1997, p. 158)

A discussion of all the women's and men's movements with their various aims and actions goes beyond the scope of this book. Instead, I briefly discuss how some of these movements have influenced counseling theories and practice. Those who wish to read more about the movements themselves can start with Susan Basow's *Gender Stereotypes and Roles* (1992), Kenneth Clatterbaugh's *Contemporary Perspectives on Masculinity* (1990), and Warren Steinberg's *Identity Conflict and Transformation* (1993).

Women: Problems with Role Stereotyping

Feminist Theories of Counseling

As women's groups crystallized in the 1960s and 1970s, feminist counselors and therapists began to criticize counseling theories developed by men, which they claimed reinforced the prevailing social and economic status of men and women. In 1970, Broverman, Broverman, Clarkson, Rosenkrantz, and Vogel alerted the mental health professions about therapist and counselor bias toward clients. In their study, equal numbers of female and male clinicians were asked to indicate characteristics of healthy men, healthy women, and healthy adults. Regardless of gender, all clinicians described healthy men and healthy women in stereotypical ways. Healthy men were described as aggressive, ambitious, decisive, independent, rational, unemotional, and worldly. Healthy women were portrayed as submissive, modest, warm, indecisive, dependent, nurturant, weak, flighty, and emotional. A key finding in the study (a finding that dismayed many women) was that a healthy adult was perceived by clinicians as having the typical characteristics of the healthy man.

On the basis of their concerns about societal and therapeutic restraints placed on women, feminists in the 1970s challenged traditional therapeutic procedures and developed feminist therapy geared specifically for women. "Feminism insists that women must have personal autonomy and both the freedom to direct and the responsibility for directing all areas of their lives; they must decide for themselves what it means to be a woman" (Faunce, 1985, p. 309).

According to Young-Eisendrath and Wiedemann (1987), the central theme in all feminist work "has been the fear of personal insignificance" (p. 8). Ballou and Gabalac (1985) say that feminist therapists focus more on developing an egalitarian relationship between therapist and client than do traditional therapists. Typically, the relationship has been unequal—a strong, authoritarian, male therapist and a weak, helpless female client.

Young-Eisendrath and Wiedemann (1987) are opposed to the medical model approach, "the symptom approach," because of, they claim, "a sense of hopelessness engendered by the illness model of psychopathology" (p. 5) that focuses on "what is absent, deficient or wrong in a person or situation" (p. 4). They propose a different model, one that enhances strengths of clients, rather than focuses on weaknesses.

Feminist therapy is a process of building a woman's sense of empowerment—not in the typical male sense of exerting power over someone else, but rather of having the authority to be one's feminine self. "The ability of a woman to validate her own convictions of truth, beauty, and goodness in regard to her self-concept and self interest is what we call *female authority*" (Young-Eisendrath & Wiedemann, 1987, p. 8).

Some of the most notable approaches to feminist therapy in recent years arose out of the feminist developmental theories proposed by women psychotherapists and researchers at the Stone Center at Wellesley College (Jordan, 1997; Jordan, Kaplan, Miller, Stiver, & Surrey, 1991; see also chap. 4 and 5). They differ from traditional developmental theorists in that they claim that forming and maintaining connections in relationships are an essential part of a woman's developmental process. According to Jordan (1991), "The Stone Center model suggests in fact that relationship, based on empathic attunement, is the key to the process of therapy, not just the backdrop for it" (p. 284).

The women at the Stone Center have recently come out more strongly with their approach to a new psychology of women (Miller & Stiver, 1997). Their theory is based on the belief that women—and all humans, for that matter—grow and develop within mutually connected relationships. This theory counteracts the prevailing belief among traditional psychological theorists that the goal of human growth and development is to achieve separation and autonomy (see chaps. 4 and 5).

Instead of the general tendency to pathologize women's proclivities to nurture relationships and develop connections, women at the Stone Center applaud these characteristics as strengths; indeed, they believe that these characteristics of mutual connections in relationships are necessary to sustain and promote human life and development.

> In reclaiming the knowledge about relationships that women in particular hold, we can begin to form a new model of psychological development *within relationships,* in which everyone participates in ways that foster the development of all people involved, something we might call "mutual psychological development." (Miller & Stiver, 1997, p. 17)

Jack (1991) applies feminist development theory to depression in women, including suggestions for therapy. In her book *Silencing the Self* (1991), which is based on a longitudinal study of 12 clinically depressed women ages 19 to 55, Jack claims that depression in women stems largely from their striving to attain intimacy through behaviors that are culturally defined as feminine—pleasing, self-sacrificing, self-silencing. Instead of creating intimacy, these behaviors lead a woman to experience a "loss of self" in relationship, to lowered self-esteem, and ultimately to depression. Jack points out that a woman's negative attitude about her "neediness" is attributable to the prevailing belief that separation and individuation are the primary goals of development. "As it currently exists, the concept of dependence . . . labels women's orientation to their relationship as weakness or pathology" (pp. 19–20). Instead, Jack argues, women's vulnerability to depression "does not lie in their 'dependence' on relationships or in their depressive response to loss, but in what happens to them within their relationships" (p. 21).

Pointing out that the quality of relationship is the key issue in women's vulnerability to depression, Jack (1991) describes forms of connection, distinguishing between "compliance in relationship" and "authentic relatedness." When, on the one hand, close relationships have high levels of mutual affection, communication, support, affection, and availability, they "create feelings of emotional security" and allow authentic forms of relating (p. 40). When, on the other hand, relationships are characterized by power imbalances, economic disparity, and a lack of sharing the real self with the other, a woman becomes "compliant in relationship" and hides her real feelings.

In her best-selling book *Women Who Run With the Wolves,* Jungian psychotherapist Clarissa Pinkola Estés (1992) also claims that women's psychic needs have been overlooked by traditional psychology:

> Traditional psychology is often spare or entirely silent about deeper issues important to women: the archetypal, the intuitive, the sexual and cyclical, the ages of women, a woman's way, a woman's knowing, her creative fire. This is what has driven my work on the Wild Woman archetype for the better part of two decades. (p. 6)

Estés's work in helping women seek their Wild Woman is similar to Robert Bly's (1990) efforts to help men recover their Wild Man. Her work is also similar to that of storyteller Michael Meade (1993) of the mythopoetic men's movement. Estés uses stories as a way for women to reach their innermost selves. A *cantadora* storyteller, Estés has been using stories therapeutically for more than 25 years:

> Although some use stories as entertainment alone, tales are, in their oldest sense, a healing art. Some are called to this healing art, and the best, to my lights, are those who have lain with the story and have found all its matching parts inside themselves and at depth. (p. 463)

Other feminists urge women to become more politically active in changing the structure of society as part of improving their emotional well-being (Basow, 1992). Ballou and Gabalac (1985) point out that whichever feminist approach one chooses, the assumption is that women have less political or economic power than men and that women's emotional problems result predominantly from external causes. In a similar view, Basow (1992) comments:

> Although there are many variations of feminist therapy, they all have in common the recognition that the social context is an important determinant of human behavior and that the gender roles and statuses prescribed by society are disadvantageous to both sexes, but especially to women. (p. 339)

Counseling Women

Women with problems associated with gender role stereotyping come to counseling for many reasons. They may be depressed or may be feeling inadequate; they may be having trouble changing their roles; they may be experiencing pathological symptoms; or they may be victims of abuse.

The strongest and most profound change in therapeutic approaches to women's psychological disorders comes from the Stone Center at Wellesley College. On the basis of their psychological theory of human development (see chaps. 4 and 5), researchers at the center believe that women's growth and development occur in mutual connections in relationships (Jordan, 1997; Jordan et al., 1991; Miller & Stiver, 1997). Their theory counteracts the prevailing cultural tendency to pathologize women's desire to seek and maintain relationships. Pathological tendencies in women thus develop from profound feelings of isolation and loneliness:

> We believe that the most terrifying and destructive feeling that a person can experience is psychological isolation. This is not the same as being alone. It is feeling that one is locked out of the possibility of human connection and of being powerless to change the situation. In the extreme, psychological isolation can lead to a sense of hopelessness and desperation. (Miller & Stiver, 1997, p. 72)

The core psychological problem for women in need of therapy, say Miller and Stiver, is that in their desperate seeking for relationships, they at the same time devise strategies to remain disconnected:

> We have suggested that the contradiction inherent in keeping large parts of one's experience and responses out of connection in order to find connections is central to many psychological troubles. (p. 82)

> We see this process as *the central relational paradox,* and we believe it is basic to understanding many psychological problems. It is also basic to understanding therapy for these problems. (p. 81)

Because I believe that their therapeutic approach is relevant to my counseling theory and practice, I refer to it in chapter 9, "Individual Counseling."

Women Who Are Depressed or Who Feel Inadequate.

Many women clients are concerned with lack of self-esteem, inability to assert themselves, and inability to exert power or control over their lives. Because they have been taught to be compliant, they tend to defer to the needs of their husbands and children and to deny their own needs. Further, because these women generally depend on men to make decisions, they tend to be unequipped to cope with such matters as finances or car maintenance. After their husbands die or leave them, these women generally feel helpless (Franks, 1986).

As Jack (1991) explains regarding feminist theories of counseling and therapy, when difficulties or conflicts arise between themselves and their husbands or children, women tend to blame themselves and to harbor mixed feelings of guilt, shame, resentment, hostility, and depression.

As the title of Jack's book *Silencing the Self* (1991) implies, the loss of a sense of self is linked to a "loss of voice in relationship" (p. 36). In helping women recover from depression, Jack emphasizes the importance of the counselor's sensitivity to bringing a woman's voice back into dialogue, first through encouraging it within the therapeutic relationship. "The therapeutic encounter must offer a quality of relatedness that hears the silenced 'I' of a depressed woman and brings it into dialogue" (p. 203). Instead of replicating the traditional hierarchical relationship of (authoritative, male) therapist and (deferential, female) client, Jack suggests that the "therapy relationship must provide a different kind of dialogue, one that challenges prevailing interpersonal and intrapsychic patterns" (p. 204). In this way, "Moving into depression can become a venture into self-knowing to understand the roots of inner division and self-alienation" (p. 193).

The counselor can help clients become aware of the anger and frustration underlying their passive behavior, assist them to assert their needs, and help them become empowered by teaching them problem-solving and competency skills (Blechman, 1984). Because these women often have not developed sufficient bonding or effective relationships with either their mothers or their fathers, helping them explore their relationships with their families of origin is often necessary. This process helps women confront their unresolved feelings about their parents and recognize that they have been modeling ineffective behaviors.

Women Who Have Trouble Changing Roles.

As with all individuals who undergo personal change, women clients experience conflicts with others when they begin to change their roles. Husbands may object if their wives plan to return to school or get a job, or they may object if their wives begin to question the husbands' authority. Even more difficult for the women, some husbands may seem to support the changes their wives are trying to make but subtly undermine them.

Many women with families who take a job outside the home become overstressed when they try to balance their domestic and job responsibilities. Similar problems occur when husbands want their wives to work to supplement family income but the wives prefer to remain home to care for the children. Some husbands may insist that their wives change their behavior; they may complain, for example, that their wives are too critical. Another role change imposed on women occurs when they suddenly become single parents. Many feel overwhelmed when the breadwinner and dual-parent roles are thrust on them. In case of role changes, counselors need to help women develop personal strengths, try new activities, and cope with resistances or anger from family members. In many cases, career counseling is necessary.

Women with Pathological Symptoms.   The overrepresentation of women patients with certain types of pathology in mental health clinics can generally be traced to stereotypical roles they and their mothers have been taught. As said earlier, Miller and Stiver (1997) emphasize that strategies of disconnections are the core of women's pathology:

> This path away from mutual connection, and simultaneously away from the truth of one's own experience, is the path to psychological problems. We believe it underlies many of the problems common to women in particular, including depression, various forms of anxiety, phobias, eating problems, and the so-called personality disorders, such as "borderline personality." (p. 81)

Approximately 85% of clients with agoraphobia and about 85% to 95% of clients with eating disorders are women (Franks, 1986). Persons with agoraphobia suffer from fear and panic when in public, which can ultimately lead to their becoming completely homebound (Brehony, 1983; Kleinknecht, 1991). Many professionals agree that these symptoms are associated with a highly developed stereotypical female sex role (Basow, 1992; Chambless & Goldstein, 1980; Richmond-Abbott, 1992).

In a summary of research on the treatment of agoraphobics, Kleinknecht (1991) discusses *in vivo,* which he considers the most effective technique. In this method, clients are helped to enter, step-by-step, increasingly anxiety-evoking situations in real life and are encouraged to stay with them until the fear drops.

Serious eating disorders include anorexia nervosa and bulimia. Anorexics eat so little that they are apt to starve to death, whereas bulimics overeat in binges and then induce vomiting to rid themselves of the food. Richmond-Abbott (1992) and Wooley and Wooley (1980) believe that the cultural expectations that women must be slender and attractive contribute substantially to these eating disorders. Others believe that women who have these disorders are resentful of significant people or circumstances in their lives whom they believe control them. These disorders are thus indirect, unconscious ways of exerting control (Le Clair & Berkowitz, 1983).

Counselors use a variety of approaches to help these women, including cognitive-behavioral, ego-development, and social-cultural techniques. They work at building self-esteem so that these women can develop responsibility for, and control over, their own lives (Baird & Sights, 1986; Hotelling, 1986; Kleinknecht, 1991).

Victimized Women.   Considerable domestic violence exists in the United States and occurs at all levels of the socioeconomic scale. The number of victimized women far exceeds that of men (Basow, 1992).

Numerous psychologists and counselors question why many women remain in violent relationships. Ibrahim and Herr (1987) believe that they remain because of low self-esteem, which causes psychological and economic dependence on the abuser. According to Resick (1983), the problem relates to sex role stereotyping, in which men are supposed to be aggressive and women submissive. Others contend that abused women either are powerless or feel powerless to change their situation.

Miller and Stiver (1997) admit that they, too,

> did not acknowledge how profoundly and extensively this violence pervaded our most intimate relationships. Only with the emergence of the women's movement has the courageous work of many survivors . . . revealed the widespread existence of incest and the sexual and physical abuse of women and children. Often still working against strong opposition from within and beyond the professions, these survivors and their allies have brought to light how large is the number of women who are battered—or killed—by their husbands or male partners and how large a number of girls are sexually or physically abused most often by male family members. (p. 58)

Shelters for battered women have proved successful in helping women leave abusers. Ibrahim and Herr (1987) believe that although such shelters are valuable, comprehensive counseling should follow, including work in improving self-esteem and developing inner strengths. In addition, the women need career planning and placement. Basow (1992) recommends that, in addition to having access to shelters, women need to become empowered in relationships by learning assertiveness skills and by developing independence.

Women benefit significantly from educational and therapeutic group work, including groups for victims of rape, incest, or sexual assault; for those struggling with eating disorders; and for those in need of career counseling (Gladding, 1997).

Men: Problems with Male Stereotyping

Although men who adhere to expected male roles are more likely to develop mental health problems, until recently they haven't, as a rule, sought counseling (Scher, Stevens, Good, & Eichenfield, 1987; Silverberg, 1986; Skovolt, 1978; Toomer, 1978; Werrbach & Gilbert, 1987). In a study in which they interviewed women and men therapists about their male clients, Werrbach and Gilbert (1987) found a consensus among the therapists that "traditional male socialization can negatively affect men's relationships and general sense of well-being" (p. 562). Moreover, they found that men are reluctant to seek help and that when they do, they tend to resist a close counseling relationship.

According to Heesacker and Prichard (1992), one aim of traditional counseling—that of trying to help men become more like women in the way they express themselves emotionally—contributes to men's reluctance to seek counseling. They recommend that counselors should perceive men as emotionally different from women, rather than as emotionally inferior. They comment, "We do not believe that men are inherently less 'therapizable.' Instead, we believe that when men's emotions are understood more accurately, men will be drawn to therapy in greater numbers and will profit from it to a greater degree" (p. 283).

Men traditionally have regarded women's tendency to develop relationships as negative, as a sign of dependency and enmeshment. Feminists such as Miller and Stiver (1997), Jack (1991), and others, as discussed earlier, explain how maintaining mutual connections with others is distinctly different from dependency and enmeshment.

Recently, professional counseling journals and books have been addressing men's problems as related to gender role stereotyping and have suggested ways of improving counseling for men. Men traditionally have been reluctant to address male issues because men tend to deny problems, seek counseling less often, and express less dissatisfaction with their roles (Silverberg, 1986). More recently, however, many men have been very dissatisfied with their lives, but instead of seeking traditional counseling services, they literally took to the woods. Beginning in the late 1980s, many men throughout the country retreated periodically to special men's gatherings in the wilderness. The most prominent of these groups, the mythopoetical men's movement, stimulated innumerable publications of new perspectives on masculinity and therapeutic approaches to men's problems, including books by Clatterbaugh,(1990), Steinberg, (1993), and Heesacker and Prichard (1992).

Mythopoetical Men's Groups

The mythopoetical men's movement was immensely popular during the late 1980s and early 1990s. As a participant at various retreats for several years, I felt the profound need, as did many others, for male bonding and a long-denied opportunity to vent inner anguish in a safe place.

This movement sprang from the vision of poet Robert Bly, whose work became popular from his best-selling book *Iron John* (1990). Through initiations by older men and close interactions with other men, Bly says, men can reach their deep masculine side. This masculine energy that Bly refers to is different from the shallow drives of the aggressive macho male. Men lost touch with this force, which Bly calls the Wild Man, when our country moved from an agrarian to an industrial society. Instead of working at home where they could maintain close relationships with their families, most fathers now work away from home and have lost touch not only with their families but also with their creative energies. Out of touch and more inhibited, they have developed stifling behaviors based on success, independence, competitiveness, and aggression (Bly, 1988).

Those mythopoetical men's group meetings that I found most successful lasted for a week and were directed by a team of leaders: a storyteller and drummer, a poet, and a Jungian analyst. Musicians who accompanied the leaders' presentations set the men in motion with their music and helped unite isolated individuals into the group (mythic) experience. Such a team provided a Jungian pattern that the leaders believed generated personal transformation (Hillman, 1989; Moore & Gillette, 1990).

Storytelling serves as a method of engaging participants in enacting dramatic events. One primary storyteller at these retreats, Michael Meade, describes in his book *Men and the Water of Life: Initiation and the Tempering of Men* (1993) the experiences generated by his storytelling. The story, the group experience, and the conflicts that arise blend and evolve into a dramatic experience for everyone involved. Seeing themselves in the context of a larger story allows men to release repressed isolated feelings and to connect with the felt community of the men gathered closely together at the retreat. Men received support from the group that enabled them to share their vulnerabilities, reexperience old buried wounds and feelings of abandonment and isolation, grieve over lost fathers, examine their flaws stemming from the patriarchal system, and anguish over their inability to connect with wives and children.

The men's movement generated considerable lively responses and debates and stimulated men to delve into new perspectives on masculinity. Through these experiences, men learned to drop their defenses and to bond emotionally with other men. This bonding contrasts sharply with the typical male bonding that is task oriented, as in team sports or the military, or that is based on superficial camaraderie in the form of joking or verbal jousting in pubs.

Evaluation of Men's Groups. The men's mythopoetical groups and other similar experiences have expanded men's emotional awareness and demonstrated that men are willing to acknowledge their need for help and respond well to counseling and therapy if they perceive the experience as inviting and meaningful.

A few cautionary remarks are needed, however, about the men's retreats. Some men who start expressing feelings of anger, pain, or tenderness for the first time are met with hostility or bewilderment from spouses, families, or colleagues who are unprepared for the men's changes in behavior. Some men behave aggressively, claiming they are expressing their Wild Man. Even worse, for some, new insights and deep feelings of emotion fade away as soon as they return home and to work, leaving them with vague feelings of depression and loss. Some men attend one retreat after another as a brief tonic without adequately following through and applying insights into their lives. For whatever reason, for many men, a huge gap exists between what they experience at these retreats and what happens after they return home.

Such a lack of follow-through after a retreat prevents one from working through newly experienced emotions. In her therapeutic work, storyteller and Jungian psychoanalyst Clarissa Pinkola Estés (1992) estimates that therapeutic work with stories, depending on the story and the individual, takes several weeks or months.

The men's mythopoetical movement has also generated a backlash from radical profeminists. The idea of males beating drums in the woods, practicing how to become warriors, has touched some raw nerves. The warrior image, however, was meant to serve as a way to explore both the use and misuse of power and the need to turn energy into constructive interactions that go beyond self-serving ends. The primary purpose at male retreats is for men to learn to contain aggressive behaviors, change traditional masculine roles and patriarchal "power over" behaviors, learn to use energies constructively, and learn to relate genuinely with loved ones.

> The hairy Wild Man, according to Bly, represents forceful energy and resolve, assertive energy that Bly contrasts to machismo and cruelty. Wild-Man energy is not focused primarily on domination and destruction, but is directed at a constructive engagement with the external world. (Steinberg, 1993, p. 126)

The theory behind the need for men to find their inner Wild Man and the danger of the misuse of one's energies is quite similar to Estés's (1992) belief, as she explains in her book *Women Who Run With the Wolves,* that women must seek their inner Wild Woman to avoid destructive behaviors that arise from neglected inner needs. Estés approaches initiation rituals differently from men's groups, however. Unlike men, who typically conduct only boy-to-manhood initiation rituals, for women, Estés says, initiation experiences occur throughout life; women are thrust into ongoing life-death-life experiences; birthing is but one example. Female initiations are thus cyclical and self-regenerative processes.

Many criticize the mythopoetical experiencing of events as too esoteric. Others are uncomfortable with the variety of interpretations possible with stories and legends:

> For those who are interested in a scientifically grounded theory of masculine development, these anachronistic Jungian theories are not the answer—nor do they claim to be. But as long as the spiritual perspective is kept at the level of spiritual or religious quest (the story that tells stories), and so long as it does not ask scientific questions, it can serve both as a therapeutic device and as a motivator for personal change. (Clatterbaugh, 1990, pp. 102–103)

Still others criticize the "relative lack of emphasis on political and social change" (Basow, 1992, p. 337). Although leaders at these men's retreats consistently emphasized that persons' inner transformational changes should be carried over into making effective social changes that benefit the community and the world as a whole, efforts to do so are left up to the individuals. One exception is Michael Meade's retreats, described later.

Many counselors have been providing bridges between men's experiences at retreats and their return to families and friends in the community. Counselors can help men who are expressing feelings of anger, pain, or tenderness for the first time understand why their spouses, families, and colleagues, unprepared for these changes in behavior, often respond with hostility or bewilderment. They can caution men who behave aggressively toward others because of a mistaken perception of the Wild Man. Counselors can also be available to some men who become depressed, frustrated, or at a loss when new deep feelings of emotion and new insights begin to fade in the light of their real world.

Some counselors and counselor educators, such as R. C. Williams and Myer (1992), refer men to these retreats because they realize the value in applying mythopoetical approaches to counseling practice with men in the community.

Heesacker and Prichard (1992), who also are professionally trained counselors, suggest that men clients be encouraged to tell stories, emphasizing that the metaphorical meanings of archetypes and myths can be useful in facilitating men's emotional development. They recommend that counselors be aware of the value of silence or brooding in counseling sessions. Instead of urging clients simply to try to verbalize their feelings, they should be encouraged to enact their emotions during counseling sessions. The authors suggest that counselors and therapists should join men's groups as a means of consciousness-raising.

Meanwhile, counselors are giving more attention to the value of group counseling with men (Gladding, 1997). A special issue of the *Journal for Specialists in Group Work* published in May 1994 addressed the particular concerns of men. In that issue,

Hetzel, Barton, and Davenport (1994) suggest that group techniques, such as the use of rituals and conflict management, can help men profit from group counseling.

Of the original team, storyteller Michael Meade continues to lead men's retreats. As his book *Men and the Water of Life* (1993) attests, Meade is convinced of his belief in the transformational experience of storytelling. His group gatherings continue to evolve. Now organized under the title Mosaic Multicultural Foundation, he has been collaborating with men from various ethnic backgrounds and persons from different cultures, such as Malidoma and Sobonfu Somé from Africa. As a husband-and-wife team, Malidoma and Sobonfu help lead Meade's workshops for men and women. Meade has also organized retreats for youths and adults, as well as for mentors and elders. In the mid-1990s, Meade formed the Mosaic Multicultural Foundation to provide scholarship and training programs for disadvantaged youths to participate in his programs (Meade, 1998).

Counseling Men

Although most men have in the past been reluctant to seek counseling, men are now increasingly willing to see counselors and therapists. Counselors should note that gender stereotyping is usually at the root of their clients' problems. Men seek counseling for many reasons: They may be experiencing personal dissatisfaction or feelings of inadequacy and wish to change; they may be exhibiting addictive behaviors that belie defenses against depression; they may be undergoing transitions in life that require changes in role that lead to friction with spouses; they may be developing physiological breakdowns or pathological patterns of violence and abuse of others.

Men Who Feel Inadequate. Some male clients who are highly successful in their jobs seek counseling because they are emotionally numb, burdened with responsibilities, and dissatisfied with themselves. They often say they think they are frauds and unworthy of their success. They usually lack the ability to develop personal relationships with both men and women.

Counseling with such men can be difficult because of their strong defenses. They have lost touch with their deep emotions because they have developed masks to cover the feelings of vulnerability that underlie their competent behaviors (Silverberg, 1986). They resist others' attempts to break through the defenses. As clients, they tend to intellectualize their problems while resisting the therapist's attempts to make them aware of their emotional vulnerability (Werrbach & Gilbert, 1987).

Clients are often troubled by the differences in how they deal with problems at work and at home. On the job, they may resolve conflicts in a constructive manner through compromise, arbitration, or consensus. But at home, when conflicts arise, they tend to control relationships either by becoming aggressive or by trying to placate and thus prevent conflict. Counselors can help such clients explore how society's expectations have contributed to these differences in their behavior.

Men with Addictive Behaviors: Defenses Against Depression. The presenting problem discussed in the previous section—men who feel inadequate—leads right into this discussion. According to Real (1997), men develop addictive behaviors to defend against depression. Addictions can take innumerable forms—compulsive drinking, gambling, eating, spending; obsessive sexual urges and behaviors; workaholism; obsessive desire to watch football and other sports, to work the computer, and so on.

These addictions are a form of self-medication. These defenses increase men's disconnection with themselves and with their loved ones and can lead to violent and destructive behaviors toward others.

Real (1997) believes that the problem of male depression is compounded because "we often fail to identify this disorder because men tend to manifest depression differently than women" (p. 23). Women, because they are permitted by the culture to experience and acknowledge their feelings, are more likely to exhibit symptoms of depression that correspond to the *DSM-IV* classification of depression (feeling worthless, immobilized, lethargic, with sudden onset of severe and long-lasting sleeping or eating disorders). Real calls this type of depression *overt* depression.

Male depression, in contrast, is masked and hidden from the person himself and from others around him. Symptoms include numbness of feelings to the extent that the man disassociates and disconnects from others, especially loved ones. Real (1997) calls this type of depression *covert* depression.

Both male and female forms of dysfunctions, Real (1997) emphasizes, are similarly caused by early socialization that forces boys and girls to acquire gender-based behavioral patterns. Boys are taught to follow stereotypical masculine patterns of self-reliance and autonomy, strength and dominance; girls are taught to be nurturers and caretakers who must become subordinate to the needs of males. As a result, both boys and girls are traumatized but in different ways: Girls who don't behave according to their expected roles are usually shamed, ridiculed, or enticed into submission. Although girls are allowed to feel anguish and shame and are allowed to cry and weep, they are expected to remain in this weak, submissive role. Consequently, they become disempowered and lose their voice and the ability to assert themselves.

Boys are traumatized even worse, Real (1997) claims, because not only are they shamed if they fail to follow expected masculine behaviors but they also cannot show hurt feelings. Boys must deny the pain, the shame, deny feelings in general. Consequently, to maintain a strong masculine image, they adopt defenses to ward off so-called feminine feelings. They are also trained to separate emotionally from their mothers as a necessary step in gaining masculine identity, whereas girls are encouraged to maintain connections with their mothers. Boys thus experience rejection and abandonment, feelings that also must be denied. To exert masculine strength, they thereby adopt a false sense of empowerment in which they assert themselves as strong and invulnerable; this aura of grandiosity gives a false sense of self, a self that can and must achieve, be the best, or as Real says, a self who always needs to "feel better than" others.

"A common defense against the painful experience of deflated value is inflated value; and a common compensation for shame, of feeling less than, is a subtle or flagrant flight into grandiosity, of feeling better than" (Real, 1997, p. 55). Thus, at an early age, boys seek to gain self-esteem through external recognition and approval of others. Real says that when boys grow up, they are like hollow men lacking feelings of intrinsic self-worth and dependent on external achievements and approval from others for feelings of self-esteem.

Boys also tend to identify with the abuser or neglectful father as another means of defending and protecting themselves. In these cases, they carry both the shame and the destructive feelings of their fathers or mothers and enact them, in turn, on their own children and spouses. These feelings are called *carried feelings* or *carried shame*. "They are the means by which the wound, the legacy of pain, is passed from father to son, mother to son, across generations. Carried feeling or carried shame are the psychological seeds of depression" (Real, 1997, p. 206).

For men to overcome covert depression, Real (1997) says, they need therapy to help them, first, let go of their addictive defenses; second, work through the painful withdrawal symptoms; and third, guide them through the long road of recovery: "First the addictive defenses must stop. Then, the dysfunctional patterns in the man's relationship to himself must be attended to. Finally buried early trauma must reemerge and, as much as possible, be reenacted" (pp. 269–270).

The first stage, letting go of addictive defenses, is exceedingly difficult for men. Most men have to be forced into taking the first step; the wife, for example, leaves him. In the second stage, after working through painful withdrawal symptoms, the client disidentifies with the abusing or neglectful parents, usually the father. In the third stage of guiding the client through recovery, the client identifies with two parts of his inner child—the injured, wounded child and the aggressive and destructive child, both of whom were introjected from parental behavior. The client learns to nurture and parent himself. At this point, Real usually assigns the client to group therapy with other men who themselves are in recovery, working through covert depression. In a form of Gestalt therapy, he uses the hot seat method, whereby the client voluntarily sits on the hot seat in the center of the group; with group support, the client is encouraged and coaxed to imagine and enact early childhood traumas and to dialogue with the abusive, neglectful parent(s) and with his injured child. The client then reestablishes a connection with his feminine side, regains a healthy connection with himself and with others, and above all, avoids passing on the toxic consequences of covert depression to his children or spouse (Real, 1997).

Men Who Have Trouble Changing Roles.   Counselors also work with men clients who are changing their career or who are undergoing a major transition in life. Men may experience uncertainty or overstress in their work if they are promoted to new and highly demanding jobs, if they lose their jobs and become dependent on their wives, or if their jobs become obsolete and they must seek jobs in fields in which they are untrained. Men who have relentlessly sought success may experience a midlife crisis in which they fear they have wasted their lives (O'Neil & Egan, 1992; Schlossberg & Entine, 1977).

Another time of particular stress for most men comes when they face retirement. A life based on achievement and power suddenly changes, and they feel useless. At the same time, they are suddenly put into close daily contact with their wives, a position unfamiliar to them.

Men also run into difficulties when their wives begin to change their own roles. Wives may decide to start careers, or they may express dissatisfaction with their husbands' preoccupation with their jobs and lack of interest in developing the relationship. Counselors note that these clients usually come to therapy depressed, anxious, frustrated, or angry with women but bewildered about what to do. Clients often say that women want too much or that they don't know what women want (Werrbach & Gilbert, 1987).

Changes in men's stereotypical gender roles have led to more men seeking and gaining custody of their children (Grief, 1985; Tillitski, 1992). Tillitski (1992) believes that counselors must be alert to an identifiable group of men with postdivorce parenting problems either as single custodial fathers or as men sharing custody of children with their former spouses.

Men with Physiological and Pathological Problems.

Skovolt (1978) and Toomer (1978) point out that physiological disorders often result when men excessively follow stereotypical roles. Skovolt says that workaholic behavior makes men more susceptible than women to ulcers, heart attacks, and high blood pressure. He also notes that more men are alcoholics and that males also outnumber females in completed suicides. Toomer believes that too much stress can be the cause of an overall shorter life span in men. Men with physical diseases caused by stress respond well to holistic counseling that emphasizes stress reduction, relaxation, and nutrition.

Some men who excessively follow stereotypical aggressive roles run into trouble with the law. Men commit a high percentage of violent crimes, including gang wars, homicides, rapes, domestic violence, assaults, child abuse, and serial murders. Most voyeurs and exhibitionists are men, as are most obscene telephone callers (Skovolt, 1978).

Special rehabilitation programs for treating men with such disorders are offered in community clinics and in prisons and parole offices. Special treatment is available in clinics and mental hospitals. Behavioral and cognitive-behavioral techniques are often used in these correctional programs. The Giarretto Institute in San Jose, California, discussed in chapter 19, works with men who have sexually abused their children. It also works with members of their families in an attempt to restore the families.

Because socialization begins in early childhood, it is important to explore one's parental relationships in the family of origin. Many of these men have modeled fathers who themselves were following stereotypical patterns or who had never bonded with their sons. Real (1997) emphasizes that it is essential to explore one's parental relationships. As discussed earlier, Real describes how men carry their fathers' shame and how boys have been taught to devalue their mothers, leaving them seriously unable to relate well to others.

Nonsexist Counselor Training

Fitzgerald and Nutt (1986) believe that special skills are needed to counsel women because of the dangers of stereotyping. Spiegel (1979) and Corey, Corey, and Callanan (1993), in contrast, believe that developing separate counseling skills for women or men becomes a new form of sexism.

Faunce (1985) discusses the importance of including principles of feminist therapy in course work and supervision that include nonsexist views, understanding of situational and cultural factors in assessing women's problems, and consciousness-raising of potential gender biases. Heesacker and Prichard (1992) and R. C. Williams and Myer (1992) make similar recommendations regarding counselor training and male gender stereotyping and counseling men.

Consciousness-raising through workshops and professional continuing education helps instructors and supervisors model nonsexist attitudes and behaviors for graduate students and interns in counseling; instructors can also alert graduate students and interns to any indications of bias or countertransference in their interactions with clients.

Regarding ethical responsibility of counselor educators, Stevens-Smith (1995) includes gender issues in counselor training programs. She notes that power and equity exist on four levels: "personal, clinical, social, and political" (p. 283). Counselors need knowledge and awareness of their own personal views and potential biases about gender roles. In clinical work, counselors must be trained to be aware of their clients' worldviews and know that these worldviews influence their perception of gender roles. The negative impact of the socialization process in our culture on the well-being and emotional maturity of both women and men must also be attended to in counselor training. And the political implications of gender cannot be ignored. "A continual refusal to address gender as a political statement may only further perpetuate inequality in power, dependence of women both economically and psychologically and growing resentment among men concerning this issue" (p. 290).

Counselor and Client Match

If counselors are aware of the negative influence of gender stereotyping, they should be better able to counsel clients of either sex (Basow, 1992; Tanney & Birk, 1976). Same-sex counseling may often be more productive, however, assuming that a qualified counselor with suitable personal qualities is available in the community, counseling center, or clinic. A woman or man searching for personal identity may respond better to a same-sex counselor. A woman who has just experienced assault, incest, or rape by a man will find it difficult to respond to a male counselor. A man will have trouble relating to a female counselor if he has just experienced a traumatic divorce. Yet, even in such cases, at times counselors of the opposite sex who are understanding, open, and unbiased may benefit clients who have had consistently negative experiences with members of the opposite sex. A warm, trusting, and productive female-male or male-female counseling relationship may ultimately lead to better relationships with members of the opposite sex.

⊸❀ GAYS, LESBIANS, AND BISEXUALS

Surveys indicate that about 10% of the population in the United States (about 22 million people) are gay or lesbian. This figure is considered conservative because some people do not publicly admit that they are gay or lesbian (Fassinger, 1991; Schliebner & Peregoy, 1998).

Reluctance to acknowledge gay or lesbian sexual orientation stems from a history of discrimination and abuse. Attitudes began to change after the gay liberation movement developed out of the civil rights and women's movements. The American Psychiatric Association in 1973 and the American Psychological Association in 1975 declassified homosexuality as a form of mental illness. Then, in the mid-1980s, after the fatal human immunodeficiency virus (HIV), the virus that causes acquired immune deficiency syndrome (AIDS), started spreading in gay communities, former prejudices against gays began to reemerge (Hoffman, 1991). Studies show that as many as 92% of gays and lesbians report being verbally threatened and that one third have been victims of violence (Fassinger, 1991; Herek, 1989).

Several professional journals have featured the counseling needs of gays and lesbians, including the September/October 1989 issue of the *Journal of Counseling & Development* and the April 1991 and September 1998 issues of *Counseling Psychologist*. In 1992, the American Counseling Association (then AACD) published the book *Counseling Gay Men and Lesbians: A Journey to the End of the Rainbow*, edited by Dworkin and Gutiérrez (1992a). These comprehensive resources cannot be covered fully in an introductory book. I have, however, drawn from them in the following discussion.

Counseling Lesbians, Gays, and Bisexuals

Browning, Reynolds, and Dworkin (1991) describe specific issues confronting lesbians who can be helped through affirmative counseling interventions. Following a similar format, Shannon and Woods (1991) do the same for gay men. Both groups have problems common to everyone, problems related to identity, interpersonal, career, and family issues. These problems are exacerbated, however, for gays and lesbians who, because of their sexual orientation, must cope with feelings of unacceptance and invisibility. Gay men face more concerns and problems related to AIDS and to victimization through violence by heterosexuals than do lesbians. Adaptation to a positive gay and lesbian identity (coming out) is often a prolonged, difficult process. Dworkin and Gutiérrez (1992b) summarize the work of O'Bear and Reynolds (1985), who found that, generally, a 16-year gap exists between awareness of gay feelings, which often occurs during adolescence, and the development of a positive gay or lesbian identity.

Integrating several other identity models, Troiden (1989) has developed a 4-stage model of gay development: (a) sensitization, (b) identity confusion, (c) identity assumption, and (d) commitment. Troiden presents these stages as a developmental process that usually starts before puberty and ends with commitment when individuals are in their 20s. Individuals who develop awareness of their gay and lesbian feelings later in life generally follow a similar sequence.

Sensitization involves feelings of difference one has from peers and feelings of social isolation. *Identity confusion* develops when individuals become aware of attitudes and behaviors that could be called gay or lesbian (O'Connor, 1992). This stage is particularly difficult for gay and lesbian adolescents, and about 20% to 35% of them attempt suicide (Herdt, 1989). In the *identity assumption* stage, individuals identify themselves as gays or lesbians. At this stage, they find new friends and support groups in the gay and lesbian communities. Concerns about stigma and family rejection are primary sources of difficulty. In the final stage of *commitment,* gays and lesbians come out to the public. Their way of life includes loving relationships and long-term commitments, rather than a focus only on sexual activities (O'Connor, 1992; Troiden, 1989).

The counselor can help gays and lesbians work through the coming-out process in several ways. The counselor can help clients work through fears and anxieties when they first acknowledge, personally or publicly, that they are gay or lesbian; help them cope with anger or rejection from family and friends; and support clients if they experience discrimination or violence in social and career interactions. Whereas heterosexuals who experience identity or interpersonal problems usually expect support from their families, gays and lesbians often experience parental rejection or withdrawal of support.

Throughout these stages, many gays and lesbians often explore and work through their own internalized, negative feelings about their sexual orientation (internalized homophobia). Those who are socially rejected or who are uninformed or misinformed about their sexual orientation often experience shame, guilt, and low self-esteem. Murphy (1989) points out that female couples who have affirmed their lesbian identities and have worked through their own internalized homophobia are able to handle parental disapproval and to maintain positive relationships with each other.

Bisexuals, whose orientation includes partners of both the same and the opposite sex, have been receiving attention in the literature. Their numbers are difficult to assess, but it is estimated that they exceed the gay and lesbian populations (Wolf, 1992).

Bisexuality has been described variously as a non-entity, a transitional stage toward or away from one's gay or lesbian tendencies, or a denial of one's gay or lesbian orientation (Wolf, 1992). Wolf (1992) says that bisexual persons come to counseling confused or anxious because they do not feel a part of gay, lesbian, or heterosexual communities. Betz (1991) expresses concern about the lack of attention to bisexuals and believes that gays, lesbians, and heterosexuals all need to give more support and understanding to bisexuals.

Career Concerns

Counselors should be aware that lesbians and gays, like heterosexuals, differ considerably among themselves in personality characteristics, abilities, and career interests. Unlike heterosexuals, however, lesbians and gays are faced with deciding whether they want to work in careers in which sexual orientation can cause discrimination or exclusion (e.g., military, federal government, public schools, child care; Orzek, 1992).

The counselor role is to help gay or lesbian clients explore occupations that suit their characteristics and then to help them assess the potential risks involved in placement. But ultimately the decisions must reside with the clients.

Interpersonal, Couple, and Family Concerns

Family and couple counseling with gays involve legal concerns that heterosexuals do not have to face (Fassinger, 1991). Because legalized gay marriages are not sanctioned in society, joint health insurance benefits, joint income tax returns, and legal custody of children are not available to gay couples. Some states prohibit gay parents from adopting children, and gay parents are often refused custody of their children from previous heterosexual marriages. Little support is given for lesbians who choose to have children within a lesbian relationship (Fassinger, 1991).

Substance Abuse

Research shows that gays and lesbians are more susceptible to substance abuse than are heterosexuals (Browning et al., 1991; Faltz, 1992; Schliebner & Peregoy, 1998). "The psychosocial stress of being a homosexual man or woman . . . in a society dominated by a heterosexual orientation, places gay and lesbian individuals at high risk for alcohol and drug abuse" (Schliebner & Peregoy, 1998, p. 205). A major contributing factor is their dependence on the gay bar as the only social place for them. Counselors need to be alert to the possibility of substance abuse with gays and lesbians who seek treatment for relationship difficulties, depression, or other symptoms of emotional stress (Faltz, 1992).

Acquired Immune Deficiency Syndrome (AIDS)

M. A. Hoffman (1991) cites statistics showing that 59% of AIDS cases resulted from male/homosexual/bisexual contact and 22% from intravenous drug use. Statistics also indicate, however, that the percentage of AIDS cases in the heterosexual population is increasing at alarming rates. Women who have sexual relationships with bisexual men or heterosexual men who have had multiple partners are at risk.

As of 1990, about 162,000 persons in the United States had AIDS. The majority of persons with AIDS (PWAs) are young: 22% in their 20s, 47% in their 30s, and 22% in their 40s. Also, 44% of males and 72% of females with AIDS are African Americans or Hispanics (Hoffman, 1991). Because of the nature of the progress of AIDS, these figures, Hoffman (1991) says, "represent only the tip of the AIDS epidemic" (p. 468). AIDS develops after a person becomes infected with the human immunodeficiency virus (HIV). It usually takes 6 to 10 years after an individual tests positive for the HIV for full-blown AIDS to appear.

Counseling with AIDS clients presents more challenges and difficulties than does counseling with clients in general (Geratz, 1995; Hoffman, 1991). Feelings of isolation and rejection are aggravated by illness and the fear of dying. AIDS victims may also deny their illness. Hoffman (1991) puts it vividly: "It is about the loss of one's health, vitality, sensuality, and career—and most profoundly, the letting go of the future as one had envisioned it" (p. 468).

Hoffman advocates a psychosocial counseling model in working with PWAs because the disease affects all aspects of the individual's life and has traumatic effects on family and friends. In her model, she includes the importance of handling the stigma attached to AIDS, the degree of interpersonal and institutional support, situational factors related to the source and progression of the disease, and client psychosocial characteristics and competence (gender, race, lifestyle).

Allers and Katrin (1988) propose an AIDS psychosocial counseling model (APCM) that involves five phases: (a) overcoming the initial fear of the disease, (b) redefining relationships, (c) modifying lifestyles, (d) reevaluating life's meaning, and (e) adjusting to the physical and social limitations (p. 235).

Price, Omizo, and Hammett (1986) recommend a psychoeducational model of treatment, similar to Allers and Katrin's (1988), in which clients are encouraged to take an active role. They suggest that clients engage in safe sex; they also recommend that clients develop emotional intimacies with partners, rather than emphasize sexual encounters. They encourage clients to refocus on activities that cut down on feelings of isolation. Especially beneficial for AIDS clients is the supportive atmosphere of group counseling that provides the feeling of family togetherness and gives an opportunity for positive role modeling. Counselors must also be familiar with social agencies to which they can refer clients for legal, medical, or economic aid.

A biopsychosocial model for counseling clients with AIDS is proposed by Geratz (1995). He believes that a comprehensive treatment program should include (a) information and education about the illness, (b) a comprehensive biopsychosocial assessment, (c) crisis intervention services when appropriate, (d) brief or long-term counseling or both, (e) group intervention, and (f) comprehensive and thorough case management with detailed follow-up procedures (p. 16).

Families of AIDS victims may also need counseling to overcome their misapprehension that the disease may be contagious, which can lead to their rejecting the patient. Grief counseling also helps them complete their relationship with the dying AIDS patient and rid themselves of the guilt and remorse that often follow the death of a loved one (Dworkin & Pincu, 1993; J. Williams & Stafford, 1991).

Parents of Gays and Lesbians

Since the late 1980s, articles have been appearing in the professional literature about counselor interaction with parents or families of gays and lesbians. Murphy (1989) has written about helping lesbians deal with parental attitudes, and Teague (1992) discusses the need for services available to families of gays and lesbians. Hammersmith (1987) proposes an interactionist sociological approach to work with families of gays. Teague and Hammersmith both discuss the importance of acknowledging family fears about stigma and the need to provide families information and resources.

Parents need emotional support and availability of counseling to work through their doubts and their concerns when their children come out as gays and lesbians. Support groups can help them share experiences and learn new attitudes and skills in relating to their children and to partners of their children.

Training Counselors

Some authors have pointed out that training programs inadequately cover counseling of gays and lesbians (Betz, 1991; Buhrke, 1989; Buhrke & Douce, 1991). They suggest that core courses in counselor training need to include discussions about the special concerns of gays and lesbians. They also recommend that some counseling theories and techniques should be modified and that courses in career counseling should include issues about discrimination of gays and lesbians. Moreover, instructors, supervisors, and graduate students in counselor training programs need to become aware of their own latent or potential biases toward their gay and lesbian clients (House & Holloway, 1992).

All counselors, whether gay, lesbian, bisexual, or heterosexual, should differentiate those clients who are expressing confusion about sexual orientation from those who have confirmed their gay or lesbian identity. In the first case, counselors should allow clients the freedom to explore their own sexual identities. In the second case, counselors should support a client's particular lifestyle.

Few counselor training programs include courses or field experiences in AIDS treatment. In a survey of APA-approved graduate programs in counseling and clinical psychology, Campos, Brasfield, and Kelly (1989) found that 75% of programs responding did not include training for counseling AIDS patients. In their study, Crawford, Humfleet, Ribordy, Ho, and Vickers (1991) found that counselors and psychotherapists were reluctant to accept AIDS patients. Crawford et al. conjecture that negative attitudes might be generated by feelings of professional inadequacy, as well as by ignorance. In any case, they recommend that training programs and in-service training include information about AIDS and skills to work with PWAs. They also recommend training counselors to be aware of countertransference that is apt to happen during counseling—times when they may tend to overidentify with the client's trauma, either by avoidance or by oversympathizing.

Because the sufferings of AIDS patients are so complex, counselors working with them need "training in cultural diversity, empowerment strategies, medical information, gay and lesbian issues, counseling clients on death and dying issues and . . . a greater degree of knowledge . . . in psychology and psychiatry disciplines" (Geratz, 1995, p. 16).

Counselor and Client Match

A majority of gay, lesbian, bisexual, and heterosexual clients choose counselors with the same sexual orientation. Even so, many mental health professionals do not believe that only gay counselors must work with gay clients or that only heterosexual counselors must work with heterosexual clients. Sexual orientation is not essential as long as the client is willing and as long as gay, lesbian, bisexual, and heterosexual counselors are aware of their own potential biases and are understanding of gay, lesbian, and bisexual difficulties. Buhrke and Douce (1991), in their guidelines for appropriate counselor training, make the following cautions: "Do not refer all gay and lesbian issues to gay or lesbian faculty or staff. Do not assume their only expertise is gay and lesbian issues. Such practice tokenizes and ghettoizes gay and lesbian people" (p. 230).

⇝ SUMMARY

Counseling professionals have been increasingly aware that they must prepare themselves to work with the complex, diverse needs of increasing numbers of multicultural individuals whose needs, values, and beliefs differ from those on which traditional counseling theories and techniques have been developed. Special attention is now being given in counselor training to increase counselors' awareness of their potential biases toward clients. The professional literature has been reflecting more understanding of diverse cultural/social characteristics, including the various ethnic minorities, men and women, gays, lesbians, and bisexuals.

Ethnic counselors and psychologists have been especially active in discussion and research about counselor attitudes, racial identity, and individual and cultural characteristics. Female counselors have developed feminine counseling theories and techniques to counter the negative impact of gender stereotyping and to help female clients develop themselves through relationships and connections with others. Professionals acknowledge that gender-based socialization processes cause dysfunctions in males as well. Male counselors are applying new theories of masculinity to counseling practice. Counselors help gays, lesbians, and bisexuals develop their own identities and cope with biases from relatives, colleagues, and society in general. For AIDS victims, counselors help clients work through feelings of isolation, denial, anger, and grief.

➛ PROJECTS AND ACTIVITIES

1. Role-play an opening counseling session with counselor and client of the opposite sex. The prospective client says she feels shy and intimidated in her interactions with the opposite sex. Then reverse roles of counselor and client. Share reactions to feelings engendered in counselor and client.

2. Invite a panel of speakers from various ethnic groups who are community mental health specialists and school counselors to speak to your class about problems in reaching ethnic clients. Invite suggestions on how to improve communication with these groups.

3. Explore traditional healing approaches of a particular ethnic group (e.g., a Native American shaman or medicine man). Invite such a traditional healer to speak to the class about her or his views of mental health and treatment.

4. Invite professionally trained female and male counselors to class to discuss the types of problems their clients present that are specifically related to sex role conflict. Ask them to discuss how they go about helping these clients.

5. Invite lesbian, gay, and bisexual persons from the campus gay liberation services and the director of the university counseling center to class, or interview each person separately. How does each think the gay liberation service and the counseling center uniquely help gays? Do they overlap? Are cross-referrals made?

6. Invite professionally trained counselors from various minority groups to discuss with your class or group the issues related to the counseling of minorities—for example, counseling by Whites, differences and similarities in minority group values and their influence on counseling, and the problem of culturally biased tests.

➛ REFERENCES

Allers, C. T., & Katrin, S. E. (1988). AIDS counseling: A psychosocial model. *Journal of Mental Health Counseling, 10,* 235–244.

Atkinson, D. R., Morten, G., & Sue, D. W. (1993). *Counseling American minorities: A cross-cultural perspective* (4th ed.). Dubuque, IA: William C. Brown.

Atkinson, D. R., Wampold, B. E., Lowe, S. M., Matthews, L., & Ahn, H. (1998). Asian American preferences for counselor characteristics: Application of the Bradley-Terry-Luce model. *Counseling Psychologist, 26,* 101–123.

Attneave, C. (1982). American Indians and Alaska Native families: Emigrants in their own homeland. In M. McGoldrick, J. K. Pearce, & J. Giordano (Eds.), *Ethnicity and family therapy* (pp. 55–83). New York: Guilford Press.

Baird, P., & Sights, J. R. (1986). Low self-esteem as a treatment issue in the psychotherapy of anorexia and bulimia. *Journal of Counseling & Development, 64,* 449–451.

Ballou, M., & Gabalac, N. (1985). *A feminist position on mental health.* Springfield, IL: Charles C Thomas.

Baruth, L. G., & Manning, L. M. (1999). *Multicultural counseling and psychotherapy: A lifespan perspective* (2nd ed.). Upper Saddle River, NJ: Merrill/Prentice Hall.

Basow, S. A. (1992). *Gender stereotypes and roles* (3rd ed.). Pacific Grove, CA: Brooks/Cole.

Betz, N. E. (1991). Implications for counseling psychology training programs. *Counseling Psychologist, 19,* 248–252.

Blechman, E. A. (1984). Women's behavior in a man's world: Sex differences in competence. In E. A. Blechman (Ed.), *Behavior modification with women* (pp. 3–33). New York: Springer.

Bly, R. (1988). The mystery of the wild man. *Resurgence, 128,* 8–10.

Bly, R. (1990). *Iron John: A book about men.* Reading, MA: Addison-Wesley.

Brehony, K. A. (1983). Women and agoraphobia: A case for the etiological significance of the feminine sex-role stereotype. In V. Franks & E. D. Rothblum (Eds.), *The stereotyping of women: Its effects on mental health* (pp. 112–128). New York: Springer.

Broverman, I. K., Broverman, D. M., Clarkson, F. E., Rosenkrantz, P. S., & Vogel, S. R. (1970). Sex-role stereotypes and clinical judgments of mental health. *Journal of Consulting and Clinical Psychology, 34,* 1–7.

Browning, C., Reynolds, A. L., & Dworkin, S. H. (1991). Affirmative psychotherapy for lesbian women. *Counseling Psychologist, 19,* 177–196.

Buhrke, R. A. (1989). Incorporating lesbian and gay issues into counselor training: A resource guide. *Journal of Counseling & Development, 68,* 77–80.

Buhrke, R. A., & Douce, L. A. (1991). Training issues for counseling psychologists in working with lesbian women and gay men. *Counseling Psychologist, 19,* 216–234.

Campos, P. E., Brasfield, T. L., & Kelly, J. A. (1989). Psychology training related to AIDS: Survey of doctoral graduate programs and predoctoral internship programs. *Professional Psychology: Research and Practice, 20,* 214–220.

Casas, J. M. & Vasquez, M. J. (1996). Counseling the Hispanic: A guiding framework for a diverse population. In P. B. Pedersen, J. G. Draguns, W. J. Lonner, & J. E. Trimble (Eds.), *Counseling across cultures* (4th ed.). Thousand Oaks, CA: Sage.

Chambless, D. L., & Goldstein, A. J. (1980). Anxieties: Agoraphobia and hysteria. In A. M. Brodsky & R. T. Hare-Mustin (Eds.), *Women and psychotherapy: An assessment of research and practice* (pp. 113–134). New York: Guilford Press.

Clatterbaugh, K. (1990). *Contemporary perspectives on masculinity: Men, women, and politics in modern society.* Boulder, CO: Westview Press.

Comas-Diaz, L. (1993). Hispanic Latino communities: Psychological implications. In D. R. Atkinson, G. Morten, & D. W. Sue (Eds.), *Counseling American minorities: A cross-cultural perspective* (4th ed., pp. 245–263). Dubuque, IA: William C. Brown.

Cook, E. P. (1990). Gender and psychological distress. *Journal of Counseling & Development, 68,* 371–373.

Copeland, E. J. (1982). Minority populations and traditional counseling programs: Some alternatives. *Counselor Education and Supervision, 21,* 187–193.

Copeland, E. J. (1983). Cross-cultural counseling and psychotherapy: A historical perspective, implications for research and training. *Personnel and Guidance Journal, 62,* 10–15.

Corey, G., Corey, M. S., & Callanan, P. (1993). *Issues and ethics in the helping profession* (4th ed.). Pacific Grove, CA: Brooks/Cole.

Crawford, I., Humfleet, G., Ribordy, S. C., Ho, F. C., & Vickers, V. L. (1991). Stigmatization of AIDS patients by mental health professionals. *Professional Psychology: Research and Practice, 22,* 357–361.

Cross, W. E., Jr., & Fhagen-Smith, P. (1996). Nigrescence and ego identity development: Accounting for differential black identity patterns. In P. B. Pedersen, J. G. Draguns, W. L. Lonner, & J. E. Trimble (Eds.), *Counseling across cultures* (4th ed., pp. 108–123). Thousand Oaks, CA: Sage.

De La Cancela, V., & Guzman, L. P. (1991). Latino mental health service needs: Implications for training psychologists. In H. F. Myers, P. Wohlford, L. P. Guzman, & R. J. Echemendia (Eds.), *Ethnic minority perspectives on clinical training and services in psychology* (pp. 59–66). Washington, DC: American Psychological Association.

Dillard, J. M. (1983). *Multicultural counseling: Toward ethnic and cultural relevance in human encounters.* Chicago: Nelson-Hall.

Draguns, J. G. (1996). Humanly universal and culturally distinctive: Charting the course of cultural counseling. In P. B. Pedersen, J. G. Draguns, W. J. Lonner, & J. E. Trimble (Eds.), *Counseling across cultures* (4th ed., pp. 1–20). Thousand Oaks, CA: Sage.

Dworkin, S. H., & Gutiérrez, F. J. (Eds.). (1992a). *Counseling gay men and lesbians: Journey to the end of the rainbow.* Alexandria, VA: American Counseling Association.

Dworkin, S. H., & Gutiérrez, F. J. (1992b). Introduction: Opening the closet door. In S. H. Dworkin & F. J. Gutiérrez (Eds.), *Counseling gay men and lesbians: Journey to the end of the rainbow* (pp. xvii–xxvii). Alexandria, VA: American Counseling Association.

Dworkin, S. H., & Pincu, L. (1993). Counseling in the era of AIDS. *Journal of Counseling & Development, 71,* 275–281.

Estés, C. P. (1992). *Women who run with the wolves: Myths and stories of the wild woman archetype.* New York: Ballantine Books.

Faltz, B. G. (1992). Counseling chemically dependent lesbians and gay men. In S. H. Dworkin & F. J. Gutiérrez (Eds.), *Counseling gay men and lesbians: Journey to the end of the rainbow* (pp. 245–258). Alexandria, VA: American Counseling Association.

Fassinger, R. E. (1991). The hidden minority: Issues and challenges in working with lesbian women and gay men. *Counseling Psychologist, 19,* 157–176.

Faunce, P. F. (1985). Tracking feminist therapies: Integrating feminist therapy, pedagogy, and scholarship. In L. B. Rosewater & L. E. A. Walker (Eds.), *Handbook of feminist therapy: Women's issues in psychotherapy* (pp. 309–320). New York: Springer.

Fitzgerald, L. F., & Nutt, R. (1986). The Division 17 principles concerning the counseling/psychotherapy of women: Rationale and implementation. *Counseling Psychologist, 14,* 180–216.

Franks, V. (1986). Sex stereotyping and diagnosis of psychopathology. *Women & Therapy, 5,* 219–231.

Garreau, J. (1988). The integration of an American dream. *Washington Post National Weekly Edition, 5,* 6–8.

Geratz, E. (1995). A biopsychosocial paradigm for counseling clients with AIDS. *Counseling Today, 37,* p. 16.

Gladding, S. T. (1997). *Community and agency counseling.* Upper Saddle River, NJ: Merrill/Prentice Hall.

Grief, G. L. (1985). *Single fathers.* Toronto: Heath.

Hammersmith, S. K. (1987). A sociological approach to counseling homosexual clients and their families. *Journal of Homosexuality, 13,* 173–190.

Heesacker, M., & Prichard, S. (1992). In a different voice revisited: Men, women, and emotion. *Journal of Mental Health Counseling, 14,* 274–290.

Herdt, G. (1989). Gay and lesbian youth: Emergent identities and cultural scenes at home and abroad. *Journal of Homosexuality, 17,* 1–42.

Herek, G. M. (1989). Hate crimes against lesbians and gay men: Issues for research and policy. *American Psychologist, 44,* 948–955.

Hetzel, R. D., Barton, D. A., & Davenport, D. S. (1994, May). Helping men change: A group counseling model for male clients. *Journal for Specialists in Group Work, 19,* 52–64.

Hillman, J. (1989). *A blue fire: Selected writings.* New York: Harper Perennial.

Hines, P. M., & Boyd-Franklin, N. C. (1982). Black families. In M. McGoldrick, J. K. Pearce, & J. Giordano (Eds.), *Ethnicity and family therapy* (pp. 84–108). New York: Guilford Press.

Ho, M. K. (1987). *Family therapy with ethnic minorities.* Newbury Park, CA: Sage.

Hoffman, M. A. (1991). Counseling the HIV-infected client: A psychosocial model for assessment and intervention. *Counseling Psychologist, 19,* 467–542.

Hotelling, K. (1986). Treating women with bulimia from a sociocultural perspective. *American Mental Counselors Association Journal, 8,* 202–210.

House R. M., & Holloway, E. L. (1992). Empowering the counseling professional to work with gay and lesbian issues. In S.

H. Dworkin & F. J. Gutiérrez (Eds.), *Counseling gay men and lesbians: Journey to the end of the rainbow* (pp. 307–324). Alexandria, VA: American Counseling Association.

Ibrahim, F. A., & Herr, E. L. (1987). Battered women: A developmental life-career counseling perspective. *Journal of Counseling & Development, 65,* 244–248.

Ivey, A. E. (1986). *Developmental therapy.* San Francisco: Jossey-Bass.

Ivey, A. E., Ivey, M. B., & Simek-Morgan, L. (1997). *Counseling and psychotherapy: A multicultural perspective* (4th ed.). Boston: Allyn & Bacon.

Jack, D. C. (1991). *Silencing the self: Women and depression.* Cambridge, MA: Harvard University Press.

Jones, E. E. (1985). Psychotherapy and counseling with black clients. In P. Pedersen (Ed.), *Handbook of cross-cultural counseling and therapy* (pp. 173–179). Westport, CT: Greenwood Press.

Jordan, J. V. (1991). Empathy, mutuality, and therapeutic change: Clinical implications of a relational model. In J. V. Jordan, A. G. Kaplan, J. B. Miller, I. P. Stiver, & J. L. Surrey (Eds.), *Women's growth in connection: Writings from the Stone Center* (pp. 283–289). New York: Guilford Press.

Jordan, J. V. (Ed.). (1997). *Women's growth in diversity: More writings from the Stone Center.* New York: Guilford Press.

Jordan, J. V., Kaplan, A. G., Miller, J. B., Stiver, I. P., & Surrey, J. L. (1991). *Women's growth in connection: Writings from the Stone Center.* New York: Guilford Press.

Kelly, K. R., & Hall, A. S. (1992). Toward a development model for counseling men. *Journal of Mental Health Counseling, 14,* 257–273.

Kiselicka, M. S. (1998). Preparing Anglos for the challenges and joys of multiculturalism. *Counseling Psychologist, 26,* 5–21.

Kitano, H. H. L., & Maki, M. T. (1996). Continuity, change, and diversity: Counseling Asian Americans. In P. B. Pedersen, J. G. Draguns, W. L. Lonner, & J. E. Trimble (Eds.), *Counseling across cultures* (4th ed., pp. 124–145). Thousand Oaks, CA: Sage.

Kleinknecht, R. A. (1991). *Mastering anxiety: The nature and treatment of anxious conditions.* New York: Plenion Insight.

La Fromboisa, T. D. (1993). American Indian mental health policy. In D. R. Atkinson, G. Morten, & D. W. Sue (Eds.), *Counseling American minorities: A cross-cultural perspective* (4th ed., pp. 123–144). Dubuque, IA: William C. Brown.

Le Clair, N. J., & Berkowitz, B. (1983). Counseling concerns for the individual with bulimia. *Journal of Counseling & Development, 61,* 352–355.

Lee, C. C., & Richardson, B. L. (1991). Promise and pitfalls of multicultural counseling. In C. C. Lee & B. L. Richardson (Eds.), *Multicultural issues in counseling: New approaches to diversity* (pp. 3–9). Alexandria, VA: American Counseling Association.

Locke, D. C. (1990). A not so provincial view of multicultural counseling. *Counselor Education and Supervision, 30,* 18–25.

Locke, D. C. (1995). Counseling interventions with African American youth. In C. C. Lee (Ed.), *Counseling for diversity* (pp. 21–40). Boston: Allyn & Bacon.

Margolis, R. L., & Rungta, S. A. (1986). Training counselors for work with special populations: A second look. *Journal of Counseling & Development, 64,* 642–644.

Markowitz, L. (1997). Ramon Rojano won't take no for an answer. *Family Therapy Networker, 21,* 24–35.

McGoldrick, M. (1982). Ethnicity and family therapy: An overview. In M. McGoldrick, J. K. Pearce, & J. Giordano (Eds.), *Ethnicity and family therapy* (pp. 3–30). New York: Guilford Press.

McGoldrick, M., Giordano, J., & Pearce, J. K., (Eds.). (1996). *Ethnicity and family therapy.* New York: Guilford Press.

Meade, M. (1993). *Men and the water of life: Initiation and the tempering of men.* San Francisco: Harper.

Meade, M. (1998). *Mosaic Multicultural Foundation brochure.* Vashon, WA: Author.

Miller, J. B., & Stiver, I. P. (1997). *The healing connection: How women form relationships in therapy and in life.* Boston: Beacon Press.

Moore, R., & Gillette, D. (1990). *King, warrior, magician, lover: Rediscovering the archetypes of the mature masculine.* San Francisco: Harper.

Multicultural counselor training [Special issue]. (1998). *Counseling Psychologist, 26.*

Murphy, B. C. (1989). Lesbian couples and their parents: The effects of perceived parental attitudes on the couple. *Journal of Counseling & Development, 68,* 46–51.

Myers, H. F., Wohlford, P., Guzman, L. P., Echemendia, R. J. (Eds.). (1991). *Ethnic minority perspectives on clinical training and services in psychology.* Washington, DC: American Psychological Association.

O'Bear, K., & Reynolds, A. (1985, March). *Opening doors to understanding and acceptance: A facilitator's guide for presenting workshops on lesbian and gay issues.* Workshop and manual presented at the American College Personnel Association Convention, Boston.

O'Connor, M. F. (1992). Psychotherapy with gay and lesbian adolescents. In S. H. Dworkin & F. J. Gutiérrez (Eds.), *Counseling gay men and lesbians: Journey to the end of the rainbow* (pp. 3–22). Alexandria, VA: American Counseling Association.

O'Neil, J. M., & Egan, J. (1992). Men's gender role transitions over the life span: Transformations and fears of femininity. *Journal of Mental Health Counseling, 34,* 305–324.

Org, P. (1993). Twenty-million in 2020. In *The state of Asian Pacific America* (pp. 11–24). Los Angeles: LEAP Asian Pacific American Public Policy Institute and UCLA Asian American Studies Center.

Orzek, A. M. (1992). Career counseling for the gay and lesbian community. In S. H. Dworkin & F. J. Gutiérrez (Eds.), *Counseling gay men and lesbians: Journey to the end of the rainbow* (pp. 23–34). Alexandria, VA: American Counseling Association.

Padilla, A. M., & DeSnyder, N. S. (1985). Counseling Hispanics: Strategies for effective intervention. In P. B. Pedersen (Ed.), *Handbook of cross-cultural counseling and therapy* (pp. 157–164). Westport, CT: Greenwood Press.

Pedersen, P. B. (Ed.). (1985). *Handbook of cross-cultural counseling and therapy.* Westport, CT: Greenwood Press.

Pedersen, P. B. (1988). *A handbook for developing multicultural awareness.* Alexandria, VA: American Counseling Association.

Pedersen, P. B. (Ed.). (1991a). Multiculturalism as a fourth force [Special issue]. *Journal of Counseling & Development, 70.*

Pedersen, P. B. (1991b). Multiculturalism as a generic approach to counseling. *Journal of Counseling & Development, 70,* 6–12.

Pedersen, P. B., Draguns, J. G., Lonner, W. J., & Trimble, J. E. (Eds.). (1996). *Counseling across cultures.* Thousand Oaks, CA: Sage.

Pleck, J. (1976). The male sex role: Definitions of problems and sources of change. *Journal of Social Issues, 32,* 155–164.

Ponterotto, J. G. (1987). Counseling Mexican Americans: A multimodal approach. *Journal of Counseling & Development, 65,* 308–312.

Ponterotto, J. G. (1998). Charting a course for research in multicultural counseling. *Counseling Psychologist, 26,* 43–68.

Ponterotto, J. G., & Casas, J. M. (1991). *Handbook of racial/ethnic minority counseling research.* Springfield, IL: Charles C Thomas.

Price, R. E., Omizo, M. M., & Hammett, V. L. (1986). Counseling clients with AIDS. *Journal of Counseling & Development, 65,* 96–97.

Real, T. (1997). *I don't want to talk about it.* New York: Fireside.

Resick, P. A. (1983). Sex-role stereotyping and violence against women. In V. Franks & E. D. Rothblum (Eds.), *The stereotyping of women: Its effects on mental health* (pp. 230–256). New York: Springer.

Richardson, B. L. (1991). Utilizing the resources of the African American Church: Strategies for counseling professionals. In C. C. Lee & B. L. Richardson (Eds.), *Multicultural issues in counseling: New approaches to diversity.* Alexandria, VA: American Counseling Association.

Richmond-Abbott, M. (1992). *Masculine and feminine: Gender roles over the life cycle.* New York: McGraw-Hill.

Sabnani, H. B., Ponterotto, J. G., & Borodovsky, L. G. (1991). White racial identity development and cross-cultural training. *Counseling Psychologist, 19,* 76–102.

Scher, M., Stevens, M., Good, G., & Eichenfield, G. A. (1987). *Handbook of counseling and psychotherapy with men.* Newbury Park, CA: Sage.

Schliebner, C., & Peregoy, J. J. (1998). Working with diverse cultures: Treatment issues and characteristics. In P. Stevens-Smith & R. Smith, *Substance abuse counseling: Theory and practice*. Upper Saddle River, NJ: Merrill/Prentice Hall.

Schlossberg, N. K., & Entine, A. D. (1977). *Counseling adults*. Monterey, CA: Brooks/Cole.

Shannon, J. W., & Woods, W. J. (1991). Affirmative psychotherapy for gay men. *Counseling Psychologist, 19*, 197–215.

Silverberg, R. A. (1986). *Psychotherapy for men: Transcending the masculine mystique*. Springfield, IL: Charles C Thomas.

Skovolt, T. (1978). Feminism and men's lives. *Counseling Psychologist, 7*(4), 3–10.

Smith, A., & Stewart, A. (1983). Approaches to studying racism and sexism in Black women's lives. *Journal of Social Issues, 38*, 1–15.

Smith, E. J. (1977). Counseling Black individuals: Some stereotypes. *Personnel and Guidance Journal, 55*, 390–396.

Speight, S. L., Myers, L. J., Cox, C. I., & Highlen, P. S. (1991). A redefinition of multicultural counseling. *Journal of Counseling & Development, 70*, 29–36.

Spiegel, S. B. (1979). Separate principles for women: A new form of sexism. *Counseling Psychologist, 8*, 49–50.

Steinberg, W. (1993). *Identity conflict and transformation*.

Stevens-Smith, P. (1995). Gender issues in counselor education: Current status and challenges. *Counselor Education and Supervision, 34*, 283–293.

Sue, D., & Sue, D. W. (1993). Ethnic identity: Cultural factors in the psychological development of Asians in America. In D. R. Atkinson, G. Morten, & D. W. Sue (Eds.), *Counseling American minorities: A cross-cultural perspective* (4th ed., pp. 199–210). Madison, WI: WCB Brown & Benchmark.

Sue, D. W. (1991). A conceptual model for cultural diversity training. *Journal of Counseling & Development, 70*, 99–105.

Sue, D. W., Arredondo, P., & McDavis, R. (1992). Multicultural counseling competencies and standards: A call to the profession. *Journal of Counseling & Development, 70*, 477–486.

Sue, D. W., Bernier, J. E., Durran, A., Feinberg, L., Pedersen, P., Smith, E. J., & Vasquez-Nuttall, E. (1982). Position paper: Cross-cultural counseling competencies. *Counseling Psychologist, 10*(2), 45–52.

Sue, D. W., & Kirk, B. A. (1972). Psychological characteristics of Chinese American students. *Journal of Counseling Psychology, 19*, 471–478.

Sue, D. W., & Sue, D. (1985). Asian Americans and Pacific Islanders. In P. Pedersen (Ed.), *Handbook of cross-cultural counseling and therapy* (pp. 141–146). Westport, CT: Greenwood Press.

Sue, D. W., & Sue, D. (1999). *Counseling the culturally different* (3rd ed.). New York: John Wiley.

Sue, S. (1977). Community mental health services to minority groups: Some optimism, some pessimism. *American Psychologist, 32*, 616–624.

Sue, S., & Morishima, J. K. (1982). *The mental health of Asian Americans*. San Francisco: Jossey-Bass.

Sue, S., & Zane, N. (1987). The role of culture and cultural techniques in psychotherapy. *American Psychologist, 42*, 37–45.

Tanney, M. F., & Birk, J. M. (1976). Women counselors for women clients? A review of the research. *Counseling Psychologist, 6*, 28–32.

Teague, J. B. (1992). Issues relating to the treatment of adolescent lesbians and homosexuals. *Journal of Mental Health Counseling, 14*, 422–439.

Thomason, T. C. (1993). Counseling Native Americans: An introduction for non-Native Americans. In D. R. Atkinson, G. Morten, & D. W. Sue (Eds.), *Counseling American minorities: A cross-cultural perspective* (pp. 171–187). Dubuque, IA: William C. Brown.

Tillitski, C. J. (1992). Fathers and child custody: Issues, trends, and implications for counseling. *Journal of Mental Health Counseling, 34*, 351–361.

Toomer, J. E. (1978). Males in psychotherapy. *Counseling Psychologist, 7*, 22–25.

Trimble, J. E. (1991). The mental health service and training needs of American Indians. In H. F. Myers, P. Wohlford, L. P. Guzman, & R. J. Echemendia (Eds.), *Ethnic minorities: Perspectives on clinical training and services in psychology* (pp. 43–48). Washington, DC: American Psychological Association.

Trimble, J. E., Fleming, C. M., Beavias, F., & Jumper-Thurman, P. (1996). Essential cultural and social strategies for counseling Native American Indians. In P. B. Pedersen, J. G. Draguns, W. J. Lonner, & J. E. Trimble (Eds.), *Counseling across cultures* (4th ed., pp. 177–209). Thousand Oaks, CA: Sage.

Troiden, R. R. (1989). The formation of homosexual identities. *Journal of Homosexuality, 17*, 43–73.

Vargas, L. A., & Koss-Chioino, J. D. (Eds.). (1992). *Working with culture: Psychotherapeutic intervention with ethnic minority children and adolescents*. San Francisco: Jossey-Bass.

Werrbach, J., & Gilbert, L. A. (1987). Men, gender stereotyping, and psychotherapy: Therapists' perceptions of male clients. *Professional Psychology: Research and Practice, 18*, 562–566.

Williams, J., & Stafford, W. B. (1991). Silent casualties: Partners, families, and spouses of persons with AIDS. *Journal of Counseling & Development, 69*, 423–427.

Williams, R. C., & Myer, R. A. (1992). The men's movement: An adjunct to traditional counseling approaches. *Journal of Mental Health Counseling, 14*, 393–404.

Wilson, L. L., & Stith, S. M. (1993). Culturally sensitive therapy with Black clients. In D. R. Atkinson, G. Morten, & D. W. Sue (Eds.), *Counseling American minorities: A cross-cultural perspective* (4th ed., pp. 101–111). Dubuque, IA: William C. Brown.

Wolf, T. J. (1992). Bisexuality: A counseling perspective. In S. H. Dworkin & F. J. Gutiérrez (Eds.), *Counseling gay men and lesbians: Journey to the end of the rainbow* (pp. 175–187). Alexandria, VA: American Counseling Association.

Wooley, S. C., & Wooley, O. W. (1980). Eating disorders: Obesity and anorexia. In A. M. Brodsky & R. T. Hare-Mustin (Eds.), *Women and psychotherapy: An assessment of research and practice* (pp. 135–158). New York: Guilford Press.

Yates, A. (1987). Current status and future directions of research on the American Indian child. *American Journal of Psychiatry, 144,* 1135–1142.

Young-Eisendrath, P., & Wiedemann, F. (1987). *Female authority: Empowering women through psychotherapy.* New York: Guilford Press.

Zane, N., & Sue, S. (1991). Culturally responsive mental health services for Asian Americans: Treatment and training issues. In H. F. Myers, P. Wohlford, L. P. Guzman, & R. J. Echemendia (Eds.), *Ethnic minority perspectives on clinical training and services in psychology* (pp. 49–58). Washington, DC: American Psychological Association.

15   Counseling Older Adults

For the first time in history, most people can expect to live well into their 70s and 80s with considerable vigor and self-sufficiency. Trends indicate that increasing numbers of people will live into their 90s and beyond. The increase in life expectancy has been truly remarkable. Whereas early in the 20th century only a small percentage of the population lived past 45 years, life expectancy now is in the mid-70s: By 1990, those over age 65 constituted 12.7% of the total U.S. population. By the year 2030, this age-group is expected to increase to over 21% (Cavanaugh, 1997). In the United States, people over 85 years of age are the fastest growing age-group.

As life expectancy has increased, developmental theorists have recognized that older adults have the potential to continue to grow and develop until they die. Stereotypes about aging, however, interfere with the recognition of the growth potential of older adults and contribute to the reluctance of older adults to seek counseling and of mental health workers to serve them.

STEREOTYPES OF OLDER ADULTS

The overriding stereotype is that as adults age, they automatically start deteriorating and declining physically, psychologically, and socially. They are thus considered an emotional and economic drain on society. Paradoxically, however, another prevalent stereotype is the belief that most older people are well heeled, wasteful spenders who indulge in frivolous activities, using up the resources of their heirs. Yet another misperception is the belief that older people live in a blissful golden age with few hassles and conflicts, contentedly reclining in rocking chairs or peacefully withdrawing from society as they wait for death. Older adults are also mistakenly perceived as being a homogeneous group very much alike in characteristics.

Of all these stereotypes, the most devastating to the welfare of older adults is equating aging with decline and deterioration. In her book *The Fountain of Age*

(1993), Betty Friedan claims that most of the faulty assessment is perpetuated by physicians, nurses, psychologists, and gerontologists. Over 75% of recently published articles and books written by health care professionals about aging deal only with those who are physically incapacitated, chronically emotionally disturbed, or victims of Alzheimer's disease. Publications about older adults generally cover only those living in nursing homes, although only 5% of older people live in these facilities (Bee, 1996; Myers, 1990; Perlmutter & Hall, 1992).

Actually, over three quarters of this age-group are self-sufficient. Relatively free of heavy responsibilities such as child rearing and career development, most older adults are able to pursue creative, self-fulfilling activities in the community. Rather than focusing on the plight of languishing through a long period of physical and mental decline, increasing numbers of older people are realizing the potentialities and possibilities of living two or three more decades of continued healthy growth and development.

Friedan (1993) emphasizes that ageism comes from society's tendency to compare older adults to an ideal-youth model. This attitude, she says, contributes to older adults trying to emulate youths and despairing as a result. She also emphasizes that the increasing numbers of active, healthy people over age 65 constitute a potentially powerful and positive social force in society—a force, however, that has not as yet been defined.

❧ NEW PERSPECTIVES ON OLDER ADULTS

New perspectives on older adults allow for a positive image of aging. Longitudinal designs by researchers and life-span developmental theories indicate older adults continue to develop. Studies about cognition and memory also indicate that one's intellectual capacities continue to develop as one gets older.

Older adults are difficult to categorize because they represent the most heterogeneous and diverse developmental group. Whereas young people are noted for looking, dressing, and acting like their peers, and those in the workplace follow certain dress codes and patterns of living, older adults tend to develop pronounced differences. They tend to go their separate ways. Some, for example, become more deeply involved in specialized hobbies, such as raising orchids or collecting miniature train sets; others become engrossed in skydiving or car racing; and some spend all their time traveling in their camper vans while others stay put in the same home and devote themselves entirely to their grandchildren. And some never retire, particularly self-employed persons and professional artists and musicians.

Developmental theorists have recently been countering the prevailing tendency to lump all older people into one age-group—the elderly—an age-group that extends over three decades (65 to 90 and beyond), the widest span of all age-groups. Those in their 60s, for instance, usually have very different concerns from those in their 80s. And those in their 70s tend to have very different concerns from those in their 90s.

A Change in Research Designs

The stereotype of the declining older adult results largely from gerontologists using cross-sectional research that compares older adult performances with those of younger people (Friedan, 1993). Moreover, the subjects of such studies were primarily older adults living in nursing homes or other caretaking institutions—a select group of persons with physical or mental incapacities (Myers, 1990; Wellman & McCormack, 1982).

Life-span developmental psychologists have since made significant methodological changes in their theoretical and research designs. Using longitudinal instead of cross-sectional approaches, they test the same subjects over a long period of time or use a sequential design that combines cross-sectional and longitudinal methods. These approaches permit one to look at changes or consistency among cohort groups—groups of individuals who were all born about the same time and who share similar contextual or historical experiences (Bee, 1996; Knight, 1996). Those who were teenagers during the Depression, for instance, grew up with attitudes different from those who were teenagers during the upheavals of the 1960s.

Longitudinal and sequential research on aging, when carried out with normally functioning older adults, shows that older persons, instead of going through a steady period of decline and deterioration as they age, continue to maintain their capacities to learn.

Emergence of Life-Span Developmental Theories

Until the 1950s, developmental psychologists theorized only about child and adolescent stages of development. With the exception of Carl Jung (1931/1968), gerontologists and psychologists believed that people started declining after they reached adulthood.

Another exception is Donald Super (1942), who, following Charlotte Buehler's life-span developmental theory, introduced a vocational development theory in which he outlined vocational tasks appropriate at different life stages (see chap. 12). In this early model, however, he followed the prevailing view that individuals over age 65 simply decline. In later years, he softened his position: For example, most recently (Super, 1990), he no longer describes older adults as being in decline. He does, however, see older adults only in non-occupational roles; moreover, "exploration" for older adults, he says, consists merely of looking for a suitable retirement home. He sees little need for society to cultivate a pool of occupational talent among older adults.

Influenced by Carl Jung, psychoanalyst Erik Erikson (1950) published an 8-stage, life-span developmental model in which he proposed that people continue to develop throughout the life span (see chap. 4). At this time, however, he included only two adult stages: (a) the *generativity* stage from age 30 through midlife and (b) the *integrity* stage for everyone over age 65. Even so, these two stages became classic models for the older adult. During the *generativity* stage, adults are in their caring, nurturing, reproductive years; during the *integrity* stage, older adults work through feelings of despair and hopelessness to achieve a renewed sense of integrity and meaning in life.

In the 1970s, Gould (1978), Levinson (1978), and Valliant (1977) elaborated on Erikson's life-span developmental theory. Their emphasis, however, was on midlife crises of 40- and 50-year-olds.

Robert Butler (1963, 1975) took the lead in focusing on developmental tasks and concerns of older adults. To challenge prevailing opinion that older adults sink into steady decline, he issued the landmark book *Why Survive* (1975), declaring that elderly persons serve a vital purpose in society. His book *Productive Aging* (Butler & Gleason, 1985) explores new roles for older adults and means by which they can best serve society.

Others suggested three substages within this span: *young-old* (ages 65–75), *old-old* (ages 75–85), and *oldest old* (age 85 on) (Bee, 1996). Unfortunately, such ageism terms imply little sense of development except for that of decline.

In the days when Erikson (1950) proposed his stages of development, the process of searching for and finding new meaning in life—gaining integrity—was considered sufficient as the last stage of life. One is then ready to die. Erikson has since revised his work many times, but his original theories stuck in the public mind. Some have criticized the integrity stage for being the so-called last stage of development. After attaining integrity, many older adults still have 20 to 30 more healthy years to live. Friedan (1993) believes there must be more to life for older persons after they reach the integrity stage; there must be another stage to go through. She believes that generativity, which Erikson proposed as occurring during the midlife period, should be continued for the rest of one's life but with a different emphasis. Whereas younger adults focus on trying to procreate, to nurture, and to influence others through bearing children, through parenting, and through career roles, older adults could somehow serve the needs of the community at large in meaningful, generative ways.

Erikson (1978, 1980, 1982) continued to revise and develop his work. Briefly, he emphasizes that older adults, as they become more reflective, draw on their resources developed in earlier stages; generativity, rather than being a stage one has left behind as one moves into the last stage, is an ongoing process but differently expressed. At the integrity stage, one reviews prior stages on an ongoing basis; one draws on one's resources—a dynamic, regenerative practice that also reaffirms one's sense of self (integrity).

Joan Erikson (1997), Erik's wife, adds a ninth and last stage to Eriksonian theory. In her 90s, she speaks eloquently about this final stage that describes those in their 80s and 90s, who, in retrospect, realize that their feelings of hope and trust, the foundations of development, are constantly being challenged as they start losing all that had been gained in previous stages—losses without hope of regaining. Paradoxically, as one relinquishes these aspects of oneself, the remaining qualities, hope and faith, enable one to transcend material needs, except for what is immediately present—enjoying a child's laughter, enjoying the scent of roses, searching for one's glasses. The final stage, wisdom, or *gerotranscendence* as she calls it, is similar to transcendent states expressed in Jungian and Eastern spiritual practices. In this seeming withdrawal from life, one becomes more keenly present:

> This type of "withdrawal," in which one deliberately retreats from the usual engagements of daily activity, is consciously chosen withdrawal. Such a stance does not necessarily

imply a lack of vital involvement; there may be continued involvement despite disengagement—as Erik says, a "deeply involved, disinvolvement." This paradoxical state does seem to exhibit a transcendent quality, a "shift . . . from a materialistic and rational vision." However, when withdrawal and retreat are motivated by a disdain for life and others, it is unlikely that such peace of mind and transcendence will be experienced. (p. 125)

Jungian psychoanalyst Alan Chinen (1989) has subdivided the latter stages into several developmental stages in which the older adult undergoes tasks and attains renewal and growth. In his book *In the Ever After,* he uses elder fairy tales as an appropriate mode of describing psychological development in the latter years. The first group of tales depicts the first stage in which older persons confront their own foibles. The next series of tales shows how older persons replace self-centered, ego-building needs essential for youth with concerns about resolving issues for the long-term benefit of others. Self-transcendence culminates in the third stage; they become elders, a stage of wisdom and compassion.

Another Jungian psychoanalyst, Clarissa Pinkola Estés (1992), proposes a series of developmental stages that continue throughout life past 100 years. Although she refers to women, similar stages, she says, can be considered for men. The stages occur at 7-year intervals, and each requires a set of tasks, which breaks the usual outlook one has of aging as passively moving through life governed only by time. "Each age represents a change in attitude, a change in tasking, and a change in values" (p. 447).

Psychological Characteristics

Cognitive Development

Recent studies show that intelligence does not decline with age. Reports in earlier studies that intelligence scores dropped in adulthood were based on the use of intelligence tests standardized to youth-oriented tasks. These tests emphasized speed-based performance and abstract reasoning unrelated to experience. Researchers then began to compare the subscores of intelligence tests between older adults and youths. They found that older adults outperformed younger adults on meaningful tasks involving knowledge, judgment, and experience (verbal reasoning, performance tests, information), whereas younger adults did better on speed tests, memory tasks, and abstract reasoning unrelated to meaningful or cultural experiences (Bee, 1996; Friedan, 1993; Schaie, 1990).

Older people generally become concerned about losing their memory—an essential component of intelligence and reasoning. Studies have tended to show a slowdown, as one gets older, in working memory, which involves the capacity to hold information in mind while at the same time using the information to solve problems or to acquire new learning (Bee, 1996; Craik & Jennings, 1992).

But research also shows that memory differences between younger and older adults are insignificant when the material to memorize is relevant and meaningful and when older adults are motivated (Knight, 1996). Younger people are quicker than older adults in memorizing nonsense syllables and digit-span recall, but older people may be insufficiently motivated because they do not sense the relevance of rote memorizing tasks.

Aside from the fact that older persons may be too wise to bother learning meaningless symbols, the question remains whether they have the cognitive capacity for rote memorization. Researchers have found that normally functioning, motivated older adults, with practice, can regain skills on speed and memory tests (Friedan, 1993; Knight, 1996).

Friedan (1993) challenges the prevailing belief among psychologists and gerontologists that human brain cells automatically deteriorate as the adult grows older. She cites the work of Diamond, Johnson, Protti, Ott, and Kajisa (1985), who studied brain cell deterioration in rats, including very old rats. Placing rats in a large cage in an enriched environment with loving care from attendants and with games and mazes to play with, the researchers compared these rats with other rats who were in an empty cage and who were fed without any loving care or enriching environment. Those in the enriched environment increased the number of brain cells, whereas the brain cells of isolated rats withered.

Rybash, Hoyer, and Roodin (1986), who support the importance of accumulated experiences over the years, believe that older adults set up a type of expert processing much like a computer. Knight (1996), commenting on this view, writes:

> With the accumulation of experience, older adults have a considerable store of knowledge about how things are and how things work, especially in their individual area of expertise, informed by work experience and family experience. In these expert domains, the more mature may tend to outperform the young. (p. 6)

Theory of Multiple Intelligences (MI).   Another issue regarding whether a person's intelligence automatically declines with age challenges the criteria for measuring intelligence itself. The standard measurement system, known as IQ, has been criticized for some time, most recently and significantly by Gardner (1993). In his book *Frames of Mind: The Theory of Multiple Intelligences*, he proposes that persons are not born with a single type of intelligence, but rather develop multiple intelligences over time through learning. His theory, described in chapter 6, explains how intelligence manifests in a variety of ways: linguistic, musical, logical-mathematical, spatial, bodily-kinesthetic, and personal. The main criteria for assessing intelligence, he claims, should apply to various cultures around the world and, moreover, should focus primarily on problem-solving abilities, abilities that entail resolving "genuine problems" and "finding and creating problems" (p. 10). Thus, older adults in certain cultures are esteemed for their high level of elder intelligence.

Psychosocial Development

Prevailing views about the aging process have held that as people get older, they become increasingly inflexible in their attitudes and behavior. Older people are stereotyped as adhering to old patterns of behavior, resisting new experiences, and being unwilling or unable to adapt to change.

In reality, however, older adults have gone through many transitions and varied relationships and upheavals throughout their lives, tasks that require considerable adaptation and flexibility. After they retire and after their children leave home, older adults experience loss of status, change in housing, loss of friends and spouses, and loss of physical agility. To cope with these many changes requires fundamental adjustments in attitudes and perspective (Chinen, 1989; Friedan, 1993; Neugarten, 1977).

Another general misconception has been that older people are expected to withdraw voluntarily from society as an inevitable step toward a new life filled with contentment and peace. This disengagement theory, developed by Cummings and Henry (1961) and considered a significant psychosocial process of aging, dominated the thinking of professionals and the general public for decades. Cummings and Henry declared that older adults who detached themselves from society were following a natural and optimally healthy process.

Recent research, however, indicates the opposite. Those who are least disengaged have higher morale, are healthier, and display more satisfaction (Adelmann, 1994; Bee, 1996). Healthy, normally functioning older adults tend to be well informed about current social issues and participate in worthwhile community activities (Cavanaugh, 1997). Having said this, many do undertake a healthy disengagement—the very old, those in their 80s and 90s, as discussed earlier, and those seeking an inner spiritual path, as discussed later.

Older adults who desire to serve the community do face barriers, however. Unlike earlier stages of development in which roles and tasks are laid out for younger generations (careers, university degree programs, raising a family), older adults must carve out roles for themselves in untracked, innovative ways and do so in a manner that keeps them maintaining a sense of freedom, independence, and control over their lives.

As an example of becoming more active and innovative participants in the community, seniors are beginning to develop and run their own programs at some senior centers, rather than merely following programs determined and administered by a younger-aged staff.

At the Whitney Senior Center in St. Cloud, Minnesota, for example, octogenarian Willis E. Dugan (1997) developed a senior activity project for the Retired and Senior Volunteer Program (RSVP). This project is an especially remarkable way of engaging seniors in a meaningful and beneficial social activity because it involves and benefits multiple generations. Senior citizens assist frail, elderly, nursing home residents in constructing wood blocks and toys for children. (This project is described more fully in chapter 19.)

In 1994, more than 285,000 older adults participated at 1,900 elderhostels worldwide—evidence that elders are eager for learning but in ways that differ from the desire to learn at conventional youth-oriented college campuses. The success of these hostels is attributable, in part, to older persons' sense of freedom to choose to learn what they want and need. It fits their personal quest, their inner journey to acquire a renewed sense of meaning in life, a zest for learning that surpasses that of the average college student.

The success of elderhostels that began in 1975 surprised even the founders' thinking. At a recent symposium on productive aging, keynote speaker and elderhostel founder Marty Knowlton (1996) said he never expected the unbelievable response and progress in the development of elderhostels worldwide. "We didn't know with whom we were dealing. They are marvelously responsive, extremely mentally alert, open, friendly, challenging." He pointed out that key to the success of the experience is how challenging older people can be to their professors. "It hones the college professor to be sharper and sharper" every time he or she engages with an older-adult student.

Permanent year-round learning institutes are forming as part of the Elderhostel Institute Network. Called the Institute for Learning in Retirement (ILR), more than 200 are located in the United States and Canada (see chap. 19 for a description of the ILR).

In their quest for meaning, older adults tend to focus on spiritual concerns and issues. The spiritual quest is necessarily done in solitude; the older person disengages from the outside world, a tendency often misunderstood in an extraverted, ego-centered, secular-minded society. Older persons who retreat into themselves are judged as fading out, losing their minds, or getting senile, not only by caring loved ones but also by most health care professionals. Even many religious organizations are unprepared to acknowledge and enhance the spiritual inner journey the older person takes. In his book *To Dance With the White Dog* (1990), Terry Kay eloquently describes such a man in his 80s who has lost his beloved wife of 60 years. When he adopts an imaginary white dog as his preferred companion for his inner journey, his overconcerned adult children believe he's not in his right mind and consider sending him to an "old folks home"; he finally convinces them to see things his way.

In their spiritual search, older persons face their own sense of mortality, part of the despair/integrity process, a difficult yet essential developmental task for older people. Schachter-Shalomi and Miller (1995) put it this way: "Release from myopic self interest brought on by the terror of death, elders can now serve others. Having acquired a broader philosophic perspective and a rootedness in the continuity of time, they can act as custodians of humanity's wisdom" (p. 91).

In many cultures other than ours, elders are honored and revered and are given special recognition as persons of wisdom. Baruth and Manning (1999) comment: "Many Japanese Americans equate old age with prestige and honor. Respect for elders is evident in the language used when addressing the elderly and in . . . bowing to them" (p. 180).

Similarly, in Native American and Hispanic families, elders are not expected to withdraw, but rather play the role of mentors to younger generations (see chap. 14).

Physical Capacities

As they age, people generally start losing physical agility and endurance; many cannot hear or see as well as they used to; and many suffer from crippling arthritis and need canes or walkers. Such physical losses, however, have been perceived as affecting all older adults. As mentioned earlier, part of the problem is society's tendency to lump all seniors together, although the older population stretches over a 30- to 40-year span. The physical capacities of 65-year-olds are usually very different from those in their 80s, and those in their 70s are usually more agile than those in their 90s.

Further misconceptions about the degree of physical deterioration in older adults may arise from misdiagnosis. The lack of mobility or agility in many older adults may result from high dosages of medications, poor nutrition, or lack of exercise. Physicians, nurses, gerontologists, psychologists, and other health care professionals may incorrectly attribute the older person's physical afflictions to the normal aging process.

On the positive side, although adults tend to acquire more physical limitations as they age, they also have more time and leisure than do younger adults to attend to good nutrition and to engage in physical fitness programs. Moreover, loss of some physical or sensory capacities tends to enhance other sensory capacities. Blind persons, for instance, are noted for their acute sense of hearing. Those persons slowed down by walkers or canes tend to observe more keenly everything around them, as is so poignantly portrayed in Terry Kay's book *To Dance With a White Dog* (1990).

⁓ COUNSELING OLDER ADULTS

Many gerontologists and other professionals have been discussing the paradox of aging in our culture: the paradox of a rapidly growing group of healthy, vigorous, older adults eager to learn and wanting to carve out new roles for themselves in a society that stereotypes them as no longer competent or as standing in the way of younger people (Butler & Gleason, 1985; Friedan, 1993; Gutman, 1987).

As scholars have become more interested in the developmental aspects of aging, the counseling profession, too, has become more interested in the counseling needs of normally functioning older people (Myers & Schwiebert, 1996). Jane Myers (1989, 1990) has been instrumental in changing attitudes and practices in mental health counseling with older adults.

> Mental health counseling with older persons is an emerging specialty stimulated by changing demographics and dramatic increases in the number of older persons during this century. Because most mental health counselors can expect to encounter older persons and their families with increasing frequency, an understanding of normative and developmental issues and transitions is imperative. (Myers, 1989, p. 245)

Largely through Myers's efforts, a national gerontological counselor certificate was established in 1990 by the National Board of Certified Counselors. Since then, more than one-third of counselor training programs have added or expanded course offerings in counseling older adults (Myers & Schwiebert, 1996).

In a review of the literature on aging and counseling, Myers (1990) notes, however, that counseling services for normally functioning older people do not meet the current need. She claims that considerable numbers of older adults have mental health concerns that could be responsive to treatment in mental health services. Whereas older persons constitute 15% of the U.S. population, older adult clients represent only 2% to 6% of mental health clients in outpatient services (Flemming, Rickards, Santos, & West, 1986; Myers, 1990). In contrast, the 10% to 15% of older adults who are chronically or severely mentally ill take up the major proportion of inpatient mental health resources. Myers (1990) comments: "Although older persons are under-represented in outpatient care, they are over-represented in inpatient mental health populations. More than 60 percent of public mental hospital beds are occupied by persons over age 65" (p. 251).

The latest viewpoints and research about older adults denote a much more optimistic view about therapeutic work with the elderly than traditionally held attitudes among professional gerontologists and other health care professionals. Increasing numbers of counseling professionals are exploring their attitudes about counseling older adults. Myers (1990) and Knight (1996) have given attention to the unique counseling needs of older adult clients; Waters and Goodman (1990) have presented counseling strategies particularly useful in empowering older adults. Knight (1996), Myers (1990), and Waters (1990b) have discussed how counselor attitudes toward older adults influence the counseling relationship.

Other counseling practitioners have presented special techniques, such as life review and reminiscing, appropriate for counseling this age-group (Crose, 1990; Knight, 1996; Sweeney, 1990; Waters, 1990a). Jungian psychiatrist Allan Chinen (1989) presents the special technique of using elder fairy tales to guide older persons through a series of developmental tasks that helps lead them through various transformational stages.

Characteristics of Older Adult Clients

Older adult clients, programmed by a society as useless, weak, or incapable of learning, generally feel despair. Many are unaware of their potentialities to learn new skills, to grow personally, and to adapt to the many transitions in their lives.

Nevertheless, older adults are potentially good prospects for counseling. They have had more complex and varied experiences in relationships, transitions, and losses than younger clients. They tend to have deeper insights and to give more considered thought to issues. They have a longer time span of past experiences to process and reflect on. They are apt to be more judicious and more contemplative about selecting a method to resolve their problems because they see more alternatives based on previous experience than do younger clients. Knight (1996) says:

> The development of expertise through life experience will, in general, be an asset when working with older adults. Older adults often have expertise that is relevant to the problem that was brought to therapy. Their accumulated knowledge of people and relationships can be brought to bear on current relationship problems. (p. 26)

Knight comments further about the rich psychological history older adults bring to counseling: "If the issue has been of concern for some time, there are probably examples of many different ways that the client has approached the problem in the past, with various patterns of success and failure" (p. 40). He perceives that the challenge for counselors and clients is to take as much as possible from these past experiences and to help clients see them from a perspective that is relevant to current needs.

Postretirement individuals often have more time and energy to explore new behaviors, interests, skills, and relationships than do younger clients. Most are no longer committed to full-time jobs, nor are they involved in raising or supporting families. (That is changing, though, with so many adult children returning home to live with their parents and with so many older adults now raising their grandchildren.)

Because older people are far more divergent in their outlook and experience and span a far broader age range, they are just as diverse in their attitudes and reactions to counseling and therapy. Elders in their 60s and 70s are usually more favorable toward counseling than elders in their 80s and 90s. Those in their 80s and 90s, who grew up at a time when counseling was considered to be only for "crazy" people, are generally reluctant to seek or accept counseling. Many in their 60s probably have had counseling of some sort or another. Some may be quite willing to seek counseling; others may be too "therapy-wise" and cynical about therapists.

With these considerations in mind, one can make some generalizations about the concerns of older adults that differ from those of younger clients. Adolescents, young adults, and midlifers are concerned by and large about strengthening their egos, developing careers, and raising families. The roles they play are fairly well established and reinforced in society.

Older adults must contend with several complex transitions and changes that are unique to the latter stage of life. Some older people think their skills are obsolete and are unaware of latent talents they may have that could be developed. Others who are eager and optimistic about applying their skills in new ways and in developing latent talents in worthwhile endeavors find resistance from employers, training institutions, family, and peers that is based on prevailing stereotypes about aging.

Transitions that older people go through require changes in long-standing habits and lifelong patterns of living in a society that offers few prescribed roles to help guide them through the necessary adaptations. When they no longer are involved in maintaining careers or no longer responsible for rearing children, many older adults are quite happy to be free from responsibility and enjoy taking trips, vacationing, or following a life of leisure. Many others, however, sensing that they are no longer needed either as parents or as valued employees, feel useless and full of despair.

Erikson (1950) believes that these feelings of despair are central to the latter stage of life-span development. He proposes that older persons faced with despair and disintegration no longer focus on outward or external connections as a way of finding meaning in life. Typically, their search for meaning turns inward. As discussed earlier, they reassess their past experiences and reintegrate them with the present to achieve new meaning. They acquire a renewed sense of self, a stage Erikson terms *integrity*. Butler (1963) elaborates on this process of integration in which one looks back on one's life, coining the term "life review."

The most valued relationships of older adults also undergo transitions. Many expect spousal relationships, parent-child relationships, and relationships with siblings to remain static, but from a developmental point of view, dynamic relationships with loved ones are necessary if the relationships are to continue to deepen and mature.

After children leave home and one or both spouses retire, the relationship between spouses often changes. The husband may hang around the house, getting in his wife's way. The wife is unaccustomed to her husband being underfoot; besides, she may be preoccupied with caring for her 90-year-old mother, who lives

50 miles away. As described more fully later in the chapter, one spouse may become seriously ill and require constant caretaking by the healthier spouse—a role the caretaker spouse may find emotionally and physically exhausting.

The death of a spouse forces changes, new responsibilities, and challenges in the life of the surviving spouse at the time when he or she is in shock and grieving over the loss. The spouse may be challenged by having to take on unfamiliar household tasks previously carried out by the other spouse. The spouse may lose contact with previous friends and be uncertain about new roles as a single person.

Older adults' relationships with their adult children also go through changes. In some instances, adult children may not know how to respond to their parents' new patterns of living. In other instances, considerable numbers of adult children in their 30s are not yet economically established and are returning to live with their parents. Older adults are unaccustomed to such a phenomenon, and many are unprepared for such interruptions in their lives. In numerous cases, older adults are having to take on full-time care of their grandchildren. According to the U.S. Bureau of the Census, 3.7 million children (18 years or younger) are living in households headed by grandparents (Morrissey, 1997).

Intergenerational relationships thus take on complicated twists unlike in earlier days when elder parents passed away soon after adult children set up their own households and started raising families. Whereas in former days certain predictable static relationships sufficed in conventional lifestyles and shorter life spans, now intergenerational relationships are as unpredictably fluid as are relationships in general. Many older adults and their adult children are in contact with each other every day. At the other extreme, many are no longer in contact with each other at all. As with any dynamic interaction, loved ones experience strain and conflicts. Working through conflicts and resolving misunderstandings is a necessary part of the developmental process.

Sibling relationships among older adults often undergo marked changes as well. A brother or sister may suddenly take on added significance in one's latter years. Sibling bonds differ from parent-child bonds. Siblings are not only peers; not only have they known each other longer than any other persons, but they are also blood relations, kinfolk who share a past more closely than with their spouses or children. Older adults often seek out siblings whom they have not seen for years. Their high expectations of bonding the way they used to may turn out to be a disappointment. Or they may develop deep, fond relationships they never had when they were young.

Physical afflictions of various kinds are a major area of concern of older adults. Although many older adults are physically fit and involved in exercise programs, run marathons, and go on long bicycle treks, 75% of older people are physically limited in one way or another (Cavanaugh, 1997). Many have had hip operations, mastectomies, or heart bypass surgery; many suffer from such chronic health problems as arthritis or back pain. Although some older adults with physical problems retreat to a sedentary, inactive lifestyle, many others partake in preventive health care programs by joining physical fitness clubs and eating healthful, nutritious meals. Many older adults learn to adapt to their physical limitations and increase activities that use other physical or sensory capacities. A once physically active older person now confined to a wheelchair may, for example, in his or her solitude turn inward, develop a vivid imagination, and become a beloved storyteller.

In most cases, older adults' financial status determines their ability to adapt successfully to the many changes of later life, to learn new skills, to keep physically fit, and to continue to be productive and self-sufficient. Whereas many older people are comfortable financially, many others, trying to survive on Social Security checks, worry about how to make ends meet. Their overriding concerns are about rising costs of medical and dental care and diminished income, and holding on to adequate housing for themselves.

Counselor Characteristics

Increasing numbers of counselors are working with older clients in mental health clinics, health centers, senior centers, and private practice (Waters, 1990b). Their earlier reluctance to work with older adults has decreased as the counseling profession has begun to dispute ageism stereotypes while giving more attention to growth and development in older adults.

Counselors who work effectively with older adult clients have additional characteristics and skills that supplement those described in chapter 8. They should be familiar with the economic, social, and political times that older adults have lived through; they should be aware that older adults have experienced many more complex transitions and have endured longer term relationships than younger adults. Counselors with this awareness help older clients (a) perceive their strengths and coping skills, which they developed over the years, and (b) apply or adapt these to resolve current dilemmas. They should also be aware of previous counseling experiences older adult clients have had and the effect of these encounters on the clients' current attitudes about counseling.

The mental health of older adult clients is very closely tied to their physical, social, and economic well-being. Counselors, when working with older clients, find it particularly important to network with other professionals and agencies serving elders in the community. For example, consultations or referrals to physicians, physical therapists, or nutritionists, with the client's knowledge, often contribute to more successful counseling results.

The Counseling Process

The counseling process for older adult clients follows the stages described in chapter 9. Although these stages parallel those that occur in the counseling process with younger clients, there generally are some differences with older clients, particularly in types of counseling goals, in transference and countertransference relationships, in encouraging client action, and in the terminating phase of counseling.

Counseling Goals

A major counseling goal is to help empower older adults to gain control over their lives. When they enter counseling, older clients typically express feelings of helplessness and hopelessness; they generally feel overwhelmed by losses, transitions, and changes in life. Such a goal can help older clients explore previously learned coping skills and learn to use them in new ways. Older clients feel empowered when counselors help them refute ageism stereotypes, a necessary first step as they strive to carve out new roles and new relationships despite resistance from society or from those close to them.

Spiritual questions and concerns are often raised by older adults when former roles and long-held commitments are no longer existent or satisfying. The older client's goal in these instances is to explore new meanings and purposes in life that transcend immediate personal needs.

Another counseling goal particularly important to older clients who generally feel isolated or lonely is that of seeking out community support groups. Persons working through grief over the death of their spouses, spouses heavily burdened with caretaking duties, or individuals cut-off from family or career relationships can profit from appropriate support groups.

Transference and Countertransference

In all counseling relationships, counselors and clients develop feelings toward each other based on unconscious attitudes arising from unresolved relationships experienced in the past. Client feelings toward counselors are called *transference;* counselor feelings toward clients are called *countertransference* (see chap. 5).

Until recently, therapists, following Sigmund Freud's original views, considered these feelings barriers to successful counseling. Transference was considered a neurosis that had to be worked through before the patient could progress in counseling. Countertransference was considered an even bigger problem. Therapists believed that they had to suppress these feelings or cut off counseling sessions.

Therapists now believe that awareness and acceptance of feelings of transference and countertransference offer opportunities for both client and therapist to work through unresolved feelings. They thereby strengthen the counseling relationship, a process that is a rehearsal for developing more effective relationships in everyday life (Corey, 1996; Gelso & Carter, 1985; Genevay & Katz, 1990).

Successfully working through transference feelings with an effective counselor can help older adults clear up unresolved power issues between themselves and their adult children; work through unrealistic or negative expectancies about relationships with grandchildren; or work through unresolved guilt feelings, jealousies, or power struggles with spouses or with siblings either living or dead (Knight, 1996).

Genevay and Katz (1990) have taken the lead in exploring countertransference with older adults. In their book *Countertransference and Older Clients,* they point out that counselors can be more effective with older clients when they recognize and make therapeutic use of these feelings. They say,

> We come face to face with thoughts, memories, feelings and unresolved issues from our own lives. . . . We can connect our feelings and experiences with those of the patients and clients we serve; and we can provide better diagnosis and treatment in the process. Out of our own observations of ourselves and our aging families we can become more effective professionals and more sensitive to the people we help. (p. 13)

Counselor countertransferences are a particularly important and complex part of the counseling process with older clients because clients are apt to be older than the counselors. Counselors may overreact to client concerns on the basis of experiences they themselves have had or are having with their own aging parents, to their own fears about aging, or to strong reactions about society's neglect of elders. At times, these counselor feelings may arise in reaction to the type of problem the older client is confronting—suicidal thoughts, declining physical or mental capacities, or death.

When older clients remind the counselor of his or her mother or father, the counselor may become oversolicitous if the clients seem frail. Or if clients disagree or take issue with what the counselor says, the counselor may feel threatened and think his or her expertise is being challenged. The counselor may become more authoritative, determined to point out the clients' faults or need to change, or the counselor may distance him- or herself from clients and become indifferent to the dynamics of the relationship. When the age differential is large, the counselor may regard the clients as grandparents; countertransference reactions may evoke protective feelings in the form of "a basically positive feeling for a somewhat fuzzily perceived older person who must be protected from the middle generation's interference" (Knight, 1996, p. 71).

Counselors need to be alert to the pressure of negative countertransference when, for example, they become convinced that a client is too old to profit from therapy, they consistently misdiagnose depression as dementia or Alzheimer's disease, they insist without evidence that medication will be more satisfactory than therapy, or they experience feelings of boredom, anxiety, or helplessness (Genevay & Katz, 1990; Knight, 1996).

Encouraging Client Action

In the final stages of counseling, counselors and clients work jointly to search out new resources or new opportunities for growth and change based on insights gained in earlier sessions. This stage is particularly important for counselors and older clients because society tends to be unprepared for, unresponsive, or even resistant to older adults developing new social and career roles.

Older clients can take action to change their lives by making use of talents and skills in new and innovative ways. Retired history or language teachers, for example, may lead tours to foreign countries; retired biologists may lead nature treks. Others might develop talents they had put aside early in life, such as playing a musical instrument, renewing their skills by taking lessons, becoming proficient, and/or joining the community orchestra. Someone who has collected antiques over the years might open an antique shop.

Terminating Counseling

Counselors working with clients considerably older than themselves tend to find terminating sessions the most difficult part of counseling. Knight (1996) says, "It is virtually always the therapist rather than the client who experiences termination as very difficult" (p. 96). Older clients, Knight says, often are reassured by termination, seeing it as an indicator of completing something successfully. They often have had more experience with endings and so are more used to them. Therapists, in contrast, tend to be more reluctant to end sessions because they fear that older persons may be too frail to deal with problems on their own or will experience loneliness or feel abandoned. Counselors do need to be alert to feelings of client sadness, fear, resentment, or anxiety that typically occur during the terminating stage of counseling. They need to address these issues to the satisfaction of their clients before counseling is concluded.

Life Review: A Special Technique with Older Adults

In 1963, Robert Butler proposed that *life review* is a natural process experienced by older adults—a process in which a person reviews and reflects on past experiences, achievements, joys, and sorrows as a way of searching for a renewed sense of meaning in life.

Butler's life review is an amplification of Erikson's original view regarding the major developmental task of older adults. Erikson proposed that when older adults feel despair, they review and reevaluate their past and gain integrity or a sense of coherence in their lives. In later writings, Erikson and other developmental theorists expanded the life review concept as a means whereby elders can develop new, productive ways of living (Erickson, Erikson, & Kivnick, 1986; Friedan, 1993; Knight, 1996; Whitbourne, 1985). Knight (1996) says that "life review is not an end in itself, but rather a process that improves the life history as a step toward creating the future" (p. 161).

Life reviews are truly meaningful if older adults use them in life-enhancing, generative ways. This focus on generativity in older adults as described earlier is emphasized by Friedan (1993). Life review has become a popular technique in counseling and therapy with older adults. Crose (1990), Disch (1988), Knight (1996), Sherman (1991), Viney (1993), Waters (1990a), and Whitbourne (1985) have written about life review and its appropriate use in counseling and therapy.

Life review activities are also led by those who are not counselors or therapists. Writers and biographers often lead such workshops for older adults. Their purpose and approach is quite different, however, because they use life review nontherapeutically. In this discussion, life review is used therapeutically by professionally trained counselors and therapists for those clients who express a need for it.

It is impossible for a counselor to expect a client to come forth with a complete life review that encompasses so many decades of life. Knight (1996) sees the counselor as a directive in helping the client through the life review process. According to Knight, counselors should note any large gaps in client stories to encourage deeper exploration through areas that clients might be avoiding. Counselors act as editors in that they help clients make choices on what areas are important to cover. He recommends that positive elements be emphasized if the goal of counseling is to help clients improve their sense of well-being. If the aim is to change long-standing behaviors, counselors may have to work on hidden negative experiences that need to be acknowledged and worked through. Consideration of how lifetime stories tie in with clients' future way of life is essential (Knight, 1996; Waters, 1990a; Whitbourne, 1985).

In contrast with Knight's directive approach, many counselors prefer to act as guides, rather than as editors, in the life review process. Rather than try to influence or shape the content of older adult recollection, they encourage clients to talk about memories that are important to them. Further, they encourage clients to do their own interpreting of these remembrances, rather than interpret them for the clients.

Life review should be done by well-trained counselors. Disch (1988) has expressed concern that mental health practitioners who are untrained in adult development might misuse or overuse life review. Waters (1990a) considers it a valuable tool for counselors but cautions that "life reviews may trigger sadness and depression for people who feel extreme dissatisfaction with their lives" (p. 277).

Knight (1996) believes that life review should not be used indiscriminately. He suggests that it is not typically appropriate or useful for problem-focused concerns related to specific situational changes that do not unduly disrupt the older adult's life. He recommends using life review when older adults are grieving and need to develop new perspectives about their lives or when they are experiencing new emotions that must be integrated into the self. Further, he sees it as a useful technique when older adults themselves raise doubtful, despairing questions about how well they have lived their lives and wonder how they can continue to live productively.

Life review techniques have been incorporated into some well-established counseling approaches—for example, Gestalt, Adlerian, personal construct, and Jungian. Gestalt techniques can be used during a life review to help delve into unfinished business (Crose, 1990). Clients are encouraged to reexperience their past stories by enacting them. The older person may be asked to dialogue with someone who is dead or otherwise unavailable and so resolve conflict with that person (empty chair technique). Alfred Adler believed that an individual's earliest recollections are essential clues to understanding their unique styles of life. Sweeney (1990) makes use of this technique in working with older adults. The client's early memories are used as a basis to encourage purposeful reminiscing that helps older adults modify lifestyles in a positive way.

Personal construct theory (see chaps. 5 and 9) can be effectively applied during the life review process (Viney, 1993). This approach is based on the assumption that elders have acquired complex constructs of meanings from the events they have experienced over the years. These constructs are reconstrued and modified during the therapeutic process, enabling clients to experience change or transformation. Commenting on a personal construct approach to elders, Viney (1993) says:

> They are also seen like all adults, as actively handling their own flaws of experience, being able to reflect on that process and to recognize that they are, themselves, agents of it. They are also able to integrate separate aspects of this experience over time in the stories they construct and to reintegrate it when events make such change appropriate by retelling their stories. (p. 9)

Viney (1993) believes that reconstruing and reintegrating experiences is at the core of psychological development. This integration can best be accomplished by listening to elders tell and retell their stories in therapy. Through this process, elders can "work through grief and guilt, getting in touch with strengths, both personal and interpersonal, and unleashing creativity and enjoyment as well as that most fulfilling sense of integrity" (p. 50).

Jungian psychiatrist Alan Chinen (1989) uses the telling of elder fairy tales as an imaginative way to help older adults review their lives. In working through the messages of the elder fairy tales, Chinen says, "The elder embraces the past, not to regress but to illuminate all of life. The end is the beginning transfigured" (p. 137).

Chinen (1989) makes a sharp distinction between youth fairy tales, in which the young hero is the protagonist in search of achievement and glory, and elder fairy tales, in which the older person is the protagonist in search of maturity and wisdom. Youth tales, on the one hand, common in our culture, focus on ego identity and achievement—essential developmental tasks in the first half of life. Heroes and heroines conquer dragons, witches, and evil older people to achieve perfect love and a kingdom. End of story. Elder tales, on the other hand, which begin where the youth-oriented tales end, are concerned with essential developmental tasks in the second half of life: self-confrontation, self-transcendence, and emancipation—tasks that lead to compassion and wisdom.

Life review can be effective in group counseling, as well as in individual counseling. When working with groups, stimuli such as music or memorabilia such as newspaper clippings or old family photographs can be used to trigger recollections (Waters, 1990a). Sharing stories is another way of evoking memories. As in any group counseling, counselors need to be certain that neither they nor any group members pressure or try to persuade another group participant to share memories that he or she is not ready or willing to share.

Special Problems of Older Adults

Depression

Counselors working with older adults need to be especially concerned about the diagnosis and treatment of depression for several reasons. First is the very high incidence of depression in the older population. Second is frequent misdiagnosis of depression as dementia or Alzheimer's disease. Third is the tendency to overprescribe antidepressant medication and to ignore the value of counseling and psychotherapy with older people.

It is estimated that 20% of the elderly have some sort of mild or moderate depression (Myers, 1990). Clinical chronic depression is relatively uncommon. Briefly, those persons suffering from chronic depression tend to have intense and persistent sadness and pessimism not obviously related to anything specific in their lives. These intense feelings interfere with their ability to function adequately socially or physically. Those with mild or moderate depression feel sad or in a down mood because they are suffering from specific losses or transitions that are stressful or unexpected. They are, however, usually able to meet daily responsibilities (Schmall, Lawson, & Stiehl, 1993).

Depression in older adults is often overlooked or misdiagnosed. Stooped posture, minimal physical activity, sleep disturbances, and reduced appetites, which are typical symptoms of depression, are also characteristic of many frail, sickly, older people who are not depressed. Misdiagnosis may also occur because many older adults who are depressed deny and cover up their feelings because they are afraid they would be diagnosed as crazy.

At times, symptoms of depression such as weakness and fatigue may be misdiagnosed as a sign of a particular physical illness. Some older depressed people exhibit temporary memory problems and confusion that mimic dementia or Alzheimer's disease. If mental health workers are unaware of this similarity, they may make incorrect diagnoses of dementia (Schmall et al., 1993). Ageism may contribute to misdiagnosis. Professionals who automatically equate older age with cognitive loss fail to consider other factors, such as feelings of depression, lack of exercise, or malnourishment.

The misuse or overuse of medication for depression has particular ramifications for older adults. Physicians and mental health workers who believe that older adults are not responsive to counseling because of their age tend to prescribe only medication. This occurs despite statistics showing that psychotherapy or counseling, along with medication, has a higher success rate than medication alone (Jakubiak & Callahan, 1996).

Suicide

If an older adult's depression goes unrecognized or is misdiagnosed as dementia, the person may become suicidal. Counselors must be particularly attentive to the possibility of suicidal intentions in depressed older adults. The average rate of suicide among those over age 65 is the highest of any age-group (Bee, 1996; Belsky, 1990).

Factors that contribute to high risk of suicide in older adults include severe losses, such as the death of a loved one; prolonged feelings of hopelessness, helplessness, or isolation; prior attempts at suicide; heavy alcohol or drug use; expressed desire to kill oneself; and availability of a lethal weapon (Schmall et al., 1993). Most of these symptoms are similar to those of suicidal younger people. In older adults, however, losses and isolation play a bigger part. Moreover, older people are more determined to follow through with the intent to kill themselves, and they are more likely to complete suicide attempts.

Elder Abuse and Neglect

Elder abuse or neglect by caretakers has only recently come to the attention of mental health counselors and other professionals. Elder abuse occurs in various ways— physical and psychological abuse, financial exploitation, and neglect. Caretakers may physically or verbally assault elders, steal or misuse elders' money or property, leave elders in unsanitary or hazardous living environments, or withhold appropriate care.

The estimate that about 4% of older adults are victims of abuse or neglect is considered much lower than the actual occurrence of abuse (Cavanaugh, 1997). Elder abuse is as prevalent as child abuse but is a well-kept secret, scarcely reported in the professional literature or public media (Callahan, 1988).

Older persons are most likely to be abused by their adult children and by their spouses. But abuse also occurs all too often in nursing homes. Pillemir and Moore

(1989) surveyed more than 500 nurses and nurse's aides working with older adults in nursing facilities. Results showed that 10% of respondents said they had physically abused a resident, and 40% reported they had psychologically abused a resident. When they were asked about their observations of how other staff members treated elderly patients, however, the levels of abuse rose dramatically: 36% reported they had observed other staff members physically abusing elderly patients, and 81% reported witnessing acts of psychological abuse.

Abuse or neglect of the elderly is more likely to be detected and prevented in long-term care facilities than in private homes. For those elderly people who live in private homes, abuse rarely gets reported. The elderly often are powerless when spouses or sons or daughters abuse or neglect them. Overcome with shame or fear of abandonment and impaired by physical disability, they are reluctant or unable to report abuse. Shelters are available where abused children or abused spouses can escape for protection, but unfortunately no such emergency facilities are available for older abused persons who need to be separated from their abusers.

Elder protective services have been mandated in all states to serve older adults who are being neglected or abused. Whenever health care professionals notice signs of elderly abuse in clinics or in long-term care facilities, they are required to report it to elder protective services.

When abuse by a caretaker is reported to protective services and the circumstances of abuse are assessed, several actions are possible. Arranging for alternative care is one option. Another is determining whether the abuse was precipitated by a caregiver who was overstressed; caretakers can be helped to assess the degree of overload and how and where to seek help when stress levels escalate.

Respite care is available in most communities to give overburdened caretakers assistance, relief, and time-out. Arrangements can be made for visiting nurses or other health care professionals to come to the home at regular intervals to bathe the patient, check on medication, change bedding, and attend to other similar tasks. These services are particularly helpful when the caretaker is physically unable to lift or move the elder. Caretakers can also get help in preparing meals or in doing household chores. These services ease stress and permit caretakers to have some time to themselves, run errands, or engage in their own social activities.

Many caretakers could benefit from counseling. Counseling can help them work through feelings of helplessness, anger, grief, or guilt when strained relationships reach a breaking point (see "Counseling Needs of Caretakers," later in the chapter).

When professionals become aware that an elderly person is being exploited financially, they can assist the elder in getting legal advice and legal protection. Reputable attorneys specialize now in elder law. In these instances, counseling can help the older person work through feelings of anger, depression, or grief at the betrayal of a trusted adviser, loved one, or caretaker.

Facing Losses; Death and Dying

Suffering from losses—loss of one's job, loss of a home, loss of a loved one, or, for the terminally ill, the imminent loss of one's own life—can happen any time during a person's life, but such losses generally occur more often in the latter stages of life. Individuals suffering from such losses as these without an opportunity to go through the process of grieving can experience emotional and physical problems (Gilliland & James, 1997; Kalish, 1985; Marino, 1996). Depression, disorientation, and anxiety disorders result from unresolved grief (Marino, 1996). Many therapists claim, however, that those suffering from losses develop new strengths as they work through the grieving process (Gilliland & James, 1997). It enables them to realize new opportunities for growth. Accepting change in life empowers and revitalizes them.

Confronting one's own mortality and facing one's own death is the ultimate stage of development (Gilliland & James, 1997; Kübler-Ross, 1974; Rando, 1984). In her classic book *On Death and Dying* (1969), Elizabeth Kübler-Ross pointed out the general denial of death among most people in our culture. She explores the need for greater understanding of the emotional problems—the fears and denials—of terminally ill patients and their families.

Through interviews with 200 terminally ill persons, Kübler-Ross found that most people go through five emotional stages: denial, anger, bargaining, depression, and final acceptance. She perceives that *denial* is a normal stage of getting ready to die. After accepting the reality of death, patients then experience *anger* and resentment, which are generally projected on family and caregivers. In the next stage, they try *bargaining* to delay or postpone death. When they realize that this is futile, *depression* sets in, followed by the *final acceptance* of the inevitability of death and a sense of peace.

In a later publication, Kübler-Ross (1974) cautions against considering these steps to be fixed stages that everyone experiences at the same time. The processes of emotional responses may differ significantly in individuals.

When working with a client who is dying, counselors need to consider the client's degree of physical pain and deterioration, psychological outlook, number and nature of interpersonal attachments, and amount of energy and degree of hope (Cavanaugh, 1997; Corr, 1991–1992). Counselors also need to take into account the setting in which the client is being cared for—whether the patient is at home, in a hospital, or in a long-term care facility.

Cavanaugh (1997) recommends using a form of life review in which counselors encourage clients and family members to write narratives about earlier life experiences that can help them work through emotional blocks to grieving.

The most valuable contribution that counselors and other mental health workers can make is to help dying individuals maintain some semblance of control and independence in their lives (Cavanaugh, 1997; Schulz & Ewen, 1993). "Dignity can be enhanced by involving the dying person in all decisions that affect him or her, including control over the end of life" (Cavanaugh, 1997, p. 508). These considerations are especially important to older adults because these people are particularly susceptible to feelings of helplessness.

Hospice Care.   Until the 1940s, most terminally ill older adults spent their last days at home being cared for by family members and friends. From the 1940s through the 1970s, most dying persons died in impersonal, clinically oriented institutions, isolated from loved ones and family and with little or no attention to their emotional and psychological needs (Cavanaugh, 1997).

In 1967, in reaction to the sterile, isolating institutional approach, St. Christopher Hospice was established. This center emphasized a more humanitarian approach for caring for the terminally ill, a method that combined institutional and home care. This movement spread quickly throughout North America and Europe. Today, there are more than 1,500 hospice programs (Bee, 1996).

The major focus in hospice care is involving family members in the care of the dying person in a warm, personal atmosphere. Hospice services generally work out of the patient's home or family home. Cared for in familiar surroundings and in significant contact with family and friends, the patient can attend to his or her impending death with less fear and apprehension. Not only are family and friends more involved in daily caretaking, but they also are able to visit with the patient more often, listen to the patient's stories, and offer comfort and reassurance in the patient's last days. Patient and loved ones have more opportunities to say good-bye and to let go of past conflicts through reconciliations and forgiveness.

Professional assistance is provided by an interdisciplinary team of professionals, which may include physicians, visiting nurses, social workers, and counselors. Assistance is also given at regularly scheduled times in such caretaking tasks as bathing the patient, preparing meals, and doing household chores.

The counselor can be particularly helpful with the family involved in hospice care when family members experience undue stress over the burdens of caretaking, express unresolved conflict with the terminally ill patient, or experience debilitating grief over losing their loved one.

Grief Process and Grief Counseling.   Kübler-Ross (1969) suggests that family members of the dying person go through similar stages of grieving: denial, anger, guilt, preparatory grief, and the final stage of saying good-bye. Their emotional reactions and behaviors, however, are quite different from those of the dying patient. Family members may shop around from physician to physician, hoping for a different diagnosis, or they may feel guilty that they did not do more for the patient. Counseling family members during the early stages of grief can help them continue to work through the grieving process after their loved one dies.

For those patients who are terminally ill, family members have some time to anticipate and begin the grief process. Sudden, unexpected deaths, however, have the additional impact of shock and lack of opportunity to say good-bye or to resolve unfinished business.

Whether death is expected or unexpected, counselors must consider various factors when assessing the intensity and duration of the client's grief. How central was the deceased in the client's life? How troubled was the client's relationship with the deceased? Has the client recently experienced other deaths or serious losses? Does the client have unresolved grief reactions from earlier stages of life?

More recently, some counselors and other mental health professionals have questioned the value of the stage model of grieving based on Kûbler-Ross's work. Grief work specialists Neimeyer and Worden believe that the stage theory implies a passive process that clients go through over a period of time. They propose instead a more active mode in which the person actively resolves grief (Marino, 1996).

Worden (1992) has developed a series of grief work stages that he believes allow clients a more active role in working through grief. Termed *emotional tasks,* the stages are (a) accepting the reality of the loss, (b) experiencing the pain of grief, (c) adjusting to an environment in which the deceased is missing, and (d) withdrawing emotional energy from the lost relationship and investing it elsewhere.

Marino (1996) describes how Robert Neimeyer has adapted Worden's approach and developed what he calls an *active adaptation model* of grieving. Neimeyer has clients face denial by encouraging them to tell the stories of their loss and to share their loss with family and friends. He helps clients acknowledge the pain, not only of the initial loss but also of the suffering afterward from the deprivation. Clients are then helped to adapt to new environments without the loved ones. In the case of loss of a spouse, this often includes taking on tasks that had been done by the partner. Suddenly faced with unfamiliar responsibilities, the survivor often has to learn quickly to manage finances, prepare meals, repair the house, or perhaps learn to drive. In the last stage of grief counseling, clients are encouraged to connect with other people and to develop new interests and activities in life.

Feelings of guilt are the most complex emotional experiences to work through for a survivor, especially if the death was sudden and traumatic or a result of suicide or if the relationship with the lost one had been troublesome. Caretakers are apt to feel guilty when they experience relief after the patients die. Or a grieving widow may believe that she had neglected the dying husband or had been unnecessarily difficult with him (Knight, 1996; Worden, 1992). In these cases, Gestalt techniques are recommended, such as role playing or empty chair dialogue, in which the client has imaginary discussions with the deceased over unresolved issues (Knight, 1996; Worden, 1992). Psychodrama also works well in a group setting in which the client enacts scripts with other group members, one of whom portrays the deceased person (Worden, 1992).

Grief specialist Gary Price believes that this active adaptation model works best in group counseling (Marino, 1996). The process of group members sharing stories of loss helps normalize the grieving process, offers mutual support to group members, and expedites the resolution of conflicts resulting from loss.

Abnormal Grief Reactions.

Sorrow, sadness, loneliness, denial, anger, disbelief, guilt, and depression are all natural and expected emotional reactions to loss. What distinguishes normal from abnormal reactions, however, is not the type of emotion being expressed but rather the intensity and duration of the response (Cavanaugh, 1997).

Persons suffering from guilt and self-blame that persist over a long time are experiencing abnormal grief reactions. These feelings disrupt the individual's life, turning into long-term depression that may manifest itself in chronic fatigue or tension or include obsessional thoughts about the deceased long after the person has died. The individual may refuse to move the deceased's belongings or resist developing new relationships long after a reasonable time of mourning has passed (Cavanaugh, 1997; Knight, 1996).

Counseling in Long-Term Care Settings

Increasing numbers of counselors are working with older adults in long-term care (LTC) settings. Counseling may occur in nursing homes, residential centers, adult day care centers, or clients' homes (Ganote, 1990). These older adults may be experiencing emotional distress related to their disability; may be experiencing grief over a loss or conflicts with caretakers or family members; or may be suffering from depression or difficulties in adjusting to the restraints of LTC settings.

For various reasons, the counseling needs of older adults in LTC have not been adequately met. Nursing homes have replaced mental hospitals as the major institution caring for older adults with mental illness. As a result, about two-thirds of the elderly in these facilities have some form of psychiatric disorder (Jakubiak & Callahan, 1996). Of the remaining elderly residents, those who do not have mental illness, their developmental concerns tend to be ignored. Furthermore, neither group receives psychiatric help or counseling. Nursing home surveys in the 1980s show that only 2% of nursing home patients received care from a mental health professional (Jakubiak & Callahan, 1996).

In the 1990s, counseling in nursing homes increased with the enactment of the Omnibus Budget Reconciliation Act (OBRA) in 1987 (Jakubiak & Callahan, 1996). Subsection C, entitled Nursing Home Reform, deals with regulation of the activities, services, and certification of nursing homes. This act calls for monitoring the quality of life in nursing homes and preadmission screening for persons with mental illness and mental retardation. The act also specifies that counseling and therapy services must be offered by trained professionals.

Counseling in LTC differs in some ways from counseling in most other settings. Most of the counselor's work is done outside the office, doing a lot of brief, intermittent counseling and often responding only as crises arise. Counselors must also work closely with physicians because older adult clients usually have medical problems accompanying their psychological concerns. It is particularly important that counselors be aware of various medications clients are taking and their side effects on the clients' physical and emotional well-being.

LTC clients generally show anxiety or depression and feel helpless as a consequence of having lost a sense of autonomy and independence. Feelings of loss are central in the lives of LTC elders. Many not only experience loss of spouses, relatives, and friends but also feel a loss of independence and control. In these instances, counselors help them work through emotions such as denial and anger—feelings that are a normal part of the grief process. Working through grief, as discussed earlier, permits clients to explore ways of adapting to life as LTC patients.

Older adults may be referred to counseling because they are striking out at caretakers or other residents or are yelling, swearing at others, or otherwise being disruptive (Ganote, 1990). The counselor's role is to provide a safe place for them to vent their feelings of helpless rage and frustration and to suggest ways they can gain some sense of control over their lives.

Counselors can help them reestablish some feelings of control by consulting with caretakers about allowing the clients to have more options and be able to make choices in their daily lives. For example, clients may be involved in menu selection, in choice of recreational activities, or in decisions about the number of visitors allowed or the timing of the visits. At the same time, counselors can encourage clients to express their feelings about their disability. They can also discuss ways clients can approach their daily activities in new ways.

Professional counselors working with LTC clients use relaxation techniques, cognitive restructuring, Gestalt techniques focused on naming and expressing emotions, and life review (Ganote, 1990; Knight, 1996; Waters, 1990a). Relaxation exercises can be effective with older adults who are overly anxious. Exercises can focus on relaxing muscles, or deep breathing, or light exercise. Clients generally find it easier to explore their feelings or concerns after therapeutic body work.

Cognitive restructuring can be helpful with clients who are depressed or who have exaggerated feelings of helplessness. A realistic appraisal of their physical and emotional concerns helps them confront their problems directly and reduces their tendency to exaggerate or overgeneralize their symptoms (Knight, 1996). For LTC clients who appear stoic, strained, and tense because of losses, Gestalt techniques can help them identify and express emotions. For example, while they bring up painful feelings, they are encouraged to notice their bodily sensations and emotional reactions.

Life review can be effective with older LTC clients who express concerns about lack of meaning in life or who express interest in exploring their past. Gestalt techniques can be helpful in the life review process. Clients can reenact past experiences as if they were in the present or can have an imaginary dialogue about an unresolved conflict with someone who has since died that will bring forth painful past experiences into the present. These activities permit new perspectives and new meanings that reshape their memories about their past experience (Crose, 1990).

Counselors can work closely with caretakers when counseling LTC clients. But as in all other settings, maintaining confidentiality between counselor and client is essential to the integrity of the counselor-client trust relationship. Only if clients are in danger of harming themselves or others may counselors share information without client consent.

Counseling Needs of Caretakers

Older adults requiring long-term intensive care generally have higher morale and more peace of mind when family members are the major caregivers. Family members who provide such care out of love and concern give generously of their time and energy.

Even so, caregivers develop stress symptoms, and many feel depressed when the demands of caretaking become overwhelming (Bee, 1996; Belsky, 1990; Gwyther & George, 1986). Factors other than actual duties of care often contribute to pressure. For instance, if caregivers feel a lack of appreciation or support from other family members, if their relationship with the older person has always been troublesome, of if they have not learned problem-solving strategies, the burden of care may become particularly overwhelming (Belsky, 1990; Gwyther & George, 1986).

Caregivers often are spouses who themselves may have some degree of physical incapacity. Many middle-aged adults also do some form of caretaking of one or more of their parents (Bee, 1996). According to Bee (1996), about 37% of middle-aged women will do some caretaking. Many of these women will be caught in a generational squeeze, having to care for both their children and their ailing parent or parents.

Counselors can help caretakers deal with the ongoing stresses of caretaking by helping them explore and work through feelings of resentment and entrapment. These feelings often result from countertransference when the patient makes unrealistic demands on the caretaker or becomes overly dependent or manipulative (Delmaestro, 1990; Katz, 1990). Counselors can also suggest ways to reduce stress, such as making arrangements for respite care. Caretakers can be encouraged to talk with health care professionals about ways to manage caretaking more efficiently. Counselors can also refer them to caretaker support groups, if available in their community, where feelings and suggestions about caretaking are shared.

During counseling, caretakers may come to realize that they are unable to continue giving personal care to loved ones. Counselors can help clients express and work through feelings of guilt or ambivalence about giving up caretaking and help them make alternative caretaking arrangements for their loved ones.

In LTC facilities, caretakers, because of frustration, at times get overly angry at residents when the residents are disruptive or unmanageable or when they curse or hit out at staff and other residents. To subdue them, staff resort to applying physical restraints (tying patients to beds or wheelchairs) or sedating them heavily with drugs.

Counselors can help caretakers acknowledge and work through countertransference feelings of anger and frustration when elderly patients make unrealistic demands or become overly dependent or manipulative (Delmaestro, 1990; Katz, 1990). When caretakers work through their own countertransference feelings with a counselor or therapist, they can better assess and understand elderly patients' feelings of helpless frustration and anger. Caretakers then are more responsive to counselor suggestions regarding ways to prevent emotional or physical outbursts of their elderly patients.

✒ CONSULTATION WITH FAMILIES OF OLDER ADULTS

In addition to offering counseling services to older adults or to caretakers of older adults, counselors offer counseling services to family members who have concerns about their aging parents. An example is helping adult children determine whether their parents are capable of living independently or whether they need care. If they need care, then the type of care needs exploration. Should the older adults live with their children, get full-time or part-time help from visiting nurses, or move to an assisted-living center or to a nursing home? The counselor can also help adult children of the elderly recognize when they may be overanxious about their parents' welfare and when they realistically need to intervene on their parents' behalf.

⇥ RESEARCH: COUNSELING OUTCOME

In a review of research on counseling outcomes with older adults, Smyer and Intrieri (1990) concluded that few studies exist and that what little research there is focuses on time-limited therapy with depressed elderly. They recommend that counselors conduct research with adults who have less severe emotional disorders, that they study the effectiveness of individual counseling with older people, and that they explore the use of preventive psychological education and support activities.

Part of the reason for the meager amount of research in gerontological counseling is that funds for research in all aspects of gerontology are inadequate. Carol Schutz (1995), executive director of the Gerontological Society of America, says that growth and support for gerontological research are increasing but that "it still remains underfunded and important, 'break-through' ideas may be languishing for lack of funds" (p. 34). As gerontological research in general increases, one can anticipate an increase in gerontological counseling research.

⇥ SUMMARY

Healthy older adults have become a significant force in society as life expectancy has increased dramatically since 1900. By the year 2030, older adults will represent more than 21% of the total population. The increased longevity of older healthy adults stimulated human development scholars to explore the unique developmental processes of people over age 65. Contrary to general belief, they found that most individuals continue to develop and grow throughout their life spans.

Stereotypes about older adults interfere with their growth potential. The most detrimental stereotype is that of equating aging with decline and deterioration. This stereotype is based on society's tendency to idealize and emulate a youth model.

As more and more older adults are living longer and healthier lives, the demand for older adult counseling services has increased. Counselors can help older adults adapt to the many changes and transitions they experience in the latter part of life. They can guide older adults in their search for new and productive roles and activities.

The counseling process with older adults is similar to that used with clients at other age levels. Some aspects, however, are unique to counseling older adults: (a) Counseling goals focus on helping clients regain control over their lives; (b) countertransference issues related to ageism and to the fear of getting old are common among counselors working with clients who are much older than they; (c) counselors also need to help clients overcome barriers in society that interfere with their carving out new roles in their lives; (d) life review, in which a person reflects on and reevaluates past experiences to gain new meaning or purpose in life, is particularly suitable for older adult clients.

Gerontological counselors must be aware of problems that are especially troublesome for older adults. Rates of depression and suicide are the highest of any age group. Elder abuse or neglect of frail elders, often unreported, occurs frequently in the elders' own homes, as well as in long-term care facilities. Losses of loved ones, careers, and family responsibilities are commonplace in older adults. The numbers of those suffering from terminal illness increase with older age. Grief work counseling helps older adults and their loved ones work through suffering and loss. In the case of terminally ill patients, counselors work with hospice services specifically developed for caring for dying persons and their families.

Gerontological counselors also offer valuable service to individuals who are long-term caretakers. They can help caretakers work through countertransference, recommend ways of reducing stress, and refer them to appropriate support groups.

✺ PROJECTS AND ACTIVITIES

1. Interview one of your grandparents or someone old enough to be your grandparent regarding his or her views about transitions, changes, or conflicts he or she has experienced in the latter years. How consistent are these views with the views discussed by developmental theorists?

2. Select an individual over age 65 who you believe is functioning optimally and another who seems to be having difficulty coping with changes in life. What factors may be contributing to differences in functioning?

3. Interview two counselors, one male and one female, regarding their views about counseling older adults. Do you notice any differences in their views about developmental processes of older adults? If so, what are they?

4. Visit a senior center. Notice whether any services are related to counseling or preventative services.

5. Check the television, newspapers, and films and note any stereotypes of older adults.

✺ REFERENCES

Adelmann, P. K. (1994). Multiple roles and physical health among older adults: Gender and ethnic comparisons. *Research on Aging, 16,* 142–166.

Baruth, L. G., & Manning, M. L. (1999). *Multicultural counseling and psychotherapy: A lifespan perspective.* Upper Saddle River, NJ: Merrill/Prentice Hall.

Bee, H. L. (1996). *The journey of adulthood* (3rd ed.). Upper Saddle River, NJ: Prentice Hall.

Belsky, J. K. (1990). *The psychology of aging* (2nd ed.). Pacific Grove, CA: Brooks/Cole.

Butler, R. N. (1963). The life review: An interpretation of reminiscence in the aged. *Psychology, 256,* 65–76.

Butler, R. N. (1975). *Why survive? Growing old in America.* New York: Harper & Row.

Butler, R. N., & Gleason, H. P. (Eds.). (1985). *Productive aging: Enhancing vitality in later life.* New York: Springer.

Callahan, J. J., Jr. (1988). Elder abuse: Some questions for policymakers. *Gerontologist, 28,* 453–458.

Cavanaugh, J. C. (1997). *Adult development and aging* (3rd ed.). Pacific Grove, CA: Brooks/Cole.

Chinen, A. B. (1989). *In the ever after: Fairy tales and the second half of life.* Willamette, IL: Cheron.

Corey, G. (1996). *Theory and practice of counseling and psychotherapy* (5th ed.). Pacific Grove, CA: Brooks/Cole.

Corr, C. A. (1991–1992). A task-based approach to coping with dying. *Omega, 24,* 81–94.

Craik, F. I. M., & Jennings, J. M. (1992). Human memory. In F. I. M. Craik & T. A. Salthouse (Eds.), *The handbook of aging and cognition* (pp. 51–110). Mahwah, NJ: Lawrence Erlbaum.

Crose, R. (1990). *Reviewing the past in the here and now: Using Gestalt therapy techniques with life review, 12,* 279–287.

Cummings, E., & Henry, W. E. (1961). *Growing old.* New York: Basic Books.

Delmaestro, S. (1990). Sharing despair: Working with distressed caregivers. In B. Genevay & R. S. Katz (Eds.), *Coun-*

tertransference and older clients (pp. 123–135). Newbury Park, CA: Sage.

Diamond, M., Johnson, P. E., Protti, A. M., Ott, C., & Kajisa, C. (1985). Plasticity in the 904-day-old male rat cerebral cortex. *Experimental Neurology, 87,* 309–317.

Disch, R. (Ed.). (1988). *Twenty-five years of the life review: Theoretical and practical considerations.* New York: Haworth Press.

Erikson, E. (1950). *Childhood and society.* New York: Norton.

Erikson, E. H. (1978). Reflections on Dr. Borg's life cycle. In E. H. Erikson (Ed.), *Adulthood* (pp. 1–32). New York: Norton.

Erikson, E. H. (1980). *Identity and the life cycle.* New York: Norton.

Erikson, E. H. (1982). *The life cycle completed.* New York: Norton.

Erikson, E. H., Erikson, J., & Kivnick, H. A. (1986). *Vital involvements in old age.* New York: Norton.

Erikson, J. M. (1997). *The life cycle completed: Erik H. Erikson.* New York: Norton.

Estés, C. P. (1992). *Women who run with the wolves: Myths and stories of the wild women archetype.* New York: Ballantine Books.

Flemming, A. S., Rickards, L. D., Santos, J. F., & West, P. R. (1986). *Report on a survey of community mental health centers* (Vol. 3). Washington, DC: Action Committee to Implement the Mental Health Recommendations of the 1981 White House Conference on Aging.

Friedan, B. (1993). *The fountain of age.* New York: Simon & Schuster.

Ganote, S. (1990). A look at counseling in long-term settings. *Generations, 14,* 31–34.

Gardner, H. (1993). *Frames of mind: The theory of multiple intelligences.* New York: Basic Books.

Gelso, C. J., & Carter, J. A. (1985). The relationship in counseling and psychotherapy: Components, consequences, and theoretical antecedents. *Counseling Psychologist, 13,* 155–243.

Genevay, B., & Katz, R. S. (Eds.). (1990). *Countertransference and older clients.* Newbury Park, CA: Sage.

Gilliland, B. E., & James, R. F. (1997). *Crisis intervention strategies.* Pacific Grove, CA: Brooks/Cole.

Gould, R. (1978). *Transformations: Growth and change in adult life.* New York: Simon & Schuster.

Gutman, D. (1987). *Reclaimed powers: Toward a new psychology of men and women in later life.* New York: Basic Books.

Gwyther, L. P., & George, L. K. (1986). Caregivers for demented patients: Complex determinants of well-being and burden. *Gerontologist, 26,* 245–247.

Jakubiak, C. H., Jr., & Callahan, J. J., Jr. (1996). Treatment of mental disorders among nursing home residents: Will the market provide? *Generations, XIX,* 39–42.

Jung, C. G. (1962). The stages of life. In *Collected works* (Vol. 8, pp. 387–403). Princeton, NJ: Princeton University Press. (Original work published 1931)

Kalish, R. A. (1985). *Death, grief, and caring relationships* (2nd ed.). Pacific Grove, CA: Brooks/Cole.

Katz, R. (1990). Using our emotional reactions to older clients: A working theory. In B. Genevay & R. S. Katz (Eds.), *Countertransference and older clients* (pp. 17–26). Newbury Park, CA: Sage.

Kay, T. (1990). *To dance with the white dog.* New York: Washington Square Press.

Knight, B. G. (1996). *Psychotherapy with older adults* (2nd ed.). Thousand Oaks, CA: Sage.

Knowlton, M. (1996, March). *Evolution of a new old age.* Speech delivered at Productive Aging Conference, Vancouver, B.C.

Kübler-Ross, E. (1969). *On death and dying.* New York: Macmillan.

Kübler-Ross, E. (1974). *Questions and answers on death and dying.* New York: Macmillan.

Levinson, D. J. (1978). *Seasons of a man's life.* New York: Knopf.

Marino, T. W. (1996). Grief counseling broadens its definition. *Counseling Today, 39,* 13.

Morrissey, M. (1997). More grandparents raising grandchildren. *Counseling Today, 39,* 1, 4.

Myers, J. E. (1989). *Adult children and aging parents.* Alexandria, VA: American Counseling Association.

Myers, J. E. (1990). Aging: An overview for mental health counselors. *Journal of Mental Health Counseling, 12,* 245–259.

Myers, J. E., & Schwiebert, V. L. (1996). *Competencies for gerontological counseling.* Alexandria, VA: American Counseling Association.

Neugarten, B. L. (1977). Personality and aging. In J. E. Birren & K. W. Schaie (Eds.), *Handbook of the psychology of aging* (pp. 311–335). New York: Van Nostrand Reinhold.

Perlmutter, M., & Hall, E. (1992). *Adult development and aging* (2nd ed.). New York: John Wiley.

Pillemir, K., & Moore, D. W. (1989). Abuse of patients in nursing homes: Findings from a survey of staff. *Gerontologist, 29,* 314–320.

Rando, T. (1984). *Grief, dying, and death.* Champaign, IL: Research Press.

Rybash, J., Hoyer, W. J., & Roodin, P. A. (1986). *Adult cognition and aging.* New York: Pergamon.

Schachter-Shalomi, Z., & Miller, R. (1995). *From age-ing to sage-ing: A profound new vision of growing old.* New York: Warner Books.

Schaie, K. W. (1990). Intellectual development in adulthood. In J. E. Birren & K. W. Schaie (Eds.), *Handbook of psychology and aging* (3rd ed., pp. 291–310). San Diego: Academic Press.

Schmall, V. L., Lawson, L., & Stiehl, R. (1993). *Depression in later life: Recognition and treatment.* Corvallis: Oregon State University.

Schulz, R., & Ewen, R. B. (1993). *Adult development and aging: Myths and emerging realities* (2nd ed.). New York: Macmillan.

Schutz, C. A. (1995). Professional organizations in aging: Where have we been and where are we going? *Generations, XIX,* 33–34.

Sherman, E. (1991). *Reminiscence and the self in old age.* New York: Springer.

Smyer, M. A., & Intrieri, R. C. (1990). Evaluating counseling outcomes. *Generations, 14,* 11–14.

Super, D. E. (1942). *The dynamics of vocational adjustment.* New York: Harper.

Super, D. E. (1990). A life-span, life-space approach to career development. In D. Brown & L. Brooks (Eds.), *Career choice and development: Applying contemporary theories to practice* (pp. 197–261). San Francisco: Jossey-Bass.

Sweeney, T. J. (1990). Early recollections: A promising technique for use with older people. *Journal of Mental Health Counseling, 12,* 260–269.

Valliant, G. E. (1977). *Adaptation to life.* Boston: Little, Brown.

Viney, L. L. (1993). *Life stories: Personal construct therapy with elderly.* Chickesler, UK: John Wiley.

Waters, E. B. (1990a). The life review: Strategies for working with individuals. *Journal of Mental Health Counseling, 12,* 270–278.

Waters, E. B. (1990b). Why counseling? *Generations, 14,* 5–6.

Waters, E. B., & Goodman, J. (1990). *Empowering older adults: Practical strategies for counselors.* San Francisco: Jossey-Bass.

Wellman, F. E., & McCormack, J. (1982). Counseling older persons: A review of outcome research. *Counseling Psychologist, 12,* 81–96.

Whitbourne, S. K. (1985). The psychological construction of the life span. In J. E. Birren & K. W. Schaie (Eds.), *Handbook of the psychology of aging* (2nd ed., pp. 594–618). New York: Van Nostrand.

Worden, J. W. (1992). *Grief counseling and grief therapy: A handbook for the mental health practitioner.* New York: Springer.

16 Counseling Programs in Elementary Schools

Children's mental health has declined sharply since the mid-1980s as a result of changing family patterns, an unstable society, rapidly changing values, and deteriorating home life. During the same time, the numbers of reported cases of alcoholism, domestic violence, and child abuse have been increasing (Gibson, Mitchell, & Basile, 1993; Myrick, 1997; Thompson & Rudolph, 1992). In 1989, after conducting a national survey, Tumas found that about 19% of children and youths need mental health services.

Children's psychological problems are most evident in elementary school classrooms, where children generally spend most of their waking hours under adult scrutiny and supervision. Emotional stress interferes with children's academic and social progress and causes children to withdraw from or disrupt classroom activities.

Although it is important to improve mental health services for children in the community, schools offer a special opportunity for children to obtain help. First, children or their parents do not have to pay fees for school counseling services, as they do for services in the community. Second, teachers who are with the same children all day are likely to spot those who are experiencing problems and to refer them to counselors.

When children request or are referred to counseling, elementary school counselors have options: They can work with children who can respond to short-term or intermittent counseling, or in more severe cases, they can contact parents and arrange for further work with the school psychologist or a child or family counselor in the community. Counselors can also be instrumental in helping improve the mental health climate in the school by offering children psychological education activities or by acting as consultants with teachers, parents, and administrators.

Although the focus in this chapter is on counseling in elementary schools, most of the activities and approaches discussed are also applicable to mental health counselors working with children in the community.

❧ HISTORY

Although high school counseling spread rapidly during the 1960s, elementary school counseling didn't get underway until the 1970s. The delay can be attributed to various factors. First, counseling initially focused primarily on vocational development. Second, it was widely believed that elementary school teachers could adequately serve as counselors because of their knowledge of their students and because special training for school counselors was not considered necessary at that time. Third, school psychological services were considered sufficiently covered by school psychologists, whose job consisted of testing children and diagnosing learning and/or emotional disabilities, and by school social workers, who were prepared to intervene in difficult family-school relations.

In 1964, the federal government, through the National Defense Education Act, authorized grants to school districts for developing elementary school counseling. In 1968, grants were authorized to fund institutes for training elementary school counselors. Such funding was previously available only for secondary school counseling. Since then, the number of elementary school counselors has increased rapidly.

❧ STRUCTURE OF ELEMENTARY SCHOOL COUNSELING PROGRAMS

Counselors are hired as part of the school staff and usually work in the school building. Their presence makes them easily available to students, teachers, and administrators. Appropriate facilities are important for effective counseling. Counselors need a soundproof office in which confidential counseling can be carried out and another room set aside for group counseling and parent or family consultation.

The American School Counselors Association (ASCA) recommends a ratio of 1 counselor to 100 to 300 elementary school students. This ratio is sufficient only if other psychological and educational specialists and community mental health resources are available to students and only if sufficient secretarial help is available to counselors. According to Baker (1996), "Universal ratios are difficult to dictate because of individual differences associated with the severity of student problems, amount of available secretarial and clerical assistance, curriculum options, and referral support" (p. 360).

❧ COUNSELING CHILDREN: ROLE, THEORIES, AND TECHNIQUES

Counselors preparing for elementary school positions have a more difficult time defining their potential counseling populations than do counselors in secondary schools. Whether children are in a K–4, K–6, or K–8 school, the difference in sophistication is much greater between the youngest and oldest ones than between the freshmen and the seniors in a high school. A freshman and a senior are more alike in overall behavior and maturity than a 5-year-old and a 9-year-old, or a 9-year-old and a 13-year-old. Elementary school children in these age ranges vary much more in independence, motivation, judgment, and developmental tasks than do adolescents between 14 and 18 years of age.

Whereas elementary counselors have the same overall functions of direct counseling, consultation, guidance, and psychological education as do counselors in other educational settings, they have more interaction with parents, families, and teachers (Gibson et al., 1993).

Elementary counselors have considerably more opportunities to engage in a counselor role consistent with that described by ASCA and ACES (direct counseling, consultation, and psychological education) than do secondary school counselors or community counselors. According to Hardesty and Dillard (1994), elementary school counselors perform fewer administrative and clerical activities than do secondary and middle school counselors. They also engage in more consultation and coordination activities and work more consistently and systematically with families, teachers, and professionals in the community. Unlike community counseling services, school counseling services do not charge fees, nor are they hampered by managed care restrictions.

Hardesty and Dillard (1994) also note, however, that counseling in elementary schools is not as widely accepted as in secondary schools. In most states, they say, only secondary schools are required to have counselors to maintain accreditation. When budgets are cut, elementary counseling programs are much more likely to be dropped than are secondary counseling programs.

Developmental Needs of Children

Awareness of the child's cognitive development is important (Franks, 1983; Thompson & Rudolph, 1992). Following Piaget's cognitive development theory (Piaget & Inhelder, 1969), children at age 5 are verbal in their thinking but usually can handle only one concept at a time. From 7 to about 11 years of age, children tend to think concretely. Then they begin to think abstractly and can consider various ways of solving problems and learning to deal with the future, as well as to focus on the present (see chap. 4). This process coincides with children's biological and physical development. As they grow, children acquire more complicated cognitive processes until they reach adulthood.

The value of Piaget's work is well known and accepted among educators:

> Understanding how children think enables counselors to choose developmentally appropriate activities for individual and group counseling and for classroom guidance. . . . Knowledge of cognitive development is also useful for counseling with teachers and parents, for example, in determining possible reasons for frustration in classrooms, lack of completion skills and low motivation. (Gibson et al., 1993, p. 29)

Counselors working with children also need to be aware of the psychosocial stages of children from ages 5 to 12 as proposed by Erikson (1950; see also chap. 4). Whereas Piaget emphasizes biological maturational cognitive development, Erikson focuses on the psychological development of individuals in their interactions and relationships with others. According to Erikson's *psychosocial theory,* 5-year-olds who are functioning adequately have passed through the development of trust and are at the stage of sensing their own individuality. They are developing a conscience and have a concept of right and wrong. From 6 to 12 years of age, children become more responsive to socially acceptable activities. Less self-centered, they become more interested in, and involved with, other people.

Some children, however, do not pass through these stages successfully. A counselor may see, for example, a child of 11 who has not developed sufficient trust, autonomy, or individuality. The counselor's job, then, is to help the child develop these qualities. Gibson et al. (1993) note that "psychosocial theory provides counselors with a useful framework for understanding the dynamic impact of the school and home settings on personal and social development" (p. 39).

The Counseling Process with Children

The counseling process for children is consistent with the process described in chapter 9. A counselor's first step is to develop trust and rapport with a client. Then, the counselor clarifies the problem, asks the child how she or he has tried to cope, and considers what new actions can be taken. Realistic plans are then made to solve the problem (Thompson & Rudolph, 1992).

Although children generally express emotions or act out emotions more easily than adults, they have difficulty labeling them. Counselors can help children become aware of and label emotions. For example, if a child says with strong feeling, "I hate my teacher," the counselor can respond, "You sound like you're very angry with your teacher, so let's talk about your anger."

The counselor should let the child control the distance between them by using a corner of a desk or table, rather than having a desk between them or sitting in opposite chairs with no barrier. The child then is free to come closer when she or he is ready (Thompson & Rudolph, 1992).

Similar to counseling with adults, counseling with children is a social interaction. Gibson et al. (1993) emphasize the importance of "non-verbal explicit behavior" in communicating with young children (p. 91). They recommend, for example, that counselors leave their own chairs and sit in smaller chairs when talking with children. Counselors should make specific suggestions to help their clients resolve their problems. They emphasize that any course of action must be made by the children.

Keat (1990a, 1990b) has modified Lazarus's multimodal counseling approach and applied it to counseling with children. As indicated in chapter 5, Lazarus (1989) defined seven problem areas (modes) of personality: **b**ehavior, **a**ffect, **s**ensation, **i**magery, **c**ognition, **i**nterpersonal relationships, and **d**rugs, which he called BASIC I.D. Keat renamed these personality modes in a manner that better describes children's problems: **h**ealth, **e**motions, **l**earning, **p**ersonal relationships, **i**magery, **n**eed, and **g**uidance of actions, behaviors, and consequences, with the acronym of HELPING (see Table 16.1).

After an initial interview, Keat outlines and ranks the child's major concerns and then proceeds to use appropriate counseling approaches or techniques to resolve them in order of their ranking. Table 16.2 shows an example of this procedure.

TABLE 16.1
Multimodel Evolution

Letter	HELPING Modes	BASIC I.D. Modes
H	Health	Drugs-Diet (D)
E	Emotions-Feelings	Affect (A)
L	Learning-School	Sensation-School (S)
P	People-Personal Relationships	Interpersonal Relations (I)
I	Imagery-Interests	Imagery (I)
N	Need to Know-Think	Cognition (C)
G	Guidance of Actions, Behaviors, and Consequences	Behavior (B)

Source: From *Child Multimodal Therapy* (p. 10) by D. B. Keat, 1990b, Norwood, NJ: Ablex.

As with Lazarus (1989), this is basically a *technically eclectic* model. While following a cognitive-behavioral model, it may also include, as *techniques,* activities borrowed from the psychodynamic model (creative arts and imagery, music, cartoons, storytelling) and approaches from the humanistic model that use a client-centered, self-actualizing approach.

Counseling Techniques for Children

Because of the large differences in age and sophistication of elementary school children, counselors serving this group use a wide repertoire of techniques, such as psychodrama, storytelling, painting (drawn from psychodynamic theories), contracts, cognitive restructuring, assertiveness training, token reinforcements (drawn from cognitive-behavioral theories); and client-centered approach and Gestalt methods—empty chair, role playing, imagery exercises—(drawn from humanistic theories); (see chap. 5).

Creative and Expressive Arts Therapy

Counselors use creative or expressive arts such as play, puppetry, storytelling, dreams, music, dance, and visual arts to help children better express their emotions, clarify their concerns, improve communication with others, and improve feelings about themselves. These activities also tend to expand their imaginations and give them new perspectives about themselves and their relationships (Allan, 1988; Gibson et al., 1993; Gladding, 1992; Thompson & Rudolph, 1992). As the value of creative and expressive arts therapy has become better known, increasing numbers of school counselors, particularly in elementary schools, have been receiving training in these areas. Creative arts therapists are also applying their skills in schools.

Counselors use expressive arts techniques to help them establish rapport with children, to help children better understand their world and gain a better perspective about how they interact with others (Allan, 1988; Gladding, 1987). For culturally

TABLE 16.2
HELPING Children Change

Mode	Rank	Concern Number	Concern	Intervention
Health	5	H1	Pain	Avoid/relief
		H2	Sickness	Wellness
Emotions	2	E1	Anxiety	Stress management
		E2	Anger	Madness management
		E3	Feeling down	Fun training
Learning	6	L1	Deficiencies	Life skills
		L2	Failing	Study skills
		L3	Sensory shallowness	Music
Personal Relationships	1	P1	Getting along (adults)	Relationship enhancement (RE)
		P2	Lacks friends	Friendship training
Imagery	4	I1	Low self-worth	IALAC (I Am Lovable and Capable); Storytelling
		I2	Coping lacks	Heroes (cartoons)
Need to Know	7	N1	Despair	Hope
		N2	Mistaken ideas	Cognitive restructuring
		N3	Lack of information	Bibliotherapy
Guidance of Actions, Behaviors, and Consequences	3	G1	Behavior deficits	Modeling
		G2	Motivation	Contracts

Source: From "Change in Child Multimodel Counseling" by D. B. Keat (1990a). *Elementary School Guidance and Counseling, 24,* p. 250.

diverse students having difficulties in school, Cochran (1996) recommends using play and art therapy. Elementary school children from different ethnic groups who have difficulties expressing themselves verbally because of language or cultural differences or both can express themselves more openly with counselors and teachers through play activities, art, music, dance, and drama.

Because they take naturally to play and to creative activities, children tend to respond spontaneously and creatively to their experiences as long as they have not been unduly inhibited. Dance helps children get in touch with their bodies and with the relationships of their physical beings to the environment, as well as allows creative ways to release their energy. Puppets help children act out dreams that manifest inner conflicts with families and with others. Music therapy can be particularly helpful with children who are withdrawn, shy, or depressed (Gladding, 1992; Keat, 1990a). Imagery increases divergent thinking and activates the imagination. Painting and drawing are nonthreatening ways for children to express suppressed feelings on paper, a tangible activity that can help children reflect on, and therefore become conscious of, unconscious aspects of their psyches. Children's literature, which abounds with fairy tales and magical realism, provides a mythic plane that reveals meaning usually unavailable with ordinary observable events.

Therapists encourage children to act out stories based on Moreno's (1946) psychodrama. With younger children, they can use such special techniques as play therapy with dolls, toys, sandboxes, and puppets; drawings of family or of feelings; and storytelling (Gibson et al., 1993; Ohlsen, Horne, & Lawe, 1988; Thompson & Rudolph, 1992).

Johnson, McLeod, and Fall (1997) conducted a study on the use of nondirective play therapy with six elementary school boys, ages 5 to 9, whose behavioral symptoms were diagnosed as attention deficit hyperactivity disorder (ADHD), mental disability, or autism. Counselors used toys of various sorts to help the boys express and control themselves. The researchers concluded, "Results of this study showed that non-directive play therapy permitted the labeled children with opportunities to express feelings, experience control and develop coping skills" (p. 33).

A successful technique in working with disturbed children is mutual storytelling (Kestenbaum, 1985). The counselor begins a story that is similar to the current circumstances. The counselor then asks the child to complete the story and intervenes only when necessary to help the flow of the story. This activity is designed to help the child look at alternative ways to resolve her or his conflict.

John Allan (1988), a Jungian counselor who has applied creative arts therapy in elementary schools, has developed a technique he calls *serial drawings*. At each meeting with the counselor, the child is asked to draw a picture. As this activity continues in regular counseling sessions over several weeks, the growth in the child's perceptions appears in successive drawings in *serial* form. These changes are acknowledged therapeutically with the child. Allan's theory is that when a child expresses images (say, by drawing them on paper), they are "concretized." When "symbolized" as well, the activity "facilitates psychological growth" (p. 22).

In the initial stages of the process of serial drawings (first to fourth sessions), the child client tends to express images that indicate feelings of helplessness. In the middle stage, painful and negative feelings appear in the drawings, with the counselor often included as a positive helper. In the last four sessions, drawings tend to show the child's self-image as central and positive, which indicates the child's emerging sense of strength. At this point, the child begins to detach from the counselor, so the counselor either is not in the drawings or is an insignificant detail in the drawings.

The value of play therapy and use of puppets in elementary counseling is presented by Carter (1987), James and Myer (1987), and Landreth (1987). Landreth discusses various types of toys designed to elicit different experiences for the child, such as developing a positive image or reducing unacceptable behavior. Play techniques help counselors establish rapport and understand children's interactions with others, help children reveal and act out feelings constructively, and help children develop socialization skills (Thompson & Rudolph, 1992).

Tests and Inventories

Standardized tests measuring intellectual ability, achievement level, and reading ability are available to elementary school counselors for use in improving students' self-understanding (see chap. 6). These tests can be obtained from well-known test-publishing companies, such as the California Test Bureau, Science Research Associates, Harcourt Brace, and Columbia University's Teachers College Press. Some commonly used tests (and the grades for which they are appropriate) are the California Short Form Test of Mental Ability (K–8), the Otis-Lennon Mental Ability Test (K–9), the Primary Mental Abilities Test (K–6), What I Like To Do (4–7), the California Test of Personality (K–8), and the Early School Personality Questionnaire (1–3).

Nonstandardized self-report techniques, such as autobiographical essays, diaries, and questionnaires, are other assessment techniques to help counselor and child client jointly participate in exploring the child's attitudes, self-esteem, and personal characteristics.

Some elementary school counselors prefer to use individual personality measures that involve drawings made by the child, such as the House-Tree-Person Test (H-T-P); Allan, 1988; Keat, 1974). In some instances, the counselor simply asks children to draw what they please and then have them tell stories about their pictures. The counselor may also ask children to draw pictures of their families.

An important distinction exists between testing for diagnostic purposes and testing for counseling. In the first case, diagnostic testing is done by the school psychologist to determine a child's learning or emotional disabilities and to help in administrative decisions about a child's placement in a school or other institution. In counseling, testing is done in confidence by counselors to help improve a child's self-understanding. Counselors use tests to help set counseling goals; to help the client make a decision, to help explore new areas of client interest, to facilitate counselor-client interactions, or to help prepare the client for future counseling sessions (see chap. 6).

Brief Counseling

Brief counseling, as discussed in chapters 5 and 9, is a method whereby the counselor meets with a client for a limited number of sessions to discuss specific problems the client is concerned about. This form of counseling seems particularly suited to elementary school counseling because conflicts of normally functioning individuals most obviously arise in school settings.

Intermittent brief counseling is particularly appropriate in elementary schools because counselors can see the same students off and on throughout the many years the students are there. Counselors can more easily follow up on their work with children, observe changes as they occur, and build on previous counseling contacts when new problems arise.

Mostert, Johnson, and Mostert (1997) explored the effectiveness of solution-focused brief counseling (SFBC) in counseling elementary students. They trained five elementary school counselors in SFBC to apply the approach to their work with clients who were having problems in school progress. They used various SFBC techniques as described in chapter 5, techniques that essentially complement student strengths, help students reframe negative attitudes, and help them make positive changes in behavior. All five counselors reported that this model was useful and efficient "not only with students, but also with parents, some of whom had been previously resistant to other therapeutic approaches" (p. 23).

Sources of Referral

Elementary school teachers generally refer more children for counseling than do secondary school teachers because they have the same children in class for most of the day for the entire school year. Elementary school teachers have a better opportunity to observe children's lack of motivation, can perceive children's uncertainties about themselves, and can often sense when children's home situations are not going well. They are more aware of children's withdrawal and more affected by children's nuisance behavior (e.g., constant fidgeting or getting out of their seats at the wrong times, lying, getting into fights). Stealing or other antisocial behavior can be observed more readily too.

Because elementary schools tend to be smaller than high schools, the principals and vice principals have more interactions with the children and the teachers. Elementary school administrators are more likely to refer children to counselors than are administrators in other schools.

If it becomes clear to children, even very young ones, that a counselor is available to them, they will begin to seek counseling on their own (Gibson et al., 1993). Administrators, teachers, and parents should encourage them to do so by letting them know that they can talk to their counselor if something is bothering them. Students who have had successful experiences with a counselor will often suggest that their friends see the counselor. It is also quite common for students to bring their friends with them to their counseling sessions because their friends need help.

Referrals also come from children and teachers as counselors make themselves more visible through informal classroom visits and by helping teachers present classroom units related to child development or mental health. Sometimes counselors teach the units themselves.

Counselors should recognize that some children who are nonverbal or resentful or whose ethnic background is different from their own may be reluctant or unwilling to see a counselor. Counselors must be visible to these children and approach them in noncoercive ways. A feeling of trust is more likely to grow under these circumstances than it would through either indifference or attempts to cajole, persuade, or force such children into counseling.

INDIVIDUAL COUNSELING: PRESENTING PROBLEMS OF ELEMENTARY SCHOOL CHILDREN

In 1968, Van Hoose perceived elementary school counseling objectives as "aiding children in (1) appropriate academic achievement, (2) furthering normal social and emotional development, (3) developing self-understanding, (4) acquiring realistic self-concepts, and (5) developing self-knowledge relative to the world of work" (pp. 98–99). In a similar vein, Ohlsen et al. (1988) specify children's needs or developmental tasks as gaining self-acceptance, gaining acceptance by significant others, loving and being loved, developing moral values, exploring career interests, coping with physical and emotional changes, clarifying sexual identity, and mastering basic learning skills.

Children's major concerns fall into three basic categories related to Erikson's (1963) psychosocial theory of development: "(1) conception of self; (2) interpersonal relations; and (3) how to gain and maintain control over their lives" (Gibson et al., 1993, p. 87).

Stern and Newland (1994) define both interpersonal and intrapersonal stressors among children. *Interpersonal stressors* result from conflicts or dysfunctions within and without the family. More specifically, the authors note that interpersonal stressors include such conditions as family divorce and family conflict, abuse, substance abuse, and homelessness. Other interpersonal stressors relate to peer conflicts, academic difficulties, and behavioral problems in school. *Intrapersonal stressors* center around children's feelings and attitudes about themselves—for example, lack of self-esteem, and confused sense of identity.

Vocational/Educational Problems: Exploration and Conflicts

Elementary school children are not likely to enter counseling with vocational concerns as the presenting problem unless the school goes to the eighth grade. During counseling sessions, however, while discussing relationships or parental expectations, children may reveal attitudes about work, occupational values, or occupational stereotypes. These discussions may contribute to children's awareness of the multiple factors in career choice and thus help the children toward more effective vocational planning in the future.

Pressure on young children about occupational choice is greater and more common than most people realize. Some adults push elementary school children to specify what they are going to be when they grow up. Counselors in these cases need to reduce the pressure by encouraging children to explore vocational options. Indeed, in these situations, dealing with parents' inappropriate pressure is usually more important than career exploration. Children may also be confused when parents express distaste for their own jobs or talk about occupations only in terms of social status.

Educational interests and abilities in earlier stages of development contribute to the vocational direction that children may take later. Their expressed interests and performance may also lead to premature parental expectations about choice of an occupation. At this stage of development, occupational stereotypes based on gender or on ethnic groups usually develop. These stereotypes cause conflict for a young child—male or female—who is showing interest in an area traditionally considered appropriate only for the other sex. Stereotyping also inhibits a young person from following natural inclinations in exploring vocational possibilities.

The concept that vocational development is part of total personality development and self-concept development has implications for elementary school counseling. Exploring and understanding one's interests, aptitudes, and values are processes that start early in life, and they should receive attention in elementary school.

Referrals for learning difficulties are usually more numerous in elementary schools than are referrals for vocational concerns. Like vocational concerns, these problems are often tied in with personal values and attitudes and interpersonal problems. Teachers tend to refer children who lack motivation to begin or complete work assignments or who are not working up to their estimated ability. Children may seek out a counselor and complain that they are bored with school or that they find the work too difficult.

The counselor can help children explore the reasons for their difficulties with schoolwork. Children may be feeling undue pressure from teachers or parents over quality of academic performance. Conversely, teachers or parents may not be paying sufficient attention to the child's work. The counselor can help a teacher determine whether a child is being expected to do work above her or his ability. If so, the teacher can modify expectations. The counselor can recommend referral to a school psychologist if the educational difficulty looks severe or puzzling enough to warrant psychological assessment for possible placement in a special education or learning disability class. If the home situation is contributing to lack of educational progress, family counseling might prove helpful. If the home situation is chaotic and children are suffering from neglect, a referral to a social worker is in order. In any case, the counselor might still continue counseling with the child or the family or both. The school psychologist or social worker and the counselor might work jointly with the child and the family.

Following are examples of problems students typically present to counselors and some possible approaches counselors could take:

Client 1: Allison is a fourth grader referred to you by her teacher because she is not working at the level her teacher believes she should. Allison has above-average ability and superior scores on reading and standardized achievement tests. She does not hand in assignments on time, is careless in her work, and generally acts bored. Allison is apparently willing to see you but seems uninterested during the first counseling session.

Client 2: Brett, a fifth grader, has asked the secretary for an appointment for counseling. When he comes in to see you, he tells you he is having trouble with mathematics and science units. He expresses little interest in them. His mother is a physicist and his father a biologist. Brett thinks they are disappointed in him. He prefers English, social sciences, and art.

Client 3: Billy is a second grader who is referred by his teacher because he does not seem to be able to comprehend the reading assignments in class. The teacher is dubious about his ability to learn second-grade material and wonders whether he belongs in a special education class. He is new in the school district, and no records of intellectual capacity or achievement are available.

Client 1: Allison has been referred by her teacher, so her motivation for counseling may be minimal. In this type of referral, I have found it helpful to clarify with the student why the referral was made, whether the student agrees with the teacher's appraisal, and whether the student believes that a problem exists. I would invite Allison to continue seeing me, but I would also tell her that she does not have to if she prefers not to. If she prefers not to continue with me, I would encourage her to see me whenever she felt she needed to. If she decides to continue, then we could discuss her classroom attitude, feelings, and behavior.

If Allison has difficulty expressing herself, I might use play media, such as free drawing or puppets, as a means of helping her relax and start talking with me. Her drawings or puppet play might give some clues to her feelings about herself and her interactions with others. If she talks freely, instead of using play media I would rely on client-centered listening to help her explore the reasons for her lack of interest in school.

Because her teacher made the referral, I would suggest to Allison that the teacher might find it useful to receive some feedback about our discussions. Allison and I could decide together what we would and would not share with the teacher. We would also determine whether Allison or I or both of us would talk with the teacher.

Client 2: In talking with Brett, it is important to help him first explore whether his belief concerning his parents' expectations about science is accurate. This exploration could include encouraging Brett to talk with his parents about their aspirations for him. Role playing a dialogue with his parents as a form of behavior rehearsal might be helpful. If his discussion with his parents indicated they would not be concerned if he did not follow scientific lines, the focus of my interviews would be on cognitive restructuring to clarify his expectations about himself. If, however, his parents proved to be set on his making top grades in mathematics and science, I would ask Brett whether it would be helpful for me to talk with them.

Client 3: Billy has been referred by his teacher for a psychological evaluation for the possibility of placing him in a special education class. The referral is inappropriate. It should have been made to the school psychologist after the teacher had consulted with the principal and obtained permission from the parents. The school psychologist is the learning specialist who is trained to make psychological evaluations and diagnoses.

Even though the referral was inappropriate, I would not immediately send Billy back to class. I would ask him whether he knew why the teacher had referred him to see me and how he felt about it. I would explain that the teacher wondered whether he was properly assigned to the right class because he is new at the school and no previous records are available. I would invite him to visit me if he wanted to talk over what was going on. In this way, I could serve as a resource to him and his parents, whether he is relocated or remains in the same class.

Personal Problems: Conflicts, Doubts, or Confusion

Children experience feelings of loneliness, inadequacy, rejection, and self-hate similar to those experienced by adolescents and adults. They have doubts about their intellectual ability and worry about their classroom or playground behavior. Some children express beliefs that they are dumb, unattractive, or worthless. Anger, disappointment, or bewilderment about themselves may be felt but not recognized or articulated. Counselors need to help children express, understand, and label these feelings and work toward more productive perceptions of themselves. Consider the following children:

Client 4: Ralph, a second grader, is referred by his teacher because he has difficulty in his interactions with other children. He is very sensitive to criticism and breaks into tears when students tease him or when the teacher corrects his work. The teacher has talked with the parents. The mother is overprotective and blames the teacher and other children for picking on Ralph. The father acts uninterested.

Client 5: Dave, a third-grader, sees you in an assembly and asks to see you in your office later in the day. When you see him, he tells you that he has been having bad dreams and that he gets stomachaches. His schoolwork is not going as well as he would like, and he is not making friends easily. His two older siblings have good academic records and seem socially secure. Dave has superior academic ability, but he calls himself dumb.

Client 4: Ralph may readily agree to talk with a counselor because he wants to do what he is asked and not risk disapproval. Because he may have strong feelings of inadequacy, however, he may find it difficult to open up about his negative feelings or impulses. At any rate, Ralph needs a non-evaluative, trusting relationship in which he can express his doubts about himself and his apprehensions about others' opinions. Play media may be useful during the sessions. I would help him explore whether his expectations and/or the expectations of his parents are unrealistic.

I would try to help Ralph become aware of and label his feelings when he cries. It is likely that his tears reflect unexpressed feelings of anger and frustration, as well as feelings of hurt and shame. If Ralph responds well, I may suggest that we arrange a conference with his parents.

Client 5: Dave apparently is undergoing depression and stress related to concerns about his capabilities and may be having some physical reactions to the pressure. As with any client expressing physical symptoms, I would recommend a medical examination to determine any physical basis for the stomachaches.

Dave has initiated counseling and is open about his concerns, so the chances of helping him are favorable. Some of Beck's techniques for breaking tasks into manageable units in which success is assured might prove helpful. Dave's teacher can cooperate in applying Beck's methods in the classroom (see chap. 5). Family consultation or counseling might be helpful.

Social Problems: Interpersonal Conflicts and Feelings of Social Inadequacy

A significant portion of referrals in elementary school result from children's problems in interactions with teachers, parents, and peers. Teachers may refer a child they constantly have to discipline. Friction may build up because of the distracting behavior of a child or a teacher's impatience or both. Teachers may be concerned by excessive shyness or may believe that a child's home situation is contributing to overdependence, nuisance behavior, or underachievement. Picking fights and calling others names are common ways for children to express their frustration and anger. Children may ask for counseling because they are unhappy, lonesome, or frustrated at school or home. Parental, sibling, or peer interactions may not be going well. Consider Carrie and Christie, for example:

> **Client 6:** Carrie, an eighth grader, comes to your office in tears. She has had a fight with her best friend. Now her friend is giving a party and has not invited her.

> **Client 7:** Christie, a third grader, runs up to you in the hallway during recess and asks to see you sometime during the day. When you see her later, she exclaims that she is both angry with, and afraid of, her teacher. She says that her teacher picks on her and blames her for things she did not do. The teacher also yells at the class, which upsets her.

> *Client 6:* Peer friction occurs frequently with children at this age and most often quickly disappears if adults do not complicate matters. If Carrie basically has good interpersonal relationships and this incident is simply a spat, I would listen sympathetically but not overreact. Carrie will probably figure out a way of resolving the conflict. If she is not invited to the party, I would help her deal with her feelings of disappointment.

> If Carrie has had persistent problems with her peers, I would explore what is contributing to the ongoing friction. Carrie might also benefit from group counseling with students who are having similar problems.

> *Client 7:* Christie presents a type of problem that requires the counselor to be diplomatic. If teachers perceive that counselors take the student's side in teacher-student conflicts, the staff will become resentful. If students perceive that a counselor is taking the teacher's side, they will probably avoid the counselor. The counselor's goal is to help improve relationships between teachers and students. This problem becomes difficult when a teacher tends to harass a child. If the teacher is not willing to consult with the counselor, the counselor may have to help the child learn strategies to minimize stress in that classroom.

> In Christie's situation, I would try to help decrease the friction. If the teacher is approachable and Christie has the ego strength, I would encourage her to discuss her concerns with the teacher. Role playing might prove useful. If Christie's behavior is contributing to the friction, I would ask her how she might change her behavior to improve the interaction.

Antisocial Behavior

Children's antisocial behavior includes stealing, defacing school property, truancy, breaking windows, cheating on tests, chronic lying, and hurting themselves or others. In the lower grades, throwing rocks at other children or at buildings or cars is a common problem. Drug or alcohol use may occur in the higher grades. When children seek out counselors to confess that they have been involved in antisocial behavior, the counselors do not necessarily turn the children over to authorities unless the children are dangerous to themselves or others. Counselors can then help the children control antisocial impulses and direct them into constructive avenues before these impulses overwhelm them. Also, if disciplinary action is not automatically meted out, other children with similar impulses would be more likely to see the counselor.

If children endanger themselves or others because of their behavior, the counselor is ethically bound to tell them that the family and other mental health professionals must be contacted so that they can get more intensive help. A case will clarify this:

Client 8: John, a fourth-grader, tells you he set a fire in the wastebasket in a lavatory. He was angry at a teacher and an administrator because he thought he was being treated unfairly. This was the first time he had set a fire. He immediately put it out. His own behavior scared him.

Client 8: Because John's behavior is not chronic and John is concerned about his own impulsive act, I would not report his behavior. I would work with him about his reasons for believing that he was treated unfairly and help him express his anger more constructively. If he has some justification for his feelings, I might arrange for a three-way conference with the teacher or administrator or both. I would explore with him his family dynamics to see whether his behavior was aggravated by poor family interactions.

If John expressed irresistible urges to set fires and had set other fires, I would discuss the need for him to receive more intensive help because that kind of behavior is potentially dangerous to others. I would contact his parents and arrange psychological or psychiatric consultation. I would still try to be a source of help to John both during and after his treatment.

Crises

Most children are faced with crises at one time or another, and some children are chronically in crises through no fault of their own. For young children, crises generally revolve around family disruptions—severe illness or death of a parent, divorce or threat of divorce, remarriage of a single parent, a parent's loss of a job, drug or alcohol abuse, or homelessness. Loss of a pet or loss of a close friend who suddenly moves away can also unduly disturb a child.

Counselors in elementary schools are often called on to work with children with diagnosed attention deficit disorder (ADD) or attention deficit hyperactive disorder (ADHD). Over 10% of children in schools (about 2 million) have ADD-ADHD. According to Erk (1995), "Counselors can be leaders in implementing multidisciplinary-multidimensional treatment for children or adolescents with ADD" (p. 295). They can coordinate the efforts of parents, school staff, and physicians; provide ADD-ADHD workshops for parents and school staff; and become advocates of ADD-ADHD children in the community. His multimodal list of interventions that counselors can use include individual and family counseling, creative arts therapy, parent education, and various types of training, such as self-esteem, social skills, and behavioral techniques, for students with ADD-ADHD.

In conjunction with these methods of treatment, Erk (1995) supports the use of Ritalin, a prescribed drug, to treat ADD-ADHD cases. Unfortunately, Erk does not mention the controversy surrounding the use of Ritalin. A growing number of health care professionals, such as psychiatrist Peter Breggin (1998), are alarmed at the unquestioned use of Ritalin without regard for serious side effects of the drug and for its long-term effects. Some are worried that teachers and counselors are encouraging its use to maintain order in classrooms. "Some parents, educators and doctors wonder if schools are encouraging students to take Ritalin because they need it or because it is easier to teach rambunctious kids if they are medicated" (Gannett News Service, 1998b, p. C1). The use of Ritalin in the United States has jumped in the past 5 years from 4.5 million to 11.4 million. As an alternative to using the drug to calm hyperactive children, Breggin suggests "de-stressing the environment—looking at ways the home, school and entertainment media may be promoting difficult behavior" (Gannett News Service, 1998a, p. C1).

Child abuse is reported more frequently in elementary school than in other counseling settings because of the teachers' close interactions with children. As indicated in chapter 3, counselors must report incidents of physical abuse, neglect, or sexual abuse. In cases where teachers discover and report abuse, counselors should not involve themselves in reporting the cases. They are freer, then, to work with the children who are traumatized by the experience and by the disruption caused when the abuse is revealed. Counselors can work with families in collaboration with community agencies to help them deal with the trauma.

Substance abuse, alarmingly, has reached elementary schools. "Substance abuse is not a problem of just the adult world or even the adult and adolescent world . . . it has already dramatically invaded the elementary school years as well" (Gibson et al., 1993, p. 103). A significant amount of pressure for elementary school children to drink alcohol comes from their peers (Roth & Friedman, 1987). Use of marijuana and other drugs also occurs at this level. Worse yet, often associated with substance abuse are extreme acts of violence, as discussed below.

The increasing numbers of elementary school children who have suicidal thoughts or who have threatened or attempted suicide have caused concern in elementary counseling circles. About 200 children younger than 14 years of age commit suicide each year (Herring, 1990). Elementary school counselors believe that family problems are the main cause of suicide attempts, followed by peer pressure (R. E. Nelson & Crawford, 1990).

Counselors need to be alert to signs of depression or suicidal thoughts of children. Standard suicidal interventions are discussed in chapter 7. Thompson and Rudolph (1992) offer detailed suggestions to counselors about how to assess the severity of depression. Parents need to be alerted to the problem, and the children should be seen by a counselor in the school or a professional therapist in the community.

During the 1990s, violence in schools escalated. Although more common in secondary schools, violence in the lower grades is increasingly being reported. The third leading cause of death of elementary and middle school children is homicide. Increasing numbers of children have been carrying weapons to school, and shootings both by outsiders and by schoolchildren are increasing. Elementary counselors must therefore be prepared to offer interventions to individuals, students, groups of students, the student body as a whole, and families.

Juhnke (1997) uses a critical incident stress debriefing (CISD) approach with elementary and middle school students suffering from postviolence emotional trauma after experiencing or witnessing a violent scene at school. Counselors first meet with parents to share feelings about the traumatic event and to introduce them to the debriefing process. Then they form joint sessions of parents and students with no more than five or six children and their parents at a time. Parents sit behind their child, sometimes putting their hands on their child's shoulders. A counselor then encourages each of the children to talk about what they remember and to express feelings as they experienced the trauma. The counselor then asks all the children to come together and share their memories and feelings about the event. Afterward, counselors arrange follow-up individual and group counseling for those who need it.

GROUP COUNSELING

Elementary school counselors offer more group counseling than do counselors in other settings (Ohlsen et al., 1988), and teachers have become increasingly aware of the value of group counseling (Wilgus & Shelley, 1988). Group counseling can be useful for children having conflicts with family or peers or whose shyness or aggressiveness interferes with social development (Ohlsen et al., 1988). Group counseling can also be effective for groups of children who are experiencing similar problems, such as anger control, grief, effects of divorce or single parenting, or alcohol and drug abuse (Gibson et al., 1993). Students having academic difficulties can also benefit from group counseling.

Group counseling methods and processes that are used for adults and adolescents apply to children as well (Ohlsen et al., 1988). But Ohlsen et al. (1988) caution that counselors must adapt techniques to fit the developmental stages of children. These authors emphasize the importance of listening to children and helping them learn to label their pain and feelings accurately and to communicate their needs and desires.

Because children have short attention spans and lack social maturity, Ohlsen and his colleagues (1988) recommend that children in primary school be scheduled for 20- to 25-minute group counseling sessions three times a week and that groups of upper grade elementary children be limited to 30 to 35 minutes twice a week.

Considerable interest in the problems of children of divorce is also shown in the literature. Results of three studies on the effects of group counseling with children of divorce showed a significant improvement in the following: (a) children's social adjustment (Tedder, Scherman, & Wantz, 1987); (b) their feelings about themselves (Omizo & Omizo, 1987); (c) their attitudes about divorce; and (d) their behavior in class (Anderson, Kinney, & Gerler, 1984).

Allan (1988) used a group creative drama approach (a form of psychodrama) for sixth and seventh graders who were chronically disruptive in classrooms. He and three graduate students were the facilitators for 30 students in separate groups of 7 or 8 children; each session lasted for 40 minutes, and the sessions ran for 7 months.

They helped each group improvise a drama, videotaping themselves as they went along. The process evolved over the months into a coherent story. This activity was based on the ideas that these children were desperate to be noticed, that excessive energy could be safely burned off, and that impulses and actions not usually permitted could be acted out, shared, and brought into consciousness. Similar to what happens during his "serial drawings," which were described earlier, Allan found that the ways in which groups expressed themselves evolved over time. In these series of psychodramas, the groups moved from chaotic behavior in the early stages of the project to organized, cooperative group experiences at the end of the 7 months. The dramas evolved from narcissistic, wild, exhibitionistic, and aggressive behavior to behavior showing consideration of others and expressions of moral and social concerns.

In evaluating this activity, facilitators thought that positive changes had occurred. Allan (1988) said, however, that the type of personal growth the children experienced through dramatization in a special setting was not immediately apparent in the regular classroom setting. He acknowledged that more work should be directed toward talking with teachers about the purpose of these groups and that more time should be spent preparing the children for reentry into the classroom.

⤞ OUTREACH

Outreach programs are designed to enhance the developmental processes for elementary school children. Some group guidance activities, such as building self-esteem, assertiveness training, career awareness, and values clarification, are tailored to personal growth. Others, such as communication skills, decision making in groups, cooperative problem solving, and making friends, are geared to social development. Both types of activities occur most frequently in classrooms, but counselors also offer them outside class for interested students.

Psychological Education

A popular activity used by counselors when they visit a classroom is *development understanding of self and others (DUSO)*. Using puppets, a counselor tells stories around eight themes, such as self-reliance, responsible choice making, and social responsibility. The puppets act out different stories relating to these themes. Discussion follows after each story (Baker & Shaw, 1987).

Counselors also use the *magic circle* in classrooms to help children become aware of feelings, gain mastery of their environment, and build social skills. Children sit in a circle and are encouraged to express both positive and negative feelings and to become aware of their impact on others.

Elementary school counselors, in line with good ethical practice, give children an option about participation and confine discussions to interactions in classrooms, rather than have children share private home problems. This ethical practice is wise for many reasons, including the fact that some programs are under fire by parents concerned about family rights to privacy.

Psychological education activities are also offered regarding child behaviors that are disruptive or destructive. J. R. Nelson, Dykeman, Powell, and Petty (1996) studied the effects of a group counseling intervention with elementary children with behavioral problems. They used a 3-step procedure. In Step 1, the purpose of the group was established. In Step 2, problems were identified by students with the help of counselors, and alternative solutions were generated. In Step 3, children were taught to monitor their own performance in school and to evaluate their improvement. Nelson et al. concluded: "The group counseling intervention resulted in clear and salutary changes in the behavioral adjustment of students" (p. 30).

In 1986, Myrick, Merhill, and Swanson studied the effects of classroom guidance activities with fourth-grade students in 67 elementary schools in Florida and 25 elementary schools in Indiana. On 13 of 20 items describing good classroom behavior, the experimental group scored higher than the control group not experiencing classroom guidance.

In a study using a life skills intervention program in two second-grade classes, Gilbert and Orlick (1996) found that children at very young ages can learn to relax and reduce stress. The classes met for 15- to 20-minute sessions for 9 consecutive weeks, learning how to control heartbeat and to relax. They used log books to record stressful experiences, coping and relaxation strategies, and their responses to stress before and after coping skills were used.

Career Development

Comprehensive career development programs proposed and funded by the National Occupational Information Coordinating Committee (NOICC) include career awareness at the elementary level. In this program, the counselor helps children become aware of their uniqueness, gives them a perspective about the role of work in society, and introduces a survey of the different occupations.

School counselors and teachers often work together to plan joint activities in the classroom that will provide career information and career self-awareness. Speakers from various occupational fields within the community may be invited to share their experiences. Field trips to local businesses may be used to supplement curriculum activities.

Social Change Activities

In elementary school, counselors can work on social changes that relate to gaps in communication between school and home or that relate to curriculum deficiencies. Sometimes these activities arise from children's complaints.

An example of helping individuals or groups become aware of their right to ask for change was given to me by an elementary school teacher. Her class complained regularly about the luncheon menu. She consulted with the counselor, who suggested that the class invite the cook to hear their complaints. The cook listened to the criticisms and explained the financial and staff limitations that were contributing to the problem. She did realize, however, that she could make some changes, and the relationship of the children with the cafeteria staff improved—as well as the menu.

When counselors gain respect from administrators, teachers, and the community, they are usually successful in having their suggestions for social change carried out. The counseling staff tend to be more successful if they begin with the assumption that administrators may be unaware they have an unfair or ineffective policy. In this way, social change becomes an educative process, rather than a pitched battle.

Consultation

Teachers in elementary schools who trust their counselors will often request consultations with them about classroom interactions with children. At times, the behavior centers on children; at times, on themselves. Following are two examples:

Teacher C: Mr. Colby, a sixth-grade teacher, complains about two disruptive children in his class. They talk out loud, answer insolently at times, and in general demonstrate rudeness and disrespect. The class laughs and becomes restless when these children act up. When one or the other or both are absent, the class works smoothly. Mr. Colby has had similar difficulties before. He prefers trying to change his behavior, rather than sending the children to the administrator for disciplinary action.

Teacher F: Mr. Fletcher drops into the counselor's office and sits down heavily. He appears to be a highly perceptive teacher but a little unsure of himself. He is being evaluated for tenure. His administrator visited his class and afterward told him that he is well organized but too distant with students. The administrator recommended that he be more outgoing and friendly—characteristics of the administrator's behavior. Mr. Fletcher senses some need to be more approachable to students but cannot see himself emulating the effervescent administrator.

Teacher C: Mr. Colby can be shown how to set limits with disruptive students and can be given guidelines on how to stick with the limits. He can be encouraged to confront students with their behavior and to set up some agreement or contract about what is acceptable classroom behavior.

Teacher F: The counselor should support Mr. Fletcher's reluctance to emulate another personality. Discussion of the reasons for his uncertainty about his professional ability and suggestions about how he can capitalize on his sensitivity to students' needs may lead him to become more approachable to students.

Liaison with Community

School counselors should develop close ties with community mental health and counseling agencies. In particular, elementary school counselors need to be aware of resources available for family and marriage counseling when problems that come to their attention are beyond the scope of services the school can offer. When a child demonstrates serious emotional difficulties or when a severe crisis leaves a child with lingering emotional problems, a referral for outside counseling is usually in order. By knowing the community's facilities, counselors will be ready when they need to report child abuse and make arrangements for cooperative efforts of treatment. They will also be better able to arrange joint outreach programs in drug education, suicide prevention, and parenting skills.

One such example is the development of a unique partnership between two elementary schools in Maryland and the Department of Counseling and Human Services at Johns Hopkins University in Manford (Keep & Bemak, 1997). The program was developed in economically disadvantaged communities with high crime rates "as a way of addressing issues of violence and aggression within the school and community" (Keep & Bemak, 1997, p. 259). A mental health team was formed, including persons from school, family, and community. Johns Hopkins faculty provided training and consultation to elementary counselors and to community participants who jointly identified student and family problems and developed cohesive prevention programs.

ADDRESSING MULTICULTURAL DIVERSITY

Special considerations for counseling ethnic groups are discussed in chapter 14. Ethnic children, especially, face many difficulties when attending a school whose student body and teachers are predominantly White middle class or when attending a school where most of the other children are from ethnic groups other than theirs. Language barriers and barriers attributed to differing family and cultural values and expectations especially affect young children.

Although it would be ideal if representative ethnic counselors served each of the various ethnic groups in every school, it's not fully possible. Counselors must develop resources to bridge the gap between cultural differences among the counselors and teachers and the schoolchildren and their families. They should have available bilingual interpreters from the community and consult regularly with respected members from various ethnic neighborhood communities.

Several authors have written or edited books on multicultural counseling that include discussions about counseling ethnic children, along with case examples (e.g., Baruth & Manning, 1999; Lee, 1995). Courtland Lee (1995), an African American counselor, edited a book whose contributors include various ethnic counselors—African American, Asian, Arab, Hispanic, and Native American. For example, Jesse Zapata (1995) describes the case of an 8-year-old immigrant Mexican boy, usually a good student, who stopped doing his schoolwork and whose attendance fell. After attempting to discipline the boy and trying to contact his home, to no avail, the teacher referred the boy to the counselor. After talking with the boy, asking about his parents, the counselor learned that the boy's mother had left him with his aunt, who spoke no English and who had returned to Mexico to attend her mother's funeral for 2 weeks. She also had taken along her older son, who usually acted as the interpreter for the family. The consultant from the Hispanic neighborhood was able to help the counselor and teacher understand that it was quite normal, in this cultural situational context, for the mother to do this. The counselor and the teacher arranged for an interpreter to work with the family during this time and for a tutor for the boy to help him catch up.

✍ WORKING WITH FAMILIES

Family Consultation

Although professionals in school counseling differ on the degree to which elementary school counselors should be involved in family counseling, all agree that effective counselor-family interaction is crucial. The recent emphasis on child development's link to the family's particular dynamics is especially pertinent to elementary school counselors. Young children are still in a relatively formative stage, so dysfunctional patterns have not fully crystallized and preventive work is possible. Remedial work is not as complex as it is when working with dysfunctional adults.

Counselors trained in family systems therapy effectively serve as consultants in elementary schools to work with school counselors and families. Counselors in a consultant role can meet with a family a few times and suggest strategies the parents might take. A follow-up consultation can be carried out by telephone. If it is apparent that family counseling is needed, a referral can be made (Dinkmeyer & Dinkmeyer, 1984; Strother & Jacobs, 1986). Amatea and Fabrick (1984) also present strategies useful for referrals to community family agencies, including collecting information about a problem, making a decision about referral, implementing the referral, and doing a case follow-up.

Family Counseling

Most elementary school counselors are trained to do family counseling in the schools. Families feel less threatened by professionals in schools than by those in community agencies. Moreover, counselors can make personal observations of a child's ongoing behavior in school that are not possible for therapists in community agencies. Also, free service in schools makes counseling available to everyone regardless of income. Nicoll (1984) recommends training counselors in the Dreikurs/Adlerian model of family counseling (now more often known as Adlerian; see chap. 10) because it emphasizes an educational model in which educational, informational, and parenting skills are paramount.

Baker (1996) stresses the necessity of family counseling in public schools because of the diminishing number of stable, intact families: "Intact traditional families have declined in number, and counselors find themselves working more and more with children and adolescents whose issues seem to require interventions that involve working with other members of the family" (p. 72).

Golden (1988) proposes that elementary school counselors do short-term family counseling and refer dysfunctional family cases elsewhere. Using the *quick assessment of family functioning*, he assesses parental strengths, determines whether the child's problem is chronic, observes the quality of communication among family members, and determines degree of parental authority and amount of rapport. If the family is functioning fairly well, he uses a Dreikurs/Adlerian approach with them. Otherwise, he refers the family to a community agency or family specialist.

Brief family counseling is recommended in elementary schools when children show behavioral or attitudinal problems in school that result from crises at home (Amatea, 1989; Hinkle, 1993; Peeks, 1993). Hinkle (1993) and Peeks (1993) recommend that elementary counselors be trained in brief family counseling based on a family systems approach and focused on short-term problems. Such counselors would be able to assess the severity of a problem and a family's strengths and willingness to change, and then determine whether to work with the family or refer the family elsewhere for longer, more intensive counseling.

A family systems approach has proved helpful in resolving conflicts within a family or between a family and school staff, conflicts that interfere with a student's progress in school. Kraus (1998) presents a case study describing a brief-problem-focused family counseling approach used with an 11-year-old boy and his parents. The boy was refusing to do schoolwork and was being aggressive with other students. Kraus concluded, "It is evident that the possibility of behavior change has improved over the other interventions used" (p. 15).

Another family systems approach, one that combines Haley's strategic therapy and Minuchen's structural approach (see chap. 10), has been described by Cerlo (1997) regarding school-phobic elementary school students. In this approach, school counselors meet with the nuclear family, have each member define the problem, and reframe the problem in more positive ways. They then work to disengage the overinvolved, overanxious parent and to engage the underinvolved parent. Parents are then encouraged to present a united front. Interventions that address child symptoms and parental anxiety are then introduced.

Parent Education

Elementary and middle school counselors offer training in parenting skills to groups of parents in basically functional families. Parent Effectiveness Training (PET; Gordon, 1975) and Systematic Training for Effective Parenting (STEP; Dinkmeyer, 1976), an Adlerian approach, are most common. Parents meet weekly for a school semester to discuss mutual problems of discipline or communication and to learn techniques in child rearing. Some schools offer similar classes for single parents, divorced parents, or parents who are recovering alcoholics.

Conroy and Mayer (1994) developed a 2-year parent education program in a primary school in Durham, North Carolina. During the first year, groups of parents met with a counselor for six sessions to discuss how the parents could help their children become more responsible and cooperative in school and at home. In the second year, through a series of evening meetings, parents discussed ways to discipline children appropriately and, at the same time, build their self-esteem. During this time, a parent resource library was available for their use. A majority of parents believed that the program had improved their parenting skills, with consequent positive changes in their children's behavior at home and at school.

⇒ SUMMARY

Duties of elementary school counselors are similar to those of counselors in other settings, except that counselors in elementary schools do more consultation with parents, families, and teachers and are more involved with crisis cases.

Counselors use special techniques, such as play media and storytelling, with nonverbal children to increase child openness and spontaneity. Psychological education activities are conducted more frequently in classrooms in elementary schools than in other educational settings. These activities focus on building self-esteem, improving personal growth, and learning communication skills. Confidentiality and rights of privacy should be honored with children in elementary schools to maintain their trust and to help them increase feelings of self-involvement in counseling. Brief intermittent counseling is well suited for elementary school counselors. Elementary school counselors have been increasing their attention to multicultural counseling and to family counseling and consultation.

⇒ PROJECTS AND ACTIVITIES

1. Interview elementary school counselors, school psychologists, and school social workers who are working in the same school district. How does each group perceive its unique responsibilities? How well do the various specialists work together?

2. A teacher tells a counselor that she wants to talk to him about a child in her class who is in counseling. The counselor explains that he wants to obtain permission from the child in order to preserve confidentiality. Later, the principal tells the counselor that the teacher is upset because he acted as though she could not be trusted. Consider how this situation could be handled to preserve confidentiality and yet not antagonize the teacher.

3. Assume that a new counselor is meeting with a group of teachers to discuss her role and to suggest guidelines for referral. A teacher tells the counselor that he is confused about to whom he should refer children who are creating discipline problems. He asks the counselor when he should refer a child to the principal

and when he should refer to the counselor. How should the counselor respond?

4. Suppose that Ralph (Client 4) has a teacher who you believe is hypercritical, but the teacher is unaware of her behavior. How might you involve the teacher to improve the classroom environment for Ralph and the other students in the class?

5. Invite an elementary school counselor and a counselor working with children in a community agency to talk with your group about the types of children's concerns with which they work. Ask them to discuss their use of play media.

6. You are asked to talk at a PTA meeting about your role as an elementary counselor. Outline what you believe would be important considerations to include. Compare your ideas with the role definitions presented in this book.

7. Compose a memo that could be sent to parents at the beginning of the academic year that defines your role and duties as a counselor. In the memo, include confidentiality

and freedom of choice as important components in counseling.

8. With another student, role-play your initial interchange with Allison (Client 1) as she walks into your office as a willing but uninterested referral.

REFERENCES

Allan, J. (1988). *Inscapes of the child's world: Jungian counseling in schools and clinics.* Dallas, TX: Spring.

Amatea, E. S. (1989). *Brief strategic intervention for school behavior problems.* San Francisco: Jossey-Bass.

Amatea, E. S., & Fabrick, F. (1984). Moving a family into therapy: Critical referral issues for the school counselor. *School Counselor, 31,* 285–294.

Anderson, R. F., Kinney, J., & Gerler, E. R., Jr. (1984). The effects of divorce groups on children's classroom behavior and attitudes toward divorce. *Elementary School Guidance and Counseling, 19,* 70–76.

Baker, S. (1996). *School counseling for the 21st century.* Upper Saddle River, NJ: Merrill/Prentice Hall.

Baker, S. B., & Shaw, M. C. (1987). *Improving consultation through primary prevention.* New York: Macmillan.

Baruth, L. G., & Manning, M. L. (1999). *Multicultural counseling and psychotherapy: A lifespan perspective* (2nd ed.). Upper Saddle River, NJ: Merrill/Prentice Hall.

Breggin, P. (1998). *Talking back to Ritalin: What doctors aren't telling you about stimulants for children.* Monroe, MA: Common Courage Press.

Carter, S. R. (1987). Use of puppets to treat traumatic grief: A case study. *Elementary School Guidance and Counseling, 21,* 210–215.

Cerlo, J. (1997). School phobia: A family systems approach. *Elementary School Guidance and Counseling, 31,* 180–191.

Cochran, J. L. (1996). Using play and art therapy to help culturally diverse students overcome barriers to school success. *School Counselor, 43,* 287–298.

Conroy, E., & Mayer, S. (1994). Strategies for consulting with parents. *Elementary School Guidance and Counseling, 29,* 60–66.

Conti, A. (1971). A follow-up study of families referred to outside agencies. *Psychology in the Schools, 8,* 338–340.

Dinkmeyer, D. (1976). *Systematic training for effective parenting.* Circle Pines, MN: American Guidance Service.

Dinkmeyer, D., & Dinkmeyer, D. (1984). School counselors as consultants in primary prevention programs. *Personnel and Guidance Journal, 62,* 464–466.

Erikson, E. H. (1950). *Childhood and society.* New York: Norton.

Erikson, E. H. (1963). *Childhood and society* (2nd ed.). New York: Norton.

Erk, R. R. (1995). A diagnosis of attention deficit disorder: What does it mean for school counselors? *School Counselor, 42,* 292–299.

Franks, J. C. (1983). Children. In J. A. Brown & R. H. Pate, Jr. (Eds.), *Being a counselor* (pp. 195–206). Monterey, CA: Brooks/Cole.

Gannett News Service. (1998a, March 12). Psychiatrist criticizes rising use of Ritalin on children. *Bellingham Herald,* p. C1.

Gannett News Service. (1998b, March 19). Ritalin worries parents, educators. *Bellingham Herald,* p. C1.

Gibson, R. L., Mitchell, M. A., & Basile, S. K. (1993). *Counseling in the elementary school: A comprehensive approach.* Boston: Allyn & Bacon.

Gilbert, J. N., & Orlick, T. (1996). Evaluation of a life skills program with Grade 2 children. *Elementary School Guidance and Counseling, 31,* 139–151.

Gladding, S. T. (1987). Poetic expression: A counseling art in elementary schools. *Elementary School Guidance and Counseling, 21,* 307–311.

Gladding, S. T. (1992). *Counseling as an art: The creative arts in counseling.* Alexandria, VA: American Counseling Association.

Golden, L. B. (1988). Quick assessment of family functioning. *School Counselor, 35,* 179–184.

Gordon, T. (1975). *Parent effectiveness training.* New York: New American Library.

Hardesty, P. H., & Dillard, J. M. (1994). The role of elementary school counselors compared with their middle and secondary school counterparts. *Elementary School Guidance and Counseling, 29,* 83–91.

Herring, R. (1990). Suicide in the middle school: Who said kids will not? *Elementary School Guidance and Counseling, 25,* 129–137.

Hinkle, J. S. (1993). Training school counselors to do family counseling. *Elementary School Guidance and Counseling, 27,* 252–258.

James, R. K., & Myer, R. (1987). Puppet: The elementary school counselor's right or left arm. *Elementary School Guidance and Counseling, 21,* 292–299.

Johnson, L., McLeod, E. H., & Fall, M. (1997). Play therapy with labeled children in the schools. *Professional School Counseling, 1,* 31–34.

Juhnke, G. A. (1997). After school violence: An adapted critical incident stress debriefing model for student survivors and their parents. *Elementary School Guidance and Counseling, 31,* 163–170.

Keat, D. (1990a). Change in child multimodal counseling. *Elementary School Guidance and Counseling, 24,* 248–262.

Keat, D. (1990b). *Child multimodal therapy.* Norwood, NJ: Ablex.

Keat, D. B. (1974). *Fundamentals of child counseling.* Boston: Houghton Mifflin.

Keep, S. G., & Bemak, F. (1997). School-family-community linked services: A school counseling role for changing times. *School Counselor, 44,* 255–263.

Kestenbaum, C. J. (1985). The creative process in child psychotherapy. *American Journal of Psychotherapy, 39,* 479–489.

Kraus, I. (1998). A fresh look at school counseling: A family system approach. *Professional School Counseling, 1,* 12–17.

Landreth, G. L. (1987). Play therapy: Facilitative use of child's play in elementary school counseling. *Elementary School Guidance and Counseling, 21,* 253–261.

Lazarus, A. A. (1989). Multimodal therapy. In R. J. Corsine & D. Wedding (Eds.), *Current psychotherapies* (4th ed., pp. 503–544). Itasca, IL: F. E. Peacock.

Lee, C. C. (Ed.). (1995). *Counseling for diversity: A guide for school counselors and related professionals.* Boston: Allyn & Bacon.

Moreno, J. L. (1946). *Psychodrama.* Beacon, NY: Beacon Press.

Mostert, D. L., Johnson, E., & Mostert, M. P. (1997). The utility of solution-focused brief counseling and schools: Potential from an initial study. *Professional School Counseling, 1,* 21–24.

Myrick, R. D. (1997). *Developmental guidance and counseling: A practical approach* (3rd ed.). Minneapolis, MN: Educational Media.

Myrick, R. D., Merhill, H., & Swanson, L. (1986). Changing student attitudes through classroom guidance. *School Counselor, 33,* 244–252.

Nelson, J. R., Dykeman, C., Powell, S., & Petty, D. (1996). The effects of group counseling intervention on students with behavioral adjustment problems. *Elementary School Guidance and Counseling, 31,* 21–33.

Nelson, R. E., & Crawford, B. (1990). Suicide among elementary school-aged children. *Elementary School Guidance and Counseling Journal, 25,* 123–128.

Nicoll, W. C. (1984). School counselors as family counselors: A rationale and training model. *School Counselor, 10,* 279–284.

Ohlsen, M. M., Horne, A. M., & Lawe, C. F. (1988). *Group counseling* (3rd ed.). New York: Holt, Rinehart & Winston.

Omizo, M. M., & Omizo, S. A. (1987). Group counseling with children of divorce: New findings. *Elementary School Guidance and Counseling, 22,* 46–52.

Peeks, B. (1993). *Revolutions in counseling and education: A system perspective in schools, 27,* 245–251.

Piaget, J., & Inhelder, B. (1969). *The psychology of the child.* New York: Basic Books.

Roth, P., & Friedman, L. (1987). Alcohol use among youths. *Educational Horizons, 65,* 121–124.

Stern, M., & Newland, L. M. (1994). Working with children: Providing a framework for the roles of counseling psychologists. *Counseling Psychologist, 22,* 402–425.

Strother, J., & Jacobs, E. (1986). Parent consultation: A practical approach. *School Counselor, 33,* 292–296.

Tedder, S. L., Scherman, A., & Wantz, R. A. (1987). Effectiveness of a support group for children of divorce. *Elementary School Guidance and Counseling, 22,* 102–109.

Thompson, C. L., & Rudolph, L. B. (1992). *Counseling children* (2nd ed.). Pacific Grove, CA: Brooks/Cole.

Tumas, J. (1989). Mental health services for children: The state of the art. *American Psychologist, 44,* 188–189.

Van Hoose, W. H. (1968). *Counseling in the elementary schools.* Itasca, IL: F. E. Peacock.

Wilgus, E., & Shelley, V. (1988). The role of the elementary-school counselor: Teacher perspectives, expectations, and actual functions. *School Counselor, 4,* 259–266.

Zapata, J. T. (1995). Counseling Hispanic children. In C. C. Lee (Ed.), *Counseling for diversity: A guide for school counselors and related professionals* (pp. 85–108). Boston: Allyn & Bacon.

17 Counseling Programs in Secondary Schools

Adolescents face developmental transitional challenges in which they struggle with their identities, make important educational and career decisions, develop intimate peer relationships, and try to become more independent and self-sufficient (Erikson, 1968; Steinberg, 1993). Because adolescents spend most of their waking hours in school, school personnel have considerable impact on their lives.

Having a well-trained staff of counselors in secondary schools is essential. Yet, counselors have been slower in establishing professional counseling services in the secondary schools than in colleges.

The first counselor role definitions and training standards for secondary school counselors as we know them today were developed in the early 1960s by APGA (ACA) and ASCA (see chap. 2). In contrast with the earlier advice-giving guidance role that prevailed in the years before World War II, these standards defined counselor role as nonjudgmental and client-centered as the counselor helps the client work through developmental, situational concerns. Since that time, these standards have served as guidelines for role definitions and training standards for counselors in all specialty areas.

In the early post-war decades, secondary school counselors had difficulty implementing effective counseling programs largely because significant numbers of counselors were not adequately trained and because administrators, parents, and teachers were resistant and confused about counselor roles. Counselors were burdened with personnel, administrative, and clerical tasks, which took precedence over counseling and counseling-related guidance activities (Nugent, 1981; Partin, 1993; Tennyson, Miller, Skovolt, & Williams, 1989).

✿ CURRENT STATUS AND WORK SETTING

In recent years, increasing numbers of certified, master's-level school counselors have had comprehensive training in developmental and family systems theories and have acquired a broader understanding of multicultural and gender issues. Increasing numbers of secondary school counselors are more involved in professional counseling and counseling-related activities and less involved in administrative and clerical duties (Hutchinson, Barrick, & Groves, 1986; Peer, 1985; Wiggins & Moody, 1987). Even so, leading counselor educators continue to emphasize the need for secondary school counselors to reduce administrative and personnel duties (S. B. Baker, 1996; Gysbers & Henderson, 1994).

Recently, counselors have been spending considerable time in crisis intervention. To alleviate this burden, counseling staffs in many schools are networking with community crisis intervention programs. High school counselors have also significantly expanded career development programs because of funding during the 1990s from federal and state grants.

Finding suitable times to counsel students who are assigned to classes throughout the school day is a problem still confronting secondary schools. Greer and Richardson (1992) tried a flexible scheduling model in a rural high school with four counselors. Instead of working the traditional hours of 9:00 a.m. to 3:00 p.m., some counselors worked from 12:00 p.m. to 7:00 p.m. or from 10:00 a.m. to 5:00 p.m. on certain days of the week (see Figure 17.1). The reactions of students, teachers, and parents were positive. Counselors saw more students and parents than when they worked the traditional hours. Parental contacts increased 62% during the first 6 months of the new schedule.

Many schools have directors of counseling who administer the counseling program, supervise new counselors and counseling interns, and deal with crises. Secretarial and clerical help is often available to the counseling staff (Gysbers & Henderson, 1994).

A minimum of 1 counselor to 300 high school students is recommended by the American School Counselor Association (ASCA). This ratio is optimal when the following other resources exist: (a) psychological specialists and community resources; (b) a registrar who deals with registration, scheduling, and student activities; and (c) career guidance specialists and substance abuse counselors who supplement the counseling staff. A few school districts in Washington State have hired registrars to oversee and manage student personnel work to free counselors for counseling.

Counselors require separate soundproof offices for confidential counseling and consultation. Counseling facilities are best placed away from administrative offices. This separation makes clear to students and teachers the distinction between referrals of students to administrators regarding student records and disciplinary action and referrals of students to counselors for help with personal concerns or decisions or academic-related problems or questions.

Effective counselors encourage students to ask for counseling on their own. They also make their services well known. They visit classrooms, publicize their services in a brochure or school newspaper, and otherwise make themselves visible to faculty, students, and parents. In this way, teachers, administrators, parents, and students become valuable referral sources because they understand the nature and availability of counseling services.

FIGURE 17.1
Sample schedule.

Source: Reprinted from "Restructuring the Guidance Delivery System: Implications for High School Counselors," by R. M. Greer & M. D. Richardson. *The School Counselor, 40,* 1992, p. 96. © ACA. Reprinted with permission. No further reproduction authorized without written permission of the American Counseling Association.

COUNSELOR A	
Monday	7 A.M.–2 P.M.
Tuesday	12 P.M.–7 P.M.
Wednesday	10 A.M.–5 P.M.
Thursday	8 A.M.–3 P.M.
Friday	8 A.M.–3 P.M.
COUNSELOR B	
Monday	8 A.M.–3 P.M.
Tuesday	7 A.M.–2 P.M.
Wednesday	12 P.M.–7 P.M.
Thursday	10 A.M.–5 P.M.
Friday	8 A.M.–3 P.M.
COUNSELOR C	
Monday	10 A.M.–5 P.M.
Tuesday	8 A.M.–3 P.M.
Wednesday	7 A.M.–2 P.M.
Thursday	12 P.M.–7 P.M.
Friday	10 A.M.–5 P.M.
COUNSELOR D	
Monday	12 P.M.–7 P.M.
Tuesday	12 P.M.–5 P.M.
Wednesday	8 A.M.–3 P.M.
Thursday	7 A.M.–2 P.M.
Friday	10 A.M.–5 P.M.

COUNSELING ADOLESCENTS: THEORIES AND TECHNIQUES

Student Developmental Needs

According to Erikson's psychosocial developmental theory, individuals go through eight developmental stages throughout their life span (see Table 4.1 in chap. 4). In adolescence, young people go through the fifth stage, during which they develop a sense of identity. Adolescents are searching for an *identity* that will enhance their feelings of self-esteem, as well as provide reassurance from others that they are valued. This stage serves as a bridge between the childhood and adult stages. Individuals must have adequately worked through and integrated challenges confronting them in earlier stages—basic *trust* in others, feeling of *autonomy,* sense of *achievement,* developing *initiative*—to be ready to develop a sense of identity in adolescence. A strong identity prepares them for the next stage, which requires that individuals develop love, *intimacy,* and caring. "The emerging ego identity, then, bridges the early childhood stages, when the body and the parent images were given their specific meanings, and the later stages, when a variety of social roles becomes available and increasingly coercive" (Erikson, 1980, p. 96).

The adolescent period is an especially appropriate time to continue to work through challenges posed in earlier stages. Building *trust* relationships involves developing caring connections with others. Strengthening feelings of *autonomy* involves persons becoming more independent, more responsible, more capable of making decisions, and more certain of the values that will shape their lives. Striving for *achievement* involves building skills and competencies necessary to function effectively in a complex, diverse, high-tech world. Taking *initiative* to explore and evaluate interests and capabilities helps develop purpose.

Feminist developmental theorists, including Gilligan (1982), Conarton and Silverman (1988), and Jordan, Kaplan, Miller, Stiver, and Surrey (1991), have taken issue with Erikson's model as a description of women's stages of development (see chaps. 4 and 5). Particularly at the adolescent stage, they claim, a girl's natural pattern of development goes unrecognized. Having to follow the male model of separation and autonomy that Erikson describes in order to compete, adolescent girls begin to feel thwarted, confused, and defeated.

Tests and Inventories

The complex and shifting labor market and the spiraling costs of college degrees pose additional problems for high school students. Innumerable tests are available to help students explore their career interests and aptitudes. Because career exploration is an important developmental task, interest inventories, aptitude tests, and personality measures are important counselor tools. These tests and inventories are described in chapter 6, along with cautions about their limitations.

Briefly, the Kuder Occupational Interest Survey (KOIS) is used in early high school, and the Strong Interest Inventory (SCII) is used in upper high school grades. Holland's Self-Directed Search (SDS) is applicable throughout high school. The Differential Aptitude Test (DAT), the Armed Services Vocational Aptitude Battery (ASVAB), and the General Aptitude Test Battery (GATB) are most often part of career exploration. Personality measures include the California Psychological Inventory (CPI), the Personality Orientation Inventory (POI), the Tennessee Self-Concept Scale, the Junior and Senior High School Personality Questionnaire, and the Mooney Problem Checklist.

Brief Counseling

Secondary school settings, like elementary schools and colleges, are well suited for brief counseling approaches that are limited in the number of sessions and based on intermittent counseling that can occur whenever problems arise. Myrick (1997) says, "More brief counseling or short-term counseling theories need to be developed and applied to school counseling" (p. 159). Brief counseling approaches that Amatea and Sherrard (1991) recommend for use in elementary school counseling are appropriate for secondary schools as well (see chap. 16).

Downing and Harrison (1992) recommend using a solution-focused, brief counseling approach in secondary schools: "Solution focused counseling fits into the time-conscious atmosphere of school counseling. . . . The basic orientation of this approach is positive and thus has great appeal for school use" (p. 331). In solution-focused counseling, clients are helped to specify the nature of their problem and to focus on goals they wish to attain to resolve their problem. They are then asked to look for a positive example in their lives in which they have been able to resolve a similar type of problem. Downing and Harrison give the example of an adolescent girl who complains that her parents are too strict about her dating. She is asked to think of a time when she successfully changed her parents' attitudes. Making use of previous positive experiences related to the problem and reinforcing client strengths, the counselor helps the client find ways to resolve the difficulty.

In my experience as a high school counselor, short-term intermittent counseling is particularly effective in school settings: Student concerns are focused on schoolwork; students miss fewer classes; and counselors are able to see students intermittently during the several years the students are in school.

➢ INDIVIDUAL COUNSELING: PRESENTING PROBLEMS OF HIGH SCHOOL STUDENTS

Secondary school counselors generally follow the individual counseling process described in chapter 9. A trusting relationship is established between client and counselor, in which the student client explores the nature of his or her problem, gains new insights, and takes steps to help resolve the problem. In their struggle for identity and independence, adolescents respond to adults with ambivalence, fears, suspicion, and rebellion. With this age-group, counselors should expect transference, resistance, and countertransference.

When problems are seen in the context of normal developmental growth that adolescents experience during this major transitional stage, counselors understand where the adolescent client is coming from. Seen in this context, the counselor can help bridge the gap that usually exists between adolescents and adults.

Adolescents who come in for counseling have value conflicts and confusions regarding who they are, what they want to be, and how to relate to others in an increasingly complex and rapidly changing society. Changes in family patterns and values contribute to their uncertainties. Peer pressures to drink or to take drugs are increasing. In a world of uncertainty, where job security is lacking, they see adults constantly anxious about losing their jobs, making ends meet, meeting rising costs of education, and obtaining adequate and affordable health care for their families.

Many adolescents come from single-parent families or suffer from domestic violence and alcohol drug abuse. Many are homeless; some have no parents. Ethnic adolescents have further complications from stereotyping and prejudicial treatment and lack of understanding from other cultural groups.

In much of the counseling literature and the media, the adolescent's most extreme problems are emphasized—alcohol and drug abuse, teenage pregnancy, depression, suicide, and violence. These important issues are discussed later in the chapter. In the following cases, the emphasis is on the normal troublesome areas of adolescent development that occur during this major transitional stage, areas that relate to career/educational, personal, and interpersonal issues.

Career/Educational Exploration and Conflicts

Students in secondary school put top priority on vocational or career exploration and choice. They are approaching the time when they must become financially independent and in so doing try to find a suitable and satisfying job or decide on and prepare for a challenging career or life work. After high school, approximately two-thirds of students will enter the labor market. The other one third will either go to college or to vocational school. While in high school, they must decide on the institutions to which they will apply and the kind of training they wish to begin.

Decisions about occupational choice or education beyond high school are more complicated than they were a few decades ago. Male students then were expected to be preoccupied with their careers because they were perceived as the primary breadwinners. Relatively few women pursued careers. The women's movement has helped change this pattern. Many women now prepare themselves for suitable jobs, whether they plan to marry or not. More complex choices about occupational and family roles of both men and women must now be made.

More career avenues have opened for minority groups. These increased options can lead to more productive and satisfying lives, but they can also lead to conflicts as new patterns replace old stereotypes. The opportunity may involve upheaval in personal relationships if individuals select options that displease people close to them. Life can become more fulfilling but also filled with more anxiety.

Career counseling is a complex process that is interwoven with total personality development and is part of total lifestyle. Students generally present their questions about vocational/career or educational plans in one of three ways: (a) They may ask for vocational/career information, (b) they may present a conflict they have with others over vocational choice, or (c) they may want to resolve some self-conflict or confusion regarding two or more occupational plans.

Career Exploration

Consider the students' concerns and approaches in the following examples:

Client 1: Gail, a sophomore, pops her head in at your door and asks for an appointment. She is trying to work out her junior year program. Her grades are very good, and she likes all subjects. She says she wants to go to college but is not sure what career to consider. She would like to explore interests and aptitudes to get some ideas about vocational direction.

Client 2: Aaron is perplexed. He is a freshman trying to decide whether to take a college preparatory curriculum or to look for apprenticeships and attend a technical school. He enjoys drafting and machine shop. He has discussed the question with his industrial arts teacher, who has given him some occupational information and recommended that Aaron talk with you.

Attempts would be made in these interviews to help the students consider and explore their perceptions about themselves and the world of work, their values about work, and the lifestyles they imagine for themselves. The counselor explores with the students their parents' views about their future. The degree to which parents support student plans and the degree of proposed financial support often determine the direction students will take.

The counselor may then suggest that the students take standardized interest inventories and aptitude tests if further exploration is necessary. I would refrain from introducing tests too quickly to allow students to explore their own feelings, attitudes, and values regarding career aspirations. In this way, students are less likely to depend on tests to provide all the answers.

Client 1: Gail appears likely to be highly responsive to tests; she may even ask for them. Her question relates to a general career exploration, so a KOIS and a DAT battery would be appropriate. If the personal and test data bring up exploratory career patterns, Gail could be given occupational reading about these occupations. If not, she would be encouraged to look into a variety of courses and be asked to return for more career consideration at a later date.

Client 2: I would probably not bring up tests and occupational material with Aaron right away. It would be preferable to have him express some of his ambivalence about life planning and lifestyle. Discussion about tests and the use of occupational information resources may be introduced later.

Conflict with Others About Career Plans

Client 3: Bob is interested in acting and has demonstrated talent performing in plays. He is thinking of directing and writing, as well as acting. He is verbal, expressive, and articulate. His father is a successful pipeline contractor who wants Bob, his only child, to come into the business. He scoffs at drama as an effeminate occupation. Bob's mother is quiet and unassuming but subtly supports Bob. His father refuses to support him in college if he persists in drama. Bob thinks he is letting his father down. At the same time, he wonders whether drama is a realistic choice economically.

Client 4: Sholanda, a senior, is referred by her social studies teacher. She is an excellent student who has a scholarship to an out-of-state college. She is thinking of law. Her boyfriend is registering at the local community college. He is distressed because she has decided to leave the state. He says she apparently does not care enough for him to change her plans. Sholanda feels guilty and wonders whether her educational plans are selfish.

These students' questions about career concerns are complicated by their interactions with, or the expectations of, significant people in their lives. They see the counselor because they are uncertain about how to cope with the differences between their own expectations and the expectations of others. An impasse often occurs between student and parents or between student and intimate friend. These conflicts have contributed to confusion or doubts about vocational planning. I probably would not begin vocational testing or appraisal with Bob or Sholanda until I explored with them any dependency/independency conflicts and ambivalences in their relationships with significant others.

Clients 3 and 4: Through increased knowledge about self, occupations, and relationships with others, Bob and Sholanda may become convinced that their career planning is correct and successfully change the minds of the dissenting persons. It is also possible that if, in either of these cases, both the student and the other party involved were to modify their positions regarding the student's future plans, a reasonable compromise could be reached. If Bob and his father are willing to met with me to discuss their differences, the chances of a compromise are enhanced. For example, Bob might continue with drama and work during the summers for his father to learn a practical trade and to explore further his interest in some phase of the business.

Sholanda's opportunities for compromise are fewer. The compromise might consist of an agreement that she and her boyfriend will visit on holidays to determine whether they will continue their relationship. Perhaps her boyfriend could decide to attend a school closer to hers because he would not lose a scholarship by changing schools.

The clients may become convinced that their choices are correct, but in either case the others may be so adamantly opposed that a breach in their relationships might occur. For Bob, this could mean a disruption in the family relationship and withdrawal of economic support. For Sholanda, the decision to persist in her action despite objections could mean the end of a love relationship.

If an impasse were to develop between Bob and his father, I would discuss with Bob the possibility of arranging counseling sessions with him and his parents using a family systems approach. Or I might refer them to a family counselor at a community agency.

Personal Conflict About Career

Students often come to a counselor about vocational planning when they have strong interests and abilities in two or three areas and are uncertain and in conflict about which path to follow. Strong interests and abilities in two or three areas become confusing, especially if it appears that one choice excludes the others. In other situations, personal values and goals seem at odds.

Client 5: Stefan is referred by a local minister who knows about you. Stefan, a senior, is expressing value conflicts related to occupations. He is a warm, outgoing person who enjoys working in social services. He is considering the ministry or YMCA work. He believes, however, that he wants to make good money in a job. His lifestyle includes material rewards that he thinks social service will not give him. Yet, business does not appeal to him. His mother is in banking, and his father is a social worker. They encourage him to make his own decisions.

Client 5: This question relates to the student's ambivalence or contradictory motivations or values. I would first explore with Stefan the alternatives he presents, the various values and motivations each choice represents, and the reasons why he is having difficulty in deciding. We would explore the extent to which external pressures are influencing the situation and consider whether these alternatives are truly mutually exclusive. I would not move too quickly in testing Stefan. That he directly expressed conflict in values is an important step for him, and therefore it should be followed up. His perception of his mother's and father's values may be contributing to his confusion. As counseling progressed, I then might give him a vocational interest inventory and a personality inventory to help him in determining the direction he wants to go.

Personal Problems: Conflicts, Doubts, and Confusion

At times, students present problems about their attitudes and behavior that are causing inner conflicts, tensions, indecision, or confusion. The central feature of this type of presenting problem is that the students are expressing ambivalence, uncertainty, or guilt about their attitudes, feelings, or behavior.

Conflict

In these situations, students raise questions about their own attitudes and behaviors that are causing inner conflicts, tension, indecision, or immobility:

Client 6: Jane is an intense person who talks rapidly. She has an impressive 3.9 grade point average. She transferred here at the beginning of her junior year and got straight A's this past semester. She wants to see a counselor about applying for scholarships. In the course of the dialogue, she says she has continual headaches and has seen her physician, who calls them tension headaches. She feels upset about herself. She says she spends all her time on her schoolwork.

Client 6: The counselor can readily help Jane regarding scholarship applications. But Jane revealed other presenting problems. How is she fitting in as a new student? The counselor might simply conclude that she needs to get more involved in social activities and to take relaxation exercises to reduce tension. But the counselor should also explore what else might be underlying her tension headaches. How does she feel about herself regarding her high achievement record? Do gender issues have any bearing on this case? According to feminist researchers, high-achieving female students tend to have lower self-esteem than high-achieving male students. What are her career aspirations? To which universities is she applying? How do her parents feel about her plans? Has she made friends in the school who have similar aspirations? Perhaps it would be helpful to arrange for her to have group counseling with other females with similar interests and abilities.

Doubts or Confusion

The presenting problems of the following clients focus either on uncertainty or on expressed dissatisfaction with their everyday behavior and attitudes. In either case, the client has doubt or confusion about how to resolve uncomfortable feelings.

Client 7: Ernest speaks his mind freely. He is the first one to volunteer answers in class and to offer opinions at meetings. He wonders whether he sounds off too much. He thinks his enthusiasm sometimes ruffles others. He asks whether he should assert himself less.

Client 8: Frank is restless. He wonders what life is all about. "Who am I? What's the purpose of it all?" he asks himself. School and life seem meaningless; courses do not make sense. He sees himself as alienated. He says he has no religious convictions, but he is curious about religion.

Client 7: Ernest needs to explore both the nature of his uncomfortable feelings when he is expressing himself in groups and the reasons why these feelings arise. If our discussions indicate that he is misperceiving the reactions of others because of his own uncomfortable feelings about assertion, cognitive restructuring may be helpful to correct his misperceptions, or client-centered techniques might help him get in touch with his lack of self-assurance. If our discussions indicate that he is dominating other group members, I would help him explore some reasons why he needs to call attention to himself. Assertiveness training could help him distinguish between aggressiveness and appropriate assertion of ideas, and role-playing communication skills might improve his group interactions. Group counseling might help him practice social skills.

Client 8: Frank's presenting problem is generally termed *existential* because he is concerned with broad questions about life or existence. If he is articulate, the interviews may involve a good deal of careful listening and reflecting by the counselor in client-centered fashion. If Frank has difficulty expressing himself, however, I would not hesitate to ask questions or make observations to help him confront the source of his concerns. Religious or spiritual questions about the meaning of life begin to surface as adolescents question the beliefs or lack of beliefs of their parents and ponder how the world is being governed. The counselor's task is to help clients with spiritual or religious concerns explore their doubts, questions, or aspirations without influencing or inhibiting these explorations because of the counselor's own religious or spiritual convictions or lack of them.

Social Problems: Interpersonal Conflicts and Feelings of Social Inadequacy

In cases of interpersonal conflicts and feelings of social inadequacy, clients are troubled by the differences between their needs or expectations and the needs or expectations of other persons in their lives. They may also indicate that they feel socially inept and ask for help in developing skills for interacting with others.

Interpersonal Conflicts

While searching for identity and working through dependency/independency relationships, adolescents can be expected to run into conflict with the usual authority figures—teachers, parents, administrators. They also feel social pressures from the groups, cliques, or gangs that form in high schools. Peer groups have varying expectations of conformity, and engaging in certain behaviors gains approval from these groups. The adolescent who decides to behave in a manner different from that of the peer group or gang often feels conflicted or anxious. Gaining independence helps adolescents develop inner strength, but it also increases the likelihood of friction, disapproval, and rejection.

Client 9: Joel stomps into your office between classes and asks to see you after school; he is angry at his social studies teacher. He complains that the teacher picks on him, criticizes him, and is sarcastic. He claims that the teacher belittled him in front of the class by calling him a clown.

Client 10: Hugh is a school leader and a good student who is popular with both sexes. He is concerned because he and his girlfriend constantly clash. She is highly independent. She refuses to let him pay her way on dates and becomes annoyed if he opens doors for her. He admires her independence yet feels irritated when she asserts herself. Hugh's friends are highly sociable, enjoy traditional male-female relationships, and see his girlfriend as an odd feminist.

When clients say they are having conflicts with others, counselors should avoid becoming their advocates in the disagreements. Counselors are not arbiters, ombudsmen, or referees. Nor are they defenders of teachers, parents, or the establishment. Rather, they help students express and clarify the conflict and explore both their own expectations, values, and feelings and the attitudes or values of those with whom they are in conflict. Alternative actions and the consequences of these actions can then be evaluated. Counselors can quickly lose effectiveness or become involved in conflict if they assume a stance of advocate one way or the other.

Client 9: It would be easy to agree with Joel if the teacher were known to be sarcastic, but if the teacher were your friend and well liked by other students, you might be tempted to defend the teacher. Rather than take sides, however, the counselor should permit students like Joel to express anger and frustration and then assess the situation with the student.

One way to start is by carefully discussing the specific behavior that Joel is complaining about, as well as assessing how he behaves in class. He might then feel able to cope in class, or he might decide that a talk with the teacher about their interactions might help. If the teacher and Joel prefer a joint consultation with the counselor, the counselor should emphasize that his or her role is to keep Joel and the teacher's dialogue open and not to act as a referee. Teachers and students are often surprised at the success of a direct discussion. If the relationship between the teacher and Joel is beyond a reasonable discussion or if the teacher has had difficulty with many students and has not been amenable to change over the years, Joel may be able to drop the course. If that is not possible, then he can be helped to cope with the teacher so as not to provoke or reinforce attacks. Rational-emotive techniques to assist him in handling unpleasant reality might prove constructive.

Client 10: Hugh is confronted with changing expectations in male and female gender roles. Here's a chance for him to examine his ambivalence about his girlfriend's independence when he puts such a high premium on his own. He appears attracted to, and yet bewildered by, her attitudes. Another factor contributing to his confusion is the difference between her behavior and the behavior of other girls in his social group. Searching out his attitudes about his girlfriend is important to his future attitudes toward, and relationships with, women and with social groups in general.

Feelings of Social Inadequacy

Students at times express feelings of inadequacy about social awareness, social ease, or social skills. Teachers also may find that a student's behavior is immature or uncertain.

Client 11: Rosa expresses concern about an inability to make friends, attract dates, or feel part of her own peer group. People do not dislike her, she says. It is worse: They are indifferent. She describes herself as shy. She wants to learn to be more outgoing.

Many students express a desire to change specific behaviors or attitudes. Because of this specificity, some counselors immediately suggest that the client take assertiveness training classes or some other kind of training in communication skills. I prefer to determine first whether the problem lies in lack of social skills or with her having a low self-image. If lack of skills is paramount, I would then proceed with assertiveness training, role playing, or some other appropriate technique. Students can practice relatively safe interactions with others between counseling sessions. At this stage, it is important for clients to realize that when they begin to assert themselves or to act differently, they may get negative reactions from others.

Client 11: If Rosa's concerns were more complicated than she originally presented, I would first explore personal and social issues. If her problem stemmed mostly from inexperience, I would help her develop social skills early in the sessions. Group counseling might be useful for Rosa to practice interacting with others in the group who are experiencing similar concerns.

Antisocial Acts

In the following situations, a student seeks out a counselor and reveals that he or she has been involved in, or is contemplating, an act that is either illegal or unethical—shoplifting, destroying school property, taking drugs, plagiarizing, cheating on an exam. The student not only admits the behavior but also expresses concern and guilt about it.

> **Client 12:** Elena is a quiet, somewhat withdrawn student who keeps to herself much of the time. She has difficulty talking about why she made the appointment. Finally, she bursts out that she has shoplifted articles in downtown stores on two occasions and given them to friends as gifts.

> **Client 13:** Gregory has been in a few times to discuss poor study habits. He received an A in a history course. You notice that he is uncomfortable. When you mention this, he stammers that he got the A by cheating on the final. He admits that this was not the only time he has cheated.

Clients 12 and 13: I would not involve parents, other authorities, or professionals in either of these situations. The behavior is not chronic, and the students are serious about seeking help. I would commend them for recognizing the need for help and give them full opportunity to express their anxieties. I would make it clear that I cannot protect them from legal or disciplinary action if their behavior continues and is discovered while they are in counseling. I would explain that if parents and the authorities discovered the behavior, they would most likely be relieved that the students had already voluntarily sought help.

I would try to help the students explore the factors contributing to the antisocial behavior. I would make no attempt to condone or excuse stealing or cheating on the basis of emotional factors. Rather, we would explore reasons for Elena's frantic efforts to buy friendship and Gregory's urgency about grades. Often in these situations, counseling brings out evidence of poor family interactions that are contributing to the behavior. Students who admit to cheating sometimes want to let the specific teacher or teachers know about the cheating. I would support the students and help them take this step. I would perceive this as part of the counseling process, however, rather than as a "confession" intended to relieve guilt and to eliminate the belief that counseling is necessary.

Crises

As teenage drug addictions, suicides, gang wars, possession of guns, and sexual assaults have become common occurrences, high school counselors have become increasingly involved in crisis cases. Figure 17.2, toward the end of the chapter, shows a log of a high school counselor's typical workday. Notice how crisis cases dominate the counselor's time.

Crises can occur when sudden, radical changes disrupt an individual's life or environment. The individual becomes seriously disoriented, depressed, or agitated. Crises require prompt and direct intervention to avoid the possibility of serious consequences or further deterioration (see chap. 7).

According to Gans (as cited in Steinberg, 1993), one out of three adolescents has considered suicide and one out of six has attempted suicide. Groups of students, as well as individuals, have crises that require intervention from school officials. It is generally known that hundreds of gangs exist in the United States. Moreover, "more than 135,000 students in this country carry handguns to school every day" (Murray, 1993, p. E1).

In schools, the counseling center is usually the first line of call when emergencies arise. Counselors generally are expected to take steps to calm the person down and to take immediate action when necessary. Counselors then determine whether to work with the student or to refer the student to a community agency (see chap. 7). With cases involving several students, such as gang-related crises, counselors might arrange conferences with those involved and perhaps their families and establish follow-up psychological education programs. Counselors also offer crisis intervention/prevention programs, which is discussed later in this chapter in the section "Outreach: Prevention and Intervention."

In crisis situations, counselors should remain calm while they talk with the students to determine whether their disorientation is caused by psychotic or drug reactions or whether they suffer from sudden, acute depression or confusion caused by upsetting circumstances, such as a sudden death in the family or the breakup of a relationship. If a student is so disoriented, depressed, or agitated as to be suicidal or dangerous to others, administrators and parents need to be informed. If a student is in a state of shock over a sudden death or breakup in the family, the counselor first needs to help the student recover from the initial shock. The counselor usually sets up counseling sessions to help the student express grief, anger, or frustration and confront the reality of the event. Psychiatric and psychological consultation should be readily available, from either a consultant hired by the school district or a consultant from a community mental health clinic. If necessary, the counselor refers the case to a community agency. It is therefore important that school counselors know the appropriate resources in the community to which a referral can be made or where consultation can be obtained (Remley & Sparkman, 1993).

GROUP COUNSELING OF ADOLESCENTS

Although adolescent group counseling is similar to adult group counseling, there are some significant differences. Counselors generally are more active with adolescents, particularly in the group's initial stages. Adolescents want to understand the structure of the group, ask about process, and raise questions about the value of the experience. They prefer an informal setting where they can sit on the floor. Adolescents in a group tend to watch and question the counselor's behavior or techniques and tend to model the counselor (Ohlsen, Horne, & Lawe, 1988).

Group counseling can be a useful technique for a wide variety of adolescent problems—girls who are pregnant, those who are having conflicts with parents, those with identity problems or concerns about sexuality, and those confused about career goals (Myrick, 1997).

Secondary school counselors generally do less group counseling than elementary school counselors (Partin, 1993). Group counseling, however, should be encouraged in secondary schools. An adolescent's strong urges to affiliate with, and be accepted by, peers and to develop intimate relations strongly suggest they would respond well to group counseling. The Jungian-based psychodrama groups that Allan (1988) developed with sixth- and seventh-grade students (see chap. 16) would work well for senior high school students.

Role playing is a particularly effective technique in adolescent groups (Ohlsen et al., 1988). Group members can role-play with the counselor to help work through feelings of transference or to rehearse an interaction with an adult. They can also role-play with one another or use the empty chair technique and play two people. In these cases, students pick out the characters and the scenario. Ohlsen et al. (1988) also encourage soliloquies and side remarks, techniques used in psychodrama, when they play characters who speak and behave one way and feel (and make asides) another way (see chap. 11).

➤ OUTREACH: PREVENTION AND INTERVENTION

Outreach, in which counselors are involved in prevention and intervention activities, continues to increase in secondary schools. Psychological education classes and workshops, social change activities, and consultation with teachers, administrators, and parents enhance and supplement the counselors' primary role of direct counseling.

In secondary schools, two forms of psychological education are offered. One type is prevention and growth oriented and follows the developmental tasks of adolescents. The other type uses intervention strategies for at-risk students who are self-destructive (substance abuse, suicidal), who are victims of physical abuse or rape, or who are in crisis, such as trying to cope with the sudden death or loss of a loved one.

Psychological Education: Developmental

Career Education

Outreach programs in career exploration and development expanded extensively in secondary schools when the National Occupational Information Coordinating Committee (NOICC, 1989a, 1989b) provided ongoing federal and state funding and guidelines to develop programs. As a result, new and expanded career programs have been developed for high schools. Freshmen and sophomores explore vocational interests and aptitudes and learn to find and use occupational information; juniors decide on certain job or career options and begin to develop specific skills necessary for these jobs; seniors learn to conduct job searches, write job résumés, practice job interviewing skills, and many also learn on the job as interns in the workplace.

Further support to career education was provided through the School-to-Work Opportunities Act passed by Congress in 1994 (NOICC, 1994). The program is administered by the National School-to-Work Office under the joint direction of the U.S. Departments of Labor and Education. States are given grants to provide career education programs to help high school students make transitions from academic training to the world of work. The program, sponsored by joint efforts of business and industry, features a work-based learning component that involves job training and on-site work experiences. Students involved in these on-the-job work experiences have two mentors—one from the school staff, the other an employee in the work setting. The school mentor works jointly with counselors, teachers, and employers to direct students' progress. The workplace mentor instructs and guides students on the job.

Participants also learn how to conduct job searches, develop résumés, practice for job interviews, and the like. Further, counselors, along with career specialists, can arrange another type of on-the-job experiences for students to observe workers firsthand. Students spend a day shadowing a particular employee in a profession to learn about characteristics of the job.

Another national career development program, Tech Prep, is designed to help students finish high school with improved marketable skills for job placement. Through joint efforts of high schools and community/technology colleges, students take course work in high school that earns community college credit.

Paralleling these federal programs, the state of Washington has developed a unique career development program called Running Start, whereby qualified junior and senior high school students take tuition-free courses at a community college and earn both high school and college credits. Qualified students are thus able to earn an A.A. degree at the community college by the time they graduate from high school.

Psychological Courses

The most common psychological courses are life skills, interpersonal skills, life planning, health, and life development. They may be required for graduation or offered as electives. Some counselors teach a unit in a social studies, English, or home economics class.

One such class, called the Lifestyle Unit, which meets for 10 sessions, is intended to increase students' awareness of their values and preferences and how such values relate to choices regarding work, marriage, and family. The class also explores gender stereotyping in careers and the influence of peers and parents on choice of lifestyles (Amatea & Cross, 1986).

Another type of classroom unit led by a counselor is one that teaches job-seeking skills and meets once a week for 7 weeks in a senior English class. Students learn to fill out job applications, write résumés, and practice job interviews through role play (G. B. Baker & Shaw, 1987).

Another such course for adolescents covers decision-making skills. Students read a fictitious newspaper article in which a person is faced with a decision or dilemma. They learn to identify and define the problem, develop possible solutions, and through role play, decide on the most appropriate solution (Gazda, Childers, & Brooks, 1987).

Group Psychological Education

Group psychological experiences are similar to the classes discussed above except that they meet outside class without credit. They may or may not have a certain time frame. Counselors usually run the groups.

Group work can be effective for a wide variety of issues. One example is a group on career guidance designed to help high school girls develop career awareness. They meet for six 45-minute sessions and discuss careers, sex stereotyping, and conflicts that women experience (G. B. Baker & Shaw, 1987).

Another example is a social communication skills training program for junior high school grades, a program that meets for ten 47-minute periods to help students in nonverbal and verbal skills, assertiveness training, cognitive restructuring, and social problem-solving activities (G. B. Baker & Shaw, 1987).

Psychological Education: Crisis Intervention

Crisis education programs have a threefold purpose: They (a) arouse awareness of administrators and staff about the serious nature of the problem and show ways of identifying the problem, (b) provide effective intervention techniques when crises arise, and (c) offer counseling and support groups after the crisis is over.

Alcohol and Drugs

The Bellingham School District in Washington State developed a program of drug and alcohol awareness, prevention, and intervention. The district hired three substance abuse counselors to serve several schools in the district.

The program was introduced into schools by counselors, who held 2- or 3-day awareness workshops for administrators, counselors, teachers, and office staff. They discussed the severity of the problems, outlined ways of identifying problems, and worked on intervention strategies and ways of making constructive referral to the substance abuse counselors.

In this program, a teacher who suspects an alcohol problem refers the student to the drug/alcohol counselor. If an assessment by the substance abuse counselor indicates that the student needs treatment, then the student may work with the substance abuse counselor. If inpatient treatment is required, the student is referred to an alcohol or drug treatment center. While students are in treatment, tutoring is available to them. After students return to school, they are offered a support class taught by the substance abuse counselor to help them resist peer pressure or environmental pressures that might lead to further drinking or drug abuse.

Suicide

Every year, 5,000 to 6,000 adolescents take their lives and another 500,000 make abortive suicide attempts (Popenhagen & Qualley, 1998). Counselors provide school-based programs that train parents, school staff, and students on how to detect early signs of suicidal behavior. One should be alert, for example, to the person who talks about committing suicide, who talks about specific plans for suicide, or who is so depressed that he or she cannot function. In these cases, a counselor should be consulted. As described earlier, counselors can intervene, make further determinations about the severity of the problem, and when necessary, refer students for more intensive help (see also chap. 7).

A suicide prevention and intervention program in the Bellingham School District demonstrates how school and community counselors and other mental health specialists can work together effectively. The program has three modes. The first mode, led by mental health counselors from the community, involves half-day workshops for all school staff to discuss recognition of suicidal symptoms and effective ways of intervening. The second mode, led by school counselors and included in the classroom curriculum, teaches students how to be aware of signs of suicidal behavior and how to bring disturbed students to the attention of adults. The third mode, led by community mental health specialists, trains suicide response teams composed of school counselors. Each team is prepared to help a school population handle the trauma of a suicide in the school.

This group is also available for other types of crises that affect total school populations, such as accidents in which several students are killed, a murder of a student, or the sudden death of a teacher.

Violence

Youth gangs are increasing in number and size throughout the United States (Omizo, Omizo, & Honda, 1997). Gang members often abuse their powers—assaults, use of guns and other weapons, destruction of property, use of drugs, and drug trafficking. Long-range effects of gang membership have shown a decrease in one's ability to develop skills necessary to ensure adulthood or to gain marketable job skills.

> The increase in the size and violence of youth gangs makes it imperative that teachers, counselors, administrators, and social service professionals recognize the variables which contribute to an adolescent's decision to join a gang. Effective preventative interventions that address these factors must be developed to deter youth from turning to gangs. These interventions should look at ways of channeling and redirecting the positive aspects of gangs into more constructive, socially acceptable outlets. (Omizo et al., 1997, p. 39)

To explore the phenomenon of youth gang membership, Omizo et al. (1997) conducted a study of eight high school male gang members in Oahu, Hawaii, a region where police have identified 45 gangs with more than 1,000 members. In a series of interviews, they found that the boys joined gangs because they felt a sense of belonging, an increase in self-esteem, protection from other gangs, and an outlet for social and recreational activities.

When counselors are aware of adolescent needs to affiliate with others, they can help channel teenagers into more constructive group activities. In addition to providing individual and group counseling to gang members, counselors offer parenting skills activities to parents. Joint school and community services can be offered to educate the general public about characteristics of youth gangs and about ways they can help gang members rechannel their energy.

Several mass killings have occurred in secondary schools in which a student shoots teachers and fellow students without warning. In these tragic cases, counselors can serve in two ways. First, with the aid of community specialists, they can work with traumatized students, families, and school staff to deal with their shock, anguish, and fears. This is called *debriefing*. Second, counselors can become trained by specialists in violence prevention to learn to detect symptoms of individuals with potential for violence so that they can intervene before disaster occurs. In turn, they can then work with other school staff and with families to alert them to danger signals in adolescents prone to violence.

Social Change

Students in secondary schools obviously are more able to change school policies and procedures they believe are inappropriate or unfair than are children in elementary schools. Counselors can help students consider options and consequences and inform them of procedures for making complaints that follow school policy.

An example of helping an individual make a change occurred in a high school in Whatcom County, Washington. A client told her counselor she was unhappy that her high school had no women's swim team. She complained that this deprived her and others of engaging in swim competition. She wanted to do something about it. She and her counselor decided that her first step would be for her to talk with the principal. The principal responded positively and suggested she talk with the superintendent. The superintendent recommended that the issue be brought before the board of education. After the student presented her rationale to the board, the board decided to hire a women's swim coach in midseason.

The same student had more difficulty when she tried to persuade the athletic director to include women's sports on a wallet-size schedule of men's sports. The director gave evasive responses and numerous rationalizations for why the change could not be made. With the counselor's encouragement, the student persisted by continuing to make appointments and telephone calls. After a year of continuous pressure, the change was made, in line with affirmative action regulations.

Consultation

Counselors serve effectively as consultants with teachers and administrators. They are particularly needed in this capacity in secondary schools because teachers who teach five or six classes to different sets of students have little opportunity to work through conflicts with students or to observe those needing help. Likewise, administrator interactions with students, especially in large high schools, are usually limited to those who are always in trouble or who are outstanding scholars, athletes, or leaders. Consider the following consultations with teachers and administrators:

Teacher A: Ms. Adams approaches a counselor in the coffee room. She asks whether he has time to talk with her. The counselor suggests taking some coffee to his office, where they can talk without being overheard. She tells the counselor that she is concerned about a student who is not handing in his assigned papers but who scores high on standardized intelligence and achievement tests. He is polite, presents no discipline problems, and promises to hand in his papers. Ms. Adams, a young, energetic, first-year teacher, feels frustrated and annoyed.

Teacher B: Mr. Baker is a high school teacher just out of college. He looks and dresses like the average student. He perceives himself as their friend and goes out of his way to show personal interest. A sophomore has a crush on him. She finds all kinds of excuses to see him. Some harmless, prank telephone calls have been made to his home. He is convinced that she made the calls.

Teacher A: Ms. Adams is trying to encourage an underachiever, and he is probably resisting because of fear of failure. Thus, encouragement to try to measure up to the teacher's expectations, which he is uncertain he can meet, is leading to further withdrawal. In this case, she might try setting smaller, achievable, sequential steps in the mode of Beck's stress theory.

Teacher B: Mr. Baker can be encouraged to explore whether he is subtly contributing to the uncomfortable relationship by his overly friendly manner. A discussion of his interactions with all students might reveal his anxieties about assuming an authority role, his awkwardness at his youthful age, and his need to be liked and approved of by the students. He would be encouraged to drop the buddy role with students and to increase social interactions with people his own age.

Administrator K: Ms. Karpinski, the principal of a high school, asks for consultation because she is considering revamping the curriculum to meet the students' needs more effectively. The town has changed from a suburban residential area to a semi-industrial one during the 10 years since the last curriculum overhaul. She wonders whether the students' vocational aims are being served.

Administrator K: A counseling staff can help the principal improve the curriculum by giving some general feedback about student requests for courses and some ideas about prospects after graduation. The counseling staff can offer to conduct a survey of students about their curriculum needs and a follow-up study of graduates.

Counselors also serve as consultants and resource persons for schoolwide testing programs mandated by the state or by school districts. In effective school counseling programs, counselors do not administer or record test scores. Rather, they are consultants helping administrators evaluate the type and quality of tests being used and set appropriate and ethical policies on appropriate administration and use of tests. They also are consultants to teachers in interpreting test results and relating scores to data in student cumulative folders.

Liaison with Community and University

Considering the large number of crisis cases now facing school counselors, it is essential that counselors develop a network of mental health professionals in the community with whom they can consult or to whom they can refer cases. The school-community joint suicide-prevention teamwork described earlier demonstrates how counseling staffs from community agencies and schools benefit from sharing resources and ideas. Because of the urgency about crises, counselor training programs should include in their course work discussions on how school counselors and community mental health counselors can work together.

In reducing the gang violence described earlier in the chapter, Omizo et al. (1997) recommend that school counselors develop ways gangs can learn to collaborate with the community. "By increasing community involvement, gang crime can be reduced or prevented. School counselors can help organize anti-gang events such as graffiti clean-ups, extracurricular social activities and neighborhood watch programs" (p. 42).

A unique collaborative program between high school counselors and university counselor educators has been developed at Pulaski County High School in Virginia, and at Radford University (Miano, Forrest, & Gumaer, 1997). After meeting together and designing a proposal, they received a grant in 1989 to develop a program to reduce dropout rates of students at risk. At-risk students include academic failures, substance abusers, those suffering from family conflicts and/or sexual abuse, pregnant girls, and those with persistent disruptive behavior.

In their collaboration, the high school and university counselors developed and implemented an innovative plan whereby they engaged the services of high school students in vocational classes to construct a school/family counseling center next to the high school. Called the School/Family Counseling Center (SFCC), it is supported by the school, families, community, and university. Comprehensive counseling services are offered to both students and their families. It is staffed by two full-time high school counselors, as well as by counseling interns from the university who are supervised by university faculty. Counseling is also provided in the evenings once or twice a week by supervised counseling interns. Initially set up for individual and family counseling, SFCC has expanded to include group and couple counseling.

✥ ADDRESSING MULTICULTURAL DIVERSITY

It is essential that counselors in schools attend to the developmental, transitional concerns of a rapidly increasing number of ethnic students. "For the first time in U.S. history, the mainstream is about to become the minority, and the group that has held the power . . . is on the verge of being outnumbered" (Markowitz, 1994, p. 20). By the year 2020, the majority of public school students in the United States will be from racial ethnic groups (Hodgkinson, 1985). Leading African American counselor and counselor educator Courtland Lee (1995) comments: "Among the contemporary issues facing school counselors and related helping professionals, addressing the developmental needs of the growing number of students from culturally diverse backgrounds, is perhaps the most challenging" (p. 3).

Increasing numbers of ethnic counselors consider it imperative that school counselors incorporate a multicultural perspective into a developmental approach underlying current counseling process (Baruth & Manning, 1999; Lee, 1995). Regarding adolescents in particular,

Adolescents often develop individual and cultural identities under difficult circumstances involving racism, discrimination, and injustice. The "culture of poverty" image may influence Native Americans' identities; similarly, African Americans, hearing repeatedly that their culture is "inferior," may develop negative identities. (Baruth & Manning, 1999, p. 90)

Lee (1995) describes how school counselors can integrate psychosocial development and multicultural diversity to benefit adolescents and children. "Children and adolescents must master psychosocial developmental tasks through their socialization within a cultural context" (p. 8). When working with adolescent development of ethnic students, counselors must learn to understand these students' particular cultural backgrounds—family and community characteristics, gender role definitions, and religious or spiritual beliefs.

The program Getting on the Right Track was developed in a North Carolina school system for African American ninth-grade students who were having difficulty reaching their academic potential (Locke, 1995). Counselors, teachers, and parents worked together to improve the students' motivation to learn through activities that strengthened their African American identity, as well as their academic skills. During a 3-year period, students met biweekly. During the first year, "they were instructed in African American history and culture; basic communication techniques (e.g., the importance of eye contact and assertiveness); study techniques; and strategies for successful interracial interactions" (Locke, 1995, p. 34). In their sophomore year, students served as peer mentors to freshmen beginning the program. Junior year activities consisted of writing their family histories, volunteering in the community, and exploring the programs of at least five colleges or universities.

In a high school in New Orleans, the counseling staff presented a unique psychological education program that developed cultural awareness of the three major ethnic groups represented in their high school (Carter & Vuong, 1997). Entitled Unity Through Diversity, the program was designed after a student survey showed that most students felt a need to understand various cultures represented in the student population. Students from the three major ethnic groups planned and presented three different assemblies at intervals throughout a semester. Social studies teachers were given cultural material to use in classroom units, materials that related both to the cultural group being highlighted and to an appreciation of multicultural diversity. Evaluation by the students afterward was highly favorable (Carter & Vuong, 1997).

❧ WORKING WITH FAMILIES

Secondary school counselors, like elementary school counselors, are in a favorable position to provide brief family counseling and family consultation based on a family systems approach (Nicoll, 1992). In high schools, this approach can be valuable in the assessment and treatment of adolescent developmental concerns, as well as of alcohol and drug abuse, eating disorders, and adolescent depression.

A remarkable example of a family counseling center for high school students and their families is the one described in the section "Liaison with Community and University" (above). The center, a combined school-family counseling center, is located next to the high school and employs two full-time school counselors and interns supervised by university faculty.

Unfortunately, however, for many young people the typical family does not exist (see chap. 10 and Figure 17.2). In response to this problem, some professional therapeutic institutes in communities throughout the country specialize in drawing together in a healing way families that have been broken by abuse. The Giarretto Institute in San Jose, California, described in chapter 19, is an example.

A DAY IN THE LIFE OF A SCHOOL COUNSELOR

A log describing the day in the life of a school counselor in Washington State, which appears in Figure 17.2, was submitted by a high school counselor in 1993 who was concerned by the preponderance of crisis cases in her daily schedule. The high school has a team of well-qualified counselors whose administrators have, over the years, responded to their requests to develop and maintain a professional counseling center in the school. This counseling center tends to draw many students who need help. The crowded daily log does not reflect, however, the considerable amount of behind-the-scenes proactive planning and work the counseling staff does.

In a recent follow-up interview, the counselor said that some significant changes have occurred: The school brought in two new counselors to ease the overload; moreover, federal and state funds have created new career development programs that allow, among other services, accelerated academic tracks for some students, including Tech Prep and Running Start (both described earlier).

Although the counselors spend more time now with student developmental concerns, the typical day still has a preponderance of similar crisis cases. Although students and families continue to come to counselors at times of crisis, an increased percentage of counselor time is now spent in execution of programs that foster academic, career, and social success and safety. More community resources outside the school are now accessible for medical, psychological, and social support of students. Leaders from various ethnic communities are becoming more actively involved with their youths and with school programs. Counselors therefore have more opportunity to focus on K–12 program planning, including methods to address more adequately the developmental needs, to create violence prevention programs, and to introduce 4-year career planning and development procedures for students from freshmen through senior years.

SUMMARY

Although secondary schools were one of the earliest places to offer counseling services, for many years school counselors had difficulty gaining a professional identity because they lacked sufficient training, were unclear about their role, and consequently were bogged down in administrative work. Recently, with increasing numbers of well-trained counselors and changed attitudes of counselors and administra-

1. Sexually abused student living away from home wants to quit school. I have talked with two of his teachers repeatedly.

2. Girl who was in a fight yesterday arrived throwing up, with bruises, scratches on face, hurt nose, swollen foot—arrangements were made for the sick room and a ride to the doctor. We called her mother. The girl's father and many relatives are Vietnam Vets. Many people close to her have died this year.

3. Student with an unusually severe sexual assault case came to make arrangements for a leave to appear in court, and also to contact her Rape Relief advocate. This girl's mother is a drug addict with AIDS. She does not live at home.

4. Student who had recently had an abortion came in with very unusual symptoms. I had her call her doctor immediately.

5. A multiple abused person who had been hospitalized for mental illness came in (after her Mom called me about her low grades and defiance). We addressed the past abuse enough to figure out how her behavior was changing and have her agree to return to her psychiatrist and later we discussed her high ability and how her grades and career plans might all fit together.

6. Got a call from special ed. about a family in emergency housing with two special ed. kids here. I have talked repeatedly for 2 years with teachers, administrators, CPS workers, police, counselors, housing admin. and drug and alcohol counselors. This move was cleared with the superintendent.

7. Talked with (a colleague) about legal issues of the assault. Gave a note to a teacher of the assaulted student about missing a test. Talked with Mom again about our plan here to resolve the dispute.

8. Discussed with (a colleague) the 9 kids who are still seriously depressed over their friend's death.

9. Laid out pamphlets for display on STD's [Sexually Transmitted Diseases] in outer office.

10. Proofread a scholarship recommendation.

11. Talked to a student about a class transfer. Sent the student to talk with his teacher.

12. The assaulted student reappeared from the doctor with a fractured bone in her foot, and perhaps in her nose. On her (and her mother's) request, we sent for her adversary and attempted to make a temporary truce. However, both girls were clearly not ready to do much more, so I sent the 1st girl home to rest (doctor's orders) and talked with the second about the incident. It appears alcohol is possibly an issue here, too. Will approach that tomorrow. We decided to resume sometime next week after some time away from each other. We established ground rules for this week to quell rumors and avoid conflict.

13. A mother came in about (her son). This student is in the middle of a bitter custody battle.

14. A new student arrived and needed to be enrolled in classes and oriented.

15. I resumed trying to find the teacher for the previous case and succeeded. Then I couldn't find the principal.

16. I checked with a student who is trying to switch her classes because of her baby, which she just put up for adoption today. This girl has been repeatedly abused and has been in the foster care system for years.

17. I talked to one of my pregnant girls—just checking in.

18. A father called after talking to his daughter's teacher at my request. We decided to drop one of her classes. I need only talk to the (missing) principal. This girl has had multiple sex abuse experiences and much loss. She does not live with her parents.

19. I talked to a student just returning from (X) for multiple suicide attempts about how he's doing, and we formed plans as to how to work with his teachers. A teacher came in later to report he missed class today.

20. I talked to a student who took 23 pills (antidepressant) and some other drugs who is in our recovery class, and recently went through treatment and extensive CPS work. This girl is protected from her mother by a court order. Her Dad is a Vietnam Vet with symptoms of PTSD [postraumatic stress disorder].

21. I brought in and changed the student's schedule whose father called me earlier. Talked with teacher about student's attendance problem.

22. We ordered 5 personal allotment books on Learning Styles, Grief Counseling in Schools, and counseling Victims of Violence.

23. Talked to a teacher about the girl who had the abortion——5 student request slips left on spindle, 20 students to see for second semester scheduling.

FIGURE 17.2

A log of a high school counselor's typical workday.

Note: To protect the people involved, names of persons and the name and location of the school district have been withheld or altered. This high school is located in a relatively stable, self-contained, small, established town. The community is surrounded by farmland with some heavy industry nearby and is made up of middle-class Whites and two ethnic minorities.

tors about counselor roles, counselors have been spending more time in professional counseling and counseling-related activities.

Adolescents go through major developmental, transitional changes, changes that naturally cause anxieties, confusion, fears, and aggression. Their developmental needs center around a search for identity. Their confusions and value conflicts relate to changing family patterns and cultural upheavals in a rapidly changing, uncertain world. In working with adolescent clients, counselors expect to encounter ambivalences, conflicts, fears, and rebellion.

During the 1990s, secondary school counselors spent an increasing amount of time dealing with student crises that involve suicide threats, gang wars, sexual abuse, and substance abuse. Special programs funded by federal and state governments during the 1990s have allowed counselors to spend more time helping students explore careers, engage in on-the-job internships, and enroll in accelerated programs.

Outreach activity programs in secondary schools include drug and alcohol education and suicide prevention programs, in addition to courses and workshops in life skills, career exploration, and gender and ethnic stereotyping.

Secondary school counselors are providing more family counseling and consultation because involving the family is often essential in helping adolescents work through both normal transitional concerns and crises such as alcohol abuse or suicide.

The need for school counselors to address the developmental needs of ethnic students has become urgent, particularly because ethnic groups will soon make up the majority of students in the United States. Counselors need to be aware of the tendency for most ethnic persons to identify closely with their particular cultures and families.

High school counselor efforts to forge liaisons with community and local colleges and universities has proved effective, and thus such liaisons are becoming more common. This is especially helpful in addressing the increase in crises cases in schools. School and community networking services for youths and their families help build community participation in working with adolescents, as well as reduce gang violence, alcohol abuse, and suicides in the adolescent population.

⊷ PROJECTS AND ACTIVITIES

1. Interview some high school counselors near you about their interest in, and use of, inventories, personality measures, and intelligence and aptitude tests.
2. Evaluate two computerized career information systems developed for use with high school students. If possible, use a computerized program yourself to explore areas of interest to you.
3. Develop a list of agencies in the community that appear to be essential as resources for the school system. Then determine how many of these agencies actually exist in nearby communities.
4. Conduct a survey of the literature or of adolescent students about adolescents' contemporary concerns. Are counselor preparation programs with which you are familiar geared to meet these needs?
5. This activity will require a tape recorder and another interested student who will team up with you for a series of role-playing counseling interviews. Use it to experiment with the different types of counselor responses possi-

ble to a client's remarks. You and the other student should each take a few minutes to work out a possible counseling situation. Then one of you acts as a client who presents your concern (with the recorder on) to the other person, who acts as the counselor. Then you will reverse roles. Role-play for at least 10 minutes so that the person playing the counselor makes several responses. Then replay the tapes and summarize what was said by the client and by the counselor. Classify the counselor's responses. Here are some suggested categories:

   a. Probing for more facts and details by questioning

   b. Giving advice or telling the client what to do

   c. Judging or interpreting responses

   d. Making responses that facilitate the expression of the client's feelings[1]

6. Role-play an interview with Sholanda, Client 4, using first a female as the counselor and then a male. What differences were felt when the counselor was a male and when the counselor was a female?

7. Explain how a client-centered counselor would work with the concerns of Gail, Client 1, about career exploration.

8. With two other students, role-play a three-way interaction with Joel (Client 9), his counselor, and his teacher.

❧ REFERENCES

Allan, J. (1988). *Inscapes of the child's world: Jungian counseling in schools and clinics.* Dallas, TX: Spring.

Amatea, E. S., & Cross, E. G. (1986). Helping high school students clarify life role preference: The Lifestyles Unit. *School Counselor, 33,* 306–313.

Amatea, E. S., & Sherrard, P. A. D. (1991). When students cannot or will not change their behavior: Using brief strategic intervention in the school. *Journal of Counseling & Development, 69,* 341–344.

Baker, G. B., & Shaw, M. C. (1987). *Improving counseling through primary prevention.* Upper Saddle River, NJ: Merrill/Prentice Hall.

Baker, S. B. (1996). *School counseling for the 21st century* (2nd ed.). Upper Saddle River, NJ: Merrill/Prentice Hall.

Baruth, L., & Manning, M. L. (1999). *Multicultural counseling and psychotherapy: A lifespan perspective.* Upper Saddle River, NJ: Merrill/Prentice Hall.

Carter, R. B., & Vuong, T. K. (1997). Unity through diversity: Fostering cultural awareness. *Professional School Counseling, 1,* 47–49.

Conarton, S., & Silverman, L. K. (1988). Feminine development through the life cycle. In M. Dutton-Douglas & H. E. Walker (Eds.), *Feminist psychotherapies and feminist systems* (pp. 37–67). Norwood, NJ: Ablex.

Downing, J., & Harrison, T. (1992). Solutions and school counseling, *School Counselor, 39,* 327–332.

Erikson, E. H. (1968). *Identity, youth, and crisis.* New York: Norton.

Erikson, E. H. (1980). *Identity and the life cycle.* New York: Norton.

Gazda, G. M., Childers, W. C., & Brooks, P. K. (1987). *Foundations of counseling and human services.* New York: McGraw-Hill.

Gilligan, C. (1982). *In a different voice: Psychological theory and women's development.* Cambridge, MA: Harvard University Press.

Greer, R. M., & Richardson, M. D. (1992). Restructuring the guidance delivery system: Implications for high school counselors. *School Counselor, 40,* 93–96.

Gysbers, N. C., & Henderson, P. (1994). *Developing and managing your school guidance program* (2nd ed.). Alexandria, VA: American Counseling Association.

Hodgkinson, H. L. (1985). The changing face of tomorrow's student. *Change, 1,* 38–39.

Hutchinson, R. L., Barrick, A. L., & Groves, M. (1986). Functions of secondary school counseling in public schools: Ideal and actual. *School Counselor, 34,* 87–91.

Jordan, J. V., Kaplan, A. G., Miller, J. B., Stiver, I. P., & Surrey, J. L. (Eds.). (1991). *Women's growth in connection: Writings from the Stone Center.* New York: Guilford Press.

Lee, C. C. (1995). School counseling and cultural diversity: A framework for effective practice. In C. C. Lee (Ed.), *Counseling for diversity* (pp. 3–17). Boston: Allyn & Bacon.

Locke, D. C. (1995). Counseling interventions with African American youth. In C. C. Lee (Ed.), *Counseling for diversity* (pp. 21–40). Boston: Allyn & Bacon.

[1]Activity 5 was written by Elvet J. Jones, professor emeritus of psychology at Western Washington University.

Markowitz, L. M. (1994). The cross-currents of multiculturalism. *Family Therapy Networker, 18,* 18–24.

Miano, G., Forrest, A., & Gumaer, J. (1997). A collaborative program to assist at-risk youth. *Professional School Counseling, 1,* 16–20.

Murray, P. (1993, May 23). Guns, kids, and pain. *Seattle Post-Intelligencer,* p. E1.

Myrick, R. D. (1997). *Developmental guidance and counseling: A practical approach* (3rd ed.). Minneapolis, MN: International Media.

National Occupational Information Coordinating Committee (NOICC). (1989a). *The national career development guidelines: Local handbook for high schools.* Washington, DC: Government Printing Office.

National Occupational Information Coordinating Committee (NOICC). (1989b). *The national career guidelines project.* Washington, DC: Government Printing Office.

National Occupational Information Coordinating Committee (NOICC). (1994). *Program guide: Planning to meet career development needs in school-to-work-transition programs.* Washington, DC: Government Printing Office.

Nicoll, W. G. (1992). A family counseling and consultation model for school counselors. *School Counselor, 39,* 351–361.

Nugent, F. (1981). *Professional counseling: An overview.* Monterey, CA: Brooks/Cole.

Ohlsen, M. M., Horne, A. M., & Lawe, C. F. (1988). *Group counseling* (3rd ed.). New York: Holt, Rinehart & Winston.

Omizo, M. M., Omizo, S. A., & Honda, M. R. (1997). A phenomenological study with youth gang members: Results and implications for school counselors. *Professional School Counseling, 1,* 39–42.

Partin, R. L. (1993). School counselors' time: Where does it go? *School Counselor, 40,* 274–281.

Peer, G. G. (1985). The status of secondary school guidance: A national survey. *School Counselor, 32,* 181–189.

Popenhagen, M. P., & Qualley, R. M. (1998). Adolescent suicide: Detection, intervention, and prevention. *Professional School Counseling, 1,* 30–36.

Remley, T. P., & Sparkman, L. B. (1993). Student suicides: The counselor's limited legal liability. *School Counselor, 40,* 164–169.

Steinberg, L. (1993). *Adolescence.* New York: McGraw-Hill.

Tennyson, W. W., Miller, G. D., Skovolt, T. G., & Williams, R. C. (1989). Secondary school counselors: What do they do? What is important? *School Counselor, 36,* 253–259.

Wiggins, J. D., & Moody, A. H. (1987). Student evaluations of counseling programs: An added dimension. *School Counselor, 14,* 353–361.

18 Counseling Programs in Colleges and Universities

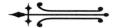

Young adults of college age are faced with developmental transitional challenges related to adjusting to academic life, developing academic skills and more specific career plans, as well as struggling with their personal identity, developing social relationships, learning to live with roommates, and forming intimate, romantic partnerships.

College counseling centers are available to students at most universities and colleges. These services are staffed by well-trained counselors who, for the most part, are available at no fee to help students work through situational conflicts that are impeding academic work. College counseling centers also offer outreach activities to help students maintain progress in school, such as consultation with faculty, psychological education courses and workshops, and crisis intervention.

Counseling centers as we know them today developed after World War II, originally to meet the needs of returning veterans. In contrast with the earlier centers that followed a diagnostic prescriptive guidance model, the new postwar counseling centers focused on the client's personal and psychosocial developmental needs. This approach was influenced by Super's (1953) view that vocational development is an intrinsic part of total personality development and by Rogers' (1942, 1951) emphasis on client-centered approaches and on personal growth. These early college counseling centers became models for the creation of role definitions and training standards for professional counselors in all settings.

College counseling centers flourished in the 1960s, expanding and spreading to colleges and universities throughout the country. To clarify counselor role, Kirk et al. (1971) published the article "Guidelines for University and College Counseling Services," based on input from counseling centers throughout the United States. These guidelines affirmed that counseling focused on student developmental situational needs as the primary function of counselors.

In the 1970s, many counselor educators became disillusioned with counseling and challenged the role of the counselor. It was a period of student unrest and growing popularity of encounter groups. Because of high demand for counselors, many college counselors were hired who had inadequately supervised internships and whose training tended to be narrowly based on one of two theoretical approaches—either on Rogerian client-centered humanism or on behaviorism. To address the problem, several counselor educators developed a series of interviewing and relationship skills based on the Rogerian approach, ones that could be measured similar to techniques of behaviorism and that could be used in counselor training programs. Armed with these sets of systematic techniques, some counselor educators proposed that psychological education replace counseling (see chap. 2).

Professional counseling as a primary role of the counselor prevailed, however. During the 1980s, more substantial, comprehensive theoretical approaches and techniques were incorporated into counseling practice—psychodynamic family systems approaches, psychosocial life-span developmental models, various cognitive theories and techniques, and new theoretical approaches to gender, ethnic, and multicultural issues (see chaps. 2, 4, 5, 10, and 19). As adjuncts to counseling, outreach and psychological education served as important secondary functions of counselors.

College counselors, in 1991, formed their own professional organization called the American College Counseling Association (ACCA). They had formerly been affiliated with the American College Personnel Association (ACPA), which focused on overall student personnel work. But when ACPA disaffiliated from the American Counseling Association (ACA), college counselors who wanted to continue to identify with ACA formed the American College Counseling Association (ACCA) as a new division of ACA. As of 1998, more than 5,000 college counselors had joined this division. In 1998, ACCA published the first issue of its new journal, *Journal of College Counseling,* with its goal, according to Benshoff (1998), "to create a professional publication that recognizes the importance and potential contributions of both research and practice to our profession" (p. 4).

ORGANIZATION AND ADMINISTRATION OF COUNSELING CENTERS

Most counseling centers are under the jurisdiction of the vice president of student affairs or the dean of students. They generally are part of university student services, which include housing, financial aid, placement, and residence halls. Some universities have merged student health services and the counseling center under one administrative head responsible to the vice president of student affairs (Gallagher, 1991; Stone & Archer, 1996).

In a 1996 survey, Gallagher found the ratio of 1 counselor to 1,600 students. The ratio generally recommended by counseling center directors is 1 counselor to 750 to 1,000 students. This ratio is minimally sufficient only if other necessary psychological personnel services are available to students. Adequate on-campus psychiatric services reduce the number of people with crises or chronic problems who would otherwise need to use the counseling center. Well-staffed minority affairs offices and alcohol or drug information and referral services also reduce pressure on college counseling centers.

≫ COUNSELING COLLEGE STUDENTS: ROLE, THEORIES, AND TECHNIQUES

Counseling services are part of student personnel services, but the counselor's role differs from that of other personnel workers. Student personnel workers help integrate students' academic work with their personal and social affairs. Although student personnel workers are involved in student affairs, their primary function is to administer such services as financial aid and resident hall management and to set and enforce disciplinary policies and procedures. Counselors at counseling centers, though, provide professional psychological counseling and counseling-related services. They are not involved in administrative duties and decisions, and they do not establish policies or regulations about student behavior.

College counseling staffs spend about 61% of their time in individual and group counseling, with brief counseling the most commonly used approach. Various outreach programs take up the rest of their time—psychological education, crisis prevention and intervention, consultation with faculty and administration, and supervision of interns and aides.

Crisis services have expanded to deal with the increasing numbers of students afflicted with traumatic crises, students addicted to alcohol, and students suffering from violence, abuse, and sexual assault.

Brief Counseling

Counseling centers have been limiting the number of counseling sessions available to clients, similar to managed care programs in the community. In 1996, about half of counseling centers surveyed reported doing so (Gallagher, 1996). According to a study conducted by Gage and Gyorky (1990), college students with specific situational developmental concerns related to academics, careers, and relationships are appropriate for time-limited counseling. Those clients who have mild disturbances and are capable of focusing on specific goals are generally able to benefit from brief counseling.

Brief counseling historically has worked well in college counseling centers ever since its inception in the early post-World War II years, the time when I started counseling in the college counseling center at Berkeley (see chaps. 1 and 2). What's different now is the limit of 10 sessions imposed in advance in all cases, as well as the focus on a single, specific goal. I first tried brief counseling with mandated limited sessions recently as a visiting counseling psychologist at the Center for Counseling and Psychological Services at Pennsylvania State University. I was dubious about its constraints. Having the agency imposing limits on my counseling sessions and having to ask permission to extend sessions for certain cases ruffled my feathers. I did find, however, that the making of specific goals at the initial stage and following them worked well for most students. Essential to the success of this system was that, for those who needed it, we could, with permission, extend the sessions. I had no trouble extending sessions at this particular center, although this may not always be the case at other centers.

Use of Tests and Inventories

Counselors use standardized tests and inventories in the counseling process when they and their clients agree that information gained from these measures can help client self-exploration (see chap. 6). They are often used to augment interviews when client concerns are related to career choice and exploration (see chap. 12), but they can also be helpful when clients are exploring interpersonal relationships or are seeking deeper self-awareness. College and university counseling centers, by and large, have been using fewer tests with clients than they did in the early days. This, in large part, is because of the decrease in centers offering career counseling.

For those students requesting career counseling, the following interest and personality inventories are generally used. The Strong Interest Inventory, the Kuder Occupational Interest Survey, and the Self-Directed Search are most often administered. The Edwards Personal Preference Schedule and the Alport Vernon Study of Values are also popular for both career and interpersonal and personal concerns. In some centers, the Minnesota Multiphasic Personality Inventory (MMPI) and the Wechsler Adult Intelligence Scale (WAIS) are used with persons experiencing personal problems or academic difficulties.

University Testing Services

Campus testing services manage a variety of tests for the university, including administering and scoring entrance examinations for applicants to various graduate programs, administering and scoring student evaluations of faculty, and scoring and making statistical analyses of classroom exams for professors. These screening and evaluative types of tests are not counseling or counseling-related functions and are not discussed here. Many counseling centers—including the one I directed—do not offer this type of testing service. Testing services such as these should be offered by a separate testing bureau that has the sole function of administering tests and evaluations and giving feedback to administrators, department heads, and faculty.

Supervising Interns and Aides

Most counseling centers serve as resources for the placement of counselor interns from departments of psychology, educational psychology, and counselor education and, less frequently, from schools of social work. At the center, counselors supervise interns at either the masters or doctoral level. College counselors may also train resident aides and counselor aides in interviewing skills so that they can interact effectively with students and instruct them in referral policies and procedures.

Maintaining Referral Networks

Most college campuses are self-contained mini-communities for students, with health services, counseling services, financial aid, housing, dining, and recreational facilities, as well as student centers and associations for various religious, cultural, ethnic, and social-political action groups. Even so, many students feel isolated and out of touch with campus student support groups. A good cross-referral system among the counseling center and other student personnel offices and student associations helps reduce student feelings of isolation.

Counseling center staffs use a variety of ways to inform the campus community about counseling services—for example, distributing brochures, featuring their services in the school newspaper, and having open houses. Excellent sources of referral to the counseling center are the directors of residence halls and their aides, student services personnel, and the various student support groups and associations.

Counseling centers can also set up guidelines for faculty and administrators to refer students to the counseling center. Faculty are in a key position to refer students whose academic difficulties seem related to signs of emotional blocking or distress. Counseling center staffs can offer faculty guidelines on when and how to refer students to the center. The University of Maryland, for example, has developed a Take a Faculty to Lunch program to orient new faculty to services offered by the center. At these sessions, counselors describe to faculty how to determine whether a student needs counseling help and how to make a referral (Westbrook et al., 1993).

Regarding administrative referrals, counseling centers must continually keep the administration informed about the center's role. Administrators responsible for students' scholastic standing and discipline may see the counseling center as a place they can refer students who are on academic probation or who have broken campus regulations. Counseling in these cases should still be voluntary. For example, a student whose grade point average has fallen below the university's minimal standards should not be required to get counseling in order to remain in school.

✥ INDIVIDUAL COUNSELING: PRESENTING PROBLEMS OF COLLEGE STUDENTS

Presenting problems of college students generally parallel those encountered in high school. Both groups are in educational settings with requirements they must fulfill to graduate and policies they must agree to follow in order to remain in school. College students differ from high school students in that most are of legal age and so are primarily responsible for their behavior; they also are not legally compelled to attend school. College students usually have more choice of instructors than do high school students.

Although they are legally adults, most undergraduates remain in a suspended state of semi-immaturity and dependence, compared with persons of the same age who do not go to college but begin careers, have a steady income, get married, and start raising families. For college students who work, jobs are usually part time and involve menial tasks. If they decide to go on to graduate school, they generally experience further delays in developing a stable economic life and permanent relationships.

Many must obtain student loans that put them into considerable debt. They are under constant stress to perform optimally in their academic work. Poor relationships with an instructor may hinder or delay graduation or jeopardize entrance into graduate school. Attending college may place strain on intimate relationships, particularly when one partner wants more time and commitment from the other.

Even with the pockets of available on-campus special interest support groups, many students feel isolated and lonely. Many come from far away, from places where they are accustomed to close identification with family and community. This may be particularly true for ethnic students and for international students (see the section "Addressing Multicultural Diversity," later in the chapter).

With the increased numbers of older students on campus and the return to college of women who left to raise children, college counselors are working now with older people. Counselors should thus be aware of issues and developmental needs of older persons, those in their 30s, 40s, and beyond. Counselors should know theories of family and marital counseling even though they work less directly with families than do counselors in other settings. Problems concerning marriage, career change, aging parents, and child care show up more often in 2-year community colleges than in 4-year colleges because the average age of students in community colleges is higher.

Career/Educational Concerns

During the period of intense student activism and the push for alternative lifestyles in the late 1960s and early 1970s, many students were less interested in exploring traditional career choices or in attaining high grade point averages than they were in personal growth and encounter groups. Some counseling centers either neglected career counseling or considered vocational concerns of students to be secondary.

A trend that started in the late 1970s and that has continued steadily throughout the years has been a continuous decline in the number of counseling centers offering career counseling. In 1996, a national survey of college counseling center directors showed that, on 30% of campuses, career counseling is offered primarily by counseling centers, 55% by career counseling and placement offices, and the remainder shared equally by counseling and career centers (Gallagher, 1996). At Western Washington University, the center I developed in 1961 and directed until 1973 no longer does career counseling.

This trend is disturbing and ironic because, in the early days, professional counseling got its start and developed its unique identity from counselors working primarily with student vocational and academic concerns. As discussed earlier (see chaps. 2 and 12), career exploration as an integral part of personal development has been the hallmark of college counseling.

Leading counseling professionals continue to insist that general counseling and career counseling are inseparable (Isaacson & Brown, 1997; Osipow & Fitzgerald, 1996; Zunker, 1994). When counseling centers abandon this heritage, they not only do an injustice to students but also take on the image of a mental health clinic—quite different from their original identity.

The cases presented here are typical of career concerns that clients bring to counseling centers still involved in career counseling. If career counseling is done in a separate career counseling center, the procedures laid out here apply as well. Further, cross-referrals between the two centers are essential to ensure that clients get the service most suitable to their needs.

Nowadays, career concerns and academic success appear to be foremost in students' minds. Many students, faced with the high-tech revolution and stiff competition, react with dismay and even panic. Jobs in some professions are not readily available at graduation, and entrance requirements at professional schools have become stiff. Specific decisions about careers are expected of students in colleges. Many students are concerned about entering graduate school; some have two or more interests that appear to conflict. Other students may have difficulty choosing majors. Some parents try to persuade a daughter or son to select a particular major whether or not she or he has any interest or ability in that direction.

Increasing numbers of women have decided to return to school after raising families. Many of them express doubts about their ability to do academic work. Some are in conflict with husbands who are ambivalent about their wives going back to school.

Some college students who made top grades in high school are flunking out of college. Requests for counseling and referrals from faculty members and deans of students can be expected regarding poor scholastic standing. Some students may want to discuss the advisability of dropping out of school.

Counselors often see students who may be in the wrong majors, may be unsuited for college, may be working too many hours, or may lack motivation because they see no purpose in attending college. Many students experience anxiety reactions and block when taking tests, doing mathematics assignments, presenting speeches before a class, or writing English themes or term papers. Consider these students' concerns:

> **Client 1:** Janet, age 32, requests counseling because she is concerned about her academic progress and her vocational goals. She has returned to college after 13 years of marriage. Her children are 11 and 9 years old; her husband is a busy executive in a local advertising agency. Janet says he supports her attending college but is too busy to give much help at home. She finds schoolwork stimulating but overwhelming, particularly because she must make arrangements for child care and assume the major responsibility for the home. She also is not sure what career she wants. Law school and environmental science are two possibilities. She looks anxious and fatigued.

> **Client 2:** Neil, a freshman, is taking a mathematics course required for graduation. He was referred to the counseling center by his mathematics teacher. Neil tells you that he does well in his homework assignments but that he blanks out on tests. He studies hard, but as soon as the test is handed out, he becomes immobilized. The teacher is sympathetic and believes that Neil understands his work, but he has no option but to fail him on tests.

> *Client 1:* The counselor needs first to help Janet reassess how she and her husband are sharing household tasks. They need to discuss the degree to which her husband is willing to share responsibility for the home and children and the degree to which she has been able to accept his help. Any residual guilt feelings about leaving the children or any doubts about her academic ability that may be

contributing to her anxiety must be worked through. After these factors are clarified, career options can be explored from the standpoint of how her interests, abilities, and values relate to law, environmental science, or other fields. Interest inventories, personality inventories, and other appropriate testing might be used. If Janet appears to need support, perhaps she might join a group for older women students on campus.

Client 2: Blocks or anxiety reactions, common among students, occur most frequently in mathematics, speech, and English classes. Neil's immobilization on mathematics exams may represent an anxiety about the consequences of failing or the need to be perfect, or it may be a fear conditioned by poor teaching in earlier mathematics classes. Ellis's rational-emotive techniques, which involve logical reasoning, are often used in these situations (see chap. 5). Some counselors might use Wolpe's (1973) desensitization techniques with Neil. I discuss Wolpe's procedures below, with Client 5.

Personal Concerns

College students have continuing questions about traditional social mores, sexual patterns, and lifestyles. Many students are exploring religious, spiritual, and philosophical beliefs. As students move away from the immediate jurisdiction of their parents, their behavior changes as they encounter new experiences.

Self-doubt and uncertainties are as frequent as in high school. Homesickness, if severe, may lead some students to drop out of school. Students may worry over why they are floundering while others their age are doing well. Anxieties may increase as students near graduation. Questions and concerns about homosexuality and bisexuality are more frequently raised by college students than by high school students.

Client 3: Vivian is a 20-year-old junior who feels attracted to some women. She has dated men and has had intimate and pleasant heterosexual relationships. In a discussion with members of the campus gay liberation group, it was suggested that she seek counseling because of her ambivalence.

Client 4: Georgia is a 20-year-old junior who describes herself as lacking motivation and self-discipline. Neither college nor social life is stimulating. She has done well academically but is beginning to have trouble in some courses. She attended a women's consciousness-raising, psychological education group jointly sponsored by the student affairs office and the counseling center. Her apathy prompted leaders of the group to refer her for counseling.

Client 5: Al says he has a phobia about going to a dentist. He has been told that further neglect of his teeth may lead to serious gum problems. He makes dental appointments and then manages to talk himself out of going.

Client 6: Gina is a freshman who was referred by a resident aide because she is experiencing severe homesickness. She feels nauseous, has periods of crying, and has missed classes. She has been thinking of dropping out of school. She has telephoned her parents, who have tried to convince her to work it out on campus.

Client 3: Vivian is expressing a need to clarify her sexual orientation in a nonjudgmental, neutral atmosphere. A client-centered approach seems appropriate in helping her sort out her feelings, attitudes, values, and concerns. I would help her confront her ambivalent feelings and explore more directly the quality and quantity of her relationships with men and women and whether she is receiving pressure one way or another from either lesbians or heterosexuals. No attempt would be made to sway her in one direction or the other.

Client 4: Georgia appears to be depressed. The counselor should notice that she has already taken two proactive steps: (a) attending a women's group session and (b) coming in for counseling. I would help her explore uncertainties she has about herself academically, personally, and socially. She can be encouraged to increase her academic input and social interactions gradually. Workshops based on behaviorally oriented theories help clients confront the degree of reality of their concerns. They also help change negative reinforcers to positive ones and use techniques to spur the depressed person into action. Beck's approach to depression (see chap. 5) is appropriate.

Client 5: Al's fear of dentists might be reduced effectively by Wolpe's desensitization techniques. I would help him develop a list of situations that elicit varying degrees of anxiety related to keeping a dental appointment. Then we would work together to rank these situations in a hierarchy of severity of anxiety, with his highest anxiety presumably being that of having his teeth worked on in a dentist's chair. Al would then be taught to relax various muscles progressively until he is capable of relaxing himself fully in a few minutes. Next, he would be taught to visualize increasingly anxious situations while relaxed, until he is able to visualize himself in a dentist's chair and remain calm. After Al becomes desensitized through imagined actions, the counselor helps him take actual steps toward seeing the dentist.

Client 6: A counselor should work closely with Gina to help reassure her and to help her stay in school. She might require more than one counseling session a week for a while. I would talk with her of her concerns about being able to do the work, feelings of inability to make friends, guilt about leaving her family, and other sources of unhappiness, such as an uncooperative roommate, an intimidating professor, or an overload of classes. In most cases, when a student is given support and reassurance, homesickness wanes. Cooperation between resident hall personnel and counseling center staff, with due regard for confidentiality, can be a plus for the student's ultimate resolution of the problem. A support group can be helpful.

Interpersonal Conflicts and Concerns

Students in dormitories often seek counseling because of friction with roommates. To get along with roommates, students must learn to accept different values and different lifestyles. They also must learn appropriate ways of asserting themselves if roommates behave in an inconsiderate way or take unfair advantage of them.

Premarriage, marriage, or couple counseling occurs fairly often. When couples break up, for instance, problems may be difficult to overcome because both may live on campus, and it would be difficult for them to avoid seeing each other. They must often contend with their roommates or acquaintances on campus who want to know about the breakup and/or help them somehow.

In many colleges, the majority of students live away from home. Even so, much of college counseling relates to parent-student relationships. Problems with parents are frequent. Parents may subtly or directly threaten to withdraw financial support or to disown a student who behaves in a way that displeases them. This displeasure can occur over anything from choice of friends or career to drinking habits to general ways of living. Many college students also worry about their parents' problems, such as divorce, illness, or loss of job. Counselors can often help students and parents work through the difficult process of confronting their differences, resolving conflicts, and developing more constructive relationships.

Client 7: Carla, a freshman, is having problems with her roommate. Unlike Carla, the roommate is friendly and sociable but is also untidy and brings in friends at all hours without checking with her. Carla expresses fondness for her roommate and wishes she could have the dates and social contacts of her friend. She dislikes her roommate's inconsiderate behavior but cannot express it directly to her. Her resident director referred her for counseling.

Client 8: Matt has an excellent grade point average but is having trouble with a professor who teaches a required course in his major field. Matt believes that his midterm grade, which was below average, was unfair. He describes the professor as belligerent. His motivation to work on assignments is low. The counseling staff has received similar complaints from other students about this professor. This professor is the only person teaching the course.

Client 9: Bert is a 26-year-old graduate student living with his mother in an apartment off campus. His mother is in her early 60s. She cooks for him, cleans house, and waits up for him when he dates. Bert wants to move out on his own. When he mentions this to his mother, she worries about being able to take care of herself and has felt this way ever since his husband's death 10 years before. Bert feels frustrated and guilty.

Client 7: Roommate problems often result from students' inability or reluctance to assert themselves with their roommates. In Carla's case, the counselor can help her confront her roommate constructively. Assertiveness training might be appropriate. Gestaltists might focus on her ambivalences about her roommate. She may need help developing social skills other than assertion. As counseling progresses, if communication between roommates reaches an impasse, Carla may decide to move. The counselor can refer her to another dorm if that plan seems appropriate.

Client 8: The counselor needs to clarify with Matt what he hopes to gain from counseling. If he wants to develop ways of interacting with the professor, then counseling is in order. The counselor could help him confront the professor in a constructive manner. Role playing might be used to help Matt practice the proposed interview. The counselor might explore why the professor has had such a bad effect on Matt's motivation. Ways of coping with similar situations could be discussed. If Matt wants to register an administrative complaint, the counselor can suggest that Matt talk with the head of the department. The counselor should not intervene; it is not the counseling center's role to report a professor's behavior to the authorities.

Client 9: The counselor can help Bert confront his mother with the importance of his developing his own life and of her developing her own. Guilt feelings must be explored. If his mother continues to express anxiety about Bert's deserting her and about her inability to take care of herself, counseling for her might be suggested. Bert could join a men's group. This experience, combined with individual counseling, would help him take constructive action that would be beneficial to both him and his mother.

Gender Issues

Gender issues are generally expressed most intensely on college campuses. Women study gender role concerns in courses and tend to join together to object to discrimination or harassment from faculty, administrators, or male students. They question social-cultural stereotyping that contributes to depression, domestic violence, and career discrimination. Gender issues are discussed at length in chapters 4, 5, and 14.

A trend that continues to raise implications for college campuses and counseling staffs is the large number of women returning to college after they have fulfilled homemaking responsibilities (Padula, 1994). A comprehensive literature review was conducted by Padula (1994) regarding women who return to college (reentry women) at a nontraditional age after prolonged absence for as much as 35 years. Studies show that these returning women tend to have significantly higher grade point averages and higher educational aspirations than do traditional students. Studies indicate, however, that they have less confidence in themselves and in their career planning, suffer from role conflict and emotional distress from family demands, and express significant dissatisfaction with advisement and counseling services. Positive attitudes and support from family, friends, and professors are particularly important (Padula, 1994).

Padula (1994) concluded that career counseling programs need to be improved for these women: Counselors need to become aware of the special needs and concerns of older women and provide counseling and support groups and psychoeducational programs that address their particular needs.

> Women reentering educational institutions do have characteristics and needs that are different from traditional students. Reentry women are also very concerned about vocational, family, and financial issues, as well as issues of personal development. These concerns underline the necessity for the development of counseling, advisement, and educational programs that will meet the needs of these reentry people. (p. 15)

Antisocial Acts and Alcohol Abuse

College students come to counseling because of antisocial, aberrant, or illegal acts similar to those of students in public schools and persons in the community. Shoplifting, drug or alcohol abuse, and sexual aberrations occur in all settings wherever counselors work. Misbehaviors and illegal acts occurring primarily on college campuses include cheating on exams, creating havoc in a dormitory or elsewhere on campus, harassing teachers, and stealing exam questions. When students voluntarily seek counseling, confidentiality is upheld. No report goes to the office of the dean of students or the vice president for student affairs unless the students are endangering others or themselves.

Antisocial behaviors generally come to the attention of a dean in the student affairs office who decides whether disciplinary action is necessary. The dean may recommend that the person receive counseling without taking disciplinary action. In these cases, it is important that the counselor let the student know that she or he cannot be protected from legal proceedings or disciplinary action if the illegal or inappropriate behavior continues.

Alcohol Counseling

Alcohol abuse increased dramatically on college campuses throughout the country during the 1990s, with serious consequences for student drinkers, fellow classmates, and school officials (Prendergast, 1994; Steenbarger, 1998).

> Recent research suggests that alcohol abuse is widespread among college students, with approximately 20% of all students qualifying as heavy drinkers and over 40% of students reporting at least one binge-drinking episode in a given two-week period. This drinking is associated with a number of adverse consequences, including sexual misconduct, damage to property, academic difficulty, drunk driving, unsafe sex, and suicidality. (Steenbarger, 1998, p. 81)

In a Carnegie Foundation survey, college presidents claimed that the biggest problem on campus is alcohol abuse (Eigen, 1991). The sharp increases in sexual assaults, date rapes, and gang rapes on college campuses are often related to alcohol abuse (Gallagher, 1997).

Steenbarger (1998) believes that the existing college counseling programs are ineffective for treating alcohol abuse because of the prevalence of brief counseling. "Even when alcohol abuse is identified, the forms of treatment offered on many campuses are too abbreviated to be effective and rely on approaches that are associated with poor outcomes" (p. 89).

Professionals recommend that counseling centers offer ongoing longer term group work, the type that has proved effective in alcohol treatment. They also recommend broadening counseling services to include motivational counseling techniques described in chapter 13 for clients in denial and teaching coping skills to clients who have stopped drinking and want to prevent relapse (Miller & Rollnick, 1991; Steenbarger, 1998).

Rutgers University, in 1989, established the first campus-based alcohol and drug rehabilitation center in the United States. Student substance abusers can now continue their education while receiving treatment. Since then, other campuses have adopted similar alcohol and drug treatment programs (Steenbarger, 1998).

Crises

Because the number of college students who are experiencing serious emotional problems has increased considerably since the mid-1980s, college counselors have been learning effective intervention procedures (Stone & Archer, 1990).

Crises arising out of suicides or suicide attempts or threats are fairly frequent. College students have a higher suicide rate than the general population (Comer, 1998). In a review of demographic studies about suicide rates in college students, Comer (1998) indicated that, since 1955, the suicide rate of adolescents and young adults has doubled. He concluded from his review that many aspects of college life are stressful: competition for grades, lack of support, indifferent or hostile reactions from professors, jockeying for academic and athletic honors, and increased use of drugs and alcohol. Further, he notes that weakening of nuclear families and rapid, volatile social and economic changes have also contributed to a dramatic upsurge in suicide.

Anxiety attacks or acute psychotic reactions requiring immediate counseling, hospitalization, or drug therapy are also common on college campuses. Students may collapse under academic pressures, the need to make too many decisions, traumatic breaks in relationships, feelings of loneliness and isolation, or the death of a relative or friend.

Cooperative emergency policies and procedures should be developed among the staffs of the counseling center, student personnel offices, student health services, residence halls, and mental health clinics. In residence halls, where emergency situations most often occur, immediate intervention is necessary to determine whether a crisis is of short duration or whether the student appears too incapacitated to continue in school. Further decisions may be necessary about hospitalization, drug therapy, and notification of the student's family. If the crisis is temporary, follow-up counseling may be appropriate. If the student needs hospitalization and the family must be informed, the student personnel officer in charge should take the necessary steps.

Psychiatric services and consultation to help counseling center staff working with clients in crisis are available on two-thirds of college campuses. These are offered in the counseling centers, student health services, or both. In addition, counseling centers average about 18 hours of psychiatric consultation per week for staff members (Gallagher, 1997).

For students experiencing crises after hours, emergency on-call services are provided by counseling centers at about three-fourths of campuses. Counselors on call are reached by beepers, by regular telephone, or through emergency lines (Gallagher, 1997).

✺ WORKING WITH GROUPS

About 85% of university counseling centers offer group counseling (Gallagher, 1997). Special characteristics of young adult groups that counselors should consider are discussed by Budman, Michael, and Wisneski (1980) and Ohlsen, Horne, and Lawe (1988). Problems tend to center on difficulties in developing intimate relationships, with consequent feelings of loneliness and isolation. Many young adults who lack the capacity to be open and trusting with others exacerbate the problem by giving up, withdrawing, or overintellectualizing. On college campuses, opportunities to socialize that are readily available may aggravate a student's feelings of isolation and loneliness.

With older students, ages 36 to 50, groups address anxieties that relate to doubts about being in school, lack of peer support, conflicts with spouses or children, pressure about changing careers, and stress as a result of separations, divorce, or broken relationships.

Personal growth groups, called *structured groups,* focus on behavioral and skills training that reduces stress, develops relationships, and handles transitions related to normal life development (Gazda, 1984). The group leader defines the problem, assesses how participants are functioning, provides a rationale for learning, and uses direct instruction, modeling, role playing, cognitive restructuring, biofeedback, and the like to accomplish goals (Ohlsen et al., 1988).

Examples of prevention groups for a college population are described by Drum (1984). He presents four comprehensive programs: Stress Awareness, Relationships, Future Forecast, and Transitions. In the latter, for instance, he outlines more than 25 panels and workshops, including academic adjustment, gender roles and relationships, coming out as a gay or lesbian, minority culture transitions, intimacy, changing religious values, and career choices.

Dendato and Diener (1986) have effectively used cognitive/relaxation techniques and training in study skills in structured groups to reduce test anxiety. In six 1-hour sessions, deep muscle relaxation and Ellis's rational-emotive strategies were taught to reduce tension and to challenge irrational beliefs about the consequences of examination grades.

Some counseling centers offer relaxation and stress reduction programs. Rhode Island University is developing a stress management laboratory using computerized EEG biofeedback, and Salisbury State College and the University of Louisville have set up relaxation rooms for clients not requiring a staff member to be present (Gallagher, 1997).

☙ OUTREACH: PREVENTION AND INTERVENTION

The outreach programs designed to improve student mental health environments in colleges and universities usually take the form of group activities or consultation with faculty and administrators. Similar to those in secondary schools, the two types of psychological education groups are developmental education and crisis prevention and intervention.

Psychological Education: Developmental

Career Education

Funding provided by the National Occupational Information Coordinating Committee (NOICC) has increased career education programs in colleges and universities.

NOICC (1992, 1994) includes guidelines for career development programs in higher education. Funding and guidelines from NOICC have enabled college counseling centers and career centers to offer a variety of programs:

> To help students/clients choose/change a major and/or identify potential occupations, colleges provide assessment of interests, aptitudes, values, and work styles . . . furnish . . . career libraries providing materials about colleges, graduate and professional schools as well as a full array of occupational data . . . provide career development classes, and individual and group counseling. (NOICC, 1994, p. 10)

NOICC has also enabled career placement offices to help students explore internships or other on-the-job experiences that provide opportunities for students to clarify their career choices. Furthermore, as a result of ongoing NOICC funding, career centers have developed programs that teach students how to write résumés, how to embark on a job search, and how to conduct themselves in job interviews (NOICC, 1994).

Counseling centers and placement office staff members often work jointly to help students explore careers related to their majors, seek employment, develop résumés, and practice job interviews. For older returning students, counselors develop workshops or group sessions about how to reenter the workforce successfully or how to explore new, more satisfying careers.

Personal Growth and Development

Despite increased demands that college counselors work with more serious psychological problems and with crisis intervention, counseling centers should continue to provide programs directed toward personal growth and development (Stone & Archer, 1990).

Westbrook et al. (1993) describe psychoeducational programs in the classroom (PEP) offered by the counseling center staff at the University of Maryland, College Park. "Psychoeducational programs in the classroom are small-group procedures that are designed to assist students in reducing stress, relieving test anxiety, relaxing or acquiring other circumscribed goals" (p. 686). Westbrook et al. emphasize the necessity for counseling centers to develop workshops and classes regarding racism.

Romano (1984) describes Psychology and Management of Stress: Theory and Application, a credit course in stress management at the University of Minnesota. After presenting psychological stress theories, he uses a combination of holistic and cognitive-behavioral approaches. Students use a holistic approach to practice progressive relaxation, breathing, and biofeedback; they learn behavioral approaches such as Meichenbaum's stress-inoculation training, assertiveness training, and some of Ellis's cognitive restructuring to reduce stress-producing attitudes and behavior (see chap. 5). In evaluation, 56% of students reported lower stress levels.

Psychological Education: Crisis Intervention

At universities and colleges, the major risk groups are students with alcohol and drug problems, adult children of alcoholics (ACOAs), suicidal students, and perpetrators and victims of violence.

Alcohol Abuse

The heavy drinking patterns of college students require that college counseling services focus on extensive prevention and intervention programs to supplement counseling and therapy alcohol abuse treatment programs discussed earlier. Steenbarger (1998) presents five steps to improve outreach alcohol prevention programs: (a) increase early screening, (b) enhance campuswide education regarding available services, (c) offer and promote more alcohol-free residence halls, (d) expand counseling services to include more and improved group preventive activities and intervention services, psychoeducational courses, and support programs, and (e) broaden services to include coping skills for those who have stopped drinking and want to prevent relapse. "A combination of targeted, educational, environmental, and programmatic structural group interventions holds significant promise in promoting the health of our campus communities" (p. 89).

In response to student heavy drinking on college campuses, Steenbarger (1998) reviewed preventive programs that have been developed on campuses throughout the country. He notes that almost 70% of college campuses have developed on-campus alcohol abuse prevention programs, many of which include policies regulating use of alcohol in fraternities and residence halls.

A comprehensive alcohol education program at the University of Cincinnati includes strategies to alert faculty, staff, and student leaders to the need to regulate alcohol consumption on campus (Coyne, 1984). Interventions are focused on groups that are the worst alcohol abusers—typically, fraternities. Counselors conduct a series of workshops with two volunteer fraternities in which they discuss alcoholism, appropriate house rules for drinking, and alternatives to alcohol.

A psychoeducational group for ACOAs at Colorado State University shared hidden family experiences, confronted denial, and retrieved and restructured suppressed feelings (Downing & Walker, 1987). Self-help strategies were included during the eight group sessions. Afterward, some members joined Al-Anon, and others sought out individual or family counseling.

Suicide

The increasing rate of suicide requires that counseling centers plan comprehensive outreach, prevention, and intervention programs. Counseling staffs have a prime responsibility to explore conditions on campus that are contributing to student suicide and to take what steps they can to ameliorate the problems. Educational programs regarding tell-tale signs of suicidal symptoms can be made available to faculty and staff. Discussions with faculty about the need for mentoring students anxious about their academic progress and consultations with administrators about the effects of faculty abuse and harassment of students can also help reduce stress. Students away from home and lacking family or community support often experience feelings of loneliness, isolation, and despair. Counselors can offer workshops regarding how to cope with such issues as broken relationships and academic pressure and encourage and develop support groups to deal with and help alleviate feelings of isolation.

At a graduate dormitory at Indiana University, after several suicides had occurred in the dorms, four friendship-development seminars were held during the year (Fondacaro, Heller, & Reilly, 1984). Problems contributing to social isolation were identified and shared.

White and Rubenstein (as cited in Gilliland & James, 1997) describe how the Cornell University Psychological Services Center collaborated with local radio stations to broadcast messages about their service aimed at high-risk suicidal students. The program was successful in increasing more high-risk student self-referrals to the center.

Violence

Some university counseling centers have set up programs related to violence prevention or intervention in response to increased numbers of sexual and physical assaults on campuses. California State College at San Francisco has developed a plan of action with academic departments to deal with potentially dangerous students on campus. Southwest Texas State University has set up a Victory Over Violence week to educate students about antiviolent activities on campus (Gallagher, 1996). To work with the aftermath of violence or tragedy on campus, the State University of New York at Cortland has developed a posttraumatic stress debriefing procedure in conjunction with the local hospital psychiatric unit (Gallagher, 1997).

Consultation

Faculty may consult with counselors about concerns or conflicts with students, administrators, or others. They may also raise questions regarding personal problems.

> **Professor D:** Professor Drake has good trust relationships in her physics class. A student confides that she thinks she is pregnant. Another confesses that he has tried cocaine and is worried about it. Still another student shares deep concerns about his alcoholic parents. Professor Drake wants to maintain openness with her students but feels overwhelmed and ill-equipped to handle the students' problems.

> *Professor D:* Professor Drake can be helped to differentiate between the roles of the caring teacher and the professional counselor. She can be given guidelines on how to refer students to a counselor when it appears necessary. She then can be a bridge for students to the counseling center.

Consultation with college administrators includes department chairs, deans of student affairs, and other student personnel workers.

> **Administrator R:** Professor Ramos, department head, asks for a consultation about a faculty member who is depressed and who has mentioned suicide. The faculty member has asked that the information be kept confidential but has also been reluctant to seek professional help. Professor Ramos is worried about the teacher and about her own responsibility for the teacher's welfare.

Administrator B: Dean Brown, dean of the School of Education, asks the counseling center director whether the center can help coordinate efforts to screen, select, and retain students who are candidates for the teacher training program.

Administrator R: The counselor can help Professor Ramos realize that the teacher in question is placing an undue burden on her. I would suggest that she tell the teacher that she cannot keep this information in confidence unless the teacher seeks help. I would offer to see the teacher and help arrange appropriate treatment. If the teacher refuses help, the administrator, with the teacher's knowledge, should be encouraged to notify the teacher's family and arrange for sick leave.

Administrator B: Dean Brown should be told that the counseling center could jeopardize its voluntary, confidential nature if it became involved in evaluations for departments. The counseling center can suggest how the department can interview prospective students and how it can set specific procedures for determining student suitability for the program. Referrals to the counseling center would be appropriate only as long as interactions between students and counselors remained strictly confidential.

Liaison with Off-Campus Community

College counseling centers should maintain good communication and effective cross-referral procedures with other services on or off campus, such as community mental health clinics, community hospitals, marriage and family centers, alcohol and drug treatment centers, rape relief centers, women's shelters, and Planned Parenthood.

ADDRESSING MULTICULTURAL DIVERSITY

College counselors are in a uniquely favorable position to work with the concerns, transitions, and issues of ethnic and multicultural students. College campuses typically draw a wider variety of multicultural groups than do many public schools or communities, where ethnic students mingle with non-ethnic students in dormitories, classes, and social activities. Moreover, diverse ethnic groups tend to come together to raise issues and discuss multiracial, multicultural problems. Ethnic and multicultural issues are thus more likely to arise and be confronted on college campuses. Although most college counseling centers include ethnic counselors on their staffs, in most cases not all major ethnic groups are represented at any one center. Counseling centers continually need to explore ways of modifying counseling to meet the divergent needs of ethnic students, work out outreach programs, and develop support groups on campus.

Effective counseling with the major ethnic groups discussed in chapter 14 applies as well on college campuses. Not covered earlier and especially evident on college campuses in concentrated numbers are multiracial and international students, whose presence on campuses raises issues that need to be attended to by college counselors.

Multiracial Students

A group of students from seven different multiracial backgrounds formed a support group at the University of Memphis. Each member of the group had a multiracial background. The special challenge or issue facing these students was studied by Nishimura (1998). She formed groups and asked them to express their concerns; from their responses, she developed common themes confronting them. The students' major concern was their difficulty establishing a racial identity that could help them define themselves and communicate that image to others. They were not comfortable in monoracial groups, often feeling "challenged to 'prove' their ethnic membership" (p. 50). They also felt a lack of models or mentors who could guide them in identity development. To them, race was an ever-present issue.

College counselors need to be aware of, and sensitive to, the complex identity issues of multiracial students. They also must examine their own attitudes and values about interracial marriage and the children of interracial marriages (Nishimura, 1998).

International Students

Increasing percentages of the college student population are from foreign countries (Pedersen, 1991). For them, the usual stresses encountered in college are compounded. When students come from different political or socioeconomic systems, the cultural or values differences they face become more complex than those of ethnic groups in the United States. These differences may show up in how faculty and students relate, how much medical care is expected, how much freedom the individual has to choose a major, and how males and females relate. Feelings of isolation and alienation may overwhelm these students when family support is not available.

The following special areas of concern for international students are specified by Orpeza, Fitzgibbon, and Baron (1991): culture shock, changes in socioeconomic status, expectations about academic performance, and family-related pressures. Many students also face worry and concern about political unrest in their home countries, fear about deportation, grief over a family death, or anxiety about family problems back home.

Overall, the theories, techniques, and attitudes discussed in chapter 14 regarding working with ethnic groups in the United States apply to students from foreign countries. Counselors must be aware of any stereotyping of clients, and they need to be alert to cultural differences without losing sight of the individual.

In a review of the literature on counseling international students, Leong and Chou (1995) concluded: "From our review, it seems particularly important to develop creative alternative modalities for international students, given some of the cultural barriers and inhibitions about seeking professional psychological help" (p. 238). They suggest as well outreach activities such as time management and language skill workshops, pretherapy orientation sessions to acquaint them with Western counseling approaches, and training of resident hall advisors.

✷ WORKING WITH FAMILIES

College counselors work with families infrequently. Because college students still have conflicts with parents, however, and because their problems may stem from earlier experiences in dysfunctional families, college counselors need to be familiar with family systems theory and family dynamics (for further discussion, see chap. 10).

Lopez (1986) describes the links between the nature of the family structure and depression in college students. He recommends that counselors assess the family structure with the depressed student and discuss troublesome family interactions, such as parental disputes and the student's role in the disputes. Different and more effective patterns of response can then be developed.

A family systems approach called *systemic theory,* based on Haley's strategic therapy (see chap. 10), is recommended for college counseling (Searight & Openlander, 1984). In this approach, counselors pay attention to family structure and use paradoxical directives to change self-defeating behavior.

A comprehensive model for counseling ACOAs in college counseling centers is described by Crawford and Phyfer (1988). They believe that ACOAs who voluntarily seek counseling have attained sufficient awareness of the problem that counselors can use Gestalt techniques (see chap. 5) to elicit feelings related to unfinished business about family interactions. They also recommend the following: family sculpting, developed by Satir (see chap. 10), so that long-denied emotions can be acted out; cognitive restructuring and behavior rehearsal to develop new ways of thinking and behaving; and counseling techniques specific to adult children who assumed roles of hero, scapegoat, lost child, or mascot in the family of origin.

More older students are requesting marital counseling. Significant numbers of students live together or consider marriage before graduation. Premarital, marital, or postmarital counseling and couple counseling for heterosexual and gay and lesbian couples are services available to students.

✷ SUMMARY

College and university counseling centers closely follow professional counseling association recommendations that well-trained professional counselors provide services geared to persons with normal developmental concerns. Students' flexible schedules and close proximity to campus services make it relatively easy for students to get counseling.

Counseling services include individual and group counseling, various outreach prevention and intervention services, supervision of interns and resident aides, and referral networking, and liaisons with health and social services on and off campus. Counselors see clients regarding concerns about careers, personal doubts about themselves and their academic ability, relationship conflicts, gender issues, antisocial behavior, especially those related to alcohol abuse, and crisis cases related to suicide and violence.

Counselor outreach psychological education programs include classes and workshops regarding career education, personal growth, and interpersonal relationships. Because gender issues arise more intensely on college campuses, more clients are likely to raise gender issues in college counseling sessions than in other counseling settings. College counselors need to continue to address the special concerns of the wide variety of ethnic, multiracial, and international students on university campuses.

Although most college students do not live with their parents, many still depend on them for financial support, and many are still suffering from residuals of earlier faulty parent-child interactions. College counselors thus need to be familiar with family theories and techniques. Marital, couple, and family counseling are becoming more common on college campuses as older married persons are returning to school.

❧ PROJECTS AND ACTIVITIES

1. A counselor in a college counseling center receives a visit from a roommate of one of her clients. The roommate tells the counselor that he is concerned the client is not leveling with the counselor about his real problem. He offers to give background information about his friend that he believes will be helpful. How should the counselor respond?

2. The director of a college counseling center notices that the proportion of minority students seeking counseling is significantly lower than that of their ratio to the student body as a whole. What steps can the director take to be sure that minority students who need help will receive it?

3. Referrals from faculty and other professionals on campus are encouraged by directors of counseling centers. Some faculty members who have referred students to the center call and ask whether the students have shown up and what has happened. What should a counselor do in these instances?

4. An official of a government agency telephones the director of a college counseling center and asks whether a certain student has had counseling, because the official wants an evaluation of the student regarding security risks. How should the director respond in a manner consistent with professional standards?

5. A residence director refers a student to a counselor. The student, who is underage, has been drinking in the dorm. The student is willing to receive counseling. After a few sessions, the resident director calls and tells the counselor that the student is still drinking and wonders what to do. How should the counselor respond?

6. A student who is a resident aide calls the counseling center to explain that a student on his floor appears to be in a serious emotional state. The student refuses to leave his room, eat meals, or attend classes; he is incoherent and seems to be hallucinating. The college has no psychiatrist on staff, and the health center offers primarily first-aid treatment. How should the counseling center staff respond?

➤❀ REFERENCES

Benshoff, J. M. (1998). On creating a new journal for college counseling. *Journal of College Counseling, 1,* 3–4.

Budman, S. H., Michael, J., & Wisneski, M. J. (1980). Short-term group psychotherapy: An adult developmental model. *International Journal of Group Therapy, 30,* 63–76.

Comer, R. J. (1998). *Abnormal psychology* (3rd ed.). New York: Freeman.

Coyne, R. K. (1984). Preliminary prevention through a campus alcohol education project. *Personnel and Guidance Journal, 62,* 524–529.

Crawford, R. L., & Phyfer, A. Q. (1988). Adult children of alcoholics: A counseling model. *Journal of College Student Development, 29,* 105–111.

Dendato, K. M., & Diener, D. (1986). Effectiveness of cognitive/relaxation therapy and study-skills training in reducing self-reported anxiety and improving the academic performance of test-anxious students. *Journal of Counseling Psychology, 33,* 131–135.

Downing, N. E., & Walker, M. E. (1987). A psychoeducational group for adult children of alcoholics. *Journal of Counseling & Development, 65,* 440–443.

Drum, D. J. (1984). Implementing theme-focused prevention: Challenge for the 1980s. *Personnel and Guidance Journal, 62,* 509–513.

Eigen, L. D. (1991). *Alcohol practices, policies, and potentials of American colleges and universities: A white paper.* Rockville, MD: U.S. Department of Health and Human Services, Office for Substance Abuse Prevention.

Fondacaro, M. R., Heller, K., & Reilly, M. J. (1984). Development of friendship networks as a prevention strategy in a university megadome. *Personnel and Guidance Journal, 62,* 520–523.

Gage, L. A., & Gyorky, Z. K. (1990). Identifying appropriate clients for time-limited counseling. *Journal of College Student Development, 31,* 476–477.

Gallagher, R. P. (1991). National survey of counseling center directors. Pittsburgh: University of Pittsburgh, University Counseling and Student Development Center.

Gallagher, R. P. (1996). *National survey of counseling center directors.* Alexandria, VA: International Association of Counseling Services.

Gallagher, R. P. (1997). *National survey of counseling center directors.* Alexandria, VA: International Association of Counseling Services.

Gazda, G. M. (1984). *Group counseling: A developmental approach* (3rd ed.). Boston: Allyn & Bacon.

Gilliland, B. E., & James, R. K. (1997). *Crisis intervention strategies* (3rd ed.). Pacific Grove, CA: Brooks/Cole.

Isaacson, L. E., & Brown, D. (1997). *Career information, career counseling, and career development* (6th ed.). Boston: Allyn & Bacon.

Kirk, B. A., Johnson, A. P., Redfield, J. E., Free, J. E., Michel, J., Roston, R. A., & Warman, R. E. (1971). Guidelines for university and college counseling services. *American Psychologist, 26,* 585–589.

Leong, F. T. L., & Chou, E. L. (1995). Counseling international students. In P. B. Pedersen, J. G. Draguns, W. J. Lonner, & J. E. Trimble (Eds.), *Counseling across cultures* (4th ed., pp. 210–242). Thousand Oaks, CA: Sage.

Lopez, F. G. (1986). Family structures and depression: Implications for the counseling of depressed college students. *Journal of Counseling & Development, 64,* 508–511.

Miller, W. R., & Rollnick, S. (1991). *Motivational interviewing: Preparing people to change addictive behavior.* New York: Guilford Press.

National Occupational Information Coordinating Committee (NOICC). (1992). *The national career development guidelines project.* Washington, DC: Author.

National Occupational Information Coordinating Committee (NOICC). (1994). *Program guide: Planning to meet career development needs.* Washington, DC: Author.

Nishimura, N. J. (1998). Addressing the issues of multiracial students on college campuses. *Journal of College Counseling, 1,* 45–53.

Ohlsen, M. M., Horne, A. M., & Lawe, C. F. (1988). *Group counseling* (3rd ed.). New York: Holt, Rinehart & Winston.

Orpeza, B. A. C., Fitzgibbon, M., & Baron, A., Jr. (1991). Managing mental health crises of foreign college students. *Journal of Counseling & Development, 69,* 280–284.

Osipow, S. H., & Fitzgerald, L. F. (1996). *Theories of career development* (4th ed.). Boston: Allyn & Bacon.

Padula, M. A. (1994). Reentry woman: A literature review with recommendations for counseling and research. *Journal of Counseling & Development, 73,* 10–16.

Pedersen, P. B. (1991). Counseling international students. *Counseling Psychologist, 19,* 10–58.

Prendergast, M. L. (1994). Substance use and abuse among college students: A review of recent literature. *Journal of American College Health, 43,* 99–114.

Rogers, C. R. (1942). *Counseling and psychotherapy.* Boston: Houghton Mifflin.

Rogers, C. (1951). *Client-centered therapy: Its current practice, implications, and therapy.* Boston: Houghton Mifflin.

Romano, J. L. (1984). Stress management and wellness: Reaching beyond the counselor's office. *Personnel and Guidance Journal, 62,* 533–536.

Searight, H. R., & Openlander, P. (1984). Systemic therapy: A new brief intervention model. *Personnel and Guidance Journal, 20,* 381–391.

Steenbarger, B. N. (1998). Alcohol abuse and college counseling: An overview of research and practice. *Journal of College Counseling, 1,* 81–92.

Stone, G. L., & Archer, J., Jr. (1990). College and university counseling centers in the 1990s: Challenges and limits. *Counseling Psychologist, 18,* 539–607.

Super, D. (1953). A theory of vocational development. *American Psychologist, 8,* 185–190.

Westbrook, F. D., Kandell, J. J., Kirkland, S. E., Phillips, P. E., Regan, A. E., Medvene, A., & Oslin, Y. D. (1993). University campus consultation: Opportunities and limitations. *Journal of counseling & Development, 71,* 684–688.

Wolpe, J. (1973). *The practice of behavior therapy* (2nd ed.). New York: Pergamon.

Zunker, V. G. (1994). *Career counseling: Applied concepts of life planning* (4th ed.). Pacific Grove, CA: Brooks/Cole.

19 Community Counseling

Before 1960, mental health care for the general population was not considered a responsibility of local communities. Persons with mental illness were placed in state-run asylums located in "rural settings, housing thousands of patients for years, sometimes decades, on end" (Wylie, 1992, p. 14). Affluent people could afford to see a psychotherapist or to seek care at a private clinic. In between, Wylie (1992) says, "there was very little in the way of health care for the vast majority of Americans" (p. 15). After humanistic, developmental, and cognitive-behavioral theories were introduced in the 1950s, 1960s, and 1970s, increasing numbers of counselors and therapists became interested in working with normal concerns of people. A national survey in the early 1960s indicated that "far more people felt they needed help with marriage and family, and 'non-job adjustment problems in the self' than any other causes, but only one person in seven ever sought such help" (p. 15).

In 1963, Congress passed the Kennedy Comprehensive Community Mental Health Act. Based on the idea that mental health care should be a community responsibility, this bill proposed setting up 2,000 mental health centers throughout the United States. It was designed to cover the full range of services for those with normal emotional problems, as well as for those with severe and chronic mental disorders (Randolph, 1978). Each center was to serve about 250,000 persons in a particular region (Wylie, 1992). Under this act, persons who were previously sent to mental institutions outside the community were to be treated in inpatient local facilities. Other proposed facilities were to include outpatient clinics that would attend to counseling concerns of the general population, halfway houses for transitional care, crisis clinics, hot lines to handle emergencies, and such preventive measures as education and consultation.

In 1965, when I served as chairman of the board of the Whatcom Community Mental Health Clinic, the psychiatric director and the board envisioned such a center in our community, and we applied for and were granted federal funds to get a start on building a community mental health center. Unfortunately, the Kennedy Act mandated that federal funding for these comprehensive programs would be cut annually, with the stipulation that states gradually take over the funding.

As we worked out plans to develop the facility, federal funds dwindled and the Washington State Legislature was unable or unwilling to provide the expected funding. As a result, completion of the facility was delayed for almost 10 years and consisted only of an outpatient clinic that served those with severe or chronic mental disorders. No provisions were made for other needed services, such as inpatient clinics, halfway houses, crisis intervention, and treatment programs for clients with normal situational problems. Our nearest state mental hospital was closed even though inpatient facilities were unavailable in the community. The local hospital eventually provided a limited number of beds for temporary inpatient care.

Similar failures to develop comprehensive community mental health services happened throughout the country, and most state-run mental hospitals were permanently closed nationwide. Local clinics thus had the extra burden of monitoring psychotropic medications and managing the chronically ill.

As a result, crisis clinics, hot lines, and halfway houses emerged to fill the gap, facilities operating on shoestring budgets by well-intentioned, overworked, and mostly untrained volunteers. These agencies have continued to grow and to improve staff and services, but no central agency coordinates them. These services have had only informal connections with the community mental health clinics and have vied with them for local funding. The degree of cooperation has depended on individual effort to develop communication networks. To supplement the limited funds from local and state governments, directors of community counseling services use alternative sources, such as the United Way, grants from local and regional corporate foundations, individual contributions, and fund-raisers. Although this type of financing draws in support from the local community, staff directors and/or their assistants must spend a great deal of their time seeking funds.

In the 1980s and 1990s, even more severe cuts in federal and state funding caused a further move away from the original idea of community mental health clinics providing comprehensive coverage for everyone. The state-funded community mental health clinics have continued to focus only on serving those with severe and chronic mental illnesses.

CURRENT STATUS AND TRENDS

Unlike counseling services in schools and colleges, community mental health services are not centralized. Instead of one place offering mental health services, community mental health is a hodgepodge of services scattered throughout the community. Moreover, individuals in the community, unlike students in schools and colleges, are not automatically eligible for free or even partially free counseling. Counseling services in the community serve mostly those who can afford to pay. For those who have health insurance, limited services are only partially covered through managed care and through employee assistance programs (EAPs; see chap. 1).

A wide variety of counseling services are available in the community, however. Unencumbered by a single institutional policy and restrictions (except for those imposed by managed care), community counseling offers a wider, more complex, and eclectic array of counseling services than in schools and colleges. Community counselors generally can work in a more flexible milieu than counselors in educational settings.

The number of professionally trained community counselors has been steadily increasing. Most states now have some form of licensing for professional counselors (see Appendix B). Moreover, increasing numbers of universities throughout the country offer master's degree programs that train counselors to work in the community.

Counseling services are also available in the workplace for those employed in large companies through EAPs. Various religious organizations, as described in chapter 1 and later in this chapter, have also taken steps to provide counseling services for those who have no insurance and who cannot afford to pay high fees.

Emerging alongside this shift are the many counselors and therapists who acknowledge the impact of the social-cultural environment on the mental and physical health of individuals, families, and communities. Some family therapists, as discussed later, have extended family relationship issues into the broader social context. Likewise, for those who have lost a loved one and for those who are terminally ill, the grief process is being shared by the community in some areas, a sharing that continues well beyond the memorial service.

Many ethnic counselors have had a significant impact on community counselor training and practice. They have successfully led the drive to incorporate multicultural counseling competencies into counselor training programs. They have raised counselor awareness about the need to consider and appreciate differences in values, customs, and lifestyles of various ethnic groups in the community. Moreover, their emphasis in their counseling on the dynamic interaction among individual, family, and community has influenced the profession as a whole (see also chap. 14).

As part of this growing community awareness, neighborhood counseling services are emerging that range from teenage counseling centers to counseling in senior centers. At the same time, in some communities, various health agencies, heretofore separate, have been combining services: Some neighborhood medical facilities include mental health services, and spiritual counseling is being combined with counseling and therapy as well as with medical care. Individual needs are being treated in conjunction with one's extended family, workplace, neighborhood, and community.

War veterans, POWs, refugees, and torture victims, as part of the therapeutic healing process, are sharing their stories with others, and their stories are being integrated into the larger social-historical context of the country as a whole. Special therapeutic clinics and support groups have also formed in the community for those with addictions, for those with attention deficit hyperactivity disorder (ADHD), and for those suffering from violence.

In previous editions of this book, I dealt with community counseling primarily in age-related categories—children, adolescents, young adults, middle-aged adults, and older adults. Nowadays, however, community counseling has burgeoned way beyond age-related boundaries.

Community counseling has come to acknowledge that people are also faced with transitions for reasons unrelated to age: marriage and family issues and transitions; loss of a job or home; a sudden death; spiritual needs; social, cultural, and economic conditions and transitions; and political upheavals. Age-related issues are still important considerations for community counselors, however. Because all these issues warrant consideration in community counseling services, each is addressed here in turn.

⨀ AGE-RELATED COUNSELING

Because community counselors work with clients of all age levels, they must be familiar with the developmental needs, conflicts, and transitional phases of children, teenagers, young adults, adults in midlife, and older adults.

Children and Teenagers

Over the years, schools have steadily improved counseling services to meet the ever-growing needs of students. In recent years, however, professionals have realized that schools should not be the only place, nor have the sole responsibility of, offering counseling services to those at-risk children whose behavior dysfunctions tend to be generated and perpetrated by malfunctioning social conditions in the community.

Joint services have successfully been developed in many communities. A noteworthy example is the family counseling and therapy center built conjointly with Radford University adjacent to the Pulaski County High School in Virginia, as described in chapter 17.

Another example of joint services between school and community is an innovative program developed by high school counselor Bob Osterman in Bellingham, Washington, to help abused youths 10 to 18 years of age with anger management problems. The program, called Creative Concepts Ice Project, which gained national attention in the ACA newsletter *Counseling Today,* teaches ice hockey to these at-risk youths to help them express their anger constructively. Osterman (as cited in Guerra, 1998b) says:

> Ice hockey releases pent-up feelings of anger and frustration in a positive way. With the penalty box time and peer review, these kids learn ways of dealing constructively with the anger they feel. . . . These penalties are not only for violating ice hockey rules like high sticking or fighting, but for not doing homework, getting into a fight at school, and so forth. (p. 32)

Osterman carries out individual counseling during the game, and group counseling after the game. When a youth is put into the penalty box for a specific time because of an infraction, Osterman goes over with him what was wrong and why it was wrong. Group counseling follows in the locker room after each game. The boys go over a videotape of the game to check on their playing skills and to review with Osterman and each other any infractions or misbehaviors that occurred in the game.

Youths who are referred by the Washington Department of Children and Family Services, private practitioners, and state juvenile probation officers are first taught ice hockey skills by a retired star professional hockey player, skills that build up their self-esteem. The program is funded by state grants and by donations of money and ice hockey equipment from business and industry.

Some community agencies offer troubled youths a full range of services unavailable in the more limited academically oriented school settings. One such example of a nonprofit neighborhood center is the Youth Eastside Services (YES) in Bellevue, Washington, a center that offers teenage counseling services. Fees are determined by use of a sliding scale. People are not refused services if they cannot afford to pay (R. Fitzgerald, personal communication, May 4, 1990).

Although its major focus is on treatment of alcohol and drug abuse with youths, YES offers services to teenagers and their parents in the community in such other areas as individual, group, and family counseling; crisis intervention; psychological education; consultation and support services; physical or sexual abuse; and general family conflicts. Groups and classes include support groups for children of alcoholics and/or drug-dependent parents, classes for families on drug/alcohol abuse, a support group for incest victims, anger management for youths, a group for adolescents with separated or divorced parents, a gay/lesbian adolescent group, and a class in building self-esteem for adolescents. YES staff, under the direction of the youth employment coordinator, also run workshops on job searches. Staff are also given in-service training workshops to work with diverse racial and cultural groups. YES staff have formed cooperative relationships with schools, consulting with school personnel and teaching courses in nearby school districts, particularly on drug and alcohol education. Casework and advocacy services are also given free to families who need help finding medical, legal, or financial services.

Young Adults

Only one-third of high school students go on to college. Thus, unlike college students, after 18 years of age most young adults lack free and easily accessible professional counseling services for exploring career possibilities and for dealing with conflicts regarding personal development and social interactions and commitments. Now that counseling and career counseling have increased significantly in the community, their services need to become more accessible and affordable to these young adults.

Persons in their mid-20s and early 30s who have finished college or graduate school are confronted with beginning a career, starting a family, developing relationships, rearing children and teenagers, and developing personally and creatively.

Career Concerns

Client 1: Maggie is 18 years old and divorced. She dropped out of school to get married when she became pregnant. She lost her baby in childbirth. After that, her marriage deteriorated. She has been working part time as a waitress and has been on and off welfare. She is discouraged about herself and her life so far and is worried about being overweight. She is looking for a full-time job but is uncertain about her job qualifications.

Client 2: Michael, who is 29 and single, is referred by the state employment office. He is a chemist who has held five jobs in the past 3 years. He is bright, energetic, and sardonic. He says that he has yet to find a good boss. He has either been fired or has left jobs because of friction with supervisors. He is not sure that chemistry is the right profession.

Client 1: Maggie has taken a positive step by seeking help. Her problem has three related facets: (a) She lacks feelings of self-esteem, (b) she is seeking vocational help, and (c) she wants to lose weight. Before exploring vocational opportunities, Maggie needs to explore family relationships that have contributed to her low self-esteem and self-defeating behavior. Another consideration is to explore whether she has worked through feelings of grief about the loss of her baby. Then vocational exploration could follow, using perhaps the Kuder Occupational Interest Survey (KOIS), the Self-Directed Search (SDS), and the General Aptitude Test Battery (GATB). I would assess with Maggie her concerns about her weight. How much overweight is she? Has her weight increased during this period of unusual stress? If it appears that her weight gain is significant and interferes with her health and that she wants to take the steps necessary to lose weight, I probably would refer her to a counselor who specializes in weight loss.

Client 2: Most noticeable in Michael's case is his difficulty with authority figures. Anticipating that he will transfer these feelings to me during counseling sessions, I would confront him constructively about his relationship problems. Helping him assert his needs and express his feelings appropriately and constructively would constitute an important part of counseling. While his relationship problems are being addressed, his career concerns can also be explored. Why did he choose chemistry? Was there any parental pressure? How competent and interested was he in his various jobs? It might be helpful for him to role-play actual conflicts he has had with his bosses. I might use interest and aptitude measures and explore occupations related to chemistry via a computerized occupational program.

Personal Concerns

Client 3: Nina is a 27-year-old lawyer. She is single, lives alone, and is a leader in the community. Her major concern relates to her uncertainties about what she wants for her future. She has made friends and enjoys their company but is reluctant to become involved in a long-term relationship. Yet, she says she would like to have children and admits to feeling lonely at times.

Client 4: Mona, 19, makes an appointment for counseling because of her inability to handle her grief over the loss of her mother and father in an automobile accident more than a year ago. She has frequent crying spells and is finding it difficult to handle her job as a clerk in a bank.

Client 3: Nina appears satisfied with her career. Her main focus is on developing constructive relationships. A key factor is her ambivalence about committing herself to a long-term relationship. Exploration of family patterns may be productive in working with clients like Nina. How does she perceive her mother and father's relationship? Did she feel enmeshed or too separate from the family? How well did the family communicate? These explorations could help reach her fears about commitment and her concerns about loneliness. Discussions about the characteristics of the friends she cultivates and about the quality of her relationships with them are appropriate.

Client 4: Mona needs help working through the feelings of loss about her parents' death. Grief counseling, which would permit release of anger and helplessness, is needed. In this process, exploring the relationship with her family and family dynamics is important. Because sharing grief with other support persons can help her work through the grieving process, I would refer her to a grief support group.

Interpersonal Conflicts and Concerns

Client 5: Mark, a 19-year-old, reveals he has recently recognized and accepted that he is gay. He is having difficulty, however, confronting his parents and friends about his sexual orientation. He is an only child and is concerned that his parents will oppose him. They are looking forward to his marriage and to future grandchildren.

Client 5: Mark needs to consider whether he is ready to confront his parents at this time because he only recently recognized and accepted that he is gay and because he is uncertain about how strongly his parents might react. I would first help him explore his relationship with his parents to evaluate how flexible they actually are and whether this is an appropriate time to tell them. I might role-play with him so that he could practice expressing his feelings authentically. I would also help him consider the consequences of rejection. If he decides to confront his parents and they do reject him, further counseling regarding his feelings of loss and abandonment is necessary. If the family is ambivalent, family counseling may be helpful.

Adults at Midlife

The developmental concerns of middle-aged individuals relate to issues regarding job changes and losses of loved ones. Individuals may suddenly be faced with losing a job. They may experience a loss of parents, divorce, and a breakup of the family. It is a time when individuals take stock of their accomplishments or lack of them and, for many persons, a time ripe for a midlife crisis.

In recent years, most persons faced with the high-tech revolution have had to be retrained or retire out of the business. Job loss has become a real concern for many individuals in midlife. In 1991-92, people over age 55 had a rate of unemployment seven times higher than individuals aged 16 through 54. In 1992, almost a million workers aged 55 and over were unable to find full-time work and either took part-time jobs or gave up looking. Periods of unemployment were longer for this group than for younger individuals (Stern, 1993).

In the late 1990s, the Asian economic crisis, the collapse of the Russian banking system, and the consequent slump in the world market led to massive layoffs of U.S. workers; corporate mergers, in an effort to downsize, caused further upheavals in the labor market and in the social and personal welfare of many people.

Adults in midlife also start evaluating their abilities as parents. They may feel guilty and troubled if their children have not become successful or happy adults or have not developed values or lifestyles compatible with their own.

Likewise, adults are troubled and anxious when they see their aging parents, who have been their model and bridge to the future, become physically disabled or senile. Thus, besides coping with the developing needs and conflicts of their own children, they are having to cope with their aging parents and to decide how best to care for them as they become more incapacitated (see the section "Working with Aging Families" later in the chapter).

Another issue of primary concern for middle-aged adults is the changes in gender roles in marriage that may begin to emerge at midlife. Men looking ahead to retirement may reduce their attention to work and begin to focus on home life. Women may show increasing interest in channeling their energies outside the home after the children leave. These reversals can lead to conflicts and friction in a marriage.

Career Concerns

Client 6: Jolene, 38, has been referred to the community counseling clinic by a friend. She has two children in school and has expressed interest in trying to develop a career. She has 1½ years of college and worked for 2 years as a cashier in a department store before marriage. She is considering college or vocational training. Her husband is supportive but ambivalent. She, too, expresses ambivalence. She is anxious about her ability to do well in school and is uneasy about whether she is being fair to the children.

Client 7: Boris, 52, has been referred to me by the counselor at the Division of Vocational Rehabilitation (DVR). He worked as a repairer of heavy equipment until he suffered a heart attack. His physician told him that he could not continue in his current job but that he would be able to handle lighter jobs. He is quite shaken by his disability and the news that he can't resume the work he had enjoyed. His despondency has affected his relationship with his wife. He expresses a need to be employed but feels hopeless about the prospects of alternative jobs.

Both Jolene and Boris have to make a career choice or career change, and their actions are complicated by factors related to this decision that arouse anxiety and apprehension. The counselor must have the professional capacity to help Jolene and Boris make decisions about career planning and must possess the background to help them confront and work through personal uncertainties about their capacities to handle new demands in life.

Client 6: Jolene may need help recognizing that her anxious feelings about getting training and her ambivalent feelings about her responsibility for her own growth and her family's welfare are not unusual. She is contemplating a significant change in lifestyle that will take cooperative effort from the whole family. I would help her explore her ambivalence about her plans. Does her uneasiness about the children have to do with what her husband and society expect from her as a mother and wife? We would discuss issues of child care and sharing of household duties, and other necessary adjustments in lifestyle. Assuming that her and her husband's ambivalence is resolved and she decides she wants to go back to school, I would help her explore career possibilities by suggesting she take vocational interest and aptitude tests.

Client 7: I would help Boris express and work through his grief, anger, and despair about having to give up a job he had enjoyed and help him express feelings of anxiety about his physical incapacity and about having to begin a new, unfamiliar job at midlife. At the same time I would help him start exploring alternative job possibilities by first asking him to describe those characteristics of his previous job that appealed to him that he could still safely do now. Discovering that he can still perform valued tasks will serve as a significant motivator; I would then help him explore occupational informational sources that match his interests and aptitudes. In his case, his job skills and interests may be clear-cut enough to match with specific job alternatives. But if doubts arise, I would suggest he take interest and aptitude tests.

After we have decided on some suitable alternative jobs, I would send the information to the rehabilitation counselor, who then arranges for appropriate job training or placement.

Personal Concerns

Client 8: Fran, a 49-year-old widow, is referred by her physician. She is a registered nurse who enjoys her work. She expresses feelings of loneliness. Her husband died suddenly 2 years ago, and her two children have left home. She has doubts about how good a parent she has been; neither child finished college, and her daughter recently went through a difficult divorce. Fran has very few women or men friends. She feels uncomfortable with the few married couples she and her husband knew.

Client 8: Fran has been left on her own after a long married life. Because she likes and functions well on her job, I would concentrate on her concerns about loneliness and relationships and would refer her to group counseling for recently widowed women. The group offers an opportunity for her to bond with other women, to work through her grief, to share her uncomfortable feelings in social situations, and to practice skills relating to others. In a group like this, her feelings of adequacy as a parent can also be shared.

Interpersonal Conflicts and Concerns

Client 9: Kirstin and Joe are a couple in their 40s. Kirstin's mother, in her late 70s, has been living by herself since her husband died 6 years before. She is losing her eyesight and her memory and sometimes becomes disoriented. Kirstin is considering taking her mother into their home. Joe believes that a retirement home or nursing home would be better. He has experienced friction over the years with his mother-in-law. He says that Kirstin has suffered headaches when she and her mother are together. Kirstin works full time as a librarian, sometimes evenings and weekends.

Client 9: The problem confronting Kirstin and Joe is very common. Although older persons typically move into assisted-living quarters, such facilities are expensive and often inadequate. Their differing attitudes about her mother need to be addressed. Kirstin's compassionate desire to care for her mother in her own home, which counters the trend of institutionalizing old people, should be recognized. Joe's emotional reactions to his mother-in-law need to be explored. Are his feelings distorted, or is he being more realistic in the light of their situation? The counselor will help them address their differences as they consider their options, including the degree of care her mother would need, suitability of retirement and nursing homes in their area, available space in their home for her mother, adjusting Kirstin's work schedule to care for her mother, availability of day care facilities for older people, and availability of visiting nurses who assist older people in their homes.

Older Adults

Older adults are the most heterogeneous of all the age-groups. They span an age range of about 30 years and represent a multitude of individual differences in socioeconomic status, experience, knowledge, skills, health, intergenerational family relationships, and motivation. For this reason, a separate chapter (see chapter 15) deals with their needs as diverse as searching for ways to lead a productive lifestyle, elder abuse, depression, dying, and grief.

Because 80% of older adults are self-sufficient and healthy enough to take care of themselves, the major concern for most older people is finding ways to keep productive and useful in a society that has retired them out of the occupational mainstream.

Unfortunately, the counseling and therapy profession and other health care professionals have not been prepared to address their needs, although that's starting to change now. But retraining is very slow. Gerontologists, for example, who are considered the specialists of older adults, by and large are trained to work primarily with long-term care patients in assisted-living facilities. Thus, they tend to view all older people as being in need of assistance in one way or another.

Goals of counseling—helping older adult clients exercise control over their lives, become empowered, find new opportunities to grow—should be the same for older adults as they are for younger people (Waters, 1984). Counselors can help older adults cope with the many transitions they go through in later life, including helping them change their relationship with a spouse when one or both retire, develop new relationships with their adult children, work with grief over the loss of spouse or friends, deal with uncertainties about new grandparent roles, move from a long-time home to a smaller apartment, and overcome fear of abandonment.

Senior centers are excellent places for counseling services for older adults. Sue Grady (1990), a certified counselor at the Mature Minglers Multipurpose Senior Center in Birmingham, Michigan, points out that the senior center is an essential part of the community and therefore can respond to clients' problems in the social context in which the seniors live. Moreover, a well-trained senior center staff can reduce the negative influence of ageism. Further, the staff can assume the roles of change agents or be advocates for seniors by encouraging community leaders to improve social services such as transportation systems and home care. They can, as well, use nontraditional counseling methods that fit the particular needs of the senior centers. For example, the staff can welcome drop-ins, carry out counseling outside the office, and set up spontaneous support groups or visit homes when necessary.

Senior centers are also the obvious place to offer group counseling, a particularly effective way for older adults to express their concerns, because in a group they can share common losses and gain intimacy with other older adults and gain a renewed sense of community spirit. Groups can be organized around specific topics, such as grieving, health, loneliness, creative expression through music or art, or life review (Corey & Corey, 1992; Thomas & Martin, 1992; see also chap. 15).

Another excellent example of a worthwhile and productive activity at a senior center is at the Whitney Senior Center in St. Cloud, Minnesota, through the Retired Senior Volunteer Program (RSVP). Retired counselor educator and octogenarian Willis E. Dugan has created a remarkable and innovative work project called the Wood Block and Toy Project. This project is designed to allow both able-bodied senior citizen volunteers and nursing home and adult care elderly engage in a productive activity—making toys for children (Dugan, 1993). "This is an example of a type of senior volunteer activity that produces feelings of belonging, a sense of contributing and improved self-esteem on the part of elderly participants" (Willis E. Dugan, personal communication, July 12, 1997).

Twice a month, senior volunteers meet at Whitney Senior Center Workshop with patients from nursing homes and adult care centers. Under supervision of retired senior volunteers, these elderly patients sand and paint precut wood blocks and toys. The toys are then distributed to children at the holiday season. "The block sets and wooden toys are distributed by United Fund to Head Start programs, libraries, church schools, Woman houses, medical clinics, welfare offices and schools" (Willis E. Dugan, personal communication, July 12, 1997).

Significantly, Dugan, who was 88 at the time of our interview, is one of the oldest living professional counselor educators, a long-time leader in the field, having served as executive director of APGA (now ACA) from 1966 to 1971. Still acting as a model elder counselor educator, he has demonstrated how retired professional counselors can continue to help others be productive and generative in the community.

Following is an example of a problem presented by an older adult that could be handled by a counselor in a senior center or in any other community counseling services:

Client 10: Fred, who is 67, makes an appointment because of feelings of restlessness, boredom, and mild depression. He retired after an active career as a salesman. He had not made any plans for retirement. He expresses general malaise and a recent sharp decrease in sexual potency. His wife, 55, is employed at a travel agency. She enjoys her job and has a great deal of contact with people. He says he is happy about her job but also feels some resentment about her constant activity.

Client 10: Fred made an appointment for counseling on his own. I perceive this decision as a positive first step. He needs an opportunity to express his feelings of loss of identity and loss of purpose in life, which generally occur to most people when they retire. He also needs an opportunity to develop attitudes and strategies for building a revised lifestyle that will include sufficient activity to help him regain self-respect. He can explore how to use the talents, attitudes, and experiences that contributed to his success as a salesman to develop activities that will give him personal satisfaction and social recognition, such as involvement in community service. He needs to confront how he can become involved in the home. Then he might more fully support his wife's activities, and she might better understand his confusion and help him work through his resentment and uncertainties. To attain this mutual understanding, Fred and his wife could profit from marital counseling as a supplement to individual counseling.

⟿ FAMILY COUNSELING AND THERAPY

Work with families and couples is paramount in community mental health services, especially because public schools and colleges do only limited amounts of family and marital counseling.

Families have a great variety of presenting problems. Persons with alcohol and drug problems, children of alcoholics and adult children of alcoholics, the aging and the adult children of the aging, children with emotional and behavioral problems, pregnant teenagers, and families of gays and lesbians may all involve family counseling or consultation. Some feminist and ethnic family counselors, as described later, approach family counseling differently than traditional family therapists.

Counseling services for normally functioning families have become increasingly available, including state and county youth and family agencies, religious-sponsored counseling centers, EAPs, HMOs, and privately sponsored family centers.

Job-Related Family Issues

Until recently, family counselors and therapists in the community have generally ignored the relationship of work issues to family breakdowns or family dysfunctions (Bielski, 1996):

Until very recently, most therapists considered the practical details of their clients' work lives not much more relevant than the color of their curtains, or only worthy of passing attention if they revealed spillover symptoms of deeper relational problems. (p. 25)

After interviewing several prominent family counselors, Bielski (1996) concluded that, during the 1990s, increasing numbers of therapists began to recognize the importance of work-related pressures on family dynamics. He writes that nationally known family therapist Betty Carter became aware of these issues in the early 1990s:

Betty Carter remembers her own dawning recognition some years ago that the lived experience of work, and the enormous social and personal pressures work encompassed in the late 20th-century America, were as important to consider in therapy as family-of-origin issues, marital interaction or substance abuse. (p. 25)

Family therapists shared with Bielski (1996) incidents from their practice in which family dysfunction or marital friction related to work issues: an executive losing a high-powered job through company downsizing with no commensurate job available; a 20-year employee being laid off with no new job in sight; individuals who overidentified with jobs at the expense of their relationships; women overworked in two-career families.

That career- and job-related issues have an impact on one's personal development and personal well-being has long been acknowledged by professional counselors and counseling associations in their definitions of counseling and counselor role. That family therapists are incorporating these ideas into family dynamics is a noteworthy occurrence in the counseling and therapy field.

Working with Aging Families

According to Sandmaier (1998), "Working with aging families is a major frontier of family therapy. It is where we ourselves must come of age" (p. 25). Many family therapists are undergoing fundamental changes in their approach to issues of adults and their aging parents. Some family therapists now advocate that it is possible to facilitate growth and development in working with aging parents and their adult children, particularly the belief in changing their relationship. "The question at hand, then is how can this juncture in the family life cycle be transformed from an emphasis on adjusting to loss and disappointments to a focus on growth and possibility?" (p. 26).

Family therapist Terry Hargrave (as cited in Sandmaier, 1998) explains that the key to counseling aging families is to shift the relationship so that there is more give-and-take, more of a mutual caregiving, where the elder person is still considered worthy of providing wisdom and nurturance to his or her adult child. "Hargrave is convinced that the recognition of an older person's continuing capacity to give to their families is absolutely critical to successful work with older families" (Sandmaier, 1998, p. 29).

Family therapist Virginia Abrams (as cited in Sandmaier, 1998) concurs. Abrams believes that this late stage in the aging parent and adult child relationship is a crucial time for engendering renewal:

> At no other juncture in life's journey . . . were children asked to so profoundly alter their roles vis-à-vis their parents. So nearly universal is the need to negotiate this shift that it is considered a bona fide adult developmental stage—achieving "filial maturity." (p. 30)

For most, she goes on, intergenerational conflicts and misunderstandings between middle-aged adults and aging parents can be attended to with effective therapeutic help. A staff clinician at a community mental health center in Manhattan called Support Program for Older People (SPOP), Abrams doesn't let long distance between parties deter her. In some cases, she reaches out by telephone to help reconnect and heal old wounds between an adult child and an elderly parent in her effort to generate last-chance attempts for renewal.

Perspectives of Ethnic Family Counselors

In working with ethnic families, counselors must be aware of differing cultural values; varying cultural expectations regarding gender roles; degree of involvement of extended family; influence of religion; whether they live in an ethnic neighborhood; whether they are first-, second-, or third-generation immigrants; and effects of their socioeconomic status.

Most African American families traditionally have had strong bonds of kinship that offer support to family members who are struggling for economic and social survival. "Therapists must . . . be willing to expand the definition of family to a more extended kinship system. Relations often live in close proximity and expect to rely on one another in time of need" (Baruth & Manning, 1999, p. 153).

Family counselors are working with increasing numbers of single-parent African American families headed by women. Conflicts between husbands and wives escalate when families move away from their kinship roots and when there is high unemployment, alcoholism, and poverty.

African American counselors recommend using pragmatic approaches in family counseling: "Therapies with the most promise for African American families set aside abstract theoretical notions of how to conduct family therapy. Models that adopt active, intervention-oriented strategies emphasizing social functioning over inner feelings are more appropriate" (Baruth & Manning, 1999, p. 153).

The insistence of Asian American families on loyalty to the family tends to make Asian families unwilling to engage in family counseling. The father is typically the spokesman for the family, so children and wives may be reluctant to bring up significant problems in the family to avoid shaming the father (Baruth & Manning, 1999).

Hispanic families tend to respond more positively to family counseling than to individual counseling because of their strong family ties and the feeling that family members have a responsibility to help each other. Close-knit Hispanic families respond well to counseling (Baruth & Manning, 1999; Garcia-Preto, 1982). Family therapist Ramon Rojano (Markowitz, 1997), as director of DSHS in Hartford, Connecticut, capitalized on his Hispanic roots and effectively extended the concept of family counseling to family community counseling (see chaps. 10 and 14).

Native American families, particularly those living on reservations, are close-knit, with considerable intergenerational bonding. Family members and extended family tend to work together to resolve their problems. They generally refrain from seeking counseling, but when they do, their close kinship tends to bring about positive results beyond that occurring in individual counseling (Baruth & Manning, 1999; Trimble, Fleming, Beauvais, & Jumper-Thurman, 1996). In a review of the literature, Trimble, et al (1996) found that counselors who work with Native Americans and who include the family's social network tend to be more effective. Baruth and Manning (1999) note:

> When the counselor is able to engage the family, he or she should proceed cautiously to allow family members to deal with problems at their own pace. Also, an overbearing or manipulative counselor will almost certainly alienate Native American clients. (p. 366)

Perspectives of Feminist Family Counselors

Back in the late 1970s, family therapists Betty Carter, Peggy Papp, Olga Silverstein, and Marianne Walters formed what came to be called the Women's Project in Family Therapy. They got together to counteract family therapy's male-dominated perspective and to develop alternative approaches to family therapy (see chap. 10). In so doing, they have, over the years, persuaded family therapists to move family issues beyond the narrow confines of a family system to include the family's social-cultural milieu. They also have encouraged family therapists to help their clients move beyond simply airing personal grievances against their parents, move beyond playing the victim, and help clients begin to take responsibility for their lives. "Therapists have been accused in recent years of encouraging a culture of grievance in which everybody blames their problems on somebody else and sees him or herself as a victim" (Simon, 1997, p. 66).

As part of this task, they have challenged family therapists who encourage clients to blame the parents, especially the mother. But it has not been easy, they say, to change long-held attitudes of most family therapists. Just at the point when they think that professional family therapists have changed the way they think about gender issues in general and mothers in particular, family therapist Marianne Walters says that "some therapists will show a tape where a mother is blamed or put down or ignored or even humiliated, and much of the audience will not even notice" (Simon, 1997, p. 60).

In working with family and relationship cases, the primary issue for these family therapists, then, is to help clients reassess their attitudes toward their mothers. Olga Silverstein says that, during counseling, she will notice the way a man relates to his wife and from that draw links to the way he relates/related to his mother: "I believe that the basic essential relationship in which a man cuts off emotionally is the one with his mother" (as quoted in Simon, 1997, p. 63).

As Betty Carter points out, males have been brought up in the culture to separate and become autonomous from their mothers. So, how can they know how to relate well, connect with their wives? Carter adds that men typically learned to block their feelings in their relationship with their parents. The father was usually wrapped up in his work, and the mother kept her distance emotionally because that was what she thought she was supposed to do. Carter generally starts with the man's relationship with his father because the man wants to, and it's easier for him too. Then, later, she shifts to his relationship with his mother, a more difficult task but more to the crux of the problem:

> Then I shift to the mother, which is a tougher deal, but that's where the real payoff comes. I've had any number of turned off men who, when they finally did go back to the mother that they were maligning or ignoring or whatever, found her eager to respond and to validate them. . . . [I]t often changes the man's whole way of relating to everyone. (as quoted in Simon, 1997, p. 63)

Child Abuse

A community-oriented treatment program for sexually abusive families is the Giarretto Institute, a privately sponsored agency in San Jose, California. Therapists, probation officers, county officials, and former patients work together to treat the family and also to create the sense of extended family. The goal is to change destructive family dynamics while reunifying or keeping the family intact (J. Szybalski, personal communication, June 12, 1993).

The core of the treatment program is its unusual type of group counseling, in which each family member joins separate groups: fathers with fathers, mothers with mothers, and children with children. Another unique feature about this institute is that former patients serve as an extended family support system. Former client families living in the community are coupled with families in treatment and act as consultants, models, and support for each family member and the family as a whole. Former clients give lectures and workshops in the community to publicize the treatment program and to raise funds.

Group treatment for mothers of incest victims is described by Landis and Wyre (1984). The group therapist is a woman, and group members are self-referred or referred by a state agency or other counselors or therapists. The women range in age from 25 to 45 and may be single, remarried, or still married to the spouses who committed the sexual abuse. Issues include anger and lack of trust toward men, poor communication with abused daughters, and difficulties developing intimate relationships. Inappropriate roles and communication styles learned in families of origin are discussed. These women confront their own passivity and its role in failing to protect their daughters. They are taught how to approach daughters about their maternal feelings. Male partners join the women in the latter stage of the group.

Pearson (1988) describes a support group for women with relationship dependency who have anxieties or stress resulting in loneliness, anger, and grief. The group focuses on sharing personal feelings, developing effective friendships, and building self-esteem.

Domestic Violence

Innovative psychoeducational programs have been developed for women who are domestic violence victims. One such program, conducted by family therapist Rhea Almeida at the Institute for Family Services in Somerset, New Jersey, breaks with traditional practice in that the abusers, as well as the abused, are involved in group psychoeducational activities (Wylie, 1996). About 60% to 70% of abusers enter the program voluntarily. The remainder are court-mandated.

> Unlike some therapeutic interventions that legal authorities and women's rights advocates alike distrust for allegedly "coddling" abusers, the Institute combines tough-minded political and social re-education with an uncompromising insistence that the mandated batterer toe the line of treatment or face expulsion from the program. (Wylie, 1996, p. 60)

The typical program, which lasts about 8 months, begins with a series of informational sessions, in the form of videos and discussions, about causes of abuse. These meetings are followed with group sessions of abusers and abused, both separately and together. Members of various ethnic groups who have successfully completed the program act as cultural consultants and sponsors to each participant throughout the program.

A different approach—a wellness model—is suggested for counselors working with battered women in shelters. Counselors aim at helping residents not only develop survivor skills but also become empowered. In this model, efforts are made to develop the social, occupational, physical, intellectual, emotional, and spiritual growth of these women (Donaghy, 1995). Staff counselor Donaghy (1995) suggests, for example: "Shelter staff can encourage women and assist them in enrollment in training programs, if desired. Staff can also offer women instruction in writing resumes and conducting employment interviews" (p. 9). Staff also provide some counseling and, when needed, refer clients to outside counseling services.

Grief Counseling

Coping with death and dying, facing the loss of a loved one, and working through the grief process are discussed in chapter 15, "Counseling Older Adults," because these experiences are more imminent and occur more often with older adults. The trauma of terminal illness, the loss of a loved one, and the need to grieve, however, occur at all stages of life. The dying and death of an individual affects family, friends, and sometimes the whole community.

When persons die early in life or in the prime of life, "before their time," their deaths are generally more traumatic to their loved ones than is the loss of an elderly person. Most distressing are a parent's loss of a young child, a child's loss of a parent, or the loss of a spouse early in the marriage. Terminal illness resulting from cancer, AIDS, or other diseases at whatever age cause emotional traumas on the dying and the family and close friends of the dying. Suicide or accidental or unexpected death also creates emotional trauma.

Taking the time to work through one's grief is crucial. Moreover, grief work, according to O'Malley (1998), should preferably be carried out and shared in the community, rather than in a therapist's office. But because community support for those mourning the death of a loved one has generally been unavailable and not even customary in our society, counselors and therapists, he says, need to fill the gap. They can do so by offering grief counseling, developing grief workshops, and encouraging and developing community efforts to attend to grieving persons.

How to determine a treatment plan depends on the individual's cultural background, particular circumstances, and developmental stage. The grief process for children, for instance, is different from that for adults because children, at their stage of cognitive development, are unable to process the loss of, say, a parent, on their own (Golden, 1998). A case described by counselor Patrick O'Malley in *Case Studies in Child and Adolescent Counseling* (Golden, 1998) concerns his work with a 9-year-old boy whose father committed suicide. According to O'Malley, the boy needed to work through grief throughout this crucial developmental period of his life. Grief counseling treatment carried him through 7 years, through most of adolescence. O'Malley describes how, during this time, he helped the boy work through depression, acting-out behaviors, and difficulty in expressing grief. O'Malley used brief, intermittent counseling with an eclectic approach based on psychodynamic therapy combined with behavioral, solution-focused, and psychoeducational techniques.

In accordance with O'Malley's (1998) emphasis on the importance of community support of families in mourning, some churches in the Seattle area sponsor grief workshops. Such workshops are helpful at Christmastime, a time that is especially difficult for individuals and families who have lost loved ones. These workshops are led by pastoral counselors or other mental health professionals who accompany church services of remembrance. In one church, different grief groups are offered for children, teenagers, and parents (Iwasaki, 1998).

✦ SPIRITUAL COUNSELING: SEARCHING FOR MEANING

Although many members of the counseling profession have considered spiritual concerns of individuals an important part of counseling, especially those who are also trained in the ministry, the counseling profession as a whole, according to Bart (1998) and Burke and Mirante (1995), has ignored, evaded, and even denied the significance of the spiritual dimension to a client's well-being.

A significant proportion of counselors and therapists now are acknowledging the importance of spiritual matters to a person's mental health. The *Diagnostic and Statistical Manual of Mental Disorders* (American Psychiatric Association, 1994), for example, added in its fourth and latest edition (*DSM-IV*) a section indicating that religious and spiritual malaise warrants treatment. The following examples bear consideration for treatment: "Examples include distressing experiences that involve loss in questioning of faith, problems associated with conversion to a new faith, or questioning of other spiritual values that may not necessarily be related to an organized church religious institution" (Burke & Miranti, 1995, p. 2).

The various ways in which spiritual concerns of individuals are being addressed in the mental health field are presented in a book of readings by Burke and Miranti called *Counseling: The Spiritual Dimension* (1995). One of its contributors, Ingersoll (1995), discusses how counselors can enhance the counseling process with those clients who have strong religious beliefs other than their own: "First, affirm the importance of the clients' spirituality in their lives. Second, attempt to enter client worldviews with congruent vocabulary and imagery . . . Last, counselors need to be willing to consult with other 'healers' in clients' lives" (p. 14).

Additional guidelines for counselors working with clients from different cultures with varying spiritual beliefs have been developed by Bishop (1995). He presents seven guidelines that can be summarized as follows: Counselors must (a) assure each client that his or her religious beliefs are an important part of the process. In so doing, religious values become part of resolving the problem. To be effective, counselors need to (b) educate themselves about different cultures and religious values and to (c) integrate them into their practice. They must also (d) interact with diverse individuals and groups in the community, (e) explore and articulate their own religious beliefs, (f) be cognizant of any resistance to religious issues that clients bring up, and (g) speak in a straightforward manner regarding their own beliefs and the beliefs of clients.

As a result of these trends, counselor educators led by Burke and Miranti (1995) have developed a set of spiritual competencies to be used in counselor training. Although no action has been taken as of this writing, the Council for Accreditation of Counseling and Related Education Programs (CACREP) has shown interest in incorporating these ideas into counselor training standards (Bart, 1998).

Most major religious groups in Seattle, Washington, offer counseling services, services that focus primarily on normal concerns of individuals and families—Jewish, Catholic, Presbyterian, Lutheran, Methodist, Baptist, Episcopalian, and Unitarian (see chap. 1). Although sponsored by specific religious faiths or denominations, these counseling centers are generally open to all faiths in terms of counseling staff backgrounds and the type of clients they serve. In an effort to network services, directors of those counseling centers sponsored by mainline Protestant churches meet monthly to share cases and to discuss mutual problems.

Counseling centers sponsored by Presbyterians in Seattle provide services throughout the city for individuals, groups, and families that are consistent with those discussed in the text (D. Anderson, personal communication, May 21, 1993). These counseling centers, which employ 23 professionals, include counselors, social workers, marriage and family counselors, pastoral counselors, and psychologists with master's or doctoral degrees. All are licensed or certified by the state of Washington and/or by appropriate professional associations. Therapists on the staff have a wide range of psychological theoretical backgrounds. They represent, as well, a wide range of religious affiliations, including Catholic and Jewish. About 25% of clients are Presbyterians, and 25% have no religious affiliations.

Counselors in religious-sponsored services such as these are ethically bound not to persuade or proselytize clients in any way. All are expected, though, to respond to clients' spiritual concerns.

Not all religious groups that offer counseling hold to these guidelines. At some places of worship, pastoral counseling is available only to members of the congregation. Moreover, the purpose in counseling includes evangelizing or trying to convert persons to that faith.

Ethnic Counselors and Spirituality

Many major ethnic groups consider spiritual and religious matters a very important part of their lives. The increasing numbers of ethnic counselors and therapists in the past decade—particularly Hispanic, Native American, and African American professionals—who have maintained strong spiritual values and close identification with family and community are affecting the counseling profession by acknowledging that spiritual values are integral to one's life.

At a meeting of the Washington Association for Spiritual Ethical and Religious Values in Counseling (WASERVIC)[1] in the autumn 1992, for example, most participants were of ethnic background. Panel members represented a broad spectrum of religious and cultural backgrounds from the Yakima community: Talulah Pinkham, a Yakima Indian and supervisor of Indian Health Services; the Reverend Mitch Weary, a black Baptist pastor; Paula Mead, a counselor at the Westside Christian Counseling Center; and Carlos Carillos, born and raised in Mexico, a counselor for the local farm workers, with a master's degree in counseling. The Yakima Valley includes the largest Indian reservation in the state and perhaps the state's largest group of Hispanic farm laborers. Their topic was "How Does Religiosity Help or Hinder the Counseling Process?"

Although they debated at length whether *religiosity* or *spirituality* was a better term, all concurred that issues of religiosity or spirituality help the counseling process. In some Black, Hispanic, and Native American communities, they pointed out, spirituality is often the *only* avenue to reach troubled persons because a negative stigma is attached to secular therapy in many of these communities (see also chap. 14, "Counseling in a Pluralistic World").

Spiritual Retreats

Innumerable retreats for spiritual guidance or reawakening have sprung up around the country, sponsored by counselors, creative arts therapists, teams of artists and therapists, and various spiritual and religious leaders and healing specialists. Many private institutes, such as Hollyhock Farm on remote Cortes Island in British Columbia, schedule ongoing May-to-October holistic and spiritual workshops and retreats. Michael Meade's (1998) Mosaic Multicultural Foundation week-long or weekend gatherings occur regularly throughout the year at various wilderness or urban centers in the Pacific Northwest and California, featuring such spiritual leaders as Jack Kornfield and Malidona Somé.

The Women of Wisdom Foundation of Seattle sponsors an annual 10-day conference in the city, featuring a variety of multicultural spiritual leaders; its February 1999 conference included Starhawk, Luisah Teish, Jeanne Achterberg, Elena Avila, and Sandra Ingerman. At this conference, seven on-site professional counselors were available free of charge or by donation. All were experienced, master's-level counselors.

---

[1]WASERVIC is a division of the Washington State Counselors Association (WSCA); WSCA is a branch of ACA. At that time, WASERVIC was called the Washington Association for Religious and Value Issues in Counseling (WARVIC).

For some people, the personal experience of spiritual transformation and communal bonding does not last once they return home and back to work, and they feel let down and vaguely disgruntled. Persons who united so closely at retreats may never see each other again. On-site counselors, such as those who were available at the Women of Wisdom conference, could serve as a means for participants to make the transition back to ordinary life.

Clinical psychologist and Tibetan Buddhist monk Jack Kornfield (1993) acknowledges the difficult transition from spiritual wilderness retreat back to frenetic urban lifestyle and offers helpful suggestions to ease the painful shift: "It requires patience. We must recognize that transitions can be long processes" (p. 180). In this process, first, one should acknowledge the loss and learn to "let go"; second, one should set aside regular periods of time alone for meditation; and third, one should arrange to meet regularly with others who have been to similar retreats. He also encourages persons to use the pain of return as a learning experience:

> When we return from a quiet contemplative period, we will often see the pain of the world, our own and others', in a more clear and undeniable way. This is actually part of our spiritual path, to see clearly and open our hearts to it all. (p. 181)

As Kornfield suggests, many persons who have been to similar retreats are arranging to meet regularly back at their hometowns. Community counselors who have been at these workshops and retreats, who understand what goes on, can help participants integrate their experiences into community counseling services and workshops. The national magazine *Wingspan,* which focuses on the mythopoetic men's movement, offers guidelines on organizing and developing groups in communities.

✒ SOCIAL, CULTURAL, AND POLITICAL TRANSITIONS

The numerous mental health services that are now focusing on social, cultural, and political concerns of a person's life have thrown a new perspective on counseling and related mental health services. Such services have broadened the profession's outlook to include developing an awareness of one's psychosocial relationship with one's community. Numerous issues are being raised and addressed that link a person's personal and interpersonal concerns with external difficulties, such as loss of job or home; death of a loved one; social, economic, or cultural barriers; and political upheavals and traumas. As a result, many individual and group counseling services specifically related to social-cultural transitions are developing in communities and neighborhoods throughout the country.

Career Development and Work Adjustment

Some counselors, including myself, have for many years emphasized that an individual's work-related concerns continue throughout life and that complex social and environmental factors affect job performance and satisfaction (Entine, 1976; Heddesheimer, 1976; Nugent, 1981; Rappoport, 1976). Thus, these are essential issues that both career counselors and other counselors need to address.

Even so, according to Hershenson (1996), most career counselors tend to focus only on career choice and give little attention to issues of job adjustment. To encourage counselors to work with these much-needed issues, Hershenson has developed a therapeutic model in which he delineates the highly complex personal and social factors that affect one's work adjustment. His model includes three components: work personality, work competencies, and work goals. He also describes how environmental and contextual factors, such as family, training, and cultural and social relationships, affect an individual's work progress:

> The first task for the counselor is one of comprehensive assessment; and the first part of that assessment is to determine whether the work adjustment problem is primarily one of work role behavior, task performance, worker satisfaction, or some combination of the three. (p. 443)

Once the assessment is made, the counselor can decide what treatment is best: If it is a personality problem, then one-to-one counseling is suggested; if it is a matter of developing competency skills, then educational skill development is in order; if the problem is with the boss, then perhaps assertiveness training would be effective. In each case, the counselor must also look into what impact the client's family life, training, and social relationships have on the problem. One's family's values and attitudes, for example, are taken into consideration to assess the degree to which they may be barriers to client effectiveness and, further, whether such barriers can be changed or resolved (Hershenson, 1996).

Life Skills Development

Life skills development is an important component of effective career development. It involves helping clients learn skills to maintain and enhance their feeling of well-being in all aspects of life. Group work, both group counseling and group instruction, is a particularly useful way to help individuals learn effective life skills. Group counseling is offered in areas such as stress management, empowerment, problem solving, anger control, coping with career transitions, sleep problems, and weight loss. These groups tend to be problem-specific with relatively homogeneous groups in which persons share emotions and experiences and receive support. Counselors often use cognitive-behavioral techniques, relaxation exercises, and assertiveness training.

Related life skills development centers offer classes and workshops on body awareness, nutrition, relaxation, assertion, yoga, tai chi, transcendental meditation, and values clarification. Holistic and wellness programs are popular and lend themselves well to courses teaching self-improvement techniques. Courses may be taught by mental health counselors, holistic counselors, psychologists, social workers, or persons specially trained in a certain discipline.

Rehabilitation Counseling

The Center for Comprehensive Care (CCC) in Seattle is an association of rehabilitation and preventive health care services on First Hill Medical Campus, the location of the city's major hospitals and medical facilities. Geared primarily to rehabilitation, the center is a federation of several association groups, including the Northwest Counseling Associates. Here, again, is an example of diverse health care groups teaming up to provide services under one facility or a confederation of facilities. Here, a wide variety of services assist and retrain patients to reenter the workforce and to resume normal life functions. Besides physical therapies, chronic care programs, and alternative therapies such as biofeedback, massage, and acupuncture, they provide psychosocial and occupational services, including individual, group, and family counseling; counseling related to physical health, work adjustment, or disability; social and family issues counseling; various specialized counseling, including career planning and adjustment issues involving legal and financial issues; stress, pain, and addictions management; and coping with trauma, including personal injury, death of a loved one, and posttraumatic stress disorder (PTSD).

Multicultural Counseling: Ethnic and Feminist Perspectives

Perspectives of Ethnic Counselors

Most ethnic individuals tend to be closely tied to their cultural roots, to family of origin, extended family, religion, and community. Their social-cultural ties have significantly influenced the approach of most ethnic counselors to their practice. The strong sense of community that many, if not most, ethnic counselors tend to have, a community sense that extends one's connections beyond self and family, is a good model for all community counselors and their clients. Thus, ethnic counseling is also described in the spiritual and family sections of this chapter.

Family therapist Ramon Rojano's Hispanic background, for example, has strongly influenced his professional practice. As director of the Department of Social and Health Services (DSHS) in Hartford, Connecticut, Rojano and his staff of 300 employees work with the hard-core inner-city poor who are primarily of mixed ethnic communities. Formerly a practicing psychiatrist and family therapist from Colombia, Rojano makes family systems therapy work in the slums by broadening the concept of family to include the community as a whole. Calling it *community family therapy,* he focuses on empowerment strategies and thus helps clients learn how to govern their own lives within their community. "His goal is to use his understanding of helping systems to reconnect his clients to their community" (Markowitz, 1997, p. 32). "Therapists too often ignore the rest of the world outside their offices—the schools, courts, public assistance programs, prisons and all other systems that shape the everyday lives of poor clients" (Markowitz, 1997, p. 29).

Rojano has also changed the image of the DSHS in Hartford, the government-funded agency whose primary function in working with the poor typically is that of managing those on welfare. Welfare agencies have gained a bad reputation: Taxpayers are disillusioned that welfare money, instead of helping people out of the ghetto, seems instead to perpetuate their remaining there, dependent and helpless (Markowitz, 1997). Rojano's answer "is to turn the large dehumanizing bureaucratic systems that can make people feel small and helpless into a kind of village that rehumanizes the helping process and ultimately makes it obsolete" (Markowitz, 1997, p. 32).

As DSHS director, Rojano incorporates the family therapy model into his community family therapy, which helps individuals become empowered within their community system, rather than tries to find ways to remove them from their community.

> The new model has to include not only finding the resources poor families need to survive, like child care, jobs, food stamps, housing, but pathways to help clients become the experts on their own lives, figuring out their own goals and developing plans to achieve them. (Markowitz, 1997, p. 29)

Rojano's convictions are based on the way he grew up within a large extended family in a close-knit community of Barranquilla, Colombia. As Markowitz (1997) points out regarding Rojano's cultural background:

> Maybe it's no coincidence that some of the most committed and passionate family therapists working in the inner cities are immigrants from Latin countries, where a person's world is first centered on family and then networked into the bonds of extended kin, neighborhoods, villages. (p. 29)

Rojano's focus on vocational training and placement seems unusual to many family therapists nowadays. Vocational counseling was the primary approach for counselors in the 1930s and 1940s, however; from this impetus, post–World War II counseling sprang into being (see chap. 2). But as Rojano points out, today's therapists think it odd that his primary therapeutic strategy is to get a client a job (Markovitz, 1997). They wonder why a counselor should aim at getting the person a job in the middle of a family crisis. As Rojano says, "Economic therapy is one of the best remedies for family problems. With a job and the emotional support of therapy, (the client) would experience more control and direction in her life" (p. 33).

He also helps parents learn how to become participants in the community by providing promising individuals with leadership training that includes such basics as civics classes and public speaking and classes that teach them how to organize and to go about creating social change. "For Rojano the biggest enemy of the poor is the isolation that living in poverty can breed" (Markowitz, 1997, p. 32).

A different aspect of ethnic counseling is emerging among some African Americans. According to Jones (1998), increasing numbers of middle-class Blacks are seeking counseling largely because more Black clergy support counseling, more Black mental health professionals are available, and successful Black lifestyles often create barriers between them and their extended families—their usual source of help.

Many concerns of both Blacks and Whites in the middle and upper classes are similar: "How do you find happiness while striving for success? How do you balance work with kids?" (Jones, 1998, p. 2a). Problems of Blacks are complicated, however, by forces related to race. Some Blacks who obtain success feel the burden of having to be exemplary representatives of their race. Others find race an impediment to getting jobs equitable to their training and skills, and an impediment, as well, to advance on the job:

> Blacks' struggles are made worse by the undercurrent of race, such as the feelings one must be a standard bearer for an entire group of people. Professional disappointments run deeper when skin color appears to be the only thing holding you back. (Jones, 1998, p. 2a)

Increasing numbers of well-trained Black counselors and psychologists and church-sponsored counseling services in Black communities are emerging in cities throughout the country. Thus, increasing numbers of middle-class Blacks feel more comfortable seeking help. They recognize, as well, that family love and support are often not enough to help them resolve problems, especially because many have moved away from family of origin. In such cases, as Jones (1998) points out, they benefit from the objective service of trained professionals.

Perspectives of Feminist Counselors

Feminist perspectives of developmental and psychological theory have made a significant impact on counseling theory and practice (see chaps. 4 and 5). The theory of mutual connections in relationship developed by women at the Stone Center at Wellesley College has provided a significant alternative approach to traditional therapeutic and counseling practice (see chaps. 9 and 14).

Similarly, as noted earlier in this chapter, the Women's Project in Family Therapy has been using its feminist perspective to develop alternative approaches to family and relationship issues. Women involved in the project urge family counselors and therapists, for example, to move beyond blaming parents, particularly the mother. Moreover, they urge each counselor to help clients consider their own responsibilities to their personal and familial relationships and their responsibilities to the larger cultural community and society as a whole.

Likewise, some male therapists are breaking traditional psychological theory that promotes the image of the dominant and autonomous male. Following the feminist approach, male therapists such as Terrence Real (1997), as discussed in chapter 14, acknowledge the value and necessity of developing and maintaining connections among loves ones, family, and community.

Traumas of Poverty and Political Upheavals

Because of adverse social, economic, or political conditions, entire groups of people are particularly vulnerable to serious emotional or behavioral disorders. At-risk factors discussed here are poverty, and traumas resulting from political upheavals. Without help, crises are apt to occur, precipitating individuals into suicide, crime, or violence.

Development of Comprehensive Neighborhood Health Centers

One of the most significant trends in mental health practice recently has been the development of comprehensive health care services for those without health insurance and those who cannot afford to pay high fees. Many of these centers combine medical health care, mental health counseling, and social services. Liaison services have also formed between universities and neighborhood communities that offer a wide variety of counseling services.

One such comprehensive neighborhood health clinic, the Pike Place Market Medical Clinic in Seattle, Washington, demonstrates the need for, and the advantages of, having mental health services combined with medical and social services in one facility to serve a particular neighborhood. It is open to all individuals regardless of age, race, religion, or gender, but because of its location near older adult retirement homes, over 75% who seek counseling are older adults (Lustbader, 1990). In her discussion of this clinic, counselor Lustbader (1990) features services to older adults because counseling services for older adults is unusual for any counseling center. A significant portion of the clinic's clients are uninsured and are charged on a sliding scale or at no fee. Private funding and grant monies are major sources of financing.

The philosophy of the clinic is that one cannot separate emotional needs from medical and social needs. Patients are typically referred for counseling by physicians in the health clinic when they think patients need counseling help. The physician brings the counselor into the examination room and explains the value of counseling help to the patient (Lustbader, 1990; personal communication, 1998). This move is intended to reduce any fear or stigma the elderly may have about counseling. "The realization that one does not have to be 'crazy' to see a counselor is an essential aspect of this introductory contact" (Lustbader, 1990, p. 22). The focus is on normal, age-related, situational concerns such as conflict with an adult child, loneliness, depression, marital conflicts, housing, and grieving.

The counselor first attends to the immediate social needs of the client, such as housing. Next, the counselor focuses on the client's emotional concerns; if appropriate, the counselor may then refer the client to group and family counseling. Because most clients are within walking distance, counselors, unlike traditional counselors, may carry out counseling through home visits if a client has difficulty coming to the clinic. Counselors also provide a variety of psychoeducational activities in the nearby senior center.

Another example of a comprehensive health care clinic established primarily for the poor and the uninsured is one developed in Bellingham, Washington, by the Interfaith Council in collaboration with St. Joseph's Hospital. Composed of representatives from the city's major religious groups, the Interfaith Council has developed the Interfaith Mental Health Center in conjunction with its Family Medical and Dental Health Center. These health centers draw on volunteer services from the town's physicians, dentists, and mental health practitioners. The Interfaith Council provides, as well, social services, such as job training links to community resources, family housing, and clothing and food. Clients are charged a $10 fee per visit, which can be waived.

The newly formed Interfaith Mental Health Center, led by Douglas Benjamin, a licensed mental health counselor, has some unique features that could well be emulated in other communities. The center provides a direct link not only between medical health care and mental health services but also between mental health services and the clergy—a group who often are the first persons sought out by individuals experiencing emotional distress. Usually, most clients are referred for counseling through their initial contact with the medical care unit, but increasing numbers are being referred directly by the clergy. Rather than serving clients who are chronically mentally ill, as is typical of public community mental health agencies, the Interfaith Mental Health Center serves clients with normal developmental concerns related to family and other relationships. The counseling focus is a holistic one in which client emotional difficulties are dealt with in the context of the client's social, economic, physical, and spiritual conditions and needs.

The Interfaith Mental Health Center, located in an old wing of St. Joseph's Hospital, rents the space from the hospital at a very low fee. D. Benjamin, the only paid staff professional, gets support from a volunteer consulting psychiatrist and 20 volunteer licensed practitioners, mostly master's-level counselors and some Ph.D. psychologists (D. Benjamin, personal communication, November 6, 1998).

Another innovative neighborhood center for at-risk people in low-income communities is the George Washington University (G.W.U.) Community Counseling Clinic in downtown Washington, DC, developed and operated by the G.W.U. counselor education program. The clinic serves individuals who are uninsured, unemployed, or unable to afford care (Guerra, 1998a).

> Stepping into the G.W.U. Community Clinic is to step into a world where people who desperately need help but traditionally have not been able to afford the fees, get competent mental health care costing as much as $28.00 and as little as $1.00 per session. (Guerra, 1998a, p. 24)

The G.W.U. Community Counseling Clinic closely follows the counseling model set by professional counseling associations in that it offers services that address individuals' developmental, career, personal, interpersonal, and family concerns. This clinic demonstrates the need for the development of similar clinics in other low-income neighborhood communities.

The community clinic is staffed by 5 counselor educator professors and about 25 master's and doctoral counseling interns. The interns are taught to use brief therapy and problem-focused counseling approaches appropriate for the developmental concerns of clients. This G.W.U. community clinic could well be emulated by counselor training programs at other universities. Such a clinic enables counselors-in-training to work with a much wider variety of clients than is usually possible in counselor training clinics located on campus.

The Homeless

The number of homeless people in the United States runs into the millions. The majority of these individuals do not fit the stereotype of the indigent "wino" sleeping it off in the streets. In the foreword to *Helping Homeless People* (Solomon & Jackson-Jobe, 1992), Jesse Jackson writes about the homeless population:

> Many were once working people—teachers, auto mechanics, veterans and construction workers. Some are highly educated. These are not just nameless and faceless people. They represent families . . . turned out because of lost jobs. Little children . . . with empty stomachs. Some are sick, physically, or mentally ill. They may be seen walking our city streets, lying under blankets on sidewalks. They are blocks from the White House. (p. v)

Cooke (1992) indicates how the helping professions can intervene to give the homeless economic, social, psychological, and institutional support. Counselors and therapists, he says, "have the skills required to empower homeless persons to take control of their environment through becoming self-aware and self-enhancing" (p. 72).

Creative arts therapist Lou Ann Nockels worked with a group of homeless people in Bellingham, Washington, in conjunction with the local chapter of the Rainbow Coalition. Using psychodrama over a period of several months, participants improvised their stories as they went along as part of the therapeutic process. Performing for the community gave them the first opportunity to express themselves about their homelessness. Their condition, when dramatized, became a social phenomenon rather than isolated, separate experiences (L. Nockels, personal communication, June 4, 1993).

Victims of Political Upheavals

PostTraumatic Stress Disorder (PTSD).   *Posttraumatic stress disorder (PTSD)* is defined in the *DSM-IV* as an anxiety disorder resulting from extreme traumatic stress. Symptoms include recurring recollections or obsessive thoughts about the traumatic event, recurring nightmares, flashbacks, denial of feelings or thoughts, outbursts of rage or irritability, difficulty in relationships, and difficulty concentrating.

Groups of individuals considered at risk for PTSD because of earlier unresolved traumas are war veterans, prisoners of war, refugees, torture victims, rape victims, and adults who were abused as children. An estimated 850,000 Vietnam veterans, who brought this disorder to attention, have been affected by PTSD (Hayman, Sommers-Flanagan, & Parsons, 1987). Assessment and treatment of PTSD started with Vietnam veterans and then generalized to other populations suffering similar symptoms. The Veterans Administration (VA) has only recently acknowledged that significant numbers of World War II and Korean War veterans have also experienced PTSD symptoms.

Hayman and his colleagues (1987) present a 4-phase treatment for PTSD in Vietnam veterans: (a) assessment and trust building, (b) stabilization, (c) processing the trauma, and (d) reintegration. In the first phase (*assessment and building trust*), counselors develop a trust relationship with clients while interviewing them about their preservice, military service, and postservice history. From these interviews, counselors assess the severity of client trauma. In the second phase (*stabilization*), counselors help the veterans bring troubling symptoms under control. Depression and rage, substance abuse, and flashbacks are addressed by using behavioral techniques. In the third phase (*processing the trauma*), counselors help the veterans process the trauma. In various ways, veterans reexperience or relive the trauma in a protective and controlled atmosphere. Hypnosis may be used to recall the trauma vividly, or psychodrama to relive or reenact the trauma. Rap groups, in which people talk openly and honestly with other veterans, may also be used. Other techniques used in individual psychotherapy are cognitive restructuring, desensitization, or flooding (Hayman et al., 1987). In the final stage (*reintegration*), veterans are helped to reintegrate themselves to employment, interpersonal relationships, and family life. Family counseling may then be helpful.

Prisoners of War (POWs).   The long-term impact of traumatic experiences of prisoners of war (POWs) results in persistent symptoms of PTSD, a disorder that is a normal response to such severe trauma (Engdahl, Dikel, Eberly, & Blank, 1997). In a study comparing POWs with combat survivors of the Korean War, researchers determined that POWs had more severe and persistent symptoms of mental and emotional dysfunctioning than did the combat survivors (Sutker & Allain, 1996).

POWs from World War II have been active in bringing public attention to the traumas they experienced during and after imprisonment. These individuals had originally returned to civilian life without an opportunity to talk through their traumatic experiences.

One such example is the plight of the World War II POW Allied Airmen who were shot down during bombing raids over Germany and were captured and held captive during the war. In a personal interview (April 20, 1991), POW Lou Loevsky, a member of the U.S. 8th Air Force, attested to the therapeutic value of sharing experiences in group work. An old friend of mine from grade school, Loevsky said very little about his war experiences until after he started attending these meetings. He invited me to attend a group counseling meeting for POWs at a VA psychological clinic in New Jersey. POWs from World War II and the Korean and Vietnam wars shared their remembrances and traumas. Loevsky said that POW emotional problems were exacerbated because the armed services denied them the opportunity after the war to talk through their traumatic experiences.

Loevsky then renewed contact with fellow POW Airmen. Consequently, the 8th and 15th Air Force POWs, along with POWs from the British Royal Air Force Bomber Command, made a video of their story, called *Behind the Wire* (Zimmerman, 1994), that described the traumatic experiences of more than 45,000 air force POWs who were shot down in enemy territory and held in four prison camps in Germany. Using a mixture of captured German film, air combat footage, and interviews with veteran POWs themselves, filmmakers integrated the POW stories into the larger historical context of the war itself. Each man's story is a harrowing tale. As his plane was going down, Loevsky risked his life to save a crewmate trapped in the plane.

Veterans and POWs all over the country have been attending group therapy sessions. At one such meeting, when the fellow crewmember told how Loevsky saved his life, someone suggested that Loevsky deserved a medal for bravery. In 1999, 55 years later, Loevsky was awarded the Distinguished Flying Cross for heroic action (personal correspondence, February 13, 1999). Besides giving lectures in schools about his war experiences, Loevsky has been helping other POW veterans and their families settle disability claims.

The value of making a dramatic replay of their experiences on video and sharing their stories with outsiders broadens their personal experiences into a larger social-political dimension. This perspective enables listeners of their stories and viewers of their video to share their suffering in the context of historical events. Their stories thus gain meaning and significance, in keeping with Victor Frankl's (1963) philosophy as expressed in his book *Man's Search for Meaning* (see chap. 5).

Refugees.   Refugees differ from other immigrants in that they are displaced persons who were forced to leave their countries because of oppression or threats of abduction, torture, and death to themselves and their families by their governments.

Many of them have experienced torture, destruction of their homes, rape, and starvation. "Leaving one's home country and the precariousness of the flight itself cause loss of family, identity, and culture; a downgrade in socioeconomic status . . . These problems have created serious mental health issues for refugees" (Bemak, Chung, & Bornemann, 1995, p. 244).

Refugees include Salvadorans, Guatemalans, Nicaraguans, Vietnamese, Cambodians, Chinese, Kurds, Bosnians, and Kosovars. Psychological symptoms are depression, anxiety, and paranoia. Difficulty in finding jobs, housing, and food contribute to feelings of hopelessness and helplessness. Brown (1987) and Leung (1991) were among the first to point out that refugees' problems are closely tied to social-political factors that contribute to and exacerbate their emotional conflicts.

To help therapists work with the special emotional needs of refugees, Bemak et al. (1995) propose a 4-level counseling and psychoeducational process called the *multilevel model approach (MLM)*. "The MLM . . . comprises cognitive, affective and behavioral interventions inclusive of cultural foundations and their relation to community and social processes" (p. 256). At Level 1 (*mental health education*), refugees are informed about individual, family, and group services and procedures that counselors use in these services. At Level 2 (*counseling*), refugees receive individual family and group counseling. At Level 3 (*cultural empowerment*), refugees are taught to use community services related to education, finances, health, employment, or other social problems. At Level 4 (*integration of Western and indigenous healing*), counselors develop a partnership with healers indigenous to the refugee's culture, in which together they help refugees express their concerns and their grief.

Torture Victims.   Many refugees are also victims of torture (Goleman, 1989, 1996; Krajik, 1986). A rehabilitation program for torture victims in the United States was first established in Minneapolis, modeled after Copenhagen's International Rehabilitation Center for Torture Victims (Holtan & Robertson, 1992). Since then, similar centers have formed in Boston, Chicago, Los Angeles, San Francisco, Tucson, and in New Jersey. Victims suffer from recurring nightmares, insomnia, paranoia, withdrawal, and violent outbursts. Treatment is similar to that for PTSD but is further complicated by cultural differences.

Dr. Inge Genefke, originator of special treatment programs for torture victims in Copenhagen, says that torture victims have a pernicious form of PTSD. They suffer from unspeakable and prolonged horrors over long periods of time, having been isolated and silenced, and are terrified of reprisals against their loved ones (Goleman, 1996).

An estimated 200,000 to 400,000 torture victims now live in the United States. More than one third of refugees who seek political asylum each year in the United States are torture victims (Goleman, 1996). The numbers are expected to increase, and the need for more treatment centers "will continue to grow because the use of torture appears to be an epidemic" (Goleman, 1996, p. C–3). According to Amnesty International spokesman Roger Rathman, "There is government condoned torture, or ill treatment of detainees verging on torture, in 114 countries" (Goleman, 1996, p. C–3).

❧ COUNSELING PERSONS AT RISK

Persons at risk are those suffering from emotional disorders interfering with their psychosocial development. Major dysfunctions include depression, addictive behaviors, and attention deficit hyperactivity disorder (ADHD).

Depression

Depression, the most common health problem in the United States, is now being treated primarily with antidepressive drugs (Yapco, 1997). Increasing numbers of counselors and therapists, however, are objecting to the overuse of medication to treat depression because, they say, drugs tend to alleviate symptoms without getting to the root of the depression. They contend that depression can best be treated by psychotherapy or counseling in which the client's social context is a foremost consideration. This view has been especially advocated by counselors Yapco (1997), Jack (1991), and family therapist Papp (1997).

Michael Yapco (1997) notes that the pharmaceutical and managed care industries have been strongly promoting the idea that depression is a disease best treated by drugs. While acknowledging that individuals who are severely or chronically depressed generally need medication along with psychotherapy, he argues that, for most individuals, depression is best treated with counseling or psychotherapy alone. Studies show, he says, that "cultural and social forces contribute more to the onset of depression than does biology" (p. 45). He also cites literature reviews that show "substantial evidence for the superior effectiveness of therapy" (p. 45).

The type of therapy Yapco (1997) recommends for depressed people is the development of relationships and social skills and the strengthening of social connections in the face of the negative and depressing events in our world:

> Our ethos of extreme individuality and personal rights for collective responsibility and social accommodation increases the likelihood that we will be lonely and depressed, without the deep ties to family and friends that can immunize us against alienation and despair. (p. 46)

Dana Jack (1991), in her book *Silencing the Self: Women and Depression,* points out that women become depressed when their healthy needs for connection and bonding have been consistently negated in our culture (see chap. 14). She recommends that therapists and counselors can best help these women by actively listening to their concerns and by validating and supporting the importance of relationships in the development of self. Her approach is to ask women directly about their feelings and to listen to their stories. In this process, she looks for and corrects distorted moral themes in their stories and then uses metaphors, fairy tales, and myths to help women activate themselves and move out of depression.

In their work with depressed couples and families, Peggy Papp (1997) and her staff at the Ackerman Institute for Family use a feminist family systems approach to help couples when either the wife or the husband is depressed. A member of the

Women's Project in Family Therapy described earlier, Papp is also director of the Ackerman Institute's Depression in Context Project. She and her staff work to "bring a systemic perspective to the treatment of depression, and to explore how issues involving gender, race, class, and sexual orientation can catalyze its onset" (p. 54).

Concurring with Jack's views about women's loss of voice, Papp (1997) and her staff encourage wives to express their feelings of loss of voice and their loss of sense of self. They also describe the influence of gender role stereotyping on the couple's expectations of each other. They explore "what effect these expectations might be having on current relationships, on their sense of power, privilege and independence" (p. 56).

Consistent with their views about the influence that social context has on depressed persons, Papp and her staff initiate discussions about the contributions of racism and sexism on one's negative self-image. For depressed men, the staff believes that helping them develop empathy and connections with their wives helps lift their depression.

Addictions

Counselors and other mental health providers have, over the years, given attention to the treatment of specific addictive behaviors such as substance abuse, eating disorders, compulsive gambling, and sex addiction. In this text, I discuss substance abuse in a separate chapter (chap. 13), as well as in the chapters on school and college counseling (chaps. 16, 17, and 18).

In their book *Facing Shame,* Fossum and Mason (1986) propose that addictive behaviors arise out of shame-based families. According to Fossum and Mason, counselors must go beyond treating a person's specific addiction; rather, the family dynamics underlying the addictive behavior must be dealt with. Otherwise, a recovering alcoholic, for example, may develop a different form of addiction to replace the alcohol that was given up, or another family member may develop a new addiction to replace what was given up by the recovering alcoholic. "We have learned that the treatment of one addictive behavior does not automatically eradicate compulsivity from the system" (p. 125). Fossum and Mason (1986) include psychosocial considerations in treating addicted families. They emphasize the importance of networks of support outside the family and often include close friends and affiliates in the therapy process.

Fossum and Mason (1986) believe that it is important for clients to give up their secretive, shame-based compulsivity when they can "share their experiences openly and honestly with one another and learn from one another" (p. 124). Using AA 12-step programs, clients admit their powerlessness and receive support and acceptance from the group; a spiritual recovery takes place, "making it possible for the client to connect on an emotional and human level with other group members" (p. 125).

Also addressing the issue of addictive behaviors as a whole, Real (1997) argues that addictions, particularly in males, are defenses to cover up depression (see chap. 14).

Attention Deficit Hyperactivity Disorder (ADHD)

Until recently, mental health professionals believed that children with attention deficit hyperactivity disorder (ADHD) outgrew it when they reached adulthood. Experts now estimate that 30% to 50% of ADHD children continue to experience disruptive behaviors throughout their lives (Jackson & Farrugia, 1997). Attention is now focused on making appropriate diagnosis of this disorder in adults and on determining the most effective treatment.

In their review of ADHD research and practice, Jackson and Farrugia (1997) concluded that the primary characteristics of adult ADHD are similar to those of childhood ADHD: inattention, hyperactivity, and impulsivity that lead to problems on the job, substance abuse, or relationship problems. "For adults affected by ADHD, the decision to seek help is often precipitated by being fired from their job, having substance abuse problems, having their spouses ask for divorce, or some other traumatic experience" (p. 318).

Researchers believe that the most effective counseling approach is a multimodal one involving educating clients about the disorder and training them in attention management skills, self-management and self-monitoring strategies, social skills and problem solving, and stress and anger management. Adult clients with ADHD need to feel a sense of empowerment and hope as they begin to use these various self-management skills (Jackson & Farrugia, 1997).

CRISES: PREVENTION AND INTERVENTION

Community counselors, like counselors in schools and colleges, must be prepared to deal with crises. They must have the knowledge, skill, and experience to know how to deal with the presenting emergency, take immediate action to help a person through the trauma, and then decide whether to refer the individual to another professional or agency.

Crisis centers staffed by volunteers trained in telephone crisis intervention are available in most large communities. In some communities, specialists form teams to work jointly with families in crises (Brammer, Abrego, & Shostrom, 1993).

Historically, community counselors have dealt with those who have attempted suicide, those with severe immobilizing depression or psychotic reactions, and those who have been traumatized by the sudden loss or death of loved ones. In recent years, severe drug reactions have become more common, as have crisis problems regarding battered wives, rape victims, abused children, and juvenile runaways.

Suicide

Community crisis workers emphasize the importance of psychosocial factors in working with suicidal clients. Crisis counselors "focus on prevention by correcting the alienated life style that cuts off the person's connectedness with others" (Gilliland & James, 1997, p. 212).

Recognizing the importance of the social context in which the client is living, crisis counselors involve family, friends, and associates of the suicidal client in prevention and support work. Counselors teach those close to the client to be aware of certain typical behaviors or feelings that suicidal persons display. They also teach family and significant others how to support suicidal persons in ways that will build their feelings of worthiness and value while making them feel accepted as fallible human beings (Gilliland & James, 1997). Crisis workers also provide clients with lists of referrals and support sources in the community. This networking not only gives suicidal clients increased feelings of security but also demonstrates to clients that individuals in the community care about them.

Counselors also help friends and family of those who have committed suicide to cope with grief or excessive feelings of guilt or blame.

Violence

When employees witness or are victims of a traumatic experience on the job, increasing numbers of companies in business and industry are calling on mental health counselors to provide help and relief (debriefing) from experiencing mass shootings, bombings of offices, mass casualties in mine disasters, violent accidents, or deaths or suicides of fellow employees. Catastrophic and traumatic incidents generally cause severe emotional reactions, and if not attended to, a delayed reaction occurs in the form of posttraumatic stress disorder (PTSD).

In these situations, mental health counselors may be called on by EAPs, may contract with or be employed by firms that specialize in crisis intervention, or may be part of a mental health group in the community that volunteers services to crisis team intervention.

An example of a business using crisis intervention specialists occurred after the bombing of the Alfred P. Murrah Federal Building in Oklahoma City in 1995. A company located close to the bombing, Kerr-McGee Corporation, whose employees witnessed the bombing, contracted Crisis Management International from Atlanta, Georgia, to debrief their employees. Eighteen counselors provided counseling support and informational services (Gladding, 1997). This task force "set up a command center, held group and individual counseling sessions, and established a phone tree to update information to its workers. Problems employees had . . . included grief, anger, depression, fatigue, nightmares, survivor guilt and trouble eating and concentrating" (Gladding, 1997, p. 242).

A volunteer crisis intervention team was formed recently in Whatcom and Skagit Counties in the state of Washington to debrief employees in businesses throughout the counties who have experienced job-related trauma. Called the Critical Incident Stress Management Program (CISM), the team is composed of a volunteer mental health professional and two volunteers from business and industry.

Mental health counselors may also be involved with government agencies designed to help victims of natural disasters such as floods, hurricanes, earthquakes, or forest fires. The federal government, for example, has established the National Organization for Victim Assistance (NOVA; Gilliland & James, 1997). After a national disaster, NOVA sends "National Crisis Response Teams (NCRTs) to . . . quickly establish crisis response teams to respond to immediate needs as well as to the extent possible, prevent crisis traumas from inflicting long-term emotional damages on disaster victims" (pp. 606-607).

⟶ SUMMARY

Many health care providers in the community are combining their services to offer more comprehensive treatment for clients. Groups are forming liaisons to meet the individual's and family's developmental, physical, psychological, spiritual, social-cultural, and economic needs. Comprehensive health care centers are emerging in some places, centers that include multicultural approaches to counseling, family and career counseling, spiritual counseling and grief work, medical care, and social services.

Community counselors work with psychosocial concerns and transitions of clients at all ages. Some community and school counselors are forming liaisons and joint services to work with at-risk schoolchildren and adolescents who live in detrimental social conditions. Young adults typically need counselor help with career planning, job adjustment, relationship issues, and raising a family. At midlife, adults have concerns about job change or job loss and changing relations with children, spouse, and aging parents. Senior centers in some places are proving to be viable places for effective counseling of older adults and for helping them carry out generative and productive activities.

Family therapists are expanding their approach in a variety of ways. Some are now acknowledging the impact of job-related issues on family dynamics. Moreover, many, particularly certain ethnic counselors and therapists, have extended family dynamics to include how the family is involved in the community, how the family is affected by social-cultural factors, and in turn, how the family can develop in relation to its community. Many family therapists have also expanded their perspective to attend to the aging family, focusing on intergenerational relationships that foster renewal and growth between adults and their aging parents. Many counselors are providing ways individuals suffering the loss of loved ones can share their grief with others through grief support groups and other community-supported healing circles.

Spiritual development is receiving increasing attention among counseling professionals. Ethnic counselors have been influential in alerting the counseling profession to the importance of spiritual concerns to one's development. In large cities, major religious organizations are providing effective and affordable counseling to the general public. Some spiritual counselors are beginning to provide ways for individuals to make effective transitions between spiritual retreats and the everyday world.

Community counselors are helping clients interact with challenging social, cultural, and political conditions and transitions, including career and work adjustment. In many cities, comprehensive health care centers are emerging in poor neighborhoods to serve the needs of those at-risk people who cannot afford health insurance or who are unemployed and homeless. Counseling centers are also emerging in major cities to care for those affected by political upheavals, such as war veterans and POWs with post-traumatic stress disorder, refugees, and torture victims. Counselors work with persons suffering from depression, addictions, and ADHD. They also provide crisis prevention and intervention services for suicidal persons and victims of violence. Some counselors provide debriefing sessions for those traumatized by violence or catastrophic events.

➢ PROJECTS AND ACTIVITIES

1. Survey your community to determine what resources are available for counseling individuals with normal developmental concerns who are not in school or in college.

2. Explore various community agencies in your vicinity from the standpoint of training. What percentage of the staff members are professionally trained counselors? How much in-service training is given? How much dependence is there on volunteers? What is the specific training of other professionals?

3. Visit community counseling agencies and read their brochures and other publicizing materials. Does the information indicate that the agencies are prepared to handle the types of client concerns discussed in this chapter?

4. Interview probation officers in your community. Do they perceive any difficulty in trying to counsel their parolees while maintaining jurisdiction over them? Do the officers have resources to whom they can refer clients?

5. What resources are available in the community for counseling elderly persons? Do these services appear satisfactory? How are they funded? What improvements would you make?

6. Survey community ethnic groups and their attitudes about and use of mental health facilities. Are ethnic groups represented on the staffs of various agencies?

7. Visit your county or regional community mental health clinic. Ask the director whether you can obtain an organizational chart of services offered under the community comprehensive mental health program in your area. Explore which needs are being met and which are being neglected. Try to determine reasons for the selection of services.

➢ REFERENCES

American Psychiatric Association. (1994). *Diagnostic and statistical manual of mental disorders* (4th ed.). Washington, DC: Author.

Bart, M. (1998). Spirituality in counseling finding believers. *Counseling Today, 41,* 1, 6.

Baruth, L. G., & Manning, M. L. (1999). *Multicultural counseling and psychotherapy: A lifespan perspective* (2nd ed.). Upper Saddle River, NJ: Merrill/Prentice Hall.

Bemak, F., Chung, R. C. Y., & Bornemann, T. H. (1995). Counseling and psychotherapy with refugees. In P. B. Pedersen, J. G. Draguns, W. J. Lonner, & J. E. Trimble (Eds.), *Counseling across cultures* (4th ed., pp. 243–265). Thousand Oaks, CA: Sage.

Bielski, V. (1996). Our magnificent obsession. *The Family Therapy Networker, 20,* 22–35.

Bishop, D. R. (1995). Religious values as cross-cultural issues in counseling. In M. T. Burke & J. G. Mirante (Eds.), *Counseling: The spiritual dimension* (pp. 59–72), Alexandria, VA: American Counseling Association.

Brammer, L. M., Abrego, P. J., & Shostrom, E. L. (1993). *Therapeutic counseling and psychotherapy* (6th ed.). Upper Saddle River, NJ: Prentice Hall.

Brown, F. (1987). Counseling Vietnamese refugees: The new challenge. *International Journal for the Advancement of Counseling, 10,* 259–268.

Burke, M. T., & Miranti, J. G. (1995). *Counseling: The spiritual dimension.* Alexandria, VA: American Counseling Association.

Cooke, A. L. (1992). The role of helping professionals: Developing a strategy. In C. Solomon & P. Jackson-Jobe (Eds.), *Helping homeless people: Unique challenges and solutions.* Alexandria, VA: American Counseling Association.

Corey, M. S., & Corey, G. (1992). *Groups: Process and practice* (4th ed.). Pacific Grove, CA: Brooks/Cole.

Donaghy, K. B. (1995). Beyond survival: Applying wellness interventions in battered women's shelters. *Journal of Mental Health Counseling, 17,* 3–17.

Dugan, W. E. (1993). *Wood Block and Toy Project: Designed for diversely-abled senior volunteers.* St. Cloud, MN: Retired Senior Volunteer Program.

Engdahl, B., Dikel, T. N., Eberly, R., & Blank, A., Jr. (1997). Post-traumatic stress disorder in a community group of former prisoners of war: A normative response to severe trauma. *American Journal of Psychiatry, 154,* 1576–1581.

Entine, A. D. (1976). Mid-life counseling: Prognosis and potential. *Personnel and Guidance Journal, 55,* 112–114.

Fossum, M. E., & Mason, M. J. (1986). *Facing shame: Families in recovery.* New York: Norton.

Frankl, V. (1963). *Man's search for meaning.* New York: Washington Square Press.

Garcia-Preto, N. (1982). Puerto Rican families. In M. McGoldrick, J. K. Pearce, & J. Giordano (Eds.), *Ethnicity and family therapy* (pp. 164–186). New York: Guilford Press.

Gilliland, B. E., & James, R. K. (1997). *Crisis intervention strategies* (3rd ed.). Pacific Grove, CA: Brooks/Cole.

Gladding, S. T. (1997). *Community and agency counseling.* Upper Saddle River, NJ: Merrill/Prentice Hall.

Golden, L. B. (Ed.). (1998). *Case studies in child and adolescent counseling* (2nd ed.). Upper Saddle River, NJ: Merrill/Prentice Hall.

Goleman, D. (1989, April 25). Grim specialty emerges as therapists treat victims of torture. *New York Times Magazine,* pp. C1, C12.

Goleman, D. (1996, July 9). A promising medical specialty emerges to help torture victims. *New York Times,* p. C3.

Grady, S. (1990). Senior centers: An environment in counseling. *Generations, 14,* 15–19.

Guerra, P. (1998a). Beyond the brick wall: Reaching a community in need. *Counseling Today, 41,* 24.

Guerra, P. (1998b). Innovative program addresses anger management through ice hockey. *Counseling Today, 40,* 32, 45.

Hayman, P. M., Sommers-Flanagan, R., & Parsons, J. P. (1987). Aftermath of violence: Post-traumatic stress disorder among Vietnam veterans. *Journal of Counseling & Development, 65,* 363–366.

Heddesheimer, J. (1976). Multiple motivations for mid-career changes. *Personnel and Guidance Journal, 55,* 109–111.

Hershenson, D. B. (1996). Work adjustment: A neglected area in career counseling. *Journal of Counseling & Development, 74,* 442–446.

Holtan, N., & Robertson, C. (1992). Scarcity among plenty: How to treat victims of torture in the USA without government assistance. *Torture, 2,* 11.

Ingersoll, R. E. (1995). Spirituality, religion, and counseling: Dimensions and relationships. In M. T. Burke & J. G. Mirante (Eds.), *Counseling: The spiritual dimension* (pp. 5–18). Alexandria, VA: American Counseling Association.

Iwasaki, J. (1998, December 11). Many bear a special grief during holidays. *Seattle Post Intelligencer,* pp. C–1, 11.

Jack, D. (1991). *Silencing the self: Women and depression.* Cambridge, MA: Harvard University Press.

Jackson, B., & Farrugia, D. (1997). Diagnosis and treatment of adults with attention deficit hyperactivity disorder. *Journal of Counseling & Development, 75,* 312–319.

Jones, C. (1998, August 21). More Blacks are turning to counselors for help. *USA Today,* pp. 1A–2A.

Kornfield, J. (1993). *A path with heart: A guide through the perils and promises of spiritual life.* New York: Bantam Books.

Krajik, K. (1986, November). Healing broken minds. *Psychology Today,* pp. 66–69.

Landis, L. L., & Wyre, C. H. (1984). Group treatment for mothers of incest victims: A step-by-step approach. *Journal of Counseling & Development, 63,* 115–116.

Leung, P. (1991). Asian Americans and psychology: Unresolved issues. *Journal of Training and Practice in Professional Psychology, 4,* 3–13.

Lustbader, W. (1990). Mental health services in a community health center. *Generations, 14,* 22–23.

Markowitz, L. (1997). Ramon Rojano won't take no for an answer. *Family Therapy Networker, 21,* 24–35.

Meade, M. (1998). *Mosaic Multicultural Foundation* [Brochure]. Vashon, WA: Author.

Nugent, F. A. (1981). *Professional counseling: An overview.* Pacific Grove, CA: Brooks/Cole.

O'Malley, P. (1998). Raising Martin. In L. B. Golden (Ed.), *Case studies in child and adolescent counseling* (2nd ed., pp. 92–102), Upper Saddle River, NJ: Merrill/Prentice Hall.

Papp, P. (1997). Listening to the system. *Family Therapy Networker, 21,* 52–58.

Pearson, J. E. (1988). A support group for women with relationship dependency. *Journal of Counseling & Development, 66,* 394–396.

Randolph, D. L. (1978). The counseling-community psychologist in the CMHC: Employer perceptions. *Counselor Education and Supervision, 17,* 244–253.

Rappoport, L. (1976). Adult development: "Faster horses . . . and more money." *Personnel and Guidance Journal, 55,* 106–108.

Real, T. (1987). *I don't want to talk about it.* New York: Fireside.

Real, T. (1997). *I don't want to talk about it.* New York: Fireside.

Sandmaier, M. (1998). Healing the family's oldest rifts. *Family Therapy Networker, 22,* 23–31, 59–60.

Simon, R. (1997). Fearless foursome: An interview with the women's project. *Family Therapy Networker, 21,* 58–68.

Solomon, C., & Jackson-Jobe, P. (Eds.). (1992). *Helping homeless people: Unique challenges and solutions.* Alexandria, VA: American Counseling Association.

Stern, L. (1993). How to find a job: New ways of winning in today's tough market. *Modern Maturity, 36,* 24–30, 32–34.

Sutker, P., & Allain, A. N., Jr. (1996). Assessment of PTSD and other mental disorders in World War II and Korean Conflict POW survivors and combat veterans. *Psychological Assessment, 8,* 18–25.

Thomas, M. C., & Martin, V. (1992). Training counselors to facilitate the transitions of aging through group work. *Counselor Education and Supervision, 32,* 51–60.

Trimble, J. E., Fleming, D. M., Beauvais, F., & Jumper-Thurman, P. (1996). Essential cultural and social strategies for counseling Native American Indians. In P. B. Pedersen, J. G. Draguns, W. J. Lonner, & J. E. Trimble (Eds.), *Counseling across cultures* (4th ed., pp. 177–209). Thousand Oaks, CA: Sage.

Waters, E. B. (1984). Building on what you know: Techniques for individual and group counseling with older people. *Counseling Psychologist, 12,* 63–74.

Wylie, M. S. (1992). Revising the dream. *Family Therapy Networker, 16,* 10–23.

Wylie, M. S. (1996). It's a community affair. *Family Therapy Networker, 20,* 58–65, 96.

Yapco, M. (1997). Stronger medicine. *Family Therapy Networker, 21,* 42–49.

Zimmerman, A. (1994). *Behind the wire: Allied airmen in German captivity* [Video]. 8th Air Force Historical Society.

Appendix A ACA Code of Ethics and Standards of Practice

⇴ PREAMBLE

The American Counseling Association is an educational, scientific, and professional organization whose members are dedicated to the enhancement of human development throughout the life span. Association members recognize diversity in our society and embrace a cross-cultural approach in support of the worth, dignity, potential, and uniqueness of each individual.

    The specification of a code of ethics enables the association to clarify to current and future members, and to those served by members, the nature of the ethical responsibilities held in common by its members. As the code of ethics of the association, this document establishes principles that define the ethical behavior of association members. All members of the American Counseling Association are required to adhere to the Code of Ethics and the Standards of Practice. The Code of Ethics will serve as the basis for processing ethical complaints initiated against members of the association.

As Approved by Governing Council

April 1997

Effective July 1, 1997

Source: "The American Counseling Association Code of Ethics and Standards of Practice," by American Counseling Association, 1997, Alexandria, VA: American Counseling Association. Copyright 1995 by American Counseling Association. No further reproduction authorized without written permission of the American Counseling Association.

Section A:
The Counseling Relationship

A.1. Client Welfare

a. *Primary Responsibility.*
The primary responsibility of counselors is to respect the dignity and to promote the welfare of clients.

b. *Positive Growth and Development.*
Counselors encourage client growth and development in ways that foster the clients' interest and welfare; counselors avoid fostering dependent counseling relationships.

c. *Counseling Plans.*
Counselors and their clients work jointly in devising integrated, individual counseling plans that offer reasonable promise of success and are consistent with abilities and circumstances of clients. Counselors and clients regularly review counseling plans to ensure their continued viability and effectiveness respecting clients' freedom of choice. (See A.3.b.)

d. *Family Involvement.*
Counselors recognize that families are usually important in clients' lives and strive to enlist family understanding and involvement as a positive resource when appropriate.

e. *Career and Employment Needs.*
Counselors work with their clients in considering employment in jobs and circumstances that are consistent with the clients' overall abilities, vocational limitations, physical restrictions, general temperament, interest and aptitude patterns, social skills, education, general qualifications, and other relevant characteristics and needs. Counselors neither place nor participate in placing clients in positions that will result in damaging the interest and the welfare of clients, employers, or the public.

A.2. Respecting Diversity

a. *Nondiscrimination.*
Counselors do not condone or engage in discrimination based on age, color, culture, disability, ethnic group, gender, race, religion, sexual orientation, marital status, or socioeconomic status. (See C.5.a., C.5.b., and D.1.i.)

b. *Respecting Differences.*
Counselors will actively attempt to understand the diverse cultural backgrounds of the clients with whom they work. This includes, but is not limited to, learning how the counselor's own cultural/ethnic/racial identity impacts her/his values and beliefs about the counseling process. (See E.8. and F.2.i.)

A.3. Client Rights

a. *Disclosure to Clients.*
When counseling is initiated, and throughout the counseling process as necessary, counselors inform clients of the purposes, goals, techniques, procedures, limitations, potential risks and benefits of services to be performed, and other pertinent information. Counselors take steps to ensure that clients understand the implications of diagnosis, the intended use of tests and reports, fees, and billing arrangements. Clients have the right to expect confidentiality and to be provided with an explanation of its limitations, including supervision and/or treatment team professionals; to obtain clear information about their case records; to participate in the ongoing counseling plans; and to refuse any recommended services and be advised of the consequences of such refusal. (See E.5.a. and G.2.)

b. *Freedom of Choice.*
Counselors offer clients the freedom to choose whether to enter into a counseling relationship and to determine which professional(s) will provide counseling. Restrictions that limit choices of clients are fully explained. (See A.1.c.)

c. *Inability to Give Consent.*
When counseling minors or persons unable to give voluntary informed consent, counselors act in these clients' best interests. (See B.3.)

A.4. Clients Served by Others

If a client is receiving services from another mental health professional, counselors, with client consent, inform the professional persons already involved and develop clear agreements to avoid confusion and conflict for the client. (See C.6.c.)

A.5. Personal Needs and Values

a. *Personal Needs.*
In the counseling relationship, counselors are aware of the intimacy and responsibilities inherent in the counseling relationship, maintain respect for clients, and avoid actions that seek to meet their personal needs at the expense of clients.

b. *Personal Values.*
Counselors are aware of their own values, attitudes, beliefs, and behaviors and how these apply in a diverse society and avoid imposing their values on clients. (See C.5.a.)

A.6. Dual Relationships

a. *Avoid When Possible.*
Counselors are aware of their influential positions with respect to clients, and they avoid exploiting the trust and dependency of clients. Counselors make every effort to avoid dual relationships with clients that could impair professional judgment or increase the risk of harm to clients. (Examples of such relationships include, but are not limited to, familial, social, financial, business, or close personal relationships with clients.) When a dual relationship cannot be avoided, counselors take appropriate professional precautions, such as informed consent, consultation, supervision, and documentation, to ensure that judgment is not impaired and no exploitation occurs. (See F.1.b.)

b. *Superior/Subordinate Relationships.*
Counselors do not accept as clients superiors or subordinates with whom they have administrative, supervisory, or evaluative relationships.

A.7. Sexual Intimacies With Clients

a. *Current Clients.*
Counselors do not have any type of sexual intimacies with clients and do not counsel persons with whom they have had a sexual relationship.

b. *Former Clients.*
Counselors do not engage in sexual intimacies with former clients within a minimum of two years after terminating the counseling relationship. Counselors who engage in such relationship after two years following termination have the responsibility to thoroughly examine and document that such relations did not have an exploitative nature, based on factors, such as duration of counseling, amount of time since counseling, termination circumstances, client's personal history and mental status, adverse impact on the client, and actions by the counselor suggesting a plan to initiate a sexual relationship with the client after termination.

A.8. Multiple Clients

When counselors agree to provide counseling services to two or more persons who have a relationship (such as husband and wife, or parents and children), counselors clarify at the outset which person or persons are clients and the nature of the relationships they will have with each involved person. If it becomes apparent that counselors may be called upon to perform potentially conflicting roles, they clarify, adjust, or withdraw from roles appropriately. (See B.2. and B.4.d.)

A.9. Group Work

a. *Screening.*
Counselors screen prospective group counseling/therapy participants. To the extent possible, counselors select members whose needs and goals are compatible with goals of the group, who will not impede the group process, and whose well-being will not be jeopardized by the group experience.

b. *Protecting Clients.*

In a group setting, counselors take reasonable precautions to protect clients from physical or psychological trauma.

A.10. FEES AND BARTERING
(See D.3.a. and D.3.b.)

a. *Advance Understanding.*

Counselors clearly explain to clients, prior to entering the counseling relationship, all financial arrangements related to professional services including the use of collection agencies or legal measures for nonpayment. (A.11.c.)

b. *Establishing Fees.*

In establishing fees for professional counseling services, counselors consider the financial status of clients and locality. In the event that the established fee structure is inappropriate for a client, assistance is provided in attempting to find comparable services of acceptable cost. (See A.10.d., D.3.a., and D.3.b.)

c. *Bartering Discouraged.*

Counselors ordinarily refrain from accepting goods or services from clients in return for counseling services because such arrangements create inherent potential for conflicts, exploitation, and distortion of the professional relationship. Counselors may participate in bartering only if the relationship is not exploitive, if the client requests it, if a clear written contract is established, and if such arrangements are an accepted practice among professionals in the community. (See A.6.a.)

d. *Pro Bono Service.*

Counselors contribute to society by devoting a portion of their professional activity to services for which there is little or no financial return (pro bono).

A.11. TERMINATION AND REFERRAL

a. *Abandonment Prohibited.*

Counselors do not abandon or neglect clients in counseling. Counselors assist in making appropriate arrangements for the continuation of treatment, when necessary, during interruptions, such as vacations, and following termination.

b. *Inability to Assist Clients.*

If counselors determine an inability to be of professional assistance to clients, they avoid entering or immediately terminate a counseling relationship. Counselors are knowledgeable about referral resources and suggest appropriate alternatives. If clients decline the suggested referral, counselors should discontinue the relationship.

c. *Appropriate Termination.*

Counselors terminate a counseling relationship, securing client agreement when possible, when it is reasonably clear that the client is no longer benefiting, when services are no longer required, when counseling no longer serves the client's needs or interests, when clients do not pay fees charged, or when agency or institution limits do not allow provision of further counseling services. (See A.10.b. and C.2.g.)

A.12. COMPUTER TECHNOLOGY

a. *Use of Computers.*

When computer applications are used in counseling services, counselors ensure that (1) the client is intellectually, emotionally, and physically capable of using the computer application; (2) the computer application is appropriate for the needs of the client; (3) the client understands the purpose and operation of the computer applications; and (4) a follow-up of client use of a computer application is provided to correct possible misconceptions, discover inappropriate use, and assess subsequent needs.

b. *Explanation of Limitations.*

Counselors ensure that clients are provided information as a part of the counseling relationship that adequately explains the limitations of computer technology.

c. *Access to Computer Applications.*

Counselors provide for equal access to computer applications in counseling services. (See A.2.a.)

SECTION B: CONFIDENTIALITY

B.1. RIGHT TO PRIVACY

a. *Respect for Privacy.*

Counselors respect their clients' right to privacy and avoid illegal and unwarranted disclosures of confidential information. (See A.3.a. and B.6.a.)

b. *Client Waiver.*

The right to privacy may be waived by the client or their legally recognized representative.

c. *Exceptions.*

The general requirement that counselors keep information confidential does not apply when disclosure is required to prevent clear and imminent danger to the client or others or when legal requirements demand that confidential information be revealed. Counselors consult with other professionals when in doubt as to the validity of an exception.

d. *Contagious, Fatal Diseases.*

A counselor who receives information confirming that a client has a disease commonly known to be both communicable and fatal is justified in disclosing information to an identifiable third party, who by his or her relationship with the client is at a high risk of contracting the disease. Prior to making a disclosure the counselor should ascertain that the client has not already informed the third party about his or her disease and that the client is not intending to inform the third party in the immediate future. (See B.1.c and B.1.f)

e. *Court Ordered Disclosure.*

When court ordered to release confidential information without a client's permission, counselors request to the court that the disclosure not be required due to potential harm to the client or counseling relationship. (See B.1.c.)

f. *Minimal Disclosure.*

When circumstances require the disclosure of confidential information, only essential information is revealed. To the extent possible, clients are informed before confidential information is disclosed.

g. *Explanation of Limitations.*

When counseling is initiated and throughout the counseling process as necessary, counselors inform clients of the limitations of confidentiality and identify foreseeable situations in which confidentiality must be breached. (See G.2.a.)

h. *Subordinates.*

Counselors make every effort to ensure that privacy and confidentiality of clients are maintained by subordinates including employees, supervisees, clerical assistants, and volunteers. (See B.1.a.)

i. *Treatment Teams.*

If client treatment will involve a continued review by a treatment team, the client will be informed of the team's existence and composition.

B.2. GROUPS AND FAMILIES

a. *Group Work.*

In group work, counselors clearly define confidentiality and the parameters for the specific group being entered, explain its importance, and discuss the difficulties related to confidentiality involved in group work. The fact that confidentiality cannot be guaranteed is clearly communicated to group members.

b. *Family Counseling.*

In family counseling, information about one family member cannot be disclosed to another member without permission. Counselors protect the privacy rights of each family member. (See A.8., B.3., and B.4.d.)

B.3 MINOR OR INCOMPETENT CLIENTS

When counseling clients who are minors or individuals who are unable to give voluntary, informed consent, parents or guardians may be included in the counseling process as appropriate. Counselors act in the best interests of clients and take measures to safeguard confidentiality. (See A.3.c.)

509

B.4. RECORDS

a. *Requirement of Records.*

Counselors maintain records necessary for rendering professional services to their clients and as required by laws, regulations, or agency or institution procedures.

b. *Confidentiality of Records.*

Counselors are responsible for securing the safety and confidentiality of any counseling records they create, maintain, transfer, or destroy whether the records are written, taped, computerized, or stored in any other medium. (See B.1.a.)

c. *Permission to Record or Observe.*

Counselors obtain permission from clients prior to electronically recording or observing sessions. (See A.3.a.)

d. *Client Access.*

Counselors recognize that counseling records are kept for the benefit of clients and, therefore, provide access to records and copies of records when requested by competent clients unless the records contain information that may be misleading and detrimental to the client. In situations involving multiple clients, access to records is limited to those parts of records that do not include confidential information related to another client. (See A.8., B.1.a., and B.2.b.)

e. *Disclosure or Transfer.*

Counselors obtain written permission from clients to disclose or transfer records to legitimate third parties unless exceptions to confidentiality exist as listed in Section B.1. Steps are taken to ensure that receivers of counseling records are sensitive to their confidential nature.

B.5. RESEARCH AND TRAINING

a. *Data Disguise Required.*

Use of data derived from counseling relationships for purposes of training, research, or publication is confined to content that is disguised to ensure the anonymity of the individuals involved. (See B.1.g. and G.3.d.)

b. *Agreement for Identification.*

Identification of a client in a presentation or publication is permissible only when the client has reviewed the material and has agreed to its presentation or publication. (See G.3.d.)

B.6. CONSULTATION

a. *Respect for Privacy.*

Information obtained in a consulting relationship is discussed for professional purposes only with persons clearly concerned with the case. Written and oral reports present data germane to the purposes of the consultation, and every effort is made to protect client identity and avoid undue invasion of privacy.

b. *Cooperating Agencies.*

Before sharing information, counselors make efforts to ensure that there are defined policies in other agencies serving the counselor's clients that effectively protect the confidentiality of information.

SECTION C: PROFESSIONAL RESPONSIBILITY

C.1. STANDARDS KNOWLEDGE

Counselors have a responsibility to read, understand, and follow the Code of Ethics and the Standards of Practice.

C.2. PROFESSIONAL COMPETENCE

a. *Boundaries of Competence.*

Counselors practice only within the boundaries of their competence, based on their education, training, supervised experience, state and national professional credentials, and appropriate professional experience. Counselors will demonstrate a commitment to gain knowledge, personal awareness, sensitivity, and skills pertinent to working with a diverse client population.

b. *New Specialty Areas of Practice.*

Counselors practice in specialty areas new to them only after appropriate education, training, and supervised experience. While developing skills in new specialty areas, counselors take steps to ensure the competence of their work and to protect others from possible harm.

c. *Qualified for Employment.*

Counselors accept employment only for positions for which they are qualified by education, training, supervised experience, state and national professional credentials, and appropriate professional experience. Counselors hire for professional counseling positions only individuals who are qualified and competent.

d. *Monitor Effectiveness.*

Counselors continually monitor their effectiveness as professionals and take steps to improve when necessary. Counselors in private practice take reasonable steps to seek out peer supervision to evaluate their efficacy as counselors.

e. *Ethical Issues Consultation.*

Counselors take reasonable steps to consult with other counselors or related professionals when they have questions regarding their ethical obligations or professional practice. (See H.1)

f. *Continuing Education.*

Counselors recognize the need for continuing education to maintain a reasonable level of awareness of current scientific and professional information in their fields of activity. They take steps to maintain competence in the skills they use, are open to new procedures, and keep current with the diverse and/or special populations with whom they work.

g. *Impairment.*

Counselors refrain from offering or accepting professional services when their physical, mental or emotional problems are likely to harm a client or others. They are alert to the signs of impairment, seek assistance for problems, and, if necessary, limit, suspend, or terminate their professional responsibilities. (See A.11.c.)

C.3. ADVERTISING AND SOLICITING CLIENTS

a. *Accurate Advertising.*

There are no restrictions on advertising by counselors except those that can be specifically justified to protect the public from deceptive practices. Counselors advertise or represent their services to the public by identifying their credentials in an accurate manner that is not false, misleading, deceptive, or fraudulent. Counselors may only advertise the highest degree earned which is in counseling or a closely related field from a college or university that was accredited when the degree was awarded by one of the regional accrediting bodies recognized by the Council on Postsecondary Accreditation.

b. *Testimonials.*

Counselors who use testimonials do not solicit them from clients or other persons who, because of their particular circumstances, may be vulnerable to undue influence.

c. *Statements by Others.*

Counselors make reasonable efforts to ensure that statements made by others about them or the profession of counseling are accurate.

d. *Recruiting Through Employment.*

Counselors do not use their places of employment or institutional affiliation to recruit or gain clients, supervisees, or consultees for their private practices. (See C.5.e.)

e. *Products and Training Advertisements.*

Counselors who develop products related to their profession or conduct workshops or training events ensure that the advertisements concerning these products or events are accurate and disclose adequate information for consumers to make informed choices.

f. *Promoting to Those Served.*

Counselors do not use counseling, teaching, training, or supervisory relationships to promote their products or training events in a manner that is deceptive or would exert undue influence on individuals who may be vulnerable. Counselors may adopt textbooks they have authored for instruction purposes.

510

g. *Professional Association Involvement.*

Counselors actively participate in local, state, and national associations that foster the development and improvement of counseling.

C.4. CREDENTIALS

a. *Credentials Claimed.*

Counselors claim or imply only professional credentials possessed and are responsible for correcting any known misrepresentations of their credentials by others. Professional credentials include graduate degrees in counseling or closely related mental health fields, accreditation of graduate programs, national voluntary certifications, government-issued certifications or licenses, ACA professional membership, or any other credential that might indicate to the public specialized knowledge or expertise in counseling.

b. *ACA Professional Membership.*

ACA professional members may announce to the public their membership status. Regular members may not announce their ACA membership in a manner that might imply they are credentialed counselors.

c. *Credential Guidelines.*

Counselors follow the guidelines for use of credentials that have been established by the entities that issue the credentials.

d. *Misrepresentation of Credentials.*

Counselors do not attribute more to their credentials than the credentials represent and do not imply that other counselors are not qualified because they do not possess certain credentials.

e. *Doctoral Degrees From Other Fields.*

Counselors who hold a master's degree in counseling or a closely related mental health field but hold a doctoral degree from other than counseling or a closely related field do not use the title, "Dr.," in their practices and do not announce to the public in relation to their practice or status as a counselor that they hold a doctorate.

C.5. PUBLIC RESPONSIBILITY

a. *Nondiscrimination.*

Counselors do not discriminate against clients, students, or supervisees in a manner that has a negative impact based on their age, color, culture, disability, ethnic group, gender, race, religion, sexual orientation, or socioeconomic status, or for any other reason. (See A.2.a.)

b. *Sexual Harassment.*

Counselors do not engage in sexual harassment. Sexual harassment is defined as sexual solicitation, physical advances, or verbal or nonverbal conduct that is sexual in nature, that occurs in connection with professional activities or roles, and that either (1) is

unwelcome, is offensive, or creates a hostile workplace environment, and counselors know or are told this; or (2) is sufficiently severe or intense to be perceived as harassment to a reasonable person in the context. Sexual harassment can consist of a single intense or severe act or multiple persistent or pervasive acts.

c. *Reports to Third Parties.*

Counselors are accurate, honest, and unbiased in reporting their professional activities and judgments to appropriate third parties including courts, health insurance companies, those who are the recipients of evaluation reports, and others. (See B.1.g.)

d. *Media Presentations.*

When counselors provide advice or comment by means of public lectures, demonstrations, radio or television programs, prerecorded tapes, printed articles, mailed material, or other media, they take reasonable precautions to ensure that (1) the statements are based on appropriate professional counseling literature and practice; (2) the statements are otherwise consistent with the Code of Ethics and the Standards of Practice; and (3) the recipients of the information are not encouraged to infer that a professional counseling relationship has been established. (See C.6.b.)

e. *Unjustified Gains.*

Counselors do not use their professional positions to seek or receive unjustified personal gains, sexual favors, unfair advantage, or unearned goods or services. (See C.3.d.)

C.6. RESPONSIBILITY TO OTHER PROFESSIONALS

a. *Different Approaches.*

Counselors are respectful of approaches to professional counseling that differ from their own. Counselors know and take into account the traditions and practices of other professional groups with which they work.

b. *Personal Public Statements.*

When making personal statements in a public context, counselors clarify that they are speaking from their personal perspectives and that they are not speaking on behalf of all counselors or the profession. (See C.5.d.)

c. *Clients Served by Others.*

When counselors learn that their clients are in a professional relationship with another mental health professional, they request release from clients to inform the other professionals and strive to establish positive and collaborative professional relationships. (See A.4.)

SECTION D: RELATIONSHIPS WITH OTHER PROFESSIONALS

D.1. RELATIONSHIPS WITH EMPLOYERS AND EMPLOYEES

a. *Role Definition.*

Counselors define and describe for their employers and employees the parameters and levels of their professional roles.

b. *Agreements.*

Counselors establish working agreements with supervisors, colleagues, and subordinates regarding counseling or clinical relationships, confidentiality, adherence to professional standards, distinction between public and private material, maintenance and dissemination of recorded information, workload, and accountability. Working agreements in each instance are specified and made known to those concerned.

c. *Negative Conditions.*

Counselors alert their employers to conditions that may be potentially disruptive or damaging to the counselor's professional responsibilities or that may limit their effectiveness.

d. *Evaluation.*

Counselors submit regularly to professional review and evaluation by their supervisor or the appropriate representative of the employer.

e. *In-Service.*

Counselors are responsible for in-service development of self and staff.

f. *Goals.*

Counselors inform their staff of goals and programs.

g. *Practices.*

Counselors provide personnel and agency practices that respect and enhance the rights and welfare of each employee and recipient of agency services. Counselors strive to maintain the highest levels of professional services.

h. *Personnel Selection and Assignment.*

Counselors select competent staff and assign responsibilities compatible with their skills and experiences.

i. *Discrimination.*

Counselors, as either employers or employees, do not engage in or condone practices that are inhumane, illegal, or unjustifiable (such as considerations based on age, color, culture, disability, ethnic group, gender, race, religion, sexual orientation, or socioeconomic status) in hiring, promotion, or training. (See A.2.a. and C.5.b.)

j. *Professional Conduct.*

Counselors have a responsibility both to clients and to the agency or institution within which services are performed to maintain high standards of professional conduct.

511

k. *Exploitive Relationships.*

Counselors do not engage in exploitive relationships with individuals over whom they have supervisory, evaluative, or instructional control or authority.

l. *Employer Policies.*

The acceptance of employment in an agency or institution implies that counselors are in agreement with its general policies and principles. Counselors strive to reach agreement with employers as to acceptable standards of conduct that allow for changes in institutional policy conducive to the growth and development of clients.

D.2. CONSULTATION (See B.6.)

a. *Consultation as an Option.*

Counselors may choose to consult with any other professionally competent persons about their clients. In choosing consultants, counselors avoid placing the consultant in a conflict of interest situation that would preclude the consultant being a proper party to the counselor's efforts to help the client. Should counselors be engaged in a work setting that compromises this consultation standard, they consult with other professionals whenever possible to consider justifiable alternatives.

b. *Consultant Competency.*

Counselors are reasonably certain that they have or the organization represented has the necessary competencies and resources for giving the kind of consulting services needed and that appropriate referral resources are available.

c. *Understanding with Clients.*

When providing consultation, counselors attempt to develop with their clients a clear understanding of problem definition, goals for change, and predicted consequences of interventions selected.

d. *Consultant Goals.*

The consulting relationship is one in which client adaptability and growth toward self-direction are consistently encouraged and cultivated. (See A.1.b.)

D.3. FEES FOR REFERRAL

a. *Accepting Fees from Agency Clients.*

Counselors refuse a private fee or other remuneration for rendering services to persons who are entitled to such services through the counselor's employing agency or institution. The policies of a particular agency may make explicit provisions for agency clients to receive counseling services from members of its staff in private practice. In such instances, the clients must be informed of other options open to them should they seek private counseling services. (See A.10.a., A.11.b., and C.3.d.)

b. *Referral Fees.*

Counselors do not accept a referral fee from other professionals.

D.4. SUBCONTRACTOR ARRANGEMENTS

When counselors work as subcontractors for counseling services for a third party, they have a duty to inform clients of the limitations of confidentiality that the organization may place on counselors in providing counseling services to clients. The limits of such confidentiality ordinarily are discussed as part of the intake session. (See B.1.e. and B.1.f.)

SECTION E: EVALUATION, ASSESSMENT, AND INTERPRETATION

E.1. GENERAL

a. *Appraisal Techniques.*

The primary purpose of educational and psychological assessment is to provide measures that are objective and interpretable in either comparative or absolute terms. Counselors recognize the need to interpret the statements in this section as applying to the whole range of appraisal techniques including test and nontest data.

b. *Client Welfare.*

Counselors promote the welfare and best interests of the client in the development, publication, and utilization of educational and psychological assessment techniques. They do not misuse assessment results and interpretations and take reasonable steps to prevent others from misusing the information these techniques provide. They respect the client's right to know the results, the interpretations made, and the basis for their conclusions and recommendations.

E.2. COMPETENCE TO USE AND INTERPRET TESTS

a. *Limits of Competence.*

Counselors recognize the limits of their competence and perform only those testing and assessment services for which they have been trained. They are familiar with reliability, validity, related standardization, error of measurement, and proper application of any technique utilized. Counselors using computer-based test interpretations are trained in the construct being measured and the specific instrument being used prior to using this type of computer application. Counselors take reasonable measures to ensure the proper use of psychological assessment techniques by persons under their supervision.

b. *Appropriate Use.*

Counselors are responsible for the appropriate application, scoring, interpretation, and use of assessment instruments whether they score and interpret such tests themselves or use computerized or other services.

c. *Decisions Based on Results.*

Counselors responsible for decisions involving individuals or policies that are based on assessment results have a thorough understanding of educational and psychological measurement including validation criteria, test research, and guidelines for test development and use.

d. *Accurate Information.*

Counselors provide accurate information and avoid false claims or misconceptions when making statements about assessment instruments or techniques. Special efforts are made to avoid unwarranted connotations of such terms as IQ and grade equivalent scores. (See C.5.c.)

E.3. INFORMED CONSENT

a. *Explanation to Clients.*

Prior to assessment, counselors explain the nature and purposes of assessment and the specific use of results in language the client (or other legally authorized person on behalf of the client) can understand unless an explicit exception to this right has been agreed upon in advance. Regardless of whether scoring and interpretation are completed by counselors, by assistants, or by computer or other outside services, counselors take reasonable steps to ensure that appropriate explanations are given to the client.

b. *Recipients of Results.*

The examinee's welfare, explicit understanding, and prior agreement determine the recipients of test results. Counselors include accurate and appropriate interpretations with any release of individual or group test results. (See B.1.a. and C.5.c.)

E.4. RELEASE OF INFORMATION TO COMPETENT PROFESSIONALS

a. *Misuse of Results.*

Counselors do not misuse assessment results, including test results, and interpretations and take reasonable steps to prevent the misuse of such by others. (See C.5.c.)

b. *Release of Raw Data.*

Counselors ordinarily release data (e.g. protocols, counseling or interview notes, or questionnaires) in which the client is identified only with the consent of the client or the client's legal representative. Such data are usually released only to persons recognized by counselors as competent to interpret the data. (See B.1.a.)

E.5. PROPER DIAGNOSIS OF MENTAL DISORDERS

a. *Proper Diagnosis.*

Counselors take special care to provide proper diagnosis of mental disorders. Assessment techniques (including personal interview) used to determine client care (e.g., locus of treatment, type of treatment, or recommended follow-up) are carefully selected and appropriately used. (See A.3.a. and C.5.c.)

b. *Cultural Sensitivity.*

Counselors recognize that culture affects the manner in which clients' problems are defined. Clients' socioeconomic and cultural experience is considered when diagnosing mental disorders.

E.6. TEST SELECTION

a. *Appropriateness of Instruments.*

Counselors carefully consider the validity, reliability, psychometric limitations, and appropriateness of instruments when selecting tests for use in a given situation or with a particular client.

b. *Culturally Diverse Populations.*

Counselors are cautious when selecting tests for culturally diverse populations to avoid inappropriateness of testing that may be outside of socialized behavioral or cognitive patterns.

E.7. CONDITIONS OF TEST ADMINISTRATION

a. *Administration Conditions.*

Counselors administer tests under the same conditions that were established in their standardization. When tests are not administered under standard conditions or when unusual behavior or irregularities occur during the testing session, those conditions are noted in interpretation, and the results may be designated as invalid or of questionable validity.

b. *Computer Administration.*

Counselors are responsible for ensuring that administration programs function properly to provide clients with accurate results when a computer or other electronic methods are used for test administration. (See A.12.b.)

c. *Unsupervised Test-Taking.*

Counselors do not permit unsupervised or inadequately supervised use of tests or assessments unless the tests or assessments are designed, intended, and validated for self-administration and/or scoring.

d. *Disclosure of Favorable Conditions.*

Prior to test administration, conditions that produce most favorable test results are made known to the examinee.

E.8. DIVERSITY IN TESTING

Counselors are cautious in using assessment techniques, making evaluations, and interpreting the performance of populations not represented in the norm group on which an instrument was standardized. They recognize the effects of age, color, culture, disability, ethnic group, gender, race, religion, sexual orientation, and socioeconomic status on test administration and interpretation and place test results in proper perspective with other relevant factors. (See A.2.a.)

E.9. TEST SCORING AND INTERPRETATION

a. *Reporting Reservations.*

In reporting assessment results, counselors indicate any reservations that exist regarding validity or reliability because of the circumstances of the assessment or the inappropriateness of the norms for the person tested.

b. *Research Instruments.*

Counselors exercise caution when interpreting the results of research instruments possessing insufficient technical data to support respondent results. The specific purposes for the use of such instruments are stated explicitly to the examinee.

c. *Testing Services.*

Counselors who provide test scoring and test interpretation services to support the assessment process confirm the validity of such interpretations. They accurately describe the purpose, norms, validity, reliability, and applications of the procedures and any special qualifications applicable to their use. The public offering of an automated test interpretations service is considered a professional-to-professional consultation. The formal responsibility of the consultant is to the consultee, but the ultimate and overriding responsibility is to the client.

E.10. TEST SECURITY

Counselors maintain the integrity and security of tests and other assessment techniques consistent with legal and contractual obligations. Counselors do not appropriate, reproduce, or modify published tests or parts thereof without acknowledgment and permission from the publisher.

E.11. OBSOLETE TESTS AND OUTDATED TEST RESULTS

Counselors do not use data or test results that are obsolete or outdated for the current purpose. Counselors make every effort to prevent the misuse of obsolete measures and test data by others.

E.12. Test Construction

Counselors use established scientific procedures, relevant standards, and current professional knowledge for test design in the development, publication, and utilization of educational and psychological assessment techniques.

SECTION F: TEACHING, TRAINING, AND SUPERVISION

F.1. COUNSELOR EDUCATORS AND TRAINERS

a. *Educators as Teachers and Practitioners.*

Counselors who are responsible for developing, implementing, and supervising educational programs are skilled as teachers and practitioners. They are knowledgeable regarding the ethical, legal, and regulatory aspects of the profession, are skilled in applying that knowledge, and make students and supervisees aware of their responsibilities. Counselors conduct counselor education and training programs in an ethical manner and serve as role models for professional behavior. Counselor educators should make an effort to infuse material related to human diversity into all courses and/or workshops that are designed to promote the development of professional counselors.

b. *Relationship Boundaries with Students and Supervisees.*

Counselors clearly define and maintain ethical, professional, and social relationship boundaries with their students and supervisees. They are aware of the differential in power that exists and the student's or supervisee's possible incomprehension of that power differential. Counselors explain to students and supervisees the potential for the relationship to become exploitive.

c. *Sexual Relationships.*

Counselors do not engage in sexual relationships with students or supervisees and do not subject them to sexual harassment. (See A.6. and C.5.b)

d. *Contributions to Research.*

Counselors give credit to students or supervisees for their contributions to research and scholarly projects. Credit is given through coauthorship, acknowledgment, footnote statement, or other appropriate means in accordance with such contributions. (See G.4.b. and G.4.c.)

e. *Close Relatives.*

Counselors do not accept close relatives as students or supervisees.

f. *Supervision Preparation.*

Counselors who offer clinical supervision services are adequately prepared in supervision methods and techniques. Counselors who are doctoral students serving as practicum or internship supervisors to master's level stu-

513

dents are adequately prepared and supervised by the training program.

g. *Responsibility for Services to Clients.*

Counselors who supervise the counseling services of others take reasonable measures to ensure that counseling services provided to clients are professional.

h. *Endorsement.*

Counselors do not endorse students or supervisees for certification, licensure, employment, or completion of an academic or training program if they believe students or supervisees are not qualified for the endorsement. Counselors take reasonable steps to assist students or supervisees who are not qualified for endorsement to become qualified.

F.2. COUNSELOR EDUCATION AND TRAINING PROGRAMS

a. *Orientation.*

Prior to admission, counselors orient prospective students to the counselor education or training program's expectations including but not limited to the following: (1) the type and level of skill acquisition required for successful completion of the training, (2) subject matter to be covered, (3) basis for evaluation, (4) training components that encourage self-growth or self-disclosure as part of the training process, (5) the type of supervision settings and requirements of the sites for required clinical field experiences, (6) student and supervisee evaluation and dismissal policies and procedures, and (7) up-to-date employment prospects for graduates.

b. *Integration of Study and Practice.*

Counselors establish counselor education and training programs that integrate academic study and supervised practice.

c. *Evaluation.*

Counselors clearly state to students and supervisees, in advance of training, the levels of competency expected, appraisal methods, and timing of evaluations for both didactic and experiential components. Counselors provide students and supervisees with periodic performance appraisal and evaluation feedback throughout the training program.

d. *Teaching Ethics.*

Counselors make students and supervisees aware of the ethical responsibilities and standards of the profession and the students' and supervisees' ethical responsibilities to the profession. (See C.1. and F.3.e.)

e. *Peer Relationships.*

When students or supervisees are assigned to lead counseling groups or provide clinical supervision for their peers, counselors take steps to ensure that students and supervisees placed in these roles do not have personal or adverse relationships with peers and that they understand they have the same ethical obligations as counselor educators, trainers, and supervisors. Counselors make every effort to ensure that the rights of peers are not compromised when students or supervisees are assigned to lead counseling groups or provide clinical supervision.

f. *Varied Theoretical Positions.*

Counselors present varied theoretical positions so that students and supervisees may make comparisons and have opportunities to develop their own positions. Counselors provide information concerning the scientific basis of professional practice. (See C.6.a.)

g. *Field Placements.*

Counselors develop clear policies within their training program regarding field placement and other clinical experiences. Counselors provide clearly stated roles and responsibilities for the student or supervisee, the site supervisor, and the program supervisor. They confirm that site supervisors are qualified to provide supervision and are informed of their professional and ethical responsibilities in this role.

h. *Dual Relationships as Supervisors.*

Counselors avoid dual relationships, such as performing the role of site supervisor and training program supervisor in the student's or supervisee's training program. Counselors do not accept any form of professional services, fees, commissions, reimbursement, or remuneration from a site for student or supervisee placement.

i. *Diversity in Programs.*

Counselors are responsive to their institution's and program's recruitment and retention needs for training program administrators, faculty, and students with diverse backgrounds and special needs. (See A.2.a.)

F.3. STUDENTS AND SUPERVISEES

a. *Limitations.*

Counselors, through ongoing evaluation and appraisal, are aware of the academic and personal limitations of students and supervisees that might impede performance. Counselors assist students and supervisees in securing remedial assistance when needed and dismiss from the training program supervisees who are unable to provide competent service due to academic or personal limitations. Counselors seek professional consultation and document their decision to dismiss or refer students or supervisees for assistance. Counselors assure that students and supervisees have recourse to address decisions made, to require them to seek assistance, or to dismiss them.

b. *Self-Growth Experiences.*

Counselors use professional judgment when designing training experiences conducted by the counselors themselves that require student and supervisee self-growth or self-disclosure. Safeguards are provided so that students and supervisees are aware of the ramifications their self-disclosure may have on counselors whose primary role as teacher, trainer, or supervisor requires acting on ethical obligations to the profession. Evaluative components of experiential training experiences explicitly delineate predetermined academic standards that are separate and not dependent on the student's level of self-disclosure. (See A.6.)

c. *Counseling for Students and Supervisees.*

If students or supervisees request counseling, supervisors or counselor educators provide them with acceptable referrals. Supervisors or counselor educators do not serve as counselor to students or supervisees over whom they hold administrative, teaching, or evaluative roles unless this is a brief role associated with a training experience. (See A.6.b.)

d. *Clients of Students and Supervisees.*

Counselors make every effort to ensure that the clients at field placements are aware of the services rendered and the qualifications of the students and supervisees rendering those services. Clients receive professional disclosure information and are informed of the limits of confidentiality. Client permission is obtained in order for the students and supervisees to use any information concerning the counseling relationship in the training process. (See B.1.e.)

e. *Standards for Students and Supervisees.*

Students and supervisees preparing to become counselors adhere to the Code of Ethics and the Standards of Practice. Students and supervisees have the same obligations to clients as those required of counselors. (See H.1.)

SECTION G: RESEARCH AND PUBLICATION

G.1. RESEARCH RESPONSIBILITIES

a. *Use of Human Subjects.*

Counselors plan, design, conduct, and report research in a manner consistent with pertinent ethical principles, federal and state laws, host institutional regulations, and scientific standards governing research with human subjects. Counselors design and conduct research that reflects cultural sensitivity appropriateness.

b. *Deviation from Standard Practices.*

Counselors seek consultation and observe stringent safeguards to protect the rights of research participants when a research problem suggests a deviation from standard acceptable practices. (See B.6.)

c. *Precautions to void Injury.*

Counselors who conduct research with human subjects are responsible for the subjects' welfare throughout the experiment and take reasonable precautions to avoid causing injurious psychological, physical, or social effects to their subjects.

d. *Principal Researcher Responsibility.*

The ultimate responsibility for ethical research practice lies with the principal researcher. All others involved in the research activities share ethical obligations and full responsibility for their own actions.

e. *Minimal Interference.*

Counselors take reasonable precautions to avoid causing disruptions in subjects' lives due to participation in research.

f. *Diversity.*

Counselors are sensitive to diversity and research issues with special populations. They seek consultation when appropriate. (See A.2.a. and B.6.)

G.2. Informed Consent

a. *Topics Disclosed.*

In obtaining informed consent for research, counselors use language that is understandable to research participants and that (1) accurately explains the purpose and procedures to be followed; (2) identifies any procedures that are experimental or relatively untried; (3) describes the attendant discomforts and risks; (4) describes the benefits or changes in individuals or organizations that might be reasonably expected; (5) discloses appropriate alternative procedures that would be advantageous for subjects; (6) offers to answer any inquiries concerning the procedures; (7) describes any limitations on confidentiality; and (8) instructs that subjects are free to withdraw their consent and to discontinue participation in the project at any time. (See B.1.f.)

b. *Deception.*

Counselors do not conduct research involving deception unless alternative procedures are not feasible and the prospective value of the research justifies the deception. When the methodological requirements of a study necessitate concealment or deception, the investigator is required to explain clearly the reasons for this action as soon as possible.

c. *Voluntary Participation.*

Participation in research is typically voluntary and without any penalty for refusal to participate. Involuntary participation is appropriate only when it can be demonstrated that participation will have no harmful effects on subjects and is essential to the investigation.

d. *Confidentiality of Information.*

Information obtained about research participants during the course of an investigation is confidential. When the possibility exists that others may obtain access to such information, ethical research practice requires that the possibility, together with the plans for protecting confidentiality, be explained to participants as a part of the procedure for obtaining informed consent. (See B.1.e.)

e. *Persons Incapable of Giving Informed Consent.*

When a person is incapable of giving informed consent, counselors provide an appropriate explanation, obtain agreement for participation and obtain appropriate consent from a legally authorized person.

f. *Commitments to Participants.*

Counselors take reasonable measures to honor all commitments to research participants.

g. *Explanations After Data Collection.*

After data are collected, counselors provide participants with full clarification of the nature of the study to remove any misconceptions. Where scientific or human values justify delaying or withholding information, counselors take reasonable measures to avoid causing harm.

h. *Agreements to Cooperate.*

Counselors who agree to cooperate with another individual in research or publication incur an obligation to cooperate as promised in terms of punctuality of performance and with regard to the completeness and accuracy of the information required.

i. *Informed Consent for Sponsors.*

In the pursuit of research, counselors give sponsors, institutions, and publication channels the same respect and opportunity for giving informed consent that they accord to individual research participants. Counselors are aware of their obligation to future research workers and ensure that host institutions are given feedback information and proper acknowledgment.

G.3. Reporting Results

a. *Information Affecting Outcome.*

When reporting research results, counselors explicitly mention all variables and conditions known to the investigator that may have affected the outcome of a study or the interpretation of data.

b. *Accurate Results.*

Counselors plan, conduct, and report research accurately and in a manner that minimizes the possibility that results will be misleading. They provide thorough discussions of the limitations of their data and alternative hypotheses. Counselors do not engage in fraudulent research, distort data, misrepresent data, or deliberately bias their results.

c. *Obligation to Report Unfavorable Results.*

Counselors communicate to other counselors the results of any research judged to be of professional value. Results that reflect unfavorably on institutions, programs, services, prevailing opinions, or vested interests are not withheld.

d. *Identity of Subjects.*

Counselors who supply data, aid in the research of another person, report research results, or make original data available take due care to disguise the identity of respective subjects in the absence of specific authorization from the subjects to do otherwise. (See B.1.g. and B.5.a.)

e. *Replication Studies.*

Counselors are obligated to make available sufficient original research data to qualified professionals who may wish to replicate the study.

G.4. Publication

a. *Recognition of Others.*

When conducting and reporting research, counselors are familiar with and give recognition to previous work on the topic, observe copyright laws, and give full credit to those to whom credit is due. (See F.1.d. and G.4.c.)

b. *Contributors.*

Counselors give credit through joint authorship, acknowledgment, footnote statements, or other appropriate means to those who have contributed significantly to research or concept development in accordance with such contributions. The principal contributor is listed first and minor technical or professional contributions are acknowledged in notes or introductory statements.

c. *Student Research.*

For an article that is substantially based on a student's dissertation or thesis, the student is listed as the principal author. (See F.1.d. and G.4.a.)

d. *Duplicate Submission.*

Counselors submit manuscripts for consideration to only one journal at a time. Manuscripts that are published in whole or in substantial part in another journal or published work are not submitted for publication without acknowledgment and permission from the previous publication.

e. *Professional Review.* Counselors who review material submitted for publication, research, or other scholarly purposes respect the confidentiality and proprietary rights of those who submitted it.

Section H: Resolving Ethical Issues

H.1. KNOWLEDGE OF STANDARDS

Counselors are familiar with the Code of Ethics and the Standards of Practice and other applicable ethics codes from other professional organizations of which they are member or from certification and licensure bodies. Lack of knowledge or misunderstanding of an ethical responsibility is not a defense against a charge of unethical conduct. (See F.3.e.)

H.2. SUSPECTED VIOLATIONS

a. *Ethical Behavior Expected.*

Counselors expect professional associates to adhere to Code of Ethics. When counselors possess reasonable cause that raises doubts as to whether a counselor is acting in an ethical manner, they take appropriate action. (See H.2.d. and H.2.e.)

b. *Consultation.*

When uncertain as to whether a particular situation or course of action may be in violation of Code of Ethics, counselors consult with other counselors who are knowledgeable about ethics, with colleagues, or with appropriate authorities.

c. *Organization Conflicts.*

If the demands of an organization with which counselors are affiliated pose a conflict with Code of Ethics, counselors specify the nature of such conflicts and express to their supervisors or other responsible officials their commitment to Code of Ethics. When possible, counselors work toward change within the organization to allow full adherence to Code of Ethics.

d. *Informal Resolution.*

When counselors have reasonable cause to believe that another counselor is violating an ethical standard, they attempt to first resolve the issue informally with the other counselor if feasible providing that such action does not violate confidentiality rights that may be involved.

e. *Reporting Suspected Violations.*

When an informal resolution is not appropriate or feasible, counselors, upon reasonable cause, take action, such as reporting the suspected ethical violation to state or national ethics committees, unless this action conflicts with confidentiality rights that cannot be resolved.

f. *Unwarranted Complaints.*

Counselors do not initiate, participate in, or encourage the filing of ethics complaints that are unwarranted or intend to harm a counselor rather than to protect clients or the public.

H.3. COOPERATION WITH ETHICS COMMITTEES

Counselors assist in the process of enforcing Code of Ethics. Counselors cooperate with investigations, proceedings, and requirements of the ACA Ethics Committee or ethics committees of other duly constituted associations or boards having jurisdiction over those charged with a violation. Counselors are familiar with the ACA Policies and Procedures and use it as a reference in assisting the enforcement of the Code of Ethics.

STANDARDS OF PRACTICE

All members of the American Counseling Association (ACA) are required to adhere to the Standards of Practice and the Code of Ethics. The Standards of Practice represent minimal behavioral statements of the Code of Ethics. Members should refer to the applicable section of the Code of Ethics for further interpretation and amplification of the applicable Standard of Practice.

SECTION A: THE COUNSELING RELATIONSHIP

STANDARD OF PRACTICE ONE (SP-1) NONDISCRIMINATION

Counselors respect diversity and must not discriminate against clients because of age, color, culture, disability, ethnic group, gender, race, religion, sexual orientation, marital status, or socioeconomic status. (See A.2.a.)

STANDARD OF PRACTICE TWO (SP-2) DISCLOSURE TO CLIENTS

Counselors must adequately inform clients, preferably in writing, regarding the counseling process and counseling relationship at or before the time it begins and throughout the relationship. (See A.3.a.)

STANDARD OF PRACTICE THREE (SP-3) DUAL RELATIONSHIPS

Counselors must make every effort to avoid dual relationships with clients that could impair their professional judgment or increase the risk of harm to clients. When a dual relationship cannot be avoided, counselors must take appropriate steps to ensure that judgment is not impaired and that no exploitation occurs. (See A.6.a. and A.6.b.)

STANDARD OF PRACTICE FOUR (SP-4) SEXUAL INTIMACIES WITH CLIENTS

Counselors must not engage in any type of sexual intimacies with current clients and must not engage in sexual intimacies with former clients within a minimum of two years after terminating the counseling relationship. Counselors who engage in such relationship after two years following termination have the responsibility to thoroughly examine and document that such relations did not have an exploitative nature.

STANDARD OF PRACTICE FIVE (SP-5) PROTECTING CLIENTS DURING GROUP WORK

Counselors must take steps to protect clients from physical or psychological trauma resulting from interactions during group work. (See A.9.b.)

STANDARD OF PRACTICE SIX (SP-6) ADVANCE UNDERSTANDING OF FEES

Counselors must explain to clients, prior to their entering the counseling relationship, financial arrangements related to professional services. (See A.10. a-d. and A.11.c.)

STANDARD OF PRACTICE SEVEN (SP-7) TERMINATION

Counselors must assist in making appropriate arrangements for the continuation of treatment of clients, when necessary, following termination of counseling relationships. (See A.11.a.)

STANDARD OF PRACTICE EIGHT (SP-8) INABILITY TO ASSIST CLIENTS

Counselors must avoid entering or immediately terminate a counseling relationship if it is determined that they are unable to be of professional assistance to a client. The counselor may assist in making an appropriate referral for the client. (See A.11.b.)

SECTION B: CONFIDENTIALITY

STANDARD OF PRACTICE NINE (SP-9) CONFIDENTIALITY REQUIREMENT

Counselors must keep information related to counseling services confidential unless disclosure is in the best interest of clients, is required for the welfare of others, or is required by law. When disclosure is required, only information that is essential is revealed and the client is informed of such disclosure. (See B.1. a.- f.)

Standard of Practice Ten (SP-10) Confidentiality Requirements for Subordinates

Counselors must take measures to ensure that privacy and confidentiality of clients are maintained by subordinates. (See B.1.h.)

Standard of Practice Eleven (SP-11) Confidentiality in Group Work

Counselors must clearly communicate to group members that confidentiality cannot be guaranteed in group work. (See B.2.a.)

Standard of Practice Twelve (SP-12) Confidentiality in Family Counseling

Counselors must not disclose information about one family member in counseling to another family member without prior consent. (See B.2.b.)

Standard of Practice Thirteen (SP-13) Confidentiality of Records

Counselors must maintain appropriate confidentiality in creating, storing, accessing, transferring, and disposing of counseling records. (See B.4.b.)

Standard of Practice Fourteen (SP-14) Permission to Record or Observe

Counselors must obtain prior consent from clients in order to electronically record or observe sessions. (See B.4.c.)

Standard of Practice Fifteen (SP-15) Disclosure or Transfer of Records

Counselors must obtain client consent to disclose or transfer records to third parties unless exceptions listed in SP-9 exist. (See B.4.e.)

Standard of Practice Sixteen (SP-16) Data Disguise Required

Counselors must disguise the identity of the client when using data for training, research, or publication. (See B.5.a.)

Section C: Professional Responsibility

Standard of Practice Seventeen (SP-17) Boundaries of Competence

Counselors must practice only within the boundaries of their competence. (See C.2.a.)

Standard of Practice Eighteen (SP-18) Continuing Education

Counselors must engage in continuing education to maintain their professional competence. (See C.2.f.)

Standard of Practice Nineteen (SP-19) Impairment of Professionals

Counselors must refrain from offering professional services when their personal problems or conflicts may cause harm to a client or others. (See C.2.g.)

Standard of Practice Twenty (SP-20) Accurate Advertising

Counselors must accurately represent their credentials and services when advertising. (See C.3.a.)

Standard of Practice Twenty-one (SP-21) Recruiting Through Employment

Counselors must not use their place of employment or institutional affiliation to recruit clients for their private practices. (See C.3.d.)

Standard of Practice Twenty-two (SP-22) Credentials Claimed

Counselors must claim or imply only professional credentials possessed and must correct any known misrepresentations of their credentials by others. (See C.4.a.)

Standard of Practice Twenty-three (SP-23) Sexual Harassment

Counselors must not engage in sexual harassment. (See C.5.b.)

Standard of Practice Twenty-four (SP-24) Unjustified Gains

Counselors must not use their professional positions to seek or receive unjustified personal gains, sexual favors, unfair advantage, or unearned goods or services. (See C.5.e.)

Standard of Practice Twenty-five (SP-25) Clients Served by Others

With the consent of the client, counselors must inform other mental health professionals serving the same client that a counseling relationship between the counselor and client exists. (See C.6.c.)

Standard of Practice Twenty-six (SP-26) Negative Employment Conditions

Counselors must alert their employers to institutional policy or conditions that may be potentially disruptive or damaging to the counselor's professional responsibilities or that may limit their effectiveness or deny clients' rights. (See D.1.c.)

Standard of Practice Twenty-seven (SP-27) Personnel Selection and Assignment

Counselors must select competent staff and must assign responsibilities compatible with staff skills and experiences. (See D.1.h.)

Standard of Practice Twenty-eight (SP-28) Exploitive Relationships with Subordinates

Counselors must not engage in exploitive relationships with individuals over whom they have supervisory, evaluative, or instructional control or authority. (See D.1.k.)

Section D: Relationship With Other Professionals

Standard of Practice Twenty-nine (SP-29) Accepting Fees from Agency Clients

Counselors must not accept fees or other remuneration for consultation with persons entitled to such services through the counselor's employing agency or institution. (See D.3.a.)

Standard of Practice Thirty (SP-30) Referral Fees

Counselors must not accept referral fees. (See D.3.b.)

Section E: Evaluation, Assessment, and Interpretation

Standard of Practice Thirty-one (SP-31) Limits of Competence

Counselors must perform only testing and assessment services for which they are competent. Counselors must not allow the use of psychological assessment techniques by unqualified persons under their supervision. (See E.2.a.)

Standard of Practice Thirty-two (SP-32) Appropriate Use of Assessment Instruments

Counselors must use assessment instruments in the manner for which they were intended. (See E.2.b.)

Standard of Practice Thirty-three (SP-33) Assessment Explanations to Clients

Counselors must provide explanations to clients prior to assessment about the nature and purposes of assessment and the specific uses of results. (See E.3.a.)

Standard of Practice Thirty-four (SP-34) Recipients of Test Results

Counselors must ensure that accurate and appropriate interpretations accompany any release of testing and assessment information. (See E.3.b.)

Standard of Practice Thirty-five (SP-35) Obsolete Tests and Outdated Test Results

Counselors must not base their assessment or intervention decisions or recommendations on

517

data or test results that are obsolete or outdated for the current purpose. (See E.11.)

SECTION F: TEACHING, TRAINING, AND SUPERVISION

STANDARD OF PRACTICE THIRTY-SIX (SP-36) SEXUAL RELATIONSHIPS WITH STUDENTS OR SUPERVISEES

Counselors must not engage in sexual relationships with their students and supervisees. (See F.1.c.)

STANDARD OF PRACTICE THIRTY-SEVEN (SP-37) CREDIT FOR CONTRIBUTIONS TO RESEARCH

Counselors must give credit to students or supervisees for their contributions to research and scholarly projects. (See F.1.d.)

STANDARD OF PRACTICE THIRTY-EIGHT (SP-38) SUPERVISION PREPARATION

Counselors who offer clinical supervision services must be trained and prepared in supervision methods and techniques. (See F.1.f.)

STANDARD OF PRACTICE THIRTY-NINE (SP-39) EVALUATION INFORMATION

Counselors must clearly state to students and supervisees, in advance of training, the levels of competency expected, appraisal methods, and timing of evaluations. Counselors must provide students and supervisees with periodic performance appraisal and evaluation feedback throughout the training program. (See F.2.c.)

STANDARD OF PRACTICE FORTY (SP-40) PEER RELATIONSHIPS IN TRAINING

Counselors must make every effort to ensure that the rights of peers are not violated when students and supervisees are assigned to lead counseling groups or provide clinical supervision. (See F.2.e.)

STANDARD OF PRACTICE FORTY-ONE (SP-41) LIMITATIONS OF STUDENTS AND SUPERVISEES

Counselors must assist students and supervisees in securing remedial assistance, when needed, and must dismiss from the training program students and supervisees who are unable to provide competent service due to academic or personal limitations. (See F.3.a.)

STANDARD OF PRACTICE FORTY-TWO (SP-42) SELF-GROWTH EXPERIENCES

Counselors who conduct experiences for students or supervisees that include self-growth or self disclosure must inform participants of counselors' ethical obligations to the profession and must not grade participants based on their nonacademic performance. (See F.3.b.)

STANDARD OF PRACTICE FORTY-THREE (SP-43) STANDARDS FOR STUDENTS AND SUPERVISEES

Students and supervisees preparing to become counselors must adhere to the Code of Ethics and the Standards of Practice of counselors. (See F.3.e.)

SECTION G: RESEARCH AND PUBLICATION

STANDARD OF PRACTICE FORTY-FOUR (SP-44) PRECAUTIONS TO AVOID INJURY IN RESEARCH

Counselors must avoid causing physical, social, or psychological harm or injury to subjects in research. (See G.1.c.)

Standard of Practice Forty-five (SP-45) Confidentiality of Research Information

Counselors must keep confidential information obtained about research participants. (See G.2.d.)

STANDARD OF PRACTICE FORTY-SIX (SP-46) INFORMATION AFFECTING RESEARCH OUTCOME

Counselors must report all variables and conditions known to the investigator that may have affected research data or outcomes. (See G.3.a.)

STANDARD OF PRACTICE FORTY-SEVEN (SP-47) ACCURATE RESEARCH RESULTS

Counselors must not distort or misrepresent research data nor fabricate or intentionally bias research results. (See G.3.b.)

Standard of Practice Forty-eight (SP-48) Publication Contributors

Counselors must give appropriate credit to those who have contributed to research. (See G.4.a. and G.4.b.)

SECTION H: RESOLVING ETHICAL ISSUES

STANDARD OF PRACTICE FORTY-NINE (SP-49) ETHICAL BEHAVIOR EXPECTED

Counselors must take appropriate action when they possess reasonable cause that raises doubts as to whether counselors or other mental health professionals are acting in an ethical manner. (See H.2.a.)

STANDARD OF PRACTICE FIFTY (SP-50) UNWARRANTED COMPLAINTS

Counselors must not initiate, participate in, or encourage the filing of ethics complaints that are unwarranted or intended to harm a mental health professional rather than to protect clients or the public. (See H.2.f.)

Standard of Practice Fifty-one (SP-51) Cooperation with Ethics Committees

Counselors must cooperate with investigations, proceedings, and requirements of the ACA Ethics Committee or ethics committees of other duly constituted associations or boards having jurisdiction over those charged with a violation. (See H.3.)

REFERENCES

The following documents are available to counselors as resources to guide them in their practices. These resources are not a part of the Code of Ethics and the Standards of Practice.

American Association for Counseling and Development/Association for Measurement and Evaluation in Counseling and Development. (1989). The responsibilities of users of standardized tests (revised). Washington, DC: Author.

American Counseling Association. (1988). American Counseling Association Ethical Standards. Alexandria, VA: Author.

American Psychological Association. (1985). Standards for educational and psychological testing (revised). Washington, DC: Author.

American Rehabilitation Counseling Association, Commission on Rehabilitation Counselor Certification, and National Rehabilitation Counseling Association. (1995). Code of professional ethics for rehabilitation counselors. Chicago, IL: Author.

American School Counselor Association. (1992). Ethical standards for school counselors. Alexandria, VA: Author.

Joint Committee on Testing Practices. (1988). Code of fair testing practices in education. Washington, DC: Author.

National Board for Certified Counselors. (1989). National Board for Certified Counselors Code of Ethics. Alexandria, VA: Author.

Prediger, D.J. (Ed.). (1993, March). Multicultural assessment standards. Alexandria, VA: Association for Assessment in Counseling.

POLICIES AND PROCEDURES FOR RESPONDING TO MEMBERS' REQUESTS FOR INTERPRETATIONS OF THE ETHICAL STANDARDS

SECTION: A
APPROPRIATE REQUESTS

1. ACA members may request that the Committee issue formal interpretations of the ACA Code of Ethics for the purpose of guiding the member's own professional behavior.

2. Requests for interpretations will not be considered in the following situations:

a. The individual requesting the interpretation is not an ACA member, or

b. The request is intended to determine whether the behavior of another mental health professional is unethical. In the event an ACA member believes the behavior of another mental health professional is unethical, the ACA member should resolve the issue directly with the professional, if possible, and should file an ethical complaint if appropriate.

SECTION B:
PROCEDURES

1. Members must send written requests for interpretations to the Committee at ACA Headquarters.

2. Questions should be submitted in the following format: "Does (counselor behavior) violate Sections _____ or any other sections of the ACA Ethical Standards?" Questions should avoid unique details, be general in nature to the extent possible, and be brief.

3. The Committee staff liaison will revise the question, if necessary, and submit it to the Committee Co-Chair for approval.

4. The question will be sent to Committee members who will be asked to respond individually.

5. The Committee Co-Chair will develop a consensus interpretation on behalf of the Committee.

6. The consensus interpretation will be sent to members of the Committee for final approval.

7. The formal interpretation will be sent to the member who submitted the inquiry.

8. The question and the formal interpretation will be published in the ACA newsletter, but the identity of the member requesting the interpretation will not be disclosed.

POLICIES AND PROCEDURES FOR PROCESSING COMPLAINTS OF ETHICAL VIOLATIONS

SECTION A
GENERAL

1. The American Counseling Association, hereafter referred to as the "Association" or "ACA," is dedicated to enhancing human development throughout the life span and promoting the counseling profession.

2. The Association, in furthering its objectives, administers the Code of Ethics and Standards of Practice developed and approved by the ACA Governing Council.

3. The purpose of this document is to facilitate the work of the ACA Ethics Committee ("Committee") by specifying the procedures for processing cases of alleged violations of the ACA Code of Ethics, codifying options for sanctioning members, and stating appeals procedures. This document is to be used as a supplement to the ACA Code of Ethics, not as a substitute. The intent of the Association is to monitor the professional conduct of its members to promote sound ethical practices. ACA does not, however, warrant the performance of any individual.

SECTION B
ETHICS COMMITTEE MEMBERS

1. The Ethics Committee, a standing committee of the Association, consists of six (6) appointed members including two (2) Co-Chairs whose terms overlap. Two members are appointed annually for three (3) year terms by the President-Elect; appointments are subject to confirmation by the ACA Governing Council. Any vacancy on the Committee will be filled by the President in the same manner, and the person appointed shall serve the unexpired term of the member whose place he or she took. Committee members may be reappointed to not more than one (1) additional consecutive term.

2. One (1) of the Committee Co-Chairs is appointed annually by the President-Elect from among the Committee members who have two (2) years of service remaining and serves as Co-Chair for two (2) years, subject to confirmation by the ACA Governing Council.

SECTION C
ROLE AND FUNCTION

1. The Ethics Committee is responsible for

a. Educating the membership as to the Association's Code of Ethics;

b. Periodically reviewing and recommending changes in the Code of Ethics of the Association, as well as Policies and Procedures for Processing Complaints of Ethical Violations;

c. Receiving and processing complaints of alleged violations of the Code of Ethics of the Association; and

d. Receiving and processing requests for interpretations.

2. The Committee shall meet in person or by telephone conference a minimum of three (3) times per year for processing complaints.

3. In processing complaints about alleged ethical misconduct, the Committee will compile an objective, factual account of the dispute in question and make the best possible recommendation for the resolution of the case. The Committee, in taking any action, shall do so only for cause, shall only take a reasonable degree of disciplinary action, shall utilize these procedures with objectivity and fairness, and in general shall act only to further the interests and objectives of the Association and its membership.

4. Of the six (6) voting members of the Committee, a vote of four (4) is necessary to conduct business. In the event a Co-Chair or any other member of the Committee has a personal interest in the case, he or she shall withdraw from reviewing the case.

5. In the event Committee members recuse themselves from a complaint and insufficient voting members are available to conduct business, the President shall appoint former ACA Committee members to decide the complaint.

Section D
Responsibilities of the Committee Members

1. The Committee members have an obligation to act in an unbiased manner, to work expeditiously, to safeguard the confidentiality of the Committee's activities, and to follow procedures established to protect the rights of all individuals involved.

Section E
Responsibilities of the Co-Chairs
Administering the Complaint

1. In the event that one of the Co-Chairs administering the complaint has a conflict of interest in a particular case, the other Co-Chair shall administer the complaint. The Co-Chair administering the compliant shall not have a vote in the decision.

2. In addition to the above guidelines for members of the Committee, the Co-Chairs, with the assistance of the Headquarters staff liaison (and legal counsel where necessary), have the responsibilities of

a. Receiving, via ACA Headquarters, complaints that have been certified for membership status of the charged member;

b. Determining whether the alleged behavior(s), if true, would violate ACA's Code of Ethics and whether the Committee should review the complaint under these rules;

c. Notifying the complainant and the charged member of receipt of the case by certified mail return receipt requested;

d. Notifying the members of the Committee of the case;

e. Requesting additional information from complainants, charged members and others;

f. Presiding over the meetings of the Committee;

g. Preparing and sending, by certified mail, communications to the complainant and charged member on the recommendations and decisions of the Committee; and

h. Arranging for legal advice with assistance and financial approval of the ACA Executive Director.

Section F
Jurisdiction

1. The Committee will consider whether individuals have violated the ACA Code of Ethics if those individuals

a. Are current members of the American Counseling Association or

b. Were ACA members when the alleged violations occurred.

2. Ethics committees of divisions, branches, corporate affiliates, or other ACA entities must refer all ethical complaints involving ACA members to the Committee.

Section G
Eligibility to File Complaints

1. The Committee will receive complaints that ACA members have violated one or more sections of the ACA Code of Ethics from the following individuals:

a. Any individuals who have reason to believe that ACA members have violated the ACA Code of Ethics.

b. ACA members, or members of other helping professions, who have reason to believe that other ACA members have violated the ACA Code of Ethics.

c. The Co-Chair of the Committee on behalf of the ACA membership when the Co-Chair has reason to believe through information received by the Committee that ACA members have violated the ACA Code of Ethics.

d. Ethics committees of divisions, branches, corporate affiliates, or other ACA entities as provided for in Section F.2. above.

2. If possible, individuals should attempt to resolve complaints directly with charged members before filing ethical complaints.

Section H
Time Lines

1. The time lines in these standards are guidelines only and have been established to provide a reasonable time framework for processing complaints.

2. Complainants or charged members may request extensions of deadlines when appropriate. Extensions of deadlines will be granted by the Committee only when justified by unusual circumstance.

Section I
Nature of Communication

1. Only written communications regarding ethical complaints against members will be acceptable. If telephone inquiries are received regarding the filing of complaints, responding to complaints, or providing information regarding complaints, the individuals will be informed of the written communication requirement and asked to comply.

2. All correspondence related to an ethical complaint must be addressed to the Ethics Committee, ACA Headquarters, 5999 Stevenson Avenue, Alexandria, VA 22304 and must be marked "confidential." This process is necessary to protect the confidentiality of the complainant and the charged member.

Section J
Filing Complaints

1. Only written complaints, signed by complainants, will be considered.

2. Individuals eligible to file complaints will send a letter outlining the nature of the complaint to the Committee at the ACA Headquarters. The complaint should include, if possible, (a) the name and address of the

complainant, (b) the name and address of the charged member, (c) the names and addresses of any other persons who have knowledge of the facts involved, and (d) a brief description of the reason why the complaint is being filed.

3. The ACA staff liaison to the Committee will communicate in writing with complainants. Receipt of complaints and confirmation of membership status of charged members as defined in Section F.1 above will be acknowledged to the complainant. Proposed formal complaints will be sent to complainants after receipt of complaints have been acknowledged.

4. If the complaint does not involve a member as defined in Section F.1., above, the staff liaison shall inform the complainant.

5. The ACA staff liaison shall assign the complaint to a Co-Chair to determine whether the complaint, if true, would violate one or more sections of the Code of Ethics or if the complaint could be properly decided if accepted. If not, the complaint will be forwarded to the other Co-Chair for review, as if a new complaint. If both Co-Chairs determine that a complaint would not violate one or more sections of the Code of Ethics or if the complaint could not be properly decided if accepted, then the complaint will not be accepted and the complainant shall be notified.

6. If the Committee Co-Chair administering the complaint determines that there is insufficient information to make a fair determination of whether the behavior alleged in the complaint would be cause for action by the Committee, the ACA staff liaison may request further information from the complainant or others. They shall be given thirty (30) working days from receipt of the request to respond.

7. When complaints are accepted, complainants will be informed that copies of the formal complaints plus evidence and documents submitted in support of the complaint will be provided to the charged member and that the complainant must authorize release of such information to the charged member before the complaint process may proceed.

8. The ACA staff liaison, after receiving approval of the Committee Co-Chair administering a complaint, will formulate a formal complaint which will be presented to the complainant for his or her signature.

a. The correspondence from complainants will be received, and the staff liaison and Committee Co-Chair administering the complaint will identify all ACA Code of Ethics that might have been violated if the accusations are true.

b. The formal complaint will be sent to complainants with a copy of these Policies and Procedures, a copy of the ACA Code of Ethics, a verification affidavit form and an authorization and release of information form. Complainants will be asked to sign and return the completed complaint, verification affidavit and authorization and release of information forms. It will be explained to complainants that sections of the codes that might have been violated may be added or deleted by the complainant before signing the formal statement.

c. If complainants elect to add or delete sections of the Code of Ethics in the formal complaint, the unsigned formal complaint shall be returned to ACA Headquarters with changes noted, and a revised formal complaint will be sent to the complainants for their signature.

9. When the completed formal complaint, verification affidavit form and authorization and release of information form are presented to the complainant for signature, he or she will be asked to submit all evidence and documents he or she wishes to be considered by the Committee in reviewing the complaint. The complainant shall submit all evidence and documentation in support of the claim within thirty (30) days of filing the formal complaint. The Committee may accept, at its discretion, evidence or documentation submitted late if good cause is shown.

SECTION K
NOTICE TO CHARGED MEMBERS

1. Once signed formal complaints have been received, charged members will be sent a copy of the formal complaint by U.S. mail, certified, with return-receipt requested, a copy of these Policies and Procedures, a copy of the Code of Ethics, notification of their right to request a hearing, (including the time limit within which to request the hearing, and that the failure to request a hearing within the time limit constitutes a waiver of the hearing), ACA's policy of disclosing adverse actions to its members and/or informing state and national licensure boards of a member's suspension or expulsion, and copies of all evidence and documents submitted in support of the complaint.

2. Charged members will be asked to respond to the complaint against them by addressing each section of the ACA Code of Ethics they have been accused of having violated. They will be informed that if they wish to respond they must do so in writing within sixty (60) working days.

3. Charged members will be informed that they must submit all evidence and documents they wish to be considered by the Committee in reviewing the complaint within sixty (60) working days.

4. After charged members have received notification that a complaint has been brought against them, they will be given sixty (60) working days to notify the Committee Co-Chair (via ACA Headquarters) in writing, by certified mail, if they wish to request a formal face-to-face hearing before the Committee. Charged members may waive their right to a formal hearing before the Committee and shall

sign a waiver of the right to a hearing. (See Section O: Hearings).

5. If the Committee Co-Chair determines that there is insufficient information to make a fair determination of whether the behavior alleged in the complaint would be cause for action by the Committee, the ACA staff liaison to the Committee may request further information from the charged member or others. They shall be given thirty (30) working days from receipt of the request to respond.

6. All requests for additional information from others will be accompanied by a verification affidavit form which the information provider will be asked to complete and return.

7. The Committee may, in its discretion, delay or postpone its review of the case with good cause including if the Committee wishes to obtain additional information. The charged member may request in writing that the Committee delay or postpone its review of the case for good cause.

SECTION L
DISPOSITION OF COMPLAINTS

1. After receiving the responses from charged members, Committee members will be provided copies of (a) the complaint, (b) supporting evidence and documents sent to charged members, (c) the response, and (d) supporting evidence and documents provided by charged members and others.

2. Decisions will be rendered based on the evidence and documents provided by the complainant and charged member or others.

3. The Committee Co-Chair administering a complaint will not participate in deliberations or decisions regarding that particular complaint.

4. At the next meeting of the Committee held no sooner than fifteen (15) working days after members received copies of documents related to a complaint, the Committee will discuss the complaint, response, and supporting documentation, if any, and determine the outcome of the complaint.

5. The Committee will determine whether each Code of Ethics the member has been accused of having violated was violated based on the information provided.

6. After deliberations, the Committee may decide to dismiss the complaint or to dismiss charges within the complaint.

7. In the event it is determined that any of the ACA Codes of Ethics have been violated, the Committee will impose for the entire complaint one or a combination of the possible sanctions allowed.

SECTION M
WITHDRAWAL OF COMPLAINTS

1. If the complainant and charged member

both agree to discontinue the complaint process, the Committee may, at its discretion, complete the adjudication process if available evidence indicates that this is warranted. The Co-Chair of the Committee, on behalf of the ACA membership, shall act as complainant.

SECTION N
POSSIBLE SANCTIONS

1. Remedial requirements may be stipulated by the Committee.

2. Probation for a specified period of time subject to Committee review of compliance. Remedial requirements may be imposed to be completed within a specified period of time.

3. Suspension from ACA membership for a specified period of time subject to Committee review of compliance. Remedial requirements may be imposed to be completed within a specified period of time.

4. Permanent expulsion from ACA membership. This sanction requires a unanimous vote of those voting.

5. The penalty for failing to satisfactorily fulfill a remedial requirement imposed by the Committee as a result of a probation sanction will be automatic suspension until the requirement is met unless the Committee determines that the remedial requirement should be modified based on good cause shown prior to the end of the probationary period.

6. The penalty for failing to satisfactorily fulfill a remedial requirement imposed by the Committee as a result of a suspension sanction will be automatic permanent expulsion unless the Committee determines that the remedial requirement should be modified based on good cause shown prior to the end of the suspension period.

7. Other corrective action.

SECTION O
HEARINGS

1. At the discretion of the Committee, a hearing may be conducted when the results of the Committee's preliminary determination indicate that additional information is needed.

2. When charged members, within sixty (60) working days of notification of the complaint, request a formal face-to-face or telephone conference hearing before the Committee, a hearing shall be conducted. (See Section K.6.)

3. The charged member shall bear all their expenses associated with attendance at hearings requested by the charged member.

4. The Committee Co-Chair shall schedule a formal hearing on the case at the next scheduled Committee meeting and notify both the complainant and the charged member of their right to attend the hearing in person or by telephone conference call.

5. The hearing will be held before a panel made up of the Committee and, if the charged member chooses, a representative of the charged member's primary Division. This representative will be identified by the Division President and will have voting privileges.

1. Purpose.

a. A hearing will be conducted to determine whether a breach of the Code of Ethics has occurred and, if so, to determine appropriate disciplinary action.

b. The Committee will be guided in its deliberations by principles of basic fairness and professionalism and will keep its deliberations as confidential as possible except as provided herein.

2. Notice.

a. The charged members shall be advised in writing by the Co-Chair administering the complaint of the time and place of the hearing, the list of any witnesses expected to testify at the hearing against the charged member (which list may not be complete), and the charges involved at least forty-five (45) working days before the hearing. A copy of the notification shall be sent to the complainant. Notice shall include a formal statement of the complaints lodged against the charged member and supporting evidence.

b. The charged member is under no duty to respond to the notice, but the Committee will not be obligated to delay or postpone its hearing unless the charged member so requests in writing with good cause received at least fifteen (15) working days in advance. In the absence of such 15-day advance notice and postponement by the Committee, if the charged member fails to appear at the hearing, the Committee shall decide the complaint on record. Failure of the charged member to appear at the hearing shall not be viewed by the Committee as sufficient grounds alone for taking disciplinary action.

3. Conduct of the Hearing.

a. Accommodations. The location of the hearing shall be determined at the discretion of the Committee. The Committee shall provide a private room to conduct the hearing, and no observers or recording devices other than a recording device used by the Committee shall be permitted.

b. Presiding Officer. The Co-Chair in charge of the case shall preside over the hearing and deliberations of the Committee. At the conclusion of the hearing and deliberations, the Co-Chair shall promptly notify the charged member and complainant of the Committee's decision in writing as provided in Section Q., Paragraphs 1 and 2, below.

c. Record. A record of the hearing shall be made and preserved, together with any documents presented in evidence, at ACA Headquarters for a period of three (3) years or until the complaint process is final, whichever is longer. The record shall consist of a summary of testimony received or a verbatim transcript at the discretion of the Committee.

d. Right to Counsel. The charged member shall be entitled to have legal counsel present to advise and represent him or her throughout the hearing. Legal counsel for ACA shall also be present at the hearing to advise the Committee and shall have the privilege of the floor.

e. Witnesses. Either party shall have the right to call witnesses to substantiate his or her version of the case.

f. The Committee shall have the right to call witnesses it believes may provide further insight into the matter. ACA shall, in its sole discretion, determine the number and identity of witnesses to be heard.

g. Witnesses shall not be present during the hearing except when testifying and shall be excused upon completion of their testimony and any cross-examination.

h. The Co-Chair administering the complaint shall allow questions of any witness by the opposition or members of the Committee if such questions and testimony are relevant to the issues in the case.

i. The Co-Chair administering the complaint will determine what questions and testimony are relevant to the case. Should the hearing be disturbed by irrelevant testimony, the Co-Chair administering the complaint may call a brief recess to restore order.

j. All expenses associated with counsel on behalf of the parties shall be borne by the respective parties. All expenses associated with witnesses on behalf of the charged member shall be borne by the charged member when the charged member requests a hearing. If the Committee requests the hearing, all expenses associated with witnesses shall be borne by ACA.

4. Presentation of Evidence

a. The staff liaison or the Co-Chair administering the complaint shall be called upon first to present the charge(s) against the charged member and to briefly describe the supporting evidence. The person presenting the charges shall also be responsible for examining and cross-examining witnesses on behalf of the complainant and for otherwise presenting the matter during the hearing.

b. The complainant or the staff liaison or the Committee Co-Chair administering the complaint shall then present the case against the charged member. Witnesses who can substantiate the case may be called upon to testify and answer questions of the charged member and the Committee.

c. If the charged member is present at the hearing, he or she shall be called upon after the case has been presented against the charged member to present any evidence which refutes the charges against him or her. This includes witnesses as in Subsection (3) above. The charged member and the complainant may submit a written statment at the close of the hearing.

d. The charged member will not be found guilty simply for refusing to testify. Once the charged member chooses to testify, however, he or she may be cross-examined by the complainant and members of the Committee.

e. The Committee will endeavor to conclude the hearing within a period of approximately three (3) hours. The parties will be requested to be considerate of this time frame in planning their testimony. If it appears that additional time will be needed to develop the issues adequately, an extension of time may be granted.

f. Testimony that is merely cumulative or repetitious may, at the discretion of the Co-Chair administering the complaint, be excluded.

g. At any time during the presentation of evidence, the presiding members of the Committee may ask pertinent questions.

5. Relevancy of Evidence.

a. The Hearing Committee is not a court of law and is not required to observe formal rules of evidence. Evidence inadmissible in a court of law may be admissible in the hearing before the Committee if it is relevant to the case. That is, if the evidence offered tends to explain, clarify, or refute any of the important facts of the case, it should be generally be considered.

b. The Committee will not consider evidence or testimony for the purpose of supporting any charge that was not set forth in the notice of the hearing or that is not relevant to the issues of the case.

6. Burden of Proof.

a. The burden of proving a violation of the Code of Ethics is on the complainant and/or the Committee. It is not up to the charged member to prove his or her innocence of any wrong-doing.

b. Although the charge(s) need not be proved "beyond a reasonable doubt," the Committee will not find the charged member guilty in the absence of substantial, objective, and believable evidence to sustain the charge(s).

7. Deliberation of the Committee.

a. After the hearing is completed, the Committee shall meet in a closed session to review the evidence presented and reach a conclusion. ACA legal counsel may attend the closed session to advise the Committee if the Committee so desires.

b. The Committee shall be the sole trier of the facts and shall weigh the evidence presented and assess the credibility of the witnesses. The act of a majority of the members of the Committee present shall be the decision of the Committee. An unanimous vote of those voting is required for permanent expulsion from ACA membership.

c. Only members of the Committee who were present throughout the entire hearing shall be eligible to vote.

8. Decision of the Committee.

a. The Committee will first resolve the issue of the guilt or innocence of the charged member on each charge. Applying the burden of proof in subsection (5) above, the Committee will vote by secret ballot unless the members of the Committee consent to an oral vote.

b. In the event a majority of the members of the Committee do not find the charged member guilty, the charges shall be dismissed. If the Committee finds the charged member has violated the Code of Ethics, it must then determine what sanctions, in accordance with Section N: Possible Sanctions, shall be imposed.

c. As provided in Section Q below, the Co-Chair administering the complaint shall notify the charged member and complainant of the Committee's decision and rights to appeal in writing.

SECTION Q
NOTIFICATION OF RESULTS

1. Charged members shall be notified of Committee decisions regarding complaints against them. Within thirty (30) days after the hearing, charged members shall be notified of the Committee's decisions and their right to appeal. The Committee's decision shall be sent by U.S. mail, certified, with return-receipt requested.

2. After the deadline for filing an appeal, or in the event an appeal is filed, after a decision on appeals has been rendered, and if a violation has been found and charged members have been suspended or expelled, counselor licensure, certification, or registry boards, other mental health licensure, certification, or registry boards, voluntary national certification boards, and appropriate professional associations will also be notified of the results. In addition, ACA divisions, state branches, the ACA Insurance Trust, and other ACA-related entities will also be notified of the results.

3. After the deadline for filing an appeal, or in the event an appeal is filed, after a decision on appeals has been rendered, and if a violation has been found and charged members have been suspended or expelled, a notice of the Committee's action that includes the sections of the ACA Code of Ethics that were found to have been violated and the sanctions imposed will be published in the ACA newsletter.

SECTION R
APPEALS

1. Decisions of the ACA Ethics Committee may be appealed by the member found to have been in violation based on one or both of the following grounds:

a. The Committee violated its policies and procedures for processing complaints of ethical violations; and/or

b. The decision of the Committee was arbitrary and capricious and was not supported by the materials provided by the complainant and charged member.

2. After members have received notification that they have been found in violation of one or more ACA Codes of Ethics, they will be given thirty (30) working days to notify the Committee in writing by certified mail that they are appealing the decision. If an appeal is not requested, the Committee shall issue its decision as the final decision as soon as the time during which an appeal may be filed expires.

3. An appeal may consist only of a letter stating one or both of the grounds of appeal listed in subsection 1 above and the reasons for the appeal. The filing of an appeal automatically stays the execution of a decision by the Committee until the appeal is completed.

4. The appealing member will be asked to identify the primary ACA division to which he or she belongs. The ACA President will appoint a three (3) person appeals panel consisting of two (2) former ACA Ethics Committee Chairs (neither of whom served on the Committee during the hearings on the matter) and the President of the identified division. The ACA attorney shall serve as legal advisor and have the privilege of the floor.

5. The three (3) member appeals panel will be given copies of the materials available to the Committee when it made its decision, a copy of the hearing record if a hearing was held, plus a copy of the letter filed by the appealing member.

6. The appeals panel will not consider evidence that was not presented to the Committee.

7. The appeals panel generally will render its decision regarding an appeal requiring a majority vote within sixty (60) working days of their receipt of the above materials.

8. The decision of the appeals panel is limited to

a. Upholding the decision of the Committee, or

b. Upholding the decision of the Committee on the finding of an ethical violation but reversing and remanding the Committee's decision on sanctions, or

c. Recommending reconsideration by the Committee of the decision providing guidance to the Committee in detail in writing for considering a new decision on remand.

9. The decision of the appeals panel need not be unanimous.

10. When a Committee decision is reversed and remanded, the complainant and charged member will be informed in writing, and additional information may be requested first from the complainant and then from the charged member. The Committee will then render another decision without a hearing.

11. Decisions of the appeals panel to uphold the Committee decision are final and binding and not subject to further hearings or appellate review.

SECTION S
SUBSTANTIAL NEW EVIDENCE

1. In the event substantial new evidence is presented in a case in which an appeal was not filed, or in a case for which a final decision has been rendered, the case may be reopened by the Committee.

2. The Committee will consider substantial new evidence and if found to be substantiated and capable of exonerating a member who was expelled, the Committee will reopen the case and go through the entire complaint process again.

SECTION T
RECORDS

1. The records of the Committee regarding complaints are confidential except as provided herein.

2. Original copies of complaint records will be maintained in locked files at ACA Headquarters or at an off-site location chosen by ACA.

3. Members of the Committee will keep copies of complaint records confidential and will destroy copies of records after a case has been closed or when they are no longer a member of the Committee.

SECTION U
LEGAL ACTIONS RELATED TO COMPLAINTS

1. Complainants and charged members are required to notify the Committee if they learn of any type of legal action (civil or criminal) being filed related to the complaint.

2. In the event any type of legal action is filed regarding an accepted complaint, all actions related to the complaint will be stayed until the legal action has been concluded. The Committee will consult with legal counsel concerning whether the processing of the complaint will be stayed if the legal action does not involve the same complainant and the same facts complained of.

3. If actions on a complaint are stayed, the complainant and charged member will be notified.

4. When actions on a complaint are continued after a legal action has been concluded, the complainant and charged member will be notified.

Appendix **B**   **American Counseling Association**
Licensure Chart
Requirements for Mental Health Counselor Credentials

This information presented pertains to the 45 U.S. states—including the District of Columbia—that regulate mental health counseling as of November 24, 1998. Twenty-eight states, including DC, issue a general practice credential, often called the "LPC," though the majority of counselors who seek this credential are mental health counselors. As for the specialties, 18 states specifically regulate mental health counseling with a credential such as an LMHC or LCPC, 16 regulate rehabilitation counseling (either as part of the LPC, which is noted in this chart, or separately in Louisiana, Massachusetts, and New Jersey), many regulate substance abuse counseling, 30 regulate career counseling with the LPC (also noted in this chart), and all 50 states and DC regulate school counseling through their state departments of education. Two other counseling specialties can be regulated, as well: geriatric and marriage & family counseling. That is, geriatric and marriage & family counseling are usually governed by the LPC, though they may not be referred to specifically.

For information on the licensure of substance abuse counseling, consult your Blue Pages' state section for that board's phone number and address (in some cases, this may be the same board that issues the LPC); for school counseling credential information, either contact your state department of education or call the ACA at 1-800-347-6647, X222, and ask for the publication called *A Guide to State Laws & Regulations on Professional School Counseling*.

When CACREP is referred to under the column "Educational Requirements," some states accept equivalent coursework. If a counseling credential title appears in bold letters (2nd column), this means that the credential is part of a "practice act," that is, a professional counselor must hold this credential in order to ply his/her trade; counseling without meeting the criteria is prohibited. This is in contrast to a "title act" that only bars the use of that credential as part of one's job title. A practice act credential is preferable, especially with regard to 3rd-party reimbursement. (All school counselor credentials are mandatory.)

A number of states grant associate licenses/certificates to persons who are working on completing certain requirements. They may grant associate licenses/certificates to persons who meet the education and exam requirements but have not yet had the supervised experience required. Please contact the state regulatory board directly for the specific curricular requirements, scope-of-practice information (*critical* scope-of-practice components: the provisions for diagnosing emotional disorders, noted by a "*Dx.*" in this chart, treating emotional disorders, noted by a " *Tx.*," and testing/assessment), specialty area criteria, if applicable, and any further information—especially for sections indicating "TBA," which means that either the ACA could not obtain these data or that the state has yet to make it public—that you may need. Following are abbreviations:

CACREP	Council for Accreditation of Counseling & Related Educational Programs (the ACA's professional counselor-training accrediting board)
CCMHC	Certified Clinical Mental Health Counselor (an NBCC professional counseling specialty title; not a required credential)
CORE	Council on Rehabilitation Education (an independent rehabilitation counselor-training accrediting board)
CRC	Certified Rehabilitation Counselor (a CRCC professional counseling specialty title; not a required credential)
CRCC	Commission on Rehabilitation Counselor Certification (an independent, non-governmental rehabilitation counselor-credentialing board)
CRCE	Certified Rehabilitation Counselor Examination (administered by the CRCC for the certification of rehabilitation counselors; also administered by a couple of states for their own credentialing process as an alternative to their *clinically* oriented exam)
NBCC	National Board for Certified Counselors (an independent, non-governmental professional counselor-credentialing board)
NCE	National Counselor Examination (administered by the NBCC for the general certification of professional counselors; also administered by most states for their own credentialing process)
NCMHCE	National Clinical Mental Health Counselors Examination (administered by the NBCC for the certification of mental health counselors; also administered by a few states for their own credentialing process)

For any questions regarding this chart, call the ACA Center for Effective Counseling Practice (CECP) at 1 (800) 347–6647, X8, or e-mail CECP at cecp@counseling.org. Especially helpful would be updates and corrections.

JURISDICTION	CREDENTIAL TITLE(S)	EDUCATIONAL REQUIREMENTS	EXPERIENTIAL REQUIREMENTS	EXAMINATION REQUIREMENTS
Alabama Board of Examiners in Counseling P.O. Box 550397 Birmingham, AL 35255 205/933-8100 205/933-6700 (FAX)	**Licensed Professional Counselor** (LPC) Note: scope-of-practice includes the practice of career counseling	Master's degree, including a minimum of 30 semester hours, from a CACREP- or CORE-accredited program, or the substantial equivalent, as defined in regulations.	3 years supervised F-T experience, 1 year of which may be obtained prior to granting of master's. May subtract 1 year of experience for every 15 graduate semester hours beyond master's (up to 2 years). F-T requirements may be modified for part-time work but must be completed within six years. Supervised experiences must include: (a) minimum of 3,000 hours of professional counseling service including 2,250 hours of face-to-face counseling and 750 hours related to counseling services in a clinical supervisory setting, (b) 150 hours of individual, face-to-face supervision by an LPC.	NCE
Alaska AK Div. of Occupational Licensing Board of Professional Counselors P.O. Box 110806 Juneau, AK 99811 907/465-2551	Licensed Professional Counselor (LPC) * Dx * Licensure passed on 6/4/98, eff. 1/1/99.	Master's degree in counseling or a related field consisting of at least 60 graduate semester hours.	3,000 hours of post-master's supervised experience (incl. 1,000 hours of direct client contact and 100 hours of face-to-face supervision) over a period of at least 2 yrs.	(TBA)
Arizona Counselor Credentialing Committee of the Board of Behavioral Examiners 1645 W. Jefferson Ave., Rm. 426 Phoenix, AZ 85007 602/542-1882 602/542-1830 (FAX)	Certified Professional Counselor (CPC) Dx Note: scope-of-practice includes the practices of rehabilitation and career counseling	Master's degree in counseling which includes 48 graduate semester hours and a supervised practicum.	2 years F-T post-master's experience or equivalent (3,200 hours), including 1 year under supervision of a CPC (if CPC eligible). May use a doctoral-clinical internship to satisfy the requirement for one year of supervised experience.	(none; already taken at CAC level)
	Certified Associate Counselor (CAC)	(same as above)	No post-degree work experience required.	NCE, CMHCE, or CRCE

credentials in **bold letters** = required credential (practice act) / $\boxed{Dx}$ = scope-of-practice allows treatment of emotional disorders

JURISDICTION	CREDENTIAL TITLE(S)	EDUCATIONAL REQUIREMENTS	EXPERIENTIAL REQUIREMENTS	EXAMINATION REQUIREMENTS
Arkansas Board of Examiners in Counseling P.O. Box 1396 Magnolia, AR 71753 870/235-4314 870/234-1842 (FAX) akthomas@saumag.edu	**Licensed Professional Counselor** (LPC) Note: scope-of-practice includes the practice of career counseling	Graduate degree in counseling w/ a minimum of 48 semester hours.	3 years post-master's supervised experience. 1 year of experience may be gained for each 30 semester hours earned beyond master's (up to 2 years).	NCE; videotape; oral exam
	Licensed Associate Counselor (LAC)	(same as above)	(none)	(none)
California (no licensing board for mental health counseling at this time) Sacramento, CA	("Licensed Marriage, Family, & Child Counselor" credential changed to "Licensed Marriage & Family Therapist," eff. 6/24/98)			
Colorado Board of Licensed Professional Counselor Examiners 1560 Broadway, Ste. 1340 Denver, CO 80202 303/894-7766 303/894-7790 (FAX) amos.martinez@state.co.us	**Licensed Professional Counselor** (LPC) $\boxed{Dx.}$ Note: scope-of-practice includes the practice of career counseling	Master's degree with 48 semester hours, or doctorate with 96 hours and 700 hours practicum and/or internship from a program offering a F-T graduate course of study in counseling.	2 years post-master's practice or 1 year post-doctoral practice under board-approved supervision.	NCE
Connecticut CT Dept. of Public Health Div. of Health Systems Reg. 410 Capitol Ave. Hartford, CT 06134 860/509-7590	**Licensed Professional Counselor** (LPC) $\boxed{Dx.}$	Master's degree (after 1/1/99: 42 semester hours or doctoral degree, in discipline of professional counseling, + other course work totaling 60 graduate semester hours altogether, including CACREP core and clinical curriculum, and preparation in principles of etiology, diagnosis, treatment-planning, and prevention of mental and emotional disorders and dysfunctional behavior).	2 yrs. experience in professional counseling (after 1/1/99: 3,000 hours supervised experience, over at least 1 year period. Minimum of 100 hours of direct supervision).	NCE

credentials in bold letters = required credential (practice act) / $\boxed{Dx.}$ = scope-of-practice allows treatment of emotional disorders

527

JURISDICTION	CREDENTIAL TITLE(S)	EDUCATIONAL REQUIREMENTS	EXPERIENTIAL REQUIREMENTS	EXAMINATION REQUIREMENTS
Delaware Board of Professional Counselors of Mental Health P.O. Box 1401 Dover, DE 19903 302/739-4522 302/739-2711 (FAX)	Licensed Professional Counselor of Mental Health (LPCMH) *Dx.*	Graduate degree, including a minimum of 48 semester hours. Must also be certified by NBCC (including as a CCMHC) or other acceptable certifying agency (therefore must meet their requirements).	3 years (4,200 hours) F-T clinical experience within a 5-year period with a minimum of 100 hours of supervision; 1 year may be obtained prior to completion of master's. May substitute 30 graduate semester hours or more beyond master's degree for 1 year of required experience but must have no less than 2 years of post- master's experience.	NCE or CMHCE
District of Columbia Board of Professional Counselors 614 H St., N.W., Rm. 108 Washington, DC 20001 202/727-9794 202/727-4087 (FAX)	**Licensed Professional Counselor** (LPC) *Dx.* Note: scope-of-practice includes the practice of career counseling	60 graduate semester hours including a master's degree in counseling or a related field.	Must complete a total of 3,500 client-contact hours in no less than 2 years, and no more than 5 years, incl. 200 hrs. of direct supervision (100 of those 200 hrs. can be group supervision).	NCE
Florida FL Agency for Health Care Admin. Board of Clinical Social Workers & Mental Health Counselors 1940 N. Monroe St. Tallahassee, FL 32399 850/488-0595 850/921-2569 (FAX)	**Licensed Mental Health Counselor** (LMHC) *Dx.*	Master's degree including a supervised practicum, internship or field experience (eff. 1/1/2001, 60 crs. will be required, almost doubling current requirement).	3 years of clinical experience; 2 years must be supervised post-master's (incl. 100 face-to-face hrs. of supervision, of which 50 hrs. can be in a group).	NCE/FL Law Exam
Georgia GA Div. of Examining Boards Composite Board of Professional Counselors & Social Workers 166 Pryor St., S.W. Atlanta, GA 30303 404/656-3933 404/651-9532 (FAX)	**Licensed Professional Counselor** (LPC) *Dx.* Note: scope-of-practice includes the practices of rehabilitation and career counseling	Master's degree or higher with a supervised practicum or a specialist degree in a program that is primarily counseling.	4 years experience, including a 1-year internship and 3 years post-master's supervision. 2 of the 3 years of supervision must be provided by an LPC (1 yr. = 600 hrs.).	NCE
	Associate Professional Counselor (APC)	Master's degree in a program that is primarily counseling.	Registration of supervision and working toward LPC credential within 5-yr. period.	(none)

credentials in bold letters = required credential (practice act) / *Dx.* = scope-of-practice allows treatment of emotional disorders

JURISDICTION	CREDENTIAL TITLE(S)	EDUCATIONAL REQUIREMENTS	EXPERIENTIAL REQUIREMENTS	EXAMINATION REQUIREMENTS
Hawaii (no licensing board for mental health counseling at this time) Honolulu, HI				
Idaho ID Bureau of Occupational Licenses State Counselor Licensure Board 1109 Main St., Ste. 220 Boise, ID 83702 208/334-3233 208/334-3945 (FAX)	**Licensed Professional Counselor - Private Practice** (LPC-PP)	Hold a current LPC license. Document direct client-contact and proficiency in diagnostic evaluation.	2,000 more hrs. supervised experience over 2 yrs. w/ at least 1,000 by an LPC-PP (remainder can be other mental health professional).	(none; already taken at LPC level)
	Licensed Professional Counselor (LPC) $\boxed{Dx.}$ Note: scope-of-practice includes the practices of rehabilitation and career counseling	Graduate degree, w/ 60 semester hours, including a 6-hour advanced practicum.	1,000 hours of experience with supervision by an LPC (can include pre-master's internship).	NCE
Illinois IL Dept. of Professional Regulation Professional Counselor Licensing & Disciplinary Board 320 W. Washington St. Springfield, IL 62786 217/785-0822 217/782-7645 (FAX)	Licensed Clinical Professional Counselor (LCPC)	Master's or doctoral degree in counseling (30 semester credits), rehabilitation counseling, psychology, or related field from a program approved by the IL Dept. of Professional Regulation.	Two years (or equivalent) of full-time supervised experience as a clinical professional counselor. One year equals 1,680 hours.	CMHCE or CRCE
	Licensed Professional Counselor (LPC) $\boxed{Dx.}$ Note: scope-of-practice includes the practices of rehabilitation and career counseling	Master's or doctoral degree in counseling (30 semester credits), rehabilitation counseling, psychology, or related field from program approved by the IL Dept. of Professional Regulation; or baccalaureate from an approved program and the equivalent of five years of full-time supervised experience.	For a baccalaureate degree, one must document the equivalent of 5 years of full-time supervised experience. One year equals 1,680 hours. No experience required for master/doctorate level. One must work under supervision with this license.	NCE

credentials in bold letters = required credential (practice act) / $\boxed{Dx.}$ = scope-of-practice allows treatment of emotional disorders

JURISDICTION	CREDENTIAL TITLE(S)	EDUCATIONAL REQUIREMENTS	EXPERIENTIAL REQUIREMENTS	EXAMINATION REQUIREMENTS
Indiana IN Health Professions Bureau Social Worker & Mental Health Counselor Board 402 W. Washington St., Rm. 041 Indianapolis, IN 46204 317/232-2960 317/233-4236 (FAX) bbuck@hpb.state.in.us	**Licensed Mental Health Counselor** (LMHC) $Dx.$ Note: scope-of-practice includes the practices of rehabilitation and career counseling	Master's degree in an area related to mental health counseling from a regionally accredited institution of higher learning. Minimum of 60 graduate semester hours in counseling in 12 specified content areas.	Not less than 1 supervised clinical practicum, internship, or field experience in a counseling setting w/ at least 1,000 hours consisting of 1 practicum of 100 hours and 1 internship of 700 hours, w/ at least 100 hours of face-to-face supervision. Applicant must have 3,000 hours of post-graduate clinical experience over a 2-year period consisting of 100 hours of face-to-face supervision under the supervision of an LMHC or equivalent supervisor (doctoral-level internship can count toward this).	(TBA)
Iowa Behavioral Science Board Lucas Bldg., 4th Fl. Des Moines, IA 50319 515/281-4413 515/281-3121 (FAX)	**Licensed Mental Health Counselor** (LMHC) $Dx.$	Master's degree in counseling with at least 45 semester hours.	1,000 hours in a 2-year period post-graduate, supervised clinical experience.	NCE or CMHCE
Kansas Behavioral Sciences Regulatory Board 712 S. Kansas Ave. Topeka, KS 66603 913/296-3240 913/296-3112 (FAX)	**Licensed Professional Counselor** (LPC) Note: scope-of-practice includes the practice of career counseling	60 graduate semester hours including a graduate degree in counseling from a university approved by the board and which includes 45 graduate semester hours distributed among core courses.	4,000 supervised hrs. as a professional counselor over a minimum of two years. At least 1,000 supervised hrs. of actual client-contact. Minimum of 200 hrs. of supervision (100 hrs. administrative supervision and 100 hrs. of clinical supervision with no more than 50 hrs. group supervision and no less than 50 hrs. individual supervision; no less than 4 hrs. of clinical supervision contact monthly.) One-half of this requirement waived for persons with a doctoral degree in professional counseling or a related field acceptable to the board.	NCE

credentials in bold letters = required credential (practice act) / $\boxed{Dx.}$ = scope-of-practice allows treatment of emotional disorders

JURISDICTION	CREDENTIAL TITLE(S)	EDUCATIONAL REQUIREMENTS	EXPERIENTIAL REQUIREMENTS	EXAMINATION REQUIREMENTS
Kentucky KY Division of Occupations & Professions 700 Louisville Rd., Ste. 2 Frankfort, KY 40602 502/564-3296, X226 502/564-4818 (FAX)	Certified Professional Counselor (CPC)	Master's or doctoral degree in counseling from an accredited institution. Minimum of 60 semester hours in 9 specified areas.	3,000 hrs. (2,000 hrs. post-master's) experience under approved supervision, which includes 1,200 hrs. direct counseling and 100 hrs. individual, face-to-face, weekly clinical supervision. Up to 1,000 hrs. of the supervised experience may be obtained from a supervised practicum or internship. 400 hrs. organized practicum or internship.	NCE
Louisiana Licensed Professional Counselors Board of Examiners 8631 Summa Ave., Ste. A Baton Rouge, LA 70809 504/922-1499 504/922-2160 (FAX)	**Licensed Professional Counselor** (LPC) Note: scope-of-practice includes the practice of career counseling	Graduate degree from a regionally accredited institution with 48 graduate semester hours including coursework in 8 specified areas, with a supervised mental health counseling practicum and supervised internship.	2 years (3,000 hours, incl. 100 hrs. of face-to-face supervision [50% can be group supervision]) post-master's experience supervised by a qualified LPC. 500 hours of supervised experience may be gained for each 30 graduate semester hours beyond master's. Must have no less than 2,000 hours of supervised post-master's experience.	NCE
Maine Board of Counseling Professionals State House, Station #35 Augusta, ME 04333 207/624-8626 207/624-8637 (FAX) dianestaples@state.me.us	**Licensed Clinical Professional Counselor** (LCPC)	Graduate degree in counseling or allied mental health field with a minimum core curriculum of at least 45 semester hours, practicum and 1,200-hour internship.	2 years post-master's experience to include at least 3,000 hours (1,500 client-contact hrs.) of supervised clinical experience. Minimum of 100 hours of personal supervision.	(none; already taken at LPC level)
	Licensed Professional Counselor (LPC) $\boxed{Dx.}$ Note: scope-of-practice includes the practice of career counseling	Graduate degree in counseling or allied mental health field with a minimum core curriculum, a practicum, and 600-hour internship.	2 years post-master's experience with a minimum of 2,000 hours of supervised experience and a minimum of 67 hours of personal supervision.	NCE or CMHCE

credentials in **bold letters** = required credential (practice act) / $\boxed{Dx.}$ = scope-of-practice allows treatment of emotional disorders

531

JURISDICTION	CREDENTIAL TITLE(S)	EDUCATIONAL REQUIREMENTS	EXPERIENTIAL REQUIREMENTS	EXAMINATION REQUIREMENTS
Maryland Board of Examiners of Professional Counselors 4201 Patterson Ave., 3rd Fl. Baltimore, MD 21215 410/764-4732 410/764-5987 (FAX)	**Licensed Clinical Professional Counselor** (LCPC) * * Upgraded from a CPC title credential, eff. 4/28/98. \boxed{Dx.} Note: scope-of-practice includes the practice of career counseling	Master's degree with 60 semester hours (or doctorate with 90 semester hours) including coursework in 9 specified areas, courses in diagnosis and substance abuse counseling, and supervised field experience.	2,000 hrs. post-master's supervision (in addition to 1,000 hrs. of an internship); all supervision may be provided by any licensed mental health professional (psychiatrist, psychologist, social worker, and/or professional counselor).	NCE
Massachusetts Board of Allied Mental Health Services 100 Cambridge St., 15th Fl. Boston, MA 02202 617/727-1716 617/727-2197 (FAX)	Licensed Mental Health Counselor (LMHC) \boxed{Dx.}	Eff. 6/1/98: minimum of 60 graduate credit hours and a master's degree in mental health counseling from an institution meeting national standards for granting a master's degree with a concentration in mental health counseling or a related field.	2 years supervised clinical experience *after* obtaining 60 credits, including not less than 200 hours of supervision, 100 of which must be individual with an approved clinician who has a master's degree or higher and experience in the specialty area. Regulations contain details on supervisors.	CMHCE
Michigan Board of Counseling P.O. Box 30670 Lansing, MI 48909 517/335-0918 517/373-3596 (FAX)	**Licensed Professional Counselor** (LPC) Note: scope-of-practice includes the practice of career counseling	Master's or higher degree in counseling, guidance, or student personnel, including a minimum of 48 semester hours, that includes specific coursework areas approved by the board.	With a master's: 2 years of post-degree experience with a minimum of 3,000 hours. For persons with 30 semester hours or 45 quarter hours beyond the master's: 1-year post-degree experience with a minimum of 1,500 hours.	NCE or CRCE
Minnesota (no licensing board for mental health counseling at this time) St. Paul, MN				

credentials in bold letters = required credential (practice act) / \boxed{Dx.} = scope-of-practice allows treatment of emotional disorders

JURISDICTION	CREDENTIAL TITLE(S)	EDUCATIONAL REQUIREMENTS	EXPERIENTIAL REQUIREMENTS	EXAMINATION REQUIREMENTS
Mississippi Board of Examiners for Licensed Professional Counselors 239 N. Lamar St. Jackson, MS 39201 601/235-8182	**Licensed Professional Counselor** (LPC)	Master's degree, 60 semester hours and courses reflecting the CACREP curriculum or equivalent.	2 years (3,500) hours of supervised experience (1,167 of these must be direct counseling), 1,750 of which must be post-master's. Minimum of 100 hours of supervision (1 hour per week); 50 hours may be group supervision. Supervisors must be LPC's or other licensed MH professionals.	NCE
Missouri Committee for Professional Counselors P.O. Box 1335 Jefferson City, MO 65102 573/751-0018 573/751-4176 (FAX)	**Licensed Professional Counselor** (LPC) *Dx.* Note: scope-of-practice includes the practices of rehabilitation and career counseling	Master's degree in counseling with 30 semester hours reflecting the CACREP core curriculum; doctorate or specialist's credential with a major in counseling.	3,000 hours post-master's experience in 24-48 months with 1 hour/week of face-to-face individual supervision (no less than 48 hours per year). May substitute 30 graduate semester hours post-master's study for 1,500 of the 3,000 hours of required experience.	NCE
Montana Board of Social Work & Professional Counselor Examiners 111 N. Jackson St. Helena, MT 59620 406/444-4285 406/444-1667 (FAX) mhainlin@mt.gov	Licensed Clinical Professional Counselor (LCPC) *Dx.* Note: scope-of-practice includes the practice of career counseling	Advanced degree, 90 quarter hours or 60 semester hours including an advanced counseling practicum.	3,000 hours of supervised experience. 50% must be post-master's. Supervision by LPC or licensed allied mental health professional.	NCE or CMHCE

credentials in bold letters = required credential (practice act) / *Dx.* = scope-of-practice allows treatment of emotional disorders

JURISDICTION	CREDENTIAL TITLE(S)	EDUCATIONAL REQUIREMENTS	EXPERIENTIAL REQUIREMENTS	EXAMINATION REQUIREMENTS
Nebraska NE Prof. & Occup. Licensure Div. Board of Examiners in Mental Health Practice P.O. Box 95007 Lincoln, NE 68509 402/471-2117 402/471-0380 (FAX)	**Licensed Mental Health Practitioner** (LMHP) `Dx.` Note: scope-of-practice includes the practices of rehabilitation and career counseling	Master's (primarily therapeutic/mental health in content) including a practicum or internship with a minimum of 300 clock hours direct client-contact under the supervision of a qualified supervisor.	Must meet requirements for CPC. 3,000 hours post-master's supervised experience in mental health practice accumulated during the 5 years immediately preceding application for licensure. Must include a minimum of 1 hour/week of face-to-face supervision with a qualified supervisor. Hours shall include 1,500 hours direct client-contact.	(none; already taken at CPC level)
	Certified Professional Counselor (CPC)	Master's from CACREP-accredited program or a counseling program from a regionally accredited institution, or meets course requirements as stated by board.	3,000 hours post-master's experience.	NCE or CMHCE
Nevada (no licensing board for mental health counseling at this time) Carson City, NV				
New Hampshire Board of Mental Health Practice 105 Pleasant St., Ste. 457 Concord, NH 03301 603/271-6762 plynch@dhhs.state.nh.us	**Licensed Mental Health Counselor** (LMHC) * * Upgrade from certification becomes eff. 10/31/98. `Dx.` Note: scope-of-practice includes the practice of rehabilitation counseling	Master's must be at least a 2-year program with minimum of 60 graduate semester hours.	3,000 hours paid, post-master's supervised clinical work in no less than 2 years and no more than 5 years. 100 hours of face-to-face supervision provided by a nationally or state certified mental health professional.	CMHCE

credentials in **bold letters** = required credential (practice act) / `Dx.` = scope-of-practice allows treatment of emotional disorders

JURISDICTION	CREDENTIAL TITLE(S)	EDUCATIONAL REQUIREMENTS	EXPERIENTIAL REQUIREMENTS	EXAMINATION REQUIREMENTS
New Jersey NJ Div. of Consumer Affairs Professional Counselor Examiners Committee P.O. Box 45033 Newark, NJ 07101 973/504-6415 973/648-3536 (FAX)	**Licensed Professional Counselor** (LPC) $\boxed{Dx.}$	Minimum of 60 graduate semester hours which includes a master's degree or doctorate in counseling from a regionally accredited institution; 45 of the 60 hours are to be distributed in at least 8 of 9 core coursework areas (through 2/99: g'fathering allowed 45 crs. w/ 5 yrs. experience).	3 years F-T supervised counseling experience in a professional counseling setting, 1 year of which may be obtained prior to the granting of the master's degree. 1 year of the experience may be eliminated by substituting 30 graduate semester hours beyond the master's degree. In no case may an applicant have less than 1 year of post-master's supervised work experience.	NCE
New Mexico Counselor Therapy & Practice Board P.O. Box 25101 Santa Fé, NM 87504 505/476-7100 505/827-7085 (FAX)	**Licensed Professional Clinical Counselor** (LPCC)	Master's or doctorate degree in counseling or a related mental health field from a nationally accredited or board-approved program or institution *that includes 60 graduate hours.*	2 years post-graduate professional clinical counseling, including 1,000 additional client-contact hours in a clinical setting with a minimum of 100 hours of supervision; supervision must come from an LPCC, licensed psychologist, and/or psychiatrist.	NCE *and* CMHCE (only CMHCE if NCE has already been taken)
	Licensed Professional Counselor (LPC) $\boxed{Dx.}$ Note: scope-of-practice includes the practice of career counseling	Master's or doctorate degree in counseling or a related mental health field from a nationally accredited or board-approved program or institution.	1,000 client-contact hours of professional post-graduate experience with a minimum of 100 hours of face-to-face supervision; supervision must come from an LPC, LPCC, licensed psychologist, and/or psychiatrist.	NCE
	Registered Mental Health Counselor (RMHC) Note: these 3 credentials are not sequential, nor are all 3 required, only 1; e.g. one may chose to obtain *only* the LPC w/o having obtained the RMHC and w/o planning to obtain the higher-level LPCC	Master's or doctorate degree in counseling or a related mental health field from a nationally accredited or board-approved program or institution.	Must have arranged for appropriate supervision, including a post-graduate experience plan which includes 1 hour of face-to-face supervision for every 10 hours of client-contact.	(none)

credentials in bold letters = required credential (practice act) / $\boxed{Dx.}$ = scope-of-practice allows treatment of emotional disorders

JURISDICTION	CREDENTIAL TITLE(S)	EDUCATIONAL REQUIREMENTS	EXPERIENTIAL REQUIREMENTS	EXAMINATION REQUIREMENTS
New York (no licensing board for mental health counseling at this time) Albany, NY				
North Carolina Board of Licensed Professional Counselors P.O. Box 21005 Raleigh, NC 27619 919/787-1980 919/571-8672 (FAX)	**Licensed Professional Counselor** (LPC) $\boxed{Dx.}$ Note: scope-of-practice includes the practice of career counseling	Master's degree in counseling including a minimum of 48 semester hours or a graduate degree in a related field supplemented with courses the board determines to be equivalent.	No less than 2 years of master's or post-master's counseling experience, or both, in a professional setting including a minimum of 2,000 hours of supervised professional practice, 100 of which must be face-to-face supervision by a board-approved supervisor.	NCE
North Dakota Board of Counselor Examiners P.O. Box 2735 Bismarck, ND 58502 701/224-8234	**Licensed Professional Clinical Counselor** (LPCC)	Master's degree in counseling, incl. 60 semester hours.	2 additional years of supervision (3,000 hrs.) by an LPCC in a clinical setting.	CMHCE + videotape of clinical skills
	Licensed Professional Counselor (LPC) $\boxed{Dx.}$ Note: scope-of-practice includes the practice of career counseling	Master's degree in counseling.	2 years of supervision by an LPCC or LPC.	(none, unless new to the state, g'fathered out of LAPC, and NCE was never taken previously)
	Licensed Associate Professional Counselor (LAPC)	Master's degree in counseling.	Written plan for obtaining the LPC credential.	NCE
Ohio Counselor & Social Work Board 77 S. High St., 16th Fl. Columbus, OH 43266 614/466-0912 614/644-8112 (FAX)	**Professional Clinical Counselor** (PCC)	Master's or doctoral degree in counseling with 60 semester or 90 quarter hours. Course content similar to CACREP core.	2 years (3,000 hrs.) of supervised clinical experience as a PC. Must already possess the PC credential.	Field Review
	Professional Counselor (PC) $\boxed{Dx.}$ Note: scope-of-practice includes the practice of career counseling	Master's or doctoral degree in counseling with 60 quarter hours or 40 semester hours. Course content similar to CACREP core. A prerequisite for the PCC credential.	2 years of (3,000 hrs.) post-master's experience. If doctorate earned, must have 2 years of supervised experience, 1 of which is paid *post-doctorate*.	Ohio Professional Counselor License Examination

credentials in bold letters = required credential (practice act) / $\boxed{Dx.}$ = scope-of-practice allows treatment of emotional disorders

JURISDICTION	CREDENTIAL TITLE(S)	EDUCATIONAL REQUIREMENTS	EXPERIENTIAL REQUIREMENTS	EXAMINATION REQUIREMENTS
Oklahoma Licensed Professional Counselors Board 1000 N.E. 10th St. Oklahoma City, OK 73117 405/271-6030 405/271-1011 (FAX)	Licensed Professional Counselor (LPC) **Dx.**	Master's degree in counseling, psychology, or a substantially equivalent field with a minimum of 45 semester hours (eff. 1/1/2000, 60 semester hours). Course work in 10 areas and a practicum.	3 years (3,000 hours) F-T *post-application* experience supervised by an approved LPC. Up to 2 years of required experience may be gained at a rate of 1 year for each 30 graduate semester hours beyond master's.	NCE; LPC Legal & Ethical Responsibilities Exam
Oregon Board of Licensed Professional Counselors 3218 Pringle Rd., S.E., Ste. 160 Salem, OR 97302 503/378-5499 lpc.lmft@state.or.us	Licensed Professional Counselor (LPC) Note: scope-of-practice includes the practices of rehabilitation and career counseling	Graduate degree, 48 semester hours in a CACREP-accredited program or the equivalent.	3 years F-T supervised experience (2,400 client-contact hours). 1 year (up to 800 hours) may be obtained prior to granting of master's degree; 120 hours of supervision, 60 of which must be individual.	NCE, CRCE, CMHCE, or other, as approved by the board.
Pennsylvania (no licensing board for mental health counseling at this time) Harrisburg, PA	Note: LPC licensure was passed by the state legislature on 11/23/98 and will be sent to the gov. sometime within the next few months			
Rhode Island RI Div. of Professional Regulation Board of Mental Health Counselors Cannon Bldg., Rm. 104 Providence, RI 02908 401/222-2827 401/222-1272 (FAX)	**Clinical Counselor in Mental Health** (CCMH) **Dx.**	NBCC-certified as a CCMHC, or graduate degree (60 semester hours or 90 quarter hours) in counseling/therapy and a minimum of 12 semester hours of supervised practicum and 1 calendar year of supervised internship consisting of 20 hours per week in mental health counseling.	2 years and 2,000 hours of direct client-contact, post-master's, and 100 hours of post-master's supervision.	CMHCE

credentials in bold letters = required credential (practice act) /   **Dx.**   =   scope-of-practice allows treatment of emotional disorders

537

JURISDICTION	CREDENTIAL TITLE(S)	EDUCATIONAL REQUIREMENTS	EXPERIENTIAL REQUIREMENTS	EXAMINATION REQUIREMENTS
South Carolina SC Dept. of Labor, Lic., & Reg. Board of Examiners for LPC's & LAC's P.O. Box 11329 Columbia, SC 29211 803/896-4658 803/734-4284 (FAX)	**Licensed Professional Counselor** (LPC)	Master's degree in counseling or the substantial equivalent (a master's degree in a counseling related field and additional graduate coursework to equal the coursework required in a master's degree program in counseling) that includes at least 48 credits.	2 years F-T post-master's experience with 1,500 hours of direct contact with clients and 150 hours of supervision provided by a board-approved Licensed Professional Counselor supervisor, at least 100 of which must be individual supervision.	(none; already taken at LAC level)
	Licensed Associate Counselor (LAC) *Dx.* Note: scope-of-practice includes the practices of rehabilitation and career counseling	(same as above)	Submission of a plan for meeting LPC requirements.	NCE
South Dakota Board of Counselor Examiners P.O. Box 1822 Sioux Falls, SD 57101 605/331-2927 605/331-2043 (FAX)	**Licensed Professional Counselor-Mental Health** (LPC-MH)	Master's degree or higher (incl. 48 semester hrs.) with emphasis on mental health counseling from a CACREP- accredited program or its equivalent.	Meet LPC requirements. 3 years post-master's experience including 150 hours of direct, face-to-face supervision under a licensed mental health professional.	CMHCE (if not already taken at LPC level)
	Licensed Professional Counselor (LPC) *Dx.* Note: scope-of-practice includes the practice of career counseling	Master's degree or higher, incl. 48 semester hours with a supervised counseling practicum.	1,800 hours of supervised F-T experience (pre-master's hours do not qualify for supervision).	NCE or CMHCE

credentials in bold letters = required credential (practice act) / *Dx.* = scope-of-practice allows treatment of emotional disorders

JURISDICTION	CREDENTIAL TITLE(S)	EDUCATIONAL REQUIREMENTS	EXPERIENTIAL REQUIREMENTS	EXAMINATION REQUIREMENTS
Tennessee State Board of Professional Counselors 126 5th Ave. N. Nashville, TN 37247 1-888-310-4650 615/532-5132 615/532-5164 (FAX)	**Licensed Professional Counselor** (LPC) Dx Note: scope-of-practice includes the practice of career counseling	60 graduate semester hours in counseling or a related field which includes a master's degree in counseling and a supervised 500-hour practicum or internship (300 hours of which must be completed in a mental health or community agency setting).	2 years post-master's experience, incl. 1,000 hrs. of direct clinical experience, not less than 10 hours per week and 50 hours of supervision as defined.	NCE; oral exam
Texas Board of Examiners of Professional Counselors 1100 W. 49th St. Austin, TX 78756 512/834-6658 512/834-6677 (FAX) jluther@licc.tdh.texas.gov	**Licensed Professional Counselor** (LPC) Dx Note: scope-of-practice includes the practices of rehabilitation and career counseling	Graduate degree in counseling or related field and 48 graduate semester hours, including 300 hour practicum.	2 years or 3,000 hours of post-master's supervised experience, of which 1,000 hours are face-to-face client time (formerly 2,000 hours; change eff. 12/97).	Texas Counseling Exam
Utah UT Div. of Occupational & Professional Licensing 160 E. 300th St., 4th Fl. Salt Lake City, UT 84145 801/530-6789 801/530-6511 (FAX) LPOE@br.state.ut.us	**Licensed Professional Counselor** (LPC) Dx	A minimum of 60 graduate semester hours in counseling, including an earned master's or doctoral degree in counseling from an accredited institution of higher education.	4,000 hours of supervised counseling experience, all of which must be completed after obtaining a master's degree between 2 and 4 yrs.	NCE *and* CMHCE; Utah Regulations/Ethics Exam
Vermont VT Office of Professional Regulation LCMHC Advisory Board 109 State St. Montpelier, VT 05609 1-800-439-8683 (in-state) 802/828-2390 802/828-2496 (FAX) dafaill@sec.st.vt.us	**Licensed Clinical Mental Health Counselor** (LCMHC) Dx Note: scope-of-practice includes the practice of career counseling	Master's degree (60 semester hrs.) including a supervised practicum.	2 years of post-master's experience including 3,000 hours of practice in clinical mental health counseling and a minimum of 100 hours of face-to-face supervision.	NCE or CMHCE

credentials in bold letters = required credential (practice act) / | Dx | = scope-of-practice allows treatment of emotional disorders

JURISDICTION	CREDENTIAL TITLE(S)	EDUCATIONAL REQUIREMENTS	EXPERIENTIAL REQUIREMENTS	EXAMINATION REQUIREMENTS
Virginia VA Dept. of Health Professions Board of Professional Counselors 6606 W. Broad St., 4th Fl. Richmond, VA 23230 1-888-817-8283 (application info) 804/662-9912 804/662-9943 (FAX) Note 1: application process is now handled by the NBCC, but the LPC board, itself, still exists and is based in Richmond, VA; contact the NBCC for application-related questions and paperwork, and for general questions, contact the LPC board NBCC address/Internet information: 3 Terrace Way, Ste. D Greensboro, NC 27403 NBCC@nbcc.org (e-mail address) www.nbcc.org (Web site)	**Licensed Professional Counselor** (LPC) $\boxed{Dx.}$ Note 2: scope-of-practice includes the practice of career counseling Note 3: certification as a "rehabilitation provider" available from the board	60 semester hours or 90 quarter hours of graduate study in counseling to include a graduate degree in counseling or a related field.	4,000 hours post-graduate supervised experience with 200 hours (at least 1 hour per week) of face-to-face supervision. Up to 100 hours of the face-to-face supervision may be group supervision. One-half of the overall 4,000 hours may be provided by a licensed psychiatrist, psychologist, and/or social worker, while remainder must come from an LPC. Post-master's externship may count for up to 2,000 hours of required experience.	Virginia Counseling Exam
Washington WA Dept. of Health Div. of Health Profession Quality Assurance P.O. Box 47869 Olympia, WA 98504 360/664-9098 360/586-7774 (FAX) tgs0303@hub.doh.wa.gov	Certified Mental Health Counselor (CMHC) $\boxed{Dx.}$	Master's degree or higher in mental health counseling or related field, or completion of 30 graduate semester hours, or 45 quarter hours, and a post-graduate supervised mental health counseling practicum or internship.	2,000 hours post-master's supervised experience, over a 24-month period, with 100 hours of face-to-face supervision.	NCE or CMHCE
West Virginia Board of Examiners in Counseling 100 Angus E. Peyton Dr., Rm. 201-D S. Charleston, WV 25303 1-800-520-3852 304/746-2512 304/746-1942 (FAX)	**Licensed Professional Counselor** (LPC) Note: scope-of-practice includes the practice of career counseling	Master's degree in counseling.	2 years professional supervised experience, 1 year of which must be post-master's (1 year post-doctorate).	NCE or CRCE

credentials in **bold letters** = required credential (practice act) / $\boxed{Dx.}$ = scope-of-practice allows treatment of emotional disorders

JURISDICTION	CREDENTIAL TITLE(S)	EDUCATIONAL REQUIREMENTS	EXPERIENTIAL REQUIREMENTS	EXAMINATION REQUIREMENTS
Wisconsin WI Dept. of Regulations & Licensing Examining Board of Social Workers & Professional Counselors P.O. Box 8935 Madison, WI 53709 608/267-7223 608/267-0644 (FAX)	Certified Professional Counselor (CPC)	Master's degree or an equivalent in counseling, including a minimum of 42 semester hours.	A minimum of 1,200 hours of post-master's supervised experience. Must be at least 2 years post-graduate supervised training.	NCE or CRCE
	Professional Counselor (PC) $\boxed{Dx.}$ Note: scope-of-practice includes the practice of rehabilitation counseling	(same as above)	Must show that appropriate training will be obtained.	(none)
Wyoming Mental Health Professions Licensing Board 2301 Central Ave. Cheyenne, WY 82002 307/777-7788 307/777-3508 (FAX)	**Licensed Professional Counselor** (LPC) $\boxed{Dx.}$ Note: scope-of-practice includes the practices of rehabilitation and career counseling	Master's degree (48 semester hrs.) from a CACREP-accredited program.	3,000 hours (incl. 1,500 post-master's) supervised clinical experience, including 100 hours of face-to-face supervision.	NCE

credentials in bold letters = required credential (practice act) / $\boxed{Dx.}$ = scope-of-practice allows treatment of emotional disorders

Appendix C   ACA Divisions

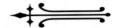

AAC	Association for Assessment in Counseling
	Publication: *Measurement and Evaluation in Counseling & Development*
AADA	Association for Adult Development and Aging
	Publication: *AADA Newsletter, Adultspan*
ACCA	American College Counseling Association
	Publication: *Journal of College Counseling*
ACEG	Association for Counselors and Educators in Government
ACES	Association for Counselor Education & Supervision
	Publication: *Counselor Education and Supervision*
AGLBIC	Association for Gay, Lesbian and Bisexual Issues in Counseling
AHEAD	Association for Humanistic Education and Development
	Publication: *Journal of Humanistic Education and Development*
AMCD	Association for Multicultural Counseling and Development
	Publication: *Journal of Multicultural Counseling and Development*
AMHCA	American Mental Health Counselors Association
	Publication: *Journal of Mental Health Counseling*
ARCA	American Rehabilitation Counseling Association
	Publication: *Rehabilitation Counseling Bulletin*
ASCA	American School Counselor Association
	Publication: *Professional School Counseling*
ASERVIC	Association for Spiritual, Ethical and Religious Values in Counseling
	Publication: *Counseling and Values*
ASGW	Association for Specialists in Group Work
	Publication: *Journal for Specialists in Group Work*
IAAOC	International Association of Addictions and Offender Counselors
	Publication: *Journal of Addictions and Offender Counseling*
IAMFC	International Association of Marriage and Family Counselors
	Publication: *The Family Journal: Counseling & Therapy for Couples & Families*
NCDA	National Career Development Association
	Publication: *The Career Development Quarterly*
NECA	National Employment Counseling Association
	Publication: *Journal of Employment Counseling*

Author Index

Subject Index